DIGITAL ADVERTISING

Digital Advertising offers a detailed and current overview of the field that draws on current research and practice by introducing key concepts, models, theories, evaluation practices, conflicts, and issues. With a balance of theory and practice, this book helps provide the tools to evaluate and understand the effects of digital advertising and promotions campaigns. New to this edition is discussion of big data analysis, privacy issues, and social media, as well as thought pieces by leading industry practitioners. This book is ideal for graduate and upper-level under-graduate students, as well as academics and practitioners.

Shelly Rodgers is Professor of Strategic Communication at the Missouri School of Journalism. With more than $18.5 million in grant support, her research focuses on advertising, health, and new technology.

Esther Thorson is Professor of Journalism at the College of Communication Arts and Sciences at Michigan State University. She spent 23 years as Associate Dean of Journalism at the University of Missouri.

DIGITAL ADVERTISING

Theory and Research

Third Edition

Edited by
Shelly Rodgers
Esther Thorson

Routledge
Taylor & Francis Group

NEW YORK AND LONDON

Third edition published 2017
by Routledge
711 Third Avenue, New York, NY 10017

and by Routledge
2 Park Square, Milton Park, Abingdon, Oxon, OX14 4RN

Routledge is an imprint of the Taylor & Francis Group, an informa business

First edition published by Lawrence Erlbaum Associates, Inc. 1999

Second edition published by Lawrence Erlbaum Associates, Inc. 2007

Library of Congress Cataloging-in-Publication Data
Names: Rodgers, Shelly (Shelly Lannette), 1965– editor. | Thorson, Esther,
    editor.
Title: Digital advertising : theory and research / edited by Shelly Rodgers,
    Esther Thorson.
Description: Third edition. | New York, NY : Routledge, 2017. | Includes
    bibliographical references and index.
Identifiers: LCCN 2016043446 | ISBN 9781138654426 (hardback : alk.
    paper) | ISBN 9781138654457 (pbk. : alk. paper) | ISBN 9781315623252
    (ebook)
Subjects: LCSH: Internet advertising.
Classification: LCC HF6146.I58 A38 2017 | DDC 659.14/4—dc23
LC record available at https://lccn.loc.gov/2016043446

ISBN: 978-1-138-65442-6 (hbk)
ISBN: 978-1-138-65445-7 (pbk)
ISBN: 978-1-315-62325-2 (ebk)

Typeset in Bembo
by Apex CoVantage, LLC

To my mother- and father-in-law, June and Joe,
who always inspire.
—Shelly
To my grandchildren, Madeline, Dominic,
Will, and Liliana Lynn.
—Esther

CONTENTS

ABOUT THE CONTRIBUTORS

Saleem Alhabash is an Assistant Professor of Public Relations and Social Media, Department of Advertising + Public Relations, Michigan State University. He researches persuasive effects of new and social media.

Fernando Angulo-Ruiz is an Associate Professor in the Department of International Business, Marketing, and Strategy, School of Business, MacEwan University. His research examines marketing capabilities, marketing performance, and international entrepreneurship.

Tae Hyun Baek is an Assistant Professor in the Department of Integrated Strategic Communication at the University of Kentucky. His research focuses on digital strategies and advertising.

Verolien Cauberghe is an Associate Professor in the Department of Communication Sciences, Faculty of Political and Social Science, Ghent University (Belgium). Her research focuses on advertising effectiveness and social marketing.

Qimei Chen is a Professor of Marketing, Jean E. Rolles Distinguished Professor, and Associate Dean for Academic Affairs, Shidler College of Business, University of Hawai'i at Mānoa. Her research examines consumer empowerment.

Shu-Chuan Chu is an Associate Professor of Advertising and Program Chair at the College of Communication at DePaul University. Her research interests include social media, electronic word-of-mouth (eWOM), and cross-cultural consumer behavior.

John P. Costello is a Graduate Research Fellow at Villanova University. Previously, he was an Associate Planner for Saks Fifth Avenue and a Merchandise Analyst for American Eagle Outfitters.

Frank E. Dardis is an Associate Professor at Penn State University. His research interests include in-game advertising, brand-communication message factors, and interactive advertising effects.

Terry Daugherty is Chair and Associate Professor of Marketing in the Department of Marketing, The University of Akron. He is Editor-in-Chief of the *Journal of Interactive Advertising*.

Vanja Djuric is Associate Instructor in the Department of Marketing and the Director of Analytics for the Taylor Institute for Direct Marketing, College of Business Administration, The University of Akron.

Judy Drennan is a Professor of Marketing at QUT Business School. Her research expertise is in digital technology and its influence on consumer behavior.

Brittany R. L. Duff is an Associate Professor of Advertising, Charles H. Sandage Department of Advertising, University of Illinois Urbana-Champaign. She researches attention to advertising, especially selective attention (ignoring ads) and divided attention (multitasking).

Ronald J. Faber is a Professor Emeritus of Mass Communication, School of Journalism and Mass Communication, University of Minnesota. His research includes compulsive buying, political advertising, cross-cultural advertising, and consumer socialization.

Andrew Gambino is a doctoral candidate at Penn State University. His research focuses on the human-technology relationship, artificial intelligence, and psychological aspects of communication technologies (http://comm.psu.edu/people/individual/andrew-gambino).

Louisa Ha is a Professor in the School of Media and Communication at Bowling Green State University and Editor of *Journalism and Mass Communication Quarterly*. Her research examines online advertising and mobile media.

Laura Herrewijn is a Post-Doctoral Researcher at Ghent University, Belgium. Her research focuses on the effectiveness of persuasive content in digital games.

Liselot Hudders is an Assistant Professor in the Department of Communication Sciences, Faculty of Political and Social Science, Ghent University (Belgium). Her research examines consumption and happiness, and advertising effectiveness.

Jisu Huh is Professor and Raymond O. Mithun Chair in Advertising, School of Journalism and Mass Communication, University of Minnesota. Her research examines DTC prescription drugs and interactive/digital/social advertising, among others.

Syed Ali Hussain is a doctoral student at the School of Journalism, Michigan State University. His research focuses on visual illness narratives on social media (photographs on Tumblr and Instagram).

Amy Rebecca Jones is a doctoral student in the Department of Marketing and Supply Chain Management at the University of Memphis. Her research focuses on sensory marketing.

Jae Min Jung is a Professor of Marketing at the California State Polytechnic University, Pomona. His research focuses on advertising and consumer psychology related to goals, judgment, persuasion, and cultural values.

Louise Kelly is a Lecturer in Advertising, Media and Digital at QUT Business School and researches in the area of advertising engagement and avoidance, online privacy, and social media platforms.

Gayle Kerr is a Professor of Advertising, IMC and Digital at QUT Business School. She researches consumer empowerment, engagement, and avoidance, examining it across platforms and in the context of advertising self-regulation.

Jinyoung Kim is a doctoral student at Penn State University. Her research focuses on psychological effects of communication technology and how technological affordances change health-related attitudes/behaviors via interactive messages.

Marian Levy is an Assistant Dean and Associate Professor in the School of Public Health at the University of Memphis. Her research focuses on social and environmental support for healthy lifestyles.

Bryan A. Liang is a Professor Emeritus at University of California, San Diego, School of Medicine and Special Advisor, Global Health Policy Institute. The focus of his work is on the systematic impact of health policy and law on providers, patients, and patient safety.

Anthony M. Limperos is an Assistant Professor in the Department of Communication, University of Kentucky. His research includes psychology of video games, media effects, new communication technology, and health communication.

Matthew Lombard is an Associate Professor in the Department of Media Studies and Production at Temple University in Philadelphia, PA. His research centers on psychological processing of media.

Yuliya Lutchyn is a Consumer Behavior and User Experience Researcher at Microsoft. Her interdisciplinary work spans the fields of consumer psychology, mediated communication, and human-computer interaction (HCI).

Tim K. Mackey is an Assistant Professor at UC San Diego School of Medicine, Associate Program Director, UC San Diego Masters Health Policy & Law Program, and Director of the Global Health Policy Institute (www.ghpolicy.org).

Drew Martin is a Professor of Marketing at the University of Hawaii, Hilo. His research explores consumer decision-making and tourism behavior and focuses on psychological, social, and cultural influences.

Francisco J. Martínez-López is a Professor of Business Administration, Department of Business Administration, Business School, University of Granada and Open University of Catalonia (Spain). His research includes e-business, consumer behavior, and management.

Daniel McDuff is Director of Research at Affectiva. He completed his Ph.D. at the MIT Media Lab in 2014 and has a B.A. and Masters from Cambridge University. His research examines psychology and computer science.

Kyeong Sam Min is the Sidney Baron Associate Professor of Marketing at the University of New Orleans. His research examines consumer judgment and decision-making, marketing communication, and cross-cultural psychology.

Marjolein Moorman is an Associate Professor in political communication in the Communication Science department at the University of Amsterdam. Her research examines advertising effect measurement, among others.

Mariko Morimoto is an Associate Professor of Marketing in the Faculty of Liberal Arts at Sophia University, Tokyo, Japan. Her research includes cross-cultural advertising, source credibility, and consumers' online privacy concerns.

Juan Mundel is a doctoral student at the Department of Advertising + Public Relations, Michigan State University. His research extends marketing practices to social media communication for vulnerable populations.

Daniël G. Muntinga is an Assistant Professor of Persuasive Communication at the University of Amsterdam. He studies historical development of advertising and branding in digital contexts.

Sifan Ouyang is a Media Executive at Neo@Ogilvy, Shanghai, China. He received his Masters degree at the Missouri School of Journalism. His research focuses on digital advertising in social media.

Patrick De Pelsmacker is a Professor of Marketing at the University of Antwerp (Belgium). His research includes advertising in new media, cross-cultural branding and advertising, and sustainable consumption.

Albena Pergelova is an Associate Professor at the School of Business, MacEwan University. Her research centers on "interactiveness" and consumer empowerment, as well as entrepreneurship.

Karolien Poels is an Associate Professor of Strategic Communication at the Department of Communication Studies, University of Antwerp. Her research includes advertising and consumer psychology, and digital games and social media.

Attila Pohlmann is a consumer behavior researcher and instructor in the Shidler College of Business, University of Hawai'i at Mānoa. He studies social identities and dynamics involved in food consumption.

Kathrynn Pounders is an Assistant Professor of Advertising and Public Relations, Stan Richards School at the University of Texas at Austin. Her research examines consumer behavior in social marketing.

Francisco Rejón-Guardia is an Assistant Professor of Marketing in the Department of Business & Economics at the University of Balearic Islands, Spain. His research includes social media and online consumer behavior.

Marla B. Royne is the Great Oaks Foundation Professor of Marketing and Chair of Marketing & Supply Chain Management at the University of Memphis. Her research examines social marketing related to health messages.

Mike Schmierbach is an Associate Professor at Pennsylvania State University. His research explores how prior media use shapes evaluations of and reactions to media, particularly video games.

Heather Shoenberger is an Assistant Professor of Strategic Communication at University of Oregon. Her research focuses on consumer decision-making and privacy issues relating to digital media.

Edith G. Smit is Dean of the Graduate School of Communication and Professor of Persuasive Communication at the Amsterdam School of Communication Research, University of Amsterdam.

Jennifer Snyder-Duch is an Associate Professor of Communication at Carlow University in Pittsburgh, PA. Her teaching, research, and community engagement focus on diversity and advocacy in traditional and digital media.

S. Shyam Sundar is Distinguished Professor and founding Director of the Media Effects Research Laboratory (http://www.psu.edu/dept/medialab) at Penn State University. His research investigates psychological aspects of new communication technologies (http://comm.psu.edu/people/individual/s.-shyam-sundar).

Charles R. Taylor is the John A. Murphy Professor of Marketing at the Villanova University of Business and Senior Research Fellow at the Center for Marketing and Consumer Insights. His research examines marketing and society issues.

Samuel M. Tham is a doctoral student at Michigan State University with research interests in advertising, decision-making, and communication technology. Prior to academia, he was a 360-degree advertising professional for over seven years.

Marijke De Veirman is a Teaching Assistant and doctoral candidate in the Department of Communication Sciences, Faculty of Political and Social Science, Ghent University (Belgium). Her research examines social media marketing.

Peeter W. J. Verlegh is a Professor of Marketing at Vrije Universiteit Amsterdam. He studies word-of-mouth, social media, and marketing communication, with a consumer focus.

Chan Yun Yoo is an Associate Professor of Integrated Strategic Communication at the University of Kentucky. His research examines digital advertising. His book is titled: *Preattentive Processing of Web Advertising*.

FOREWORD

Someone who knew me well once described me as being "an analogue person in a digital world." It may, therefore, be somewhat ironic for me to be writing the foreword for this book. However, having spent a long career studying advertising and mass communication, I can recognize when a seismic change in advertising is occurring and appreciate the need for insight and direction to help guide advertising theory and research through this transition. This is clearly such a time in the development of advertising, and *Digital Advertising* promises to be a book to provide some of the needed guidance.

Although some trace the beginning of mass media back as far as the development of movable type in 1440, it wasn't until the advent of the penny press in the 1830s and 40s that the media could truly be called a mass medium (Rogers, 1986). Since that time we have experienced a major change in the nature of mass media and media advertising at the rate of only once or twice in every lifetime. Radio and radio networks came into prominence in the late 1920s and early 1930s, changing the nature and focus of advertising messages and a blurring the lines between entertainment and advertising (Fox, 1985). Television became the dominant medium in the early 1950s (Dominick, 1983) and brought with it an increased importance on image and visual messages and the realization of the value of achieving brand recall (Samuel, 2001; Sivulka, 2012). In the past 15–20 years, digital media have begun to revolutionize communications and advertising. Beginning in 2016 or 2017, digital advertising is expected to overtake television in terms of advertising spending (Ember, 2015; Kroll, 2016).

With each dynamic shift in media dominance, we have seen a corresponding change in where advertising dollars are allocated, and this was eventually followed by a major change in the focus of advertising and communication research and theory. Typically, with the start of any new medium, researchers re-examine previous questions and issues to see if they still hold for the new medium. It is typically only after this that we begin to develop new questions and theories based on crucial characteristics of the new medium. We are now at this time in developing our understanding of digital advertising, and this book, *Digital Advertising*, is perfectly positioned to begin this effort by identifying what we currently know and suggesting directions for future research and theory.

The editors of *Digital Advertising*, Shelly Rodgers and Esther Thorson, are among the leading scholars in advertising and are well qualified to help us identify the changes needed to improve and expand research and theory in these changing times. I have had the pleasure of knowing them both for many years and have seen how highly regarded they are by their peers. Shelly was elected and served as President of the *American Academy of Advertising (AAA)*, and Esther was named as a Fellow of *AAA*, the organization's most prestigious honor. Both, together and independently, have already produced many important works in driving our understanding of digital advertising and promoting scholarly understanding of advertising in general. Together, they co-edited *Advertising Theory*, which has played an important role in updating and advancing theory building in advertising (Rodgers & Thorson, 2012). Esther also co-authored one of the first important volumes exploring digital advertising (Schumann & Thorson, 1999), while Shelly has authored or co-authored numerous groundbreaking articles on various aspects of digital advertising. Together they also co-authored "The Interactive Advertising Model: How Users Perceive and Process Online Advertising" (Rodgers & Thorson, 2000). This work has served as an important framework for research on digital advertising, and an updated version of this model serves as a useful starting point for this book.

In *Digital Advertising*, they have once again brought together an excellent group of prominent advertising researchers to explore, expand, and direct the development of advertising research and theory. Contributors to this volume include several current and past editors of the top journals in advertising and mass communication such as Terry Daughtery (*Journal of Interactive Advertising*), Marla Royne (*Journal of Advertising*), Ray Taylor (*International Journal of Advertising*), and Louisa Ha (*Journalism & Mass Communication Quarterly*). Many other chapter authors have been among the leaders of research on digital advertising since its inception, while others represent some of the best up-and-coming minds in the field.

The development and growth of digital advertising will call for many changes in the models, critical concepts, and methods we use to understand the impact of advertising on consumers and society. The growth of Instagram, Twitter, Facebook, Google, YouTube, Snapchat, and numerous other vehicles is highlighting and altering the notion of who creates, distributes, and controls advertising and brand messaging. Donald Trump's 2016 presidential campaign has demonstrated how a new two-step flow from Twitter or Instagram to media outlets and then on to the public can be every bit as effective, or more so, than traditional media advertising. These changes may enhance the importance of concepts such as trust, message/brand salience, and strength of belief. Emerging technologies such as virtual reality and holographic imaging may increase our focus of concepts like presence and emersion. They are also likely to alter our reliance on various methods of analysis, increasing the importance of tools like multi-level modeling and network analysis. The ability of digital media to provide seamless feedback on media use, advertising exposure, and purchase behavior provides huge amounts of information for exploration, enhancing the importance of techniques such as database management, web analytics, and data mining, making information and computer science more integral to advertising.

It is an interesting and exciting time for advertising theory and research. However, we are still in the early stages of this media evolution. Digital advertising is likely to grow in ways still unimagined and with it, our theories and models will also need to change. *Digital Advertising* is a book to help start us on this journey.

Ronald J. Faber

Professor Emeritus

University of Minnesota

References

Dominick, J. R. (1983). *The dynamics of mass communication*. Reading, MA: Addison-Wesley Publishing Company.

Ember, S. (2015, December 7). Digital ad spending expected to soon surpass TV. *New York Times*, B-6. Retrieved May 28, 2016 from http://www.nytimes.com/2015/12/07/business/media/digital-ad-spending-expected-to-soon-surpass-tv.

Fox, S. (1985). *The mirror makers: A history of American advertising and its creators*. New York, NY: Random House.

Kroll, S. (2016, May 12). European digital ad spend surpasses TV; 57% ads in-view in Q1 2016. *Exchange Wire*. Retrieved May 28, 2016 from https://www.exchangewire.com/blog/2016/05/12/european-digital-ad-spend-surpasses-tv-57-ads-in-view-in-q1–2016.

Rodgers, S., & Thorson, E. (2000). The interactive advertising model: How people perceive and process interactive ads. *Journal of Interactive Advertising, 1*(1), 42–61.

Rodgers, S., & Thorson, E. (2012). *Advertising theory*. New York, NY: Routledge.

Rogers, E. M. (1986). *Communication technology: The new media in society*. New York, NY: The Free Press.

Samuel, L. R. (2001). *Brought to you by: Postwar television and the American dream*. Austin, TX: University of Texas Press.

Schumann, D. W., & Thorson, E. (1999). *Advertising and the world wide web*. Mahwah, NJ: Lawrence Erlbaum Associates.

Sivulka, J. (2012). *Soap, sex, and cigarettes: A cultural history of American advertising*. Boston, MA: Wadsworth.

PREFACE

Digital Advertising

With an almost infinite number of digital possibilities, communication fields are in chaos. There's a lot that brands can do, but how do brands decide which avenues to pursue? Our response is to begin with sound theory about targeted, intentional messages combined with the recognition that customers have become extremely active in this process.

Building on this premise, *Digital Advertising*—co-edited by Shelly Rodgers and Esther Thorson—updates two previous editions:

> Schumann, D., & Thorson, E. (2007). *Internet advertising: Theory and research* (2nd Ed.). Hillsdale, NJ: Lawrence Erlbaum Associates, Inc.
>
> Schumann, D., & Thorson, E. (1999). *Advertising and the World Wide Web*. Hillsdale, NJ: Lawrence Erlbaum Associates, Inc.

Our primary objective was to offer a wide-ranging text that draws on current research and practices in digital advertising by introducing key concepts, models, theories, evaluation practices, conflicts, and issues for individuals interested in this area.

So what prompted this 3rd edition? For starters, the prior editions of the text were written during a time when internet advertising was synonymous with banner ads and pop-ups, and interactivity consisted of connecting with consumers via email, instant message, or blogs. And much of the scholarly research at that time focused on testing traditional concepts online, such as segmenting or using clicks to determine the effectiveness of internet ads.

A lot has changed since then, starting with the terminology and, to some degree, the metrics used. *Digital Advertising* provides a detailed and current view of what might be considered digital advertising theory. The book provides readers with a working knowledge of the primary theoretical approaches and will help readers synthesize the vast literature on digital advertising. The book also helps to provide the critical tools necessary to evaluate and understand the effects of digital advertising with emphasis on mobile and social media. Chapters are authored by leading scholars from around the globe, and several leading industry practitioners provide their thoughts about theory, metrics, and a host of other issues related to digital advertising. To put theories into action, practical examples are provided.

Who will benefit from this book? Given our focus is on scholarly research, *Digital Advertising* is intended to address the need for a current scholarly text that spans the digital advertising literature. Thus, the book is an essential reading for graduate and upper-level undergraduate students, as well as academics and practitioners wanting to understand how to carry out effective digital advertising.

Theoretical Premise

To better orient the reader, the theoretical premise of *Digital Advertising* is that the crucial mechanism is a network of message movements across platforms, with frequent message curation, manipulation, and even creation (e.g., user-generated advertising) by participants (formerly known as the audience).

The current media landscape is moving at such a fast pace, fueled by digital technologies and media, one might question whether it is possible to document this dynamic environment in a thorough and detailed manner. We believe it is not only possible, but with the right theoretical premise, such a book may get ahead of the debate by articulating a forward thinking research agenda with staying power, even within a fast-changing digital environment.

Many of the strategies and tactics of advertising are understood in the limited theoretical perspective of message distribution to individuals (e.g., targeted behavioral advertising) or to aggregates (TV primetime audiences).

However, most brand campaigns now employ combinations of paid, earned, social, and owned media tools. Further, advertising agencies and advertising researchers have long considered their main task to be distributing television, print, or digital ads, and then measuring how consumers respond to them. More and more, however, the movement of advertisements through what Henry Jenkins (2008) calls a "spreadable media model" has become the central focus for advertising campaigns.

We call this process "promotional radiating." Indeed, radiation through a network involves many examples of message functionalities significantly different from those intended by message creators. This large and complex movement and development involves participants passing along or endorsing messages, viral phenomena in which reach skyrockets, and what promotion professionals call electronic word-of-mouth (eWOM).

Big data analysis tools have made it possible to track and analyze brand-related activities in this complex network of message movement. This is critically important to professional persuaders because it is a new view of consumer response, and because that flow and patterning itself can be joined and influenced by persuaders.

Brand "fandom," trans-media branding, image recognition, real-time social media analysis, and content marketing are tools that have become crucial for effective brand campaigns. Many of these concepts are relatively new. *Digital Advertising* aims to fill a void in the literature by bringing together an elite group of "forward thinkers," who lay the groundwork for these and other current issues in digital advertising scholarship. And each chapter provides suggestions for future research.

How the Book is Organized

Drawing from the book's theoretical premise, *Digital Advertising* is organized into six main parts: 1) Research Foundations, 2) Theory Breakthroughs, 3) New Approaches to Research, 4) Digital Media—Radiating Voices, 5) Evaluating Digital Advertising, and 6) Future Research Trends and Opportunities.

To add cohesion throughout the text, each section draws from and builds on Chapters 1 and 2, which provide a theoretical premise for the book.

Part I—Research Foundations

Part I sets the stage for the entire book by providing four chapters that lay a foundation for understanding key theories and concepts presented in the book.

Chapter 1

To demonstrate the utility of the original IAM and to illustrate uses of the new IAM, Chapter 1, by Rodgers, Ouyang, and Thorson, provides the findings of a content analysis of 385 articles that cite the IAM. The purpose was twofold: 1) show how the original IAM has been used by scholars worldwide, 2) set the stage for an updated version of the IAM that accounts for changes in emerging technology since the introduction of the original IAM.

Chapter 2

Building on Chapter 1, Chapter 2, by Thorson and Rodgers, presents a new model that encapsulates and extends the IAM. Called the Networking Advertising Model, or NAM, Chapter 2 provides the beginnings of a theory that takes networking and "spreadability" into account, and suggests examples that help to illustrate how the new model may operate with regard to advertising.

Chapter 3

The purpose of Chapter 3, co-authored by Tham, Rodgers, and Thorson, is to map industry trends in digital advertising. The primary question to be addressed is which areas of industry could provide further advancement by scholars? The chapter involves a close analysis of trends as identified in the last few years of the industry publication *Advertising Age*.

Chapter 4

Chapter 4, by Daugherty and Djuric, report the results of a systematic analysis of interactive advertising research using the paradigm funnel and based on the *Journal of Interactive Advertising*. The results provide a useful starting point for scholars wanting to understand what research has been conducted—as witnessed through the pages of JIAD—and where their research may fit into this growing body of research.

Part II—Theory Breakthroughs

To help readers navigate the vast literature on digital advertising and promotion, Part II articulates current breakthroughs in theories. Chapters are written on a broad range of topics ranging from psychological processing of message types (e.g., video ads, native ads, user-generated content), digital channels (e.g., social media, mobile), and advertising clutter.

Chapter 5

Ha's Chapter 5 reviews the evolution of research on advertising clutter in three different contexts: traditional media, online media, and mobile platforms.

Chapter 6

Chapter 6, by Sundar, Kim, and Gambino, presents the theory of interactive media effects (TIME) and analyzes seven recent trends in digital advertising via two proposed theoretical routes, i.e., cue route and action route.

Chapter 7

Using the theory of psychological reactance, Morimoto (Chapter 7) examines the relationship between consumer privacy online and negative responses to digital advertising. This includes perceived intrusiveness, irritation and avoidance, and the role of advertising personalization in easing negative responses to digital advertising.

Chapter 8

Jung, Min, and Martin, in Chapter 8, draw on reversal theory to offer a compelling approach to explain complex consumer behaviors that fluctuate between meta-motivational states in consumers' cyber journeys. The authors review the digital advertising literature on reversal theory and conclude by providing possible avenues for future research.

Chapter 9

Chapter 9, by Duff and Lutchyn, looks at how consumers exert control over their media and ad environment by limiting their exposure to advertising through avoidance, engaging with other content simultaneously, or meta-engaging with ads by being aware that those ads are supporting the media content that the ad is placed in.

Part III—New Approaches to Research

Part III drills down into the various approaches to digital advertising. Researchers and practitioners have always been concerned with how to get people to pay attention to, and how to keep attention focused on advertising—and digital advertising is no different. YouTube's attempt to get people to watch ads by forcing an ad prior to the viewing of a video is one example. Digital advertising has also influenced the way in which people view advertising in traditional media. As shown in Part II, competing ad clutter in digital advertising environments necessitates research to determine how or what researchers and practitioners can do to enhance attentiveness and persuasion in digital and traditional environments. Thus, this section is devoted to highlighting key factors that can influence digital advertising strategies.

Chapter 10

Chapter 10, by Lombard and Synder-Duch, introduces the concept of presence (or telepresence) and offers a theoretical framework and research paradigm that is relevant to advertising in the digital age.

Chapter 11

With the changing nature of the healthcare environment, Chapter 11, by Royne, Pounders, Levy, and Jones, provides an overview of some of the pressing healthcare issues and discusses various digital media that may be used to provide health information, followed by a discussion of how message strategies may be used to more fully engage with consumers who require a deeper knowledge of health issues.

Chapter 12

De Veirman, Cauberghe, Hudders, and De Pelsmacker (Chapter 12) discuss social networking sites (SNS) brand communities and provide an overview of previous research and an empirical study on how people interact with brands on SNSs and what motivates them to do so.

Chapter 13

Yoo and Baek, in Chapter 13, present the event study method and demonstrate how it can be used to explain digital advertising's accountability. The authors then examine the effect of digital advertising on a firm's financial value to demonstrate the method's utility.

Chapter 14

Kelly, Kerr, and Drennan (Chapter 14) examine advertising avoidance by building on the theoretical premise of promotional radiation and applying an approach/avoidance framework to define advertising avoidance and identify types of antecedents.

Part IV—Digital Media—Radiating Voices

Now, more than ever, consumers in a digital environment actively participate in the message creation/dissemination process. The world is changing, and the continued growth of global commerce and the advertising industry in emerging markets will increasingly change the ways that global marketers do business (Taylor, 2013). Part IV examines digital promotional techniques and channel selection with a focus on current research and literature on social media, the role of search, segmenting and targeting, mobile, in-game advertising, and emerging markets, to name a few.

Chapter 15

Chapter 15, by Muntinga, Moorman, Verlegh, and Smit, demonstrates why brand-related content creation is the consequence of various factors working in concert. Different consumers are shown to have different motivations to create brand-related content, and the influence of consumer characteristics on brand content creation is mediated by intrinsic motivations.

Chapter 16

With the proliferation and prevalence of social media and social networking sites, Chapter 16, by Alhabash, Mundel, and Hussain, provides the landscape of social media usage patterns in advertising, marketing, and public relations. The chapter draws on classical advertising/persuasion theories to better understand social media's fit in the chain of processes leading to persuasion.

Chapter 17

In Chapter 17, Shoenberger reviews the concept of privacy in the digital context and outlines the privacy paradox.

Chapter 18

Herrewijn and Poels (Chapter 18) discuss in-game advertising, provide a definition of the practice, and give an overview of its benefits and drawbacks. They present the results of a case study that examines how players respond to different types of ads in digital games.

Chapter 19

McDuff's chapter (Chapter 19) illustrates how measurement of emotion, in addition to cognitive responses to advertising, are not only possible with digital technology but necessary, and shows how these practices have been applied to evaluating digital advertising effectiveness.

Part V—Evaluating Digital Advertising

Measuring the impact of advertising efforts has been the focus of advertising researchers and practitioners for decades. New approaches in social media enable advertisers to target consumers with highly personalized content, product placements are used to enhance gaming experiences, and the integration of traditional with digital advertising has changed the way that people interact with and use traditional media. Advertisers are challenged to create new and novel ways to compose a seamless brand experience, changing the way that people engage with brands. But do these novel approaches work? As our authors demonstrate in this section, more studies are needed that examine the effectiveness of various evaluation approaches, including the use of new metrics designed to capture meaningful brand experiences and advertising value.

Chapter 20

Chapter 20, by Taylor and Costello, discusses factors that have led to the rise of digital advertising internationally. The authors examine digital advertising research from three perspectives, propose general principles related to digital advertising internationally, and conclude by summarizing major findings and outlining future areas to guide international digital advertising research.

Chapter 21

In Chapter 21, Rejón-Guardia and Martínez-López provide an extensive literature review on online advertising, emphasizing traditional forms of internet ads and social network ads. The chapter concludes with recommendations for managers and academics for improving the efficacy of online advertising.

Chapter 22

Pergelova and Angulo-Ruiz (Chapter 22) synthesize the digital advertising effectiveness literature and propose a model that incorporates a broader set of metrics, including consumer empowerment, and outlines an efficiency methodological measurement approach that captures a diversity of input and outputs.

Chapter 23

Mackey and Liang (Chapter 23) review the health advertising literature as it relates to digital advertising and identify trends and challenges, such as health and pharmaceutical advertising, direct-to-consumer advertising, the growing role of social networking in health, and the need for reliable data on health marketing expenditures.

Part VI—Future Research Trends and Opportunities

The majority of the book is devoted to updating what has changed in the digital realm since the first and second editions of this text. Our final section, Part VI, is devoted to projecting ahead about what else may change or what we might expect to see coming down the proverbial pipeline. Thus, the final section draws on the collective wisdom of veteran and beginning scholars, who provided "think pieces" about where research on digital advertising and promotion has been and where it might be headed. Our purpose in this final section is to leave readers with tangible ideas for their own studies and research on digital advertising.

Chapter 24

Chu, in Chapter 24, examines the role of culture in electronic word-of-mouth (eWOM), noting that the majority of studies on eWOM have been conducted in the U.S. and Western contexts, leaving a lot of questions regarding the role of eWOM in cross-cultural settings.

Chapter 25

Schmierbach (Chapter 25) presents and defines the concept of immersion, arguing that the term is vague, and findings do not yet account for how this relationship may be nonlinear or moderated by the content of the ad.

Chapter 26

Dardis (Chapter 26) discusses in-game advertising and argues there are many under-examined variables that can affect brand-related outcomes, specifically related to virtual direct experience (VDE).

Chapter 27

Limperos (Chapter 27) also examines advertising in video games but with a focus on understanding key factors that may affect how people process and recall ads that appear in video games, followed by suggestions about how researchers might continue to study the effectiveness and overall value of this form of digital advertising.

Chapter 28

Chapter 28, by Pohlmann and Chen, explores how social media has disrupted traditional measurement of affect. They discuss challenges with the traditional hierarchy of effects models and propose a new interactive response model to better understand and manage consumers' interactions with social media advertising.

Chapter 29

Chapter 29, by Huh, argues that computational social science research that uses big data has great potential for examining consumers' interactions with and responses to digital advertising, and for contributing to advertising theory building. She presents important considerations for multidisciplinary computational advertising research and provides several new directions for future research in this area.

References

Jenkins, H. (2008). *Convergence culture: Where old and new media collide.* New York, NY: New York University Press.

Taylor, C. R. (2013). Editorial: Hot topics in advertising research. *International Journal of Advertising, 32*(1), 7–12.

ACKNOWLEDGMENTS

We are so deeply indebted to all our contributors, without whom this book would not be possible. Your creative and forward-thinking chapters have inspired us, and we feel lucky to have the privilege to edit your works!

A huge thanks goes out to our two detailed and highly organized editorial assistants—Frances Gordon and Dani Myers. Thank you!

We also thank our publisher friends, Christina Chronister and Julie Toich, for their organization and assistance—you were a sheer delight to work with throughout the entire process.

There were many, many colleagues who were kind enough to discuss the book with us in preparing the proposal, identifying potential contributors, and finalizing chapters—you know who you are—thank you for your great ideas and generosity!

Shelly is glad to have another chance to work with her long-time friend and colleague, Esther.

Esther thinks that Shelly is the most organized human she knows, and as always, learns so much working with Shelly!

PART I
Research Foundations

1

REVISITING THE INTERACTIVE ADVERTISING MODEL (IAM) AFTER 15 YEARS

An Analysis of Impact and Implications

Shelly Rodgers, Sifan Ouyang, and Esther Thorson

Introduction

The Interactive Advertising Model (IAM), developed by Rodgers and Thorson (2000), was one of the first models that theorized about the interactions between internet users and online advertisements. In the 15+ years since its inception and initial publication, the model has been widely referenced by scholars from various academic disciplines (advertising, marketing, IT, etc.), and is recognized as an effective model for understanding how interactive advertising "works" (Kim, Hayes, Avant, & Reid, 2014).

Despite the growing number of scholarly publications and articles citing the IAM, it is both necessary and beneficial to evaluate the IAM's impact and influence on scholarship by examining how scholars have used and critiqued the IAM over the past 15 years. This examination allows quantification of the impact of the IAM and enhances further understanding of the explanatory power of the model in digital advertising, as well as other contexts. This analysis also sheds insights on how the IAM may be revised and adapted to the fast-changing landscape of digital advertising.

The objectives of the present chapter are two-fold: First, we quantitatively assess the impact of the IAM by analyzing all peer-reviewed articles citing the IAM over a 15-year period (2000 to 2015). Second, we use the content analysis findings to identify themes, trends, and potential challenges associated with the IAM. Chapter 2 then builds on the results of this chapter by presenting an extended version of the IAM that attempts to fill gaps identified by research reported in Chapter 1.

The remainder of this chapter is organized as follows. First, we briefly review the IAM and its various components. Next, we provide an explanation of the methodology used to analyze articles that cite the IAM. Then, results of our analysis are provided, followed by a discussion of theoretical implications going forward. Based on our results, we conclude that the IAM remains useful for understanding how people perceive and process advertising in a Web 1.0 environment; however, the model may need to be revised and updated to reflect the current and dynamic Web 2.0 and even Web 3.0 technologies.

Overview of the IAM

Rodgers and Thorson (2000) conceptualized the Interactive Advertising Model, or IAM, as an integrative process, based on three dominant paradigms or schools of thought: functional, structural, and information processing (see Figure 1 from Rodgers & Thorson, 2000). The authors argued that a theoretical integration of multiple paradigms could serve to better understand and interpret the complex nature of the interactive environment, as the internet itself was an "integrated medium" (Rodgers & Thorson, 2000, p. 43).

Both function and structure could determine the internet users' information processing of advertising in cyberspace. The functionalist view explains how (mode) and why (motive) users use the internet, as well as the various stages of information processing (attention, brand liking, etc.), consumer's attitudes (e.g., form attitudes toward the ad), and behaviors (e.g., click on the ad) as outcomes influenced by online ads. The structural view, on the other hand, helps to understand the basic components (ad types, formats, and features) of the stimulus environment primarily controlled by advertisers at the time of the model's inception.

Function

From a functionalist perspective, the IAM proposed that internet users control the initiation of internet activity, as they enter cyberspace with specific goals in mind and constantly adjust to the interactive environment to fulfill these goals. Internet motives, the inner drive to carry out the internet activity, can explain why individuals use the internet. Four categories of reasons were identified as the primary motives for entering cyberspace (Rodgers & Sheldon, 2002): researching, communicating, surfing, and shopping. The categories of internet motives were suggested to not only influence consumer responses to online ads differently, but also to help advertisers determine the most effective ad appeal and ad type. However, users could have more than one internet motive in mind before entering cyberspace and switch motives during their online activities when seeing an unexpected stimulus, or for some other reason.

Mode, the extent of a user's goal-directedness of internet activities, conjointly determines the level of ad processing with motive, as internet motive will influence the mode in which users use the internet. For example, researchers tend to be "serious" with a highly goal-directed mode, while surfers tend to be "playful" without a specific goal in mind.

As discussed, individuals are also expected to experience several stages of information processing of online ads: attend to, remember, and develop attitudes toward internet ads, as well as actions taken in response to internet ads. In terms of evaluating consumer responses to online ads, almost all measures used in traditional advertising could be applied to interactive advertising, such as attitude toward the ad or purchase intention. In addition, new types of measures were available to examine effects of online ads, e.g., hits, click-through rates, and time spent on websites.

Structure

The IAM argued that information processing of online ads would be influenced by the presentation of the interactive ad, as well as characteristics of the stimulus environment. Thus, the structural view was provided to complement the functional view in terms of understanding how physical features could interact with users' motive or mode. As a result, the IAM provided a classification of all the "then available" ad types and formats 15+ years ago and discussed some common ad features at that time.

Ad Type

Ad type represents the general structure of any advertisement and was classified into five main categories according to Thorson (1996): product/service, PSA, issue, corporate, and political. The IAM argues that ad type can predict whether, or how much, cognitive effort is involved in processing online ads and how different ad types can often indicate consumer responses to the ad.

Ad Format

Ad format is the manner in which the online ad appears. The IAM argued that different formats would result in differential processing and outcomes. Several then-popular interactive ad formats were examined using the IAM model: banners, interstitials (pop-ups), sponsorships, hyperlinks, and websites.

Ad Feature

The internet was conceptualized as having more ad features than broadcast or print media because the medium itself was more complex than traditional media. The IAM provides a comprehensive list of two subjective ad features, structures based on consumer responses (e.g., "attitude towards the website" and "interest"), and objective ad features (e.g., color, size, or typeface) across print, broadcast, and the internet. The IAM suggests that both objective and subjective ad features would have an impact on consumer responses and would interact with users' motives as well. In addition, interactivity was seen as the most salient ad feature made possible by the internet, and it would allow users to be involved in the persuasion process by changing the structural elements.

Methodology

Now that the basic components of the IAM have been reviewed, the next step was to conduct a search of the literature to collect scholarly articles that cite the IAM. This was accomplished with a literature search on Google Scholar with the aim to collect peer-reviewed literature citing the IAM. Compared to other databases, Google Scholar not only has relatively accurate citation counts, but also covers a larger collection of conference proceedings and international journals (Meho & Yang, 2007). A total of 385 citing articles were found, at the writing of this chapter, using a "cited-by" search in Google Scholar, and the citation details (i.e., author, publication, title, and year) were exported using Zotero for further content analysis.

Of the 385 articles identified by a Google Scholar search, 243 were scholarly journal articles (63.1%), 71 were theses or dissertations (18.4%), 39 were book chapters or sections in books (10.1%), and 32 were conference proceedings (8.3%). We report results from all sources citing the IAM, as presented; however, several sources were not read for this analysis because they were written in languages other than English.

A codebook was then developed for a content analysis of all 385 cited articles. There were five main coding categories, adapted from Kim et al. (2014, p. 1): 1) basic information (title, item type, publication, year, author, university, and locale); 2) methodology (research approach, reasoning, method type, method, theory presence, and theory); 3) data collection (sampled population, unit of analysis, data collection method, big data, and technology); 4) research details (independent variables, dependent variables, phenomenon, topic area, media effect type, ad format examined, and social media examined); and 5) IAM contribution (IAM use, IAM citing aspect, IAM citing detail, implications of broader research, and implications of IAM).

Two graduate students were the coders. Inter-coder reliabilities were taken at the beginning and ending of the content analysis, and an overall intercoder reliability of .788 (Scott's pi) was achieved.

Results

IAM Citation Trends

As shown in Figure 1.1, the past five years have seen an increase in citations of the IAM, particularly between 2011 and 2014, during which more than 160 articles

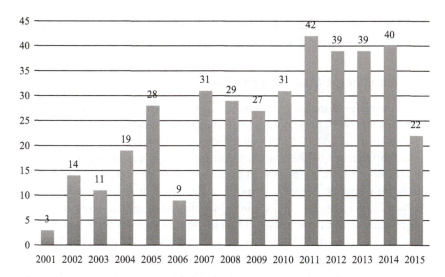

FIGURE 1.1   Number of Journal Articles Citing the IAM Since 2000 (Total *N*=385)

TABLE 1.1 List of Journals that Frequently Referenced the IAM

Publication	No. Of Citing Articles
Journal of Interactive Advertising	23
Journal of Advertising	9
International Journal of Advertising	9
Int. Journal of Internet Marketing and Advertising	5
Journal of Marketing Communications	3
Advances in Consumer Research	3
Journal of Current Issues & Research in Advertising	3

were published citing the IAM. The number of citing articles appears to peak in 2011 (42 articles).

Three journals that contributed the most in terms of the number of published citing articles include *Journal of Interactive Advertising* (23 articles), *Journal of Advertising* (9 articles), and *International Journal of Advertising* (9 articles). In addition, the IAM appeared three or more times in the following advertising journals: *International Journal of Internet Marketing and Advertising* (5 articles), *Journal of Marketing Communications* (3 articles), *Advances in Consumer Research* (3 articles), and *Journal of Current Issues and Research in Advertising* (3 articles).

In terms of international impact, first authors affiliated with non-U.S. institutions contributed to more than 65% of the 372 articles linked to a known university. International scholars represent 75 countries and regions, among which scholars from Spain, South Korea, Germany, China, and Taiwan authored more than 100 citing articles combined. In addition, more than 50 journal articles citing the IAM were written in languages other than English.

Evaluation of the IAM's Contribution

To accurately evaluate the contribution of the IAM, the content analysis examined the extent to which the articles referenced the IAM (IAM use), how other scholars used the IAM (IAM citing aspects), and what specific topics were discussed in reference to the IAM (IAM citing detail). Results showed that over 35 percent of all citing articles used the IAM to provide evidence to support the discussion of two main aspects: hypothesis development and/or research results. About 12 articles (4.3%) applied the IAM as a theoretical framework to develop a hypothesis or test prepositions and make predictions from the original article (Rodgers & Thorson, 2000). For example, the study by Burns (2006) looked at how audience attitudes varied by six different digital ad formats, which was supported by a major implication of the IAM regarding the variation of processing outcomes of different ad formats. The rest of the articles (60.6%) briefly mentioned or referenced the IAM to inform the background or discussion of internet advertising.

Most Cited Aspects of the IAM

The original IAM model proposed two ways of looking at the interactive processing of online ads: consumer-controlled aspects or advertiser-controlled aspects. The results from the content analysis suggest that about 35.3 percent of citing articles focused on consumer-controlled aspects, while 25.2 percent focused on advertiser-controlled aspects of online ads. The remainder of the articles did not have a clear emphasis on either consumer- or advertiser-controlled aspects.

Several citing aspects emerged as themes that were frequently referenced by the articles: internet motives and modes (30.3%), ad formats and ad features (23.0%), consumer responses and outcomes (21.1%), and interactivity (9.6%).

Internet Modes and Motives

The aspect of the IAM that has received the most scholarly attention relates to the functional aspects presented by the model, i.e., internet motives and modes. Among the 384 citing articles, "mode" was mentioned in 123 articles and "motive" was mentioned in 68 articles.

As discussed, motive and mode are two concepts dealing with "drive" and "goal-directedness" of web users' surfing behavior, respectively, both of which can influence the information processing of advertising stimuli. Rodgers (2002) examined the moderating role of internet motives on processing of banner ads when there was a match of ad appeal and individuals' motive. The same study also

TABLE 1.2 Primary Aspects of the Interactive Advertising Model

Primary Aspects of the IAM	Count of Adjusted IAM Citing Details	Percentage of Adjusted IAM Citing Details
Internet motive	61	23.37%
Consumer responses/outcomes (forget the ad, purchase the product, etc.)	55	21.07%
Ad formats	41	15.71%
Model	29	11.11%
Interactivity	25	9.58%
Ad features	19	7.28%
Mode	18	6.90%
Cognitive tools (attention, memory, attitude, etc.)	7	2.68%
Ad type	6	2.30%
Grand Total	**261**	**100.00%**

provided a review of the original concept of motive to complement the IAM and also suggested the necessity of looking at motives and modes conjointly to account for individual variation.

Following this study, scholars started to research how motives can impact consumer behavior from various aspects upon receiving an advertising stimulus. For example, Yang (2006) examined how information versus entertainment motive can moderate search patterns of product information; Zanjani, Diamond, & Chan (2011) evaluated ad recall of congruent e-magazines by information seekers versus surfers. While the classification of the originally proposed four basic motives proved to be valid, a cross-cultural study suggested internet motives differed by country (Rodgers, Jin, Rettie, Alpert, & Yoon, 2005).

Other studies looked at mode, or the goal-directedness of the internet users. The IAM suggested that users with a higher level of goal-directedness would be more defensive against online advertising. Hupfer and Grey (2005) found that highly goal-directed individuals perceived banner ads with a sample offer as a distraction, while the same incentive generated positive attitudes from experiential users. Other studies incorporated the IAM to examine some negative "side effects" of internet advertising, such as banner blindness, advertising avoidance (Duff & Faber, 2011), and advertising clutter (Ha & McCann, 2008). Likewise, goal-orientated users were found to be more responsive to website design elements and customized features (Kabadayi & Gupta, 2011).

Consumer Responses to Exposure of Different Ad Formats

The IAM provided a framework for understanding ad processing, which made it easier for researchers to compare consumer responses to different formats of digital advertising. Among different ad formats, banners (15.8%) and websites (24.8%)

received the most extensive examination from scholars that cite the IAM. Attitudes toward a specific ad format were not only found to significantly influence attitudes toward the ad (Burns & Lutz, 2006), but also could implicitly impact attitudes toward the advertised brands due to the intrusive nature of some ad formats, such as pop-ups (Madhavaram & Appan, 2010). General attitudes toward online advertising were also found to influence behavioral intentions toward brands (Lee & Miller, 2006). More studies evaluated antecedents and consequences of processing online ads of different formats: social factors (Zeng, Huang, & Dou, 2009), persuasion knowledge (Tutaj & van Reijmersdal, 2012), and advertising device or medium (Tutaj & van Reijmersdal, 2012) played a significant role in influencing reactions to different advertising formats. In addition to affective outcomes, internet advertising credibility (Choi & Rifon, 2002) was also investigated.

Regarding types of media effects, the results of the content analysis showed that approximately 86.1 percent of citing articles ($N = 251$) evaluated one or more aspects of cognitive, affective, and behavioral effects to ad exposure. Attitudes toward ads, attitudes toward a specific ad format or ad medium, and attitudes toward brands were the most common affective measures examined in articles that cited the IAM (21.1%, $N = 251$); ad recall, recognition, and level of information processing were among the measures of cognitive effects examined (7.1%, $N = 251$); purchase intention and intent to revisit the websites were examined frequently for behavioral aspects of ad effects (17.8%, $N = 251$).

New Ad Formats and Promotional Techniques

Some recent studies have examined several of the newer trends in digital advertising to better understand the underlying mechanism of ad processing, such as the investigation of brand recall of in-game advertising (Siemens, Smith, & Fisher, 2015), attitudes toward branded flash mob video ads (Grant, Botha, & Kietzmann, 2015), and psychological effects of ad-video congruency on YouTube (Kononova & Yuan, 2015). Interactive television advertising was also examined from cognitive, affective, and behavioral aspects (Benning & Ang, 2002; Levy & Nebenzahl, 2007; Aymerich-Franch, Delgado, Reina, & Prado, 2010; Levy, 2010).

For new ad formats made possible by new technologies, social media advertising and mobile advertising were two emerging trends due to the widespread use of smartphones. Advertising on Facebook, YouTube, and Twitter received the most extensive scholarly attention.

While most citing articles examined the effects of exposure to online ads, an increasing number of recent studies have gone beyond the traditional definition of "advertising" and extended implications from the 2000 IAM to examine other interactive promotional techniques. For instance, approximately 10 percent of all citing articles that focused on media effects ($N = 202$) involved evaluation of interactive applications. These studies examined both online and offline promotional techniques, such as an online product tour or demo (Gao, 2011;

Park, Park, & Rhee, 2013), public display applications (Alt, Schneegass, Girgis, & Schmidt, 2013), digital menu boards (Peters, 2011), and humanlike navigation (Yang, 2006). It should also be noted that the majority of the research in this stream came from outside the advertising discipline.

Evaluation of Interactivity and Other Ad Features and Technologies

Rodgers and Thorson (2000) argued that interactivity was a unique feature of internet advertising that added complexities beyond what traditional advertising experiences account for when examining processing of online ads, and that subjective and objective interactivity should both be investigated thoroughly.

With the progress of web technologies over the years, there has been a call for a distinction of users' perception of interactivity and what constitutes interactive features. Tremayne (2005) argued that functional aspects and perceptual aspects of interactivity should be examined independently, and that the users' role, rather than technological manipulation, should be emphasized in terms of cognitive processing patterns and individual traits related to interactivity. Wu (2005) found that perceived interactivity mediated the role of actual interactivity on influencing attitudes toward the websites. Broekhuizen and Hoffmann (2012) found perceived interactivity influenced low-skilled individuals more prominently in terms of information processing quality, despite the fact that high-skilled users were more involved with interactivity features on websites (Rodgers & Thorson, 2000). Gender (McMahan, Hovland, & McMillan, 2009) and need for cognition (Sicilia, Ruiz, & Munuera, 2005) were also found to impact perceived interactivity. Animation is another ad feature that has received a lot of attention in articles citing the IAM, especially when animated banner ads were first popular. Scholars have looked at how animation speed (Sundar & Kalyanaraman, 2004) can positively impact recall and attention, as well as potential positive attitudinal outcomes resulting from animation (Yoo, Kim, & Stout, 2004).

Discussion

The purpose of the chapter was to assess the impact of the Interactive Advertising Model (IAM) on the literature by examining scholarly articles that cited the model over a 15-year period (2000 to 2015) with the goal to draw on results to update the model and improve the model's utility. Citing articles were identified with a Google Scholar search, yielding 385 articles at the writing of this chapter. A content analysis was undertaken to understand who is citing the IAM, what aspects of the IAM are being cited, and what potential criticisms or gaps are apparent in the IAM.

The results of the content analysis show that the IAM has been widely cited by scholars as a conceptual framework to understand web users' information processing of online advertising. Advertising researchers were the primary citers of the IAM, but researchers from disciplines other than advertising (e.g., marketing, consumer behavior, information technology, etc.) have also cited the IAM in their research. Although advertising journals were the primary outlets for articles that cited the IAM, peer-reviewed publications in marketing, business and management, psychology, and information technology have also published articles that referenced the IAM. The IAM received broad international citation from scholars overseas, and there were quite a number of articles citing the IAM that were written in languages other than English.

The IAM presents a number of components, but the most cited component was the consumer-controlled aspects of the model, particularly related to internet motives/modes (i.e., functionalist school of thought) and, to some extent, ad formats/features (i.e., structural school of thought). Consumer responses (i.e., information processing school of thought) were examined to a lesser degree, and interactivity aspects of the model were the least cited component of the IAM. Although most of the research that cited the IAM cited it "in passing," a growing number of articles appear to use the IAM to develop or test theory, or to explain research results. Several "themes" arose in our analysis that deserve further discussion.

Mixed Motives

First, the analysis revealed that some scholars disagreed with the classification of four internet motives, arguing that the IAM failed to include phenomena like "mixed motives." For example, some argued that "seeking information" can be a "fun" experience for some users (e.g., Huang, 2003) or that an individual who starts off seeking information may stop to shop after seeing an ad related to the information being sought.

Of course, internet motives were initially proposed by the IAM to deal with how a specific type of internal drive, or reason, for surfing the internet can impact the integrative processing of online ads. Motives are neither the consumer evaluation of the activity or ads (e.g., "fun experience") or the appeals or purposes associated with an ad (e.g., using humor to promote a product). The IAM, instead, was concerned with the motivated state containing energy and direction (Deci & Ryan, 1985) that drives users to switch on the computer and surf the web. So by identifying basic motives, we can better predict web-related attitudes and other consumer responses. In other words, the basic classification of internet motives does not intend to isolate nor simplify the dynamic process of users' encounters with ads, but serves to provide predictions of differential processing patterns that can lead to different consumer responses.

Moreover, what scholars in our analysis seemed to be interested in learning was how to interpret motives when people had several goals or purposes in mind during or before an internet activity. Based on the foregoing discussion, it is perhaps better to conceptualize this phenomenon as "multiple agenda" rather than mixed motives, as a motive deals with the primary motivation to surf the internet at the specific moment instead of a careful deliberation about why to surf. This was part of the reason why "motive-switching" was included in the IAM to better reflect the process. In this sense, motive-switching was meant to capture the dynamic and interactive process that occurs between consumers and advertisers in an online environment (for a new interactive response model specific to social media, see Chapter 28).

Fortunately, several of our authors expound upon this idea. For example, drawing on reversal theory, Chapter 8 describes metamotivational states that range from telic (serious-minded) to paratelic (playfulness) to explain how complex consumer behaviors fluctuate in digital environments. Chapter 12 elaborates on the relationship between motivations and brand-related activities and then illustrates how this relationship works by sharing the results of a very interesting empirical study. Chapter 15 focuses on consumers who are motivated to create content about products and brands using three characteristics (mavenism, connectivity, and persuasiveness) and five types of intrinsic motivations. They present the results of an empirical study using 2,495 respondents on SNSs and 100 brands to illustrate how brand-related content creation is the consequence of various factors working in concert, painting a much more complex picture than originally proffered by the IAM.

Control of the Online Environment

Second, our analysis revealed that more research citing the IAM has focused on the consumer-controlled (versus the advertiser-controlled) aspects of the IAM. Perhaps this is because internet users were once suggested as the "control center," as they were able to more easily avoid internet advertising compared to blocking traditional mass advertising on TV, radio, or print media. However, new technologies have enabled advertisers to intrude into consumers' online territory by using contextual targeting and geo-targeting to place ads according to users' interests, preferences, and purchase history. Additionally, new technologies can exert new pressures on online audiences to ensure the delivery of ads, such as inserting multiple forced viewing ads inside one episode of a TV show. Additionally, and as shown in Chapter 2 and the subsequent chapters of this book, new technologies have added extra complexities to the advertising delivery process, which may significantly influence the processing of digital advertising (and maybe even change the very meaning of what constitutes a "digital ad").

Several authors in our review brought up an excellent point: the original IAM did not account for social media. That is true because social media—in their current form—did not exist when the IAM was first published. The closest things we had to social media in 2000 were online discussion boards and chat rooms, though social networking services were beginning to surface, such as classmates.com, which helped people find former school classmates (Digital Trends Staff, 2016). To fill this gap, Chapter 16 offers a systematic review of best uses of social media for persuasive brand-related communication, and Chapter 21 explores the main aspects of advertising effectiveness in an SNS setting and provides a theoretical framework for understanding ad effects in SNSs as well as other digital contexts. As shown in Chapter 12, SNSs allow brands to interact with consumers, and this interaction is considered beneficial to brands. Some of the by-products of this interaction include strengthening the brand's online visibility, enhancing brand equity, and ultimately leading to better brand performance.

New Measures of Advertising Effectiveness

Third, the content analysis revealed reliance on traditional advertising effectiveness measures with a call for new measures that were unique to digital spaces. For instance, Russell (2009) argued that there should be more creativity of metrics to adapt to the increasingly complex environment of digital ads. While most traditional measures in advertising may be valid for measuring psychological processes of web advertising such as memory, recall, and attention (Rodgers & Thorson, 2000), industry measures such as click-through rates (CTRs) could provide unexpected results perhaps taken for granted in the traditional realm. For example, design characteristics of banner ads like size, color, and message length were found to positively impact CTRs, while animation did not have a significant effect on CTR (Robinson, Wysocka, & Hand, 2007; Khalifa, 2014). Chapter 22 provides a new way to measure efficiency of digital advertising that incorporates a broader set of metrics, including consumer empowerment, and proposes an efficiency model that captures inputs and outputs that are relevant to digital advertising campaigns. Chapter 19 outlines measures related to physiological response and behaviors that are highly scalable due to internet-based frameworks and computer vision technology.

Additionally, as Chapter 8 argues, most measures available today are focused on positive performance with little attention devoted to understanding what may harm performance measures. Chapter 14 applies an approach/avoid framework to define ad avoidance and investigates antecedents to avoidance. A number of our authors discuss the effectiveness of in-game and video advertising; for example, Chapter 18 provides an introduction to in-game advertising, outlines its benefits and drawbacks, and highlights what may constitute "effective" in-game advertising. The authors then provide the results of a case study to illustrate the impact that interactivity (defined in terms of in-game brand placements) can have on ad effectiveness. Several of our chapters on in-game advertising or video advertising are brief "think pieces" that present some of the most pertinent factors being explored. For example, Chapter 25 examines immersion and argues that the vague use of the term has resulted in findings that do not account for a nonlinear relationship or one that is moderated by ad content. Chapter 26 is on virtual direct experience (VDE) in video games, and Chapter 27 outlines some common types of in-game ads and reviews video game advertising research that is sure to spark new research ideas for those interested in advancing the gaming and advertising literature.

As Chapter 20 notes, much of the reported measures on digital advertising have been based on U.S. samples, yet digital advertising has become increasingly important for brands globally. Thus, Chapter 20 argues that consumers from different countries may have different consideration sets and executional factors related to digital advertising, which researchers must account for. Likewise, a lot has been written and researched on electronic word-of-mouth (eWOM) but, as Chapter 24 points out, few studies have examined eWOM in an international context. The author goes on to demonstrate how eWOM research from a cross-cultural perspective is necessary since different countries may have different cultural values that can have varied effects on eWOM outcomes. With more than 3.2 billion people online searching for health information, there is enormous opportunity to explore the role of advertising in this unique and highly important context. Chapters 11 and 23 are devoted to doing just that.

New Ways to Spread Information

Fourth, and finally, when the IAM was introduced more than 15 years ago, advertising was a much more clearly defined process of persuading people to pay for branded products using professionally designed messages and paying to have the messages placed in a variety of media, like television, radio, or newspapers. To put this into perspective, the model was designed in a world without Facebook, Google, LinkedIn, Snapchat, Pinterest, or Twitter. There was email, and one could forward messages via email. There was, however, "interactivity," meaning consumers could go to brand websites and make comments or participate in games, etc. So this was truly one of the earliest stages of advertising in which it was easy for a consumer to provide feedback to marketers about their messages. Of course, prior to the birth of the interactive world, one could call or write marketers or even write comments that would appear in news media about marketers and their messages, but the effort and time required for this was great, and few consumers bothered with it.

But once advertising messages became common via the internet, there came to be lots of ways for consumers to respond to them. This was the Web 1.0 technology world into which the IAM was proffered. Ads, however, no longer need paid media to be "spread." There are now thousands of ways ads can reach people, and there are thousands of ways people can "use" ads. Targeting is presumed to enhance the opportunity for "spread" of brand-related content, but as Chapter 17 illustrates, targeting is a double-edged sword, as consumers can sometimes see it as an invasion of privacy. Chapter 2 presents a new model—the Network Advertising Model, or NAM—that builds on the IAM and uses the results reported in Chapter 1. The idea of "spreadability" is a central feature of NAM. As argued in

Chapter 2, the IAM can be extended into Web 2.0 and even Web 3.0 technologies by taking the findings of Chapter 1 as well as other factors into consideration.

Conclusion

The Interactive Advertising Model (IAM) (Rodgers & Thorson, 2000) has been widely referenced by scholars from various disciplines around the world. The IAM offers an integrated way to evaluate advertising effects from both consumer-controlled and advertiser-controlled viewpoints; however, despite the seeming utility of the model, our analysis revealed several shortcomings that need to be addressed by future scholars if the model is to be kept current. While the IAM's initial purpose was to serve as a general model to examine information processing of ad exposures online, the implications of the results of this review also shed light on research related to interactivity-related phenomena outside the scope of advertising. Several themes with regard to the model's use were identified, while a number of challenges for using the model also emerged among the citing articles. While this is by no means an exhaustive review, this examination of and reflection on the IAM after 15+ years supports an important notion proposed by Rodgers and Thorson in 2000: that methodologies and theories applied to traditional advertising can be adapted to interactive advertising, regardless of changes in advertising technologies, as long as the unique characteristics of users and ads are taken into consideration.

References

Alt, F., Schneegass, S., Girgis, M., & Schmidt, A. (2013). Cognitive effects of interactive public display applications. In *Proceedings of the 2nd ACM International Symposium on Pervasive Displays* (pp. 13–18). ACM.

Aymerich-Franch, L., Delgado Reina, M., & Prado, E. (2010). Actitud y motivación hacia la publicidad interactiva en televisión: Influencia de la complejidad de la aplicación y del tip de incentivo. *Questiones publicitarias*, *1*(15), 1–18.

Benning, P. E., & Ang, L. (2002). Interactive advertising: The development of a model for interactive television. In *ANZMAC 2002 Conference Proceedings*.

Broekhuizen, T., & Hoffmann, A. (2012). Interactivity perceptions and online newspaper preference. *Journal of Interactive Advertising*, *12*(2), 29–43. doi: 10.1080/15252019. 2015.1021432.

Burns, K., & Lutz, R. (2006). The function of format: Consumer responses to six online advertising formats. *Journal of Advertising*, *35*(1), 53–63. doi: 10.2753/joa0091–3367350104.

Choi, S., & Rifon, N. (2002). Antecedents and consequences of web advertising credibility. *Journal of Interactive Advertising*, *3*(1), 12–24. doi: 10.1080/15252019.2002.10722064.

Deci, E. L., & Ryan, R. M. (1985). The general causality orientations scale: Self-determination in personality. *Journal of Research in Personality*, *19*(2), 109–134. doi: 10.1016/0092–6566(85)90023–6.

Digital Trends Staff. (2016, May 14). The history of social networking. *Digital Trends*. Retrieved from http://www.digitaltrends.com/features/the-history-of-social-networking.

Duff, B., & Faber, R. (2011). Missing the mark. *Journal of Advertising, 40*(2), 51–62. doi: 10.2753/joa0091–3367400204.

Gao, Y. (2011). An experimental study of the effects of interactivity and humor in e-commerce. *Review of Business Information Systems (RBIS), 15*(1), 9–14.

Grant, P., Botha, E., & Kietzmann, J. (2015). Branded flash mobs: Moving toward a deeper understanding of consumers' responses to video advertising. *Journal of Interactive Advertising, 15*(1), 28–42. doi: 10.1080/15252019.2015.1013229.

Ha, L., & McCann, K. (2008). An integrated model of advertising clutter in offline and online media. *International Journal of Advertising, 27*(4), 569–592. doi: 10.2501/S0265048708080153.

Huang, M. H. (2003). Designing website attributes to induce experiential encounters. *Computers in Human Behavior, 19*(4), 425–442. doi: 10.1016/S0747-5632(02)00080-8.

Hupfer, M. E., & Grey, A. (2005). Getting something for nothing: The impact of a sample offer and user mode on banner ad response. *Journal of Interactive Advertising, 6*(1), 149–164.

Kabadayi, S., & Gupta, R. (2011). Managing motives and design to influence web site revisits. *Journal of Research in Interactive Marketing, 5*(2/3), 153–169. doi: 10.1108/17505931111187785.

Khalifa, A. (2014). Measuring the effectiveness of online advertising: The Tunisian context. *International Journal of Management Excellence, 3*(1), 354. doi: 10.17722/ijme.v3i1.139.

Kim, K., Hayes, J. L., Avant, J. A., & Reid, L. N. (2014). Trends in advertising research: A longitudinal analysis of leading advertising, marketing, and communication journals, 1980 to 2010. *Journal of Advertising, 43*(3), 296–316.

Kononova, A., & Yuan, S. (2015). Double-dipping effect? How combining YouTube environmental PSAs with thematically congruent advertisements in different formats affects memory and attitudes. *Journal of Interactive Advertising, 15*(1), 2–15. doi: 10.1080/15252019.2015.1009524.

Lee, K., & Miller, K. (2006). Internet users' attitude and behavioural intention on ebranding. *International Journal of Internet Marketing and Advertising, 3*(4), 335–354. doi: 10.1504/ijima.2006.012687.

Levy, S. (2010). ITV viewers' attitudes towards iTV advertising and their influence on interactive behavior. *Innovative Marketing, 6*(2), 82–90.

Levy, S., & Nebenzahl, I. D. (2007). The influence of product involvement on consumers' interactive processes in interactive television. *Marketing Letters, 19*(1), 65–77.

Madhavaram, S., & Appan, R. (2010). The potential implications of web-based marketing communications for consumers' implicit and explicit brand attitudes: A call for research. *Psychology & Marketing, 27*(2), 186–202. doi: 10.1002/mar.20326.

McMahan, C., Hovland, R., & McMillan, S. (2009). Online marketing communications: Exploring online consumer behavior by examining gender differences and interactivity within internet advertising. *Journal of Interactive Advertising, 10*(1), 61–76. doi: 10.1080/15252019.2009.10722163.

Meho, L. I., & Yang, K. (2007). Impact of data sources on citation counts and rankings of LIS faculty: Web of Science versus Scopus and Google Scholar. *Journal of the American Society for Information Science and Technology, 58*(13), 2105–2125.

Park, J., Park, W., & Rhee, C. (2013). Perceived vividness and consumers' perception in e-commercial websites. In *Proceeding of Thirty Fourth International Conference on Information Systems*.

Peters, A. N. (2011). The role of dynamic digital menu boards on consumer decision-making and healthy eating (Order No. 1505962). Available from ABI/INFORM Complete; ProQuest Dissertations & Theses A&I; ProQuest Dissertations & Theses Global. (920300336). Retrieved from http://search.proquest.com/docview/920300336?accountid=14576.

Robinson, H., Wysocka, A., & Hand, C. (2007). Internet advertising effectiveness: The effect of design on click-through rates for banner ads. *International Journal of Advertising, 26*(4), 527–541. doi: 10.1080/02650487.2007.11073031.

Rodgers, S. (2002). The interactive advertising model tested: The role of motives in ad processing. *Journal of Interactive Advertising, 2*(2), 22–33. doi: 10.1080/15252019.2002.10722059.

Rodgers, S., Jin, Y., Rettie, R., Alpert, F., & Yoon, D. (2005). Internet motives of users in the United States, United Kingdom, Australia, and Korea: A cross-cultural replication of the WMI. *Journal of Interactive Advertising, 6*(1), 79–89. doi: 10.1080/15252019.2005.10722108.

Rodgers, S., & Sheldon, K. M. (2002). An improved way to characterize internet users. *Journal of Advertising Research, 42*(5), 85–94.

Rodgers, S., & Thorson, E. (2000). The interactive advertising model: How people perceive and process interactive ads. *Journal of Interactive Advertising, 1*(1), 42–61.

Russell, M. G. (2009). A call for creativity in new metrics for liquid media. *Journal of Interactive Advertising, 9*(2), 44–61. doi: 10.1080/15252019.2009.10722155.

Sicilia, M., Ruiz, S., & Munuera, J. (2005). Effects of interactivity in a web site: The moderating effect of need for cognition. *Journal of Advertising, 34*(3), 31–44. doi: 10.1080/00913367.2005.10639202.

Siemens, J., Smith, S., & Fisher, D. (2015). Investigating the effects of active control on brand recall within in-game advertising. *Journal of Interactive Advertising, 15*(1), 43–53. doi: 10.1080/15252019.2015.1021432.

Sundar, S. S., & Kalyanaraman, S. (2004). Arousal, memory, and impression-formation effects of animation speed in web advertising. *Journal of Advertising, 33*(1), 7–17. doi: 10.1080/00913367.2004.10639152.

Thorson, E. (1996). Advertising. In M. B. Salwen & D. W. Stacks (Eds.), *An integrated approach to communication theory and research* (pp. 211–230). Hillsdale, NJ: Lawrence Erlbaum.

Tremayne, M. (2005). Lessons learned from experiments with interactivity on the web. *Journal of Interactive Advertising, 5*(2), 40–46.

Tutaj, K., & van Reijmersdal, E. (2012). Effects of online advertising format and persuasion knowledge on audience reactions. *Journal of Marketing Communications, 18*(1), 5–18. doi: 10.1080/13527266.2011.620765.

Wu, G. (2005). The mediating role of perceived interactivity in the effect of actual interactivity on attitude toward the website. *Journal of Interactive Advertising, 5*(2), 29–39. doi: 10.1080/15252019.2005.10722099.

Yang, K. C. (2006). The influence of humanlike navigation interface on users' responses to Internet advertising. *Telematics and Informatics, 23*(1), 38–55.

Yoo, C. Y., Kim, K., & Stout, P. A. (2004). Assessing the effects of animation in online banner advertising: Hierarchy of effects model. *Journal of Interactive Advertising, 4*(2), 49–60. doi: 10.1080/15252019.2004.10722087.

Zanjani, S. H., Diamond, W. D., & Chan, K. (2011). Does ad-context congruity help surfers and information seekers remember ads in cluttered e-magazines? *Journal of Advertising, 40*(4), 67–84. doi: 10.2753/JOA0091–3367400405.

Zeng, F., Huang, L., & Dou, W. (2009). Social factors in user perceptions and responses to advertising in online social networking communities. *Journal of Interactive Advertising, 10*(1), 1–13. doi: 10.1080/15252019.2009.1072215.

2

NETWORK ADVERTISING MODEL (NAM)

Esther Thorson and Shelly Rodgers

Introduction and Background

Advertising today exists in a multiple channel (or "source"), multiple media, multiple device interactive communication network—a massively interconnected set of nodes and a variety of "connections" among those nodes. This reality implies major changes in how advertising can influence people to buy brands (or vote for a candidate, or think more highly of a corporation, or adopt better health habits). Before the creation and expansion of the digital communication network, advertisers often turned to theories of "integrated marketing communication" (IMC), where a number of media (e.g., radio, TV, newspapers) were combined to bring integrated messages about a brand to people, thus reaching customers with different frequencies, at different times, and under different circumstances. IMC carried with it the assumption that paid media (advertising) would integrate with unpaid ways of reaching people, like public relations tools, e.g., brands being featured in news stories, brands seen as sponsors of events, and brands being linked with games and contests (e.g., Schultz, Tannenbaum, & Lauterborn, 1993). An advertisement or PR event that led people to talk about the ad or the brand (word-of-mouth) was also considered to be one of the "voices" of the integrated effort (Thorson & Moore, 1996).

But in the mid-1990s the internet started to come of age, and as its structures and functions developed over the next 20 years, scholars came to realize that communication was moving toward being less "mass" and more "network" oriented. Because culture is mediated and enacted through communication, a networked culture came into dominance (Castells, 2000, p. 356).

The model introduced here—called the Network Advertising Model, or NAM—is quite different from the Interactive Advertising Model (IAM) (Rodgers & Thorson, 2000) as described in Chapter 1, although, in fact, the NAM subsumes significant components of the IAM. In the new model, we continue to use the word "advertising"—a decision motivated because we are maintaining the central idea of creatively and intentionally structured messages that would be called "ads" as opposed to messages that have different names and kinds of structures, e.g., tweets, shares, press releases, Facebook sites, events. Ads, however, no longer need paid media to be spread. There are now thousands of ways ads can reach people, and there are thousands of ways people can "use" ads and spread them into more nodes of the communication network, but now linked with the consumer's own unique "input" attached. That is, ads "spread" into the digital communication network are not the same as when they were initially constituted, if only because now some individual has "liked," "shared," or "posted" them so they arrive at the next node with that addition. Note that we refer to consumers "using ads," instead of "responding to ads." This is purposeful, meant to indicate the high degree to which consumers can control and influence what happens to ads as they spread throughout the network. Of course, consumers can be directly persuaded by ads (Thorson, 1996), but they can also turn them into memes, post them in any number of social media, email them, make fun of them, screen them out, or make their own "ads" (user-generated ads or sometimes "mash-ups" of ads).

The reason for the massive increase in what can be done with ads is due to what has been called "spreadability" (Jenkins, 2008; Jenkins, Ford, & Green, 2013). In a network characterized by spreadability, movement of messages continues to include what is traditionally known as "distribution," that is, the placement of messages into media sites that are consumed by people (e.g., old media like television and newspapers, but now also new media like Google searches or Facebook posts). And the internet itself involves many media. It includes online sites of old media (CNN Online), social media like Facebook and Twitter, as well as sites built by individuals (e.g., blogs) or corporations (e.g., brand sites). Many devices including laptop computers, tablets, smartphones, and smartwatches can access all of these sites. What this complex structure means is that there can be huge spin or spread of messages once they enter the network space. And messages that "look like ads" can enter the space from any source, not just via professional distribution. At almost any point of encounter with a message, people or organizations can curate, that is, decide what to do with the message—pass it along, critique it, mash it up into something else, recommend it, etc. And of course, people can still be "persuaded" by the message, as posited by the original IAM (Rodgers & Thorson, 2000). But let us review for a moment the historical context into which the IAM evolved.

When the IAM was published in 2000, only about 50 percent of Americans owned a smartphone; Google was three years old (founded 1998); there was no Facebook (founded 2004), no Twitter (founded 2006), no Instagram (founded 2010), and no Snapchat (founded 2012). Most digital advertising was located on websites that brands owned or on news websites. The major feature that digital ads shared was that people could interact with them (Coyle & Thorson, 2001). Indeed, it was the powerful feature of "interactivity" that led to the IAM's construction, and as seen in the pages of this book, interactivity remains a central concept to digital advertising as noted so persuasively by our chapter authors.

However, what was present in 2000 is what Castells (2000) refers to as an "electronic communication system characterized by its global reach, its integration of all communication media, and its potential interactivity" (p. 329). In 1999, the internet connected 63 million computer hosts, contained 3.6 million websites, and was used by 179 million people in more than 200 countries (Castells, 1996, p. 375). This was the "network" in its infancy. Along with the internet, the network brought integration of different communication platforms where written, oral, audio, and visual communication became part of the same system; now people could interact in a variety of ways (Castells, 1996). The internet was to completely change communication, and along with it, all communication industries: news, advertising, marketing, business, health, and politics. The internet created the concept of digitally networked communication, but the next 15 years would bring mass changes to how that network operated and the influence it had.

In 2000, certainly in terms of advertising expenditures, but also in terms of audience size, media culture was TV-dominated, meaning advertising operated in a mass communication system, where there was largely one-way flow of messages from producers to a mass audience. There had already occurred a proliferation of channels, such that people had lots of sources to choose from, but only when they went to the internet for content could they interact with sources and content immediately and fairly extensively (see Rodgers, Thorson, & Jin, 2009; Thorson & Rodgers, 2012). Therefore, when the IAM first appeared, it conceptualized even interactive advertising in a basically mass communication world, not as Castells (2000) puts it, a "networked world" (p. xxxix).

Figure 2.1 shows a simple diagram of advertising in a mass communication world. An advertiser created a message, media experts designed a combination of media channels to employ to distribute the message, and legacy media were

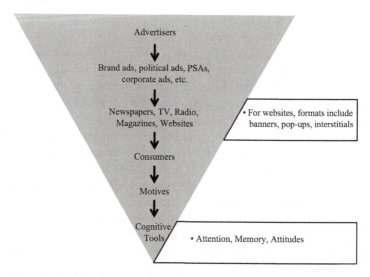

FIGURE 2.1   Advertising Processes in a Mass Communication System

paid for the time and space to run the ad. Payment for advertising's appearance in digital media varied. Working from a primarily nonlinear perspective, the IAM (see Figure 2 in Rodgers & Thorson, 2000) focused on digital media and posited that five categories of variables should be taken into account when the goal was to predict the efficacy of the ad. First, what motivations (information, entertainment, etc.) led the consumer to go to the internet in the first place (recall that the only way to access the internet was with a computer as there were no smartphones and no tablets)? The consumer possessed long theorized psychological processing modes (attention, memory, and attitudes) and encountered an ad designed by the advertiser. The ad could have different persuasive intentions (like promoting a corporation, selling a brand, or selling a political candidate), and it could be of the various structural types available to digital professionals at that time (e.g., banners, interstitials, pop-ups, or a brand website). Responses from the consumer might include the usual ones of processing the ad (remembering it, paying attention to it, liking it), but the big change was that the consumer could interact with the ad—click on it, explore the website it was located on, leave a message, or email the advertiser—and sometimes even make a purchase. Scholars have explored the attribute of interactivity in many and important ways, as exemplified in Chapter 1. At the same time, however, much advertising research continued to attend to the performance of advertising in legacy media and mostly assumed a mass communication process.

In the 15+ years since the IAM was published, mass communication has fast become over-shadowed by digital communication networks of great complexity and range. Figure 2.2 shows some of the processes involved in network-based advertising, where an n-dimensional graph is used to represent the communication networks of today (although this representation is vastly less extensive and populated than the real digital network of today). People receive input and provide output, which then becomes input to others carried by a host of digital sources, devices, and message types.

Let us think about a Macy's ad spreading through the digital communication network. It can appear in a newspaper, magazine, or on television, that is, non-digital devices, but then can be inserted into the digital network in all kinds of forms by consumers—email, blogs, tweets, Facebook posts, etc. It is likely to also appear on websites of the legacy media where advertisers place it—or the media may publish a QR Code so that consumers can scan a link with their smartphones, going from print to digital. The ad can appear as a tweet or a Facebook advertisement. It can be part of Macy's website. It can be in a smartphone app. Or it can be used by anyone as something they share with others, that they like or that they use as raw material for producing something creative of their own—a UGA ad, or part of a meme, or something they insert into a YouTube video or post in a blog.

Furthermore, the consumer who is exposed to any of these Macy's ads is him/herself broadly interconnected in the digital communication network. The person

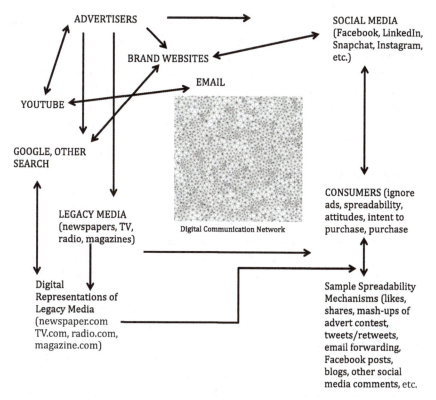

FIGURE 2.2 Advertising Processes in the Communication Network

may be a Macy's digital Fanclub member and may be connected to everyone else in the Fanclub, along with Macy's employees who create the content of that website. The person may follow many Twitter accounts and has many followers of his/her own, and thus is connected to all of those people, *plus* all of the followers of the people they are connected to. The person is likely to have a Facebook account where he/she is connected to hundreds of friends, colleagues, and family members, plus links with any other Facebook dwellers chosen. For example, he/she may have Liked a Macy's ad for athletic shoes and, as a result, now receives Macy's ads on his/her news feed. Or he/she may have Macy's ads follow him/her around through the internet because somewhere, sometime, he/she showed an interest in a product sold by Macy's and, thus, is being targeted with behaviorally targeted ads. Individuals may receive Macy's ads in their mailboxes or email accounts. Or they may have an ad forwarded to them by a friend—who actually received the ad from a friend who had received it from Macy's.

In a network communication system, the possible ways of linking with a piece of information—like "Macy's carries a brand of athletic shoes"—are almost endless. Furthermore, there are so many ways that a person can respond to each of those links—sharing, liking, going to Macy's website and purchasing, going to a retail Macy's store, and there, getting an in-store message on his/her cellphone. Of course, a person can—in spite of all this connectivity—still avoid the ad, (see the approach/avoid framework in Chapter 14), react negatively to the ad (see Chapter 7 on reactance theory), or block the ad and/or not even have it enter his/her conscious attention (see Chapter 10 by Lombard and Snyder-Duch and Chapter 17 by Shoenberger).

As a result of the network approach, there are both desirable and undesirable consequences, such as negative brand reviews and ad avoidance that digital advertising theories must account for. As Chapter 22 shows, a networked perspective also requires a very different, albeit complex metric or set of metrics, involving mindset metrics; consumer empowerment appears to be a crucial factor, along with identification of long-term performance outputs.

In short, we have attempted to represent the complexity of how advertising processes look in a digital community network in the diagram in Figure 2.2. We have not attempted to put all the players in the diagram because the diagram would quickly become unreadable. At the top of the diagram are advertisers who, as always, have messages they wish consumers to receive. Note the outgoing arrows, to YouTube, search engines (primarily Google), legacy media and their dot-com versions, the brand's own website, consumers' emails, and social media. Note that many of the arrows are bi-directional, representing interactivity, that is, two-way flow. Just as in the IAM (Rodgers & Thorson, 2000), consumers have many psychological or behavioral responses they can make to the ads, and of course, these will vary by how they encountered the ad in the digital network or whether they encountered it in legacy media. Also note that the consumer has many tools for spreading the ad (or news of their attitudes about the brand, or their shipping experience, or how much they like their new athletic shoes). They can like, share, create a mash-up, tweet or re-tweet, and so on. This means that for every single consumer, the opportunity to spread advertising content is massive. And everyone they share with has exactly the same opportunities. The number of possible contact nodes in a digital communication network is, therefore, potentially astronomical. Further, the content "spread" can be a plus for the advertiser (Likes) or they can be damaging (low star-ratings, bad consumer comments, boycotting and encouragement of others to do so).

So how does conceiving of advertising as operating in a digital communication network help us theorize about how digital advertising works? First, many of the chapters of this volume can be seen to fit closely into this conception (as noted in the discussion below). Second, the Network Advertising Model (NAM) has some important features that are critical for both understanding how advertising will operate in the future, and how it will have to adjust as the network continues to change in important ways. We explore these aspects next.

Articulating Aspects of the NAM

In spite of the massive complexity and extensiveness of the digital communication network, there are some important, common denominators about ad encounters and consumer uses of them. First, unlike in the pre-digital communication world, the advertiser has a lot less control over where its messages go. Indeed, once ad messages are released into the network, they can, as we have seen, go absolutely anyplace in the network—and the advertiser has little or no control over that activity. This means that development of network "listening processes" is critical. And those listening processes are often where "big data" come into relevance, e.g., tracking Tweet mentions of a brand through millions of Tweets, tracking movement of brand messages through millions of Facebook postings, and observing trending Tweets about topics of relevance to an advertising campaign (see Huh's Chapter 29). Listening to relevant messages travel and observing as they are transformed as they go allows the advertiser to get ahead of problems before the cost to the brand becomes damaging, and to measure how much added value is accruing to the advertising as a result of its travels and manifestations in the network.

Second, as two enormous companies, Google and Facebook have come to rule much of the digital communication network. However, the algorithms that are so influential in determining what and where information is spread are hugely challenging to advertisers. Because advertising is so important to the development of the Google/Facebook "duopoly" (Levy, 2015, n.p.), we look closely at recent statistics and behaviors concerning the two companies and what those statistics suggest for understanding advertising in the digital communication network.

First, we do this in the context of how money is being spent today for advertising and what projections look like for future spending. In 2015, in the U.S., $180 billion was spent on advertising: $73 billion on television, $24 billion on newspapers, and $67 billion on digital advertising. Of the digital $67 billion, $13 billion (19%) was spent on social media, and of that $13 billion, Facebook absorbed fully 45 percent of it (Statista, 2016). Indeed, in 2015 Google and Facebook together accounted for 75 percent of all digital advertising spending. Digital advertising spending is expected to overtake television in the next year or so, with accompanying large increases in the proportion that goes to social media. It is clear that to remain relevant to advertising, research must focus on digital advertising and its operation in the communication network, specifically as that network is dominated by Google and Facebook. What this means is that considerable attention must be paid to how advertising operates within the context of Google and Facebook algorithms for advertising venues, and their costs. For example, an advertiser can buy space for an ad on Facebook, either in people's news feeds or as a sponsored ad on the periphery of the feed. But Facebook has algorithms that determine what consumers will be exposed to with those ads, and that information is not shared with advertisers. Indeed, the nature of both Google search and Facebook posting algorithms is proprietary.

In June 2016, Facebook published a list of priorities for how it will post messages in news feeds. The posting algorithm will put top priority on the posts of consumers' friends and family. Only after those posts will come paid news and advertising posts. This suggests that Facebook has data that indicates people do not like getting a lot of news and advertising in their feeds, and when they do, they are probably lessening or even curtailing use of those feeds. So although Facebook makes money with more posting of stories and advertising, they nevertheless must operate as a "platform," i.e., an organization that serves a number of different customers, and must balance the desires of those customers against each other to maximize revenues (Sridhar, Mantrala, Naik, & Thorson, 2011). That is, Facebook must maintain and grow its 1.65 billion monthly active users (Facebook, 2016) by keeping them happy, even though their revenues derive from news organizations and advertisers who are vying to fill news feeds with their own postings.

Google similarly determines where advertisements and news stories go in the order of what comes up from a search. Advertisers can buy sponsored ads that link with search words and appear at the top of search content, but Google's algorithms determine to whom and where they appear in searches. Thus, for both Google- and Facebook-based advertising, there is limited control by advertisers over where their advertising goes and to whom. Furthermore, as noted, Google and Facebook consider detailed information collected about Google and Facebook users proprietary. Although some consumer information is shared with advertisers, both companies claim that maintaining the privacy of individuals who use their services is a fundamental priority (Google, 2016; Facebook, n.d.). Of course, many advertisers suggest that the privacy argument is just a cover for maintenance of full data control (Rutenberg, 2016).

Thus, when we think about the network of digital communication in which advertising must operate, we need to keep in mind—and do research on how—advertising is represented by these two very different companies (and, of course, search and social media companies in general, even though Google and Facebook are the most powerful). The Network Advertising Model (NAM) suggests that search and social media environments set up very different challenges for advertising and must be examined separately. For Google, the key variable appears to be "the intent of the consumer" that does the search (Cox Target Media, 2016). For example, when a person initiates a search, if an advertiser can suggest a brand that might fulfill that search needed at the time of the search, there is a greater likelihood of purchase, or at least the development of stronger purchase intent. For this type of situation, much of the "marketing funnel," or "consumer decision journey," of effects is missing. Usually the funnel consists of consumer processes like a build-up of brand awareness, development of a brand consideration set, evaluation of competing brands, and finally a brand choice and subsequent purchase. But under circumstances of detailed, personal targeting, stimulating desire for the product is skipped, and sometimes size of brand sets has already been reduced. At other times, a brand has already been chosen, so the only job for advertising is to provide price and place information. Given behavioral targeting methods available today, data about what the person has already been looking at can be used to determine at just what point he/she is in the decision-making funnel and deliver an ad appropriate to that of the decision-maker (see Chapter 6 by Sundar, Kim, & Gambino). Also, when searching for a product or a brand begins, the person is most likely operating cognitively rather than emotionally or impulsively. And ads designed to accommodate central processing of ad arguments (Petty & Cacioppo, 1986) and systematic processing (Chaiken, 1980) would seem most appropriate. Indeed, there is already a large existing literature on rational processing of ads that may be a particularly useful theoretical guide.

The situation is much different for advertising via social media. Because the primary objective for most Facebook users is a social one, all the variables of social norms, injunctive norms, and descriptive and subjective norms may be particularly important to understanding how the consumer processes the ad. When you Like a brand ad or Share it, you are not only expressing yourself, but you are deciding whether those in your network will approve of the product in general or the brand specifically. If the product is a designer handbag, will you be seen as a high status person of excellent taste, or a person who is superficial and selfish enough to spend $5000 on such a bag? In social networks, the kind of theorizing that Alhabash and his co-authors (Chapter 16) do would appear particularly important. Further, in this kind of environment, virality and word-of-mouth (WOM) may become particularly important (e.g., Wang & Rodgers, 2011). While on Facebook, it is easy to check with others about a brand—and just as easy to share with others that you are making or have made the purchase decision, so again the literature on eWOM becomes highly relevant. It should be noted that that "influencer marketing" (Adweek, 2016, n.p.) becomes much more important when social media are essential components of the advertising plan. As Chapter 20 by Taylor and Costello and Chapter 24 by Chu note, culture also plays an important role in this regard.

Of course, there is digital advertising that does not depend directly on Google and Facebook. Categories of such advertising include locations such as brand websites, news websites, and email, and types of ads like banners, sponsorships, interstitials and superstitials, pop-ups, and hyperlinks, among others (see Chapter 21 by Rejon-Guardia and Martinez-Lopez that does an excellent job detailing these and other types of digital advertising). As a result, there will continue to be a need to determine how efficacious and efficient these modes of advertising are—a subject that is undertaken in a number of our chapters, such as McDuff's Chapter 19 that looks at new ways of measuring digital advertising efficacy, and Pergelova's Chapter 22 that proposes a new way to think about digital advertising efficiency.

Another insight the NAM provides is that, in the digital communication network, the distinctions among paid, owned, and earned media become more fluid. Purchase of Google or Facebook ads is clearly "paid advertising," but once the content of those ads spreads into the network, being exposed to and influencing people beyond what was "paid for," it becomes "earned." By the same logic, the impact of a brand's website (owned media) can also become transformed as it spreads into the network. If advertising is mostly one-way communication between advertiser (i.e., message sender) and consumer (i.e., message receiver), mediated via a paid channel and designed to enhance attitude and purchase of a brand, then what is a re-tweeted ad? Is a user-generated ad (UGA), which is created by the consumer and not the advertiser, an advertisement? Is a banner that connects a brand with a social cause an advertisement? Is a company that specializes in designing Twitter and Facebook presences for a brand an advertising company or a public relations company? So much of what message designers and media planners/buyers do continues to look at the beginning of the process like they would advertising; however, as illustrated in Figure 2.2, as the messages spread throughout the network, they are transformed into other persuasive entities. Thus, perhaps theories of network advertising will need to be considered theories of networked messaging or networked persuasion.

Another result of moving to a digital network communication model of advertising is that it provides a framework for understanding how the processing of multiple channels or devices during the same sitting provides opportunities and challenges for advertisers. There is evidence (Nagy & Midha, 2014) that processing of television programs, including both entertainment and live programming like sports, political debates, and contests, is enhanced when people use social media and search engines while they watch live TV. If ads during the TV programs are commented on in social media, or relevant search activity is engaged in, it is more likely the ads will yield an impact. Indeed, in a related effort at creating theory, Chapter 12 looks at how entertainment programming itself can influence people to be interactive with the embedded ads and experience telepresence.

Another insight provided by conceptualizing advertising operating in a communication digital network is that it vastly increases the complexity and uncertainty for advertisers to engage in integrated marketing communication (IMC). First, of course, there are just so many more "voices" that can be employed. While some work has been done on such IMC topics as combining public relations and advertising tools (Rose & Miller, 1994; Duncan & Caywood, 1996), and with combining traditional media channels (e.g., advertising with print or radio advertising), there has been little examination of how digital strategies can best be combined with non-digital ones, or how digital strategies themselves are best combined to produce impact. The uncertainty in IMC work in the digital communication network is due to the fact that, as discussed, so much of what happens with an advertising campaign depends on what consumers *do* with the ad. Chapter 9 by Duff and Lutchyn articulates this nuance in terms of *inattention* toward advertising.

And where is mobile advertising in the terms of the network? Mobile advertising today can come via text messages, embedded in apps, or occur in social media or news sites. Further, mobile advertising can appear in smartphone searches. At a recent gathering of advertising professionals, it was discussed that how to deliver advertising on mobile platforms has not yet been solved. In early 2016, fully 80 percent of Facebook's advertising revenue came from mobile. In thinking about the impact of advertising in mobile, it is important to consider how the digital network, along with access to it via smartphones, has so completely changed communication. With additional access points comes additional clutter, which Ha in Chapter 5 argues is one of the key challenges affecting digital advertising spaces.

As Wellman and Rainie (2012) point out, before the mid-1990s, nearly all phones were place-bound. Today, 90 percent of Americans have a smartphone (Wellman & Rainie, 2012), and they are the key way that people participate in networked communication. At first, cell phones were mostly about talking, but between 2006 and 2011, texting went from being common for 31 percent to 59 percent of Americans. In 2012, a Pew study reported that American teens texted an average of 50 texts a day (Lenhart, 2012), and now that number is far greater. Thus, a very significant challenge to an overall networked theory of advertising will be an understanding of when and in what format people will accept advertising messages on their smartphones—and privacy is certainly part of the theorizing (see Chapter 17). Beyond that, which kind of mobile delivery will be the most efficient for what brands? As addressed in Chapter 11 by Royne et al., and Chapter 23 by Mackey and Liang, health and pharmaceutical advertising further complicate these and other issues presented here.

In short, digital network communication is a social science area that itself has much to offer the advertising field. The Network Advertising Model (NAM) articulated here is but a "baby step" toward thinking about the fundamental problems that advertising faces as an industry, and for guidance to scholars about how to think about the problem and what kinds of studies to engage in. The chapters in this book provide excellent progress toward understanding the role of theory as it relates to digital advertising. In the next chapter, we again try to place advertising into the larger societal changes that have led us to today's digital network.

References

Adweek. (2016). Topic: Influencer marketing. Retrieved from http://www.adweek.com/topic/influencer-marketing.

Castells, M. (2000). *The rise of the network society* (2nd ed.). Malden, MA: Blackwell Publishing.

Chaiken, S. (1980). Heuristic versus systematic information processing and the use of source versus message cues in persuasion. *Journal of Personality & Social Psychology, 39*(5), 752–766.

Cox Target Media. (2016, March 15). A day in the life of your customer: Understanding the new path to purchase. Retrieved from http://www.coxtarget.com/insights/a-day-in-the-life-of-your-customer-understanding-the-new-path-to-purchase/

Coyle, J., & Thorson, E. (2001). The effects of progressive levels of interactivity and vividness in web marketing sites. *Journal of Advertising, 30*(3), 65–77.

Duncan, T. R., & Caywood, C. L. (1996). The concept, process, and evolution of integrated marketing communications. In E. Thorson & J. Moore (Eds.), *Integrated communication: Synergy of persuasive voices* (pp. 13–34). Mahwah, NJ: Lawrence Erlbaum.

Facebook. (2016). Stats. Retrieved from http://newsroom.fb.com/company-info/

Facebook. (n.d.). How to keep your account secure. Retrieved from https://www.facebook.com/about/basics/how-to-keep-your-account-secure/how-youre-protected/

Google. (2016, June 28). Privacy & terms. Retrieved from https://www.google.com/policies/privacy/

Jenkins, H. (2008). *Convergence culture: Where old and new media collide*. New York, NY: New York University Press.

Jenkins, H., Ford, S., & Green, J. (2013). *Spreadable media: Creating value and meaning in a networked culture*. New York, NY: New York University Press.

Lenhart, A. (2012). Teens, smartphones and texting. *Pew Research Center: Internet, Science & Tech.* Retrieved from http://www.pewinternet.org/2012/03/19/teens-smartphones-texting/

Levy, A. (2015, April 17). In online ads, it's Google, Facebook and then who? Retrieved from http://www.cnbc.com/2015/04/17/after-google-and-facebook-the-fight-to-be-no-3.html.

Nagy, J., & Midha, A. (2014). The value of earned audiences: How social interactions amplify TV impact. *Journal of Advertising Research, 54*(4), 448–453.

Petty, R. E., & Cacioppo, J. T. (1986). The elaboration likelihood model of persuasion. *Advances in Experimental Psychology, 19*, 123–205.

Rodgers, S., & Thorson, E. (2000). The interactive advertising model: How people perceive and process interactive ads. *Journal of Interactive Advertising, 1*(1), 42–61.

Rodgers, S., Thorson, E., & Jin, Y. (2009). Social science theories of traditional and internet advertising. In D. W. Stacks & M. B. Salwen (Eds.), *An integrated approach to communication theory and research* (2nd ed., pp. 198–219). New York, NY: Routledge.

Rose, P. B., & Miller, D. A. (1994). Merging advertising and PR: Integrated marketing communications. *Journalism & Mass Communication Educator, 49*(2), 52.

Rutenberg, J. (2016, May 22). Facebook's troubling one-way mirror. Retrieved from http://www.nytimes.com/2016/05/23/business/facebooks-troubling-one-way-mirror.html?_r=0.

Schultz, D. E., Tannenbaum, S. I., & Lauterborn, R. F. (1993). *Integrated marketing communications: Putting it together and making it work*. Chicago, IL: NTC Business Books.

Sridhar, S., Mantrala, M. K., Naik, P. A., & Thorson, E. (2011). Dynamic marketing budgeting for platform firms: Theory, evidence, and application. *Journal of Marketing Research, 48*(6), 929–943.

Statista. (2016). Digital market outlook: Digital advertising. Retrieved from https://www.statista.com/outlook/216/109/digital-advertising/united-states#

Thorson, E. (1996). Advertising. In M. B. Salwen & D. W. Stacks (Eds.), *An integrated approach to communication theory and research* (pp. 211–230). Hillsdale, NJ: Lawrence Erlbaum.

Thorson, E., & Moore, J. (1996). *Integrated communication: Synergy of persuasive voices*. Mahwah, NJ: Lawrence Erlbaum Associates, Publishers.

Thorson, E., & Rodgers, S. (2012). A theory of advertising as a field. In S. Rodgers & E. Thorson (Eds.), *Advertising theory* (pp. 3–17). New York, NY: Routledge, Taylor & Francis Group.

Wang, Y., & Rodgers, S. (2011). Electronic word of mouth and consumer generated content: From concept to application. In M. S. Eastin, T. Daugherty, & N. M. Burns (Eds.), *Handbook of research on digital media and advertising: User generated content consumption* (pp. 212–231). Hershey, PA: Information Science Reference.

Wellman, B., & Rainie, L. (2012). *Networked: The new social operating system*. Cambridge, MA: The MIT Press.

3

TRENDS AND OPPORTUNITIES FOR DIGITAL ADVERTISING RESEARCH

A Content Analysis of *Advertising Age*, 2000–2015

Samuel M. Tham, Shelly Rodgers, and Esther Thorson

In this chapter, we map the digital trends within the advertising industry since the inception of Rodgers and Thorson's (2000) Interactive Advertising Model (IAM). The digital advertising landscape has evolved dramatically over the last decade and a half, both in terms of technology and infrastructure influences. To understand how these changes have influenced the development of digital advertising, we will examine the emergent and dominant interactive advertising trends from 2000 to 2015 juxtaposed with major technological milestones. As we have seen in recent years, the rise of social media and mobile advertising has greatly impacted the development and direction of digital advertising. By understanding the role of society and the evolution of technology, we can better understand how society is shaped by technology, and how technology is influenced by society.

The relationship of modern society and technology is interesting in itself. Technological determinists have long suggested that society is shaped and controlled by the evolution of technology. On the other hand, social determinists have argued that society itself determines what forms of technology becomes popular and useful. The concept of mutual shaping has emerged as a hybrid of both deterministic viewpoints—acknowledging the impact of technological and social influences, which embraces the notion that both viewpoints mutually shape one another (Quan-Haase, 2013). The concept of mutual shaping suggests that the adoption and usage of technology is an intricate process that involves complex human communication systems and decision-making processes within a social system. Put simply, the evolution of technology will impact peoples' lived experiences. This, in turn, will change and reshape society. Advertising sits in the wake of these technological and societal changes and adapts to new challenges.

The evolution of interactive advertising over the years is a result of pushing the technical and creative boundaries of web browsing, digital platforms, and infrastructure limitations to which consumers were bound. As technological adoption advanced, the role of advertising adapted to be relevant within the societal framework. To understand these major components of development and change and how they fit together, we break this chapter into three parts. The first part highlights technological milestones by examining various industry trends and digital innovations over the past 15 years. The second part reviews the major digital advertising types, followed by the third part, which provides a discussion that attempts to combine both elements in the context of social and technological determinisms as well as highlights some key areas pertaining to the future of digital advertising.

Industry Trends and Digital Innovations

The new millennium saw unprecedented and precarious growth in the technology industry, with companies such as Amazon and Google cementing their place in the dotcom era, despite initial losses. The first half of the decade saw significant investment and expenditure, with a growing number of investors focusing on the future payoff of the industry. This was quickly stifled when the dotcom bubble burst in March 2000, with many businesses taking on a more pragmatic and focused approach toward online advertising, striving to be more efficient and effective when spending in the realm of digital advertising.

The dotcom crisis, along with the Sept. 11, 2001 terror attacks, forced the industry to address two growing concerns: consumer privacy and audience measurement. The newness of the technology sparked a furor of privacy issues as cookie tracking data led to discussions over what forms of consent were needed by those whose information and browsing habits were being accessed. Ethical concerns aside, companies also began to debate the best way to measure audience engagement. While click-through rate (CTR) was the dominant form of measurement, industry insiders began to propose new ways of measurement due to the abuses and inaccuracies of CTR.

The early 2000s also saw the introduction of several well-known companies that changed the landscape of the internet. Early social media sites, Friendster and MySpace, were created, Apple introduced the world to the iTunes store, and Skype revolutionized video chatting for those with a fast enough internet connection. As a result of these new innovations, digital advertising also improved with rich media in the form of ultramercials, skyscraper advertisements, and advergames.

By the end of 2003, the number of users on the internet rose to 719 million from 248 million at the end of 1999 (Internet World Stats, 2016). The widespread growth of users led to advancements in the infrastructure to efficiently deal with growing bandwidth issues. As a result, new infrastructure allowed internet companies to provide consumers with high-speed internet access. This evolution continued as the functionality of web use transformed. Online shopping became a common practice and search engines dominated. Google became a leader in the industry with the launch of AdWords, leading to Google fetching $85 a share when it went public in 2004 (La Monica, 2004).

This era, coined Web 2.0, was characterized by video advertising, user-generated content (UGC), and the proliferation of high-speed broadband connections (Pew Research Center, 2016). Video advertising gained popularity as streaming technology became more efficient; YouTube was founded in February 2005 as a result of this growing phenomena. UGC in the form of personal blogs and social media also became more commonplace and grew in popularity, with social media becoming particularly popular after the creation of Facebook in 2004 and Twitter in 2006. The social nature of the web also led to an explosive start toward online gaming with the opening of the massive multiplayer online role playing game World of Warcraft in 2004.

The mid-2000s saw the first serious consideration of mobile as a source of advertising. Despite picking up the moniker "third screen," mobile services were dominated by an oligopoly of phone companies that had mixed feelings when it came to advertising on their networks. While mobile advertising was touted to have tremendous potential as the next big thing, there were concerns due to lack of capabilities for video streaming, as well as small screen sizes. Instead, video streaming became a mainstay of online advertising in spite of UGC issues surrounding intellectual property and copyright infringement.

The end of the decade saw two key trends: the rise of search, and the dominance of mobile and social media. Developments in search engines had seen an increase in functionality, including the creation of Google's video search after its acquisition of YouTube. At the same time, mobile and social media also grew exponentially. Apple launched its first iPhone in 2007 (Apple Press Information, 2007), and it followed up with the Apple App Store in 2008. By 2008, 19 percent of cell phone owners had gone online with their phones (Pew Research Center, 2008). Despite the popularity of social media, advertisers struggled to adapt to it and were unsure how best to use it. Some advertisers used it as a tool for broadcast and some as a form of initiating two-way communication with consumers. As social media rose in popularity, so did the prevalence of UGC (e.g., wiki websites, podcasts, YouTube videos). The increase in UGC encouraged speculation and concerns about the effectiveness of earned media versus paid media on the internet.

The issue of privacy again came to the forefront as data mining became openly available for advertisers. The over-proliferation of organic Facebook ads on users' feeds led to consumer fatigue, resulting in blocking, unfriending, and unfollowing brands. Facebook and other social media websites have had to balance the interests of advertisers and consumers ever since. As a result, Facebook decided to reduce the number of organic articles for brands that showed up on their users' pages. Consequently, there was a backlash from advertisers, who did not want to pay more for the same amount of reach they previously had before.

By 2013, 56 percent of Americans were owners of smartphones (Pew Research Center, 2013). This was mirrored in digital advertising, with 5.5 percent of total advertising dollars being spent on mobile platforms. Bigger screens, video streaming, and updated infrastructure all led to greater usability for consumers. The rise of mobile advertising saw a larger growth in the number of advertisements than in the rate of prices.

Types of Digital Advertising

Since the goal of the present chapter is to understand the evolution of interactive advertising in the industry from 2000 to 2015, one way to go about this is to conduct a content analysis by reviewing one of advertising industry's top publications, *Advertising Age*. However, *Advertising Age* over these 15 years changed its publication frequency from a weekly publication from 2000 to 2007 to just 45 to 47 issues per year from 2008 to 2013. To account for an uneven distribution of content for the 15 years, stratification was employed in the sampling of the issues. A monthly, 12-issue-per-year stratified sampling strategy was deemed the most effective and was employed in this study (Riffe, Lacy, & Drager, 1996). Subsequently, a total of 184 weeks of *Advertising Age* issues were randomly selected for analysis from January 2000 to April 2015.

Articles were systematically selected from each issue based on two main criteria. First, the articles had to be of editorial content (i.e., not an advertisement, headline, or blurb) and longer than one paragraph. Second, articles had to be in the interactive or digital advertising section of the issue or employ keywords that referred to "digital advertising." Based on these criteria, 592 articles were selected. The three main categories of these articles were opinion pieces, case studies, and industry trends.

Each article was then further analyzed to determine the specific type of interactive advertising discussed. These were then sorted into data "bins" for further analysis. Other information—such as the characteristics of the type of interactive advertising, the organization that was involved, authorship, and impact of the advertising—was also recorded. This analysis resulted in seven key trends in digital advertising: banner advertising, advergames, video advertising, search advertising, mobile advertising, social media advertising, and native advertising. Each will be discussed briefly below.

Banner Advertising

While banner advertising was one of the major types of digital advertising early on, it soon had to adapt as rich media became popular. Rich media allowed users to click, drag, scroll, and interact in multiple ways. In 2000, Microsoft's MSN tested and reported that the CTR for Unilever's Dove brand's rich media banner ad—featuring an enhanced version of a banner ad that unfurled, after a two-second rollover, to resemble a print ad—was twice the number of regular banner ads (Elkin, 2000). However, the introduction of superstitials featuring Flash technology, greater interactivity, and less static graphics was thought to lead to the decline of regular banner ads. Additionally, as metrics evolved, it was thought that CTR was not a good measure, because awareness was thought to be a more important metric that could not be measured by clicks alone. While banner ads did not completely die down, they were carefully cultivated for effective use in promotions such as Samsung's 2008 Olympic gold medal treasure hunt campaign that had consumers look for clues in emails, banner ads, and text messages in order to have a chance to win prizes.

Advergames

The advergame format started in 2000 with the intent to allow consumers to engage within a game while learning more about the advertised product as they play. Companies like McDonalds, the U.S. Army (with its America's Army game), and Coca-Cola (Championship Run game) are examples of companies that used advergames to increase traffic and online subscriptions for their websites. On some occasions, advertisers used games to get followers to go to specific websites for more information. In 2005, a study identified that women were avid gamers, and several womens'-interest websites used advergames as a tactic to target women to visit their sites (see Oser, 2005). By the mid-2000s, advergames had gained tremendous traction, with executive vice president of Wild Tangent, Dave Maden, observing that marketers needed a videogame strategy (Oser, 2005).

Video Advertising

Video advertising had steadily risen and is now the mainstay of online advertising. While recognized for its early potential, there were technical concerns in the early 2000s due to the general populace mostly having only a dial-up connection that could not effectively handle video feeds. By 2005, with technological improvements to allow better video quality compression and high-speed internet, videos playing online became more common. This led to short video ads progressively becoming longer since they no longer needed to be preloaded and could be streamed efficiently. While online video ads initially were made identical to the television spots, creative executives realized that to set the online environment apart, unique video clips needed to be created. Video ads were initially thought as the most effective way to reach teenagers. However, they were quickly adopted by other industries, such as automakers, which used video to showcase the functionality of their vehicles to adults. Advertisers also teamed up collaboratively online in video advertising, such as when Pontiac and Maxim magazine partnered for cross-promotional purposes to reach an adult target audience.

With the introduction of sharing on social media, advertisers have sought to reach viral status with their messages and videos. At the time, the number of views thought to indicate campaign success was "one million" (Cutler, 2009, n.p.). To do this, advertisers employed metrics to analyze how the videos were received and shared. However, advertisers had noted that even though a campaign may have achieved virality, it might not mean commercial success since it did not guarantee viewers being customers. An example cited was Miller's TV channel that was largely popular, but the channel's popularity did not convert into alcohol sales. Additionally, commentators have noted that the chase for virality had also resulted in a slew of low-quality ads that sought to win consumers' attention and achieve viral status.

Video ads were monetized in different ways. On websites like Hulu, users got to watch a free episode in return for watching a few advertisements. As video advertising became more popular, advertisers had started to create their own spots, with the belief that brands should not rent entertainment but should own it (Hampp, 2008).

The success of video advertising had seen YouTube sell video ad space on a real time exchange. Sites like Buzzfeed had switched to video ads and greatly reduced banner ads, while Facebook launched its own video ads and noticed a 360 percent increase in video news feeds in 2014.

Search Advertising

Search advertising was developed when search engines and portal sites (e.g., MSN, AOL, Yahoo!) were used as the starting points during a user's web session. In order to get information or go to a specific web destination, users typed what they were looking for in the search bar. The search results were accompanied by ads to offer the consumer various purchase options that might complement their search term. While this quickly became a popular option for advertisers due to its effectiveness, it has faced criticism due to the lack of rich media support. The earliest and most well-known company to utilize search advertising was Google.

One of the earliest ethical concerns was the inability to differentiate between what was paid and unpaid content. By 2004, search advertising was a $2.6 billion market with the biggest players being Google and Yahoo! search engines. With the advancement of video advertising, the concept of video search was thought to be an avenue in which search could grow beyond just text. By 2007, with the advent of mobile devices, Google, Yahoo!, and Microsoft all announced mobile search products on the horizon. Social media had also joined the fray, with Facebook announcing a social graph search that had, to that point, received mixed reviews.

Mobile Advertising

While mobile's potential was recognized from the early onset, it never truly took off until the latter part of 2000 in part due to the lack of agreement from advertisers, carriers, and consumers as to what advertising on this platform should look like. In the early days, it was thought that mobile marketing was not a strategy in itself but was part of the media mix (Cuneo, 2003). Part of the reason for this was because of the challenges faced by advertisers with the technological affordances of mobile devices in 2005, which typically had smaller screen sizes and limited bandwidth.

The mobile ascendency saw the experimental development of apps that became widely adopted. Each app served a unique purpose and was primarily used on mobile phones. However, in 2009, the primary feature for smartphones was still talking, followed by text and email. As a medium for digital advertising, mobile was continually growing, particularly alongside the growth of video streaming and social media usage.

Social Media Advertising

Social networking sites (SNSs) were developed in 2003. The earliest forms, such as Tribe, allowed users to build networks mixed with Craigslist-style classifieds. By 2005, social media and music collided through the creation of MySpace. One of the hallmarks of social media sites was the creation of UGC in the form of posts, videos, and likes or product promotion.

One of the reasons for using social media for advertising was that opinions generated by peers were thought to be the most influential form of recommendations (Hanlon, 2008). However, there were still concerns from advertisers over the best way to use the medium. In 2008, social media campaign advertising became highly popular and was thought to be more effective than advertising in a legacy medium (e.g., TV, newspapers, magazines, and radio). Typical campaigns attempted to get users to share ads through various forms on social media in hopes of tapping into more consumers' social networks. Advertising on Facebook looked quite different from advertising in legacy media since Facebook advertising, at the time, allowed brands to sponsor channels or take over a homepage (Lee, 2011).

One of the foundational building blocks of such campaigns was to build communities for advertisers as a way to engage with their consumers. An effect of building a base of loyal customers was the belief that their love for the brand would see these customers organically recommend the product by sharing and spreading the word online. Social media advertising was also thought to be efficient in connecting with hard-to-reach groups that may not see most ads but could be reached through their friends. It provided a way for advertisers to reach niche markets and consumers to find such products based on keyword searches and interests. Despite its utility, CPM (Cost Per Thousand) for social media ads in 2010 were revealed to be much lower compared to other online media ($0.56 versus $2.43). Additionally, in 2009, there were plans to develop a brand social score—a social media metric that provided a magnitude score (e.g., 0–10) indicating the level of chatting about your brand in a given week, which shared traits of the then-popular Net Promoter Score but was easier to understand (Klaassen, 2009). The original users of Facebook as of September 2006 were U.S. college students, but news of the SNSs quickly spread worldwide (Phillips, 2007) and, as of January 2009, more than 50 percent of Facebook users and 44 percent of MySpace users in the United States were over 35 years of age. In 2011, Google joined the social media bandwagon by announcing the launch of Google +. That same year, Twitter reached its own milestone, celebrating 200 million registered accounts.

Native Advertising

In 2012, native advertising started gaining popularity. Much like advertorials in print, native advertising utilized similar principles for online advertising. Websites started featuring sponsored content disguised in the form of editorials or sponsored created content. Essentially, different models of reinforcement to the advertisement were used within a page in a non-obvious manner. This has created ethical issues in terms of identifying what content was editorial and what content was sponsored. Social media subsequently has adopted similar styles of native ads due to its presumed effectiveness.

Evolution of Interactive Advertising/Impact of Digital Innovations

Reviewing the last 15 years of technological evolution and the development of interactive advertising, we see three major advertising trends and innovations that stood out as key players. These three major digital innovations are search, social media, and mobile.

Search

Search engines began as a way for users to seek out content online. The original purpose of search allowed users to quickly and easily find content online through clever use of keywords using Boolean logic. As the web grew and more content became available, the importance of search increased, and companies sought to find ways to monetize this digital innovation. In 2000, Google started to monetize search using a CPM model, where it allowed advertisers to display ads based on keyword searches. This model eventually evolved into Google AdWords, where advertisers on average spent $1 for every $2 of revenue they earned (Gabbert, 2012). In a time where traditional advertisements were dominated primarily by banner advertisements, advertising appearing in the form of searches highlighted a picture of the flexibility of advertising adapting to a digital milestone.

Social Media

The growth of social networking sites, from Friendster to MySpace to Facebook, highlights a period of online interactivity between users in an online virtual space.

This virtual connectivity created a series of networks for individuals to communicate with each other using the web. The social aspect of the web also led to a rise of virtual online games that helped connect users. Advertising in this space had taken many twists and turns. For example, early versions of online gaming led many advertisers to believe that the future of advertising lay in product placement within virtual worlds. As the user experience of social media evolved, developers found new ways to best monetize their product. Through a combination of building on stepwise technological innovations, such as the success of search, social media combined previous search successes with behavioral advertising targeting models.

Mobile

Mobile as a form of digital advertising was recognized early on in the articles we read and was viewed by industry as the "up and coming" technology. The idea behind the name, "the third screen," alludes to the amount of time users would spend on their phones just like they would on television and computers. However, many factors such as technology (e.g., bandwidth, screen size), government regulations, and the desire for phone companies to protect their interests inhibited the anticipated growth explosion of advertising on mobile. However, as those challenges were overcome, at least in part, mobile transitioned from part of a meta-media to one that stood by itself. The development of apps and digital browsing created new avenues in which advertising was presented to users. In addition to how mobile dovetails with social media and different applications, it allowed users to turn to their mobile devices throughout the day for entertainment, information, and socialization. This, in turn, brought new avenues for advertising as users engaged in those activities.

Summary of Content Analysis

The results of our 15-year content analysis of *Advertising Age* reveal a number of trends involving advertising types and technological changes (that are, incidentally, inextricably linked) including emphasis on traditional forms of online advertising, as well as mobile and social advertising. The primary types of digital advertising that surfaced in the articles included banners, advergames, video, search, mobile, social media, and native. These results share similarities with the results presented in Chapter 1's content analysis of articles that cited the Interactive Advertising Model (IAM) over the past 15 years, and the analysis of articles from the *Journal of Interactive Advertising* cited in Chapter 4. Although scholars are sometimes criticized for not keeping pace with industry, these results at least suggest that scholars are covering essentially the same topics (in terms of types of digital ads) that were highlighted by industry in the pages of *Advertising Age*.

However, much of the *Advertising Age* articles that focused on display advertising seemed to be concerned with how best to use the forms of advertising to *get* consumers to pay attention to the brands, products, and services being advertised. As Chapter 9 shows, increased control and consumer participation with digital media content has brought about new ways for people to engage with ads and brands so consumers are likely to pushback on digital advertising shown in traditional forms, which can affect basic exposure and attention.

Issues arose in our review of *Advertising Age* that have always interested both practitioners and scholars. For example, measurement of digital advertising efficacy has been a big issue of interest and concern. Industry is criticized for over-reliance on the tried and true "click-through rate" (CTR) to determine ad effectiveness for online display ads, which still comprise about 50 percent of digital advertising budgets in the U.S. (Rajeck, 2016). Several of our chapters offer alternative measures for ad effectiveness: Chapter 22 provides a new way to measure efficiency of digital advertising that incorporates a broader set of metrics, including consumer empowerment, and Chapter 19 outlines measures related to physiological response.

With the dizzying speed with which technology changes and innovates, there is a real need for well-established theories that can describe, explain, and predict outcomes, and that stand the test of time regardless of what new innovation comes down the proverbial pipeline. Numerous chapters in this volume present models and frameworks for understanding digital advertising, and paint a complex picture of important factors, how these factors operate under certain circumstances, and how various factors work in concert to influence common (and not so common) advertising outcomes. Advertisers are being blocked, ignored, flamed, and unfollowed, and consumers—as was true in 2000—are in charge of the digital space now more than ever before. Consumers are banning advertisers from their email, mobile phones, etc., and access to social media entrances and exits are being blocked too. To address this, Chapter 14 applies an approach/avoidance framework to help us understand potential antecedents to avoidance in an effort to overcome such hindrances.

Just as industry can learn from academics, *academics can learn from industry*. From the content analysis of *Advertising Age*, it was suggested that ad blocking or ad avoidance might occur as a result of consumer fatigue from receiving too many advertisements. Subsequently, to avoid receiving so many ads online, consumers may take additional steps to communicate their impatience (or irritation) with brands, such as "unfollow" a brand or "opt out" of email promotions. Here, the lesson is that scholars can learn something from industry, and industry can help scholars identify relevant concepts of study. Ad blocking seems to be a ripe area of study, as digital advertising takes on metrics and measurements that include cognitive, emotional, and behavioral outcomes that can occur when consumers receive too much advertising.

Additionally, we saw a lack of coverage in *Advertising Age* on what we consider to be up and coming topics in digital advertising, such as 3D displays, virtual reality, holographic product displays, and virtual shopping environments. As

Chapter 10 explains, it is critically important to understand virtual reality (VR) in the context of digital advertising, since VR offers advertisers a way to engage with consumers by transporting them to, for example, travel destinations where consumers can interact with brands via a range of technologies, such as an interactive head mount that can track motions made while engaged with the brand.

We have highlighted just a few of the chapters in this volume to give readers a sense of how examination of industry trends is a useful exercise in informing scholarship. To close out this chapter, we offer a brief explanation of what is meant by "mutual shaping of technology" and attempt to illustrate how this may play out based on examples seen in the articles we read in *Advertising Age* in preparing this chapter.

Mutual Shaping of Technology

With 15 years of technological milestones and advertising trends explained, we can start to better understand how advertising has been revolutionized by the technology that precedes it and the people that use it. In order to understand the implications of these technological milestones and the development of interactive advertising, we turn to the concept of technological and social determinism that is often combined today to form the concept of mutual shaping (Quan-Haase, 2013). To better understand the mutual shaping of technology in the case of the World Wide Web, we need look no further than the early halcyon days of the internet where both users and developers were new to the industry.

One of the early issues that users faced was the credibility of the information on the websites they visited online. The modality, agency, interactivity, and navigability (MAIN) model explains that in lieu of a standardized system for veracity of information online, users turn to cues and use heuristics as a way to determine credibility online. Take, for example, if a user found a web page easy to navigate, it could be perceived as benevolence from the part of the web site and made the information seem more credible (Sundar, 2008). The MAIN model also highlights how technology changed the way users think about using the web based on perceptions of credibility and heuristics. In doing so, users helped shape the environment of the online sphere through feedback. Feedback in turn became the drivers of what the public wanted and served a social function of the public's desires. These social functions from using the technology based on the feedback from the users allow developers to customize and edit their content appropriately to conform to the demands of their users (Moschella, 2003). In this manner, we see both the adoption of certain technology and platforms even though they do not always necessarily invoke pragmatism.

Another example is the development of MP3 files. MP3 can be regarded as an innovation driven by both technological and social reasons. Technologically, the MP3 was a new form of sound compression that allowed audio files to be portably contained on computers. As a result, this portability led to the social trend of music sharing (Sterne, 2006). MP3 files therefore initially changed the way people listened to music because users had to get MP3 players to open those music files. As a result of the device changing the way people listened to music, the listening habits of people changed as they moved away from traditional radio and CD listening. As habits change, advertising, too, adapts with the innovations. In the case of MP3, the Apple Store and other music streaming sites, like Spotify, were developed and enabled new forms of advertising.

The advancement of technological progress and adoption does not always guarantee sophistication in use. Social media is another example of mutual shaping of technology as users' preferences lead to developers engaging their users through their feedback. Some have regarded social media as a regression in communication. For example, Twitter has a limitation of just 140 characters, and Snapchat only allows a photo to have an 80-character message. The argument is that this results in people becoming decoders of information and not interpreters of textual information (Fuchs, 2009). Despite that, the popularity of social media has not only led to high adoption and technological changes, but also the way people use the media. Interactive advertising therefore has had to adapt appropriately with these changes.

Looking at the present day, we see a gradual increase and popularity of online streaming through major networks like Netflix and Amazon Prime (Gibbs, 2015). As users continue to make the switch from legacy media to on-demand services, such as Amazon Prime, Hulu, and Netflix, questions arise as to how advertisers will continue to stay relevant and reach consumers that are paying a premium price to avoid advertising (Forbes, 2015). For example, what theory or theories help to explain the need to empower consumers while protecting their privacy online? How can advertisers have flexibility and be proactive in becoming part of the digital landscape?

From this review, it is clear that practitioners are grappling with some of the same issues that scholars are grappling with, including consumer privacy, data management, mobile, social media, efficacy of display advertising, inappropriate ad placement, viewability, and standardized metrics (Rajeck, 2016). The contributors of this volume offer a diversity of theories, models, and approaches to tackle these and other issues and provide detailed explanations along with vivid and current (as well as historical) examples that bring the theories to life. As you read on, you'll see how contributors reflect on where digital advertising research has been over the past 15+ years and project ahead to where it might be going.

References

Apple Press Information. (2007, January 9). Apple reinvents the phone with iPhone. Retrieved from https://www.apple.com/pr/library/2007/01/09Apple-Reinvents-the-Phone-with-iPhone.html.

Cuneo, A. (2003, April 10). Mobile media chiefs' pitch falls on death ears. *Advertising Age*. Retrieved from http://adage.com/article/news/mobile-media-chiefs-pitch-falls-deaf-ears/108406/

Cutler, M. (2009, March 30). How to make your online video go viral. *Advertising Age*. Retrieved from http://adage.com/article/digital/digital-marketing-make-online-video-viral/135629/

Elkin, T. (2000, October 30). Microsoft's MSN fattens banners with rich media. *Advertising Age*. Retrieved from http://adage.com/article/focus-design/microsoft-s-msn-fattens-banners-rich-media/56376/

Forbes. (2015, August 20). Netflix saves users from watching 130 hours of commercials per year. Retrieved from http://www.forbes.com/sites/insertcoin/2015/08/20/netflix-saves-users-from-watching-130-hours-of-commercials-per-year/#44f788ad38e0.

Fuchs, B. (2009, August 26). Is Twitter making you stupid? *CNBC*. Retrieved from http://www.cnbc.com/id/32569284.

Gabbert, E. (2012, August 12). Google adwords facts and stats. Retrieved from http://www.wordstream.com/blog/ws/2012/08/13/google-adwords-facts.

Gibbs, A. (2015). Awards season: The rise of streaming networks. *CNBC*. Retrieved from http://www.cnbc.com/2015/12/15/awards-season-the-rise-of-streaming-networks-amazon-and-netflix.html.

Hampp, A. (2008, March 18). Ogilvy's Scott: Brands should own entertainment. *Advertising Age*. Retrieved from http://adage.com/article/digital/ogilvy-s-scott-brands-entertainment/125792/

Hanlon, P. (2008, January 7). Expand your brand community online. *Advertising Age*. Retrieved from http://adage.com/article/cmo-strategy/expand-brand-community-online/122867/

Internet World Stats. (2016). Internet growth statistics. Retrieved from http://www.internetworldstats.com/emarketing.htm.

Klaassen, A. (2009). What's your brand's social score? *Advertising Age*. Retrieved from http://adage.com/article/digital/razorfish-ogilvy-net-promoter-social-media-model/137867/

La Monica, P. (2004). Google goes low. *CNN Money*. Retrieved from http://money.cnn.com/2004/08/18/technology/googleipo/

Lee, E. (2011, June 20). Display's new kingpin: Facebook's No.1. *Advertising Age*. Retrieved from http://adage.com/article/digital/display-s-kingpin-facebook-s-1/228290/

Moschella, D. C. (2003). *Customer-driven IT: How users are shaping technology industry growth*. Boston, MA: Harvard Business Press.

Oser, K. (2005, April 11). Meridith rolls games on mag sites. *Advertising Age*. Retrieved from http://adage.com/article/digital/meredith-rolls-games-mag-sites/102846/

Pew Research Center. (2008, March 5). Mobile Access to data and information. Retrieved from http://www.pewinternet.org/2008/03/05/questions-and-data-5/

Pew Research Center. (2013, June 5). Smartphone ownership. Retrieved from http://www.pewinternet.org/2013/06/05/smartphone-ownership-2013/

Pew Research Center. (2016). Broadband vs. dial-up adoption over time. http://www.pewinternet.org/data-trend/internet-use/connection-type/

Phillips, S. (2007). A brief history of Facebook. *The Guardian*. Retrieved from http://www.theguardian.com/technology/2007/jul/25/media.newmedia.

Quan-Haase, A. (2013). *Technology and society: Social networks, power, and inequality*. Oxford: Oxford University Press.

Rajeck, J. (2016, January 5). Three display advertising issues to watch in 2016. *eConsultancy.com*. Retrieved from https://econsultancy.com/blog/67366-three-display-advertising-issues-to-watch-in-2016/

Riffe, D., Lacy, S., & Drager, M. W. (1996). Sample size in content analysis of weekly news magazines. *Journalism & Mass Communication Quarterly*, 73(3), 635–644.

Rodgers, S., & Thorson, E. (2000). The interactive advertising model: How users perceive and process online ads. *Journal of Interactive Advertising*, 1(1), 41–60.

Sterne, J. (2006). The mp3 as cultural artifact. *New Media & Society*, 8(5), 825–842.

Sundar, S. S. (2008). The MAIN model: A heuristic approach to understanding technology effects on credibility. In M. J. Metzger & A. J. Flanagin (Eds.), *Digital media, youth, and credibility* (pp. 73–100). The John D. and Catherine T. MacArthur Foundation Series on Digital Media and Learning. Cambridge, MA: The MIT Press. doi: 10.1162/dmal.9780262562324.073.

4

A SYSTEMATIC ANALYSIS OF INTERACTIVE ADVERTISING RESEARCH THROUGH A PARADIGM FUNNEL

Terry Daugherty and Vanja Djuric

> *The internet has been the most fundamental change during my lifetime and for hundreds of years.*
>
> —*Rupert Murdoch, Media Mogul*

During the past 20 years, technology (e.g., the internet, broadband, smartphone, etc.) has altered our lives and ushered in a new age of interactivity capable of transforming how we communicate and use media. As a result, interactive media have brought information, entertainment, and commerce together in a period of media convergence unparalleled throughout human history and given rise to digital technologies that allow consumers to participate, create, and control media. Likewise, the creation and delivery of advertising has also evolved because of its symbiotic relationship with media, leading to the concept of interactive advertising. Interactive advertising is capable of moving beyond simply identifying how much or how often a persuasive message is delivered and, instead, presents opportunities for two-way, many-to-many exchanges between consumers, brands, and the media (Eastin, Daugherty, & Burns, 2011).

Because advertising is an applied discipline capable of being shaped and influenced by research, the *Journal of Interactive Advertising* (JIAD) was founded in the fall of 2000 in recognition of the need to explore and understand this fast-developing digital age (Leckenby & Li, 2000). The *Journal's* primary focus is to put into practice the concepts of interactivity in our academic discourse; to emphasize that interactive media are changing all aspects of advertising, marketing, communication, and society; and to provide a forum to address the enormous challenges and complexity of interactive advertising. In essence, JIAD has helped to establish and record a paradigm of interactive advertising research. Therefore, the purpose of this chapter is to provide a systematic analysis of the research published by JIAD to understand how the practice of interactive advertising has emerged and changed over time. More specifically, we begin by defining interactive advertising within a scholarly framework and apply the concept of a paradigm funnel to provide structure and insight within this body of work. We then identify various research trends that have manifested in the pages of the *Journal* and discuss future directions for interactive advertising in general.

Defining Interactive Advertising as a Paradigm

The notion of a paradigm in the social sciences has come to reflect the deep beliefs and assumptions involving knowledge within a particular research community (Nairn, Berthon, & Money, 2007). Kuhn (1962) first introduced the concept in *The Structure of Scientific Revolutions* subsequently resulting in a plethora of paradigm classifications (Willmott, Jackson, & Carter, 1993; Lewis & Grimes, 1999). While the concept has led to an influx of disciplines jockeying for theoretical superiority, Kuhn's (1962, 1970) original work was focused on understanding how research changes over time, with one paradigm displacing another (Berthon, Nairn, & Money, 2003). Meaning, as scientists discover new knowledge that fundamentally expands or changes their theoretical assumptions, an alternative paradigm emerges, such as interactive advertising.

Leckenby and Li (2000) first defined interactive advertising as any paid or unpaid promotion of products, services, or ideas by an identified sponsor to consumers through mediated means. They recognized that the digital age was significantly changing the world and that interactivity would soon permeate society while exceeding the boundaries (i.e., passive observer) of traditional advertising. At its core, interactivity occurs between humans and machines through communication, interaction, control, change, and creation via computer-mediated experiences (see Hoffman & Novak, 1996; Rafaeli & Sudweeks, 1997; Bezjian-Avery, Calder, & Iacobucci, 1998; Heeter, 2000), with JIAD launched as an outlet for multidisciplinary interactive advertising scholarship.

Paradigm Funnel

The paradigm funnel represents a systematic technique for exploring, classifying, and analyzing a body of literature (Berthon et al., 2003). By following a structured approach in synthesizing a stream of research, the goal is to identify where observed differences exist between the explicit purposes and underlying assumptions of a study. Because science is comprised of empirical observation, the merging of fact with conjecture, and the articulation of theory (Kuhn, 1970, p. 25), the dynamics of any research paradigm will range from an explicit and observable scientific structure to the implicit and unobservable (Nairn et al., 2007).

Subsequently, a paradigm funnel is comprised of four levels, with shifts between levels stemming from the observation of data, the way data are interpreted, and the theoretical approach. If data is observationally based (Level 1), then explanations are sought through structured analysis (Level 2). However, if scientific solutions are not found at this level, specific theory is questioned (Level 3) leading to the challenging of deep assumptions (Level 4) and ultimately a new paradigm (see Figure 4.1). This is not to say that the evolution of a research paradigm over time is linear. Rather, this structure allows for ordered comparisons to be made within complex literature that is often fragmented.

For the purpose of this chapter, the aforementioned criteria were applied to all research articles published in JIAD to identify the paradigm structure and gain insight into how interactive advertising scholarship has developed. A census of the *Journal* was taken for research published between January 1, 2000 and June 1, 2016 using the EBSCO database. Excluding editorials and point-of-view articles, a total of 180 manuscripts were reviewed. The articles were evaluated based on the aforementioned paradigm funnel criteria and assigned to one of the four levels. Two coders independently analyzed all of the manuscripts, resulting in only 12 intercoder disagreements, indicating an acceptable reliability of 93 percent and Scott's Pi accounting for chance agreement of 0.97 (Riffe & Lacy, 2014). The articles assigned to each funnel level are illustrated in Table 4.1.

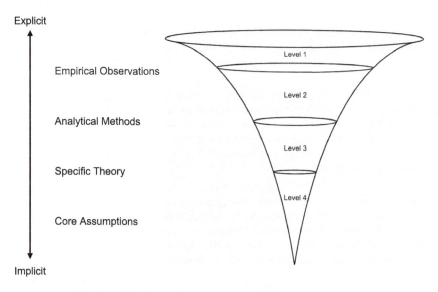

FIGURE 4.1   The Paradigm Funnel

Source: Nairn et al., 2007

TABLE 4.1 Interactive Advertising Paradigm Funnel

Level	Study
1. Empirical Observations 38 articles	Katz (2000); Richards (2000); Jeandrain (2001); Dahlen (2002); Gould & Coyle (2002); McMillan (2002); Ang, Zhou, and Jiang (2003); Chan-Olmsted and Kang (2003); Chou (2003); Liu (2003); Patwardhan and Yang (2003); Ryu, Kim, and Kim (2003); Seounmi, Lee, and Doyle (2003); Taniwaki (2003); Lee, Lee, Kim, and Stout (2004); Macias, Lewis, and Shankar (2004); Nelson, Keum, and Yaros (2004); Phillips, Tandoh, Noble, and Bush (2004); Bailey (2005); Kim, McMillan, and Hwang (2005); Rosenkrans (2005); Barton (2006); Fong and Burton (2006); Cheong and Morrison (2008); Hanley, George-Palilonis, and Tanksale (2008); Jansen, Hudson, Hunter, Liu, & Murphy (2008); Troutman and Timpson (2008); Hansen (2009); Okazaki (2009); Chen and Haley (2010); Fagerstrøm and Ghinea (2010); Huang and Tsang (2010); Katz (2010); Kelly, Kerr, and Drennan (2010); Atkinson, Driesener, and Corkindale (2014)
2. Analytical Methods 114 articles	Wells and Chen (2000); Choi, Miracle, and Biocca (2001); Edwards and Gangadharbatla (2001); Brown (2002); Choi and Rifon (2002); Daugherty and Reece (2002); Jee and Lee (2002); Luo (2002); Rodgers (2002); Yoon, Cropp, and Cameron (2002); Ha (2003); Hwang, McMillan, and Lee (2003); Macias (2003); Bellman and Rossiter (2004); Chaney, Lin, and Chaney (2004); Ferguson and Perse (2004); Grigorovici and Constantin (2004); Hernandez, Chapa, Minor, Maldonado, and Barranzuela (2004); Ko, Jung, Kim, and Shim (2004); Wan and Youn (2004); Xie, Donthu, Lohtia, and Osmonbekov (2004); Yoo, Kim, and Stout (2004); Chen, Griffith, and Shen (2005); Hupfer and Grey (2005); Nicovich (2005); Patwardhan and Ramaprasad (2005); Rodgers, Jin, Rettie, Alpert, and Yoon (2005); Sundar and Kim (2005); Swain (2005); Benedicktus and Andrews (2006); Chen and Rodgers (2006); Goldsmith and Horowitz (2006); Morimoto and Chang (2006); Porter and Golan (2006); Steyer, Garcia-Bardidia, and Quester (2006); Thorson and Rodgers (2006); Acar (2007); Berneburg (2007); Bruner and Kumar (2007); Drossos, Giaglis, Lekakos, Kokkinaki, and Stavraki (2007); Glass (2007); Merisavo et al. (2007); Nasco and Bruner (2007); Sicilia and Ruiz (2007); Unni and Harmon (2007); Wu (2007); Chu and Kamal (2008); Daugherty, Eastin, and Bright (2008); Gangadharbatla (2008); Im, Lee, Taylor, and D'Orazio (2008); Micu and Thorson (2008); Wise, Bolls, Kim, Venkataraman, and Meyer (2008); Xia and Bechwati (2008); Bellman, Schweda, and Varan (2009); Cha (2009); Edwards, Lee, and Ferle (2009); Jin and Bolebruch (2009); McMahan, Hovland, and McMillan (2009); Rosenkrans (2009); Zeng, Huang, and Dou (2009); Chang, Yan, Zhang, and Luo (2010); Cui, Wang, and Xu (2010); Eckler and Bolls (2011); Hoy and Milne (2010); Lewis and Porter

Level	Study
	(2010); Mabry and Porter (2010); Ahrens and Coyle (2011); Cauberghe and Pelsmacker (2011); Chi (2011); Chu (2011); Elias, Appaih, and Gong (2011); Kwon and Sung (2011); Lin and Peña (2011); Park, Rodgers, And Stemmle (2011); Dardis, Schmierbach, and Limperos (2012); Cortés and Vela (2013); Kamal, Chu, and Pedram (2013); Kim, Lin, and Sung (2013); Lee and Ahn (2013); Lee, Ham, and Kim (2013); Moon, Kim, Choi, and Sung (2013); Morrison, Cheong, and McMillan (2013); Pentina and Taylor (2013); Tsai and Men (2013); Wise, Alhabash, and Eckler (2013); Carr and Hayes (2014); Duff, Yoon, Wang, and Anghelcev (2014); Evans (2014); Jeong and Coyle (2014); Logan (2014); López and Sicilia (2014); Hayes and King (2014); Muk and Chung (2014); Sokolik, Magee, and Ivory (2014); Alhabash, McAlister, Lou, and Hagerstrom (2015); Chen, Lin, Choi, and Hahm (2015); De Keyzer, Dens, and De Pelsmacker (2015); Kinney and Ireland (2015); Kononova and Yuan (2015); Limpf and Voorveld (2015); Sashittal and Jassawalla (2015); Schulz, Dority, and Schulz (2015); Shan and King (2015); Siemens, Smith, and Fisher (2015); Wang, Cunningham, and Eastin (2015); Alhabash et al. (2016); Maslowska, Smith, and van den Putte (2016); van Riet et al. (2016); Wu (2016); Yaoyuneyong, Foster, Jounson, and Johnson (2016); Yoon and Youn (2016)
3. Specific Theory 21 articles	Heeter (2000); Rodgers and Thorson (2000); Ang (2001); Coffey (2001); Lombard and Snyder-Duch (2001); Pennington (2001); Roberts and Ko (2001); Schumann, Artis, and Rivera (2001); Sheehan (2002); Steinfield (2002); Mitra (2003); Fortunato and Windels (2005); McMillan (2005); Spurgeon (2005); Townsend (2005); Tremayne (2005); Murdough (2009); Russell (2009); Liang (2010); Martin and Todorov (2010); Ohme, Matukin, and Pacula-Lesniak (2011)
4. Core Assumptions 7 articles	Pavlou and Stewart (2000); Cannon (2001); Wu (2005); Vilpponen, Winter, and Sundqvist (2006); Sheehan and Morrison (2009); Mallia and Windels (2011); Wagler (2013)

Empirical Observation—Level 1

Level 1 of the funnel constitutes research focused on observing and document-ing criteria or events within a paradigm. The purpose is the recognition and acknowledgment of the phenomenon in a descriptive manner proclaiming to the scientific world something is happening and to identify this as fact. A total of 21 percent of JIAD's articles were classified in this part of the funnel with most designed to explore an emerging area of interactive advertising (Figure 4.2). For instance, scholars early on investigated the implications of interactivity, websites,

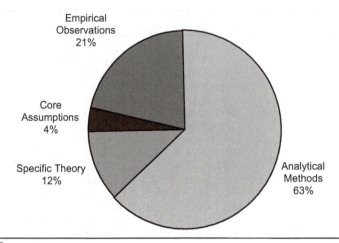

N=180

FIGURE 4.2 Percentage of Articles at Each Level of the Funnel

and online advertising (Katz, 2000; Gould & Coyle, 2002; McMillan, 2002; Rosenkrans, 2005), but this continuously changed to focus on new consumer behaviors, tactics, and/or technologies. Another group sought to examine consumer acceptance of advergames and brand messages within games (Chou, 2003; Seounmi et al., 2003; Nelson et al., 2004) from both a user perspective as well as evaluating the marketing viability of such strategies, while others looked to define the emergence of the Web 2.0 by exploring electronic word-of-mouth (eWOM), social media, and user-generated content (UGC) (Fong & Burton, 2006; Kelly, Kerr, & Drennan, 2010; Fagerstrøm & Ghinea, 2010). Overall, the top of the funnel often reflects first observations by researchers in an effort to call attention to phenomenon, which research in JIAD supports. In addition, the Level 1 interactive advertising funnel of research published by JIAD provides more breadth than depth in that the number of topics (e.g., interactivity, internet advertising, mobile, etc.) is greater compared to only a few focal areas.

Analytical Methods—Level 2

Level 2 of the funnel represents research determined to connect data to theory using analytical approaches. Research at this level moves beyond categorizing facts to testing relationships and identifying patterns for enhancing predictive power. While the use of advanced techniques is a defining characteristic of this level, order and structure associated with correct theory is critical. Subsequently, the amount of research at this level increased significantly, reaching 63 percent. Whereas Level 1 provided breadth, Level 2 delivers depth across a number of interactive advertising topics. For instance, testing the effectiveness of common forms of internet advertising (e.g., display, search) is consistent throughout and a tactic researchers continuously seek to understand (Choi & Rifon, 2002; Rodgers, 2002; Yoo, Kim, & Stout, 2004; Rosenkrans, 2009), with more recent trends examining video advertising (Lee, Ham, & Kim, 2013; Kononova & Yuan, 2015). Similarly, web use and online behavior remain key areas of research with articles testing message structure (Luo, 2002; Hwang, McMillan, & Lee, 2003), interactivity (Jee & Lee, 2002; Wu, 2005), and consumer characteristics (McMahan, Hovland, & McMillan, 2009; Elias, Appiah, & Gong, 2011; Wise, Alhabash, & Eckler, 2013; Schulz, Dority, & Schulz, 2015).

The importance of social media is also readily apparent as articles examining motivational use (Gangadharbatla, 2008; Tsai & Men, 2013; Logan, 2014; Sashittal & Jassawalla, 2015), cultural differences (Chen & Haley, 2010), and advertising strategy (Chen et al., 2015; Kinney & Ireland, 2015; Alhabash et al., 2016) are introduced. Furthermore, the continued growth of gaming manifests with research exploring brand placement (Grigorovici & Constantin, 2004; Glass, 2007; Siemens et al., 2015), in-game advertising (Chaney, Lin, & Chaney, 2004; Chang et al., 2010; Lewis & Porter, 2010), and information processing (Acar, 2007; Dardis et al., 2012).

More recent work in Level 2 of the funnel assesses various approaches for analyzing eWOM and the timing associated with message reception, third-party influences (Carr & Hayes, 2014), interpersonal relationships (Shan & King, 2015), and message characteristics (Wang et al., 2015). The prominence of this topic area is also related to the growth of research examining mobile devices and advertising (Drossos et al., 2007; Cortés & Vela, 2013; Kim et al., 2013; Limpf & Voorveld, 2015).

Specific Theory—Level 3

Level 3 of the funnel is comprised of research specifically designed to articulate theory generation and test empirical propositions, with 12 percent of the articles classified accordingly. The intent at this level is to conceptually organize and propose new beliefs within the interactive advertising paradigm through a theoretical lens. To this end, the concept of interactivity has drawn most of the attention, with articles identifying antecedents associated with interactive experiences (Heeter, 2000; Lombard & Snyder-Duch, 2001; Schumann et al., 2001; McMillan, 2005; Tremayne, 2005). Similarly, new frameworks for how interactive advertising is processed by consumers have emerged to make positive contributions to the literature (Rodgers & Thorson, 2000; Roberts & Ko, 2001; Martin & Todorov, 2010). Further, immersive computer-mediated environments such as virtual reality (VR) (Pennington, 2001) and cybernetic virtual existences (Mitra, 2003) have also been explored, challenging interactive advertising researchers to move beyond the present and look to the future. In turn, e-commerce models designed around integrating both online and offline businesses have been presented (Steinfield, 2002) and extended to international markets (Liang, 2010). The limited breadth and depth of research identified within this level could be a symptom of the adolescence of interactive advertising as a paradigm. However, this also suggests many opportunities for scholars to make a significant theoretical contribution.

Core Assumptions—Level 4

Finally, Level 4 of the funnel challenges deep assumptions established by previous research, questioning the core framework, knowledge, and/or methods associated within the values and beliefs of a paradigm. Only 4 percent of the articles were categorized at this level, which is not necessarily surprising given the abbreviated window of interactive advertising research. Early work at this level sought to challenge existing media strategies by evaluating both the effectiveness (Pavlou & Stewart, 2000) and differences (Cannon, 2001) of interactive advertising relative to traditional offline media. Another article (Wu, 2005) challenged the concept of interactivity as failing to account for mediated differences between what is perceived versus what is real, and beliefs were also contested involving what is known about eWOM (Vilpponen et al., 2006). Surprisingly, the most depth in opposition to core assumptions stems from the industry classified area of "creativity," with researchers questioning current practices for the approaches used within computer-mediated environments (CMEs) (Sheehan & Morrison, 2009; Mallia & Windels, 2011; Wagler, 2013). Ultimately, as scholars continue to participate in a continuously evolving digital media landscape, the prospect of challenging assumptions is more than likely diminished when the rate of change negatively affects the necessary learning curve to effectively develop interactive advertising. Yet, as the research paradigm matures and technology evolves, more challenges of existing core assumptions will emerge.

Paradigm Funnel Discussion

The application of a paradigm funnel to the articles published in JIAD provides a distinct approach for examining this growing body of research while offering several benefits. First, we assessed the body of work in the *Journal* using a broad interpretation of Kuhn's (1962) paradigm, defined in terms of interactive advertising. This resulted in analyzing 180 research articles used to identify patterns or trends that could potentially provide scholarly insight. Second, the evaluation process encouraged the separation of facts, methodology, analysis, and theory for a greater understanding of the type of contribution each research article provides. This categorical breakdown serves to remind scholars of the importance of properly framing any research. Third, because the research is analyzed over time, the approach affords an understanding of how a research paradigm evolves. For instance, over half of the research in JIAD across a 16-year period was classified as Level 2 (analytical methods). While an uneven distribution of levels is expected (Nairn et al., 2007), emerging and developing paradigms would more than likely appear top heavy across the first two levels. At the same time, a significantly disproportionate funnel level could signal a paradigm shift. Given the recency of many of the articles in Level 2, this could be a sign that the interactive advertising paradigm is beginning to mature.

In the end, the analysis provides a starting point for understanding how research conducted within a paradigm can help scholars identify gaps or new opportunities. This structured perspective serves to facilitate the cataloging of empirical work using critical analysis while enabling researchers to question existing knowledge. For example, the breadth of research topics examined in JIAD seems connected to the emergence of new interactive media and/or technology and appears to be negatively associated with research depth. While the delineation of funnel levels plays a role in this fact, there are no structural limitations preventing greater breadth and depth within the literature. This is more than likely a product of the broad paradigm definition of interactive advertising and the set number of articles published by the *Journal* each year. Regardless, it appears that opportunities exist for researchers to make significant contributions to interactive advertising through theory development and testing.

Impact and Contribution

Given the volume of interactive advertising research published in a relatively short period of time, JIAD is making a positive contribution to the body of literature. As a result, the *Journal* has been recognized as a leading academic outlet for advertising scholarship (Kim, Hayes, Avant, & Reid, 2014; Wang, Rodgers, Wang, & Thorson, 2016) while publishing work from more than 300 authors in 23 different countries. This external validation is qualified by the Google Scholar citation count of the *Journal* (Figure 4.3). For instance, with 11,000+ citations overall, the interactive advertising research presented to the academic community via JIAD is obviously considered valuable by many.

Perhaps the greatest contribution of the *Journal* is the diversity of research topics explored under the umbrella of *interactive advertising*. In fact, it is the multiplicity of subject matter through a focused lens that makes JIAD unique. To better understand the range of issues examined, the published articles ($N = 180$) were reviewed post-hoc and broadly classified according to their primary interactive advertising topics. Categories were derived a priori (e.g., social media, interactivity) as well as inductively; intercoder reliability was not assessed because the purpose was to identify organic research themes independent of the previous paradigm funnel analysis.

Not surprising, the majority of research articles in the *Journal* (29.4%) examine some general form of internet advertising with other prominent themes identified, such as social media (15%), gaming (9.4%), and interactivity (5.6%) (see

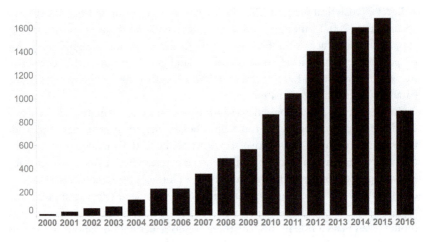

FIGURE 4.3 JIAD Google Scholar Citations per Year

Figure 4.4). In all, 15 topics were discovered that reflected many of the most important issues within the industry, such as mobile (6.7%), eWOM (5.6%), and consumer behavior online (4.4%). To further extrapolate this data, a timeline of published articles was constructed (see Figure 4.5) revealing interesting patterns. For example, there have been consistent trends with about 35 percent of internet advertising articles published from 2000 to 2006. Although internet advertising has certainly evolved since the first banner ad appeared in 1994, the increasing importance of online advertising to reach consumers is clear. In fact, it was not until around 2006 when social media research began to emerge when we started to see a slight decline. The use of social media for viral marketing, engagement, and brand exposure has raised many questions with advertisers resulting in an increase in the quantity of articles published. While there is no reason to expect a slowdown currently, this research is starting to see a shift to mobile communication, which has been surprisingly sporadic. Nonetheless, gaming and mobile tend to follow a similar trend in that both started in the early 2000s with a steady flow along with pulses of increased activity. Interestingly, a linear connection does appear between interactivity, eWOM, and mobile. This perhaps reflects the convergence of social media and smartphones (see 2005–2007 in Figure 4.5).

Pockets of "hot topics" do appear for gaming, interactivity, UGC, and high-speed internet access between 2003 and 2005, yet have not seen much growth since. Other topics such as e-commerce and virtual reality have appeared throughout the years but have a low publishing quantity overall. Perhaps this demonstrates the continuous evolving nature of interactive advertising and the need for researchers to further observe, confirm, and postulate in this area. A clear pattern does emerge for some topics when examining the midpoint of the timeline as

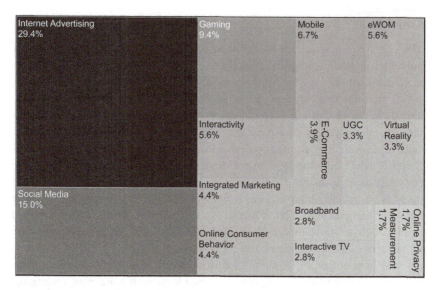

FIGURE 4.4   General Interactive Advertising Research Topics in JIAD

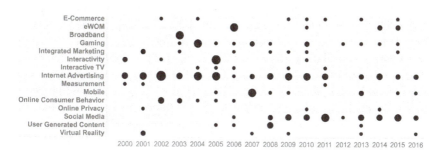

FIGURE 4.5   Timeline of JIAD Publications by Topic

we see a cluster of interactive advertising topics that were once mainstream (e.g., interactivity, IMC, consumer behavior, etc.) displaced in the literature.

The most surprising observation is the scarcity of published research examining digital measurement and consumer privacy within the *Journal*. These topics remain critical issues in the industry but have failed to manifest scholarly interest in the pages of JIAD. While a spattering of articles appear, the quantity does very little to move the literature toward knowledge saturation. Obviously, measurement and privacy have been explored in other scholarly outlets so the absence of this type of work could reflect subject matter bias, which is even more concerning. At a very minimum, this should serve as a call to action among the community of interactive scholars supporting JIAD.

Conclusion

This chapter presents a systematic review of the interactive advertising literature published in JIAD through the application of a paradigm funnel approach. As such, much of the body of work appears within Levels 1 and 2 of the funnel, which attempts to document factual observations and manipulate data for the articulation of theory. The preponderance of research at these two levels reflects the early development of a paradigm. Consequently, as the paradigm matures, additional research is required to develop unique interactive advertising theories (Level 3) while questioning core assumptions (Level 4). It is our belief that the construction of specialized theory that embraces the unique characteristics and qualities of interactive advertising is not only needed, but is necessary for the future of the paradigm. This is not to say that there is no need for continued empirical observations in interactive advertising research. The broad classification of interactive advertising means that innovations of computer-mediated technologies will present almost continuous demand for the discovery and observation of facts. Yet, more mature areas within the paradigm, such as internet advertising, social media, and gaming, are ready for rich theoretical propositions and models.

The field of interactive advertising is interdisciplinary, with research obviously appearing beyond the pages of JIAD and within a multitude of scholarly outlets. As a result, the scope of our findings are limited and are not intended to generalize outside the examined unit of analysis. Rather, our intent was to critically analyze the scholarly contribution JIAD has made to the field of interactive advertising. The uniqueness of the *Journal* stems from its inextricable connection with our digital world and a proclivity for interactive scholarship. Leckenby and Li (2000) originally sought, 16 years ago, to provide a forum for the development of interactive scholarship and to put into practice the knowledge gained. Without a doubt, the exploration, classification, and analyses in JIAD are examining critical aspects of interactive advertising and expanding our understanding of this paradigm.

References

Acar, A. (2007). Testing the effects of incidental advertising exposure in online gaming environment. *Journal of Interactive Advertising, 8*(1), 45–56.

Ahrens, J., & Coyle, J. R. (2011). A content analysis of registration processes on websites: How advertisers gather information to customize marketing communications. *Journal of Interactive Advertising, 11*(2), 12–26.

Alhabash, S., McAlister, A. R., Kim, W., Lou, C., Cunningham, C., Quilliam, E. T., & Richards, J. I. (2016). Saw it on Facebook, drank it at the bar! Effects of exposure to Facebook alcohol ads on alcohol-related behaviors. *Journal of Interactive Advertising, 16*(1), 44–58.

Alhabash, S., McAlister, A. R., Lou, C., & Hagerstrom, A. (2015). From clicks to behaviors: The mediating effect of intentions to like, share, and comment on the relationship between message evaluations and offline behavioral intentions. *Journal of Interactive Advertising, 15*(2), 82–96.

Ang, P. H. (2001). The role of self-regulation of privacy and the internet. *Journal of Interactive Advertising, 1*(2), 1–9.

Ang, P. H., Zhou, Q., & Jiang, Y. (2003). Lessons in broadband adoption from Singapore. *Journal of Interactive Advertising, 4*(1), 33–38.

Atkinson, G., Driesener, C., & Corkindale, D. (2014). Search engine advertisement design effects on click-through rates. *Journal of Interactive Advertising, 14*(1), 24–30.

Bailey, A. A. (2005). Consumer awareness and use of product review websites. *Journal of Interactive Advertising, 6*(1), 68–81.

Barton, B. (2006). Ratings, reviews & ROI: How leading retailers use customer word of mouth in marketing and merchandising. *Journal of Interactive Advertising, 7*(1), 5–50.

Bellman, S., & Rossiter, J. R. (2004). The website schema. *Journal of Interactive Advertising, 4*(2), 38–48.

Bellman, S., Schweda, A., & Varan, D. (2009). A comparison of three interactive television ad formats. *Journal of Interactive Advertising, 10*(1), 14–34.

Benedicktus, R. L., & Andrews, M. L. (2006). Building trust with consensus information: The effects of valence and sequence direction. *Journal of Interactive Advertising, 6*(2), 3–25.

Berneburg, A. (2007). Interactive 3D simulations in measuring consumer preferences: Friend or foe to test results? *Journal of Interactive Advertising, 8*(1), 1–13.

Berthon, P., Nairn, A., & Money, A. (2003). Through the paradigm funnel: A conceptual tool for literature analysis. *Marketing Education Review, 13*(2), 55–66.

Bezjian-Avery, A., Calder, B., & Iacobucci, D. (1998). New media interactive advertising vs. traditional advertising. *Journal of Advertising Research, 38*, 23–32.

Brown, M. (2002). The use of banner advertisements with pull-down menus: A copy testing approach. *Journal of Interactive Advertising, 2*(2), 57–65.

Bruner, G. C., & Kumar, A. (2007). Attitude toward location-based advertising. *Journal of Interactive Advertising, 7*(2), 3–15.

Cannon, H. M. (2001). Addressing new media with conventional media planning. *Journal of Interactive Advertising, 1*(2), 28–42.

Carr, C. T., & Hayes, R. A. (2014). The effect of disclosure of third-party influence on an opinion leader's credibility and electronic word of mouth in two-step flow. *Journal of Interactive Advertising, 14*(1), 38–50.

Cauberghe, V., & Pelsmacker, P. D. (2011). Adoption intentions toward interactive digital television among advertising professionals. *Journal of Interactive Advertising, 11*(2), 45–59.

Cha, J. (2009). Shopping on social networking web sites: Attitudes toward real versus virtual items. *Journal of Interactive Advertising, 10*(1), 77–93.

Chaney, I. M., Lin, K. H., & Chaney, J. (2004). The effect of billboards within the gaming environment. *Journal of Interactive Advertising, 5*(1), 37–45.

Chang, Y., Yan, J., Zhang, J., & Luo, J. (2010). Online in-game advertising effect: Examining the influence of a match between games and advertising. *Journal of Interactive Advertising, 11*(1), 63–73.

Chan-Olmsted, S., & Kang, J. W. (2003). The emerging broadband television market in the United States: Assessing the strategic differences between cable television and telephone firms. *Journal of Interactive Advertising, 4*(1), 13–24.

Chen, H., & Haley, E. (2010). The lived meanings of Chinese social network sites (SNSS) among urban white-collar professionals: A story of happy network. *Journal of Interactive Advertising, 11*(1), 11–26.

Chen, K. J., Lin, J. S., Choi, J. H., & Hahm, J. M. (2015). Would you be my friend? An examination of global marketers' brand personification strategies in social media. *Journal of Interactive Advertising, 15*(2), 97–110.

Chen, Q., Griffith, D. A., & Shen, F. (2005). The effects of interactivity on cross-channel communication effectiveness. *Journal of Interactive Advertising, 5*(2), 19–28.

Chen, Q., & Rodgers, S. (2006). Development of an instrument to measure web site personality. *Journal of Interactive Advertising*, 7(1), 4–46.

Cheong, H. J., & Morrison, M. A. (2008). Consumers' reliance on product information and recommendations found in UGC. *Journal of Interactive Advertising*, 8(2), 38–49.

Chi, H. H. (2011). Interactive digital advertising vs. virtual brand community: Exploratory study of user motivation and social media marketing responses in Taiwan. *Journal of Interactive Advertising*, 12(1), 44–61.

Choi, S. M., & Rifon, N. J. (2002). Antecedents and consequences of web advertising credibility: A study of consumer response to banner ads. *Journal of Interactive Advertising*, 3(1), 12–24.

Choi, Y. K., Miracle, G. E., & Biocca, F. (2001). The effects of anthropomorphic agents on advertising effectiveness and the mediating role of presence. *Journal of Interactive Advertising*, 2(1), 19–32.

Chou, Y. (2003). G-commerce in East Asia: Evidence and prospects. *Journal of Interactive Advertising*, 4(1), 47–53.

Chu, S. C. (2011). Viral advertising in social media: Participation in Facebook groups and responses among college-aged users. *Journal of Interactive Advertising*, 12(1), 30–43.

Chu, S. C., & Kamal, S. (2008). The effect of perceived blogger credibility and argument quality on message elaboration and brand attitudes: An exploratory study. *Journal of Interactive Advertising*, 8(2), 26–37.

Coffey, S. (2001). Internet audience measurement: A practitioner's view. *Journal of Interactive Advertising*, 1(2), 10–17.

Cui, N., Wang, T., & Xu, S. (2010). The influence of social presence on consumers' perceptions of the interactivity of web sites. *Journal of Interactive Advertising*, 11(1), 36–49.

Dahlen, M. (2002). Learning the web: Internet user experience and response to web marketing in Sweden. *Journal of Interactive Advertising*, 3(1), 25–33.

Dardis, F. E., Schmierbach, M., & Limperos, A. M. (2012). The impact of game customization and control mechanisms on recall of integral and peripheral brand placements in videogames. *Journal of Interactive Advertising*, 12(2), 1–12.

Daugherty, T., Eastin, M. S., & Bright, L. (2008). Exploring consumer motivations for creating user-generated content. *Journal of Interactive Advertising*, 8(2), 16–25.

Daugherty, T., & Reece, B. B. (2002). The adoption of persuasive internet communication in advertising and public relations curricula. *Journal of Interactive Advertising*, 3(1), 46–55.

De Keyzer, F., Dens, N., & De Pelsmacker, P. (2015). Is this for me? How consumers respond to personalized advertising on social network sites. *Journal of Interactive Advertising*, 15(2), 124–134.

Drossos, D., Giaglis, G. M., Lekakos, G., Kokkinaki, F., & Stavraki, M. G. (2007). Determinants of effective SMS advertising: An experimental study. *Journal of Interactive Advertising*, 7(2), 16–27.

Duff, B. R. L., Yoon, G., Wang, Z., & Anghelcev, G. (2014). Doing it all: An exploratory study of predictors of media multitasking. *Journal of Interactive Advertising*, 14(1), 11–23.

Eastin, M. S., Daugherty, T., & Burns, N. M. (2011). *Handbook of research on digital media and advertising: User generated content consumption*. Hershey, PA: IGI-Global.

Eckler, P., & Bolls, P. (2011). Spreading the virus: Emotional tone of viral advertising and its effect on forwarding intentions and attitudes. *Journal of Interactive Advertising*, 11(2), 1–11.

Edwards, S. M., & Gangadharbatla, H. (2001). The novelty of 3D product presentations online. *Journal of Interactive Advertising*, 2(1), 10–18.

Edwards, S. M., Lee, J. K., & Ferle, C. L. (2009). Does place matter when shopping online? Perceptions of similarity and familiarity as indicators of psychological distance. *Journal of Interactive Advertising*, 10(1), 35–50.

Elias, T., Appiah, O., & Gong, L. (2011). Effects of strength of ethnic identity and product presenter race on black consumer attitudes: A multiple-group model approach. *Journal of Interactive Advertising, 11*(2), 13–29.

Evans, N. J. (2014). Pinpointing persuasion in children's advergames: Exploring the relationship among parents' internet mediation, marketplace knowledge, attitudes, and the support for regulation. *Journal of Interactive Advertising, 14*(2), 73–85.

Fagerstrøm, A., & Ghinea, G. (2010). Web 2.0's marketing impact on low-involvement consumers. *Journal of Interactive Advertising, 10*(2), 67–71.

Ferguson, D. A., & Perse, E. M. (2004). Audience satisfaction among TiVo and ReplayTV users. *Journal of Interactive Advertising, 4*(2), 1–8.

Fong, J., & Burton, S. (2006). Electronic word-of-mouth: A comparison of stated and revealed behavior on electronic discussion boards. *Journal of Interactive Advertising, 6*(2), 7–62.

Fortunato, J. A., & Windels, D. M. (2005). Adoption of digital video recorders and advertising: Threats or opportunities. *Journal of Interactive Advertising, 6*(1), 93–104.

Gangadharbatla, H. (2008). Facebook me: Collective self-esteem, need to belong, and internet self-efficacy as predictors of the iGeneration's attitudes toward social networking sites. *Journal of Interactive Advertising, 8*(2), 5–15.

Glass, Z. (2007). The effectiveness of product placement in video games. *Journal of Interactive Advertising, 8*(1), 23–32.

Goldsmith, R. E., & Horowitz, D. (2006). Measuring motivations for online opinion seeking. *Journal of Interactive Advertising, 6*(2), 2–14.

Gould, J. R., & Coyle, S. J. (2002). How consumers generate clickstreams through web sites: An empirical investigation of hypertext, schema and mapping theoretical explanations. *Journal of Interactive Advertising, 2*(2), 42–56.

Grigorovici, D. M., & Constantin, C. D. (2004). Experiencing interactive advertising beyond rich media: Impacts of ad type and presence on brand effectiveness in 3D gaming immersive virtual environments. *Journal of Interactive Advertising, 5*(1), 22–36.

Ha, L. (2003). Crossing offline and online media: A comparison of online advertising on TV web sites and online portals. *Journal of Interactive Advertising, 3*(2), 24–35.

Hanley, M., George-Palilonis, J., & Tanksale, V. (2008). Research-informed development for interactive media: Enhancing learning by engaging students with users. *Journal of Interactive Advertising, 9*(1), 56–64.

Hansen, S. S. (2009). Brands inspiring creativity and transpiring meaning: An ethnographic exploration of virtual world play. *Journal of Interactive Advertising, 9*(2), 4–17.

Hayes, J. L., & King, K. W. (2014). The social exchange of viral ads: Referral and coreferral of ads among college students. *Journal of Interactive Advertising, 14*(2), 98–109.

Heeter, C. (2000). Interactivity in the context of designed experiences. *Journal of Interactive Advertising, 1*(1), 3–14.

Hernandez, M. D., Chapa, S., Minor, M. S., Maldonado, C., & Barranzuela, F. (2004). Hispanic attitudes toward advergames: A proposed model of their antecedents. *Journal of Interactive Advertising, 5*(1), 74–83.

Hoffman, D. L., & Novak, T. P. (1996). Marketing in hypermedia computer-mediated environments: Conceptual foundations. *The Journal of Marketing, 6*(3), 50–68.

Hoy, M. G., & Milne, G. (2010). Gender differences in privacy-related measures for young adult Facebook users. *Journal of Interactive Advertising, 10*(2), 28–45.

Huang, M., & Tsang, A. S. (2010). Development and current issues related to Internet marketing communications in China. *Journal of Interactive Advertising, 11*(1), 1–10.

Hupfer, M. E., & Grey, A. (2005). Getting something for nothing: The impact of a sample offer and user mode on banner ad response. *Journal of Interactive Advertising, 6*(1), 105–117.

Hwang, J. S., McMillan, S. J., & Lee, G. (2003). Corporate web sites as advertising: An analysis of function, audience, and message strategy. *Journal of Interactive Advertising, 3*(2), 10–23.

Im, S., Lee, D. H., Taylor, C. R., & D'Orazio, C. (2008). The influence of consumer self-disclosure on web sites on advertising response. *Journal of Interactive Advertising, 9*(1), 37–48.

Jansen, B. J., Hudson, K., Hunter, L., Liu, F., & Murphy, J. (2008). The Google online marketing challenge: Classroom learning with real clients, real money, and real advertising campaigns. *Journal of Interactive Advertising, 9*(1), 49–55.

Jeandrain, A. C. (2001). Consumer reactions in a realistic virtual shop: Influence on buying style. *Journal of Interactive Advertising, 2*(1), 2–9.

Jee, J., & Lee, W. N. (2002). Antecedents and consequences of perceived interactivity: An exploratory study. *Journal of Interactive Advertising, 3*(1), 34–45.

Jeong, Y., & Coyle, E. (2014). What are you worrying about on Facebook and Twitter? An empirical investigation of young social network site users' privacy perceptions and behaviors. *Journal of Interactive Advertising, 14*(2), 51–59.

Jin, S. A. A., & Bolebruch, J. (2009). Avatar-based advertising in second life: The role of presence and attractiveness of virtual spokespersons. *Journal of Interactive Advertising, 10*(1), 51–60.

Kamal, S., Chu, S. C., & Pedram, M. (2013). Materialism, attitudes, and social media usage and their impact on purchase intention of luxury fashion goods among American and Arab young generations. *Journal of Interactive Advertising, 13*(1), 27–40.

Katz, H. (2000). Interactivity in 2000: An industry viewpoint. *Journal of Interactive Advertising, 1*(1), 78–85.

Katz, H. (2010). The pool lane one: Making a splash with online video. *Journal of Interactive Advertising, 10*(2), 72–77. Kelly, L., Kerr, G., & Drennan, J. (2010). Avoidance of advertising in social networking sites: The teenage perspective. *Journal of Interactive Advertising, 10*(2), 16–27.

Kim, K., Hayes, J. L., Avant, J. A., & Reid, L. N. (2014). Trends in advertising research: A longitudinal analysis of leading advertising, marketing, and communication journals, 1980 to 2010. *Journal of Advertising, 43*(3), 296–316.

Kim, E., Lin, J. S., & Sung, Y. (2013). To app or not to app: Engaging consumers via branded mobile apps. *Journal of Interactive Advertising, 13*(1), 53–65.

Kim, J., McMillan, S. J., & Hwang, J. S. (2005). Strategies for the super bowl of advertising: An analysis of how the web is integrated into campaigns. *Journal of Interactive Advertising, 6*(1), 46–60.

Kinney, L., & Ireland, J. (2015). Brand spokes-characters as Twitter marketing tools. *Journal of Interactive Advertising, 15*(2), 135–150.

Ko, H., Jung, J., Kim, J., & Shim, S. W. (2004). Cross-cultural differences in perceived risk of online shopping. *Journal of Interactive Advertising, 4*(2), 20–29.

Kononova, A., & Yuan, S. (2015). Double-dipping effect? How combining YouTube environmental PSAs with thematically congruent advertisements in different formats affects memory and attitudes. *Journal of Interactive Advertising, 15*(1), 2–15.

Kuhn, T. S. (1962). *The structure of scientific revolutions.* Chicago: University of Chicago Press.

Kuhn, T. S. (1970). *The structure of scientific revolutions* (2nd ed.). Chicago: University of Chicago Press.

Kwon, E. S., & Sung, Y. (2011). Follow me! Global marketers' Twitter use. *Journal of Interactive Advertising, 12*(1), 4–16.

Leckenby, J. D., & Li, H. (2000). From the editors: Why we need the Journal of Interactive Advertising. *Journal of Interactive Advertising, 1*(1), 1–3.

Lee, J., Ham, C. D., & Kim, M. (2013). Why people pass along online video advertising: From the perspectives of the interpersonal communication motives scale and the theory of reasoned action. *Journal of Interactive Advertising, 13*(1), 1–13.

Lee, S. J., Lee, W. N., Kim, H., & Stout, P. A. (2004). A comparison of objective characteristics and user perception of web sites. *Journal of Interactive Advertising, 4*(2), 61–75.

Lee, Y. J., & Ahn, H. Y. (2013). Interaction effects of perceived sponsor motives and Facebook credibility on willingness to visit social cause Facebook page. *Journal of Interactive Advertising, 13*(1), 41–52.

Lewis, B., & Porter, L. (2010). In-game advertising effects: Examining player perceptions of advertising schema congruity in a massively multiplayer online role-playing game. *Journal of Interactive Advertising, 10*(2), 46–60.

Lewis, M. W., & Grimes, A. I. (1999). Metatriangulation: Building theory from multiple paradigms. *Academy of Management Review, 24*(4), 672–690.

Liang, C. (2010). The present situation of and prospects for e-business in China. *Journal of Interactive Advertising, 11*(1), 74–81.

Limpf, N., & Voorveld, H. A. (2015). Mobile location-based advertising: How information privacy concerns influence consumers' attitude and acceptance. *Journal of Interactive Advertising, 15*(2), 111–123.

Lin, J. S., & Peña, J. (2011). Are you following me? A content analysis of TV networks' brand communication on Twitter. *Journal of Interactive Advertising, 12*(1), 17–29.

Liu, Y. L. (2003). Broadband demand, competition, and relevant policy in Taiwan. *Journal of Interactive Advertising, 4*(1), 39–46.

Logan, K. (2014). Why isn't everyone doing it? A comparison of antecedents to following brands on Twitter and Facebook. *Journal of Interactive Advertising, 14*(2), 60–72.

Lombard, M., & Snyder-Duch, J. (2001). Interactive advertising and presence: A framework. *Journal of Interactive Advertising, 1*(2), 56–65.

López, M., & Sicilia, M. (2014). eWOM as source of influence: The impact of participation in eWOM and perceived source trustworthiness on decision making. *Journal of Interactive Advertising, 14*(2), 86–97.

Luo, X. (2002). Uses and gratifications theory and e-consumer behaviors: A structural equation modeling study. *Journal of Interactive Advertising, 2*(2), 34–41.

Luna Cortés, G., & Royo Vela, M. (2013). The antecedents of consumers' negative attitudes toward SMS advertising: A theoretical framework and empirical study. *Journal of Interactive Advertising, 13*(2), 109–117.

Mabry, E., & Porter, L. (2010). Movies and Myspace: The effectiveness of official web sites versus online promotional contests. *Journal of Interactive Advertising, 10*(2), 1–15.

Macias, W. (2003). A preliminary structural equation model of comprehension and persuasion of interactive advertising brand web sites. *Journal of Interactive Advertising, 3*(2), 36–48.

Macias, W., Lewis, L. S., & Shankar, V. (2004). Dr. Mom and Dr. Web: A qualitative analysis of women's use of health information on the web. *Journal of Interactive Advertising, 4*(2), 9–19.

Mallia, K. L., & Windels, K. (2011). Will changing media change the world? An exploratory investigation of the impact of digital advertising on opportunities for creative women. *Journal of Interactive Advertising, 11*(2), 30–44.

Martin, K., & Todorov, I. (2010). How will digital platforms be harnessed in 2010, and how will they change the way people interact with brands? *Journal of Interactive Advertising, 10*(2), 61–66.

Maslowska, E., Smit, E. G., & van den Putte, B. (2016). It is all in the name: A study of consumers' responses to personalized communication. *Journal of Interactive Advertising, 16*(1), 74–85.

McMahan, C., Hovland, R., & McMillan, S. (2009). Online marketing communications: Exploring online consumer behavior by examining gender differences and interactivity within internet advertising. *Journal of Interactive Advertising, 10*(1), 61–76.

McMillan, S. J. (2002). Longevity of websites and interactive advertising communication. *Journal of Interactive Advertising, 2*(2), 11–21.

McMillan, S. J. (2005). The researchers and the concept: Moving beyond a blind examination of interactivity. *Journal of Interactive Advertising, 5*(2), 1–4.

Merisavo, M., Kajalo, S., Karjaluoto, H., Virtanen, V., Salmenkivi, S., Raulas, M., & Leppäniemi, M. (2007). An empirical study of the drivers of consumer acceptance of mobile advertising. *Journal of Interactive Advertising, 7*(2), 41–50.

Micu, A. C., & Thorson, E. (2008). Leveraging news and advertising to introduce new brands on the web. *Journal of Interactive Advertising, 9*(1), 14–26.

Mitra, A. (2003). Cybernetic space: Bringing the virtual and real together. *Journal of Interactive Advertising, 3*(2), 1–9.

Moon, J. H., Kim, E., Choi, S. M., & Sung, Y. (2013). Keep the social in social media: The role of social interaction in avatar-based virtual shopping. *Journal of Interactive Advertising, 13*(1), 14–26.

Morimoto, M., & Chang, S. (2006). Consumers' attitudes toward unsolicited commercial e-mail and postal direct mail marketing methods: Intrusiveness, perceived loss of control, and irritation. *Journal of Interactive Advertising, 7*(1), 1–11.

Morrison, M. A., Cheong, H. J., & McMillan, S. J. (2013). Posting, lurking, and networking: Behaviors and characteristics of consumers in the context of user-generated content. *Journal of Interactive Advertising, 13*(2), 97–108.

Muk, A., & Chung, C. (2014). Driving consumers to become fans of brand pages: A theoretical framework. *Journal of Interactive Advertising, 14*(1), 1–10.

Murdough, C. (2009). Social media measurement: It's not impossible. *Journal of Interactive Advertising, 10*(1), 94–99.

Nairn, A., Berthon, P., & Money, A. (2007). Learning from giants: Exploring, classifying and analysing existing knowledge on market research. *International Journal of Market Research, 49*(2), 257–274.

Nasco, S. A., & Bruner, G. C. (2007). Perceptions and recall of advertising content presented on mobile handled devices. *Journal of Interactive Advertising, 7*(2), 51–62.

Nelson, M. R., Keum, H., & Yaros, R. A. (2004). Advertainment or adcreep game players' attitudes toward advertising and product placements in computer games. *Journal of Interactive Advertising, 5*(1), 3–21.

Nicovich, S. G. (2005). The effect of involvement on ad judgment in a video game environment: The mediating role of presence. *Journal of Interactive Advertising, 6*(1), 29–39.

Ohme, R., Matukin, M., & Pacula-Lesniak, B. (2011). Biometric measures for interactive advertising research. *Journal of Interactive Advertising, 11*(2), 60–72.

Okazaki, S. (2009). Mobile finds girls' taste: Knorr's new product development. *Journal of Interactive Advertising, 9*(2), 32–39.

Park, H., Rodgers, S., & Stemmle, J. (2011). Health organizations' use of Facebook for health advertising and promotion. *Journal of Interactive Advertising, 12*(1), 62–77.

Patwardhan, P., & Ramaprasad, J. (2005). Rational integrative model of online consumer decision making. *Journal of Interactive Advertising, 6*(1), 2–13.

Patwardhan, P., & Yang, J. (2003). Internet dependency relations and online consumer behavior: A media system dependency theory perspective on why people shop, chat, and read news online. *Journal of Interactive Advertising, 3*(2), 57–69.

Pavlou, P. A., & Stewart, D. W. (2000). Measuring the effects and effectiveness of interactive advertising: A research agenda. *Journal of Interactive Advertising, 1*(1), 61–77.

Pennington, R. (2001). Signs of marketing in virtual reality. *Journal of Interactive Advertising,* *2*(1), 33–43.

Pentina, I., & Taylor, D. G. (2013). Regulatory focus and daily-deal message framing: Are we saving or gaining with Groupon? *Journal of Interactive Advertising, 13*(2), 67–75.

Phillips, J., Tandoh, M., Noble, S., & Bush, V. (2004). The value of relationship strength in segmenting casino patrons: An exploratory investigation. *Journal of Interactive Advertising,* *5*(1), 60–73.

Porter, L., & Golan, J. G. (2006). From subservient chickens to brawny men: A comparison of viral advertising to television advertising. *Journal of Interactive Advertising, 6*(2), 4–33.

Rafaeli, S., & Sudweeks, F. (1997). Networked interactivity. *Journal of Computer-Mediated Communication, 2*(4). doi: 10.1111/j.1083–6101.1997.tb00201.x.

Richards, J. I. (2000). Interactive advertising concentration: A first attempt. *Journal of Interactive Advertising, 1*(1), 15–22.

Riffe, D., & Lacy, S. (2014). *Analyzing media messages: Using quantitative content analysis in research.* New York, NY: Routledge.

Roberts, M. S., & Ko, H. (2001). Global interactive advertising: Defining what we mean and using what we have learned. *Journal of Interactive Advertising, 1*(2), 18–27.

Rodgers, S. (2002). The interactive advertising model tested: The role of motives in ad processing. *Journal of Interactive Advertising, 2*(2), 22–33.

Rodgers, S., Jin, Y., Rettie, R., Alpert, F., & Yoon, D. (2005). Internet motives of users in the United States, United Kingdom, Australia, and Korea: A cross-cultural replication of the WMI. *Journal of Interactive Advertising, 6*(1), 61–67.

Rodgers, S., & Thorson, E. (2000). The interactive advertising model: How users perceive and process online ads. *Journal of Interactive Advertising, 1*(1), 41–60.

Rosenkrans, G. (2005). Online auctions as advertising revenue in the media mix. *Journal of Interactive Advertising, 6*(1), 14–28.

Rosenkrans, G. (2009). The creativeness and effectiveness of online interactive rich media advertising. *Journal of Interactive Advertising, 9*(2), 18–31.

Russell, M. G. (2009). A call for creativity in new metrics for liquid media. *Journal of Interactive Advertising, 9*(2), 44–61.

Ryu, C. R., Kim, D. H., & Kim, E. M. (2003). Diffusion of broadband and online advertising in Korea. *Journal of Interactive Advertising, 4*(1), 3–12.

Sashittal, H. C., & Jassawalla, A. R. (2015). Why do college students use Pinterest? A model and implications for scholars and marketers. *Journal of Interactive Advertising, 15*(1), 54–66.

Schulz, H. M., Dority, B. L., & Schulz, S. A. (2015). Individual differences in online consumer behaviors in relation to brand prominence. *Journal of Interactive Advertising, 15*(1), 67–80.

Schumann, D. W., Artis, A., & Rivera, R. (2001). The future of interactive advertising viewed through an IMC lens. *Journal of Interactive Advertising, 1*(2), 43–55.

Seounmi, Y., Lee, M., & Doyle, K. O. (2003). Lifestyles of online gamers: A psychographic approach. *Journal of Interactive Advertising, 3*(2), 49–56.

Shan, Y., & King, K. W. (2015). The effects of interpersonal tie strength and subjective norms on consumers' brand-related eWOM referral intentions. *Journal of Interactive Advertising, 15*(1), 16–27.

Sheehan, K. B. (2002). Online research methodology: Reflections and speculations. *Journal of Interactive Advertising, 3*(1), 56–61.

Sheehan, K. B., & Morrison, D. K. (2009). The creativity challenge: Media confluence and its effects on the evolving advertising industry. *Journal of Interactive Advertising, 9*(2), 40–43.

Sicilia, M., & Ruiz, S. (2007). The role of flow in web site effectiveness. *Journal of Interactive Advertising, 8*(1), 33–44.

Siemens, J. C., Smith, S., & Fisher, D. (2015). Investigating the effects of active control on brand recall within in-game advertising. *Journal of Interactive Advertising, 15*(1), 43–53.

Sokolik, K., Magee, R. G., & Ivory, J. D. (2014). Red-hot and ice-cold web ads: The influence of web ads' warm and cool colors on click-through rates. *Journal of Interactive Advertising, 14*(1), 31–37.

Spurgeon, C. (2005). Losers and lovers: Mobile phone services advertising and the new media consumer/producer. *Journal of Interactive Advertising, 5*(2), 47–55.

Steinfield, C. (2002). Understanding click and mortar e-commerce approaches: A conceptual framework and research agenda. *Journal of Interactive Advertising, 2*(2), 1–10.

Steyer, A., Garcia-Bardidia, R., & Quester, P. (2006). Online discussion groups as social networks: An empirical investigation of word-of-mouth on the Internet. *Journal of Interactive Advertising, 6*(2), 6–52.

Sundar, S. S., & Kim, J. (2005). Interactivity and persuasion: Influencing attitudes with information and involvement. *Journal of Interactive Advertising, 5*(2), 5–18.

Swain, W. N. (2005). Perceptions of interactivity and consumer control in marketing communications: An exploratory survey of marketing communication professionals. *Journal of Interactive Advertising, 6*(1), 82–92.

Taniwaki, Y. (2003). Emerging broadband market and the relevant policy agenda in Japan. *Journal of Interactive Advertising, 4*(1), 25–32.

Thorson, K. S., & Rodgers, S. (2006). Relationships between blogs as eWOM and interactivity, perceived interactivity, and parasocial interaction. *Journal of Interactive Advertising, 6*(2), 5–44.

Townsend, L. (2005). The status of wireless survey solutions: The emerging "power of the thumb." *Journal of Interactive Advertising, 6*(1), 40–45.

Tremayne, M. (2005). Lessons learned from experiments with interactivity on the web. *Journal of Interactive Advertising, 5*(2), 40–46.

Troutman, M., & Timpson, S. (2008). Effective optimization of web sites for mobile access: The transition from eCommerce to mCommerce. *Journal of Interactive Advertising, 9*(1), 65–70.

Tsai, W. H. S., & Men, L. R. (2013). Motivations and antecedents of consumer engagement with brand pages on social networking sites. *Journal of Interactive Advertising, 13*(2), 76–87.

Unni, R., & Harmon, R. (2007). Perceived effectiveness of push vs. pull mobile location based advertising. *Journal of Interactive Advertising, 7*(2), 28–40.

van't Riet, J., Hühn, A., Ketelaar, P., Khan, V. J., Konig, R., Rozendaal, E., & Markopoulos, P. (2016). Investigating the effects of location-based advertising in the supermarket: Does goal congruence trump location congruence? *Journal of Interactive Advertising, 16*(1), 31–43.

Vilpponen, A., Winter, S., & Sundqvist, S. (2006). Electronic word-of-mouth in online environments: Exploring referral networks structure and adoption behavior. *Journal of Interactive Advertising, 6*(2), 8–77.

Wagler, A. (2013). Embracing change: Exploring how creative professionals use interactive media in advertising campaigns. *Journal of Interactive Advertising, 13*(2), 118–127.

Wan, F., & Youn, S. (2004). Motivations to regulate online gambling and violent game sites: An account of the third-person effect. *Journal of Interactive Advertising, 5*(1), 46–59.

Wang, S., Cunningham, N. R., & Eastin, M. S. (2015). The impact of eWOM message characteristics on the perceived effectiveness of online consumer reviews. *Journal of Interactive Advertising, 15*(2), 151–159.

Wang, Y., Rodgers, S., Wang, Z., & Thorson, E. (2016). A seventeen-year study of graduate student authorship in advertising journals. *Journalism & Mass Communication Educator*, *71*(1), 69–83.

Wells, W. D., & Chen, Q. (2000). The dimensions of commercial cyberspace. *Journal of Interactive Advertising*, *1*(1), 23–40.

Willmott, H., Jackson, N., & Carter, P. (1993). Breaking the paradigm mentality. *Organization Studies*, *14*(5), 681–719.

Wise, K., Alhabash, S., & Eckler, P. (2013). "Window" shopping online: Cognitive processing of general and specific product windows. *Journal of Interactive Advertising*, *13*(2), 88–96.

Wise, K., Bolls, P. D., Kim, H., Venkataraman, A., & Meyer, R. (2008). Enjoyment of advergames and brand attitudes: The impact of thematic relevance. *Journal of Interactive Advertising*, *9*(1), 27–36.

Wu, G. (2005). The mediating role of perceived interactivity in the effect of actual interactivity on attitude toward the website. *Journal of Interactive Advertising*, *5*(2), 29–39.

Wu, G. (2007). Applying the Rossiter-Percy grid to online advertising planning: The role of product/brand type in previsit intentions. *Journal of Interactive Advertising*, *8*(1), 15–22.

Wu, L. (2016). Understanding the impact of media engagement on the perceived value and acceptance of advertising within mobile social networks. *Journal of Interactive Advertising*, *16*(1), 59–73.

Xia, L., & Bechwati, N. N. (2008). Word of mouse: The role of cognitive personalization in online consumer reviews. *Journal of Interactive Advertising*, *9*(1), 3–13.

Xie, T., Donthu, N., Lohtia, R., & Osmonbekov, T. (2004). Emotional appeal and incentive offering in banner advertisements. *Journal of Interactive Advertising*, *4*(2), 30–37.

Yaoyuneyong, G., Foster, J., Johnson, E., & Johnson, D. (2016). Augmented reality marketing: Consumer preferences and attitudes toward hypermedia print ads. *Journal of Interactive Advertising*, *16*(1), 16–30.

Yoo, C. Y., Kim, K., & Stout, P. A. (2004). Assessing the effects of animation in online banner advertising: Hierarchy of effects model. *Journal of Interactive Advertising*, *4*(2), 49–60.

Yoon, D., Cropp, F., & Cameron, G. (2002). Building relationships with portal users: The interplay of motivation and relational factors. *Journal of Interactive Advertising*, *3*(1), 1–11.

Yoon, D., & Youn, S. (2016). Brand experience on the website: Its mediating role between perceived interactivity and relationship quality. *Journal of Interactive Advertising*, *16*(1), 1–15.

Zeng, F., Huang, L., & Dou, W. (2009). Social factors in user perceptions and responses to advertising in online social networking communities. *Journal of Interactive Advertising*, *10*(1), 1–13.

PART II
Theory Breakthroughs

5

DIGITAL ADVERTISING CLUTTER IN AN AGE OF MOBILE MEDIA

Louisa Ha

What is clutter? Is all advertising clutter? These are the basic questions that we need to ask before embarking on research on advertising clutter. Clutter has been defined as "a large amount of non-editorial content in an editorial medium" (Ha & McCann, 2008, p. 570). It is more about density than quantity of such non-editorial content. If the non-editorial content refers to advertisements, then it is advertising clutter. Clutter is described as a "difficult media environment" (Webb, 1979, p. 225). The key to this definition of advertising clutter is that the advertising is placed in a *third-party* editorial media vehicle, such as magazines or television programs (Ha, 2008). Some important characteristics of clutter are that clutter is unwanted, undesirable, and excessive, and interferes with the consumption of editorial content.

Relevance of the ads to the individual is one major factor of whether the advertising is considered desirable (Kim & Sundar, 2010). The entertainment value of the ad also affects the consumer's receptiveness of the ads (Ducoffe, 1995; Ko, Cho, & Roberts, 2005). In addition, the goal of the user in the media consumption process moderates clutter perception (Ha & McCann, 2008; Heinz, Hug, Nugaeva, & Opwis, 2013; Seyedghorban, Tahernejad, & Matanda, 2015). Hence, perceived clutter levels vary by individuals (Ha, 1996). When advertising has a high level of ad-context congruity (Zanjani, Diamond, & Chan, 2011) or high compatibility with editorial content (Ha, 1996) being seen as relevant (Kim & Sundar, 2010), then advertising is not clutter but is considered desirable and useful content to the audience. Hence, advertising clutter is a complex concept, as it varies by individuals.

Evolution of the Research on Clutter

Research on advertising clutter can be dated back to the late 1970s and had focused primarily on TV advertising clutter from Webb (1979) to Mord and Gilson (1985), Brown and Rothschild (1993), Pieters and Bijmolt (1997), and Zhao

(1997) to more recent researchers, such as Hammer, Riebe, and Kennedy (2009). The captivity of television as a mass medium and the high stakes TV advertising poses to the TV and advertising industry are the main reasons for such focus on TV advertising clutter. However, Ha (1996) demonstrates that the effect of clutter is not limited to TV but can affect any media outlet, including self-paced media such as magazines.

The online and digital media context presents new challenges because the passive and captive environment of traditional offline media is replaced by the active and self-paced environments in digital media. The competition for users' attention online is fierce, as users can easily move to another web page at the click of a mouse or the touch of a finger in mobile media. Theoretically, users are less subject to advertisers in digital media with the abundance of choices at their fingertips. Yet, online advertising formats range from complete control by advertisers, such as pre-roll video ads, that show the TV commercial before the display of an online video users want to watch, and pop-up ads that block the whole screen for several seconds before the user can move to anything else, to ads as non-intrusive as a sponsored link on a Google search page and banners along the edges or bottom of a web page.

Burns and Lutz's (2006) experiment compared different consumer responses to six online advertising formats: banners, floating ads, large rectangles, interstitials, skyscrapers, and pop-ups. Their experiment showed that pop-up ads and floating ads scored highest on the annoyance factor, while interstitial ads scored highest on the entertainment factor. Banner ads scored highest on the information factor and received the highest overall positive attitude from consumers and performed the best on all behavioral measures, such as click-through percentage, percent visit later, and click-through frequency. Cho and Cheon (2004) developed a model of online advertising avoidance prompted by perceived goal impediment, perceived ad clutter, and prior negative experience using a student sample. Perceived ad clutter was found to be the most important predictor of advertising avoidance. This result was replicated in a recent study of a general consumer sample in Iran (Seyedghorban, Tahernejad, & Matanda, 2015).

Causes of Advertising Clutter

One fundamental issue challenging advertisers is that some consumers have an overall negative attitude toward advertising in general due to its profit-making persuasion motive and its negative effect on society. Advertising is seen by some to lower the quality of content and sacrifice the independent nature of the news media. The use of ad-blocker software on computers and subscriptions to ad-free premium program packages, such as YouTube Red and Hulu Plus, are examples of overt manifestations of those online users who do not like to see any ads at all. The Adobe Page Fair Ad Blocking Report shows that 16 percent of U.S. online users and up to 198 million users worldwide used ad blockers (PageFair, 2015). The report also indicates that a large increase in the quantity of online ads will stimulate interest in using ad blockers among U.S. online users. The trade association for digital advertising, the Interactive Advertising Bureau (IAB), views ad-blockers as a threat to the digital advertising industry, especially condemning those who replace the blocked ads with their own programmatic ads (Tribbey, 2016).

Three Dimensions of Clutter as Advertising Environment

Unlike the extreme of complete hatred toward advertising and total ad avoidance, complaints about advertising clutter are more commonly caused by the ways advertisements are presented to the audience in an editorial media unit, be it as an issue of a magazine, a TV program, a newspaper, or a web page. Ha (1996) proposed three dimensions of advertising clutter, or essentially three ways that advertisements can constitute clutter to the audience: quantity, competitiveness, and intrusiveness. Quantity is the large number of ads or proportion of ads (degree of commercialization) in the space of an editorial media unit, or the so-called "list length effect," and commercial load (Bellman, Treleaven-Hassard, Robinson, Rask, & Varan, 2012). Competitiveness is the degree of similarity of the product categories in the ads in an editorial media unit, causing confusion and perceived duplication among the audiences. Intrusiveness is the degree to which the ads interfere with the audience's consumption of editorial content. So a commercial inserted in between two programs would be considered less intrusive than the one inserted in an unexpected commercial break that interrupts the flow of a program. Although Ha's (1996) study showed that both the quantity and intrusiveness dimensions had the most negative impact on advertising effectiveness in terms of recall, recognition, and attitude toward the ad, the competitiveness dimensions of clutter could still be a concern when researchers examine ads that are of similar product categories in a more captive medium such as television and not in a self-paced medium such as magazines. The many similar product/service sponsored links in a Google search is a common example of highly competitive digital ad clutter, as they can be confused by the highly similar product listings.

Effects of Clutter

Approaches to Clutter Effects

Despite the interest of advertisers and researchers in the effects of clutter, the results are inconclusive due to several reasons. First is the difference in the captivity of media, which is the degree to which the user can control the pace of flow of content of the medium. Captive media, such as TV and radio, usually result in higher recall than self-paced media, such as print and online. For example, Hammer, Riebe, and Kennedy (2009) found that there is no difference in the recall of ads and ad avoidance in radio and TV with more or fewer ads. Creative execution is a better predictor of recall than clutter. Second is the difference in user task orientations. If users have a clear task, their tolerance of clutter is lower. If they are in a leisure/surfing mode, they are less resistant toward clutter. Third is the difference between laboratory and field research settings. The lab environment that controls many variables and forces ad/editorial exposure to participants could result in higher recall and recognition than the many distractions the audience would be faced with in field settings.

Ha and McCann (2008) proposed an integrated model of advertising clutter to provide a comprehensive model of understanding perception formation and its effects in both the digital and traditional media environments. Their model includes: 1) the structural approach, 2) the information processing approach, and 3) the goal impediment (functional) approach in examining the effect of advertising clutter. The difference between online and offline advertising clutter is mainly in the increase in advertiser control of advertising display time/customization, and variety in ad formats for user control (see Figures 5.1 and 5.2).

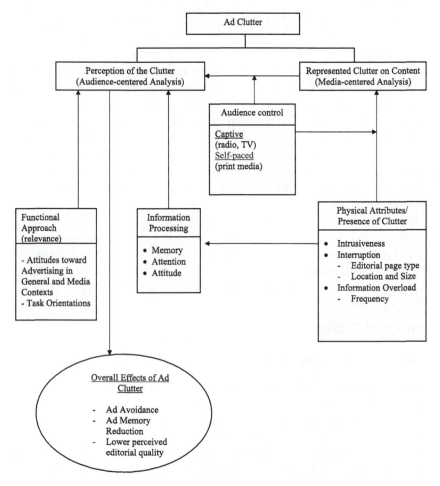

FIGURE 5.1 A Conceptual Framework of Advertising Clutter in Offline Media

Reprinted with permission. Ha, L. & McCann, K. (2008). An integrated model of advertising clutter in offline and online media environment. *International Journal of Advertising*, 27(4), 569–592. http://www.tandfonline.com/doi/abs/10.2501/S0265048708080153

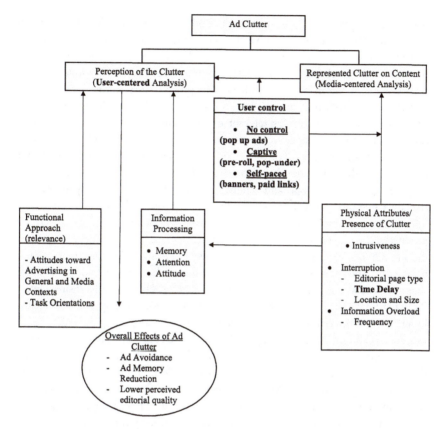

FIGURE 5.2 A Conceptual Framework of Advertising Clutter in Online Media (Bold faces indicate differences from offline media.)

Reprinted with permission. Ha, L. & McCann, K. (2008). An integrated model of advertising clutter in offline and online media environment. *International Journal of Advertising*, 27(4), 569–592. http://www. tandfonline.com/doi/abs/10.2501/S0265048708080153

As noted in Chapter 1, the structural approach is about the physical attributes of ads and, in this case, advertising clutter, which are controllable by advertisers and the media firm. These include the duration of ads, number of ads, location and visibility of ads, ad-context/editorial congruity, and the execution (production quality) of the ads. These factors can affect the perception of clutter level among the audiences.

Although physical attributes as a media-centered analysis can influence perception of clutter, there are other information processing factors affecting perception of clutter such as overall attitudes toward advertising (e.g., Muehling, 1987) and persuasion knowledge or the awareness of a persuasive intent in advertising (e.g., Campbell & Kirmani, 2000). Capability of processing advertising messages among the audiences (perceived message overload) can also affect the perceived advertising clutter level. Reactance theory and overload theory are the common theories used to explain the negative effects of clutter. Reactance theory argues that audiences resist external control over them and react negatively toward efforts to persuade them (Brehm & Brehm, 1981; Edwards, Li, & Lee, 2002), while overload theory explains the inability of audiences to process large amounts of messages in a cluttered situation (Malhotra, Jain, & Lagakos, 1982). In addition, users select advertising that is perceived as relevant or interesting for them to process based on selective attention theory to save their attention resources (Smith & Buchholz, 1991). Finally, the consumer's involvement in the advertised product will affect their processing of the advertising based on the Elaboration Likelihood Model (ELM) proposed by Petty, Cacciopo, and Schumann (1983). Consumers highly involved in the advertised product will use a central processing route and pay attention to the information contained in the advertising. Consumers not involved in the advertised product will use peripheral cues such as advertising execution elements to process the ads. When advertising clutter consists largely of products that consumers are not involved in, then the entertainment value of the ads becomes a critical factor for them to process and remember the ads. Hence, researchers on advertising clutter should also take into consideration the information processing approach in examining effects of advertising clutter on the processing of advertising messages.

There is also the functional approach that can be applied to the study of clutter by examining how clutter affects the editorial content consumption process and the goal or user task in media content consumption. Similar to the user mode in Rodgers and Thorson's (2000) Interactive Advertising Model (IAM), Ha and McCann's (2008) integrated model proposed that user task orientations affected perceived clutter levels. Informational searches and task-oriented consumers had a higher perceived level of ad clutter than entertainment, exploration, and shopping-oriented consumers. Subsequent empirical research by Zanjani et al. (2011) confirmed that information seekers were more likely to be affected by ad clutter than surfers. Their experiment shows that advertising clutter has little effect on surfers who have no particular purpose in consuming the e-magazine. But those who have the task of seeking information found the ad clutter intrusive and avoided the ads. Their recognition and recall of ads was lower when the ad-context congruity increased.

Segev, Wang, and Fernandes's (2014) study of advertising on blogs found that importance of ad-context congruency was contingent upon consumers' issue involvement. Ad-context congruency was especially important to those who feel the issue in the editorial content is very relevant to them. But to those who were less involved with the issue, ad-context incongruence was better perceived. In contrast, Seyedghorban, Tahernejad, and Matanda (2015) found that paratelic users (surfers) were more likely to perceive higher advertising clutter than telic users (task performers) because they were more likely to have prior negative experiences with online advertising, e.g., they had clicked on ads that were not useful to them.

Types of Clutter Effects

Cognitive Effects of Advertising Clutter

There are three types of clutter effects on audiences: cognitive, affective, and behavioral. The most common measures of the effects of clutter are its negative cognitive effect on memory of advertisements. For memory of ads, unaided and aided recall, and recognition of ads with choices are common measures. Lee and Cho's (2010) experiment found that there is an interactive effect between frequency of the ads and online advertising clutter. In a highly cluttered web page, frequency of the target ad facilitated memory, but not recognition, of the banner ad. Bellman et al.'s (2012) experiment found that beyond three minutes of commercials within the primetime shows online, there was a marked decline in ad recall and recognition. Usually a negative cognitive effect is related to the quantity of advertising but not the intrusiveness of advertising.

Affective Effects of Advertising Clutter

Affective effects of clutter include attitude toward the advertisement (A_{ad}) in the medium/media vehicle, attitude toward advertising in general, attitude toward the brand (A_{br}), perceived editorial quality, and enjoyment of media content.

It is a well-known fact that consumers have different expectations and attitudes toward advertising in different media. For example, in the 2012 Millward Brown Global AdReactions Report of 6000 mobile media users worldwide (Statista, 2016a), results showed that consumers have much more favorable attitudes toward TV (51%), radio (50%), and magazine ads than online media such as online video ads (28%), mobile ads (23%), and email ads (18%). Hence, Elliot and Speck (1998) found different receptiveness toward advertising clutter for different media. The attitude transfer process can explain how negative attitudes toward advertising that appears in media may affect attitude toward the ad (A_{ad}), attitude toward a specific brand (A_{br}), and/or attitude toward advertising in general (i.e., advertising that appears in a media vehicle, such as magazines) (Ha, 1996).

It is also important to understand that ad clutter as a measurement of commercialization can also affect perceived editorial quality of the media vehicle. For example, too many ads in a magazine will adversely affect the audience's perception of the quality of the magazine and lower the value of the advertisement to the advertiser (Ha & Litman, 1997). Kim and Sundar's (2010) experiment also found that subjects who saw relevant ad clutter evaluated the website that displayed the ads significantly more positively than the website that had irrelevant ad clutter. So it is not just amount, but *relevancy*, that determine the affective effect of clutter. Hence, advertising clutter does not only threaten efficacy of advertising but also the editorial media that carry the advertising as well.

Clutter can also affect the enjoyment of editorial content. Disengagement and adaptation are two psycho-physiological responses to the video programs resulting from ad clutter (Bellman et al., 2012). Disengagement is a decline in autonomic arousal after watching commercials in a video. Adaptation is the disruption and welcome break of the hedonic experience of media content through commercials that led to increasing enjoyment. According to Bellman et al.'s (2012) experiment, adding commercials to prime-time type of programs online did not increase enjoyment of programs, instead audiences adapted to the program.

Behavioral Effects of Advertising Clutter

Behavioral effects of advertising clutter include advertising avoidance and reactance, such as not clicking through the ads. One commonly studied behavioral effect of ad clutter is advertising avoidance. Many advertising avoidance studies, including Cho and Cheon's (2004) model, include perceived advertising clutter as a factor causing advertising avoidance. Almost all advertising avoidance studies included one or more clutter dimension in their studies to explain why people avoid advertising (Rejón-Guardia & Martínez-López, 2014; Seyedghorban, Tahernejad, & Matanda, 2015).

Another behavioral effect is advertising reactance, that is, the resistance to be persuaded by the advertisement after exposure to the ads. When consumers feel overwhelmed by advertisements and cannot avoid them for whatever reasons (such as loud noise, blocked screen), they will resist the advertising and purposely reject the advertising messages they are exposed to. They can ignore or refuse to follow the suggestions and actions recommended by the advertisers, such as clicking through the link/ad. Schumann, von Wangenheim, and Groene (2014) found lower click-through rates (CTRs) among consumers who reported higher ad clutter in their experiment of receptiveness toward digital advertising.

Attention to Advertising in Multiple Web Pages

How do online users process ads in a cluttered environment? Goodrich's (2011) study used a dual attitude model to explain users' processing of ads in a cluttered environment by comparing mere exposure versus conscious processing of online advertising shown in a sequence of eight web pages with some containing banner ads. Her experiment found interaction effects of ad types and ad locations. Visual ads on the right side of a web page and text ads on the left side of the page resulted in higher attention. However, high attention was negatively correlated with brand attitude. The tested product, an electric shaver, did not have a contextual fit with the web pages. The Goodrich (2011) study showed that attention to the ad due to structural factors such as advertising types and location may not result in liking of the brand. Breaking through the clutter is not just about generating attention to the ad, but also creating a positive brand attitude.

In the following section, clutter-related issues in several major digital advertising formats are examined.

Digital Advertising Clutter in Different Ad Formats

Search Advertising and Competitiveness of Ads

Search advertising revenue in the U.S. reached $27.6 billion in 2015, which is more than one half of the total revenue of all digital advertising types (Statista, 2016b). Despite this, relatively little research has been published about search ads (Ha, 2008). Even when it was studied, it was mainly for relevance (ad contextual congruity), rather than competitiveness in relation to ad clutter. Dou, Linn, and Yang's (2001) study examined the online ad industry's use of smart banners by typing in 345 keywords for 115 product categories in 11 search engines. They found that many smart banners did not find relevant results. Kim and Sundar's (2010) experiment using a small student sample ($N = 13$) found that advertising clutter could be reduced by increasing the relevance of ads to the website context without reducing the number of ads. Haans, Raassens, and van Hout (2013) found that evidence type used (i.e., expert, statistical, or causal evidence) in the text affected the CTR of the sponsored links (search ads) in low involvement products. Expert and statistical evidence were considered the most credible and attractive to the searchers. An interaction effect was found in Yoo's (2011) experiment between positivity of advertising message frame and presence of keywords in the search results in facilitating the sponsored link click-through.

One main assumption in search advertising is that when consumers type in a keyword or a phrase into a search engine, such as Google, they are interested in the product/service and, subsequently, are in a shopping mode. But if the consumer tries to research specific information on a topic rather than shopping, then these so-called "smart" ads become an impediment to completing that goal because shopping is not a goal at that time. The consumer has to browse through all the paid listings to find relevant listing to their search. This extra effort will not lead to more use of the ads, but may add to the consumers' resentment toward the advertisers (and search engines) that serve the ads.

Even with the smart ads or personalized ads, there is another issue of trust in the advertisers. Those advertisers to whom the consumers are unfamiliar but who used personalized ads will create a backlash effect because they are seen as violating privacy and stealing personal data from the consumer, i.e., they will be considered less trustworthy and manipulative by consumers (Bleier & Eisenbeiss, 2015). There are also ethical and legal concerns about targeted online behavioral advertising (Nill & Aalberts, 2014). Hence, adding the relevance of the ads is not as effective as it seems. Schumann, von Wangenheim, and Groene's (2014) experiment showed that normative reciprocity, i.e., reminding consumers that receiving targeted advertising as a return for getting free services, was more effective in gaining consumer acceptance than emphasizing the utility value of the targeted advertising to the consumers. The CTR of the targeted ads was higher even in higher perceived clutter level when the reciprocity argument was presented.

Banner Blindness Effects

Banner blindness refers to the overlooking of banner ads on a web page. Several studies about consumers' attention to banner ads (Benway, 1998) have found a banner blindness effect if the banners are placed in an F shape on a screen (i.e., too high or on the edges) or for users who have to perform a goal-directed search for information (Pagendarm & Schaumburg, 2001). Banner ads on Face-book attracted much lower attention levels than the friends' recommendations of the user (Barreto, 2013). Consumers easily overlook these banner ads. However, these banner blindness studies did not vary the number of banners (quantity) or whether the banners pop up or animate on the users' screen (intrusiveness) to examine if banner blindness still occurred. Frequency of banner ads has been shown to positively relate to recall in clutter situations (Zanjani, Diamond, & Chan, 2011). Prior studies have shown that pop-up ads (Edwards, Li, & Lee, 2002; Cho & Cheon, 2004) caught the consumers' attention despite the negative effect of stimulating their intention to avoid the ads. Animated ads can arouse consumers and draw attention to the ads (Sundar & Kalyanaraman, 2004; Yoo, Kim, & Stout, 2004). Hence, the manner of how banners are presented to consumers is critical for them to be viewed as clutter.

Pre-Roll Ads vs. Mid-Roll Commercials in Online Videos and TV Shows

Despite the increasing use of in-stream video advertising in online videos, not many published studies examine video advertising from a clutter perspective. One major concern of clutter in online in-stream video ads is the position of the ads that can affect the intrusiveness of the ads. There are three types of positions: pre-roll (before the video is shown), mid-roll (inserted in the middle of the video content similar to TV commercial breaks), and post-roll ads (shown after the video is over or between episodes). Krishnan and Sitaraman's (2013) study of Akamai's video delivery network with 65 million unique viewers watching 362 million videos and 257 million ad videos of 33 video providers found that mid-roll ads were 18.1 percent more likely to complete when placed as a mid-roll than as a pre-roll. Bellman et al.'s (2012) study comparing different levels of mid-roll adver-tising clutter in TV shows online revealed that the optimal level of online video advertising was three minutes per hour with six different ads and was similar to research on traditional TV advertising clutter. They also found a primacy order effect in that only the first ad being shown had a greater advantage in getting attention and was better remembered than other ads.

Li and Lo's (2015) experiment showed that mid-roll ads led to better brand name recognition than pre-roll and post-roll ads and to the interaction effect of ad position and ad context congruity. They explained that the mid-roll ads performed better due to attention spillover from the video when editorial content for ads were congruent with the content of the media, such as watches shown in fashion programs. But when the ad was unrelated to the video content, the audiences simply ignored the ads with no benefit of brand recognition even if they were put as mid-roll ads (Li & Lo, 2015). They found that incongruent ads with content worked best in post-roll ads. However, it should be noted that all these studies about online video ads only measured their effects on memory and brand recognition, rather than attitude toward the ad or brand. The author argues that the latter are more important measures of advertising effectiveness if we consider the main purpose of advertising is persuasion.

With these lab-based experimental findings supporting the effectiveness of mid-roll ads, it is interesting that YouTube, the largest online video provider, still employs pre-roll full ads and TrueView ads, which allow users to skip ads after five seconds. It is because pre-roll ads can capture the most viewers and must be viewed for consumers to watch the video (and can even include those consumers who did not finish the video). Hence, the provision of choice may reduce consumers' resistance toward the ads, but how much this is viewed positively as a consumer choice needs further study. Even if there is only one commercial, which is typical in a YouTube video, consumers may view it as unwanted or an obstacle to the use of the video content, which puts it squarely in the realm of an ad clutter effect study.

Measures of Digital Editorial Unit and Digital Advertising Clutter

A critical need for researchers of digital advertising clutter is to determine the editorial unit. The editorial unit may vary by the type of display device in which the digital advertising is placed. Nonetheless, the first screen visible to the user without scrolling down probably is the most conservative and standardized measure of editorial unit. It is because scrolling down a page will become another page of content on the screen and that requires extra effort by users of the content. It is hard to estimate how many users scroll down the screen to view the entire page. Other deep-link destination pages of a website is a further step for a user to explore the site, and more research is needed to estimate the likelihood of users to scroll further down a website. In a digital video setting, the duration of the video should be an editorial unit. A smartphone screen is much smaller than a tablet or a computer screen, so the likelihood of perceived clutter level is higher in a smartphone screen than its bigger screen counterparts when advertising is displayed as a proportion of space. It is important that advertisers prepare different versions of ads for different versions of the page. Many web pages now have a computer version and a mobile version. Advertisers should also prepare their ads accordingly for the mobile version and computer version to minimize the physical presence of advertising clutter.

If we still use the conceptualization of three dimensions of clutter as the advertising environment presented to the audiences, then we need to develop measures of the digital advertising clutter corresponding to the three dimensions with regard to different advertising formats. For example, the clutter level from a quantity dimension would be the proportion of the screen or number of advertisement/sponsored links or both, depending on the ad format of interest. If sponsored links and small buttons/banners are used for comparison, then the number of ads will be a better measure. But if prominence or size is the key issue of concern, then the proportion of screen devoted to digital banner ads/sponsored links should be a measure of digital ad quantity. If the digital ad is in the form of in-stream video, the proportion of the duration of the commercial over the actual video can be used to measure the quantity of ads in addition to commercial load.

As for the competitiveness dimension, the degree of similar product categories being shown on a screen should be a measure of competitiveness. Hence, in a Google search page, the proportion of sponsored links from the same product/service categories among all the sponsored links will be the competitiveness measure. In fact, judging from this perspective, even though the sponsored links occupy little physical space of a page because of their high similarity in product categories, its competitiveness clutter level is likely quite high. Yet, because of the high ad-context congruity in the search algorithm and display of the sponsored links, the perceived competitiveness may be viewed as favorable instead of confusing. But whether users may be confused or more willing to try different sponsors in more sponsored links in different search settings will require more research.

For the intrusive dimension, whether the user is forced to view the ad on a screen or per video/podcast will be the main measure. The most intrusive one is the total blocking of the use of editorial content until the ad is fully displayed, such as pop-up ads and non-skippable video ads on online videos. The moderately intrusive one will be the TrueView type of skippable ads (after five seconds of compulsory display, the users can opt out of the ad) and the mid-roll ads. The non-intrusive one will be banner ads or sponsored links on the side of the screen that users can easily ignore and where no editorial content is blocked from the users. As new digital formats emerge with either higher or lower levels of intrusiveness, researchers should continue to monitor advertising formats and measure the perceived intrusiveness of digital ads to consumers.

Mobile Advertising and New Levels of Ad-Context Congruity

Now, mobile media represents a large portion of online access. eMarketer reported that 75 percent of internet users used their mobile devices to access the internet

(Statista, 2016c). Hence, digital ads are much more likely to be displayed on mobile media, which have smaller screens. The GPS (Global Positioning System) and other access of data of mobile users allow even more possibility of customization for advertisers. These so-called location-based advertising and targeting created more opportunities for ad-context congruity. It raises ad-context congruity to a much higher level by the sheer ability to put the ad in close proximity to the actual purchase time and location. Indeed, Bauer and Strauss's (2016) review of location-based advertising studies on mobile devices identified at least 12 types of contextual information from mobile phones that can aid advertisers: 1) users' location, 2) the time the ad can be delivered when users use the device, 3) users' profiles, 4) users' interests, 5) users' preferences, 6) users' behaviors, 7) users' demographics, 8) weather at the users' locations, 9) characteristics of the surrounding environment, 10) type of mobile device the user is using, 11) users' needs (related to search), and 12) users' activities. There are many more possibilities depending on the point of access for information. Despite all these possibilities, an important concern is how much the advertiser should take advantage of such contextual information without being seen as violating the privacy of the individual user. Weather is public information while user demographic information is not. Some types of relevancy may be more welcomed than others. For example, location may be a welcome customization. When someone searches a restaurant, a local restaurant ad display would be more relevant than a restaurant at a far distance from the user unless the user specifies the location of the restaurant. Or when someone is in a shopping mall, ads and sales discount offers from stores in the shopping mall would be highly relevant. Okazaki, Molina, and Hirose (2012) argue that the perceived ubiquity of mobile ads to the consumers led to the avoidance of mobile ads. Yet, how many of the customized mobile ads they would like to receive and how these ads should be displayed (pointers on maps, text messages, banners, buttons, or videos) should be further studied.

Future of Digital Advertising Clutter Research

Differences Between Pull and Push advertising

A final factor to be considered in clutter research is whether the advertising is requested by the consumer (on-demand) or given to the consumer. Ads may not be perceived as clutter when consumers are the ones who request the information/ads (pull), such as a product search on a shopping site such as Amazon.com. But when ads are presented without consumers requesting it (push), they are more easily perceived as clutter (Grusell, 2007; Brettel & Spilker-Attig, 2010). Consumers are much more likely to find the ads helpful when they choose to receive the ads (pull), and they resent misleading ads that do not deliver what they were promised (Truong & Simmons, 2010). It is easy to push digital targeted ads to consumers using computer programming, but consumers' reactance can be much higher if the ads interrupt the consumption of other digital content. Digital ads, while they are relatively easy to customize to the consumer based on their location, use time and other contextual information available in mobile devices, so are also more likely to be seen as clutter impeding the consumption of editorial content if the customization is seen as illegitimate (e.g., advertisers should not know the user's information, such as an advertiser with no prior relationship with the user). In other words, customization is a double-edged sword that advertisers need to be aware of. A research hierarchy will need to be developed by researchers to determine an acceptable level of relevance and customization to determine how consumers trust and view the utility value of such information. Such questions that would guide this inquiry include: How many ads (quantity) and how many ads from companies from the same category (competitiveness) interrupt the flow of editorial content (intrusiveness)? And, in different usage situations (pull vs. push), what effect (e.g., ad avoidance, ad blocking, flaming, etc.) do customized ads have on consumer responses (e.g., avoidance, anger, resentment, ad blocking, etc.)?

One important question in digital advertising is the blurring boundaries between ads and editorial content. The increasing call for "native advertising," such as product brand placement and sponsored content, to combat avoidance of clearly identified advertisements (Verhellen, Dens, & De Pelsmacker, 2013) may push the concept of clutter to another level. Should we include native ads in the measurement of clutter level? If yes, then we need to first determine what is pure editorial content and what is sponsored content. All sponsored content should be considered clutter including product placement, which is part of the editorial content. Hence, it may be better to put advertising clutter in perspective by limiting it to third-party editorial media, such as a mobile app or a web page (either regular or mobile version) not owned by the advertiser, and exclude subtle brand placements.

Although the chapter has proposed measurements of digital editorial units and clutter levels, it would also be helpful for researchers to examine the degree of discrepancy between the physical attributes of advertising clutter and perceived levels of clutter by varying each functional and individual information processing factor to see which factor(s) affect the perceived clutter level most. It should be noted that creativity in advertising would facilitate the acceptance of ads as entertainment instead of clutter.

Ultimately, optimizing the advertising environment will reduce the perceived advertising clutter level and maximize receptiveness toward advertising and sponsored content in editorial media. It is the joint responsibility of the industry and the academic researchers to come up with the most acceptable digital advertising environment. As we learn more about the antecedents and consequences of perceived clutter, advertisers may want to create ads that include both high information and entertainment value that reflects consumers' needs. Once this is done, advertising will not viewed as clutter, but as a welcome, integral part of media consumption.

References

Barreto, M. A. (2013). Do users look at banner ads on Facebook? *Journal of Research in Interactive Marketing*, 7(2), 119–139.

Bauer, C., & Strauss, C. (2016). Location-based advertising on mobile devices: A literature review and analysis. *Management Review Quarterly*, 66(3), 159–194.

Bellman, S., Treleaven-Hassard, S., Robinson, J. A., Rask, A., & Varan, D. (2012). Getting the balance right. *Journal of Advertising*, 41(2), 5–24. doi: 10.2753/JOA0091–3367410201.

Benway, J. P. (1998, October). Banner blindness: The irony of attention grabbing on the World Wide Web. *Proceedings of the Human Factors and Ergonomics Society Annual Meeting*, 42(5), 463–467.

Bleier, A., & Eisenbeiss, M. (2015). The importance of trust for personalized online advertising. *Journal of Retailing*, 91(3), 390–409.

Brehm, S. S., & Brehm, J. W. (1981). *Psychological reactance: A theory of freedom and control.* New York, NY: Academic Press.

Brettel, M., & Spilker-Attig, A. (2010). Online advertising effectiveness: A cross-cultural comparison. *Journal of Research in Interactive Marketing*, 4(3), 176–196.

Brown, T. J., & Rothschild, M. L. (1993). Reassessing the impact of television advertising clutter. *Journal of Consumer Research, 20*, 138–146.

Burns, K. S., & Lutz, R. J. (2006). The function of format: Consumer responses to six online advertising formats. *Journal of Advertising*, 35(1), 53–63.

Campbell, M. C., & Kirmani, A. (2000). Consumers' use of persuasion knowledge: The effects of accessibility and cognitive capacity on perceptions of an influence agent. *Journal of Consumer Research*, 27(1), 69–83.

Cho, C., & Cheon, H. J. (2004). Why do people avoid advertising on the internet? *Journal of Advertising, 33*(4), 89–97.

Dou, W., Linn, R., & Yang, S. (2001). How smart are 'smart banners'? *Journal of Advertising Research*, 41(4), 31–43.

Ducoffe, R. H. (1995). How consumers assess the value of advertising. *Journal of Current Issues & Research in Advertising*, 17(1), 1–18.

Edwards, S. M., Li, H., & Lee, J. H. (2002). Forced exposure and psychological reactance: Antecedents and consequences of the perceived intrusiveness of pop-up ads. *Journal of Advertising, 31*(3), 83–96.

Elliot, M. T., & Speck, P. S. (1998). Consumer perceptions of advertising clutter and its impact across various media. *Journal of Advertising Research, 38*(1), 29–41.

Goodrich, K. (2011). Anarchy of effects? Exploring attention to online advertising and multiple outcomes. *Psychology & Marketing, 28*(4), 417–440.

Grusell, M. (2007). Advertising? Yes please, but only when it's my choice. *Journal of Media Business Studies, 4*(3), 87–101.

Ha, L. (1996). Advertising clutter in consumer magazines: Dimensions and effects. *Journal of Advertising Research, 36*(4), 76–85.

Ha, L. (2008). Online advertising research in advertising journals: A review. *Journal of Current Issues and Research in Advertising, 30*(1), 33–50.

Ha, L., & Litman, B. (1997). Does advertising clutter have diminishing returns? *Journal of Advertising, 26*(1), 31–42.

Ha, L., & McCann, K. (2008). An integrated model of advertising clutter in offline and online media environment. *International Journal of Advertising, 27*(4), 569–592. http://www.tandfonline.com/doi/abs/10.2501/S0265048708080153.

Haans, H., Raassens, N., & van Hout, R. (2013). Search engine advertisements: The impact of advertising statements on click-through and conversion rates. *Marketing Letters, 24*(2), 151–163.

Hammer, P., Riebe, E., & Kennedy, R. (2009). How clutter affects advertising effectiveness. *Journal of Advertising Research, 49*(2), 159–163.

Heinz, S., Hug, M., Nugaeva, C., & Opwis, K. (2013, April). Online ad banners: The effects of goal orientation and content congruence on memory. In *CHI'13 Extended Abstracts on Human Factors in Computing Systems* (pp. 1875–1880). ACM.

Kim, N. Y., & Sundar, S. S. (2010). Relevance to the rescue: Can "smart ads" reduce negative response to online ad clutter? *Journalism & Mass Communication Quarterly, 87*(2), 346–362. doi: 10.1177/107769901008700208.

Ko, H., Cho, C. H., & Roberts, M. S. (2005). Internet uses and gratifications: A structural equation model of interactive advertising. *Journal of Advertising, 34*(2), 57–70.

Krishnan, S. S., & Sitaraman, R. K. (2013, October). Understanding the effectiveness of video ads: A measurement study. In *Proceedings of the 2013 Conference on Internet Measurement Conference* (pp. 149–162). ACM.

Lee, S. Y., & Cho, Y. S. (2010). Do web users care about banner ads anymore? The effects of frequency and clutter in web advertising. *Journal of Promotion Management, 16*(3), 288–302. doi: 10.1080/10496490903582594.

Li, H., & Lo, H. Y. (2015). Do you recognize its brand? The effectiveness of online in-stream video advertisements. *Journal of Advertising, 44*(3), 208–218.

Malhotra, N. K., Jain, A. K., & Lagakos, S. W. (1982). The information overload controversy: An alternative viewpoint. *Journal of Marketing, 46*, 27–37.

Mord, M. S., & Gilson, E. (1985). Shorter units: Risk-responsibility-reward. *Journal of Advertising Research, 25*, 9–19.

Muehling, D. D. (1987). An investigation of factors underlying attitude-toward-the-advertising in general. *Journal of Advertising, 16*(1), 32–40.

Nill, A., & Aalberts, R. J. (2014). Legal and ethical challenges of online behavioral targeting in advertising. *Journal of Current Issues & Research in Advertising, 35*(2), 126–146.

Okazaki, S., Molina, F. J., & Hirose, M. (2012). Mobile advertising avoidance: Exploring the role of ubiquity. *Electronic Markets, 22*(3), 169–183.

PageFair (2015, August). The 2015 ad blocking report. Retrieved from https://blog.pagefair.com/2015/ad-blocking-report/

Pagendarm, M., & Schaumburg, H. (2001). Why are users banner-blind? The impact of navigation style on the perception of web banners. *Journal of Digital Information, 2*(1). Retrieved from https://journals.tdl.org/jodi/index.php/jodi/article/view/36/38.

Petty, R., Cacciopo, J. T., & Schumann, D. (1983). Central and peripheral routes to advertising effectiveness: The moderating role of involvement. *Journal of Consumer Research, 10*(3), 135–146.

Pieters, R. G. M., & Bijmolt, T. H. A. (1997). Consumer memory for television advertising: A field study of duration, serial position, and competition effects. *Journal of Consumer Research, 23*, 362–372.

Rejón-Guardia, F., & Martínez-López, F. J. (2014). Online advertising intrusiveness and consumers' avoidance behaviors. In F. Rejón-Guardia & F. J. Martínez-López (Eds.), *Handbook of strategic e-business management* (pp. 565–586). Berlin Heidelberg: Springer.

Rodgers, S., & Thorson, E. (2000). The interactive advertising model: How users perceive and process online ads. *Journal of Interactive Advertising, 1*(1), 41–60.

Schumann, J. H., von Wangenheim, F., & Groene, N. (2014). Targeted online advertising: Using reciprocity appeals to increase acceptance among users of free web services. *Journal of Marketing, 78*(1), 59–75. doi: http://dx.doi.org/10.1509/jm.11.0316.

Segev, S., Wang, W., & Fernandes, J. (2014). The effects of ad–context congruency on responses to advertising in blogs: Exploring the role of issue involvement. *International Journal of Advertising, 33*(1), 17–36.

Seyedghorban, Z., Tahernejad, H., & Matanda, M. J. (2015). Reinquiry into advertising avoidance on the internet: A conceptual replication and extension. *Journal of Advertising, 45*(1), 120–129.

Smith, R. E., & Buchholz, L. M. (1991). Multiple resource theory and consumer processing of broadcast advertisements: An involvement perspective. *Journal of Advertising, 20*(3), 1–8.

Statista. (2016a). Millward Brown AdReaction 2012—global report. Retrieved from http://www.statista.com/statistics/247891/mobile-users-attitudes-towards-different-advertising-formats-worldwide/

Statista. (2016b). Digital market outlook. Retrieved from https://www.statista.com/outlook/216/digital-advertising#market-revenue.

Statista. (2016c). eMarketer 2015 worldwide internet and mobile users. Retrieved from http://www.statista.com/statistics/284206/north-america-mobile-phone-internet-user-penetration/

Sundar, S. S., & Kalyanaraman, S. (2004). Arousal, memory, and impression-formation effects of animation speed in Web advertising. *Journal of Advertising, 33*(1), 7–17.

Tribbey, C. (2016, February 1). Ad-blocking remains high hurdle for digital video. *Multichannel News* (p. 15).

Truong, Y., & Simmons, G. (2010). Perceived intrusiveness in digital advertising: Strategic marketing implications. *Journal of Strategic Marketing, 18*(3), 239–256.

Verhellen, Y., Dens, N., & De Pelsmacker, P. (2013). Consumer responses to brands placed in YouTube movies: The effect of prominence and endorser expertise. *Journal of Electronic Commerce Research, 14*(4), 287–303.

Webb, P. H. (1979). Consumer initial processing in a difficult media environment. *Journal of Consumer Research, 6*, 225–236.

Yoo, C. Y. (2011). Interplay of message framing, keyword insertion and levels of product involvement in clickthrough of keyword search ads. *International Journal of Advertising, 30*(3), 399–424. doi: 10.2501/IJA-30-3-399–424.

Yoo, C. Y., Kim, K., & Stout, P. A. (2004). Assessing the effects of animation in online banner advertising: Hierarchy of effects model. *Journal of Interactive Advertising, 4*(2), 49–60. Retrieved from http://jiad.org/vol4/no2/yoo/index.htm.

Zanjani, S. H. A., Diamond, W. D., & Chan, K. (2011). Does ad-context congruity help surfers and information seekers remember ads in cluttered e-magazines? *Journal of Advertising, 40*(4), 67–84. doi: 10.2753/JOA0091–3367400405.

Zhao, X. (1997). Clutter and serial order redefined and retested. *Journal of Advertising Research, 37*(5), 57–74.

6

USING THEORY OF INTERACTIVE MEDIA EFFECTS (TIME) TO ANALYZE DIGITAL ADVERTISING

S. Shyam Sundar, Jinyoung Kim,
and Andrew Gambino[1]

Advertising in digital media is conceptually different from advertising in any of the older media. Historically, whenever a new medium becomes popular, advertisers adapt their messages to fit that medium (print ads to radio ads to television ads), but the central concept would remain the same: mass communication of persuasive content. But, with digital advertising, that concept has undergone a dramatic change. Persuasive messages are no longer disseminated to the masses but tailored to individual consumers. What's more, those consumers have unprecedented agency in dictating the nature of the messages they receive as well as the manner and frequency with which they receive them. As a result, digital advertising is not simply about piping ad content through a new set of channels but a negotiated transaction between advertisers and consumers.

There are many digital technologies and trends underlying the negotiation between advertisers and consumers. The large-scale adoption and diffusion of mobile and social media technologies, coupled with advances in user tracking, data mining, and big-data analyses, have served to provide advertisers with more opportunities to reach consumers as well as to better target their efforts. Concurrently, advances in interface technology have enabled users of modern digital media to make intricate decisions about the nature, duration, and format of advertising appeals to which they will attend. On most internet-based media, ranging from cable television to mobile apps, consumers can pay to avoid advertisements altogether. In some platforms, such as YouTube, they can limit their exposure to ads that precede the content they are seeking to watch. On search engines, such as Google, they can shape the nature of ads they receive by entering keywords that are of personal interest and utility. The many algorithms that advertisers use to target consumers can be co-opted by the latter to tailor their information environment.

At the heart of this negotiation between advertisers and consumers is the concept of *interactivity*. Digital advertising is uniquely characterized by the interactivity offered by modern media. Interactivity can be theoretically defined as the functionality that affords user input, which can shape output by the medium. It has been operationally defined in various ways—as ability to have a conversation (Rafaeli, 1988), exercise choice (Heeter, 1989), and manipulate interface features and content (Steuer, 1992), to mention three classic approaches. With newer technologies, interactivity has transcended simple notions of having a conversation (e.g., Skype), exercising choice (from menu options on a website), and controlling the flow of communication (e.g., joystick in a game) to customization and assertion of human agency (Sundar, 2008a). In the current context of personal and social media, interactivity can range from the swiping action that we perform so often on our mobile devices to customizing the apps on our smartphones to clicking the "Like" button in Facebook to following a brand on Twitter to sharing content on Pinterest to writing about our feelings on blogs. These activities involve a range of user activity, from customization of one's environment to curation of information for the benefit of others in one's network to creation of original content, as in user-generated content, or UGC.

Theory of Interactive Media Effects (TIME)

The theory of interactive media effects (TIME) was formulated to understand the psychological consequences of all these interactive possibilities afforded by modern digital media. It is a combination of four models of technology-effects and draws upon the media-effects research tradition in emphasizing a variable-centered, rather than object-centered, approach to studying the psychological effects of media (Sundar, Jia, Waddell, & Huang, 2015). That is, instead of studying a given technology or medium as a whole, this approach advocates disaggregating it into its constituent variables and investigating the distinct effects of those variables as well as common or logical combinations of those variables.

The variables underlying interactivity are treated as *affordances* (Sundar & Bellur, 2010), which are possibilities for action suggested visually by environmental stimuli (Gibson, 1977). The notion of *possibilities* is important because media users may not always engage with all the interactive tools offered on an interface. Oftentimes, interactivity serves as a visual cue that users notice but do not actively use. An example is the live-chat option on an e-commerce site, which one may not use if one can complete the transaction without consultation. Another example would be the rating associated with a hotel on TripAdvisor.com. We may not necessarily use the interactive tool that gathers our own rating but simply observe the metric generated based on entries by other users of the site. In both these examples, interface affordances are simply cues to action, which are not necessarily undertaken by the user. Yet, these cues can have important effects. It is quite common for us to evaluate a website based on the features it has, even though we

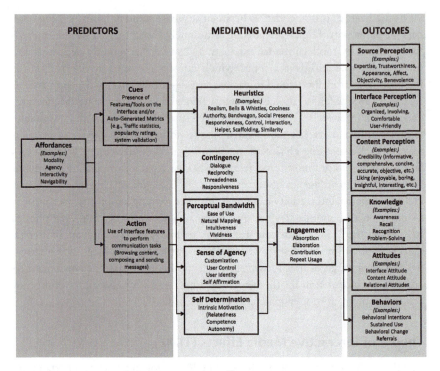

FIGURE 6.1 Theory of Interactive Media Effects (TIME)

Sundar (2015, p. 51, Figure 3.1). © Wiley Blackwell. Reprinted with permission.

may not use all those features. Likewise, it is common for us to make decisions about which hotel to stay at based on metrics generated by interactive actions of other users rather than our own. TIME categorizes these types of effects, due primarily to cues on the interface, as belonging to the Cue-route, which is the top pathway in Figure 6.1.

Cue-Route of TIME

Affordances of interactive media can serve as cues on the interface, triggering cognitive heuristics (or mental shortcuts) about the nature of the underlying content, thereby shaping user judgments of the quality and credibility of that content. This is the fundamental premise of the MAIN Model (Sundar, 2008b), which focuses on cues embedded in four classes of affordances—Modality, Agency, Interactivity, and Navigability. For example, the sheer presence of video modality in an otherwise textual medium can cue the *realism heuristic* (that which you can see is credible, based on the mental shortcut "seeing is believing"). Likewise, the agent or source of communication could cue a number of heuristics, including the *bandwagon heuristic* (if others think it is good, then it's good for me, too), which could be triggered when you encounter content accompanied by metrics suggesting a large number of endorsements, such as likes, shares, and ratings. Interactive affordances can cue the *contingency heuristic* (what I receive is contingent upon what I send), leading to heightened perceptions of message relevance. Navigability tools on the interface, such as convenient toolbars and warnings before critical actions, could cue the *scaffolding heuristic* (it's looking out for me, so it can be trusted) and thereby have a positive halo effect on the content presented through the interface. In this way, the various affordances related to modality, agency, interactivity, and navigability trigger distinct cognitive heuristics that shape user judgments of the interface and its content. The MAIN model identifies over two-dozen specific heuristics. Other newer heuristics triggered by interface cues have also been identified, especially in the context of online privacy and security, such as *fuzzy boundary heuristic* and *bubble heuristic* (Gambino, Kim, Sundar, Ge, & Rosson, 2016; Sundar, Kim, Gambino, & Rosson, 2016).

As Sundar, Xu, & Dou (2012) note, the MAIN Model can be applied to the context of advertising and marketing by changing the dependent variable from credibility to consumer attitudes toward the advertisements and products. Digital advertising is rife with cues that can trigger heuristics pertaining to the quality of the product or service being advertised. For example, a just-in-time advertisement, such as in location-based advertising (LBA), can cue the *helper heuristic* (it's trying to help, so it can be trusted) or the *intrusiveness heuristic* (it's hijacking my attention, so it can't be trusted) depending upon how it manifests itself on the user's smartphone and which affordance of LBA is highlighted on the interface to serve as a salient cue to users. When we apply the cue-route of TIME to analyzing digital advertising, principal consideration is given to the visually suggestive cues conveyed by the advertisement on the digital interface. These cues are likely to dictate the success of the ad by determining whether users will receive the ad. In some cases, users may be sufficiently persuaded by the cues and their superficial reception of the ad, without feeling the need to explore further. This is where the heuristics can help us understand the effects of digital advertising. But, in other cases, users may go further and attend to the ad with greater involvement. This is where the action-route of TIME takes over, the bottom pathway in Figure 6.1.

Action-Route of TIME

By definition, interactive media encourage user action. TIME incorporates mechanisms from three theoretical models (interactivity effects model, agency model of customization, and motivational technology model) to propose that actions engendered by affordances of interactive media—actions such as manipulating the interface, browsing content and sending messages—will lead to greater user engagement with media content, via four sets of potential mediators: 1) by expanding users' "perceptual bandwidth," i.e., breadth and depth of their sensory experience of the interface; 2) by cueing perceptions of contingency (or relatedness) in message exchange; 3) by imbuing in users a sense of agency, that they can control the course of the interaction; and, 4) by enhancing self-determination or intrinsic motivation among users, accruing from feelings of greater competence, relatedness, and autonomy in their online interactions.

Not every action afforded by interactive media leads to all four of these predictors of user engagement. The expansion of perceptual bandwidth is caused primarily by the modality-interactivity affordance, which refers to the variety of interaction techniques available for users to manipulate the interface, ranging from clicking, sliding, zooming, swiping, and dragging on the screen (Sundar, Bellur, Oh, Xu, & Jia, 2014) to manipulating virtual environments that can create a vivid alternate reality (Sundar, Oeldorf-Hirsch, & Garga, 2008). Perceptions of contingency are primarily promoted by the message-interactivity affordance (Sundar, Bellur, Oh, Jia, & Kim, 2016), which refers to tools that offer back-and-forth, interdependent message exchanges, such as an instant messenger (where it is abundantly clear that the messages received are a direct consequence of messages sent), as well as to tools that offer tailored content based on prior user behaviors (where it may be less clear that messages received are contingent upon prior user actions). Sense of agency is driven by the source-interactivity affordance, which permits users to serve as agents or sources of communication, either by customizing, curating, or creating content. Self-determination is predicted by competence, relatedness, and autonomy, which are influenced by navigability, message-interactivity, and customization (or source-interactivity) affordances respectively, according to the motivational technology model (Sundar, Bellur, & Jia, 2012).

The engagement generated by user action in interactive media environments can range from absorption in content to elaboration of that content to self-expression by making new content contributions. It can also mean repeated visits to the site or sustained use of the interface. These different forms of user engagement will in turn dictate the cognitive, attitudinal, and behavioral outcomes of using interactive media.

Applying TIME to Digital Advertising

Considering the centrality of interactivity in digital advertising, TIME is an obvious choice for theorizing about its psychological effects. Many, if not most, digital ads are likely to have cue effects, by instantly triggering cognitive heuristics about the advertised product or service. These effects can be understood by investigating the role of specific cognitive heuristics that govern user judgments and, thereby, drive the persuasive success of the ads. The cue-route of TIME, which is based on the MAIN model, has already identified several heuristics at play in digital media interactions. Research could investigate the role of these heuristics in the particular domain of digital advertising, while also discovering new heuristics that may be specific to this domain.

When consumers do engage with digital ads, the action-route of TIME offers a variety of concepts with which to analyze the psychological mechanisms of online persuasion. While interacting with some ads contributes to enhanced sense of contingency, interacting with others may make the user feel more agentic. Some interactive marketing campaigns, especially in the health domain, could enhance self-determination among users while others may succeed in transporting users to a virtual environment. The action-route of TIME provides the vocabulary as well as mechanisms for understanding these outcomes of digital advertising and their consequent effects on persuasion.

We illustrate the use of TIME by analyzing seven recent trends in digital advertising: Mobile Video, VR/AR Ads, Chatbots, Behavioral Advertising (BA), Location-based Advertising (LBA), Search-Engine Advertising (SEA), and Native Advertising (NA). We begin each section by defining the trend (or type of digital advertising) and reviewing the emerging literature on its psychological effects. We then identify one or more core affordances of interactivity, in keeping with the variable-centered approach of TIME. Next, we describe the potential effects of these affordances on persuasion, both via the cue-route and via the action-route, as applicable.

Mobile Video Advertising

Coupled with the explosive growth of mobile device usage and improvements in network speeds, mobile video is seen as the future of advertising. Experts project that revenue from mobile video advertisements will grow from $3.54 billion in 2015 to $13.3 billion by 2020 (PWC, 2015). Mobile video is simply video viewed on a mobile device (e.g., smartphone, tablet). However, there are many distinct features or affordances of mobile video that separate it from its predecessors (e.g., internet video, television). Advertisers must take into account both the form of the device itself and the application platform on which the video will be viewed. For example, we know that screen size matters. In a study by Kim, Sundar, and Park (2011), individuals who viewed the same content on a larger screen rated it as more enjoyable. Additionally, Kim and Sundar (2016) showed that when exposed to mobile video advertisements on larger mobile screens, the content was better received (higher trust in ad) and processed more heuristically than text-based advertisements. An effective mobile video advertising campaign will consider these modality affordances, and TIME can be a useful framework for assessing its impact.

The cue-route of TIME, which is based on the MAIN model, offers guidance in explaining many of the psychological effects of mobile video advertisements. For example, screen size may serve as a salient modality cue, which leads to the triggering of a relevant cognitive heuristic. As previously mentioned, larger screen sizes can lead to a more immersive experience (Detenber & Reeves, 1996; Kim &

Sundar, 2016). The positive outcomes attributed to this type of immersion may be due to the *being-there heuristic*, when sensory information leads to an authentic and intense feeling of being a part of the universe portrayed in the digital media.

More generally, video modality, compared to text, is known to trigger heuristic processing of mobile advertising content, with positive persuasion outcomes (Kim & Sundar, 2016). One explanation for these positive effects is the *realism heuristic* (if something seems real, then it must be credible), triggered by the relative ease with which video content is decoded by consumers compared to textual content. However, heuristics can also lead to negative attitudes toward products. Particularly relevant to mobile advertising are the *intrusiveness* and *distraction heuristics*, which may be cued by flashy or unsolicited content (Sundar & Kalyanaraman, 2004; Zhang, Wu, Kang, Go, & Sundar, 2014; Gambino et al., 2016).

Such negative impressions via the cue-route may be exacerbated when users attempt to engage with mobile video ads. The static nature of video advertisements, especially forced advertisements (Hegner, Kusse, & Pruyn, 2016), leave the user with very little opportunities for interaction with the interface, let alone the brand or product. As a result, the action-route of TIME would predict that mobile video ads would decrease users' sense of agency. When the user is provided an opportunity to select the ad that he/she would like to watch, there is a semblance of source-interactivity, but once the ad starts playing, the user is essentially held hostage as he/she is forced to view a non-interactive video advertisement. Therefore, the action-route of TIME would predict negative effects for mobile video ads, whereas the cue-route predicts a combination of positive and negative effects, as discussed earlier.

Virtual Reality and Augmented Reality Advertising

With affordable VR devices attracting content producers in a number of domains, advertisers have begun deploying virtual reality advertising campaigns (Ellis, 2016). Earlier in the year, Oreo utilized the Google Cardboard technology to offer a 360-degree flythrough of an Oreo-inspired virtual world, and it appears that many other firms are attempting to deploy advertisement strategies in the VR realm. While consumers are excited about these VR experiences (the Oreo "Wonder-Vault" currently has over 3 million views), there are still major doubts and questions regarding how to effectively utilize the VR platform for advertising purposes (Harwell, 2016).

VR/AR platforms hold a lot of promise for digital advertising, considering the compelling user experience provided by them. An experiment by Jin (2009) showed that the role of a modality-rich experience, such as a virtual environment, was most effective on consumers unfamiliar with the product being advertised. In terms of AR, utilizing layover images (the display of digital images over relevant real-world spaces) and super-imposed visuals, advertisers can showcase their products in and supplement them with additional information that is relevant or personalized to the consumer to increase positive consumer attitudes and purchase intentions (Stoyanova, Brito, Georgieva, & Milanova, 2015). While this technology is new, research has found that consumers enjoy these AR advertisements more so than traditional print advertisements, with users showing higher perceptions of informativeness, novelty, and effectiveness and less irritation than a QR-code-based ad, as well as less time-effort than a traditional advertisement (Yaoyuneyong, Foster, Johnson, & Johnson, 2016).

The cue-rich environments of both AR and VR present many possibilities for their effects, making it difficult for the practitioner to correctly identify the key elements of VR and AR. For advertisers, the very newness of the technology can be utilized and lead to outcomes such as engagement and increased feelings of presence (Limperos, Waddell, Ivory, & Ivory, 2014). These positive effects may be explained by the *coolness heuristic*, which is an acknowledgement of the hipness of a product based on its newer, stylish modality cues (Sundar, Tamul & Wu, 2014). However, at times when the new modality causes uncertainty in the user, it can have negative effects on involvement. In this case, the user may be so involved with the technology, they will pay little attention to the content of the advertisement and rank it very low on credibility. This phenomenon is termed the *novelty heuristic* (Sundar, 2008b; Sundar & Limperos, 2013). Additionally, when superfluous interactive features are included but do not trigger the positive *coolness heuristic*, they can lead to disappointment in the user and yield negative evaluations via the *bells-and-whistles heuristic*, that a feature is all flash and no substance (Oh, Robinson, & Lee, 2013).

In terms of interactive action, VR and AR systems hold possibilities to be truly immersive, reactive, and user-action centered. Because of these elements, user experience of VR and AR technologies can be examined via TIME's action-route, particularly in increasing a user's perceptual bandwidth, or expanding a user's sensory breadth and depth in an interaction, encouraging more exploration of the interface and freeing up cognitive resources (Steuer, 1992; Sundar et al., 2015). Identified as a key mechanism in the modality-interactivity action-route, perceptual bandwidth can be increased in VR through immersive affordances within 3D environments that increase a user's feelings of vividness, intuitiveness, and natural mapping, such as a 3D object that responds instantaneously to the user's interaction with it.

According to TIME, increases in perceptual bandwidth via these mechanisms can lead to heightened levels of engagement, especially absorption in the narrative, with positive effects on brand awareness, recognition, recall, attitudes toward content, and even behavioral change. Additionally, these outcomes can be achieved in VR and AR through the source-interactivity affordance. By allowing the user to be the central actor in an immersive, reactive mediated experience, especially since the entire environment responds to user action, VR and AR ads afford users a high sense of control, which can lead to positive agency effects through self-determination and feelings of competence.

Because of the user-action rich environments of VR and AR, TIME predicts many positive outcomes for VR and AR advertisements. However, cue-route effects for these technologies may be the key, especially given how important peripheral cues have been in similar advertising environments (Peters & Leshner, 2013). It is important to be mindful of the double-edged, modality-based heuristics such as *coolness* and *bells and whistles*, which depend on the user's interpretation of the affordances as being either interesting or superfluous. These cue-based effects may immediately turn the user on or off to the experience and promote or prevent the positive action-route effects from taking hold, or they may enhance the experience and be additive to the action-route effects.

Chatbot Advertising

While it once seemed like a convenience to "have an app for that," many tech companies are betting on users growing tired of the clutter and attempting to package services in a single platform. Apple has Siri, Amazon has Alexa, and now with over 900 million users, Facebook's Messenger application is attempting to meet all of its users' needs through its M messenger bot (Moses, 2016). Unlike Siri, which serves as a sole personal assistant, Facebook has allowed for outside developers to build their own chatbot based on M's technology. That means that within the messenger service, any company can develop its own chatbot that can interact personally with a user to take orders and respond directly to them. Over 30,000 companies have already taken the plunge, from Kayak.com for your travel needs, to 1–800-flowers, to Poncho (weather), to Fusion (emoji-based news), chatbots are becoming more prevalent and diverse in their services every day (Moses, 2016; Oremus, 2016). With M and Messenger, Facebook is attempting to streamline and deploy a single communication tool for all user needs, cutting down on the time spent navigating through multiple applications. The technology is ambitious but has already shown benefits, particularly in attracting users (generally young adults) who would not normally interact with the brand.

By utilizing this technology, a brand can make itself visible and interactive, and instantly responsive to the input and needs of the consumer. Visibility and interactivity with a brand can be utilized to build a personal relationship with the consumer. As brand interactivity in the form of communication has been suggested as the causal link between consumer brand attitudes and activity (Beukeboom, Kerkhof, & de Vries, 2015), the direct line of communication that a chatbot affords advertisers is a great opportunity. However, the basis for positive effects in a chatbot interaction may lie in effective, contingent interactions. Contingent interactions are defined by reactive, interdependent message exchanges, and perception of contingency has been shown to determine levels of engagement and attitudes and intentions toward websites (Sundar et al., 2014). As most current chatbots rely on a scripted question and answer system without drawing back on previous communication, they may not actually be achieving contingent interactions nor reaping its positive effects.

Even within a simple messenger interface, there are opportunities for chatbots to utilize cues and heuristics to positively influence their brand. For chatbots making recommendations, the *machine heuristic*, that non-human agents will provide more objective information (Sundar & Nass, 2001), can be triggered by simply reminding the user that she/he is interacting with a robot. An experiment in an educational setting has shown that the perception that the machine is the source can lead to heightened learning outcomes, and a telepresent agent was rated high in credibility (Edwards, Edwards, Spence, Harris, & Gambino, 2016). The triggering of the *machine heuristic* can be done through simple graphic cues or communication choices, but awkward communication may lead to negative, communication flow-disrupting outcomes. The Facebook Messenger platform also provides developers the opportunity to give user's responsive buttons with options such as "If you would like to read more about this story, click here." These navigability cues can trigger positive heuristics such as the *helper heuristic* and *scaffolding heuristic*, which can increase perceptions of content credibility and brand attitude due a user's feelings of the features being provided by a benevolent designer (Sundar, 2008b).

In addition to cue-based effects, chatbot ads can have action-route effects due to message-interactivity. Attitudes toward the brand and product can be increased by going beyond a simple question-answer system and increasing the level of contingency in the interaction. For example, hierarchical hyperlinks, buttons, and navigational tools that logically arrange the order in which content appears can give the user the perception that the system is responding personally to them, thus increasing their perceived contingency (Sundar, Kalyanaraman, & Brown, 2003; Sundar & Kim, 2005). Additionally, showing and utilizing the history of an interaction will lead to heightened perceptions of contingency and positive attitudes (Sundar et al., 2014).

Behavioral Advertising

Thanks to technological developments in user tracking and dynamic data mining, advertisers are now able to de-massify their campaigns based on consumers' preferences and needs, and target individuals with highly personalized advertising, whereby online and mobile campaign messages perfectly match their personal background and preferences. For instance, Amazon.com automatically reminds its customers to place new orders for household products (e.g., laundry detergent, dish soap) when they are about to run out, or sends discount offers for high-priced items that have been placed in their online shopping cart without being checked out. Many restaurant chains, including Panera, email their customers coupons for sandwiches if a regular customer does not visit one of its branches for a while. In general, advertisers have been quick to capitalize on the substantial benefits of personalized advertising, with tailored campaigns becoming increasingly common (Chen & Stallaert, 2014).

In order for BA to reflect each user's needs, advertisers first collect exhaustive information about each customer, once they decide what messages to display that fit his or her needs (McStay, 2012). Such user information comes in diverse formats, including basic demographics, IP address, browsing activities within specific websites (e.g., the number of clicks, frequency and recency of visits, total time), and purchase records (Bilenko, Richardson, & Tsai, 2011). All of these extensive details about individual customers are saved in *cookies*, small files that are stored in a web browser, containing information about the individual's personal tastes and preferences (McStay, 2012). Based on the accumulated data, a multitude of user profiles are built, from which the consumer's likely interests are inferred. In particular, the rich data that embodies each customer's taste can be compiled from two distinct sources—from a single website (*first*-party BA) or from multiple websites that a user has visited (*third*-party BA) (Sableman, Shoenberger, & Thorson, 2013).

Given the prominent usage of BA on various online and mobile venues, increasing research attention has been paid to capturing its psychological impact on consumers. For instance, Yan et al. (2009) found that when the commercial messages were directed to each user, users' click-through of online ads increased quite dramatically (670%). Similarly, Sa and his colleagues (2013) reported that not only did a user's perceived relevance to the online ad lead to more pleasant and interesting experience with the commercial website, but also the perceived relevance of BA to the page's content improved recall of the campaign messages. Yet, Summers, Smith, and Reczek (2014) revealed the positive impact of diverting consumers' attention to online ads is conditional upon their prior positive attitudes toward BA.

Despite the positive influence of BA on users' experiences with commercial websites, automatic presentation of various BA based on consumers' background information has triggered privacy concerns. In fact, Ur and his colleagues (2012) reported that the majority of consumers perceive online advertising as manipulative when based on their personal data, implying avoidance of BA. They tended to believe, erroneously, that they could prevent their data from being tracked by using anti-virus software and ad-blocking functions on their internet browsers. Along similar lines, Kelly, Kerr, and Drennan (2010) showed user distaste for BA in the context of social networking sites. BA avoidance was more pronounced if customers had negative experience with online advertising, the content of BA was irrelevant to their tastes, and the consumers were generally skeptical of information from the internet. In fact, Okazaki and his colleagues (2012) showed that perceived ubiquity of BA leads customers to disapprove of BA.

The basis for such positive, as well as negative attitudes toward BA, with their consequent effects on advertising success, can be analyzed by applying the cue-route of TIME, which explains that various cues in BA content might trigger both positive and negative heuristics that influence customers' stance toward the messages. For example, advertisers can run online campaign messages based on the frequency of a user's visit to a specific retailer's website such that the more frequently the consumer visits the brand's site (e.g., a young female college student's daily visit to Forever21.com for clothing and accessory shopping), the more likely she is to receive individualized online advertising, such as "Check out this exclusive discount offer for VVIP customers like you!" Since this kind of targeted message presents the most acceptable and relatable content to customers by analyzing their previous browsing history, the *similarity heuristic* (if there is similarity between my interests and what this ad offers, it is credible) might play a role in increasing their liking of brands and products. When brands provide commercials based on a customer's recent browsing activities on specific websites, they might trigger the *helper heuristic* (this ad is here to help me, so I trust it). Not all heuristics triggered by BA's affordance of personalized advertising is positive however. Considering that the individualized content includes explicitly or implicitly identifiable personal information of customers, BA messages might trigger the *intrusiveness heuristic* (it's intruding into my activities, so it cannot be trusted) or the *online security heuristic* (the internet is not safe, thus risky to reveal personal information). Moreover, some unsolicited BA that matches with customers' background information might imbue an impression that there exist algorithms operating behind the scenes that save such information and generate targeted advertising messages, thus triggering the *fuzzy boundary heuristic* (the boundaries between systems are fuzzy, resulting in information leakage across them) (Sundar, Kang, Wu, Go, & Zhang, 2013).

Different from the cue-based effects that shape customers' online experiences with BA, the action-route of TIME would predict that the interactive nature of BA triggers actions that lead to psychological engagement with the advertising messages. Given that many corporate online websites and mobile applications serve as tools that provide personalized content directed to each customer, customers are likely to perceive contingency of such content. In line with this prediction, De Sa, Navalpakkam, and Churchill (2013) showed that BA messages that were contingent upon users' personal interests resulted in more a pleasant and interesting experience with the brand's website. When customers perceive such high levels of contingency afforded by personalized commercials, it then leads to engagement with the commercial messages (e.g., repeated visits to websites, clicks of BA messages), and they form positive attitudes toward the brands. In fact, Yan et al. (2009) found that the BA messages that reflect customers' needs produced more click-throughs. In all, the action-route of TIME theorizes that customers' perceived responsiveness afforded by BA would increase engagement with not only the given campaign messages but also the linked online and mobile websites. This kind of engagement is a critical determinant of consumer attitudes and purchase intentions of the promoted products and services.

Location-Based Advertising

As the vast majority of consumers carry their mobile devices with wireless connection to the web, location-based advertising (LBA) has emerged as an increasingly popular advertising platform. With the aid of location-tracking technologies (e.g., the Global Positioning System), LBA allows advertisers to pinpoint each consumer's location and propagate real-time personalized commercial messages immediately (Aalto, Göthlin, Korhonen, & Ojala, 2004), which realizes the ideal of just-in-time marketing. In particular, LBA is characterized by its four strengths that other direct advertising technologies might lack: 1) real-time, 2) context (location)-specific, 3) immediately replaceable, and 4) individually tailored commercial messages (Bauer & Strauss, 2016). As an example, Facebook might run a mobile ad on a user's newsfeed, suggesting a visit to a well-known local restaurant that is located near the user at that moment.

In order to run LBA, *beacons*, small-sized devices that transmit and receive data via Bluetooth technology to mobile devices in the vicinity (a maximum of 50 meters) are used (Bessler, 2007). Specifically, beacons emit their own data to nearby devices, which are detected by smartphones and other mobile devices (Bessler, 2007). Some pre-installed mobile applications on smartphones then respond to the beacons' signal by showing a push message to users, such as "Welcome to Nike! Check out our new summer shorts!" or "Greetings from Walmart! You just got a $1 coupon for Ben & Jerry's chocolate ice cream!" In addition to push messages, some promotional deals can be requested by customers via their smartphones as they walk into a retail store.

Given its popularity with advertisers, LBA has generated several empirical studies that document its psychological influence on various persuasion outcomes (Bruner & Kumar, 2007). A recent study by Lee, Kim, and Sundar (2015) showed that customers who received ads that matched with their current location expressed more positive attitudes toward the messages and showed greater behavioral intentions to visit the promoted store. Similarly, Banerjee and Dholakia (2008) found that LBA positively affected consumers' perceptions of usefulness of the ad, store evaluations, and willingness to respond to the offer. However, this effect is by no means universal. There has been an increasing realization that customers avoid such context-congruent advertising due to privacy concerns (Dhar & Varshney, 2011). As Lee and Hill (2013) found, many consumers tend to perceive that their control over their private information is violated. Moreover, as Lin, Paragas, and Bautista (2016) noted, push-based LBA are oftentimes perceived as disruptive and intrusive to customers, inducing psychological disturbance (Edwards, Li, & Lee, 2002; Bruner & Kumar, 2007).

Nonetheless, the real-time presence of benefits to customers in the form of available coupons and promotional deals present many opportunities for advertisers. In particular, as the cue-route of TIME predicts, multiple cues embedded in LBA messages can trigger a set of heuristics that help customers evaluate the quality of products and their brands being promoted by LBA. When users receive mobile coupons that can be readily used at the right time and place, such presence of advertising messages might trigger the *instant gratification heuristic* (immediate service is better than delay in satisfaction of needs) with positive effects on purchase. In addition, automatic delivery of usable coupons and other useful promotional information to their mobile devices when they walk into its branch might encourage customers' further information disclosure to advertisers, which facilitates direct and tailored marketing to their audience by triggering the *reciprocity heuristic* (if retailers provide their information to me, I will do the same in return). Moreover, pull-based messages that deliver multiple coupons and sale information based upon consumers' requests can trigger the *interaction heuristic* (the more calls for interaction, the better) and the *responsiveness heuristic* (this stores attends to my request and responds immediately). Since GPS-based systems track a user's location every second, LBA systems can also change the advertising content instantly based on changes in the user's location. If a user visits a grocery store, an LBA system delivers relevant coupons for that store, and it can automatically change its promotional messages if the user is taking a break in a coffee shop. Such expedient change of content might not only trigger the *responsiveness heuristic*, but also the *coolness heuristic* (if it is cool, then it is credible) and the *flow heuristic*, arising from an optimal match between user expectations and system actions.

The action-route of TIME would focus on customers' actions with LBA, such as turning on/off GPS function of mobile devices and customization of the frequency and timing of location-based notifications, which would determine their level of engagement with LBA content. More specifically, the source-interactivity aspect of LBA, whereby the users can customize the options of location-based notifications, would imbue in them a sense of agency. As a result of perceiving agency, consumers can better engage with the brands, which ultimately leads to positive attitudes and behavioral intentions toward the advertised products. Extant research has shown that the perceived agency engendered by LBA increases engagement with the campaign messages. For instance, Banerjee and Dholakia (2008) showed that LBA that allowed customers to share their locations and express their needs for instant shopping enhanced their perceived usefulness of the ad, store evaluations, and willingness to buy their products. However, such active usage of LBA needs to be employed with great care. As previous literature on the personalization paradox (Awad & Krishnan, 2006; Aguirre, Mahr, Grewal, Ruyter, & Wetzels, 2015) showed, customers worry about losing their privacy although they want more tailored services based on locations. Hence, it is important to alleviate privacy concerns by giving more granular interactive tools that consumers can customize when, where, and how often they would receive push notifications. Such tools should even allow users to opt out of the services, if necessary, preventing them from receiving unwanted marketing notifications. By providing this level of agency to users, it might relieve their privacy concerns while using location-based services.

Search Engine Advertising

In addition to BA and LBA, search engine advertising (SEA) is another form of online advertising that consumers readily experience as they search for specific brand or product-related information on search engines, such as Google, Bing, and Yahoo. In fact, SEA accounts for the largest portion of online advertising (Haans, Raassens, & Van Hout, 2013), serving as one of the largest advertising platforms (Yao & Mela, 2011) in the U.S. market (Bucklin & Sismeiro, 2009).

SEA includes commercial texts next to general online search results where advertisers pay a premium for consumers' clicks on the URL of their websites (Ghose & Yang, 2009; Haans, Raassens, & Van Hout, 2013). SEA generally consists of two parts: a link to advertiser's website and a short description of the linked site, often without any pictures. When users enter specific keywords in a search engine, a list of sponsored links and short descriptions show up on the results page, which are ranked based on each advertiser's payment for a single click (Zenetti, Bijmolt, Leeflang, & Klapper, 2014). With prepaid keywords relevant to certain products/services and their brands, advertisers can directly reach their audience who are interested in knowing more about them (Varian, 2007).

There exist three mechanisms that serve to evaluate the value and effectiveness of SEA (Zenetti et al., 2014). For example, if a user searches for "Apple" (a technology company headquartered in Cupertino, CA) on Google, the first search result located on the top of the page is a sponsored link to the company's official website (www.apple.com), not generic search results on the fruit. This is because the company has paid for a set of predefined keyword listings related to the company and their products. The first mechanism that simply shows prioritized results with a sponsored link is called an "impression." Yet, not all impressions lead to an actual click of the sponsored URL. Rather, a majority of users ignore the promoted link and proceed to the non-sponsored content lower down on the page. Hence, what advertisers actually pay for search engine advertising is calculated based on the number of actual clicks on a promoted website, which denotes "click-through." Moreover, if the user subsequently spends money on purchasing products and/or services through their visit, then advertisers pay for such committed action on the part of the user, called "conversion."

As SEA grew into a powerful and influential platform in online advertising, many empirical studies have documented its effectiveness in augmenting click-throughs and conversion rates. For instance, Zenetti et al. (2014) revealed that SEA significantly increased the level of awareness of both ad messages and brands. Moreover, they showed increased intention to purchase products from the sponsored brand even without clicking the provided website URL. Yet, not all studies have shown support for the positive effect of displaying the sponsored search results at the top. Ghose and Yang (2009) found that higher click-through and conversion rates did not come from placing the sponsored link at the forefront on result pages. Instead, links located at the middle positions led to greater user interactions with the advertisers' websites. Further, it is important to note that a growing body of literature shows users' avoidance of SEA on the web. A survey by Hotchkiss, Garrison, and Jensen (2004) reported that 77 percent of respondents did not favor sponsored search results. Similarly, Lo, Chiu, and Hsieh (2013) showed that users clicked the sponsored links much less than the non-sponsored ones and spent less time viewing the SEA than the neutral information on the results page, echoing the findings of Hotchkiss et al. (2004).

Despite consumers' tendency to avoid SEA, however, the cue-route of TIME would presume that the presence of sponsored links might trigger both the *prominence heuristic* (privileging the first search result) and the *helper heuristic* (the sponsored link is there to help me, so it can be trusted). However, if too many links are present, the *browsing heuristic* (encouraging users to check out the various offers) or the *elaboration heuristic* (encouraging users to make sense of the relationship between the offers and the search keyword) might be triggered, depending upon how integrated the links are to the search results.

The action-route of TIME provides a slightly different approach to explaining how SEA influences consumers' evaluations of various brands and products. SEA is generated based on a set of key words provided by online users, which reflect their informational needs. That is, a list of sponsored links on the results page is an outcome of message-interactivity affordances. This would imbue in users a sense of contingency (and also agency) since the information comes from their own request. Whenever consumers change their key words entered on search engines, the search engine refreshes the page with new results, thereby signaling the contingent nature of its operation. The more sponsored links correspond to their interests, the greater the feeling of contingency. This will likely encourage their active engagement with the sponsored links, with consequent effects on their attitudes and behaviors, as already noticed in research. Zenetti et al. (2014) showed that customers' actions of search and subsequent review of search results significantly improved their recognition of SEA messages. Moreover, these messages led to greater purchase intention even without visiting the promoted website. In sum, given active user involvement in the search process, SEA can benefit from the positive effects proposed by the action-route of TIME.

Native Advertising

One of the biggest trends in mobile and digital advertising in general is the move toward native advertising (Cohen, 2016). Native advertising refers to a long-used tactic of embedding an advertisement within the "native" frame of content (e.g., a pinned tweet, a "story" on Gawker, or a sponsored video in a user's Facebook newsfeed). From a story in GQ to a status update on Facebook, a native advertisement looks like a typical article or post, but it is actually an advertisement. In the push to properly monetize digital advertising, and especially mobile applications, native advertising has shown to be one of the most effective strategies (Fulgoni &

Lipsman, 2014). Facebook (2016) boasts about how their native advertising has shown engagement scores up to 60 percent higher than banner advertisements, with up to three times higher retention. While it seems like a sure-fire hit for advertisers, when we think about what constitutes a native advertisement, it is difficult to pinpoint exactly what might make it successful.

In essence, a native advertisement is just an advertisement embedded in an interface with which a user is familiar. For the most part, research on native advertising has focused on consumers' recognition of whether a native advertisement is content or advertisement, as this is a concern amongst content producers and consumers (IAB, 2013). However, Wojdynski and Evans (2016) showed that despite a disclosure cue, very few participants recognized the content as an advertisement, and overall, the content was perceived as more negative when it was recognized as an advertisement. Simply, one reason for the effectiveness of native adverting may lie in its ability to effectively blend in with its ecosystem.

As native advertising depends very much on the entire interface in which the content is embedded, the cue-route of TIME is particularly useful in explaining the mechanisms behind effective native ads. When embedded in social media, native ads are accompanied by the same kind of metrics relating to popularity as regular user-generated content. Perhaps the most ubiquitous of all cues in social media platforms is the bandwagon cue, a cue that conveys to the user information about the crowd's opinion and often triggers the *bandwagon heuristic* (if others think this is good (content), then I should think so, too) (Sundar, Oeldorf-Hirsch, & Xu, 2008). In an experiment in an e-commerce setting, Sundar et al. (2008) showed that merely varying the star rating of a product in an Amazon web page led to higher attitudes toward the product as well as purchase intentions. In a study of alcohol marketing, Alhabash, McAlister, Quilliam, Richards, and Lou (2015) found that when a Facebook brand status update had more Likes or Shares, participants were more willing to share it themselves (viral behavior) and express greater behavioral intentions. These studies demonstrate the power of bandwagon cues on user psychology in an environment similar to native advertising. Additionally, given that native advertising is generally embedded within a trusted medium (e.g., Facebook), it can trigger the *authority heuristic*, where users infer credibility based on perceived endorsement by a trustworthy or well-established source.

Successful native advertisements appearing in social-media depend heavily on user-generated content that signal its popularity or relevance to other users (Alhabash et al., 2015). Social media interfaces allow the user to interact with native advertisements, which appears just like a normal post in the news feed (with a small "sponsored" mark), by taking actions such as "liking," "sharing," "commenting," and now "reacting" to them. When users see these native ads and are compelled to "like," "share," or "comment," on them, they are directly interacting with the brand and signaling their intention to join their network. These are manifestations of the source-interactivity affordance, and therefore, are likely to enhance consumers' sense of agency. Increasing feelings of "self-as-source" via such interactive actions can lead to heightened feelings of involvement and identification with the brand.

Concluding Remarks

In sum, a variety of theoretical mechanisms derived from TIME can be used to explain the positive, as well as negative effects, of different forms of digital advertising. As Table 6.1 shows, seven major types of digital advertising can be analyzed

TABLE 6.1 List of the Cue-route Heuristics and the Action-route Mechanisms

Type of Digital Advertising	Cue-route Heuristics	Action-route Mechanisms
Mobile Video Advertising	*being-there* heuristic *realism* heuristic *intrusiveness* heuristic *distraction* heuristic	Lack of User Control ➔ Decreased Sense of Agency
Virtual Reality, Augmented Reality Advertising	*coolness* heuristic *novelty* heuristic *bells-and-whistles* heuristic	Vividness ➔ Increased Perceptual Bandwidth Intuitiveness ➔ Increased Perceptual Bandwidth Natural Mapping ➔ Increased Perceptual Bandwidth User Control ➔ Increased Sense of Agency Competence ➔ Increased Sense of Agency
Chatbot Advertising	*machine* heuristic *helper* heuristic *scaffolding* heuristic	Threadedness ➔ Increased Contingency Reciprocity ➔ Increased Contingency Responsiveness ➔ Increased Contingency
Behavioral Advertising	*similarity* heuristic *helper* heuristic *intrusiveness* heuristic *online security* heuristic *fuzzy boundary* heuristic	Reciprocity ➔ Increased Contingency Responsiveness ➔ Increased Contingency
Location-based Advertising	*instant gratification* heuristic *reciprocity* heuristic *interaction* heuristic *responsiveness* heuristic *coolness* heuristic *flow* heuristic	Customization ➔ Increased Sense of Agency User Control ➔ Increased Sense of Agency

(Continued)

TABLE 6.1 (Continued)

Type of Digital Advertising	Cue-route Heuristics	Action-route Mechanisms
Search Engine Advertising	*prominence* heuristic *helper* heuristic *browsing* heuristic *elaboration* heuristic	Threadedness ➜ Increased Contingency Responsiveness ➜ Increased Contingency
Native Advertising	*bandwagon* heuristic *authority* heuristic	Involvement ➜ Increased Sense of Agency User Control ➜ Increased Sense of Agency Identification ➜ Increased Sense of Agency

via both the cue-route and the action-route. The former is distinguished by the heuristics that are triggered by affordances embedded in the digital ads, often at first glance, whereas the latter is determined by the psychological states induced when consumers act on those affordances.

The heuristics pertain to user impressions of the central affordance of a given type of digital ad and convey their assignment of both value proposition as well as their perceptions of downsides to that type of advertising. For example, mobile video can be seen as being higher on credibility because of its realism of portrayal and transportability; it can also be seen as intrusive and distracting, leading to negative effects. The central modality affordance in VR/AR advertising can evoke the *coolness* and *novelty heuristics* for generating positive effects, but can also invoke the negative *bells-and-whistles heuristic* if the content of the ad is unmatched by the novel modality of presentation. Likewise, data-based advertising techniques like BA, LBA, and SEA all have distinct positive heuristics triggered by their respective affordances but also raise concerns about privacy and security of the user data that they collect and share with other systems.

The conclusions drawn by users based on heuristics are quite different from the outcomes of the action-route, as evident from the mechanisms listed in the third column of Table 6.1. The action-route is dominated by the three types of interactivity identified by TIME. While VR/AR affords modality interactivity; chatbot, SEA, and BA afford message-interactivity; and LBA and native advertising afford source-interactivity. User actions on these affordances serve to enhance perceptual bandwidth, sense of contingency, and sense of agency respectively, with positive effects on user engagement with digital advertising. These principles of the action-route cannot only help us understand the success of certain forms of digital advertising but can also be applied to understand why some forms of advertising (such as mobile video) are unable to engage users in a positive manner. The secret to success in digital advertising is the affordance of interactivity, in some form. Denying users an opportunity to interact, especially when their attention is hijacked as in the case of traditional media, will only lead to negative reactions. This lesson emerges very clearly when one analyzes digital ads using the TIME framework.

Note

1   This research is supported by the U.S. National Science Foundation (NSF) via Standard Grant CNS-1450500.

References

Aalto, L., Göthlin, N., Korhonen, J., & Ojala, T. (2004). Bluetooth and WAP push based location-aware mobile advertising system. In *Proceedings of the 2nd International Conference on Mobile Systems, Applications, and Services* (pp. 49–58).

Aguirre, E., Mahr, D., Grewal, D., de Ruyter, K., & Wetzels, M. (2015). Unraveling the personalization paradox: The effect of information collection and trust-building strategies on online advertisement effectiveness. *Journal of Retailing, 91*(1), 34–49.

Alhabash, S., McAlister, A. R., Quilliam, E. T., Richards, J. I., & Lou, C. (2015). Alcohol's getting a bit more social: When alcohol marketing messages on Facebook increase young adults' intentions to imbibe. *Mass Communication and Society, 18*(3), 350–375.

Awad, N. F., & Krishnan, M. S. (2006). The personalization privacy paradox: An empirical evaluation of information transparency and the willingness to be profiled online for personalization. *MIS Quarterly, 30*(1), 13–28.

Banerjee, S., & Dholakia, R. R. (2008). Mobile advertising: Does location-based advertising work? *International Journal of Mobile Marketing, 3*(2), 68–74.

Bauer, C., & Strauss, C. (2016). Location-based advertising on mobile devices: A literature review and analysis. *Management Review Quarterly, 66*(3), 159–194.

Bessler, S. (2007). A system for locating mobile terminals with tunable privacy. *Journal of Theoretical and Applied Electronic Commerce Research, 2*(2), 82–91.

Beukeboom, C. J., Kerkhof, P., & de Vries, M. (2015). Does a virtual like cause actual liking? How following a brand's Facebook updates enhances brand evaluations and purchase intention. *Journal of Interactive Marketing, 32*, 26–36.

Bilenko, M., Richardson, M., & Tsai, J. (2011). Targeted, not tracked: Client-side solutions for privacy-friendly behavioral advertising. *TPRC*. Retrieved from http://papers.ssrn.com/sol3/papers.cfm?abstract_id=1995127.

Bruner, G. C., & Kumar, A. (2007). Attitude toward location-based advertising. *Journal of Interactive Advertising, 7*(2), 3–15.

Bucklin, R. E., & Sismeiro, C. (2009). Click here for internet insight: Advances in clickstream data analysis in marketing. *Journal of Interactive Marketing, 23*(1), 35–48.

Chen, J., & Stallaert, J. (2014). An economic analysis of online advertising using behavioral targeting. *MIS Quarterly, 38*(2), 429–449.

Cohen, D. (2016, April 5). Native advertising dominate Facebook audience network. *Adweek*. Retrieved from http://www.adweek.com/socialtimes/native-advertising-facebook-audience-network-study/637217.

De Sa, M., Navalpakkam, V., & Churchill, E. F. (2013, April). Mobile advertising: Evaluating the effects of animation, user and content relevance. In *Proceedings of the 2013 Annual Conference on Human Factors in Computing Systems (CHI'13)* (pp. 2487–2496).

Detenber, B. H., & Reeves, B. (1996). A bio-informational theory of emotion: Motion and image size effects on viewers. *Journal of Communication, 46*(3), 66–84.

Dhar, S., & Varshney, U. (2011). Challenges and business models for mobile location-based services and advertising. *Communications of the ACM, 54*(5), 121–128.

Edwards, A., Edwards, C., Spence, P. R., Harris, C., & Gambino, A. (2016). Robots in the classroom: Differences in students' perceptions of credibility and learning between "teacher as robot" and "robot as teacher." *Computers in Human Behavior, 63*, 304–310, doi: http://dx.doi.org/10.1016/j.chb.2016.06.005.

Edwards, S. M., Li, H., & Lee, J. H. (2002). Forced exposure and psychological reactance: Antecedents and consequences of the perceived intrusiveness of pop-up ads. *Journal of Advertising, 31*(3), 83–95.

Ellis, S. S. (2016, March 23). Immersive advertising is becoming a (virtual) reality for brands. *The Huffington Post*. Retrieved from http://www.huffingtonpost.com/advertising-week/immersive-advertising-is_b_9534484.html.

Facebook. (2016). The future of mobile advertising is native. *Facebook*. Retrieved from https://www.facebook.com/business/news/mobile-native-advertising.

Fulgoni, G., & Lipsman, A. (2014). Numbers, please: Digital game changers: How social media will help usher in the era of mobile and multi-platform campaign-effectiveness measurement. *Journal of Advertising Research, 54*(1), 11–16.

Gambino, A., Kim, J., Sundar, S. S., Ge, J., & Rosson, M. B. (2016). User disbelief in privacy paradox: Heuristics that determine disclosure. In *Proceedings of CHI'16 Extended Abstracts on Human Factors in Computing Systems (CHI EA '16)* (pp. 2837–2843).

Ghose, A., & Yang, S. (2009). An empirical analysis of search engine advertising: Sponsored search in electronic markets. *Management Science, 55*(10), 1605–1622.

Gibson, J. (1977). The theory of affordances. In R. E. Shaw & J. Bransford (Eds.), *Perceiving, acting, and knowing: Toward an ecological psychology* (pp. 67–82). Hillsdale, NJ: Lawrence Erlbaum Associates.

Haans, H., Raassens, N., & Van Hout, R. (2013). Search engine advertisements: The impact of advertising statements on click-through and conversion rates. *Marketing Letters, 24*(2), 151–163.

Harwell, D. R. (2016, March 10). The creepy, inescapable advertisements that could define virtual reality. *The Washington Post*. Retrieved from https://www.washington post.com/news/the-switch/wp/2016/03/10/the-creepy-inescapable-advertisements-that-could-define-virtual-reality/

Heeter, C. (1989). Implications of new interactive technologies for conceptualizing communication. In J. L. Salvaggio & J. Bryant (Eds.), *Media use in the information age: Emerging patterns of adoption and consumer use* (pp. 217–235). Hillsdale, NJ: Lawrence Erlbaum Associates, Inc.

Hegner, S. M., Kusse, M. D. C., & Pruyn, A. T. (2016). Watch it! The influence of forced pre-roll video ads on consumer perceptions. In P. Verlegh, H. Voorveld, & M. Eisend (Eds.), *Advances in Advertising Research* (pp. 63–73). New York, NY: Springer.

Hotchkiss, G., Garrison, M., & Jensen, S. (2004). Search engine usage in North America. Retrieved from http://www.enquiro.com/research.asp.

IAB. (2013). The native advertising playbook. *IAB*. Retrieved from https://www.iab.com/wp-content/uploads/2015/06/IAB-Native-Advertising-Playbook2.pdf.

Jin, S. A. A. (2009). The roles of modality richness and involvement in shopping behavior in 3D virtual stores. *Journal of Interactive Marketing, 23*(3), 234–246.

Kelly, L., Kerr, G., & Drennan, J. (2010). Avoidance of advertising in social networking sites: The teenage perspective. *Journal of Interactive Advertising, 10*(2), 16–27.

Kim, K. J., & Sundar, S. S. (2016). Mobile persuasion: Can screen size and presentation mode make a difference to trust? *Human Communication Research, 42*(1), 45–70.

Kim, K. J., Sundar, S. S., & Park, E. (2011). The effects of screen-size and communication modality on psychology of mobile device users. In *Proceedings of the 2011 Annual Conference Extended Abstracts on Human Factors in Computing Systems (CHI EA'11)* (pp. 1207–1212).

Lee, H. H., & Hill, J. T. (2013). Moderating effect of privacy self-efficacy on location-based mobile marketing. *International Journal of Mobile Communications, 11*(4), 330–350.

Lee, S., Kim, K. J., & Sundar, S. S. (2015). Customization in location-based advertising: Effects of tailoring source, locational congruity, and product involvement on ad attitudes. *Computers in Human Behavior, 51*, 336–343.

Limperos, A., Waddell, T. F., Ivory, A. H., & Ivory, J. D. (2014). Psychological and physiological responses to stereoscopic 3D presentation in handheld digital gaming: Comparing the experiences of frequent and infrequent game players. *Presence, 23*(4), 341–353.

Lin, T. T. C., Paragas, F., & Bautista, J. R. R. (2016). Determinants of mobile consumers' perceived value of location-based mobile advertising and user responses. *International Journal of mobile communications, 14*(2), 99–117.

Lo, S. K., Chiu, Y. P., & Hsieh, A. Y. (2013). Photograph and model use within an online auction page for influencing buyer's bidding behavior. *Online Information Review, 37*(3), 354–368.

McStay, A. (2012). I consent: An analysis of the cookie directive and its implications for UK behavioral advertising. *New Media & Society, 15*(4), 596–611.

Moses, L. (2016, June 21). How fusion, complex and other publishers are using Facebook messenger bots. *Digiday*. Retrieved from http://digiday.com/publishers/4-publishers-using-facebook-messenger-bots/

Oh, J., Robinson, H. R., & Lee, J. Y. (2013). Page flipping vs. clicking: The impact of naturally mapped interaction technique on user learning and attitudes. *Computers in Human Behavior, 29*(4), 1334–1341.

Okazaki, S., Li, H., & Hirose, M. (2012). Benchmarking the use of QR code in mobile promotion: Three studies in Japan. *Journal of Advertising Research, 52*(1), 102–117.

Oremus, W. (2016, June 28). Facebook thinks it has found the secret to making bots less dumb. *Slate*. Retrieved from http://www.slate.com/blogs/future_tense/2016/06/28/facebook_s_ai_researchers_are_making_bots_smarter_by_giving_them_memory.html.

Peters, S., & Leshner, G. (2013). The effects of advergames on game players' processing of embedded brands. *Journal of Advertising, 42*(2–3), 113–130.

PWC. (2015). Global entertainment and media outlook 2016–2020. Retrieved from http://www.pwc.com/gx/en/industries/entertainment-media/outlook.html.

Rafaeli, S. (1988). Interactivity: From new media to communication. In R. P. Hawkins, J. M. Wieman, & S. Pingree (Eds.), *Advancing communication science: Merging mass and interpersonal processes* (pp. 110–134). Newbury Park, CA: Sage.

Sableman, M., Shoenberger, H., & Thorson, E. (2013). Consumer attitudes toward relevant online behavioral advertising: Crucial evidence in the data privacy debates. *Media Law Resource Center Bulletin, 1*, 93–110.

Steuer, J. (1992). Defining virtual reality: Dimensions determining telepresence. *Journal of Communication, 42*(4), 73–93.

Stoyanova, J., Brito, P. Q., Georgieva, P., & Milanova, M. (2015). Comparison of consumer purchase intention between interactive and augmented reality shopping platforms through statistical analyses. In *Innovations in Intelligent Systems and Applications (INISTA), 2015 International Symposium on* (pp. 1–8). IEEE.

Summers, C., Smith, R. W., & Reczek, R. W. (2014). Learning about the self through advertising: The effect of behaviorally-targeted advertising on consumer self-perceptions and behavior. *Advances in Consumer Research, 42*, 693–694.

Sundar, S. S. (2008a). Self as source: Agency and customization in interactive media. In E. Konijn, S. Utz, M. Tanis, & S. Barnes (Eds.), *Mediated interpersonal communication* (pp. 58–74). New York, NY: Routledge.

Sundar, S. S. (2008b). The MAIN model: A heuristic approach to understanding technology effects on credibility. In M. J. Metzger & A. J. Flanagin (Eds.), *Digital media, youth, and credibility* (pp. 72–100). Cambridge, MA: The MIT Press.

Sundar, S. S., & Bellur, S. (2010, June). *Measuring media use as affordances: A heuristics approach to interactivity.* Paper presented at the 60th annual conference of the International Communication Association, Singapore.

Sundar, S. S., Bellur, S., & Jia, H. (2012). Motivational technologies: A theoretical framework for designing preventive health applications. In M. Bang & E. L. Ragnemalm (Eds.), *Proceedings of the 7th International Conference on Persuasive Technology (PERSUASIVE 2012), LNCS 7284* (pp. 112–122).

Sundar, S. S., Bellur, S., Oh, J., Jia, H., & Kim, H. S. (2016). Theoretical importance of contingency in human-computer interaction: Effects of message interactivity on user engagement. *Communication Research, 43*(5), 595–625.

Sundar, S. S., Bellur, S., Oh, J., Xu, Q., & Jia, H. (2014). User experience of on-screen interaction techniques: An experimental investigation of clicking, sliding, zooming, hovering, dragging and flipping. *Human Computer Interaction, 29*(2), 109–152.

Sundar, S. S., Jia, H., Waddell, T. F., & Huang, Y. (2015). Toward a theory of interactive media effects (TIME): Four models for explaining how interface features affect user psychology. In S. S. Sundar (Ed.), *The handbook of the psychology of communication technology* (pp. 47–86). Malden, MA: Wiley Blackwell.

Sundar, S. S., & Kalyanaraman, S. (2004). Arousal, memory, and impression-formation effects of animation speed in web advertising. *Journal of Advertising, 33*(1), 7–17.

Sundar, S. S., Kalyanaraman, S., & Brown, J. (2003). Explicating website interactivity: Impression-formation effects in political campaign sites. *Communication Research, 30*(1), 30–59.

Sundar, S. S., Kang, H., Wu, M., Go, E., & Zhang, B. (2013). Unlocking the privacy paradox: Do cognitive heuristics hold the key? In *Proceedings of CHI'13 Extended Abstracts on Human Factors in Computing Systems (CHI EA '13)* (pp. 811–816).

Sundar, S. S., & Kim, J. (2005). Interactivity and persuasion: Influencing attitudes with information and involvement. *Journal of Interactive Advertising, 5*(2), 6–29.

Sundar, S. S., Kim, J., Gambino, J., & Rosson, M. R. (2016). *Six ways to enact privacy by design: Cognitive heuristics that predict users' online information disclosure.* Paper presented at the Bridging the Gap between Privacy by Design and Privacy in Practice workshop in the 34th annual conference on Human Factors in Computing Systems (ACM SIGCHI), San Jose, SD.

Sundar, S. S., & Limperos, A. (2013). Uses and grats 2.0: New gratifications for new media. *Journal of Broadcasting & Electronic Media, 57*(4), 504–525.

Sundar, S. S., & Nass, C. (2001). Conceptualizing sources in online news. *Journal of Communication, 51*(1), 52–72.

Sundar, S. S., Oeldorf-Hirsch, A., & Garga, A. (2008). A cognitive-heuristics approach to understanding presence in virtual environments. In A. Spagnolli & L. Gamberini (Eds.), *PRESENCE 2008: Proceedings of the 11th Annual International Workshop on Presence* (pp. 219–228). Padova, Italy: CLEUP Cooperativa Libraria Universitaria Padova. Retrieve from http://www.temple.edu/ispr/prev_conferences/proceedings/2008/sundar.pdf.

Sundar, S. S., Oeldorf-Hirsch, A., & Xu, Q. (2008). The bandwagon effect of collaborative filtering technology. *Proceedings of CHI'08 Extended Abstracts on Human Factors in Computing Systems, 26,* 3453–3458.

Sundar, S. S., Tamul, D., & Wu, M. (2014). Capturing "cool": Measures for assessing coolness of technological products. *International Journal of Human-Computer Studies, 72,* 169–180.

Sundar, S. S., Xu, Q., & Dou, X. (2012). Role of technology in online persuasion: A MAIN model perspective. In S. Rodgers & E. Thorson (Eds.), *Advertising theory* (pp. 355–372). New York, NY: Routledge.

Ur, B., Leon, P. G., Cranor, L. F., Shay, R., & Wang, Y. (2012, July). Smart, useful, scary, creepy: Perceptions of online behavioral advertising. In *Proceedings of the 2012 Annual Conference on Usable Privacy and Security* (pp. 4–18).

Varian, H. R. (2007). Position auctions. *International Journal of Industrial Organization, 25*(6), 1163–1178.

Wojdynski, B. W., & Evans, N. J. (2016). Going native: Effects of disclosure position and language on the recognition and evaluation of online native advertising. *Journal of Advertising, 45*(2), 157–168.

Yan, J., Liu, N., Wang, G., Zhang, W., Jiang, Y., & Chen, Z. (2009, April). How much can behavioral targeting help online advertising? In *Proceedings of the 2009 International Conference on World Wide Web* (pp. 261–270).

Yao, S., & Mela, C. F. (2011). A dynamic model of sponsored search advertising. *Marketing Science, 30*(3), 447–468.

Yaoyuneyong, G., Foster, J., Johnson, E., & Johnson, D. (2016). Augmented reality marketing: Consumer preferences and attitudes toward hypermedia print ads. *Journal of Interactive Advertising, 16*(1), 16–30.

Zenetti, G., Bijmolt, T. H., Leeflang, P. S., & Klapper, D. (2014). Search engine advertising effectiveness in a multimedia campaign. *International Journal of Electronic Commerce, 18*(3), 7–38.

Zhang, B., Wu, M., Kang, H., Go, E., & Sundar, S. S. (2014). Effects of security warnings and instant gratification cues on attitudes toward mobile websites. In *Proceedings of the 2014 Annual Conference on Human Factors in Computing Systems (CHI'14)* (p. 111).

7

PERSONALIZATION, PERCEIVED INTRUSIVENESS, IRRITATION, AND AVOIDANCE IN DIGITAL ADVERTISING

Mariko Morimoto

Introduction

With the convenience and speed afforded by the digital age of marketing, business conducts and consumer expectations have altered greatly. These changes have benefited both advertisers and consumers, but have also raised concerns for consumer privacy. Generally referred to as "an individual's right to be let alone" (Warren & Brandeis, 1890, *supra* note 1 at 195), privacy in the context of advertising is often associated with consumers' concern over their ability to control personal information in situations such as market transactions and consumption activities (Foxman & Kilcoyne, 1993). A report from Pew Research Center revealed that the majority of Americans believe that being able to maintain privacy and confidentiality in their lives is important. In the report, over 93 percent stated that control over *who* can collect information is important, and 90 percent responded that control over *what* information can be collected is also important (Madden & Raine, 2015).

In recent years, consumers have come to own multiple technological devices, which connect to the internet, causing increased concerns about advertisers using cross-device tracking methods to obtain personal information. With the control over the flow of information out of their hands, consumers have developed concern and skepticism toward ads delivered in a digital environment. These issues in multi-device tracking practices in digital advertising continue to grow so rapidly that even legislators such as the Federal Trade Commission (FTC) struggle to adapt regulations to keep up (Kaye, 2015).

On the other hand, there is past research supporting the use of advertising personalization to reduce the likelihood that individuals will respond negatively toward digital advertising (e.g., Baek & Morimoto, 2012). This is at the expense of collecting personal information from consumers, which may also increase consumers' privacy concerns. Thus, the key to creating successful digital advertising campaigns is to identify the degree of personalization in advertising that does not threaten the consumers' ability to control personal information.

The purpose of this chapter is to elaborate the relationship between consumer concerns over their online privacy and negative responses they may have to digital advertising using the framework of Brehm's (1966) psychological reactance theory. Consumers may feel perceived intrusiveness, irritation, and avoidance toward digital advertising. A certain degree of advertising personalization, however, has the potential to ease negative responses and may even enhance its effectiveness. Hence, this framework aims to initiate discussion for discovering a balance between personalization in digital advertising and consumer online privacy protection.

Consumer Online Privacy Concerns from Psychological Reactance Perspective

Consumer privacy is an ever-present issue in marketing and advertising. Obtaining accurate consumer information to target prospective customer groups is essential for an effective promotional campaign. From a consumer's standpoint, however, the collection of personal information to create a better targeting strategy may be interpreted as an encroachment of their privacy, creating adverse effects that all advertisers wish to avoid: negative perceptions, negative attitudes, and negative reactions to ads and brands.

Consumer Online Privacy in the Context of Consumers' Information and Activity Control

To overcome consumer's potential negative response to digital advertising, the theory of psychological reactance helps to explain the relationship between targeted advertising and online privacy. However, subsequent advertising outcomes must first be defined, which has been done in previous research in marketing and advertising (e.g., Foxman & Kilcoyne, 1993; Phelps, Nowak, & Ferrell, 2000; Sheehan & Hoy, 2000). First, privacy law generally consists of four areas, including: 1) *appropriation* of name or likeness, 2) *intrusion* into solitude of an individual, 3) *disclosure* of private information, and 4) placing an individual in *a false light* (Pember & Calvert, 2008; Morimoto & Macias, 2009). Of the four, the subcategory of *intrusion* is relevant in the context of digital advertising.

Foxman and Kilcoyne (1993) defined consumer privacy on the basis of who controls consumer data and whether consumers are informed of the collection and their privacy rights. The concept of a social contract, which is formed when a consumer provides a marketer with their personal information (Dunfree, Smith, & Ross, 1999), provides helpful insights. This contract is breached when consumer information is rented or sold to a third party without permission, non-consented information collection is conducted, or consumers are not offered an opportunity to limit the dissemination of their information (Culnan, 1995; Phelps et al., 2000). Phelps et al. (2000) found that consumers want control over the types and volume of commercial solicitations depending on the marketers' use of their personal information. Based on the consumers' idea of control, Morimoto and Macias (2009) have conceptualized issues on consumer online privacy to revolve around intrusion into consumer solitude, physical spaces, and activities; control over private information; and control over marketer and advertiser interactions on digital platforms. Hence, a good predictor of consumers' subsequent attitudes and behavioral intent toward digital advertising is the degree of control they perceive to have over their online activities and information. The theory of psychological reactance (Brehm, 1966) illustrates the process well.

Psychological Reactance and Its Relationship with Consumers' Information and Activity Control

Psychological reactance occurs when individuals become agitated due to a threat to their behavioral freedom (Brehm, 1989). In this situation, individuals are motivated to change, modify, or alter attitudes and behaviors to re-establish their threatened freedom and autonomy (Baek & Morimoto, 2012). Reactance is likely to take place when: 1) an individual regards the threatened freedom as important, 2) the severity of the threat escalates, 3) the particular threat restricts other freedoms, and 4) the individual enjoys the freedom (Brehm, 1966; Edwards, Li, & Lee, 2002, p. 85). To be more specific, Clee and Wicklund (1980) have explained reactance to occur when an individual perceives reduction of their freedom. This repels them from the behaviors and attitudes forced upon them, consequently moving the individual in the opposite direction of the influence, which is called a "boomerang effect" (p. 390).

Individuals must expect to have freedom of choice—to freely engage in controlling their information and behavior—for reactance to occur (Clee & Wicklund, 1980). Consumers feel a loss of freedom when they realize that control of their information and behaviors is in the hands of advertisers. The fear of further removal from control of personal information may spark psychological reactance and yield unintended responses from the consumer such as the development of negative attitudes toward advertised brands and advertisers, as well as negative behavioral outcomes. Consumers can freely expect to have control over their exposure to different types of digital ads and dissemination of their information such as past purchases, locations, and activities. The theory of psychological reactance can effectively explain possible consequences of digital advertising and help advertisers understand consumers' negative reactions.

Empirical research on advertising responses based on psychological reactance is extended to digital environments. Edwards et al. (2002) focused on consumers experiencing forced exposure to pop-up ads and reported that perceived intrusiveness could cause reactance, irritation, and ad avoidance. In regard to unsolicited commercial emails, the more consumers view promotional messages as obtrusive, the stronger their reactance will be. The end result is ad avoidance and negative attitudes toward ads (Morimoto & Macias, 2009). White, Zahay, Thorbjørnsen, and Shavitt (2008) also suggested that click-through intentions could be affected by consumers' reactance to personalization in commercial email messages. Reactance can be also triggered by lack of trust toward advertisers. Bleier and Eisenbeiss (2015) discovered that personalized banner ads based on the consumer's purchase interests provoked reactance and privacy concerns when the marketers and advertisers were less trusted. As these examples show, psychological reactance can be the root to predicting consumer responses to digital advertising and the consequences of efforts by advertisers.

Potential Outcomes of Psychological Reactance in Digital Advertising

Hierarchy of effects models (e.g., Ray, 1982; Park & Salvendy, 2012) explain the effects of cognition, affect, and behavior on the consumer's responses to product offerings, and are often used to understand consumer information processing and advertising responses. Ray (1982) suggested that consumers first obtain an understanding of the information, which then shapes their attitudes and finally leads to behavioral intentions. This model can also describe potential consequences of psychological reactance triggered by digital advertising. The three factors that have been identified as possible outcomes of reactance are further elaborated in the following sections.

Perceived Ad Intrusiveness

The first outcome is a cognitive evaluation called perceived ad intrusiveness. Yoo and Kim (2005) explain cognitive evaluations as "thoughts that consumers produce when they are exposed to advertising" (p. 21). Perceived intrusiveness is one of the key influencers of attitude formation among audiences of digital advertising (Morimoto & Chang, 2009), alongside emotional reactions such as irritation (Edwards et al., 2002).

There are two attributes that constitute ad intrusiveness. The first attribute is a function of interruption to one's task. In Ha's (1996) research on advertising clutter, the nature of advertising to seek the audience's attention was found to be obtrusive in editorial content in media (see also Chapter 5 of this text). Consequently, this shows that ads may be seen as intrusive, as they can interfere with the goals of the audiences (Edwards et al., 2002). The situation can be replicated in a digital environment as well. Edwards et al. (2002) conceptualized perceived ad intrusiveness as the point that a person finds presented information contradictory to his/her own goals, as in the context of internet ads. This type of intrusiveness can be seen in various digital advertising ranging from more traditional contexts, such as pop-up ads (e.g., Edwards et al., 2002) and unsolicited commercial email messages (e.g., Morimoto & Chang, 2009), to newer forms like online videos (Goodrich, Schiller, & Galletta, 2015) and location-based ads (e.g., Gazley, Hunt, & McLaren, 2014). Regardless of the advertisement's format, any degree of perceived intrusiveness generally affects the consumer's subsequent emotions, attitudes, and behavioral intent and provokes psychological reactance when they feel it hinders their freedom to complete online tasks, enjoy media content, etc.

The second attribute revolves around the issue of information control, particularly the disclosure of personal information. Baek and Morimoto (2012) have defined the point of threat to consumer privacy as the moment when the consumer becomes worried about "the potential invasion of the right to prevent the disclosure of personal information to others" (p. 63). Consumers may find the use of personal information and browsing data in digital advertising as intrusive if they have not given marketers permission for its collection. Greater levels of intrusiveness are felt among consumers if the use of their personal information is for commercial purposes or if its transfer to a third party is unsanctioned. In other words, the freedom of being able to control the distribution of one's information plays an important role in whether the individual undergoes psychological reactance.

The control aspect of perceived ad intrusiveness in digital advertising is explored in more recent research. Van Doorn and Hoekstra (2013) have argued that when an online ad requires personal identification or transaction information, it tends to trigger ad intrusiveness and leads to decreased purchase intentions. A study of short message service (SMS) advertising by Cortés and Vela (2013) have shown that sending SMS ads to the consumer's mobile phone without permission can also fuel perceived ad intrusiveness; if a consumer feels that his/her mobile phone is a personal and private object, the likelihood of perceiving intrusiveness through SMS ads is greater. Other research has also generally indicated that perceived ad intrusiveness is related to irritation (e.g., Ying, Korneliussen, & Grønhaug, 2009) and negative attitudes toward ads (e.g., Gazley et al., 2014), a concept known to negatively influence various factors and behaviors including attitudinal variables.

Ad Irritation

Ads that stimulate the consumer's senses can bring out feelings of irritation (Edwards et al., 2002). Perceived ad intrusiveness due to interruptions to tasks caused by the volume of ads on screen and/or lack of control of personal information can be considered excessive stimuli. Thus, ad intrusiveness can be denoted as an antecedent of ad irritation, making it a crucial factor to study since it can impact the effectiveness of advertising executions (Aaker & Bruzzone, 1985).

Ad irritation can be described as the negative, impatient, and displeasing feelings that consumers experience due to advertising stimuli (Aaker & Bruzzone, 1985; Morimoto & Chang, 2009). Previous scholars have identified influencers of irritation in perceived ad intrusiveness (e.g., Greyser, 1973; Edwards et al., 2002; Cortés & Vela, 2013), in product categories (e.g., Bauer & Greyser, 1968; Aaker & Bruzzone, 1985) and in the amount of ads and ad appearances (e.g., Edwards et al., 2002). It is not difficult to imagine that the data collected from the consumer's digital activities are also used to develop cross-media promotional strategies. For effective media planning, the same ads are likely to appear across multiple digital devices and social media platforms, but repeated exposure to the ads may invoke irritation within the consumer. Psychological reactance theory also predicts that people tend to respond to persuasive messages in a negative manner if they appear to dissatisfy the consumer's needs for self-determination and control (Brehm, 1966; Burgoon, Alvaro, Grandpre, & Voulodakis, 2002). According to this idea, the reception of commercial messages sent using personal information can be also taken as unwanted communication (Baek & Morimoto, 2012). As a result, ad irritation may cause affective responses such as attitudes toward advertising (e.g., Hernandez, Chapa, Minor, Maldonado, & Barranzeula, 2004), consumer skepticism (e.g., Obermiller & Spangenberg, 1998), and behavioral outcomes, like avoidance (e.g., Speck & Elliott, 1997; Cho & Cheon, 2004).

Empirical research on irritation in the digital context illustrates the trend explained above. In the mobile phone context, Park and Salvendy (2012) identified ad irritation as one of the three factors that shapes attitudes toward ads. By comparing multiple media formats, Baek and Morimoto (2012) found that the effect of ad irritation on attitudinal variables is magnified in digital media in comparison to traditional ad media; unsolicited commercial email appears to trigger more irritation than traditional telemarketing does. Another study on unsolicited commercial email has also shown a strong relationship between perceived ad irritation and attitudes toward the medium (Morimoto & Chang, 2009). Although these examples mostly exhibit the influence of irritation on affective factors rather than behavioral intentions/outcomes, advertisers should be aware that some behavioral outcomes seen in reactions toward traditional ads are also expected to be in the digital advertising environment due to psychological reactance.

Ad Avoidance

Negative perceptions toward advertising practices can subsequently lead to negative behavioral outcomes (Ray, 1982), and avoidance is one of the major negative changes in the consumer's behavior. Ad avoidance is defined as "all actions by media users that differentially reduce their exposure to ad contents" (Speck & Elliott, 1997, p. 61) and regarded as a remedy to intrusion by ads (Morimoto & Macias, 2009). Cho and Cheon (2004) have proposed three dimensions of ad avoidance in the internet context: cognitive, affective, and behavioral. *Cognitive* ad avoidance is when consumers intentionally ignore ads, *affective* ad avoidance is when consumers dislike the ads and avoid the source of the ads, and *behavioral* ad avoidance is the actual physical action taken to avoid ads (Cho & Cheon, 2004). Hence, according to psychological reactance theory, consumers may avoid ads to regain the freedom to resume their online tasks. The tendency of avoidance is expected to be greater for digital advertising since the internet is a more goal- and task-oriented medium than traditional media (Chen & Wells, 1999). Also, by avoiding digital ads, consumers regain control of personal information since avoidance can terminate the dissemination of personal information, such as locations and activities. Thus, this behavioral outcome is likely to remain as the consumer's remedy to ad intrusiveness and irritation.

Ad avoidance takes place in several patterns: consumers can select opt-out options from mailing lists to avoid future reception of ads (e.g., Milne & Rohm, 2004), individuals can attempt to minimize time spent viewing ads by closing pop-ups ads (Edwards et al., 2002), viewers can switch channels to avoid ads while watching TV (Heeter & Greenberg, 1985; Speck & Elliot, 1997), and ads can also be avoided cognitively, meaning, they are not paid attention to (Fransen, Verlegh, Kirmani, & Smit, 2015). Consumers can install ad-blocking software, services, and applications to avoid ads in the internet environment. Although there are relatively fewer consumers who are willing to pay to avoid receiving digital ads, particularly on their mobile phones (Sterling, 2015), than those who attempt to avoid ads through other techniques, marketers can use paid services to show their ads even to ad-blocker users (Welch, 2015). The "chase" between these two parties—consumers escaping from ads and marketers catching up with them—seems to continue regardless of ad media formats.

Previous scholars throughout the years have also identified factors associated with ad avoidance. For example, Speck and Elliot's (1997) study on broadcasting and print media has suggested attitudes toward media categories and perceived annoyance as strong predictors of ad avoidance. Perceptions like intrusiveness, irritation, informativeness, and ad utilities toward ad executions can increase the possibility of ad avoidance (e.g., Edwards et al., 2002; Morimoto & Chang, 2009). In addition, past negative experiences with ads can affect the likelihood of ad avoidance (Cho & Cheon, 2004). These examples illustrate the Learning Hierarchy Model (Ray, 1982), which suggests a relationship between perceptions, affects, and behavioral outcomes.

In digital advertising, consumers tend to physically avoid more traditional forms of digital ads such as pop-up ads (Edwards et al., 2002) and unsolicited commercial email messages (Morimoto & Chang, 2009) by installing ad blocking software or by closing/deleting them. Sheehan and Hoy (2000) pointed out that consumers might even react to ads more actively and send negative messages back to advertisers, called "flaming" (p. 46), when their concerns for privacy become significant. Such elaborated responses, however, appear less often among young consumers who have grown up with internet technology and have been surrounded by digital ads. Instead, young consumers appear to cognitively avoid ads on social media as they find these ads irrelevant and social media as a less credible source (Kelly, Kerr, & Drennan, 2010). Although ad avoidance is usually paired with negative reactions to ads, it is possible to reduce the chance of such reactions by providing more freedom to consumers via opt-out options that can be easily completed online by consumers themselves. For instance, a study on YouTube viewers revealed that viewers showed strong preference for "skippable" ads; an option to skip midstream ads can reduce negative responses from consumers and enhance their viewing experiences (Pashkevich, Dorai-Raj, Kellar, & Zigmond, 2012). For digital advertisers, while avoidance is not necessarily a preferred consumer outcome, negative responses can be minimized through proactive strategies to reach appropriate audiences, one of which is personalization of ad contents used to effectively target customers.

Personalization and Reactance to Digital Advertising

Personalization of Digital Advertising

Advertising personalization has been a popular topic; however, scholars have not come to a concrete conclusion that fully endorses its effectiveness in consumer attitude and behavioral formation. White et al. (2008) define personalization as "a specialized flow of communication that sends different recipients distinct messages tailored to their individual preferences or characteristics" (p. 40). The definition is accepted in academia, but it does not clearly reflect the nature of advertising as a form of commercial speech. Baek and Morimoto (2012) suggested in their study that although the distinction between personalized promotions and advertising is ambiguous, personalized advertising gives more weight on *commercial* messages with a sale of a product in mind compared to other promotional offers. By combining both approaches, personalized advertising can be defined as distinctive commercial messages tailored to individual preferences and/or characteristics and sent to different recipients. Digital advertising can take advantage of information-processing technology to target well-defined audiences.

Personalized advertising has both pros and cons. The most notable advantage is better targeting efforts with preferred outcomes. Using personal data to match consumer preferences and interests, advertisers can make ads more useful to consumers and achieve a higher potential for purchase (Wang, Yan, Chen, & Zhang, 2015a). Additionally, greater relevance in personalized advertising can make the information search process more efficient for consumers (Van Doorn & Hoekstra, 2013). Because of its relevance, personalized advertising can receive more information processing capacity from consumers and end up with better encoding results (Bright & Daugherty, 2012).

On the other hand, personalized advertising has raised concerns due to data collection. Specifically, privacy concerns tend to increase when consumers believe that advertisers keep tabs of their online behaviors to obtain data on their preferences, which can be perceived as privacy disclosure (Wang et al., 2015a). When ad messages include personal information, consumers may also feel as if they cannot escape from the observation of unknown advertisers (White et al., 2008). Moreover, consumers can feel manipulated by advertisers or view personalized advertising as a threat to their privacy if the ad appears too close to their preference (Bleier & Eisenbeiss, 2015). Even with this ambivalence, the popularity of personalized advertising in a digital environment will probably remain, the key to overcoming consumers' concern being able to identify the types and tolerable degrees of personalization. The big question is: where exactly is this balance?

Types of Personalization

Demographic and Psychographic Information

Researchers have attempted to identify the types and degrees of personalization that could maximize advertising effectiveness. Demographic and psychographic information is a frequently used variable in personalized advertising. Of the two, demographic information such as gender (excluding age) tends to be a commonly used factor. Therefore, consumers' responses can be negative when they encounter ads with elements of stable personal information. White et al. (2008) indicated that when personalized information such as name, location, and lifestyle in commercial messages clearly identifies, characterizes, and/or distinguishes the recipient, it could trigger personalization reactance, i.e., reactance in response to inappropriate personalization, because such communication is too personal for the recipient. Consumers may think that once this type of information is in the hand of marketers, they will have permanent access to the information. Although laws in many countries require marketers to provide consumers with an option to opt-out from mailing/contact lists (e.g., CAN-SPAM Act in the U.S. and EU Opt-In Directive in EU), it does not guarantee that the information will be discarded by advertisers upon opt-out requests. Consequently, personalization reactance is provoked, followed by negative consumer reactions.

Previous Online Browsing & Purchase Histories

The second type of personalization uses the consumer's shopping and online activities. In this practice, ads are tailored to reflect their most recent shopping behavior (recorded via clickstream data), for instance, at an online store (Bleier & Eisenbeiss, 2015). The monitoring is administrated through cookies: small text files installed on users' devices for data collection (Smit, Edith, Noort, & Voorveld, 2014). While the consumer's geolocational information may be protected if they refuse cookies, advertisers can still track their online activities because they leave digital footprints in other ways. Thus, browsing histories can be monitored and used for more tailored advertising (Van Doorn & Hoekstra, 2013). However, even if the created ads better fit the customer's interests, personalized ads with this information are likely to provoke perceived intrusiveness (Van Doorn & Hoekstra, 2013). The degree of personalization with this type of information, combined with other advertising creative and media decisions, should be carefully administrated in practice.

Location-Based Information

With the development of mobile communication and positioning technologies, location-based advertising (LBA) has become an important practice for advertisers because information on places that are relevant and interesting to consumers based on proximity is helpful when trying to approach consumers (Limpf & Voorveld, 2015). LBA can be classified into either a push or pull format: pull LBA is initiated by the consumer when they request ads or promotions from marketers close to their geographic locations (Limpf & Voorveld, 2015) while push LBA is initiated by advertisers when they push location-based ads to consumers' devices (Wang, Yang, & Zhang, 2015b). Although these ads are convenient for consumers and make their shopping experiences easier, they may also raise a serious privacy concern if receivers find the ads intrusive (Limpf & Voorveld, 2015; Wang et al., 2015b). Because this information type is closely related to consumers' actual behavior and physical location, commercial messages sent without the consumer's permission might be taken as aggressive and/or as a threat to privacy.

Solutions to Ease Reactance for Digital Advertisers

Building Trust with Consumers

Consumers have become more concerned about digital advertising due to lack of trust with online advertisers. Their fears are caused by internet hackers' and legitimate businesses' uses of detailed consumer profiles (Rapp, Hill, Gaines, & Wilson, 2009). Consumers are less willing to disclose personal information to advertisers without a preexisting relationship with them (Milne, Culnan, & Greene, 2006). This phenomenon can be explained by a mere exposure effect (Zajonc, 1968), a tendency that individuals prefer objects/ideas that they have become familiar with. Thus, advertisers who have made prior connections with consumers may be able to better enhance the acceptance and effectiveness of personalized digital advertising.

To approach new consumers, it is essential to inform them of the ethical conducts in information handling. Lack of explicit privacy policies from advertisers can result in perceived loss of control (Rapp et al., 2009), an antecedent of psychological reactance. To prevent this from happening, advertisers should make maximum effort to avoid hindering consumers from trusting ads, as it is known to influence their perception of the usefulness of marketing efforts (Bleier & Eisenbeiss, 2015).

Providing Sense of Control to Consumers

Another way to ease reactance is to provide consumers with a sense of control over advertising and information flow. According to the idea of psychological ownership, an individual develops a sense of ownership over objects/items because of a strong attachment, and later the sense of right to gain information and have a voice in related decisions. Vulnerability arises if the individual feels a loss of control (Pierce, Kostova, & Dirks, 2001; Aguirre, Mahr, Grewal, Ruyter, & Wetzels, 2015). Thus, digital advertisers should offer options that consumers can take to initiate control over their ad exposure and personal information. Tucker (2014) stated that when consumers feel they have control over their privacy, they tend to click on personalized ads more. The sense of control will assure consumers' psychological ownership and encourage acceptance of digital ads. The balance between advertisers' access to consumer information and consumers' ability to control information and ad flow will play a significant role in enhancing the usability and effectiveness of digital advertising.

Striking a Balance between Effective Personalization in Digital Advertising and Privacy Concerns

This chapter has discussed the process of how negative responses toward digital advertising are formed using the theory of psychological reactance. As digital advertisers begin to develop and find more efficient ways to collect and utilize consumer data, consumers may start to form defense mechanisms or strong tendencies to ignore advertising efforts. This scenario is unfavorable for advertisers who seek utilization of personal information to create relevant ads. Hence, the goal for digital advertisers is to identify the fine line between personalization in advertising and invasion of consumer privacy to create beneficial ads.

To understand the balance between these two issues, scholars have a responsibility to further investigate this subject. Many researchers are already actively pursuing the topic of consumer privacy concerns, and more research will continue to cultivate the path in the digital environment. Possible research areas include, but are not limited to, testing different degrees of advertising personalization on consumer perceptions, attitudes, and behaviors and interaction effects between personalization and different media formats and products. Because digital advertising transgresses national boundaries, it is also worthwhile to conduct research from a global perspective. The world of digital advertising is infinite and offers enormous opportunities, where both practitioners and researchers will hopefully continue to explore more to serve consumers better in the digital age.

References

Aaker, D. A., & Bruzzone, D. E. (1985). Causes of irritation in advertising. *Journal of Marketing, 49*(2), 47–57.

Aguirre, E., Mahr, D., Grewal, D., Ruyter, K. D., & Wetzels, M. (2015). Unraveling the personalization paradox: The effect of information collection and trust-building strategies on online advertisement effectiveness. *Journal of Retailing, 9*(1), 34–49.

Baek, T. H., & Morimoto, M. (2012). Stay away from me: Examining the determinants of consumer avoidance of personalized advertising. *Journal of Advertising, 41*(1), 59–76.

Bauer, R. A., & Greyser, S. A. (1968). *Advertising in America: The consumer view.* Boston, MA: Harvard University Press.

Bleier, A., & Eisenbeiss, M. (2015). The importance of trust for personalized online advertising. *Journal of Retailing, 91*(3), 390–409.

Brehm, J. (1966). *A Theory of psychological reactance.* New York, NY: Academic Press.

Brehm, J. W. (1989). Psychological reactance: Theory and applications. *Advances in Consumer Research, 16*(1), 72–75.

Bright, L. F., & Daugherty, T. (2012). Does customization impact advertising effectiveness? An exploratory study of consumer perceptions of advertising in customized online environments. *Journal of Marketing Communication, 18*(1), 19–37.

Burgoon, M., Alvaro, E., Grandpre, K., & Voulodakis, M. (2002). Revisiting the theory of psychological reactance. In J. P. Dillard & M. Pfau (Eds.), *The persuasion handbook: Developments in theory and practice* (pp. 213–232). Thousand Oaks, CA: Sage.

Chen, Q., & Wells, W. D. (1999). Attitude toward the site. *Journal of Advertising Research, 39*(September/October), 27–37.

Cho, C. H., & Cheon, H. J. (2004). Why do people avoid advertising on the internet? *Journal of Advertising, 33*(4), 89–97.

Clee, M. A., & Wicklund, R. A. (1980). Consumer behavior and psychological reactance. *Journal of Consumer Research, 6*(4), 389–405.

Cortēs, G. L., & Vela, M. R. (2013). The antecedents of consumers' negative attitudes toward SNS advertising: A theoretical framework and empirical study. *Journal of Interactive Advertising, 13*(2), 109–117.

Culnan, M. J. (1995). How did they get my name? An exploratory investigation of consumer attitudes toward secondary information use. *MIS Quarterly, 17*(3), 341–363.

Dunfree, T. W., Smith, N. C., & Ross, W. T. Jr. (1999). Social contracts and marketing ethics. *Journal of Marketing, 63*(July), 14–32.

Edwards, S. M., Li, H., & Lee, J. H. (2002). Forced exposure and psychological reactance: Antecedents and consequences of the perceived intrusiveness of pop-up ads. *Journal of Advertising, 31*(3), 83–95.

Foxman, E. R., & Kilcoyne, P. (1993). Information technology, marketing practice, and consumer privacy: Ethical issues. *Journal of Public Policy & Marketing, 12*(1), 106–119.

Fransen, M. L., Verlegh, P. W. J., Kirmani, A., & Smit, E. G. (2015). A typology of consumer strategies for resisting advertising and a review of mechanism for countering them. *International Journal of Advertising, 34*(1), 6–16.

Gazley, A., Hunt, A., & McLaren, L. (2014). The effects of location-based-services on consumer purchase intention at point of purchase. *European Journal of Marketing, 49*(9), 1686–1708.

Goodrich, K., Schiller, S. Z., & Galletta, D. (2015). Consumer reactions to intrusiveness of online-video advertisements: Do length, innovativeness, and humor help (or hinder) marketing outcomes? *Journal of Advertising Research, 55*(1), 37–50.

Greyser, S. A. (1973). Irritation in advertising. *Journal of Advertising Research*, *13*(1), 3–10.

Ha, L. (1996). Advertising clutter in consumer magazines: Dimensions and effects. *Journal of Advertising Research*, *36*(July/August), 76–83.

Heeter, C., & Greenberg, B. S. (1985). Profiling the zappers. *Journal of Advertising Research*, *25*(2), 15–19.

Hernandez, M. D., Chapa, S., Minor, M. S., Maldonado, C., & Barranzeula, F. (2004). Hispanic attitudes toward advergames: A proposed model of their antecedents. *Journal of Interactive Advertising*, *4*(3), 117–131.

Kaye, K. (2015, November 16). Cross-device tracking creates new level of concerns, FTC says. *Advertising Age*. Retrieved from http://adage.com/article/datadriven-marketing/cross-device-tracking-creates-new-privacy-concerns-ftc/301383/

Kelly, L., Kerr, G., & Drennan, J. (2010). Avoidance of advertising in social networking sites: The teenage perspective. *Journal of Interactive Advertising*, *10*(2), 16–27.

Limpf, N., & Voorveld, H. A. M. (2015). Mobile location-based advertising: How information privacy concerns influence consumers' attitude and acceptance. *Journal of Interactive Advertising*, *15*(2), 111–123.

Madden, M., & Raine, L. (2015, May 20). Americans attitudes about privacy, security and surveillance. *Pew Research Center*. Retrieved from http://www.pewinternet.org/2015/05/20/americans-attitudes-about-privacy-security-and-surveillance/

Milne, G. R., Culnan, M. J., & Greene, H. (2006). A longitudinal assessment of online privacy notice readability. *Journal of Public Policy & Marketing*, *255*(Fall), 238–249.

Milne, G. R., & Rohm, A. J. (2004). Consumers' protection of online privacy and identity. *Journal of Consumer Affairs*, *38*(2), 217–232.

Morimoto, M., & Chang, S. (2009). Psychological factors affecting perceptions of unsolicited commercial e-mail. *Journal of Current Issues and Research in Advertising*, *31*(1), 63–73.

Morimoto, M., & Macias, W. (2009). A conceptual framework for unsolicited commercial e-mail: Perceived intrusiveness and privacy concerns. *Journal of Internet Commerce*, *8*(3–4), 137–160.

Obermiller, C., & Spangenberg, E. R. (1998). Development of a scale to measure consumer skepticism toward advertising. *Journal of Consumer Psychology*, *7*(2), 159–186.

Park, T., & Salvendy, G. (2012). Emotional factors in advertising via mobile phones. *Journal of Interactive Advertising*, *28*(9), 597–612.

Pashkevich, M., Dorai-Raj, S., Kellar, M., & Zigmond, D. (2012). Empowering online advertisements by empowering viewers with the right to choose. *Journal of Advertising Research*, *52*(4), 451–457.

Pember, D. R., & Calvert, C. (2008). *Mass media law*. New York, NY: McGraw-Hill.

Phelps, J., Nowak, G., & Ferrell, E. (2000). Privacy concerns and consumer willingness to provide personal information. *Journal of Public Policy & Marketing*, *19*(1), 27–41.

Pierce, J., Kostova, T., & Dirks, K. (2001). Toward a theory of psychological ownership in organizations. *Academy of Management Review*, *26*(2), 298–310.

Rapp, J., Hill, R. P., Gaines, J., & Wilson, R. M. (2009). Advertising and consumer privacy. *Journal of Advertising*, *38*(4), 51–61.

Ray, M. (1982). *Advertising and communication management*. Englewood Cliffs, NJ: Prentice-Hall.

Sheehan, K. B., & Hoy, M. G. (2000). Dimensions of privacy concern among online consumers. *Journal of Public Policy & Marketing*, *19*(1), 62–73.

Smit, Edith G., Noort, G. V., & Voorveld, H. A. M. (2014). Understanding online behavioural advertising: User knowledge, privacy concerns and online coping behaviour in Europe. *Computers in Human Behavior*, *32*, 15–22.

Speck, P. S., & Elliott, M. T. (1997). Predictors of advertising avoidance in print and broadcast media. *Journal of Advertising, 26*(3), 61–76.

Sterling, G. (2015, July 10). Most users would reject opportunity to pay to avoid mobile ads. *Marketing Land*. Retrieved from http://marketingland.com/most-users-would-reject-opportunity-to-pay-to-avoid-mobile-ads-134777.

Tucker, C. E. (2014). Social networks, personalized advertising, and privacy controls. *Journal of Marketing Research, 51*(5), 546–562.

Van Doorn, J., & Hoekstra, J. C. (2013). Customization of online advertising: The role of intrusiveness. *Marketing Letters, 24*(4), 339–351.

Wang, W., Yang, L., Chen, Y., & Zhang, Q. (2015a). A privacy-aware framework for targeted advertising. *Computer Networks, 79,* 17–59.

Wang, W., Yang, L., & Zhang, W. (2015b). Privacy preservation in location-based advertising: A contract-based approach. *Computer Networks, 93,* 213–224.

Warren, S. D., & Brandeis, L. D. (1890). The right of privacy. *Harvard Law Review, 4*(5), 1–23.

Welch, C. (2015, September 24). Best-selling iOS ad blocker crystal will let companies pay to show you ads. *The Verge*. Retrieved from http://www.theverge.com/2015/9/24/9393941/clear-ios-ad-blocker-offering-paid-whitelist.

White, T. B., Zahay, D. L., Thorbjørnsen, H., & Shavitt, S. (2008). Getting too personal: Reactance to highly personalized email solicitations. *Marketing Letters, 19*(1), 39–50.

Ying, L., Korneliussen, T., & Grønhaug, K. (2009). The effect of ad value, ad placement and ad execution on the perceived intrusiveness of web advertisements. *International Journal of Advertising, 28*(4), 623–638.

Yoo, C. Y., & Kim, K. (2005). Processing of animation in online banner advertising: The role of cognitive and emotional responses. *Journal of Interactive Marketing, 19*(4), 18–34.

Zajonc, R. (1968). Attitudinal effects of mere exposure. *Journal of Personality and Social Psychology Monographs, 9*(2), 1–27.

8

THE ROLE OF REVERSAL THEORY IN DIGITAL ADVERTISING

Jae Min Jung, Kyeong Sam Min, and Drew Martin

Inevitably, companies increasingly use interactive marketing tools to engage customers and remain relevant in the marketplace (Stone & Woodcock, 2013; Rodriguez, Dixon, & Peltier, 2014). As the prevalence of the internet and digital media ushers in an era of unprecedented, two-way communication between companies and consumers, the value of popular websites that provide interactive features has skyrocketed (Jung, Hui, Min, & Martin, 2014). At the heart of interactive marketing is digital advertising. This chapter introduces a relatively under-researched theory called reversal theory (Apter, 2007, 2015) that offers promising utility in understanding consumer behavior (Cummins, Peltier, Schibrowsky, & Nill, 2013) in the era of social media and digital marketing.

While much research demonstrates that interactive advertisements are effective (Kim & Forsythe, 2008; Köhler, Rohm, de Ruyter, & Wetzels, 2011), relatively little attention has been devoted to identifying the conditions under which the interactivity may harm persuasion (Schlosser, 2003; Jung, Min, & Kellaris, 2011; Seyedghorban, Tahernejad, & Matanda, 2016). For instance, Schlosser (2003) found that interactivity is effective for casual internet browsers who do not have specific goals in mind, but that it is ineffective for searchers with specific goals. Jung et al. (2011) further advanced the notion of contingency to game advertising. Specifically, they found that for casual internet browsers, interactivity enhances persuasion regardless of the user's need for cognitive closure. For information searchers, interactivity's persuasive effect is contingent upon the searchers' need for cognitive closure. Under high need for cognitive closure, interactivity tends to harm persuasion for searchers (see Schlosser, 2003); however, under low level of need for cognitive closure, interactivity still facilitates persuasion, even for searchers. Thus, Jung et al. (2011) showed that consumer characteristics, such as the need for cognitive closure, can determine the effectiveness of interactivity. However, these studies assume that consumers remain static and they pursue only one goal.

According to reversal theory, individuals' metamotivational modes fluctuate between telic (i.e., serious-minded) and paratelic (i.e., playful-minded) states due to situation, frustration, and satiation (Apter, 2007). Taking this multi-static, non-rational view of consumers (Holbrook, 1994), Rodgers and Thorson's (2000) Interactive Advertising Model (IAM), as explained in Chapter 1, could encapsulate reversal theory's potential role in explaining consumers' online behaviors insofar as motivational states are concerned, explained below. However, to date, the advertising and marketing literatures are slow in adopting reversal theory. This chapter introduces reversal theory, discusses the theory's relevance to online consumer behavior, reviews the interactive digital advertising literature from the reversal theory perspective, and suggests areas for future research.

A Review of Reversal Theory and Implications for Online Consumer Behavior

What is Reversal Theory?

In the mid-1970s, Drs. K. C. T. Smith and Michael Apter proposed reversal theory to explain the structure of mental life. Reversal theory relates to motivation, emotion, and personality (Apter, 1981, 2007). Apter further developed the theory in the 1980s that has generated sustained interests in various fields of psychology and other disciplines including marketing and advertising (e.g., Davis, 2009). Surprisingly, the theory remains relatively undeveloped by marketing scholars. Apter rejects the notion that people's motivational states remain static (homeostatic) and contends that people's motivational states fluctuate in two opposite states instead. Thus, most individuals display bi-stability such as "serious-mindedness" and "playfulness." Sometimes, people are motivated to achieve goals by minimizing their felt arousal and engaging in a goal-directed way, which often involves planning for the future. Other times, behaviors are directed by pleasurable feelings at the present state. Basically, everyone experiences the same universal set of states differently not only from each other, but also from within a person at different moments. These universal common experiences are metamotivational states operationalized as four pairs of opposites: 1) telic and paratelic (means-end dimension), 2) conformist and negativistic (rules dimension), 3) mastery and sympathy (transaction dimension), and 4) autic and alloic (relationship dimension) (Apter, 2015). Each pair of states has basic psychological value and a different range of emotions. The outcome is seeing the world from a particular perspective. Among them, the telic and paratelic states are the most widely researched (Apter, 2013) and arguably the most relevant for understanding consumer behavior in the digital world.

An Overview of Telic and Paratelic States

Telic and paratelic metamotivational states display interesting contrasting features. Telic states (from Greek, *telos* meaning a "goal") refer to a serious-minded state in which individuals prefer a low level of arousals and seriously engage in a purposeful way to achieve a goal. They also plan carefully and rationally, and do not pay attention to emotions. In contrast, paratelic states (*para* from Greek, meaning "alongside") refer to a playful state. Individuals in a paratelic state engage in an activity seeking immediate enjoyment, spontaneously. They prefer a high level of arousal and seek to maintain this level as long as possible. Thus, telic and paratelic states are polar opposite metamotivational states representing a means–ends domain (Apter, 1981).

Whereas the telic state focuses on important future goals and planning ahead, the paratelic state focuses only on the present. As a result, a telic state seeks achievement and progress, and a paratelic state prefers fun and immediate gratification. Further, telic and paratelic states have a range of emotions associated with the arousal level (see Figure 8.1).

Figure 8.1 shows that telic emotions vary from relaxation to anxiety as the arousal level individuals feel changes from low to high. Heightened arousal induced by a demanding task causes individuals in a telic state to become anxious, but they

Reversal Theory

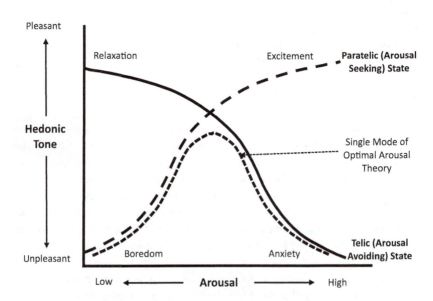

FIGURE 8.1 The Relationship Between Arousal and Hedonic Tone According to the Reversal Theory. The solid line and dashed line presents bi-stable metamotivational state, a telic state and a paratelic state, respectively, according to the reversal theory. The dotted line is the inverted U-shape that represents the single mode of optimal arousal theory.

Adapted from *Reversal theory: The dynamics of motivation, emotion, and personality* by M. J. Apter, 2007, p. 19.

become pleasantly relaxed once the task is completed. In contrast, paratelic emotions vary from boredom to excitement as the arousal level changes from low to high. When individuals in a paratelic state are highly involved and psychologically aroused with an activity, they will be pleasantly excited. When the activity lacks enough stimulation, the person in a paratelic state becomes bored. As a result, individuals experiencing the same level of arousal may have completely opposite emotions depending on the person's metamotivational state. For example, the same high arousal level can be a source of anxiety or excitement, depending on the person's bi-stable state or mode interpreting the motivational experience. This condition provides a unique perspective for reversal theory, which differs from optimal arousal theory (Hebb, 1955), which posits an inverted u-shaped curve with a medium level of arousal showing greater pleasantness than either low or high arousal levels (Apter, 2007).

Reversal theory employs a bi-stability concept; both high and low arousal levels are viewed as two opposite points that are optimal at a given time, and either arousal level can be effective under certain situations (Apter, 2007). Lastly, telic-paratelic states provide a different experiential structure. The paratelic state creates a "protective frame" (not in a telic state) that helps individuals feel immune from the consequences of failure. This feature helps explain why some people engage in dangerous sports such as parachuting and rock-climbing (Apter & Batler, 1997). While this behavior initially creates anxiety, overcoming the danger creates a protective frame and induces switching of the person's mental state from telic to paratelic mode. The outcome is excitement as intense as the initial anxiety.

Causes of Reversals in Telic-Paratelic States

According to Apter (2007), psychological conditions including 1) contingency, 2) frustration, and 3) satiation may cause reversals in metamotivational states.

Contingency

Contingent conditions refer to situations that give rise to reversals. Specifically, faced with a threat or duty, individuals normally switch to a telic state, if not already in this mode. Removing a threat or absence of duty leads to a paratelic state (Apter, 2007). In addition to this obvious situational condition, other enduring conditions induce the metamotivational mode. For example, different locations can prompt contingent reversals (Kerr & Tacon, 1999; Tacon & Kerr, 1999). A university library and a lecture hall were shown to foster a telic state, whereas a university sports center and a student union building triggered a paratelic state. Students in a lecture hall, who were in a telic mode, were switched to paratelic mode when they were given a surprise break in the middle of a lecture (Kerr & Tacon, 2000). Prior studies of competitive sports demonstrate reversals by recording the activities and interviewing the players (Cox & Kerr, 1990; Males, 1999;

Bellew & Thatcher, 2002). Manipulations of metamotivational state in laboratory experiments also reveal reversals. When participants were presented with a financial reward, a telic state was induced, but when they were presented with comedy films, a paratelic state was induced (Svebak & Apter, 1987).

Reversals likely occur due to contingency in the digital world too. Filling out an online purchase order form presumably would create a telic state, as the consumer feels relaxed or anxious. Once the form is completed, the same person switches to a paratelic state feeling either bored or excited. In addition to random events, online or offline retail or service establishments can produce rather enduring conditions that evoke either telic or paratelic modes.

Frustration

Frustration is the second condition for reversal to occur. When individuals become frustrated, they switch from a paratelic to a telic mode (Apter, 2007). For instance, a person who simply wants to have fun playing a game online may become increasingly frustrated if unable to improve a personal best score. If the person fails to achieve a higher score, the player becomes increasingly frustrated as the game continues. At a certain point, improving the score outweighs the fun of just playing the game. The game's excitement gives way to the anxiety of not achieving the goal. Frustration results in a reversal from arousal-seeking to arousal-avoidance and a concomitant reversal from paratelic to telic states.

Further, frustration can motivate individuals to switch from telic to paratelic modes. Suppose Bob wants to buy an air purifier to use at home for his family. As Bob searches for product information online, he discovers many brands and technologies with prices varying from less than $100 to over $1,000. Each manufacturer has a website complete with videos and testimonials claiming superior product technology. Information overload leads to simply too many evaluative criteria. "What should I look for? What would be the right size? Which technology is better for me? Is there any unknown harmful effect of the technology?" Yet, he has a limited time to make an informed decision. Bob becomes frustrated and gives up searching. He thinks to himself, "Let me just try a product that is priced at below median price with an acceptable star rating at a popular ecommerce site. How bad could it be? Having any purifier would be better than not having anything at all." Bob suddenly finds himself thinking about goal achievement for the family's welfare. At the start of information search, Bob was in a serious mode, but his telic mode is now switched to a playful, paratelic mode as he visualizes goal achievement. The unachievable goal of buying the best air purifier loses centrality and is replaced by immediate gratification and excitement of anticipating positive responses from his family.

An empirical study demonstrates both types of reversals due to frustration (Barr, McDermott, & Evans, 1993). The stimulus was a kind of jigsaw puzzle in which there were over 300,000 ways of combining the pieces incorrectly and only one way of combining the pieces correctly. The participants' metamotivational states were measured using telic/paratelic state scales before and after they attempted to assemble the puzzle. Surprisingly, six out of 30 participants (50 percent female) successfully solved the difficult puzzle. None of these puzzle masters showed reversals in their metamotivational state probably due to the absence of frustration. Most participants (79.2%) who experienced frustration, however, experienced reversals. Whereas 41.7 percent reversed from a paratelic to a telic state, 37.5 percent reversed from a telic to a paratelic state. Further, the researchers confirm that participants' arousal seeking tendency changed accordingly reflecting their telic/paratelic state before and after the puzzle task.

Satiation

A third reason for reversal could be metamotivational satiation—an internal dynamic that leads naturally to reversal unless something else happens. According to the theory, satiation is a kind of underlying rhythm that moves forward and backward between telic and paratelic states (Apter, 2007). People make a gratuitous switch from one state to another for no apparent reason other than being "fed up" with current trivial daily activities such as gardening, interior decoration, and browsing on social media sites (Apter, 2007). Many consumers spend a significant portion of their time on computers almost every day, reading newspapers, searching for information on products, visiting blogs about topics of personal interest from cooking to politics, and checking their news feeds on social media. During the course of these mundane activities, satiation can kick in, and consumers may experience reversals in their metamotivational states. Lafreniere, Cowles, and Apter (1988) confirm that indeed such satiation can explain reversals. Students from statistics classes were recruited to participate in a study of personality and attitudes to computers. Participants were asked to spend for two hours on a computer. All participants were given a set of teaching programs on statistics and a varied set of video games. Results showed that 80.6 percent of participants changed either from a statistics program to video games or vice versa, suggesting reversals in metamotivational states. Subsequent questionnaires and interviews revealed that participants offered no reason for wanting to change the materials.

State Dominance and Individual Difference

Walters, Apter, and Svebak (1982) found that some participants' preferences for arousal seeking or avoidance remain unchanged considerably longer than others, typically toward one of two polar ends. This behavior does not imply, however, that those traits are stable because metamotivational states did reverse in all participants despite the differences in duration that the one mode lasted (Apter, 2007). This form is so-called state dominance. Individuals can be telic dominant or paratelic dominant. However, this condition does not mean that those individuals never experience the opposite state. State dominance differs from many personality traits such as extraversion or introversion.

Murgatroyd, Rushton, Apter, and Ray (1978) developed the Telic Dominance Scale (TDS). Their scale used 42 items to operationalize state dominance of individuals in terms of telic dominance. Scale instructions asked participants to choose one of the two courses of action, telic- versus paratelic-related actions, based on which one they would most usually prefer or most closely apply to them. The telic dominance scale consisted of three subscales, namely *serious-mindedness* (14 items), *planning-orientation* (14 items), and *arousal-avoidance* (14 items). Although these three dimensions likely correlate, they represent three distinctive phenomena. In addition, Cook and Gerkovich (1993) developed the Paratelic Dominance Scale that consists of 30 items. These items primarily employed temporal components (e.g., "I often take risks," "I usually take life seriously").

Svebak and Murgatroyd (1985) compared extremely telic-dominant individuals with extremely paratelic-dominant individuals in in-depth interviews. Paratelic-dominant individuals tend to be engaged in a greater variety of activities, act more flexible and spontaneous, and appear less well-organized than telic-dominant individuals. In contrast, telic-dominant individuals tended to execute their planned activities more carefully, spend more time carefully monitoring their activities and performance, and showed concerns about achieving their longer-term goals. When describing their account of activities, the two groups were also quite different. Telic-dominant individuals were detailed and described events in a more systematic way, whereas paratelic-dominant individuals described events more generally. In addition, the two groups differed in their language use. Telic-dominant people tended to use descriptive language, whereas the paratelic-dominant group tended to use evaluative language (Apter, 2007).

State Balance, State Dominance, and Change

According to reversal theory, personality is about patterns over a period of time rather than fixed traits. Thus, individuals are flexible and change in their metamotivational states. A consumer might spend more time in a paratelic state than in a telic state over the weekend. This same person might spend more time in a telic state than in a paratelic state on a weekday. Thus, the balance of time spent on one state rather than the other can change. This weekday versus weekend partitioning is referred to as a "state balance" and the state balance changes over time (Apter & Larsen, 1993). State balance differs from state dominance. State balance refers to the actual time spent in one state rather than the other. State dominance refers to the individual's innate bias or tendency to be in one state than the other. State balance and dominance tend to associate strongly; however, they do not necessarily move in the same direction all the time (Apter, 2007). Girodo (1985) reports generally paratelic-dominant individuals changed to telic-dominance after undergoing dramatically serious and potentially traumatic training (e.g. undercover police training). Further, some evidence suggests consumers' state dominance changes toward telic dominance over the span of their lives. Prior studies find strong, positive correlations between age and telic dominance; the older consumers are, the more they exhibit telic dominance (Murgatroyd, 1985; Tacon & Abner, 1993).

Summary

In sum, the telic state is goal-oriented, serious-minded, and arousal-avoiding, whereas the paratelic state is spontaneous, playful, and arousal-seeking (Apter, 1981). Reversal theory is primarily concerned about how consumers interpret experiences (e.g., arousal) rather than the specific content (Apter, 1981). A lot of complex and inconsistent behaviors of consumers that traditional psychological theory fails to account for can be explained by acknowledging the fact that consumers reverse between those psychological states depending on the particular motive they felt at a particular time (Apter & Batler, 1997). Researchers have adopted reversal theory to explain individuals' complex and inconsistent behaviors in various contexts such as stress-moderating effects (Martin, Kuiper, Olinger, & Dobbin, 1987), design (Fokkinga & Desmet, 2014; Gielen & van Leeuwen, 2014), sports (Sit & Lindner, 2006), behavioral counseling (Blaydon, Lindner, & Kerr, 2004), management (Carter, 2005), and digital advertising (Rodgers & Thorson, 2000; Davis, 2009; Jung et al., 2014; Seyedghorban et al., 2016).

The Role of Reversal Theory in Digital Advertising

Interactivity in Digital Advertising and Reversal Theory

Online advertising or communication between firms and consumers can be characterized as interactive (Yadav & Varadarajan, 2005). A computer-mediated environment allows consumers to control online media and communicate back to the sender of the message any time of the day. With digital technology advancing, new and innovative interactive technologies extend the capability of computer-mediated communication to a whole new level. The literature on online advertising shows several researchers investigating how online interactivity affects persuasion (Schlosser, 2003; Jung et al., 2011). These studies manipulate goal types (e.g., information vs. entertainment) and observe effectiveness of the interactivity in the ads from a rather homeostatic, traditional consumer behavior perspective. Traditional models such as the integrative attitude formation model (MacInnis & Jaworski, 1989) may be adequate in a static environment. However, some evidence suggests that internet users are different from traditional consumers. Internet consumers tend to be more active searching for information (Hoffman, Novak & Schlosser, 2000; Rosenkrans, 2009). Consumers appear to be multi-static and non-rational (Holbrook, 1994), especially when using technology (Mick & Fournier, 1998). Rodgers and Thorson (2000) integrate the psychological reversals into the consumer-controlled aspect "internet user mode" as part of their Interactive Advertising Model (IAM).

According to the IAM, internet users' motives (e.g., research vs. entertainment) interact with the likely user mode, which in turn transpires information processing (i.e., attention, memory, and attitude). The user's motives also interact directly with information processing because motives encourage that the user puts effort into carrying out any online activity. Based on motives such as researching, shopping, entertaining, communicating, or socializing, online users differentially attend to, comprehend, and form attitudes about interactive advertisements (Rodgers & Thorson, 2000). Further, an internet user's motives closely relate to user mode (e.g., serious vs. playful). An internet user searching for product information arguably is serious-minded. In contrast, a user seeking entertainment is playful. Because the user's motive changes more frequently while using the internet than traditional media, an online user's mode likely changes frequently as well. Hence, the IAM incorporates reversal theory and classifies an internet user mode as "telic" (high goal-oriented, seriousness, and present-oriented) and "paratelic" (low goal-oriented, playfulness, and future-oriented) along the goal-directedness continuum. Further, building on multi-stability (Apter, 1981; Mick & Fournier, 1998), Davis (2009) tests reversal theory and finds coexistence of two reversal states, such as telic and paratelic states, when consumers encounter multimedia messaging services.

Online Consumers' Mode and Advertising Interactivity

Despite its presumed importance (Rodgers & Thorson, 2000), few studies investigate the relationship between online consumer mode and advertising interactivity. Li and Bukovac (1999) found that larger banner ads invited a higher click-through rate from playful versus serious mode online users. The IAM suggests that paratelic users may respond more positively to interactive online advertising, whereas telic users may respond more negatively to interactive online advertising because interactive features interfere with telic users' goal pursuit process.

Drawing on reversal theory and the IAM, Jung et al. (2014) conducted a field experiment to examine how online consumers' user mode influences their evaluation of advertisements that vary in its interactivity. They used a 2 (advertising interactivity: high vs. low) x 2 (user mode: telic vs. paratelic) between-subjects design. Advertising interactivity was manipulated with a banner ad embedded on a cell phone section of a fictitious online retailer. Under the high interactivity condition, each banner component came to life as the banner expanded to a larger size and each component appeared one at a time when participants moved the mouse over the banner. Under the low interactivity condition, the banner remained static without any interactive components activated. The user mode was measured using an adapted version of the Telic/Paratelic Statement Instrument (T/PSI) (O'Connell & Calhoun, 2001). Jung et al. (2014) modified this seven-item, serious-mindedness/playfulness subscale of the T/PSI into a 10-item, 7-point semantic differential scale: five items for serious-mindedness and five items for playfulness. Before responding to the scale, participants read the instructions, "Please click on the number that best indicates how you were feeling in the last few minutes, just before you started this survey." Since the telic and paratelic states should be mutually exclusive (Apter, 2007) and dichotomization determines the two states (O'Connell & Calhoun, 2001), the authors dichotomized the sample on each dimension based on the neural point of four, and determined telic users (those who score high on serious-mindedness and low on playfulness) and para-telic users (those who score high on playfulness and low on serious-mindedness).

In addition, Jung et al. (2014) measured perceived advertising interactiv-ity using a four-item modified scale from McMillan and Hwang (2002). They also measured arousal-seeking tendency using 19 items adopted from Xie and Lee (2008). Some of the arousal-seeking tendency scale items were: "I prefer an unpredictable life full of change to a more routine one," "I sometimes like to do things that are a little frightening," and "I like to experience novelty and change in my daily routine."

Results of Jung et al. (2014) showed that an interactive effect exists between user mode and advertising interactivity such that telic state online viewers formed a more favorable attitude toward the low interactivity ad, whereas paratelic state online viewers formed a more favorable attitude toward the high interactivity ad. Further, the study finds that when exposed to the low (high) interactive ad, the telic (paratelic) state online viewers formed a more positive ad attitude than the paratelic (telic) state online viewers. Consistent with a mediation hypoth-esis, the study confirms that the impact of user mode (telic vs. paratelic) on ad attitude is mediated through an arousal seeking tendency. When exposed to a low interactivity ad, paratelic state consumers, compared with telic consumers, formed a less favorable attitude toward the ad because paratelic state consumers had a greater level of arousal seeking tendency, which made them evaluate the ad with low interactivity less favorably. When exposed to a high interactivity ad, however, paratelic state consumers, compared with telic state consumers, formed a more favorable attitude toward the ad because paratelic state consumers had a greater level of arousal seeking tendency, which prompted them to evaluate the ad with high interactivity more favorably.

Conclusion

This chapter argues that reversal theory provides a valuable framework relevant to online consumer behavior in general, and digital advertising in particular. While reversal theory is a well-established psychological theory, historical background, causes, state dominance, and state balance demonstrate applications to consumer behavior. Reviewing the interactive advertising literature from a reversal theory perspective, the results of the present chapter were to show how only a paucity of research using reversal theory has been applied to digital advertising (e.g., Li & Bukovac, 1999; Rodgers & Thorson, 2000; Davis, 2009; Jung et al., 2014). Jung et al.'s (2014) research is one of the first empirical studies rooted on the reversal theory in marketing and contributes to the literature by incorporating the meta-motivational state's role in the context of an interactive ad. This research demonstrates that the users' metamotivational state and arousal seeking tendency affect persuasiveness of digital advertising that varies in interactivity.

Results also have significant implications for practitioners. Since online consumers' metamotivational state changes from telic to paratelic or vice versa during the course of their digital experience, and the user mode at the time of their exposure to an ad influences the persuasiveness of an interactive ad, digital advertising professionals should include both high and low interactivity advertisements available (Jung et al., 2014). Advancements in digital technology potentially help to identify the metamotivational state of online consumers. Enlightened digital advertisers can show either high or low interactive advertising that match online consumers' modes to maximize ad effectiveness.

Despite reversal theory's relevance and the importance to digital advertising, adoption of this approach remains limited. Since Rodgers and Thorson (2000) incorporate telic versus paratelic user modes as an important part of the IAM, surprisingly few known researchers employ reversal theory in exploring the effectiveness of digital advertising. As the relationship between digital advertising and firm success continues to grow, researchers need to pay more attention to the value of reversal theory as a plausible explanation for changeable bi-stability of human behavior. This chapter only examines one dimension, telic-paratelic dimension, but three more dimensions (conformity-negativity, autocentric-allocentric, mastery-sympathy) remain unexplored in this context. An essential first step is developing scales to measure these constructs. Further, more experiments are needed to show different types of metamotivational states that affect different types of advertisements beyond interactivity.

References

Apter, M. J. (1981). The possibility of a structural phenomenology: The case of reversal theory. *Journal of Phenomenological Psychology, 12*, 173–187.

Apter, M. J. (2007). *Reversal theory: The dynamics of motivation, emotion, and personality* (2nd ed.). Oxford, England: Oneworld.

Apter, M. J. (2013). Developing reversal theory: Some suggestions for future research. *Journal of Motivation, Emotion, and Personality, 1*(1), 1–8.

Apter, M. J. (2015). Exploring the concept of focus in reversal theory. *Journal of Motivation, Emotion, and Personality, 4*(4), 1–8.

Apter, M. J., & Batler, R. (1997). Gratuitous risk: A study of parachuting. In S. Svebak & M. J. Apter (Eds.), *Stress and health: A reversal theory perspective* (pp. 119–129). Washington, DC: Taylor & Francis.

Apter, M. J., & Larsen, R. (1993). Sixty consecutive days: Telic and paratelic states in everyday life. In J. H. Kerr, S. Murgatroyd, & M. J. Apter (Eds.), *Advances in reversal theory* (pp. 107–122). Amsterdam, The Netherlands: Swets & Zeitlinger.

Barr, S. A., McDermott, M. R., & Evans, P. (1993). Predicting persistence: A study of telic and paratelic frustration. In J. H. Kerr, S. Murgatroyd, & M. J. Apter (Eds.), *Advances in reversal theory* (pp. 123–136). Amsterdam, The Netherlands: Swets & Zeitlinger.

Bellew, M., & Thatcher, J. (2002). Metamotivational state reversals in competitive sport. *Social Behavior and Personality, 30*(6), 613–624.

Blaydon, M. J., Lindner, K. J., & Kerr, J. H. (2004). Metamotivational characteristics of exercise dependence and eating disorders in highly active amateur sport participants. *Personality and Individual Differences, 36*, 1419–1432.

Carter, S. (2005). Reversal theory: Changing you and your organization for the better. *Training Journal, 2*, 20–22.

Cook, M. R., & Gerkovich, M. M. (1993). The development of a paratelic dominance scale. In J. H. Kerr, S. Murgatroyd, & M. J. Apter (Eds.), *Advances in reversal theory* (pp. 177–188). Amsterdam, The Netherlands: Swets & Zeitlinger.

Cox, T., & Kerr, J. H. (1990). Self-reported mood in competitive squash. *Personality and Individual Differences, 11*, 199–203.

Cummins, S., Peltier, J. W., Schibrowsky, J. A., & Nill, A. (2013). Consumer behavior in the online context. *Journal of Research in Interactive Marketing, 8*(3), 169–202.

Davis, R. (2009). Do consumers experience a reversal state when encountering mobile commerce services? In *Proceedings from ANZMAC '09: Australian and New Zealand Marketing Academy Annual Conference*. Melbourne: Australia and New Zealand.

Fokkinga, S., & Desmet, P. (2014). Reversal theory from a design perspective. *Journal of Motivation, Emotion, and Personality, 2*(2), 12–26.

Gielen, M. A., & van Leeuwen, L. (2014). Found in translation: Bringing reversal theory to design for play. *Journal of Motivation, Emotion, and Personality, 2*(2), 27–40.

Girodo, M. (1985, May). *Telic and paratelic modes in operational undercover and field narcotics agents*. Paper presented at the Second International Conference on Reversal Theory, York University, Toronto.

Hebb, D. O. (1955). Drives and the C.N.S. (Conceptual nervous system). *Psychological Review, 62*, 243–254.

Hoffman, D. L., Novak, T. P., & Schlosser, A. E. (2000). *Consumer control in online environments*. Nashville, TN: Owen Graduate School of Management, Vanderbilt University.

Holbrook, M. B. (1994). The nature of customer value. In T. R. Roland & L. O. Richard (Eds.), *Service quality: New directions in theory and practice* (pp. 21–71). Thousand Oaks, CA: Sage Publications.

Jung, J. M., Hui, H. C., Min, K. S., & Martin, D. (2014). Does telic/paratelic user mode matter on the effectiveness of interactive Internet advertising? A reversal theory perspective. *Journal of Business Research, 67*, 1303–1309.

Jung, J. M., Min, K. S., & Kellaris, J. J. (2011). The games people play: How the entertainment value of online ads helps or harms persuasion. *Psychology & Marketing, 28*(7), 661–681.

Kerr, J. H., & Tacon, P. (1999). Psychological responses to different types of locations and activities. *Journal of Environmental Psychology, 19*, 287–294.

Kerr, J. H., & Tacon, P. (2000). Environmental events and induction of metamotivational reversals. *Perceptual and Motor Skills, 91*, 337–338.

Kim, J., & Forsythe, S. (2008). Adoption of virtual try-on technology for online apparel shopping. *Journal of Interactive Marketing, 22*(2), 45–59.

Köhler, C. F., Rohm, A. J., de Ruyter, K., & Wetzels, M. (2011). Return on interactivity: The impact of online agents on newcomer adjustment. *Journal of Marketing, 75*(2), 93–108.

Lafreniere, K. D., Cowles, M. P., & Apter, M. J. (1988). The reversal phenomenon: Reflections on a laboratory study. In M. J. Apter, J. H. Kerr, & M. P. Cowles (Eds.), *Progress in reversal theory* (pp. 247–254). Amsterdam, The Netherlands: Elsevier Science.

Li, H., & Bukovac, J. L. (1999). Cognitive impact of banner ad characteristics: An experimental study. *Journalism and Mass Communication Quarterly, 76*(2), 341–353.

MacInnis, D. J., & Jaworski, B. J. (1989). Information processing from advertisements: Toward an integrative framework. *Journal of Marketing, 53*(4), 1–23.

Males, J. R. (1999). Individual experience in slalom canoeing. In J. H. Kerr (Ed.), *Experiencing sport: Reversal theory* (pp. 189–208). Chichester, England: Wiley Publications.

Martin, R. A., Kuiper, N. A., Olinger, L. J., & Dobbin, J. (1987). Is stress always bad? Telic versus paratelic dominance as a stress-moderating variable. *Journal of Personality and Social Psychology, 53*(5), 970–982.

McMillan, S. J., & Hwang, J. (2002). Measures of perceived interactivity: An exploration of the role of direction of communication, user control, and time in shaping perceptions of interactivity. *Journal of Advertising, 31*(3), 29–42.

Mick, D. G., & Fournier, S. (1998). Paradoxes of technology: Consumer cognizance, emotions, and coping strategies. *Journal of Consumer Research, 25*(2), 123–143.

Murgatroyd, S. (1985). The nature of telic dominance. In M. J. Apter, D. Fontana, & S. Murgatroyd (Eds.), *Reversal theory: Applications and developments* (pp. 20–41). Cardiff: University College Cardiff Press.

Murgatroyd, S., Rushton, C., Apter, M. J., & Ray, C. (1978). The development of the telic dominance scale. *Journal of Personality Assessment, 42*(5), 519–528.

O'Connell, K. A., & Calhoun, J. E. (2001). The telic/paratelic state instrument (T/PSI): Validating a reversal theory measure. *Personality and Individual Differences, 30*, 193–204.

Rodgers, S., & Thorson, E. (2000). The interactive advertising model: How users perceive and process online adv. *Journal of Interactive Advertising, 1*(1), 42–61.

Rodriguez, M., Dixon, A. L., & Peltier, J. W. (2014). A review of the interactive marketing literature in the context of personal selling and sales management. *Journal of Research in Interactive Marketing, 8*(4), 294–308.

Rosenkrans, G. (2009). The creativeness and effectiveness of online interactive rich media advertising. *Journal of Interactive Advertising, 9*(2), 18–31.

Schlosser, A. E. (2003). Experiencing products in the virtual world: The role of goal and imagery in influencing attitudes versus purchase intentions. *Journal of Consumer Research, 30*, 184–198.

Seyedghorban, Z., Tahernejad, H., & Matanda, M. J. (2016). Reinquiry into advertising avoidance on the Internet: A conceptual replication and extension. *Journal of Advertising, 45*(1), 120–129.

Sit, C., & Lindner, K. J. (2006). Situational state balances and participation motivation in youth sport: A reversal theory perspective. *British Journal of Educational Psychology, 76*(2), 369–384.

Stone, M. D., & Woodcock, N. D. (2013). Interactive, direct and digital marketing: A future that depends on better use of business intelligence. *Journal of Research in Interactive Marketing, 8*(1), 4–17.

Svebak, S., & Apter, M. J. (1987). Laughter: An empirical test of some reversal theory hypotheses. *Scandinavian Journal of Psychology, 28*, 189–198.

Svebak, S., & Murgatroyd, S. (1985). Metamotivational dominance: A multimethod validation of reversal theory constructs. *Journal of Personality and Social Psychology, 48*(1), 107–116.

Tacon, P., & Abner, B. (1993). Normative and other data for the telic dominance and negativism dominance scales. In J. H. Kerr, S. Murgatroyd, & M. J. Apter (Eds.), *Advances in reversal theory* (pp. 165–176). Amsterdam, The Netherlands: Swets & Zeitlinger.

Tacon, P., & Kerr, J. H. (1999). Metamotivational states in sport locations and activities. In J. H. Kerr (Ed.), *Experiencing sport: Reversal theory* (pp. 175–187). Chichester, England: Wiley Publications.

Walters, J., Apter, M. J., & Svebak, S. (1982). Colour preference, arousal and the theory of psychological reversals. *Motivation and Emotion, 6,* 193–215.

Xie, G. X., & Lee, M. J. (2008). Anticipated violence, arousal, and enjoyment of movies: Viewers' reactions to violent previews based on arousal-seeking tendency. *The Journal of Social Psychology, 148*(3), 277–292.

Yadav, M. S., & Varadarajan, R. (2005). Interactivity in the electronic marketplace: An exposition of the concept and implication for research. *Journal of the Academy of Marketing Science, 33*(4), 585–603.

9

ADVERTISING (IN)ATTENTION IN THE DIGITAL ENVIRONMENT

Brittany R. L. Duff and Yuliya Lutchyn

Introduction

New technologies and media are making access, interaction, and creation of media content increasingly under audience control. Similarly, advertising is trying to integrate into new formats with video pre-roll ads, native advertising, fan communities and consumer reviews, photo filters, emoji creation, apps, etc. As noted in Chapter 2, these ads and ad formats are intended to enable consumers to become active participants—curators, creators, and disseminators—of advertising messages in the same way that they are with other media content. However, messages may not be perceived the same way when they initially come from advertisers. Greater involvement can lead to greater feelings of ownership, control, and satisfaction, but could also lead to pushback on advertising.

Consumers increasingly expect control of their media experience and along with that comes control over the advertising experience. At the most basic level, this means having control over one's own exposure and attention to advertising. Before higher levels of message engagement can occur, exposure and awareness of the advertiser must occur. Thus, the role of attention in media effects, particularly in terms of brand messages, is more important than ever. In fact, at the 2016 Cannes Lions advertising festival, generally a celebration of advertising, there was a focus beyond the award-winning ads. According to *The Wall Street Journal*, "One of the biggest topics at Cannes this week has been how to win consumers' attention amid a swiftly changing technology landscape and backlash against a perceived overload of advertising" (Perlberg, 2016, n.p.).

So why might an old topic—attention to advertising—turn into such an important topic in the advertising industry? In the past, media content was more clearly a product to be consumed. Companies created content, and to help pay for the cost of creating and distributing this content, advertising was placed in it. Thus, there was an understanding of an exchange between audience and media companies that, in order to have free or subsidized content, the audience would give their attention, or at least the possibility of attention, to ads. Ad placement costs are based largely on the size of an audience, with terms such as CPM (cost per thousand) and reach being used, or discussions about how many people will be exposed to an ad in a particular buy. However, increased audience control over media content and experiences means that this *exchange* has become less clear. Consumers might be asking themselves the following questions: If I am an active participant in creating content then why should I also subsidize my access to that content with my attention? Whereas attention may have operated like a discount on media content in the past, if I help to create that content, why should I also be paying with my attention to ads?

As people have more ways to access media on their own time and in varied formats (different screens, devices), they are finding new ways to exert control over content. In social media and many online venues, people are the active creators of the content, and little content is actually created beyond what the audience is creating. Thus, the role of creator and consumer of content is blurred. As illustrated in Figure 2.2 of Chapter 2, technology is also making it possible to alter or change even content that is created in a more traditional manner for consumption. For example, if you do not want to see the name "Trump" in news articles online, you can install a browser extension that will change "Trump" to "Drumpf" each time that it appears, thus automatically changing media content to fit personal preferences (Romano, 2016, n.p.).

Along with the new ways of interacting with media content generally has come a broader range of ways to engage with advertising. Traditionally, this trend is interpreted in terms of increased user abilities and greater engagement with advertising. However, increased control and interaction also mean that consumers are now better able to control how they *do not* interact with ads. Of course, consumers' desire to control exposure and attention to ads is not new. People have flipped past magazine ads or turned the channel during a TV commercial for decades. However, the use and the ease of consumers' ad control tactics have increased dramatically. With participation, content creation, and manipulation increasingly becoming a part of the media experience, it is more critical than ever to understand the role of control over ad exposure and attention to advertising. Researchers need to understand the changes to media, look at what is truly new, and use theory to conduct research and predict outcomes for advertising.

In this chapter, we will discuss advertising exposure and attention in the new digital environment, particularly media multitasking and advertising avoidance. What we currently know, as well as critical questions that remain unanswered, will be discussed. Additionally, the potential for disruptive new technologies could again throw into question how we think of audience and attention to ads.

Attention

Attention forms the base of how advertising "works" and is often seen as occurring before any other effects of advertising can happen. The influential advertising hierarchy of effects model has been used in various forms for over 100 years (see Barry, 1987). Hierarchy of effects models generally follow a series of "steps" that begin with attention/awareness of the advertisement. Once one has been exposed to an ad and is aware of it, then they are able to form an interest or attitude toward the subject of the ad message. This interest/attitude then forms the basis for action toward the product. While this model has been debated, it forms the basis of how we think of more modern models of customer journeys to action or sales funnels, which specify a series of steps after awareness that eventually lead to taking an action toward the product. There are a number of critiques of specifying advertising effects as occurring in a linear manner or across all types of products (e.g., Ehrenberg, 1974), and newer critiques in light of media flexibility and consumer control (John, 2016). However, this debate about the process of advertising effects is largely about what occurs *after* ad exposure/awareness/attention. Because exposure and attention are widely acknowledged as being crucial base steps for any message effects that follow (Slater, 2004), a better understanding of those serve as a base for effects in a digital environment—where control, access, and interaction with media are rapidly changing—which is key to understanding how ads might (not) work.

It is important to begin by looking at what attention is, to understand what it might mean in new media contexts. In 1890, William James defined attention as "the taking possession of the mind, in clear and vivid form, of one out of what may seem several simultaneously possible objects or trains of thought" (p. 403). In the time since this definition, not much has changed. Currently, the American Psychological Association's term glossary defines attention as "a state of focused awareness on a subset of the available perceptual information" (Attention, 2016, n.p.). While there are some minor differences in these definitions, attention can be seen as a cognitive processing response that is selective (a focus on some things to the exclusion of others). For example, think about all that is going on around you right now. You may be focused on reading this chapter but there are many, many other perceptual inputs competing for your attention. If you are sitting comfortably, you might not be thinking about how it feels to be in contact with the chair, but you can focus on it now. There are also many things you can see in your visual field and probably many sounds competing for attention. Turning your focus to any one of them can move it to the forefront and push other things (like this chapter) to the background. Thus, attention helps us more systematically process our world by limiting the amount of information we are processing at any given time.

In terms of the perceptual information that we may attend to, we can look at both bottom-up and top-down attention. Top-down attention is goal-directed, "internally driven" attention (Johnston & Dark, 1986, p. 44). Essentially, top–down attention imposes your goals like a filter on how the perceptual environment is perceived by you. If you are searching for an app on your phone screen that has a blue and white logo, you also might seem to notice those apps that look similar (blue and white logo). Because you are selecting items that match your goal item, you may not even notice other apps that look different (e.g., brown and white logos). For an excellent video illustration of top–down selective attention, please see Dan Simons' (n.d.) video, "The Monkey Business Illusion."

Bottom–up, or "data-driven" (Johnston & Dark, 1986, p. 44) attention is happening at some level at all times; all of those perceptual inputs that you *are not* focusing on while reading this chapter are still monitored at a low level. However, for media research, it is most important to think about bottom–up attention when something in the perceptual environment attracts or "grabs" your attention. Bottom–up processing can occur when you are browsing without a direct goal (looking for interesting images), or it can also occur when something in the environment attracts attention (e.g., a flashing ad). When something unusual, different, or relevant to you (like your name) gains attention, this is an example of operating in a more bottom–up manner, which comes from the perceptual environment and is up to you for processing.

Attention can be categorized as selective, divided, switching, or sustained. Selective attention is when a person focuses on one input while filtering out others; divided attention involves focusing on more than one input at the same time; attention switching involves multiple inputs but with a focus on only one input at a time while switching focus between inputs; and sustained attention, which involves simply monitoring an input for a sustained length of time (McDowd & Birren, 1990). At its most basic level, it is useful to think of attention to media as being either selective or divided/switching. For example, you might be in a lecture taking notes on your computer when a chat window pops up with a message from a friend. You might be trying to concentrate exclusively on the class content and, thus, ignore the chat window, or you might try to type a response to your friend while also watching the lecture. In the first case, you have a goal of concentrating only on the lecture and thus you will *selectively* attend only to that goal and try to ignore everything else, including the chat. However, if you have goals of both concentrating on the lecture and also chatting with your friend, you will be *dividing* attentional focus between the two. There is some debate on the role of switching versus dividing attention, whether we are really able to divide focus or if we switch very rapidly in a way that makes it seem as if we are focusing on more than one thing. For media research, the distinction is more important in terms of whether there is a physical switching, such as if you must look at a tablet screen and also a television screen while they are in different locations.

As we have discussed, attention to advertising is seen as an important basic response. However, the digital media environment has created many shifts that have placed particular importance on how audience members are avoiding ads and also how they might be exposed to them in more competitive media environments than previously thought.

Media Multitasking and Advertising

Avoidance in the digital domain has, thus far, largely evolved in terms of the mechanical means that people have for eliminating advertising. However, shifts in media technology and access have also changed the way that people behave and interact with media and content. One such change that has presented a challenge for advertisers is the rise of media multitasking. Changes in audience measurement and shifts in how ads might be perceived and received under varied levels of attention are now being explored by practitioners and researchers alike.

The Growth of Multitasking

Media multitasking is growing quickly as a behavior. Simultaneous media use now adds six hours to the average mediated day; a 30-hour "extended" day would be needed to sequentially try and fit in all of the media content being consumed (Ipsos MediaCT & IAB, 2012). In 2015, adults spent 27 percent more time on their computers and mobile devices than they had two years previously (Nielsen, 2012). Deloitte (2015) found that 90 percent of people now multitask while watching TV, and people ages 14 to 48 were doing an average of three additional activities during that multitasking. A survey of 12,000 people in 30 countries showed that we now spend an average of 109 minutes each day simultaneously watching TV and another digital screen (Millward Brown, 2014). Additionally, with content fluidity, more people may complete multiple tasks within a single media device but with additional screens (e.g., multiple computer monitors; Richtel, 2012) or multiple windows open in a single screen that are dedicated to different media tasks.

The rising prevalence of media multitasking has resulted in anxiety by advertisers about the accuracy of reach and effectiveness metrics, as well as questions about what it might mean for advertising now that it is often exposed in a competitive media environment. According to Google, 81 percent of internet users multitask to avoid ads (Heussner, 2012). Media measurement companies are now trying to measure multiscreen media use in order to better understand how it affects advertising (GfK MRI, 2012; Nielsen, 2012). Ipsos MediaCT and the IAB (2012) have said that to guide ad content and format recommendations, understanding multitasking mind-sets and motives will be crucial; similar calls for increased research have been issued by media scholars (e.g., Roberts & Foehr, 2008).

To date, most studies on how consumers experience media content and ads have primarily looked at exposure to one medium/message, in isolation or as part of a sequential media experience. However, this is no longer how many message exposures are actually experienced.

Defining Media Multitasking

Increased portability of devices and ease of accessing content on demand are making it easier to multitask with media and content. Because this area of research is relatively new and is growing at a rapid pace, it is necessary to think about how to conceptually define media multitasking to provide a solid foundation for future research to draw upon. Past definitions of media multitasking have included distinctions between media and/or devices as a criteria for engaging in the behavior of media multitasking. These definitions include Consuming two or more media simultaneously (Roberts & Foehr, 2008; Ophir, Nass, & Wagner, 2009), or using a medium while engaging in a non-mediated task (e.g., watching TV while cleaning; Jeong & Fishbein, 2007). Others have defined it in terms of number of devices and the properties of devices such as "multiscreening," or the simultaneous use of multiple screens (Segijn, Voorveld, & Smit, 2016). While these definitions have been useful to help begin research on media multitasking, they all define media multitasking with an emphasis on the medium, content, or device (the media) rather than on the process (the multitasking). A definition based on the process that occurs during media multitasking could help bridge existing and future advertising research, even as media change.

Media used to be largely delivered in distinct formats and disseminated through separate channels so that the medium was the delivery system. Media multitasking can now just as easily occur within a medium as between media. If a person has a computer with multiple windows open (e.g., TV show and social media) they might not be considered to be media multitasking based on past definitions because they are only using one computer and one screen. For example, in the Media Multitasking Index (Ophir, Nass, & Wagner, 2009), the amount of media multitasking that a person engages in is determined by how often they use 12 different media forms (e.g., print-based media) at the same time as other media (e.g., television). Because media devices are becoming more flexible in terms of content access, people may be multitasking with different mediated content within a device or between devices. The perceptions of media format might then change based on the perceptions of the people answering the multitasking question: would they consider reading an e-book to be print media? Thus, the concept of "media multitasking" may now actually be "mediated multitasking."

Media and interactions with media are changing quickly, particularly in regard to content fluidity, so a person-centered definition may be more useful and more able to evolve as media change. Sanbonmatsu, Strayer, Medeiros-Ward, and Watson (2013) defined multitasking as concurrent performance of at least two tasks with each task having its own unique goal (see also Duff & Sar, 2015). Past definitions of media multitasking depend on distinctions between devices and media that may be blurred by changes in media. For this reason, we will define multitasking as simultaneously engaging in more than one task (at least one of which is mediated) that each have separate goals. Note that with this definition, a person should be involved in more than one task, but this definition does not specify that there needs to be more than one medium or device used. Also note that the *task* is defined by the goals of the person. Thus, one could have a task of being entertained or alleviating boredom. Using this definition in the context of media lets us as researchers focus on the process and motives of the person doing the media multitasking while leaving it open to fit new ways of multitasking with media. This could also allow people to be multitasking within or between devices. In a fluid media environment, conceptualizing this definition can help us to better specify similarities and differences in media multitasking studies and findings.

It is important to think about how a broader, process-focused definition of media multitasking means that there is also a need to be specific about the media, content, people, and processes being studied. For example, different content utilizes different modalities. A study on the medium of television used to be able to assume audio/visual elements based on the device capabilities and design of television content. However, with device flexibility, we should now look at the elements of the mediated content or interaction. You could use your smartphone to access social media, play a video game, text friends, look up directions, read a book, etc. You could even do more than one of these things at the same time on that same device. Therefore, content and the use of the content is somewhat divorced from thinking of the mode of access.

A study in which a person is reading a blog while also listening to the radio would utilize separate modalities (hearing vs. seeing), and there is evidence that there may be separate pools of processing resources for different modalities (Navon & Miller, 1987). Therefore, the results of that study may point to a far different conclusion about how multitasking affects ads placed on that blog than a study about reading a blog while also watching a video. Additionally, the motivation and goals of the person matter. What are the simultaneous goals that they hold for their tasks? Are they trying to find a specific news story (top-down) or perhaps they are just browsing around to see if anything interesting is happening (bottom-up). Are they using media to do some work, to find information, or to be entertained? The various aspects of the person, their goals, and the content will need to be identified in order for work in media multitasking to provide meaningful predictions.

Media Multitasking and Advertising Effects

Despite the increasing importance of media multitasking there have been few advertising studies in the context of multitasking and divided attention (see Kazakova & Cauberghe, 2013). Researchers have begun to identify some of the potential advertising effects under conditions of media multitasking, mostly using predictions based on the limited capacity framework (Lang, 2000). Additionally, we are beginning to explore media multitaskers as an audience, looking at traits and preferences that might predict heavy media multitasking. However, there are still a very limited number of studies that have been conducted in an advertising context and, as you will see, there are conflicting findings even among the few studies that exist. After reviewing the existing literature, we will discuss reasons why some results might seem to conflict and also identify a few of the many avenues for media multitasking research that remain unexamined.

Limited Capacity

Because limited capacity processing is the dominant framework used in research on the effect of multitasking on advertising, it is useful to understand the basis of limited capacity as it applies to multitasking. Divided attention has been the most widely used construct to explain performance in simultaneous task research (Craik, Govoni, Naveh-Benjamin, & Anderson, 1996; Konig, Buhner, & Murling, 2005). It is thought that mental resources are shared by tasks competing for attention and action (Kahneman, 1973), and thus multiple tasks may interfere with one another (Pashler, 1994; Monsell, 2003). Divided attention usually leads to a decrease in the performance on at least one task because less attention is likely to be allocated to each task due to people's limited resource capacity (Lang, 2000). These interference effects are thought to be most pronounced when the tasks utilize the same sensory resources, such as two visual tasks (Navon & Miller, 1987).

Lang's (2000) limited capacity model of mediated message (LC4MP) is the most widely used processing model in advertising studies of media multitasking. This model posits that there are three sub-processes in the processing and storing of information: encoding, storage, and retrieval processing (Lang, 2000). Because there are limited resources available at each stage, a distraction from your target could require some of those limited processing resources, and thus, take them away from processing the target at any stage. This would then result in a failure to encode, store, or retrieve that information.

For example: You are looking at a map on your phone for the street you need to turn at and just as you spot the street name ("Sa ... "), you hear a loud crash and look up. Because you were interrupted before you could fully read it, you were not able to successfully encode it. If you look at the street name and as you are repeating it to yourself (rehearsing it in working memory; "Sawyer Avenue, Sawyer, Sawyer"), and you suddenly hear a loud crash, you might turn your attention to the crash instead of trying to remember the street name. So while you initially encoded the street name, you forgot it before it could enter long-term memory, and therefore, failed at storing it. Or perhaps you see the name, repeat it to yourself, successfully remember the street, and get to your destination. An hour later your friend messages you and asks what street they need to turn on to meet you. You remember that it started with an "S" but not much more. Thus, while you encoded it and stored it, you did not process it sufficiently to immediately retrieve it from long-term memory.

Each sub-process is thought to be indexed by a specific memory measure. If you were able to recognize the street name when asked if "Sawyer Avenue" was the street that you need to turn at, you encoded it successfully. If you were given a hint or cued recall to remember it (e.g., "It started with an 'S'") and successfully named it, we would know that you had stored the name in working memory. If you were asked simply to recall the name of the street and replied that it was "Sawyer," you would have successfully retrieved it. Because the process is thought to be hierarchical, knowing at what stage the process was disrupted and whether the information was easily accessible can be ascertained. For example, if I asked you to recall the name of the street and you could not remember, I would know that you were not able to retrieve it, but that does not mean that there is not some level of memory for the name. If I follow up by reminding you that it started with an "S" and you then remember that the street was "Sawyer," we would know that you encoded and stored the name, so you did process it enough to have some memory of it; however, it is not highly accessible in your memory so it is difficult to retrieve on command.

Memory

Using a limited capacity cognitive framework, it is not surprising that many of the studies that have been conducted on media multitasking have looked at how multitasking might affect memory for ads. Because multitasking involves more inputs to be processed (compared to single-tasking) it would seem to be a straightforward prediction that media multitasking would lead to decreased memory for ads, particularly if the ad is exposed during the multitasking (during encoding).

Studies that have used memory for the ads have generally found what was expected: decreased explicit memory compared to single-task performance. Findings from multitasking research indicate that when secondary tasks are cognitively demanding, individuals' explicit memory for ad messages generally decreases (Naveh-Benjamin, Craik, Parretta, & Tonev, 2000; Shapiro & Krishnan, 2001; Zhang, Jeong, & Fishbein, 2010). This is assumed to be due to the competition for limited cognitive resources.

Others have also found that adding tasks can decrease explicit memory. Duff and Sar (2015) found a main effect of decreased recognition memory for groups multitasking with either one, two, or three windows open to different tasks on a large computer screen. Voorveld (2011) showed banner ad recall and recognition was lower for a group that listened to the radio while browsing the web page compared to a group that just browsed the web page. Likewise, Segijn, Voorveld, and Smit (2016) found that ad recognition memory decreased with simultaneous use of a tablet and TV compared to single tasking. In addition to the lab studies, Angell, Gorton, Sauer, Bottomley, and White (2016) used a survey the day after a televised soccer match to look at recognition and recall for billboard ads that appeared in the game. They found that for people who were doing multitasking with tasks unrelated to the game or that had low social interaction and accountability (e.g., looking at a website) showed impaired recall and recognition of the ads.

While these results present a general pattern of decreased performance on memory tests for ads exposed while multitasking, it might be that there is still an effect of the ad during multitasking, but it is not shown through explicit memory tests. Implicit memory is memory without conscious awareness that can be evidenced by changing task performance (Schacter, 1987) or affective response (Zajonc, 2001). It is thought to be free from some of the limits of explicit memory in that it does not need to be stored and retrieved in the same way. The exposure might simply prime or activate an association that is shown through behavior but even without any ability to remember the exposure (Shapiro & Krishnan, 2001).

Shapiro and Krishnan (2001) asked participants either to pay attention to both an audio message and print advertisements at the same time (divided attention) or to just pay attention to the print message while ignoring the audio message (selective attention). While both conditions had multiple media exposed simultaneously, only one group had goals of attending to both, making them the multitasking group. Explicit memory, measured by the number of correctly identified brands, was lower for the multitasking group compared with the single task group. Implicit memory, measured by asking participants to select from several brands as if they were making a purchase in a store, did not differ between the multi- and single-task groups. However, Segijn, Voorveld, and Smit (2016) also looked at implicit memory, measured by having people try to identify as quickly as possible degraded images of the brand name, and found that it decreased with simultaneous screen tasks compared to a single task.

Affect, Evaluation, and Attitude

Using the same framework of limited cognitive processing resources, several studies have looked at affective or evaluative outcomes for the ad or brand. While memory was expected to be impaired due to increased use of processing resources, it has generally been predicted that people would have a more positive reaction to ads exposed during multitasking. This has been thought to be due to a lack of resources available that would normally be used to generate counterarguments against the persuasive message.

Chowdhury, Finn, and Olsen (2007) looked at people's ability to either support or counter argue with the message in an ad. In their study, people watched a TV program and, for one group, ads played during a commercial break (sequential presentation) while for the other group, the ads played at the same time as the program via a split screen (simultaneous presentation). Participants made the same number of support statements or counterarguments when the arguments in the ads were weak. However, for strong argument ads, participants made fewer support statements in the simultaneous presentation group compared to the sequential group.

Other researchers have also found that media multitasking leads to less counter arguing (Petty, Wells, & Brock, 1976) and also more positive attitude toward the persuasive message seen during multitasking compared to single-tasking (Jeong & Hwang, 2012, 2015). While these studies found fewer counterarguments and higher attitude toward the ad, Segijn, Voorveld, and Smit (2016) found a relationship between the two and showed that the decrease in counter arguing serves as a mediator of the effects of multitasking on increased ad attitude and purchase intent.

Other studies have also looked at the effects of information overload on processing of product messages. These studies used a non-mediated cognitive load manipulation to change processing (high cognitive load participants rehearse something in working memory, such as remembering an 8-digit number while doing the task) but their similar theoretical background, utilizing limited capacity, helps to connect these studies with the media multitasking studies. Amongst the findings are that high cognitive load (dual task) participants respond more positively to intrusive brand placements in a movie whereas low cognitive load participants find the placements too obvious and distracting (Yoon, Choi, & Song, 2011). Others have found that high cognitive load leads to lowered ability to imagine product use (Shiv & Huber, 2000) and decreases the effectiveness of ads that engage multiple senses due to lessened ability to think about the sensory message in the ad (Elder & Krishna, 2010).

Individual Differences and Audience Level Factors

The increasing use of data in advertising means that targeting will be used more than ever. While demographic data was generally used in the past, individual interests, motivations, and personality are now more easily used to define an audience. Most advertising research on media multitasking has focused on the performance aspects of multitasking; however, there are some important implications for understanding media multitaskers as an audience. Media multitasking is growing at a fast pace, but why do people multitask? Why do some people prefer multitasking while some find it aversive or overwhelming? In advertising, understanding your audience is important in decisions of placement, format, and content, and, as noted previously, industry has identified the need to explore and understand multitaskers' "mindset and motivation" (Ipsos MediaCT & IAB, 2012, n.p.). Additionally, it is important for us to understand both the predictors of this behavior as well as potential downstream effects. In particular, people who tend to engage in more frequent media multitasking may also have identifiable traits that help to understand them as people in a media context as well as show how they may respond and attend to tasks differently than people who are less likely to multitask. Beyond implications for ads, it is important for multitasking researchers to know potential differences that could affect their research outcomes.

Age and Gender

One of the more studied predictors of multitasking is age. Many studies on media multitasking are carried out on college students, but studies looking at groups beyond college students consistently find that age predicts media multitasking propensity (Carrier, Cheever, Rosen, Benitez, & Chang, 2009; Duff, Yoon, Wang, & Anghelcev, 2014). This makes sense at an intuitive level; generations differ in the media environment that they grew up in and therefore what seems natural or standard in terms of media use is different. However, it is also possible that another cause is cognitive elements of aging that affect ability to multitask. Older adults may have increased disruption in working memory due to multitasking and may have lowered flexibility in attention allocation (Prakash et al., 2009). It could also be a combination, where the current media environment is actually altering the ability of young people to split their attention (Yap & Lim, 2013). If the difference is due to the media environment that one grows up in, we would expect there to be fewer age-related differences when people who grew up with a flexible media environment are themselves older. On the other hand, if it is due to cognitive changes that occur to everyone as they age, we would expect to continue to see differences by age, even as people who grew up with media multitasking become older. It is clear that this is an important area and one that deserves further exploration. It also points to the need to do media multitasking research on groups outside of college students.

The majority of studies on media multitasking have failed to find differences in preferences or performance based on gender (Ophir, Nass, & Wagner, 2009; Zhong, Hardin, & Sun, 2011; Sanbonmatsu, Strayer, Medeiros-Ward, & Watson, 2013). One study did find a difference in 14 to 16 year olds, where females self-reported more media multitasking than did males (Jeong & Fishbein, 2007). In a survey comparing a national sample and a college student sample, it was found that gender predicted multitasking in the national sample but not in the college sample (Duff et al., 2014). Some unpublished data from our lab suggests that this gender difference might exist when asked to say how often one multitasks with various media (e.g., "Never-Always") but disappears when the measure assesses how many hours each week one multitasks with those same media. However, it is unclear why gender differences only appear on on one of the self-report measures. Thus, more work is needed in this area.

Traits and Preferences

Most work on traits that predict media multitasking has been done with college students. These studies have found several predictive traits, such as technology innovativeness and use of SNS (Zhong et al., 2011), neuroticism (Poposki, Oswald, & Chen, 2009; Wang & Tchernev, 2012), and attentional impulsiveness (Sanbonmatsu et al., 2013). Duff et al. (2014) found that creativity, personal control, and need for simplicity were also predictors of media multitasking in college students. However, of those three, only creativity was a predictor of multitasking in a national sample. Even in the subset of the national sample that was matched for age to the college sample (18–29), personal control and need for simplicity were not predictors. This means that we might need to be careful about generalizing results from college students to the larger population.

The trait most consistently found to correlate with high levels of media multitasking is sensation seeking. Sensation seeking is "the need for varied, novel, and complex sensations and experiences" (Zuckerman, 1979, p. 10). It has been found to be a significant predictor of media multitasking in college students (Strayer & Watson, 2012; Sanbonmatsu et al., 2013; Duff et al., 2014), 14 to 16 year olds (Jeong & Fishbein, 2007), and a U.S. national sample (Duff et al., 2014). It is interesting that sensation seeking is a consistent predictor even outside of college-age students because sensation seeking tends to generally decline with age (Roth, Hammelstein, & Brähler, 2007). It has been found that the sensation value of message content should match with the need for sensation in the audience (Donohew, Lorch, & Palmgreen, 2006) thus sensation seeking could be an important area for future work in advertising.

Only one study that we are aware of has looked at advertising-specific behaviors with media multitaskers. Duff et al. (2014) found that higher media multitasking was a predictor of belief in advertising utility. Both a college student sample and a national sample showed a significant correlation between multitasking propensity and the belief that advertising could be useful. Because this is a correlation, it is not possible to know if this is due to increased exposure to media and advertising or if it is due to a separate factor that underlies both. We will discuss this finding later but it is clear that more work needs to be done connecting advertising and message-specific variables to media multitasking.

Task Performance

In addition to work identifying traits that may contribute to, or be outcomes of, media multitasking, there is research identifying whether there are behavioral and performance differences in heavy media multitaskers (HMM) versus light media multitaskers (LMM), particularly in terms of attention. This work can be thought of in terms of limited capacity in that it generally takes the perspective that media multitasking will overwhelm or overload users and thus deplete learning or performance.

Educational performance is one area that has been studied in connection with multitasking. In an observational study of middle, high school, and college students during a 15-minute session of studying, those who were more likely to move off-task from their homework were also more likely to have stated a preference for task switching (Rosen, Carrier, & Cheever, 2013). Another study found that multitasking with social technologies during class time was negatively related to GPA (Junco, 2012).

In terms of performance ability, perhaps the most influential study on media multitaskers showed that heavy media multitaskers (HMM) actually perform worse on focusing and attention-switching tasks compared to light media multitaskers (LMM), though the authors note that HMM should have more practice with switching attention (Ophir et al., 2009). Slower, less efficient task switching and less ability to focus on a target while ignoring distractors may be a result of HMMs' inability to filter out task-irrelevant information and involuntary attentional breadth (Lin, 2009; Ophir et al., 2009). Other research has also shown HMMs perform worse on tasks that involve focusing and blocking out distractions, suggesting lowered executive control (Sanbonmatsu et al., 2013). Other research has shown potential interventions such as mindfulness training that can help HMM increase their short-term ability to focus on a single task (Gorman & Green, 2016).

Unanswered Questions and Future Research

While limited capacity is clearly a useful framework for multitasking research, this is not the only way to think about it. The interactions between people and media are complex, and there are multiple facets that need to be understood. An overreliance on limited capacity as the guiding force behind media multitasking research is concerning in that it creates a narrative that may lead to accepting the findings from those studies as *the* way that multitasking affects persuasive messages. However, using other perspectives and frames could lead to future research using different manipulations, or different outcome variables and considering other factors in media and people and provide a more full picture of multitasking causes and effects.

A few studies have used additional variables or perspectives outside of limited capacity and have found outcomes that would not necessarily be predicted using a one-size-fits-all version of limited capacity. Angell et al. (2016) conducted a survey to look at memory for soccer sponsor ads during multitasking. They found the typically expected lowered ad memory for people who multitasked during the game, except in one group who multitasked with media that were relevant to the game and had high social accountability (e.g., tweeting about the game). For this group, memory for the ads exposed during the game was actually improved. The authors note that it might be because the content of both tasks was congruent so it reinforced, rather than detracted from, memory formation.

Other factors may also change ad memory while multitasking. People who tend to be analytic processers tend to focus on the features of specific items and divorce them from context. Holistic processers tend to focus more on context and the relationship between objects and their field (Masuda, Gonzalez, Kwan, &

Nisbett, 2008). In terms of perceptual processing, holistic processors tend to distribute visual attention more broadly (McKone et al., 2010) whereas analytic processors show more concentrated eye movements on focal items (Masuda & Nisbett, 2001). Analytic and holistic processing is a trait in that people have a tendency to process more one way or another. This difference is largely studied in terms of differences between cultures, but processing can also change temporarily with context. For example, people in a positive mood tend to process more holistically, while people in a negative mood process more analytically (Gasper, 2004).

In a study using multiple windows with separate tasks, it was shown that while analytic processors performed as would be expected, showing a decrease in ad memory when adding tasks, holistic processors showed no decrease in memory when adding tasks. A follow-up study found that people in a positive mood who were processing the screen more holistically showed no drop off in ad memory whether they had one, two, or three tasks on screen (Duff & Sar, 2015). In this case, the difference was found when multitasking was thought of as a perceptual process and not just a cognitive process. Processing style is just one factor that may change how people respond in a multitasking situation; there are likely many more that will affect how people process ads while multitasking. Differences in the type of ad message, the goals of the person in why they are engaging with media, the properties of the media, and myriad other unexplored areas are in need of research.

Similar to memory outcomes, a focus on limited capacity may not reveal factors in improved liking for ads exposed during multitasking. The current work shows a strong pattern of increased evaluation of ads, with the explanation that overloaded capacity keeps people from being able to generate counterarguments against a message. However, this would also seem to imply that the ads themselves are highly persuasive and people simply accept things that they do not generate conscious counterarguments against. Yet there are likely many other reasons as well. The only study to look specifically at the connection between the lack of counterarguments and increased evaluation (Segijn, Voorveld, & Smit, 2016) noted that the model only explained 11.5 percent of the variance. Just a few other studies have looked at alternative explanations.

Voorveld (2011) found more positive attitude toward ads exposed in more than one medium simultaneously (radio and web display ad) with the rationale that they prime one another, and similar messages in different formats could contribute to complexity. Chinchanchokchai, Duff, and Sar (2015) looked at multitasking as increasing overall task enjoyment. Multitaskers focused less on the passage of time and felt that time was passing more quickly than did people who did a single task. This feeling of time passing quickly led to greater task enjoyment and more positive attitude toward the ads exposed to during the task. We are exposed to thousands of brand messages each day and likely do not form counterarguments against most of them, so what else might be happening during multitasking that could lead to improved liking of ads?

Limited Capacity

The application of limited capacity to media multitasking can be problematic when there is an assumption of multiple task demand, i.e., that any two tasks would be worse than performing any single task. This ignores the reality of media in which any given experience or content varies widely on how perceptually complex it is, what senses are engaged, how much interaction there is, if it is active or passive to use, motivation to use, etc. Additionally, it can be tempting to think of the resource pool as starting with a baseline of all resources free and ready to devote to a task and that adding task demand creates a linear shift up to a depleted pool with no resources left to devote to tasks. Media content varies widely in terms of cognitive demand as well as perceptual demand. Motivation and ability will interact with this demand from the media being used. For example, if you are a chemist and see an academic article on your area of chemistry, you would eagerly dive in. If another person with no interest and/or knowledge in chemistry had to read the same thing, it would feel like a chore. In these two cases, the same amount of resources are not likely to be utilized, and it is also likely that one may more eagerly embrace a secondary task.

While it is common to see the term "overload" in the context of media multitasking, it is interesting to think about drivers of media use to begin with. In fact, it is likely that "underload" is a more apt driver of much media use, including media multitasking. In one psychology study, people had to listen to a long phone message about who would be attending an upcoming event (Andrade, 2009). One group simply listened to the message and did nothing else while the other group was told that they should copy shapes while listening. Even though the listening-only group had more spare resources, they had worse memory for the names from the message. In this case, adding a small additional task actually helped people keep their focus on the uninteresting primary task (Andrade, 2009).

One study on motivations for task switching while doing homework showed that boredom was one of the most common reasons given (Rosen et al., 2013). This is important because it highlights that we cannot assume that any single task is a baseline of optimal load and anything above it is overload. In fact, people may be using media in a very active and intentional way, multitasking in order to reach optimal processing or engagement when the first task is not interesting or engaging enough. Adding tasks in this context may mean that the additional tasks are actually improving the situation from underload to optimal load.

Optimal stimulation levels (e.g., Mehrabian & Russell, 1974) could speak to the idea of both low and high load being experienced as aversive. One study found that people would rather administer electric shocks to themselves rather than be alone in an empty room with nothing else to do (Wilson et al., 2014). Multitasking is one way to increase stimulation, and as noted earlier, higher need for sensation or stimulation is correlated with heavier media multitasking (Sanbonmatsu et al., 2013; Duff et al., 2014), indicating that they may be self-correcting the lack of stimulation from single tasks.

When doing a dull or unengaging primary task, people may also turn inward to mind-wandering or task-unrelated thought. Mind wandering is "a shift in the focus of attention away from the here and now toward one's private thoughts and feelings" (Smallwood, O'Connor, Sudberry, & Obonsawin, 2007, p. 818). Mind wandering can actually use a large amount of cognitive resources when it occurs (Smallwood et al., 2007). There is some evidence that memory for an unengaging ad is improved by adding a second task, thus decreasing the mind wandering that occurred while sitting through the uninteresting ads. This is particularly true when those secondary tasks were perceptual rather than cognitive (Chinchana-chokchai, 2013).

Breadth vs. Depth

The other area that will be useful to rethink for multitasking research is the idea of desired outcomes. Media multitasking often means that there are fewer resources available for a task and that attention may be diffused rather than focused. Much of the current work in the field looks at what resources that might take away from a specific primary task; however, it is also possible that there are positives to that distributed attention, that instead of just one thing losing, that other things could gain.

Heavy media multitaskers (HMM) tend to be slower and less efficient at task switching, (Ophir et al., 2009) and this may be due to their inability to filter out irrelevant or distracting information (Sanbonmatsu et al., 2013). This means that HMM are worse at focusing on a single task because they have a hard time ignoring non-task information (distracters). However, while this implies that they might be worse at "depth" tasks, their "breadth" sampling of information may be a more democratic information processing in that any information could potentially be of use rather than selectively processing only certain goal items (Lin, 2009). This can hurt performance on goal-directed tasks of focus, but it might be useful in other ways. In one study, people were told to complete a task and not to focus on an "irrelevant" sound which actually helped to predict when the target would appear (Lui & Wong, 2012). This sound was used better by the HMM, giving them better performance than LMM; however, when the sound was not present, HMM performed worse on the task than LMM (Lui & Wong, 2012).

For advertising, this could mean that ads, which are not the focus of most people, could be better used by HMM. Indeed, perceptions of the usefulness of advertising in general are higher for HMM than LMM (Duff et al., 2014). Additonally, sampling broadly (versus deeply) could have other benefits. For example, high creative achievement has been shown to negatively correlate with ability to screen out irrelevant stimuli (Carson, Peterson, & Higgins, 2003). This has been similarly shown with creative mentality being a predictor of heavy media multitasking (Duff et al., 2014). The role of creativity, content, and multitasking could be an interesting area for advertising researchers to explore in the future. There are likely other benefits, drawbacks, and overall implications for media in considering breadth versus depth approaches to media interactions.

Technology and Advertising Avoidance: The "Adpocalypse"

People are finding new ways to do old things. One growing response to advertising is to avoid it through ad blocking (Sloane, 2015). While one could previously limit exposure to advertising by fast forwarding past the ads in a recorded TV show or quickly turning the page of a magazine, there was usually some minimal level of exposure to the ad, and it took effort to reduce ad exposure each time ads were presented. Now selective exposure to advertising can be accomplished through more automatic and complete means such as using ad-blocking software or by paying premium prices for ad-free content. Use of these methods to avoid ads means that the ads are never even presented to the audience, and avoidance is complete so there is no exposure. As the use of these methods grows, anxiety on the part of advertisers has grown as well.

Whether using an automated or mechanical way to limit exposure or how much attention is given to an ad, this response to advertising is termed "advertising avoidance" and has been defined as all the actions that media users employ to reduce exposure to ad content (Speck & Elliott, 1997, pp. 61–62). In addition to more mechanical means of limiting exposure to ads, such as using ad-blocking software or hitting the Skip button a few seconds into a video pre-roll ad, people can also selectively attend to and ignore ads to which they are exposed. When exposure is completely avoided (such as when the ad is blocked), an ad cannot have any effect. When exposure exists but avoidance occurs by selective attention, there is the potential for effects, but there is debate about whether those effects may be positive or negative for ads.

When Apple announced that their iOS would support ad-blocking apps, the ad world exploded with concern. Headlines read, "Confusion reigns as Apple puts the spotlight on mobile ad blocking" (Morrison, 2015) and "Advertisers sweat as ad blockers proliferate" (Gillies, 2015). In the U.S. it has been estimated that more than 25 percent of internet users have downloaded ad-blocking software (Sloane, 2015), and additional ad-blocking capabilities for mobile browsing could further facilitate adoption of ad blocking. Some websites, such as *The Washington Post*, have responded to this by blocking content for those users who were using ad blockers (Zeitlin, 2015). The Interactive Advertising Bureau (IAB) has considered multiple options, including suing ad-blocking companies. Others have suggested that consumers see ads as a distraction and that education about how the revenue from ads is used to support the individuals who create the content or run the site could be a way to stem the tide of ad blocking (Peterson & Fishman, 2015). In fact, the most popular ad-blocking app, Peace, was pulled from the iTunes store after the developer said that he realized how it might hurt the revenue of smaller online content creators who depend on ad dollars (Hern, 2016). The ad industry has suggested that more meaningful content, more creativity, and relevance will help stem the problem (Perlberg, 2016).

Ignoring Ads

Seeing an ad is usually not the primary reason to access content. Rather, there are other reasons to use media: to watch a show, read a blog, post an update for friends, etc. So an ad that is not directly part of the content could be seen as distracting the audience from the purpose for using that media. Limiting exposure or attention to ads could help limit that distraction and free up the audience for their intended purpose of the media use, engaging with the primary content. Speck and Elliott (1997) found that search hindrance is a significant predictor of ad avoidance in all media. A similar variable, perceived goal impediment, was also found to explain ad avoidance on the internet (Cho & Cheon, 2004). Edwards, Li, and Lee (2002) also found that perceived intrusiveness leads viewers to avoid ads. However, most of this research relied only on a consumer's retrospective self-reports of why they think that they avoid ads. While this is useful for us to begin understanding the reasons why people might avoid ads, if they are not always aware of the ads that they are ignoring, there might be effects that are not connected to the conscious choice to ignore ads. Instead, it might be that people simply ignore the ads without processing them because they are not what they want to see.

While completely eliminating exposure to an ad would lead to no effects of the ad, exposure to the ad while concentrating on other content should lead to some outcome for the exposed advertisement. Most studies looking at ads that appear without being a part of the main content looked at the ads as being incidental or passive exposures. The idea being that they were not actively being processed or attended to, but they may gain some effect simply by being present and processed at a very low level. Ads are sold based on exposure, and the current main concerns for digital ads are ad-blocking and viewability, both of which are related to basic exposure of the ad (Peterson & Fishman, 2015). Ads that are exposed but not fully processed have been thought to potentially lead to positive outcomes through the mere exposure effect or perceptual fluency.

Passive Exposure or Active Avoidance?

So what happens when an ad appears, but the person is trying to do something that does not involve that ad? For example, if they are playing a game on their phone and a banner appears at the bottom of the screen, do they notice the ad and process it? Do they simply not notice it, or do they actively fight paying attention to it, knowing that it could cause them to lose focus on the game? The literature would suggest that the positive or negative outcome could depend on the response, even at a pre-conscious level.

The first response, consciously noticing the ad (in our example, noticing the banner at the bottom of the videogame screen) has been the most commonly studied response. This assumes attention has been directed toward the ad and the person is consciously processing the ad. Because we are more interested in exploring inattention, we will not go into detail of these responses. However, research using the persuasion knowledge model (PKM) might suggest that the person would register the ad as being put there to persuade them, and they may then have a negative or positive attitude toward the ad based on their judgment of the ad's appropriateness, etc. (see Ham, Nelson, & Das, 2015 for an overview of measuring persuasion knowledge). Others have used reactance theory to look at whether ads that are unable to be avoided (e.g. pop-ups) cause a feeling of lack of control and backlash against the ad/brand (e.g. Edwards, Li, & Lee, 2002). However, there is evidence that people do not look directly at most display ads and are often not consciously aware of the ads that appeared.

The mere exposure effect (MEE) and perceptual fluency are used to explain why we might expect effects for ads that are exposed but not attended to by the audience. MEE suggests that simply by being exposed, a stimulus becomes more familiar and this increased familiarity increases feelings of approach that is attached to the object at a pre-conscious level (Zajonc, 2001). Similarly, perceptual fluency predicts positive exposure effects but through an increased ease in processing the exposed item. This increased ease in processing the next time the object is encountered is interpreted as "liking." In fact, positive effects have been found for ads incidentally exposed in magazines, product placements, and online (Janiszewski, 1990; Shapiro, MacInnis, & Heckler, 1997; Matthes, Schemer, & Wirth, 2007).

However, another line of work, distractor devaluation and inhibition, suggests opposite effects. Objects that are ignored are rated as less liked than objects that were attended to or never seen before (Raymond, Fenske, & Tavassoli, 2003). This is thought to be due to the inhibition of items that are not part of the goal; thus, an ad that appeared on a web page might not be liked, it might actually be disliked more after the exposure even without awareness of having been exposed to the ad before. Indeed, Duff and Faber (2011) found that people who had goals of finding specific information on a news site disliked ads that had appeared on those pages even though they did not have a conscious memory of them (they could not recognize them). So when might there be positive effects, and when might there be negative effects of ad exposure? One thing to look at is the goal of the user. If they have no specific goal, they are simply browsing or looking for whatever might catch their interest in a bottom-up way, the ad will more likely to have a positive outcome. However, if they had a specific goal, they are engaging in a top-down manner, the ad is more likely to have a negative outcome. In that case, the user's goals would dictate the outcome even for the same content. Additionally, properties of the media also matter; a more perceptually complex video game led to negative ratings for display ads whereas a perceptually simple video game led to more positive ratings. Many other factors might also help to predict what the outcome could be, and hopefully future research will continue to shed light on these factors.

Tech Trends

How we think about attention in advertising—from the consumers', the researchers', and the practitioners' perspectives—will likely change in the near future due to some dramatic developments in the technology (i.e., proliferation of smart devices, and increasing adoption of personal digital assistants powered by artificial intelligence). Smart objects are products that are equipped with sensors and are able to modify their performance based on their environment, task, and various user-related parameters, such as mood, arousal, and many others. More and more objects, in our everyday lives—from phones to cars, refrigerators, and even entire homes—are re-engineered to become "smart" and able to capture many types of rich data in real time, from the user's location, vitals and posture, to his mood, gaze, and speech (Darwish & Hassanien, 2011).

Smart interconnected objects—both public and personal—will produce a very large volume of data in real time, all of which will need to be integrated, interpreted, and presented to the consumer in a usable format. This task is mainly imposed on personal digital assistants powered by artificial intelligence. The efficiency and quality of the data analysis made by artificial intelligence can be very impressive. For example, Cortana, Microsoft's virtual agent powered by artificial intelligence, correctly predicted the winners of the first 14 matches of the 2014 FIFA World Cup knockout stage, including the semi-finals (Backaitis, 2014).

Virtual agents like Cortana, Apple's Siri, Google Now, and Amazon's Alexa will serve as a primary interface through which consumers will interact with their smart devices and, more broadly, the world around them (Nadella, 2015). At the writing of this chapter, virtual assistants have relatively limited capabilities. For example, Cortana can help you set a reminder, find files on your PC, manage your calendar, send a message or dial a number for you, solve a mathematical equation, convert currency, search the internet, and select news based on your interests. Admittedly, these are rather simple actions. However, due to massive ongoing efforts in sensing, connectivity, and machine learning, agents will eventually turn into a true gateway to the internet of things and people, relatively independent and able to make decisions. Ultimately, an agent will be able to not only respond to its owner's needs, but it will even anticipate them and be proactive in presenting information and services to its owner.

A world full of smart connected devices and curated by personal intelligent agents will bring dramatic changes to how consumers interact with the media, with the ads, and the products—affecting the issues we discussed above. If the objects around us, including media-viewing devices, recognize who we are, understand our speech, can continuously read our mood and vitals, know our likes and needs, obtain similar information from other smart objects, and then act upon this knowledge, the relevance and timeliness of the promotional content presented to consumers can become unprecedented.

Consider the following scenario: A consumer enters a supermarket, her smartphone automatically recognizes the location, and compiles a shopping list from several sources. It sends a request to the smart refrigerator for information on what is needed. Then it retrieves information about the upcoming child's birthday party from its calendar, and adds "cake and party supplies" to the list. Finally, it also checks the consumer's daily vitals and the doctor's notes, and then recommends foods that meet certain criteria (e.g., are rich in iron or low in sodium). As the consumer is walking between the aisles, the display ads around her change in real time, and her smartphone immediately receives coupons for the most relevant products. At the same time, the digital assistant alerts the consumer that the prices in another grocery store are lower and calculates how much the consumer would save if she shops elsewhere.

Of course, the idea of the personalized just-in-time message is not new; most e-commerce websites (e.g., Amazon, Netflix) already use technology that allows them to identify and track individual shoppers to provide them with a personalized service and shopping suggestions. However, smart products and personal digital assistants are taking this experience to a new level. First, information collected by the digital agent will not be limited to options available from a single retailer, like those at Amazon or Netflix. Second, new technologies will be more timely or even proactive in their suggestions, anticipating needs rather than waiting for a consumer to start shopping ("I see that you are in the retail store. Ron's birthday is coming. Do you want to buy him a card?"). Third, they will be significantly more insightful, as they can access and integrate additional information about the consumer that is usually not available to e-commerce websites (or even to the consumer's self-introspection), e.g., current location, mood, calendar, family needs, dietary restrictions, vitals, and so on.

Finally, because digital assistants can communicate with a number of smart objects and then integrate all relevant information about the user, they can potentially modify our overall media consumption experience, e.g., stop and resume video based on the user's (in)attention, display ads based on the user's current needs or interests, select the ad version to match the person's mood, and so on. When the promotional content is highly relevant, tailored and timely, advertising becomes much less intrusive, and the consumer is less motivated to avoid it. However, it is also possible that this makes advertising more integrated and more difficult to ignore, leading people to work harder to eliminate its effects. Additionally, if every ad one sees is relevant, timely, and engaging, on what basis will a person ultimately make their decision? In this way, advertising would be more akin to information and much less like persuasion.

Avoidance of advertising, especially by mechanical means, will continue to grow along with technology and should be kept in mind. As advertising messages are seen in different places, from different sources, and as a source of media content (instead of just being placed in that content), there is an element of increased engagement and interest on behalf of the user. However, it is likely that there will also be increased pushback as people find it more difficult to escape from ads. For example, one augmented reality app allows users to block ads from their everyday environment—a friend's bottle of Coca-Cola would simply look like a bottle with a blurry red label (Cuthbertson, 2015)

Advertising formats are changing and will continue to become more engaging, relevant, and integrated into content. However, many people do not consider ads to be the main thing that they want to interact with. Media multitasking as a way to control and shift attention will continue to rise, though it is likely that we will see new technologies that will allow for that attention management to be done in a more intentional way, alerting the user when attention seems to wane or even switching for the person. Understanding how indirect and partial attention change advertising effects will continue to be important.

References

Andrade, J. (2009). What does doodling do? *Applied Cognitive Psychology, 24*(1), 100–106.

Angell, R., Gorton, M., Sauer, J., Bottomley, P., & White, J. (2016). Don't distract me when I'm media multitasking: Toward a theory for raising advertising recall and recognition. *Journal of Advertising, 45*(2), 198–210.

Attention. (2016). American psychological society's glossary of psychological terms. Retrieved from http://www.apa.org/research/action/glossary.aspx.

Backaitis, V. (2014, July 11). Why Microsoft's Cortana is 14 for 14 calling World Cup matches. *CMS Wire.* Retrieved from http://www.cmswire.com/cms/big-data/why-microsofts-cortana-is-14-for-14-calling-world-cup-matches-025853.php.

Barry, T. E. (1987). The development of the hierarchy of effects: An historical perspective. *Current Issues and Research in Advertising, 10*(2), 251–296.

Carrier, L. M., Cheever, N. A., Rosen, L. D., Benitez, S., & Chang, J. (2009). Multitasking across generations: Multitasking choices and difficulty ratings in three generations of Americans. *Computers in Human Behavior, 25*(2), 483–489.

Carson, S. H., Peterson, J. B., & Higgins, D. M. (2003). Decreased latent inhibition is associated with increased creative achievement in high-functioning individuals. *Journal of Personality and Social Psychology, 85*(3), 499–506.

Chinchanachokchai, B. (2013). *Where was my mind? The role of perceptual load on mind wandering and consumer memory for advertising content.* Unpublished Doctoral Dissertation. Urbana, IL: University of Illinois at Urbana-Champaign.

Chinchanachokchai, S., Duff, B. R., & Sar, S. (2015). The effect of multitasking on time perception, enjoyment, and ad evaluation. *Computers in Human Behavior, 45*, 185–191.

Cho, C. H., & Cheon, H. J. (2004). Why do people avoid advertising on the internet? *Journal of Advertising, 33*(4), 89–97.

Chowdhury, R., Finn, A., & Olsen, D. G. (2007). Investigating the simultaneous presentation of advertising and television programming. *Journal of Advertising, 36*(3), 85–96.

Craik, F. I. M., Govoni, R., Naveh-Benjamin, M., & Anderson, N. D. (1996). The effects of divided attention on encoding and retrieval processes in human memory. *Journal of Experimental Psychology: General, 125*(2), 159–180.

Cuthbertson, A. (2015, January 23). Brand Killer: Augmented reality goggles create real-world AdBlock. *International Business Times.* Retrieved from http://www.ibtimes.co.uk/brand-killer-augmented-reality-goggles-create-real-world-adblock-1484844.

Darwish, A., & Hassanien, A. E. (2011). Wearable and implantable wireless sensor network solutions for healthcare monitoring. *Sensors, 11*(6), 5561–5595.

Deloitte. (2015). Digital democracy survey: A multi-generational view of consumer technology, media and telecom trends. Retrieved from http://www.deloitte.com/us/tmttrends.

Donohew, L., Lorch, E. P., & Palmgreen, P. (2006). Applications of a theoretic model of information exposure to health interventions. *Human Communication Research, 24*(3), 454–468.

Duff, B. R. L., & Faber, R. J. (2011). Missing the mark: Advertising avoidance and distractor devaluation. *Journal of Advertising, 40*(2), 51–62.

Duff, B. R. L., & Sar, S. (2015). Seeing the big picture: Multitasking and perceptual processing influences on ad recognition. *Journal of Advertising, 44*(3), 173–184.

Duff, B. R. L., Yoon, G., Wang, Z., & Anghelcev, G. (2014). Doing it all: An exploratory study of predictors of media multitasking. *Journal of Interactive Advertising, 14*(1), 1–13.

Edwards, S. M., Li, H., & Lee, J. H. (2002). Forced exposure and psychological reactance: Antecedents and consequences of the perceived intrusiveness of pop-up ads. *Journal of Advertising, 31*(3), 83–95.

Ehrenberg, A. S. C. (1974). Repetitive advertising and the consumer. *Journal of Advertising Research, 14*(2), 25–34.

Elder, R. S., & Krishna, A. (2010). The effects of advertising copy on sensory thoughts and perceived taste. *Journal of Consumer Research, 36*(5), 748–756.

Gasper, K. (2004). Do you see what I see? Affect and visual information processing. *Cognition and Emotion, 18*(3), 405–421.

GfK MRI. (2012). Tablets and multi-tasking. The GfK MRI iPanel reporter: A quarterly report on consumers, tablets and e-readers. Retrieved from http://www.gfkmri.com/assets/PDF/iPanelReporter_Tablets%20&%20Multitasking.pdf.

Gillies, T. (2015, October 25). Advertisers sweat as ad blockers proliferate. *CNBC.* Retrieved from http://www.cnbc.com/2015/10/23/advertisers-sweat-as-ad-blockers-proliferate.html.

Gorman, T. E., & Green, C. S. (2016). Short-term mindfulness intervention reduces the negative attentional effects associated with heavy media multitasking. *Scientific Reports, 6,* 24542.

Ham, C. D., Nelson, M. R., & Das, S. (2015). How to measure persuasion knowledge. *International Journal of Advertising, 34*(1), 17–53.

Hern, A. (2016, January 1). A proxy war: Apple ad-blocking software scares publishers but rival Google is target. *The Guardian.* Retrieved from https://www.theguardian.com/technology/2016/jan/01/publishers-apple-ad-blockers-target-google.

Heussner, K. M. (2012, February 28). Americans are the biggest mobile multitaskers. *Adweek.* Retrieved from http://www.adweek.com/news/technology/americans-are-biggest-mobile-multitaskers-138593.

Ipsos MediaCT & IAB. (2012). Screens: What are people doing… and why? Presentation of findings. Retrieved from http://www.iab.net/media/file/Simultaneous-screen-IAB-Innovation-Day-v19.pdf.

James, W. (1890). *Principles of psychology.* New York, NY: Dover.

Janiszewski, C. (1990). The influence of nonattended material on the processing of advertising claims. *Journal of Marketing Research, 27,* 263–278.

Jeong, S., & Fishbein, F. (2007). Predictors of multitasking with media: Media factors and audience factors. *Media Psychology, 10*(3), 364–384.

Jeong, S., & Hwang, Y. (2012). Does multitasking increase or decrease persuasion? Effects of multitasking on comprehension and counterarguing. *Journal of Communication, 62*, 571–587.

Jeong, S., & Hwang, Y. (2015). Multitasking and persuasion: The role of structural interference. *Media Psychology, 18*(4), 451–474.

John, J. (2016, March 29). In today's digital world, the sales funnel is dead. *Advertising Age*. Retrieved from http://adage.com/article/digitalnext/today-s-digital-world-sales-funnel-dead/303301/

Johnston, W. A., & Dark, V. J. (1986). Selective attention. *Annual Review of Psychology, 37*(1), 43–75.

Junco, R. (2012). In-class multitasking and academic performance. *Computers in Human Behavior, 28*(6), 2236–2243.

Kahneman, D. (1973). *Attention and effort*. Englewood Cliffs, NJ: Prentice-Hall.

Kazakova, S., & Cauberghe, V. (2013). Media convergence and media multitasking. In S. Diehl & M. Karmasin (Eds.), *Media and convergence management* (pp. 177–188). Berlin: Springer.

Konig, C. J., Buhner, M., & Murling, G. (2005). Working memory, fluid intelligence, and attention are predictors of multitasking performance, but polychronicity and extraversion are not. *Human Performance, 18*(3), 243–266.

Lang, A. (2000). The limited capacity model of mediated message processing. *Journal of Communication, 50*(1), 46–70.

Lin, L. (2009). Breadth-biased versus focused cognitive control in media multitasking behaviors. *Proceedings of the National Academy of Sciences, 106*(37), 15521–15522.

Lui, K. F., & Wong, A. C. N. (2012). Does media multitasking always hurt? A positive correlation between multitasking and multisensory integration. *Psychonomic Bulletin & Review, 19*(4), 647–653.

Masuda, T., Gonzalez, R., Kwan, L., & Nisbett, R. E. (2008). Culture and aesthetic preference: Comparing the attention to context of East Asians and Americans. *Personality and Social Psychology Bulletin, 34*(9), 1260–1275.

Masuda, T., & Nisbett, R. E. (2001). Attending holistically versus analytically: Comparing the context sensitivity of Japanese and Americans. *Journal of Personality and Social Psychology, 81*(5), 922–934.

Matthes, J., Schemer, C., & Wirth, W. (2007). More than meets the eye: Investigating the hidden impact of brand placements in television magazines. *International Journal of Advertising, 26*(4), 477–503.

McDowd, J. M., & Birren, J. E. (1990). Aging and attentional process. In J. E. Birren & K. W. Schaie (Eds.), *Handbook of the psychology of aging* (3rd ed., pp. 222–233). New York, NY: Academic Press.

McKone, E., Davies, A. A., Fernando, D., Aalders, R., Leung, H., Wickramariyaratne, T., & Platow, M. J. (2010). Asia has the global advantage: Race and visual attention. *Vision Research, 50*(16), 1540–1549.

Mehrabian, A., & Russell, J. A. (1974). *An approach to environmental psychology*. Cambridge, MA: MIT Press.

Millward Brown. (2014). AdReaction: Marketing in a multiscreen world. Retrieved from https://www.millwardbrown.com/AdReaction/2014/#/

Monsell, S. (2003). Task switching. *Trends in Cognitive Sciences, 7*(3), 134–140.

Morrison, M. (2015, September 8). Confusion reigns as Apple puts the spotlight on mobile ad blocking. *Advertising Age*. Retrieved from http://adage.com/article/digital/confusion-reigns-apple-spotlight-mobile-ad-blocking/300167/

Nadella, S. (2015, May). Speech presented at Lenovo Tech World 2015 conference in Beijing, China.

Naveh-Benjamin, M., Craik, F. I., Perretta, J. G., & Tonev, S. T. (2000). The effects of divided attention on encoding and retrieval processes: The resiliency of retrieval processes. *The Quarterly Journal of Experimental Psychology: Section A, 53*(3), 609–625.

Navon, D., & Miller, J. (1987). Role of outcome conflict in dual-task interference. *Journal of Experimental Psychology: Human Perception and Performance, 13*(3), 435–448.

Nielsen Cross Platform Report. (2012). The cross-platform community: A new connected community. *Nielsen*. Retrieved from http://www.nielsen.com/us/en/insights/news/2012/the-cross-platform-report-a-new-connected-community.html.

Ophir, E., Nass, C., & Wagner, A. D. (2009). Cognitive control in media multitaskers. *Proceedings of the National Academy of Sciences, 106*(37), 15583–15587.

Pashler, H. (1994). Dual-task interference in simple tasks: Data and theory. *Psychological Bulletin, 116*(2), 220–244.

Perlberg, S. (2016, June 22). Advertising isn't dead, but market is changing. *The Wall Street Journal*. Retrieved from http://www.wsj.com/articles/advertising-isnt-dead-but-market-is-changing-1466610850.

Peterson, T., & Fishman, C. (2015, June 19). Ad blocking is a growing problem. What's the fix? *Advertising Age*. Retrieved from http://adage.com/article/media/publishers-weigh-ways-fight-ad-blocking/299116/

Petty, R. E., Wells, G. L., & Brock, T. C. (1976). Distraction can enhance or reduce yielding to propaganda: Thought disruption versus effort justification. *Journal of Personality and Social Psychology, 34*(5), 874–884.

Poposki, E., Frederick Oswald, F., & Chen, H. (2009). Neuroticism negatively affects multitasking performance through state anxiety. *Navy Personnel Research, Studies and Technology, 9*(3), 29. Retrieved from http://www.nprst.navy.mil/Reports/NPRST-TN-09–3.pdf.

Prakash, R. S., Erickson, K. I., Colcombe, S. J., Kim, J. S., Voss, M. W., & Kramer, A. F. (2009). Age-related differences in the involvement of the prefrontal cortex in attentional control. *Brain and Cognition, 71*(3), 328–335.

Raymond, J. E., Fenske, M. J., & Tavassoli, N. T. (2003). Selective attention determines emotional responses to novel visual stimuli. *Psychological Science, 14*(6), 537–542.

Richtel, M. (2012, May 29). Wasting time is new divide in digital era. *The New York Times*. Retrieved from http://www.nytimes.com/2012/05/30/us/new-digital-divide-seen-in-wasting-time-online.html?_r=0.

Roberts, D. F., & Foehr, U. G. (2008). Trends in media use. *The Future of Children, 18*(1), 11–37.

Romano, A. (2016, February 29). Truly American Chrome extension will change "Trump" to "Drumpf." *Mashable*. Retrieved from http://mashable.com/2016/02/29/donald-drumpf-chrome-extension/#bsMRD0LkBaq0.

Rosen, L. D., Carrier, L. M., & Cheever, N. A. (2013). Facebook and texting made me do it: Media-induced task-switching while studying. *Computers in Human Behavior, 29*(3), 948–958.

Roth, M., Hammelstein, P., & Brähler, E. (2007). Beyond a youthful behavior style: Age and sex differences in sensation seeking based on need theory. *Personality and Individual Differences, 43*(7), 1839–1850.

Sanbonmatsu, D. M., Strayer, D., Medeiros-Ward, N., & Watson, J. (2013). Who multi-tasks and why? Multi-tasking ability, perceived multi-tasking ability, impulsivity, and sensation seeking. *PloSONE, 8*(1), e54402.

Schacter, D. L. (1987). Implicit expressions of memory in organic amnesia: Learning of new facts and associations. *Human Neurobiology, 6*(2), 107–118.

Segijn, C. M., Voorveld, H. A., & Smit, E. G. (2016). The underlying mechanisms of multiscreening effects. *Journal of Advertising*, 1–12, doi: 10.1080/00913367.2016.1172386.

Shapiro, S., & Krishnan, H. S. (2001). Memory-based measures for assessing advertising effects: A comparison of explicit and implicit memory effects. *Journal of Advertising, 30*(3), 1–13.

Shapiro, S., MacInnis, D. J., & Heckler, S. E. (1997). The effects of incidental ad exposure on the formation of consideration sets. *Journal of Consumer Research, 24*(1), 94–104.

Shiv, B., & Huber, J. (2000). The impact of anticipating satisfaction on consumer choice. *Journal of Consumer Research, 27*(2), 202–216.

Simons, D. (n.d.). The invisible gorilla. Retrieved from http://www.theinvisiblegorilla.com/videos.html.

Slater, M. D. (2004). Operationalizing and analyzing exposure: The foundation of media effects research. *Journalism & Mass Communication Quarterly, 81*(1), 168–183.

Sloane, G. (2015, April 9). As ad blocker usage explodes, can YouTube win back scofflaws with a subscription model? Users revolt against pre-roll. *AdWeek*. Retrieved from http://www.adweek.com/news/technology/how-ad-blocking-could-affect-youtubes-subscription-model-163983.

Smallwood, J., O'Connor, R. C., Sudbery, M. V., & Obonsawin, M. C. (2007). Mind wandering and dysphoria. *Cognition & Emotion, 21*, 816–842.

Speck, P. S., & Elliott, M. T. (1997). Predictors of advertising avoidance in print and broadcast media. *Journal of Advertising, 26*, 61–76.

Strayer, D., & Watson, J. (2012). Supertaskers and the multitasking brain. *Scientific American Mind, 23*(1), 22–29.

Voorveld, H. (2011). Media multitasking and the effectiveness of combining online and radio advertising. *Computers in Human Behavior, 27*, 2200–2206.

Wang, Z., & Tchernev, J. (2012). The "myth" of media multitasking: Reciprocal dynamics of media multitasking, personal needs, and gratifications. *Journal of Communication, 62*, 493–513.

Wilson, T. D., Reinhard, D. A., Westgate, E. C., Gilbert, D. T., Ellerbeck, N., Hahn, C., Brown, C., & Shaked, A. (2014). Just think: The challenges of the disengaged mind. *Science, 345*(6192), 75–77.

Yap, J. Y., & Lim, S. W. H. (2013). Splitting visual focal attention? It probably depends on who you are. In *Proceedings of the 2nd Annual International Conference on Cognitive and Behavioral Psychology*, Singapore.

Yoon, S., Choi, Y. K., & Song, S. (2011). When intrusive can be likable. *Journal of Advertising, 40*(2), 63–76.

Zajonc, R. B. (2001). Mere exposure: A gateway to the subliminal. *Current Directions in Psychological Science, 10*(6), 224–228.

Zeitlin, M. (2015, September 9). Washington Post declares war on ad blockers. *Buzzfeed*. Retrieved from https://www.buzzfeed.com/matthewzeitlin/the-washington-post-begins-blocking-ad-blockers?utm_term=.stOok9LbKY#.puwAK9xGbD.

Zhang, W., Jeong, S. H., & Fishbein, M. (2010). Situational factors competing for attention: The interaction effect between multitasking and sexual explicitness on TV recognition. *Journal of Media Psychology, 22*(1), 2–13.

Zhong, B., Hardin, M., & Sun, T. (2011). Less effortful thinking leads to more social networking? The associations between the use of social network sites and personality traits. *Computers in Human Behavior, 27*(3), 1265–1271.

Zuckerman, M. (1979). *Sensation seeking: Beyond the optimal level of arousal.* Hillsdale, NJ: Lawrence Erlbaum Associates Inc.

PART III

New Approaches to Research

10

DIGITAL ADVERTISING IN A NEW AGE

The Power of (Tele)Presence

Matthew Lombard and Jennifer Snyder-Duch

Introduction

Using what Sharp is calling "eye-catching software" on their digital advertising displays, [the device] creates the illusion that a passer-by's reflection can be seen in the image as they walk near or past it. On top of this, the displays are also able to understand the type of person approaching and choose an advert befitting to his/her demographic. . . . [The device] makes advertising a more personalised experience; something that businesses could soon be snapping up in an attempt to engage the public.

—(Humans Invent, 2013)

"Our goal with *Quantico* from a VR standpoint was to make sure the storytelling was front and center," [Jerry] Weinstock [vice president and creative director at ABC Integrated Marketing] says. "With VR, the viewer is in the car with our actors. It's a much deeper level of engagement for a sponsor while still remaining organic and true to the storyline."

—(Gaudiosi, 2016)

This new [#LookingForYou] campaign for Battersea Dogs & Cats Home, the U.K. rescue and rehoming charity, features the very sweet pup, Barley, on a series of digital billboards at Westfield shopping mall in Stratford, London. People entering the mall are handed leaflets but, unbeknownst to them, the leaflet contains an RFID chip. As they walk round the mall, the chip activates videos on digital billboards when they pass by. Barley appears to interact directly with the shoppers and his antics apparently get increasingly cute with every step. (Jack, 2015); The campaign generated 2,500 unique visits to the campaign's microsite, 320,000 video views, 99% positive social sentiment, new visitors to the site, and 200 new inquiries about rehoming dogs.

—(Warc, n.d.)

Advertising in the traditional media environment is defined as "a form of controlled communication that attempts to persuade consumers, through use of a variety of strategies and appeals, to buy or use a particular product or service" (Defleur & Dennis, 1996, p. 564) and relatedly, "paid nonpersonal communication from an identified sponsor using mass media to persuade or influence an audience" (Wells, Burnett, & Moriarity, 1998, p. 13). As the examples above suggest, we have entered a new age in which advertising is much more interactive and personalized to consumers. In addition, advances in technology have prompted users to engage much differently in their media environment, and this has presented advertisers with substantial challenges and opportunities in developing the relationship between consumers and brands.

In this chapter, we describe key characteristics of advertising today, and explain how the concept of telepresence, or presence, in which media users overlook or misperceive the role of technology in their experience, offers a valuable framework for the study and practice of advertising today and in the future.

The Changing Nature of Advertising

In 2001, we argued that advertisers had an opportunity to take advantage of emerging technologies to provide a new advertising experience:

> The internet and other interactive technologies make it possible to create ads that are not only more targeted, but more personal, in which advertising is an experience in which the consumer participates and is engaged. Thus, the model of advertising as communication that is nonpersonal and controlled exclusively by the sponsor seems to be evolving into one in which advertising is personal and interactive. Interactive advertising gives consumers more control by giving them a range of choices in their experience with product information. And it produces a sense that the communication is more personal than traditional media ads because it creates or simulates a one-on-one interaction.
>
> *(Lombard & Snyder-Duch, 2001, p. 56)*

Over the past 15 years, advertising has certainly evolved in the ways that we predicted. The ultimate goal of consumer advertising—to persuade individuals to purchase a product or service—remains the same. However, technological advances have drastically changed the nature of ads. Based on academic and industry literature, three characteristics strongly distinguish digital advertising from advertising in traditional media: interactivity, personalization, and engagement.

Interactivity

Interactivity is perhaps the most prominent attribute of media in the digital age (Kim & McMillan, 2008) and can be defined simply as "a characteristic of a medium in which the user can influence the form and/or content of the mediated presentation or experience" (Lombard & Snyder-Duch, 2001, p. 57). Related to advertising, Bezjian-Avery, Calder, and Iacobucci (1998) explain, "Whereas in traditional advertising, the presentation is linear and the consumer is passively exposed to product information, for interactive advertising, the consumer instead actively traverses the information. The pieces of information the consumer sees depends on where the consumer wants to go" (p. 24). Lombard and Snyder-Duch (2001) explain that media interactivity is not dichotomous, but can vary in degree from not interactive to highly interactive based on several variables. While a banner ad is interactive in that it allows a user to click through for more information, the ads described in the opening of this chapter allows users to enter a real-time, realistic experience where they feel as if they are using the product (see Table 10.1 for a description and examples of variables that affect degree of interactivity).

TABLE 10.1 Variables that Influence the Degree of Interactivity of a Mediated Experience

Variable	Examples
The number of inputs from the user that the medium accepts and to which it responds.	*A basic website accepts cursor movement and selection via keyboard/mouse while virtual reality may accept head movement via tracking sensors, movement and selection via position, and button-presses via a controller/joystick, and even audio/voice input, text via virtual keyboard, body movement, hand and finger movement, haptic pressure, eye movement, facial expression, or physiological inputs such as heart rate, muscle tension, and skin conductance.*
The number and type of characteristics of the mediated presentation or experience that can be modified by the user.	*A viewer of streaming video (e.g., on YouTube) can modify image size and resolution, amount of text on the screen, volume and pace. A videogame player can modify these, along with their avatar's appearance, content (e.g., the course of the adventure, which parts of the game-world are explored, etc.), and duration.*
The range or amount of change possible in each characteristic.	*Users of basic videogames can select among a small set of generic virtual representations (avatars) and environment while users of virtual worlds such as Second Life can select and modify many elements of their avatar and environment.*
The speed at which the medium responds to user inputs (asynchronous vs. synchronous, long vs. short lag).	*Responses to an email message may take hours or days (asynchronous) while responses in a chatroom are immediate (synchronous). Responses to actions in an operating system or other software while using an older, slower computer can be noticeably slower than the responses to the same actions while using a modern, faster computer.*
The degree of correspondence between the type of user input and the type of medium response (natural mapping).	*Using a combination of keystrokes or moving a joystick to cause a player to kick a soccer ball in a basic video game represents unnatural mapping while making a kicking movement with one's leg and foot to cause the same action represents natural mapping.*

Research and commentary about interactive advertising are ultimately about control: the amount and nature of control given to the consumer in the digital environment. The literature makes it clear that digital media allows for a level of interactivity that has changed the relationship between the advertiser and the consumer (Jenkins, Ford, & Green, 2013; Turow & Draper, 2014), and research suggests that interactive ads promote more positive attitudes toward products and brands (Sundar & Kim, 2005) and contribute to ad effectiveness (Arroyo-Cañada & Gil-Lafuente, 2012). In fact, ads that disrupt a consumer's media use—as traditional television and radio ads did—are often judged as annoying and may cause negative attitudes toward a brand (Edwards, Li, & Lee, 2002; Bright, 2011; Smith, 2012; Tanyel, Stuart, & Griffin, 2013). Rodgers and Thorson (2000) offer a model to explain interactive advertising. Their model is useful in that it moves beyond ad structure to integrate function: the motives (research, shopping, communication, entertainment, etc.) and mode (serious versus playful) of users as they encounter advertising messages (Rodgers & Thorson, 2000).

Personalization

Personalization can be described broadly as the "tailoring of message content and delivery based on data collection or covert observation of users, to increase the personal relevance of the message" (Bang & Wojdynski, 2016, p. 868). Personalization has long been central to consumer advertising strategy. Advertisers want consumers to feel that ads are meant specifically for them. For decades, they have aimed to make advertising appeals seem personal through their media placement and through storytelling that addresses consumers' specific needs and depicts how products fit perfectly into their lives. But digital technology has provided the marketing and advertising industries with sophisticated new methods to assess consumers' demographics, media habits, and lifestyles and use the information to personalize messages. "As a consumer travels in the virtual, or digital world, everywhere he or she goes, and everything he or she does, leaves a trail of bits of information because almost all actions and activities are recorded" (Dickey & Lewis, 2011, p. 25).

The strong trend, then, has been toward more and more personal advertising. Today we find companies investing in sophisticated and expensive tracking and creative techniques such as "real-time bidding," which allows online advertisers to adapt content—including price, product details, and product variations—at the moment when users interact with the ad (Minsker, 2013). As another example, Sharp's eye-catching software described in the opening of this chapter incorporates passers-by into the content of a digital display ad and adapts content based on their demographics.

The research on the effectiveness of personalization is still in its early phase. Some research indicates that such techniques are perceived as off-putting. For example, Turow, King, Hoofnagle, Bleakley, and Hennessy (2009) surveyed

American adults and found that a majority are not in favor of personalized advertising, and the percentage of those who report that they do not want personalized ads is even higher when they are made aware of the techniques used by marketers and advertisers to gather personal data. Other studies indicate that personalization is effective but is mediated by other variables including the user's personal disposition, in particular the need for cognition (Tam & Ho, 2005), congruency between media content and ad content (Simola, Kivikangas, Kuisma, & Krause, 2013), the clarity and strength of product attributes in the ad (Howard & Kerin, 2004), consumer trust in the retailer (Bleier & Eisenbeiss, 2015), and the cognitive demand of the user's primary task when encountering the ad (Bang & Wojdynski, 2016).

Engagement

In addition to the changes in consumers' experiences as individual ads become more interactive and personalized, advertisers realize that changes in the media environment at large provide challenges and opportunities. In the advertising industry, *engagement* has come to describe consumers' interactions with brands through social media, a measure that goes beyond the traditional measure of advertising *reach* or *impressions*. As Gangadharbatla (2012) explains, engagement:

> roughly translates to some evidence that the individual, i.e., the audience member, an advertiser is trying to reach is responding in some way to the message, e.g., by clicking the Like button or by commenting on the advertisers' wall on Facebook or by writing a review or by retweeting (RT) or downloading an app.
>
> *(p. 409)*

It can be described as "a two-way conversation between the brand and its fans" (Schoenfeld, 2012, para. 8). How the industry should measure this kind of engagement in order to determine ROI is still being debated. Advertisers can certainly count clicks and retweets, but further research is needed to understand what causes those behaviors and what they indicate. It seems that some combination of information processing and emotional response variables characterizes consumers' engagement with a brand (Wang, 2006; Brandow, 2016).

Jenkins et al. (2013) also use the term engagement. They argue that an "appointment model" no longer characterizes consumer media use, where content is offered at particular times. Rather, the user experience can be described as "engagement," where media users are "a collective of active agents whose labor may generate alternative forms of market value" (Jenkins et al., 2013, p. 116). This approach to engagement acknowledges that audiences interact with content across multiple channels. "Such models value the spread of media texts as these engaged audiences are more likely to recommend, discuss, research, pass along, and even generate new material in response" (Jenkins et al., 2013, p. 116). This means that advertisers have to work differently to understand and shape the relationship between consumers and products or brands.

What is needed—in both academic research and industry practice—is a framework to better understand and take advantage of the interactivity, personalization, and engagement of modern (and future) digital advertising. The concept and phenomena of (tele)presence provide such a framework.

Digital Advertising: The Role of Presence

The term presence (short for telepresence) emerged in technology studies as early as 1980 (Minsky, 1980) as virtual reality and teleoperation (operation of technology at a distance) emerged, and to some extent in the public sphere in the mid-2000s as companies including Cisco launched high-end teleconferencing equipment designed to replicate the in-person meeting experience (Cisco, 2006). Among academics, the idea of mediated experiences that mimic non-mediated ones extends back many more decades, to at least Horton and Wohl's (1956) work on parasocial interaction and relationships with radio and television personalities. The term is often used imprecisely to refer to one or more different related phenomena, but in 2000 a panel of scholars associated with what would become the International Society for Presence Research (ISPR) developed a detailed definition and explication, which begins this way:

> Presence (a shortened version of the term "telepresence") is a psychological state or subjective perception in which even though part or all of an individual's current experience is generated by and/or filtered through human-made technology, part or all of the individual's perception fails to accurately acknowledge the role of the technology in the experience. Except in the most extreme cases, the individual can indicate correctly that s/he is using the technology, but at "some level" and to "some degree", her/his perceptions overlook that knowledge and objects, events, entities, and environments are perceived as if the technology was not involved in the experience.
> *(ISPR, 2000)*

Since then, many authors have developed variations of this definition, describing different subsets of types or dimensions of presence (see Lombard & Jones, 2015 for a detailed review). A current project (Lombard & Sun, 2016) designed to assess presence experiences as they occur in the course of peoples' everyday lives presented ten of these different but overlapping types of presence (see Table 10.2).

Despite these disparate forms of presence, most scholars (see ISPR, 2000) seem to agree that the primary and most inclusive forms are spatial (a sense of being in the media-created physical environment) and social (a sense of being in the media-created social environment). A third form of presence particularly relevant in the context of advertising is presence as engagement: "'Engagement,' 'involvement,'

TABLE 10.2 Types of Presence (adapted from Lombard & Sun, 2016)

Presence Type	First-person descriptor	Spatial vs. Social Emphasis
Spatial Presence	I felt like I was in the *space or environment* created by the technology.	Spatial
Transportation	I felt like I *went* somewhere else, people or things *came* to me, or we went somewhere else *together.*	Spatial and social
Engagement	I felt *mentally immersed*; I was focused on or absorbed in the experience.	Spatial and social
Perceptual Realism	The people, things, and events I experienced through the technology *looked, sounded, and/or felt* as they would in the real world.	Spatial and social
Inverse Presence	Even though *I wasn't using technology, I felt like I was* (for example: I felt like I was in a movie when I was really walking in the street).	Spatial and social
Social Presence	I felt I was actually *with the people* who were available via technology.	Social
Social Realism	The people, things, and events I experienced through the technology *could (or did) occur* in the real world.	Spatial and social
Medium As Social Actor	The technology itself *seemed to have a personality* (including computers, phones, robots, mannequins, etc.).	Social
Actor Within Medium	Even though I *couldn't interact with them, I felt I was actually with the people or characters* who were available via the technology.	Social
Self-Presence	I felt connected to the *avatar or other representation of me* in the world created by the technology.	Social

Note: These types of presence are identified in the literature as distinct, but they are not mutually exclusive—most presence experiences involve more than one and sometimes many of them.

and 'psychological immersion' occur when part or all of a person's perception is directed toward objects, events, and/or people created by the technology, and away from objects, events, and/or people in the physical world" (ISPR, 2000). This form of presence is measured in presence questionnaire items that ask media users to rate how much they felt "involved" and "enjoyed" their experience and how intense it was (Lessiter, Freeman, Keogh, & Davidoff, 2001, p. 293), and how much they felt "mentally immersed," had their "senses engaged," and felt a "sensation of reality," how "relaxing or exciting" it was, and how "engaging [the story] was" (TPI; Lombard, Weinstein, & Ditton, 2011, pp. 293–294). This type of engagement is distinct from the behavioral-based and more nuanced accounts of engagement from the advertising industry and literature as discussed above, but it is clearly related, since presence as engagement is likely to be associated with user responses to advertising messages within and across media (see Mollen & Wilson, 2010 for a detailed explication of how interactivity, telepresence, and engagement have been defined and measured in different contexts and may be related).

A common view among scholars has been that presence, especially spatial presence, requires sophisticated and expensive technology that as nearly-as-possible reproduces our non-mediated experience. Much of the early scholarly work on the topic focused on nascent virtual reality and teleoperation systems that were most often only available in laboratories and specialized industry settings (note the subtitle of the MIT Press journal founded in 1992, *Presence: Teleoperators and Virtual Environments*). But researchers observed that even a good novel can produce sensations of spatial and social presence, which they identified as "the book problem" (Schubert & Crusius, 2002; Biocca, 2003). And as far back as the 1950s, Horton and Wohl (1956) wrote about radio and television audience members experiencing a "simulacrum" of social interaction with presenters and entertainers. Today, some of the most compelling social presence experiences come from text and images in social media, including ephemeral, low-production value live-streaming video (e.g., via Snapchat). A logical explanation for the seeming contradiction is the fact that we do not respond directly to our sensory inputs but to our mental recreations of those inputs.

Regardless of the sophistication of the technology, any mediated experience, including an advertising experience, that evokes strong spatial and social presence features vivid and compelling places, people and events that create a sense of psychological, and even physiological, connection for the user. But technology that allows advertising to become more interactive, personal, and engaging, for example giving them the experience of shopping in an interesting (virtual) store environment; examining and trying out a product they care about; talking to a real or artificial salesperson or favorite person; being the main character in an event or story related to the product, service, or brand; and any of the scenarios at the beginning of this chapter, is likely to evoke stronger presence.

Research on Digital Advertising and Presence

From telling vivid stories by firelight and in novels, to painting and sculpture, photography, the electronic media of the 20th century, and today's rapidly evolving immersive, social, and hyper-realistic digital media, humans have always sought to make mediated experiences seem more direct and non-mediated. Reeves and Nass (1996) are among those who argue that our responses to these technologies are based in evolution; others point to aspects of our embodied experience (Haans & IJsselsteijn, 2012). In any case it's clear that presence is both an important motivator and goal in human experience, and that presence experiences lead to a series of responses many of which are valuable to advertisers.

Even though the definitions and measures of presence and the impacts of presence experiences examined have varied across studies, the results of disparate research point to an important mediating role of (tele)presence in advertising effects. When ad messages and experiences are designed to evoke presence, those presence responses lead to a variety of cognitive, affective, and behavioral effects desired by advertisers, including enjoyment, attitude toward the ad and product, product knowledge, and purchase intention. This is the case with manipulations of different types of presence in different contexts. Researchers have examined media contexts including online advertising (Choi, Miracle, & Biocca, 2001; Li, Daugherty & Biocca, 2002; Klein, 2003; Hopkins, Raymond, & Mitra, 2004; Fortin & Dholakia, 2005; Yang, 2006; Debbabi, Daassi, & Baile, 2010), indoor (Yim, Cicchirillo, & Drumwright, 2012) and outdoor (de Boer, Verleur, Heuvelman, & Heynderickx, 2010) 3D displays, noninteractive (Russell & Stern, 2006) and interactive (Cauberghe, Geuens, & De Pelsmacker, 2011) television, video games (Nelson, Yaros, & Keum, 2006), and virtual worlds (Grigorovici, 2003; Jin, 2009; Tikkanen, Hietanen, Henttonen, & Rokka, 2009). A consistent pattern in the results is the fact that presence plays a key role in the positive effects of interactivity, anthropomorphic agents, modality (audio vs. text), and the use of 3D displays.

Presence-Evoking Marketing and Advertising Experiences

As presence-evoking technologies become more effective, practical, and widespread (at least in developed nations), they will present important opportunities for digital advertisers. The exact nature of these opportunities, especially in the far term, is difficult to predict, but we can look to examples (including the ones at the beginning of this chapter) of how advertisers are utilizing emerging presence technologies now, and consider research findings and technology forecasts to predict how they may be utilized in the distant future. These technologies can be distinguished by their emphasis on evoking spatial and social presence as well as presence as engagement.

Spatial Presence

Home and Public Virtual Reality

VR, from 360-degree navigable spaces to fully interactive motion-tracked head-mounted displays at home or in public spaces (malls, hotels, bars, etc.), can be used to transport users to travel destinations and allow them to interact with and customize products (e.g., cars, appliances, home decor, make-up, fashion, etc.) (e.g., Robertson, 2015; Johnson, 2015a; Li, 2016). Longer-form virtual experiences centered on a product or brand (e.g., Johnson, 2015b) can be used to engage, entertain, and persuade.

Holographic Product Displays and Demonstrations

In interactive signage and in store displays, these can be personalized based on information provided actively or passively via sensors (as in Minority Report) (see Genuth, 2013).

Virtual Shopping Environments

Virtual and augmented reality can allow users to have a version of the brick-and-mortar shopping experience. The shopping cart icon used by most retail websites can be made more literal, as the separate web pages for lists of products and product details and reviews can be made to match the physical space of a retail store (e.g., Buss, 2012).

Product Placement

Widely used in film and television, and more recently in videogames, this technique in which a product or brand appears as a major or minor part of the story or environment is being extended to other presence-evoking experiences including virtual reality (Takahashi, 2014). The specific products/brands displayed are likely to be personalized based on information provided actively or passively by users, and even the prominence of the appearance might be adjusted based on such knowledge.

Social Presence

Customer Service Via Real or Virtual Agents

The evolution of video conferencing services such as Skype and FaceTime and the rise of mobile media will continue to make it easier and less expensive to communicate with customers and potential customers from home, brick-and-mortar stores, or anywhere in ways that create a sense of face-to-face interaction. Given the power of these interactions, especially for high-involvement products and services, advertisers and businesses will likely make available and initiate more of them. Some banks are already experimenting with ATMs with telepresence equipment that connects users to remote human tellers (Ginovsky, 2013), and the logic can be extended to other financial services, luxury purchases, and many others. The "person" at the other end of the conversation need not be human; Amtrak has used an artificially intelligent voice-based agent named Julie to take rail reservations (Amtrak, n.d.). Given the rise of Siri and other audio AI agents, the public will likely become more accustomed to these interactions, and it's extremely likely that realistic images will soon accompany the voices (see Kolbe, Salomann, & Brenner, 2006).

Robots and Androids as Product/Brand/Retail Representatives

Service robots like Lowe's OSHbot (Rodriguez, 2014) are already helping customers find and buy the right products, while other service robots guide airport visitors (Blackman, 2012) and serve hotel guests (Lewis-Kraus, 2016). Robots and androids evoke not only delight and interest, but presence scholars have established that we cannot help responding to them in many of the ways we respond to humans and animals (Reeves & Nass, 1996; Xu & Lombard, 2016). Robots and androids can therefore be used to advise and persuade customers and prospective customers in a variety of settings.

Engagement

Engaging Form: Virtual/Mixed Reality and Theme Parks

Technologies that require users' complete attention and shut out distractions are more likely to evoke presence as engagement. Virtual reality that utilizes head-mounted displays to replace the sights and sounds from the non-mediated world encourages users to become mentally immersed in messages, including advertising messages. Mixed reality technology such as Microsoft's Hololens (n.d.), in which virtual objects seem to interact with real ones in interesting ways and users can interact with either, should produce a similarly high level of engagement presence. Theme parks such as Disneyland, sections of other parks devoted to "Harry Potter," "Star Trek," and many others (Thorpe, 2016), and individual theme park rides create a cohesive, immersive world for attendees to engage with and represent a logical context for sponsored messages (see Olson, 2004). Of course, the technologies must work properly and not draw attention to their operation to fully engage users.

Engaging Content: Supplementary and Transmedia

Media products are increasingly deemed successful not just because they reach a large audience, but because the audience members they do reach are devoted and passionate about the products (Napoli, 2011; Jenkins et al., 2013; Arvidsson & Bonini, 2015). Indicators of this passion include posting comments, images, and reviews to social media, in real-time or otherwise; producing fan fiction based on content characters and storylines; etc. Media, and specifically advertisers, can encourage and take advantage of this type of passion first with compelling storylines, characters, and dialogue in media products and then by providing additional opportunities to interact with the media content. It is common to provide behind-the-scenes and outtake videos, "extra" content online, and fan convention appearances; increasingly producers are creating content-related experience-based promotions across media platforms from websites to VR (e.g., Knowles, 2016; Lazzaro, 2016). These techniques within and across media should increase audience mental immersion (engagement), loyalty, and receptiveness to (appropriately designed and placed) advertising messages.

Parasocial Interaction and Authenticity

As noted above, an effective presence experience need not rely on expensive technology and high production values. Low-fi, raw, imperfect but intimate first-person videos, as from news/weather/sports presenters, actors, program creators/ writers, gamers, and others can be extremely engaging because they evoke a sense of authenticity and personal connection. These represent key opportunities to enhance engagement and, if used wisely, promote products and services.

Presence in the More Distant Future

We can imagine all three types of presence reaching their full potential in the context of advertising in the more distant future. Here is one possible scenario:

> You return home and enter your ironically named "Reality Room," an otherwise empty space containing the well-hidden holography generator technology that can create or recreate vivid, interactive representations of any combination of places, objects, people, and events. You ask the virtual assistant (who has a human name) to put you in the living room of your favorite dramedy series with your favorite fictional character from your collection of stories. The father of the series' family appears on the couch next to you. Both the physical environment and your companion are utterly realistic, and you begin to relax as you and he carry on a warm conversation. The topic eventually turns to the latest models of transport vehicle; the character describes the model he thinks you should consider purchasing. He makes a compelling argument, and though you realize he's likely been programmed to persuade you, it's hard to resist him given your fondness for him and his (fictional) family. Together you visit a virtual showroom where you take a test ride, feeling every aspect of being inside the vehicle as it speeds down familiar sun-drenched streets, as onlookers smile in admiration. On returning to the living room, you thank your companion and say

goodbye. Your virtual assistant asks you if you enjoyed your experience and where you would like to go next, and as the room becomes a restful nature scene, you sit by the mountain stream, listen to the birds happily chirping back and forth with each other, and decide that you will buy the vehicle your friend introduced you to.

Ethical Considerations

It is important to acknowledge that the incredible possibilities created by emerging technologies also produce a number of ethical considerations. First, our environment is increasingly cluttered with persuasive media messages, including consumer advertisements. Advertisers and media owners must act responsibly in avoiding interruptive ads (Manluccia, 2015). Secondly, beyond the inconvenience and invasiveness of clutter, the interactivity of new media allows advertisers access to our personal information. A condition to using media content today, it seems, is giving up our rights to privacy. Turow et al. (2009) found that consumers do not accept this invasion of privacy for the sake of personalized ads, as the industry argues. At the same time, media users—citizens—often find it difficult to know the extent to which they are being monitored (Stole, 2014). Transparency should be the guiding principle, along with giving users the ability to establish the scope and parameters of the personalization. Finally, the power of presence to blur the line between reality and fiction could be easily abused, with potential serious effects on individuals and even cultures (see Olson, 2004). Again, transparency is critical; users need to be reminded before and after high presence experiences about the nature of the illusions.

Conclusion

Presence is not a new phenomenon, but emerging technologies are bringing it to the forefront of media experiences as they allow a range of possibilities for media users to enter more and more interesting, realistic, personalized, and interactive environments. Much of the industry and academic research on digital advertising does not adequately examine the complexity of users' perceptual experience with media and how this might impact advertiser-consumer interactions. Presence adds a layer of understanding by addressing the ways that people are socially and spatially immersed in all types of mediated experiences. Further, presence may help explain the appeal of interactive and personalized ads, as research indicates that people desire a sense of connection with the people and places they encounter in media.

Of course, the causes and consequences of presence experiences depend in complex ways on the form and content of the media presentation, attributes, and motivations of the viewer or user; the type of product or service (or idea) being promoted; and likely, many other factors (see Lombard & Ditton, 1997).

Researchers are just beginning to catalog, much less understand, the role of each of these factors (see Cummings & Bailenson, 2015). At the same time the technologies that evoke presence are changing: Advertisers have moved from a relatively few, distinct options (print ads featuring combinations of text and image, radio ads featuring voice and music, and network and local television ads featuring all of these) to a complex, fragmented, digital media environment with a vast array of options including everything from social media apps to immersive virtual worlds. In many cases the presence-evoking technologies and the experiences they create are novel (at this writing, VR headsets have just begun to enter the consumer market), and their ability to maintain their power to delight and persuade is unknown. But the evidence suggests (Reeves & Nass, 1996) and we strongly believe that because presence itself is a basic motivation, even as we adjust to each technology, a new "better" one will take its place. And advertisers, and all content producers, will need to adjust.

References

Amtrak. (n.d.). Meet Julie: Your virtual assistant. Retrieved May 1, 2016 from https://www.amtrak.com/about-julie-amtrak-virtual-travel-assistant.

Arroyo-Cañada, F. J., & Gil-Lafuente, J. (2012). Considerations of interactive digital television as advertising media. *Journal of Promotion Management, 18*(3), 306–318. http://doi.org/10.1080/10496491.2012.696456.

Arvidsson, A., & Bonini, T. (2015). Valuing audience passions: From Smythe to Tarde. *European Journal of Cultural Studies, 18*(2), 158–173. doi: 10.1177/1367549414563297.

Bang, H., & Wojdynski, B. W. (2016). Tracking users' visual attention and responses to personalized advertising based on task cognitive demand. *Computers in Human Behavior, 55*, 867–876. http://doi.org/10.1016/j.chb.2015.10.025.

Bezjian-Avery, A., Calder, B., & Iacobucci, D. (1998). New media interactive advertising vs. traditional advertising. *Journal of Advertising Research, 38*(4), 23–32.

Biocca, F. (2003, May). Can we resolve the book, the physical reality, and the dream state problems? From the two-pole to a three-pole model of shifts in presence. In *EU Future and Emerging Technologies, Presence Initiative Meeting.*

Blackman, S. (2012, August 21). Rise of the holograms: The next generation of airport employees. *Airport Technology.* Retrieved May 1, 2016 from http://www.airport-technology.com/features/featureholograms-next-generation-airport-employees/

Bleier, A., & Eisenbeiss, M. (2015). The importance of trust for personalized online advertising. *Journal of Retailing, 91*(3), 390–409. http://doi.org/10.1016/j.jretai.2015.04.001.

Brandow, M. (2016, March 14). Engagement matters. Emotion sells. Data fuels [Web log post]. Retrieved from http://www.mediapost.com/publications/article/271175/engagement-matters-emotion-sells-data-fuels.html.

Bright, L. F. (2011). Media evolution and web 2.0 technologies. In M. S. Eastin, T. D. Daugherty, & N. M. Burns (Eds.), *Handbook of research on digital media and advertising: User generated content consumption* (pp. 32–51). Hershey, PA: IGI-Global. Retrieved from Ebscohost ebook collection.

Buss, D., (2012, May 10). Peapod expands virtual grocery shopping to Chicago. *Brand Channel.* Retrieved from http://brandchannel.com/2012/05/10/peapod-expands-virtual-grocery-shopping-to-chicago/

Cauberghe, V., Geuens, M., & De Pelsmacker, P. (2011). Context effects of TV programme-induced interactivity and telepresence on advertising responses. *International Journal of Advertising, 30*(4), 641–663. doi: 10.2501/IJA-30-4-641-663.

Choi, Y. K., Miracle, G. E., & Biocca, F. (2001). The effects of anthropomorphic agents on advertising effectiveness and the mediating role of presence. *Journal of Interactive Advertising, 2*(1), 19–32. doi: 10.1080/15252019.2001.10722055.

Cisco. (2006, October 23). Cisco announces the Cisco telepresence meeting solution—A breakthrough "in-person" experience for real-time, remote, business communication and collaboration [Press release]. Retrieved from http://www.cisco.com/cisco/web/UK/news/archive/2006/102306.html.

Cummings, J. J., & Bailenson, J. N. (2015). How immersive is enough? A meta-analysis of the effect of immersive technology on user presence. *Media Psychology, 19*(2), 272–309. doi: 10.1080/15213269.2015.1015740.

Debbabi, S., Daassi, M., & Baile, S. (2010). Effect of online 3D advertising on consumer responses: The mediating role of telepresence. *Journal of Marketing Management, 26*(9–10), 967–992. doi: 10.1080/02672570903498819.

de Boer, C. N., Verleur, R., Heuvelman, A., & Heynderickx, I. (2010). Added value of an autostereoscopic multiview 3-D display for advertising in a public environment. *Displays, 31*(1), 1–8. http://dx.doi.org/10.1016/j.displa.2009.09.001.

DeFleur, M. L., & Dennis, E. E. (1996). *Understanding mass communication.* Boston, MA: Houghton Mifflin Company.

Dickey, I., & Lewis, W. (2011). An overview of digital media and advertising. In M. S. Eastin, T. D. Daugherty, & N. M. Burns (Eds.), *Handbook of research on digital media and advertising: User generated content consumption* (pp. 1–31). Hershey, PA: IGI-Global. Retrieved from Ebscohost ebook collection.

Edwards, S. M., Li, H., & Lee, J. H. (2002). Forced exposure and psychological reactance: Antecedents and consequences of the perceived intrusiveness of pop-up ads. *Journal of Advertising, 31*(3), 83–95. http://doi.org/10.1080/00913367.2002.10673678.

Fortin, D. R., & Dholakia, R. R. (2005). Interactivity and vividness effects on social presence and involvement with a web-based advertisement. *Journal of Business Research, 58*(3), 387–396. doi: 10.1016/S0148-2963(03)00106-1.

Gangadharbatla, H. (2012). Social media and advertising theory. In S. Rodgers & E. Thorson (Eds.), *Advertising theory* (pp. 402–416). New York, NY: Routledge.

Gaudiosi, J. (2016, March 5). ABC and Lexus launch "Quantico" virtual reality experience. *Fortune.* Retrieved from http://fortune.com/2016/03/05/abc-and-lexus-launch-quantico-vr/

Genuth, I. (2013, April 11). Nike launched a holographic 3D advertising campaign. *The Future of Things.* Retrieved May 1, 2016 from http://thefutureofthings.com/5069-nike-launched-a-holographic-3d-advertising-campaign/

Ginovsky, J. (2013, August 27). Banks need to rethink telepresence approach: Use it to improve customer engagement, not reinvent teller experience. *Banking Exchange.* Retrieved May 1, 2016 from http://www.bankingexchange.com/news-feed/item/3898-banks-need-to-rethink-telepresence-approach.

Grigorovici, D. (2003). Persuasive effects of presence in immersive virtual environments. In G. Riva, F. Davide, & W. A. Ijsselsteijn (Eds.), *Being there: Concepts, effects and measurement of user presence in synthetic environments.* Amsterdam, The Netherlands: IOS Press. Retrieved from http://www.neurovr.org/emerging/book4/4_13GRIGOR.PDF.

Haans, A., & IJsselsteijn, W. A. (2012). Embodiment and telepresence: Toward a comprehensive theoretical framework. *Interacting with Computers, 24*(4), 211–218. doi: 10.1016/j.intcom.2012.04.010.

Hopkins, C. D., Raymond, M. A., & Mitra, A. (2004). Consumer responses to perceived telepresence in the online advertising environment: The moderating role of involvement. *Marketing Theory, 4*(1), 137–162. doi: 10.1177/1470593104044090.

Horton, D., & Wohl, R. (1956). Mass communication and para-social interaction: Observations on intimacy at a distance. *Psychiatry, 19*(3), 215–229. doi: 10.1521/00332747.1956.11023049.

Howard, D. J., & Kerin, R. A. (2004). The effects of personalized product recommendations on advertisement response rates: The "try this. It works!" technique. *Journal of Consumer Psychology, 14*(3), 271–279. doi: 10.1207/s15327663jcp1403_8.

Humans Invent. (2013, February 11). The future of advertising will stop you in your tracks. *Gizmodo UK*. Retrieved from http://www.gizmodo.co.uk/2013/02/the-future-of-advertising-looks-creepy/

International Society for Presence Research. (2000). *The concept of presence: Explication statement*. Retrieved from https://ispr.info/about-presence-2/about-presence/

Jack, L. (2015, May 4). An adorable homeless dog follows people around, via a new interactive billboard. *Fast Company*. Retrieved from http://www.fastcocreate.com/3045876/an-adorable-homeless-dog-follows-people-around-via-a-new-interactive-billboard.

Jenkins, H., Ford, S., & Green, J. (2013). *Spreadable media: Creating value and meaning in a networked culture*. New York, NY: New York University Press.

Jin, S. A. (2009). Modality effects in second life: The mediating role of social presence and the moderating role of product involvement. *Cyberpsychology & Behavior, 12*(6), 717–721. doi: 10.1089/cpb.2008.0273.

Johnson, L. (2015a, April 9). Is virtual reality the next big form of in-bar entertainment? Jim Beam and Dos Equis have been quick to embrace the trend. *AdWeek*. Retrieved from http://www.adweek.com/news/technology/virtual-reality-next-big-form-bar-entertainment-163963.

Johnson, L. (2015b, May 1). Drones are filming seriously jaw-dropping virtual reality video for brands: Patrón goes inside the agave field. *AdWeek*. Retrieved from http://www.adweek.com/news/technology/drones-are-filming-seriously-jaw-dropping-virtual-reality-video-brands-164433.

Kim, J., & McMillan, S. J. (2008). Evaluation of internet advertising research. *Journal of Advertising, 37*(1), 99–112. http://doi.org/10.2753/JOA0091–3367370108.

Klein, L. R. (2003). Creating virtual product experiences: The role of telepresence. *Journal of Interactive Marketing, 17*(1), 41–55. doi: 10.1002/dir.10046.

Knowles, K. (2016, April 27). Step into a spy's shoes: Top TV series launches first virtual reality spin-off. *The Memo*. Retrieved from http://www.thememo.com/2016/04/27/vr-le-bureau-des-legendes-virtual-reality-le-bureau-des-legendes-360-video/

Kolbe, L., Salomann, H., & Brenner, W. (2006). Self-services in customer relationships: Balancing high-tech and high-touch today and tomorrow. *e-Service Journal, 4*(2), 65–84. doi: 10.2979/esj.2006.4.2.65.

Lazzaro, S. (2016, March 28). 7 movies you can experience in virtual reality. *Observer*. Retrieved from http://observer.com/2016/03/7-movies-you-can-experience-in-virtual-reality/

Lessiter, J., Freeman, J., Keogh, E., & Davidoff, J. (2001). A cross-media presence questionnaire: The ITC-sense of presence inventory. *Presence, 10*(3), 282–297. doi: 10.1162/105474601300343612.

Lewis-Kraus, G. (2016, March 2). Check in with the velociraptor at the world's first robot hotel. *Wired*. Retrieved from http://www.wired.com/2016/03/robot-henna-hotel-japan/

Li, S. (2016, April 10). How retail stores are using virtual reality to make shopping more fun. *Los Angeles Times*. Retrieved from http://www.latimes.com/business/la-fi-retail-vr-20160410-story.html.

Li, H., Daugherty, T., & Biocca, F. (2002). Impact of 3-D advertising on product knowledge, brand attitude, and purchase intention: The mediating role of presence. *Journal of Advertising, 31*(3), 43–57. doi: 10.1080/00913367.2002.10673675.

Lombard, M., & Ditton, T. B. (1997). At the heart of it all: The concept of presence. *Journal of Computer-Mediated Communication, 3*(2), n.p. doi: 10.1111/j.1083–6101.1997.tb00072.x.

Lombard, M., & Jones, M. T. (2015). Defining presence. In M. Lombard, F. Biocca, W. A. Ijsselsteijn, J. Freeman, & R. Schaevitz (Eds.), *Immersed in media: Telepresence theory, measurement and technology* (pp. 13–34). London: Springer.

Lombard, M., & Snyder-Duch, J. (2001). Interactive advertising and presence: A framework. *Journal of Interactive Advertising, 1*(2), 56–65. doi: 10.1080/15252019.2001.10722051.

Lombard, M., & Sun, W. (2016). Outside the lab: A direct, mixed-method approach to examining telepresence experiences in everyday life. Unpublished manuscript.

Lombard, M., Weinstein, L., & Ditton, T. (2011, October). Measuring telepresence: The validity of the Temple Presence Inventory (TPI) in a gaming context. In *Proceedings of the 2011 Annual Conference of the International Society for Presence Research (ISPR)*, Edinburgh, Scotland. Retrieved from http://astro.temple.edu/~lombard/ISPR/Proceedings/2011/Lombard_etal.pdf.

Manluccia, N. (2015, October 30). How to avoid the potential horrors of virtual reality marketing: Don't let virtual reality ads become virtual prisons for consumers. *Advertising Age*. Retrieved from http://adage.com/article/digitalnext/avoid-horrors-virtual-reality-marketing/301135/

Microsoft HoloLens (n.d.). Official site. Retrieved on May 4, 2016 from https://www.microsoft.com/microsoft-hololens/en-us.

Minsker, M. (2013). Digital advertising gets personal. *CRM Magazine, 17*(10), 22–26. Retrieved from Ebscohost Academic Search Premiere database.

Minsky, M. (1980). Telepresence. *OMNI Magazine*. Retrieved from http://web.media.mit.edu/~minsky/papers/Telepresence.html.

Mollen, A., & Wilson, H. (2010). Engagement, telepresence and interactivity in online consumer experience: Reconciling scholastic and managerial perspectives. *Journal of Business Research, 63*(9/10), 919–925. doi: 10.1016/j.jbusres.2009.05.014.

Napoli, P. M. (2011). *Audience evolution: New technologies and the transformation of media audiences*. New York, NY: Columbia University Press.

Nelson, M. R., Yaros, R. A., & Keum, H. (2006). Examining the influence of telepresence on spectator and player processing of real and fictitious brands in a computer game. *Journal of Advertising, 35*(4), 87–99. doi: 10.2753/JOA0091–3367350406.

Olson, S. R. (2004). The extensions of synergy: Product placement through theming and environmental simulacra. *Journal of Promotion Management, 10*(1–2), 65–87. doi: 10.1300/J057v10n01_06.

Reeves, B., & Nass, C. (1996). *The media equation: How people treat computers, televisions, and new media as real people and places*. Cambridge, UK: Cambridge University Press.

Robertson, A. (2015, September 10). What virtual reality postcards can tell us about the future of travel. *The Verge*. Retrieved from http://www.theverge.com/2015/9/10/9289073/marriott-virtual-reality-postcard-samsung-gear-vr.

Rodgers, S., & Thorson, E. (2000). The interactive advertising model: How users perceive and process online ads. *Journal of Interactive Advertising, 1*(1), 42–61. doi: 10.1080/15252019.2000.10722043.

Rodriguez, A. (2014, October 28). Meet Lowe's newest sales associate—OSHbot, the robot. *Advertising Age.* Retrieved from http://adage.com/article/cmo-strategy/meet-lowe-s-newest-sales-associate-oshbot-robot/295591/

Russell, C. A., & Stern, B. B. (2006). Consumers, characters, and products—a balance model of sitcom product placement effects. *Journal of Advertising, 35*(1), 7–21. doi: 10.2753/JOA0091–3367350101.

Schoenfeld, A. (2012, February 1). 5 ways to report on engagement [Web log post]. Retrieved from http://simplymeasured.com/blog/5-ways-to-report-on-engagement/

Schubert, T., & Crusius, J. (2002). Five theses on the book problem: Presence in books, film and VR. In *PRESENCE 2002-Proceedings of the Fifth International Workshop on Presence.* Porto, Portugal: Universidad Fernando Pessoa.

Simola, J., Kivikangas, M., Kuisma, J., & Krause, C. M. (2013). Attention and memory for newspaper advertisements: Effects of ad-editorial congruency and location. *Applied Cognitive Psychology, 27*(4), 429–442. doi: 10.1002/acp.2918.

Smith, K. T. (2012). Longitudinal study of digital marketing strategies targeting millennials. *The Journal of Consumer Marketing, 29*(2), 86–92. http://doi.org/10.1108/07363761211206339.

Stole, I. L. (2014). Persistent pursuit of personal information: A historical perspective on digital advertising strategies. *Critical Studies in Media Communication, 31*(2), 129–133. http://doi.org/10.1080/15295036.2014.921319.

Sundar, S. S., & Kim, J. (2005). Interactivity and persuasion: Influencing attitudes with information and involvement. *Journal of Interactive Advertising, 5*(2), 5–18. http://dx.doi.org/10.1080/15252019.2005.10722097.

Takahashi, D. (2014, December 8). MediaSpike creates cool in-game native ads for virtual reality. *VentureBeat.* Retrieved from http://venturebeat.com/2014/12/08/mediaspike-creates-cool-in-game-native-ads-for-virtual-reality/

Tam, K. Y., & Ho, S. Y. (2005). Web personalization as a persuasion strategy: An elaboration likelihood model perspective. *Information Systems Research, 16*(3), 271–291. http://dx.doi.org/10.1287/isre.1050.0058.

Tanyel, F., Stuart, E. W., & Griffin, J. (2013). Have "millennials" embraced digital advertising as they have embraced digital media? *Journal of Promotion Management, 19*(5), 652–673. http://doi.org/10.1080/10496491.2013.829161.

Thorpe, V. (2016, April 30). BBC in race with theme park giants to build hi-tech visitor attractions. *The Guardian.* Retrieved from http://www.theguardian.com/media/2016/apr/30/bbc-theme-park-doctor-who-visitor-attractions.

Tikkanen, H., Hietanen, J., Henttonen, T., & Rokka, J. (2009). Exploring virtual worlds: Success factors in virtual world marketing. *Management Decision, 47*(8), 1357–1381. http://dx.doi.org/10.1108/00251740910984596.

Turow, J., & Draper, N. (2014). Industry conceptions of audience in the digital space. *Cultural Studies, 28*(4), 643–656. http://doi.org/10.1080/09502386.2014.888929.

Turow, J., King, J., Hoofnagle, C. J., Bleakley, A., & Hennessy, M. (2009, September 29). Americans reject tailored advertising and three activities that enable it. Retrieved from http://ssrn.com/abstract=1478214 or http://dx.doi.org/10.2139/ssrn.1478214.

Wang, A. (2006). Advertising engagement: A driver of message involvement on message effects. *Journal of Advertising Research, 46*(4), 355–368. doi: 10.2501/S0021849906060429.

Warc. (n.d.). Case study summary: Battersea cats and dogs home: Looking for you. Retrieved from http://www.warc.com/Pages/Taxonomy/Marketing%20Intelligence/Brands/Battersea%20Dogs%20and%20Cats%20Home/Results.Index?DVals=4294633669&Sort=ContentDate|1&Filter=All.

Wells, W., Burnett, J., & Moriarity, S. (1998). *Advertising principles & practices* (4th ed.). Upper Saddle River, NJ: Prentice Hall.

Xu, K., & Lombard, M. (2016, June). *Media are social actors: Expanding the CASA paradigm in the 21st century*. Paper presented at the International Communication Association conference, Fukuoka, Japan.

Yang, K. C. (2006). The influence of humanlike navigation interface on users' responses to internet advertising. *Telematics and Informatics, 23*(1), 38–55. http://dx.doi.org/10.1016/j.tele.2005.03.001.

Yim, M. Y. C., Cicchirillo, V. J., & Drumwright, M. E. (2012). The impact of stereoscopic three-dimensional (3-D) advertising. *Journal of Advertising, 41*(2), 113–128. http://dx.doi.org/10.2753/JOA0091-3367410208.

11

USING DIGITAL MEDIA TO IMPROVE PUBLIC HEALTH COMMUNICATION

Marla B. Royne, Kathrynn Pounders, Marian Levy, and Amy Rebecca Jones

As our society is increasingly plagued by a plethora of chronic diseases, effective health communication appears more important than ever. For example, obesity runs rampant across the U.S. among both adults and children (Ogden, Carroll, Kit, & Flegal, 2014), and diabetes is on the rise (CDC, 2014). Many Americans do not exercise on a regular basis and often fail to adhere to a healthy diet. These problems and others are often caused by unhealthy lifestyle choices, sometimes due to a lack of knowledge about the importance of healthy behaviors and how to more easily integrate them into busy lives. As such, it is important for health messages to be more effective in message and media strategies, as well as in reaching the target audience.

With these diseases becoming more prevalent in society, it requires consumers to become more engaged in their own healthcare. To accomplish this, they will need deeper knowledge of health issues. One way this may be done is for public health professionals to begin to market public health information in the same way corporations market their products (Royne & Levy, 2011). While corporations have had great success implementing sound persuasion strategy, such approaches have not been utilized as effectively in public health (Royne & Levy, 2011). Although marketing is used by corporations as a potentially powerful tool that can influence consumers' purchase behaviors, creative marketing approaches are less common in public health (Royne & Levy, 2011). If public health were to use more effective corporate marketing techniques by using contemporary digital media and creative messages to reach those in need of important information, it could help to improve individuals' lives and well being.

Based on this premise, the purpose of this chapter is to discuss how digital media can be used to effectively deliver health communications in a world of changing healthcare and increased chronic disease. Specifically, this chapter provides an overview of some pressing healthcare issues in our society and discusses various digital media and how they may be used to provide health information. This is followed by a discussion of message strategies and how message strategies may be used by digital media to further improve the provision of important health information.

Intractable Problems Related to Lifestyle

The U.S. currently faces a public health crisis that has critical personal, societal, and economic implications. Four of the 10 leading causes of death in the U.S. (i.e., heart disease, cancer, diabetes, and stroke) are due to chronic diseases, with heart disease and cancer accounting for nearly one-half of all deaths (CDC, 2011; CDC, 2013). More than one-half of all Americans suffer from at least one preventable chronic condition (Ward, Schiller, & Goodman, 2014), and the cost of seven major chronic diseases (i.e., cancer, heart disease, hypertension, stroke, diabetes, pulmonary, and mental conditions) has been estimated at $1.3 trillion annually in human capital, medical expenditures, and loss of economic productivity (Devol & Bedroussian, 2007).

Many chronic diseases share risk factors related to three modifiable lifestyle behaviors: tobacco use, unhealthy diet, and physical inactivity (Arbeit, Johnson, & Mott, 1992). Obesity is a significant and underlying factor in these conditions, and has been fueled by substantial increases in food intake and sedentary behavior over the past few decades. Currently, 35 percent of U.S. adults are obese (Ogden, et al., 2014), and the direct and indirect cost of adult obesity is estimated at $209 billion, representing more than one-fifth of U.S. healthcare expenditures (Cawley & Meyerhoefer, 2012). Further, nearly 17 percent of U.S. children and adolescents aged 2–19 are obese (Ogden, et al., 2014). This is cause for concern because obesity in childhood often continues into adulthood (Ogden, Carroll, Kit, & Flegal, 2012), and childhood obesity is associated with a number of negative health consequences (Freedman, Mei, Srinivasan, Berenson, & Dietz, 2007; Puhl & Latner, 2007; Sutherland, 2008; Han, Lawlor, & Kimm, 2010). Moreover, few Americans consume a healthy diet. The typical food intake of 80–99 percent of Americans fails to meet recommended levels of fruits, vegetables, whole grains, and reduced-fat dairy products (Krebs-Smith, Guenther, Subar, Kirkpatrick, & Dodd, 2010).

Unhealthy lifestyles fueled by poor consumer choices are the result of a myriad of social and environmental influences, including television viewing habits (Dietz & Gortmaker, 1985), sweetened beverages (Malik, Schulze, & Hu, 2006), and diets consisting of fast food (Rosenheck, 2008), all of which have been examined in the larger, ecological context of social, physical, and media environments (Reisch et al., 2013). Clearly, environment is a major influence on individual behaviors, and today's environment includes a significant digital component that permeates all levels of society.

Targeted Marketing of Unhealthy Products to Vulnerable Populations

The advertising industry has played a substantial role in creating an environment that can adversely affect health behaviors (Royne & Levy, 2011). For example, the successful marketing of unhealthy food and beverages, as well as tobacco and alcohol products (Moore, Williams, & Qualls, 1996), has contributed to the development of adverse health outcomes (Grier & Kumanyika, 2008). Vulnerable populations, such as children and minorities, have been targeted by food marketers in the form of popular characters on packaging, product placement, toys, interactive marketing, and more recently, digital media (Story & French, 2004; Grier & Kumanyika, 2008; Culp, Bell, & Cassady, 2010; IOM, 2013). In 2009, the food industry spent $1.79 billion on marketing to youth aged 2–17 (FTC, 2012). Even with the proposed guidelines of Interagency Working Group on Foods Marketed to Children, the "IWG," designed to regulate the nutritional quality of foods advertised to children, only 1.4 percent of television advertisements comply with all aspects of IWG guidelines (Hingle, Castonguay, Ambuel, Smith, & Kunkel, 2015).

Not surprisingly, national data indicate that adolescents obtain an increasingly higher proportion of calories through snacking (Piernas & Popkin, 2010), and a recent study found disparities persist in snacking patterns among vulnerable populations (Larson, Story, Eisenberg, & Nuemark-Sztainer, 2016). For example, consumption of energy dense, nutrient-poor snacks and sugary beverages were highest among low-income, African American, Native American, and adolescents of mixed origin (Larson et al., 2016). Substantial disparities also exist in the prevalence of childhood obesity by socio-demographic characteristics including age, sex, race/ethnicity, and socioeconomic status. For instance, the largest disparities in childhood obesity occur between non–Hispanic black girls (22%) compared to non–Hispanic white girls (13%) and between Mexican American boys (24%) compared to non–Hispanic white boys (15%) (CDC, 2013).

The public health community points out the detrimental impact of food and beverage marketing to children adversely affecting food knowledge, dietary intake, consumption behaviors, and health, including obesity (WHO, 2009). In response to the finding that television advertisements market foods high in nutrients that promote chronic disease (e.g., fat, saturated fat, sodium) and undersupply protective nutrients (e.g., fiber, vitamins, antioxidants), health professionals suggest strategies related to education, coalition building with the food industry, and policy change (Mink, Evans, Moore, Calderon, & Degar, 2010). However, this approach fails to capitalize on the potential of marketing and emphasizes the need for alternative approaches to traditional health communication strategies.

As noted by the Centers for Disease Control and Prevention, health communication "includes using multiple behavioral and social learning theories and models to advance program planning, and identifying steps to influence audience attitudes and behavior" (CDC, 2016, n.p.). With this definition in mind, we provide a brief discussion of a social-ecological model that is useful for health promotion.

Social-Ecological Model for Health Promotion

The social-ecological model for health promotion is based on the understanding that behavior change is a function not only of educational activities, but also advocacy, organizational change, policy development, economic support, environmental change, and multi-method strategies (see McLeroy, Bibeau, Steckler, & Glantz, 1988; Stokols, 1996). Specifically, individuals interact within multiple levels of influence; they exist within social networks, which in turn exist within surrounding environments (McLeroy et al., 1988).

This ecological perspective focuses attention on both individual *and* social environmental factors as targets for health promotion interventions. It highlights the importance of approaching public health problems at multiple levels and advocates the simultaneous, concurrent change across five more complex levels of influence: individual, interpersonal, organizational, community, and public policy (McLeRoy, Bibeau, Steckler, & Glantz, 1988; Stokols, 1996). The model assumes that appropriate changes in the social environment will produce changes in individuals, and that mutual and interdependent support of individuals within the population is essential for implementing environmental changes (McLeroy et al., 1988).

According to McLeroy et al. (1988), the first level of influence is comprised of individual factors. This includes specific personal characteristics that influence behaviors, such as knowledge, attitudes, beliefs, and preferences. The second level includes interpersonal factors and involves interpersonal processes and primary relationships with family, friends, and peers that provide social identity, support, and role definition (McLeroy et al., 1988). For example, parents help shape youth attitudes and behaviors by modeling food behaviors. The next level, organizational factors, includes rules, policies, environmental, and informal structures within an institution or system, such as schools, worksites, and neighborhoods, in which social relationships occur. Community factors refer to the social networks, norms, standards, and practices that exist formally or informally in relationships among organizations, such as church groups. Finally, public policy factors include local, state, and federal policies and laws that regulate or support desired behaviors (McLeroy et al., 1988). And, of course, all of these factors may inhibit or promote desirable behaviors.

In sum, although the social-ecological model briefly reviewed here was conceptualized long before digital media, it can still be used for understanding health communication that relates to digital advertising. First, the social-ecological perspective of effective health communication stresses the interaction and integration of factors both within and across all five levels (McLeroy et al., 1988). Second, the theoretical framework recognizes behavior is influenced by the complex and interwoven relationships that exist between an individual and his/her environment. Last, the model acknowledges that while consumers are responsible for their lifestyle choices, consumer behavior is also largely influenced by social and environmental influences related to community norms, regulations, and policies. As such, health messages from health practitioners should start at the individual level of the social-ecological model and capitalize on digital tools and appropriate messages to reach the social networks at a greater level, several of which are reviewed next.

Digital Media and Public Health Messages

The growth and acceptance of digital media along with the increased need for public health information suggests the use of today's newest marketing techniques may be highly appropriate for health communication in today's society. About 92 percent of all adults use digital media (Pew Internet, 2015). At the same time, vulnerable populations and ethnic groups, who at one time were less likely to use technology, are now regular users of digital media. For example, the Pew Research Center (2015) notes, "Blacks and whites are on more equal footing when it comes to . . . mobile platforms" (n.p.). About 92 percent of African Americans, 93 percent of Hispanics, and 91 percent of whites have a cell phone (Pew Internet, 2015). Moreover, 68 percent of African Americans, 64 percent of Hispanics, and 66 percent of whites have a smartphone (Pew Internet, 2015).

Clearly, digital media continue to evolve, and a wide range of digital tools is available to reach the public and provide informative messages that can encourage healthy lifestyles. Digital tools, such as exercise apps and digital personal assistants that send doctors' reminders, represent an intersection between interpersonal communication and mass media. This is noteworthy because interpersonal communication has been related to health behavior change (Seo & Matsaganis, 2013). Thus, using digital media platforms and technologies such as Facebook, YouTube, and FitBit to communicate health information has the potential to result in improved health outcomes. For example, in 2011 the Canadian agency ReThink created a digital multi-platform, cutting-edge breast cancer campaign that focused on encouraging women to do self-checks with a twist (Rethinkbreastcancer.com, n.d.). Because digital media interpersonal communication channels ultimately lead to mass communications channels as part of the shared social network, digital tools (e.g., Facebook, Twitter, Snapchat) seem particularly appropriate for the social ecological model, which is grounded in individual, environmental, and social levels.

Through use of analytics and targeting software, the digital environment allows for effective dissemination of public health messages (e.g., Cohen et al., 2010; Park, Rodgers & Stemmle, 2013). By being able to tailor and target health messages to consumers based on their demographic, psychographic, and behavioral data, it offers the ability for today's public health professionals to get persuasive messages out to their intended market. Public health professionals can also gain specific knowledge of their audiences, ranging from demographics, behavioral data, and psychographic information in the form of product and brand likes and dislikes, activities and interests, as well as the use of social media and other digital tools.

With the growth of the internet and social media networks, users are able to find more information and connect with individuals to discuss issues more than ever before. For example, the internet provides resources for chronic disease self-management through provision of specialized health information, social support, and psychosocial benefits (e.g., Dobransky & Hargittai, 2012; Househ, Borycki, & Kushniruk, 2014) via online communities. Fox (2010) reports that about one in four consumers engage regularly with an online health community. These communities provide emotional support and shared knowledge to consumers by engaging with similar individuals online (Frost & Massagli, 2008). This is consistent with Seo and Matsaganis (2013), who find that interpersonal channels are more successful in changing both attitudes and behaviors. Moreover, existing work shows the power of mass media in reaching and informing large audiences (Wakefield, Loken, & Hornik, 2010). That is, online health communities are essentially an intersection of mass media and interpersonal communication (Walther et al., 2010), offering a digital alternative for activating health behavior change (Webb, Joseph, Yardley, & Michie, 2010) through online interaction.

Along with online communities, it is important for healthcare providers to use online tools to provide consumers with updated information and enhance services. For instance, a healthcare provider (e.g., physician's office, pharmacy) could use various outlets, such as patient portals, text messages, or social media to communicate information about flu immunization and/or tips on how to reduce illness risk. These outlets could also be used to introduce new doctors, update the community on relevant health issues, and provide wellness tips to patients.

When it comes to social media, Facebook leads the way with more than 1.65 billion monthly active users across the globe (Facebook, 2016), a total population larger than most countries. Other popular social media include Twitter, known for people sharing 140-character text messages as well as photos and videos, which provides opportunities for sharing short bursts of information; Instagram, which launched in 2010, is a social media resource where pictures and short video clips can be shared by users; and YouTube, a popular digital tool used to post videos (for a review of social media use for health, refer to Koteyko, Hunt, & Gunter, 2015; Lefebvre & Bornkessel, 2016).

Underlying the use of all of these social media is the ability for health information to "go viral." Virality may be explained by comparing it to emotional contagion, where the emotions of one individual are transferred to another via some type of communication. This emotion may be positive or negative, and the concept has been tested in a number of social sciences including psychology, sociology, and marketing (Hatfield, Cacioppo, & Rapson, 1994). Although the emotional contagion research has been examined primarily within the context of personal interactions, it has been suggested that the transfer of emotions does not necessarily demand physical contact (Hasford, Hardesty, & Kidwell, 2015), and as such these emotional effects may be experienced via online communications.

Although typically associated with brand placement, advergames represent another contemporary approach to digital media (also see more perspectives on advertising in games, Chapters 18 and 25). Advergames are specifically designed interactive online games that contain embedded brand messages to promote a product, brand, or service (Bellman, Kemp, Haddad, & varan, 2014) via gaming and entertainment (Vashisht & Sreejesh, 2015). Advergames are believed to be more effective advertising tools as compared to traditional media (Wade, 2004) because advergames can engage consumer attention for longer time spans (Edwards, 2003), generate more involvement compared to traditional television programming (Nicovich, 2005), have potentially more viral marketing ability, and are more cost effective (Ipe, 2008). Additionally, consumers are less susceptible to the effects of suspicion and persuasion knowledge of advergames as compared to traditional advertising formats (Friestad & Wright, 1994; Obermiller, Spangenberg, & MacLachlan, 2005). Finally, as compared to traditional advertising, advergames may become hypnotic or enthralling in nature as the game becomes more important to the player (Nicovich, 2005).

Digital devices such as smartphones, smartwatches, and tablets, also link consumers to a variety of health-related apps designed for tasks such as monitoring calorie intake, calories burned, steps per day, blood glucose, pulse rate, and sleep patterns. These apps, often free or available for a minimal charge, have a potentially huge impact on consumers and their physical health (see Garcia-Gomez et al., 2014).

In addition to self-monitoring, many apps allow consumers the opportunity to share information with their social network and/or others who are using the same app. Interacting with others may serve as a source of motivation for some consumers. Social comparison theory (Festinger, 1954) states that self-evaluation, self-improvement, and self-enhancement are primary motivations for social comparisons. Making an upward comparison to a referent that is perceived to be better than oneself on a specific attribute may motivate a person to improve on the attribute. For example, if a consumer has the Nike App and realizes that most people in the network are more active than they are, they may be inspired to increase their level of physical activity. Social comparisons can be particularly motivating when consumers compare themselves to peers or friends (Lockwood & Kunda, 1997).

Message Strategies for Digital Media

Effective communications will result if an effective message strategy is in place. At its most basic level, advertising messages fall within a broad two-level categorization model: rational and emotional messages. Rational messages focus more on functional benefits, facts, and statistics to communicate the information. This approach appeals to the consumer's logic. In contrast, emotional messages appeal to a person's feelings with the goal of eliciting an emotional response such as humor, happiness, fear, or guilt. The belief is that emotional appeals provide a connection at a visceral level. Both rational and emotional appeals can be effective. Considerable research has focused on the situations that might prove one appeal to be more effective than the other. While a review of this body of literature is outside the scope of this chapter, we do provide an overview of rational and emotional appeals in health messages that may prove effective in digital media. This distinction is important for two reasons.

First, in digital media, and social media in particular, engagement is extremely important, and the message content directly affects consumer engagement. Second, consumers respond to emotional appeals and rational appeals differently, and the various types of appeals within these two broad categories will generate different responses. Moreover, reactions to digital media will be digital in nature by virtue of their characteristics. For example, people will share information online more quickly and more readily than sharing a printed newspaper story because of the ease of communication. Further, people share content online for many different reasons, but generally, more emotional content leads to more arousal (Heilman, 1997), and high arousal emotions (Berger, 2011) such as anxiety (Gross & Levenson, 1995) lead to more sharing than low arousal emotions such as sadness.

Recognizing the different emotional reactions among consumers, earlier this year Facebook expanded their traditional "Like" button to include an additional five animated emoji reactions: Love, Haha, Wow, Sad, and Angry. This allows individuals to specifically express their emotional response to the posted message when a simple thumbs up is just not enough.

Finally, different types of digital media may be more relevant for emotional versus rational messages. For instance, certain rational messages might be best communicated via Twitter, because it is a verbally based platform. However, effective emotional messages may require visual elements and hence, may be more suited to Facebook and YouTube than Twitter.

Rational Appeals

Health messages typically utilize common message elements. For example, most health communication advertisements convey risk, advocate a healthy action or unhealthy inaction, and appeal to the self or one's family. It is important to understand how combining these elements influence the efficacy of health communication. Accordingly, this section will focus on these various message elements and identifying when they are most efficacious. Provided that health messages typically illustrate the undesired outcome of contracting an illness or disease and advocate an action (or inaction) to obtain a healthy outcome, a large body of work has examined regulatory focus.

Regulatory Focus Theory suggests people are motivated to minimize the discrepancy between actual and desired end states (Higgins, 1997, 1998). Specifically, people seek pleasure and avoid pain (Higgins, 1997, 1998). To achieve this goal, Regulatory Focus Theory suggests two types of self-regulation systems: promotion-focused and prevention-focused. A promotion-focused regulation system is associated with emphasizing aspirations and achievements and focuses on the presence and absence of positive outcomes. Additionally, a promotion-focused regulation system uses an approach strategy of goal attainment. A prevention-focused regulation system is associated with emphasizing safety and protection and focuses on the presence of negative outcomes. A prevention-focused regulation system is associated with an avoidance strategy of goal attainment.

A large stream of research in persuasion has focused on regulatory fit, which refers to the notion that although a goal may be pursued with either a promotion or prevention focus, some goals are more compatible with a specific self-regulatory strategy, resulting in a higher level of "fit" (Higgins, 2002b). For example, approach goals that strive toward a desirable end state tend to be more compatible with a promotion focus, whereas avoidance goals that seek to deter an undesirable end state tend to be more compatible with a prevention focus (Higgins, 2002a; Cesario, Grant, & Higgins, 2004). The fit occurs because striving for a gain involves more eagerness than guarding against a non-gain, and guarding against a loss involves more vigilance than striving for a non-loss (Idson, Liberman, & Higgins, 2000).

Although regulatory focus was initially conceptualized as a relatively stable chronic trait (Higgins, 1997, 1998, 2002a), it can be situationally induced (Higgins, 1997, 1998; Lee & Aaker, 2004). For example, messages can emphasize the positive outcomes of targeted behaviors (e.g., "regular exercise can promote a healthy heart!") and encourage audiences to pursue gains. In contrast, messages can focus on negative outcomes resulting from noncompliance of targeted behaviors and focus on the prevention of those outcomes (e.g., "regular exercise can prevent heart disease!"). Thus, much work on regulatory focus has concentrated on understanding the effectiveness of promotion-focused and prevention-focused messages.

A large stream of prior research has focused on the effects of regulatory fit in persuasion. That is, when the regulatory focus of a message is consistent with individuals' dispositional tendency or primed goal direction, the persuasive effects are increased. Promotion-focused messages are more persuasive among those with promotion goals, while the opposite holds true for those with prevention goals (e.g., Cesario, Grant, & Higgins, 2004). Such regulatory fit has been shown to result in positive persuasion outcomes. Kim (2006) examined how message framing influenced the effectiveness of antismoking messages. Results showed that when regulatory goals were congruent with the antismoking message frame participants perceived lower benefits related to smoking and indicated they were less likely to smoke in the future.

Lee and Aaker (2004) found that regulatory focus moderates message framing on persuasion. Their work demonstrated gain frames are more persuasive when the message is promotion-focused, whereas loss frames are more persuasive when the message is prevention-focused. Additionally, this work showed increased eagerness toward positive outcomes and increased vigilance against negative outcomes when there was a match between the message frame and the regulatory focus of the message. This was attributed to fluency and "feeling" right when processing the message. This has implications for health communications in terms of pairing message frame with the appropriate type of message.

Self-efficacy and response-efficacy have long been central components of health communication strategy. Generally speaking, self-efficacy refers to the ease of the advocated behavior and response-efficacy refers to the effectiveness of the advocated behavior. Keller (2006) identified a match effect between regulatory focus and the type of efficacy (self-efficacy or response-efficacy) conveyed in communication about health behaviors. Findings from two studies demonstrate greater regulatory-efficacy fit and higher intention to perform the advocated healthy behaviors when self-efficacy features are paired with a promotion focus and when response-efficacy features are paired with a prevention focus.

A substantial number of health messages convey risk of a health hazard. Prior work has examined the effectiveness of various temporal frames in regard to conveying risk. Much of the work is rooted in Construal Level Theory, which proposes that people use higher-level construals to represent information about future distant events and lower-level construals to represent near future events (Liberman & Trope, 1998; Trope & Liberman, 2003). Higher-level construals are conceptualized as abstract and schematic, whereas lower-level construals are conceptualized as concrete and contextualized (Trope & Liberman, 2003). Chandran and Menon (2004) found that conveying risk in a proximal frame (i.e., every day) is more effective than conveying risk in a distal frame (i.e., every year) because the risk is construed as more proximal. This results in increased self-risk perceptions, intentions to exercise cautionary behaviors, concern about the health hazard, and overall effectiveness of the risk communication.

However, recent work has identified that self-construal influences the impact of temporal frame. Self-construal is described as an assembly of thoughts, feelings, and behaviors concerning the self as distinct from others (Singelis, 1994). Research in self-construal focuses on the distinction between an independent and interdependent construal of the self (Markus & Kitayama, 1991). People with an accessible independent self tend to place high value on independence and are associated with promotion goals. On the other hand, people with an accessible interdependent self-view tend to place importance on relationships with others and belonging. They tend to think and behave under the consideration of "we" rather than "I," and group interests often override individual concerns (Kitayama, Markus, & Matsumoto, 1995). While self-view has been considered a chronic trait dependent on culture, several studies have revealed that one's accessible self-view can be situationally manipulated (e.g., Aaker & Lee, 2001). Thus, self-construal can be a form of message framing utilized in health communication advertising. Oftentimes, self-construal is primed using both copy and imagery in the ad. For example, a PSA about depression may focus on how depression can influence the self versus one's family. In addition, a PSA promoting mammograms may focus on consequences for the self versus one's family.

Pounders, Lee, and Mackert (2015) found temporal frame interacts with self-construal in the contexts of heart disease and skin cancer prevention. Specifically, a proximal frame is more effective when paired with an interdependent self, whereas a distal frame is more effective when paired with an independent self. They suggest this is the result of consistent cognitive processing. People with an interdependent self-view construe information concretely and specifically, while people with an independent self-view construe information more schematically and abstractly (Spassova & Lee, 2013). Further, they find that the mediating process differs for those with an interdependent versus independent self-view. For those with an interdependent self-view, message concreteness mediates the relationship between temporal frame and message persuasiveness, and message persuasiveness then mediates the impact of message concreteness on intention to engage in healthy behaviors. However, for those with an independent self-view, only message persuasiveness plays a mediating role in understanding the impact of temporal frame on intention to engage in healthy behaviors. This finding is consistent with the different ways that interdependent versus independent people construe information.

A substantial body of work has focused on the relationship between self-construal and regulatory focus. For example, Aaker and Lee (2001) found that people with an accessible interdependent self-view are more persuaded by prevention-focused information consistent with an avoidance goal, whereas people with an accessible independent self-view are more persuaded by promotion-focused information consistent with an approach goal. When there is a match between self-view and regulatory focus of the message, people demonstrated greater message recall. Lee, Keller, and Sternthal (2010) extended this work by establishing promotion-focused people are more likely to construe information at abstract, high levels, whereas prevention-focused people are more likely to construe information at concrete, low levels. A fit between one's regulatory focus and the construal level of the information resulted in enhanced attitude due to processing fluency. Specifically, a PSA that features what one has to gain by engaging in a healthy behavior should also focus on the self, whereas a PSA that features what one has to lose by not engaging in a healthy behavior should focus on one's family. This serves as yet another example of match effects between message elements in persuasion.

Emotional Appeals

The use of emotional appeals in health messages is not a new concept. Health communication research has long investigated discrete emotions such as fear and humor. Multiple theoretical frameworks exist in the area of health and fear appeals. These include the health belief model, theory of reasoned action, protection motivation theory, and extended parallel process model. In the advertising arena, protection motivation theory has been widely used to understand consumer response to fear appeals in the context of conveying risk of health hazards. Fear is defined as a negative emotional response to a perceived threat (Rogers, 1983). The general premise of protection motivation theory is that a threat message includes four components: probability of the threat, magnitude of the threat, effectiveness of the recommended response (response efficacy), and one's ability to perform a recommended response (self-efficacy) (Rogers, 1983). The first two components refer to the threat appraisal, whereas the latter two components refer to the coping appraisal. High levels of all four components result in the greatest amount of change in behavior (Rogers, 1983). However, work on fear appeals has demonstrated divergent findings. Generally, research has found that fear appeals can work until a certain point, beyond which it creates anxiety and is ineffective (Keller & Block, 1996; Keller, 1999).

Berger and Milkman's (2012) work shows that negative emotions can also generate arousal and virality, and the authors point to the success of an anxiety building campaign. Powerful fear appeals also have the potential to generate the needed arousal to activate engagement and create online activity. Hence, advertisers must develop the appropriate ad campaign, and to generate the desired emotions they seek to effectively communicate health information with the intended target audience.

Recently, researchers have shifted focus to guilt and shame appeals. Guilt and shame are negative self-conscious emotions because the internal attribution is the self (Tangney & Dearing, 2002). Although much of the existing literature refers to guilt and shame interchangeably, guilt and shame are two different emotions with unique cognitive appraisals and coping mechanisms (Tangney & Dearing, 2002; Tracy, Robins, & Tangney, 2007). Guilt is a negative emotion that occurs when individuals appraise information about their behavior that violates some social or moral standard (Izard, 1997; Tangney & Dearing, 2002). Shame is a negative emotion that arises when an individual appraises negative information about the global self. Therefore guilt is associated with the notion "I did something bad," while shame is associated with the notion "I am a bad person" (Tangney & Dearing, 2002; Tracy, Robins, & Tangney, 2007). Guilt and shame also differ in coping mechanisms. Guilt is associated with adaptive or approach coping, whereas shame is associated with maladaptive or avoidance coping (Tracy, Robins, & Tangney, 2007).

Recent work in the arena of consumer behavior and marketing has examined the impact of guilt and shame in the context of motivating healthy behaviors (Agrawal & Duhachek, 2010; Duhachek, Agrawal, & Han, 2012; Boudewyns, Turner, & Paquin, 2013). Agrawal and Duhachek (2010) investigated how the two emotional states influence the effectiveness of messages that highlight the socially undesirable consequences of binge drinking. They find that compatible appeals, or appeals which are the same elicited by the manipulated message frame, are less effective. This is due to defensive processing; specifically, consumers discount the negative consequences because they are motivated to reduce the negative emotion (Agrawal & Duhachek, 2010).

Additionally, Duhachek, Agrawal, and Han (2012) found that guilt appeals are more effective when paired with gain frames, and shame appeals are more effective when paired with loss frames. This finding is attributed to coping mechanisms. Specifically, gain frames elicit the use of problem-solving coping strategies, which are accompanied with feelings of guilt. In addition, loss frames elicit the use of emotion-focused coping strategies, which are accompanied with feelings of shame (Duhachek, Agrawal, & Han, 2012).

Health communication research has also examined positive emotions, such as humor. The use of humor in advertising has a long history, yet there is still not a universal agreement about the definition. Speck (1987) offered a broad perspective of humor arguing that humor is multi-dimensional, a concept consistent with the idea that humor has many types. Specifically, Speck notes that humor is "a family of related phenomena made up a several distinct humor species" (p. 61). There are also questions about the underlying mechanism that drives humor and its success in the advertising arena, with a number of different theories proposed to explain how it works. However, the success of humor in the commercial marketplace has led to a call for health communications that offers more than basic information and education. Rather, edutainment, or the integration of educational messages with entertaining approaches including humor, have been advanced (e.g., Lister et al., 2014). Lister et al. (2014) propose the Laugh Model as one method to reach the public with an entertaining and somewhat humorous approach. Specifically, they found that implementation of their model in the Utah Partnership for Healthy Weight campaign produced successful results, and as such, argue for moving toward this model to improve health communications in society.

Interestingly, recent research has examined the interplay between shame and humor. Yoon (2015) found that the individual factor, fear of negative evaluation, moderates the interplay between shame and humor. Those with low fear of negative evaluation favored humor ads when the level of shame was low and preferred no-humor ads when shame induction was high. However, for those with high fear of evaluation, the results demonstrate humor is important when shame induction is high.

When utilizing digital media, emotional appeals are often more effective when portrayed in platforms that utilize pictures and/or videos such as Instagram and YouTube. This may be particularly true for positive emotions, such as humor, as suggested by Lister et al. (2014), who also indicate that emotional content may be more likely to be shared on social media.

Conclusion

With the considerable influence of advertising, it is imperative that the best practices of research and technology be considered to confront adverse influences on health by effectively communicating important health information to consumers. With continuing advances in technology, digital advertising represents an opportunity to promote healthy lifestyles by augmenting current actions of public health.

There are numerous digital tools that offer enormous resources to health practitioners. Social media, apps, and wearables all offer vast information about consumers to healthcare providers and also serve as tools for healthcare providers to communicate with consumers. In addition, big data and other information provided on social media offer a unique lens by which healthcare providers can better understand and target consumers. As important as it is to use digital tools in the arena of health communication, it is also necessary to use sound message strategy when creating health messages for those tools.

A final consideration is the need to tailor digital tools and messaging to the target audience. Considering the lifestyle factors that contribute to pervasive chronic diseases, messages related to food intake, physical activity, and tobacco will likely make the most impact on improving health outcomes and containing healthcare costs. Moreover, further specialized content should be developed to support positive health behaviors in vulnerable populations: underserved minorities, limited English speaking, low-income, children, and the elderly, all of whom are at increased health risk. Perhaps most important is the need for collaboration between marketing and public health professionals. Marketing experts are needed to help shape the format and develop the content of digital advertising to realize the true potential of digital advertising to improve public health.

References

Aaker, J. L., & Lee, A. Y. (2001). "I" seek pleasures and "We" avoid pains: The role of self-regulatory goals in information processing and persuasion. *Journal of Consumer Research*, *28*(1), 33–49.

Agrawal, N., & Duhachek, A. (2010). Emotional compatibility and the effectiveness of antidrinking messages: A defensive processing perspective on shame and guilt. *Journal of Marketing Research*, *47*(2), 263–273.

Arbeit, M. L., Johnson, C. C., & Mott, D. S. (1992). The heart smart cardiovascular school health promotion: Behavior correlates of risk factor change. *Preventive Medicine*, *21*, 18–32.

Bellman, S., Kemp, A., Haddad, H., & Varan, D. (2014). The effectiveness of advergames compared to television commercials and interactive commercials featuring advergames. *Computer in Human Behavior*, *32*, 276–283.

Berger, J. (2011). Arousal increases social transmission of information. *Psychological Science*, *22*, 891–893.

Berger, J., & Milkman, K. L. (2012). What makes online content viral? *Journal of Marketing Research*, *49*(2), 192–205.

Boudewyns, V., Turner, M. M., & Paquin, R. S. (2013). Shame-free guilt appeals: Testing the emotional and cognitive effects of shame and guilt appeals. *Psychology and Marketing*, *30*(9), 811–825.

Cawley, J., & Meyerhoefer, C. (2012). The medical care costs of obesity: An instrumental variables approach. *Journal of Health Economics*, *31*(1), 219–230.

Centers for Disease Control and Prevention. (2011). National diabetes fact sheet: National estimates and general information on diabetes and prediabetes in the United States. Retrieved from https://www.cdc.gov/diabetes/pubs/pdf/ndfs_2011.pdf.

Centers for Disease Control and Prevention. (2013). Death and mortality. *NCHS FastStats web site.* Retrieved from http://www.cdc.gov/nchs/fastats/deaths.htm.

Centers for Disease Control and Prevention. (2014). National diabetes statistics report, 2014. *CDC.com.* Retrieved from https://www.cdc.gov/diabetes/pubs/statsreport14/national-diabetes-report-web.pdf.

Centers for Disease Control and Prevention. (2016). What is health communications. Gateway to health communication & social marketing practice. Retrieved from http://www.cdc.gov/healthcommunication/healthbasics/whatishc.html.

Cesario, J., Grant, H., & Higgins, E. T. (2004). Regulatory fit and persuasion: Transfer from "feeling right." *Journal of Personality and Psychology, 86*(3), 388–404.

Chandran, S., & Menon, G. (2004). When a day means more than a year: Effects of temporal framing on judgments of health risk. *Journal of Consumer Research, 31*(2), 375–389.

Cohen, E. L., Caburnay, C. A., Len-Ríos, M. E., Cameron, G. T., Luke, D. A., Poor, T., Powe, B., Stemmle, J., & Kreuter, M. W. (2010). Engaging ethnic media to expand the reach and effectiveness of communication strategies to reduce health disparities. *Health Communication, 25*(6), 569–571.

Culp, J., Bell, R. A., & Cassady, D. (2010). Characteristics of food industry websites and advergames targeting children. *Journal of Nutrition Education and Behavior, 42*(3), 197–201.

DeVol, R., & Bedroussian, A. (2007). An unhealthy America: The economic burden of chronic disease—Charting a new course to save lives and increase productivity and economic growth. Retrieved from http://www.milkeninstitute.org/publications/view/321.

Dietz, W. H., & Gortmaker, S. L. (1985). Do we fatten our children at the television set? Obesity and television viewing in children and adolescents. *Pediatrics, 75*(5), 807–812.

Dobransky, K., & Hargittai, E. (2012). Inquiring minds acquiring wellness: Uses of online and offline sources of health information. *Health Communication, 27*(4), 331–343.

Duhachek, A., Agrawal, N., & Han, D. (2012). Guilt versus shame: Coping, fluency, and framing in the effectiveness of responsible drinking message. *Journal of Marketing Research, 49*(60), 928–941.

Edwards, E. (2003, January 26). Plug (the product) and play. *Washington Post.* Retrieved from https://www.washingtonpost.com/archive/politics/2003/01/26/plug-the-product-and-play/4d6dc386-d032-4854-8b16-524ca455b5d6/

Facebook News Room. (2016). Company info-stats. Retrieved from http://newsroom.fb.com/company-info/

Federal Trade Commission. (2012). Review of food marketing to children and adolescents—Follow-up report.

Festinger, L. (1954). A theory of social comparison processes. *Human Relations, 7*(2), 117–140.

Fox, S. (2010) Patients and online communities. *Pew Research Center.* Retrieved from http://www.pewinternet.org /2010/04/06/patients-and-online-communities/?beta=true&utm_expid=53098246-2.Lly4CFSVQG21phsg=KopIg.1&utm_referrer=http%3A%F%2Fwww.pewinernet.org% 2Fsearch%2Bcommunity%2F.

Freedman, D. S., Mei, Z., Srinivasan, S. R., Berenson, G. S., & Dietz, W. H. (2007). Cardiovascular risk factors and excess adiposity among overweight children and adolescents: The Bogalusa heart study. *Journal of Pediatrics, 150*(1), 12–17.

Friestad, M., & Wright, P. (1994). The persuasion knowledge model: How people cope with persuasion attempts. *Journal of Consumer Research, 21*(1), 1–31.

Frost, J. H., & Massagli, M. P. (2008). Social uses of personal health information within PatientsLikeMe, an online patient community: What can happen when patients have access to one another's data. *Journal of Medical Research, 10*, e15.

Garcia-Gomez, J. M., de la Torre-Diez, I., Vicente, J., Robles, M., Lopez-Coronado, M., & Rodrigues, J. J. (2014). Analysis of mobile health applications for a broad spectrum of consumers: A user experience approach. *Health Informatics Journal, 20*(1), 74–84.

Grier, S. A., & Kumanyika, S. K. (2008). The context for choice: Health implications of targeted food and beverage marketing to African Americans. *American Journal of Public Health, 98*(9), 1616–1629.

Gross, J., & Levenson, R. (1995). Emotion elicitation using films. *Cognition & Emotion, 9*, 87–108.

Han, J. C., Lawlor, D. D., & Kimm, S.Y. (2010). Childhood obesity. *Lancet, 375*(9), 1737–1748.

Hasford, J., Hardesty, D. M., & Kidwell, B. (2015). More than a feeling: Emotional contagion effects in persuasive communication. *Persuasive Communication, 52*, 836–847.

Hatfield, E., Cacioppo, J. T., & Rapson, R. L. (1994). *Emotional contagion*. New York, NY: Cambridge University Press.

Heilman, K. (1997). The neurobiology of emotional experience. In S. Salloway, P. Malloy, & J. L. Cummings (Eds.) *The neuropsychiatry of limbic and subcortical disorders*, (pp. 133–142). Washington, DC: American Psychiatric Press.

Higgins, T. E. (1997). Beyond pleasure and pain. *American Psychologist, 52*(December), 1280–1300.

Higgins, T. E. (1998). Promotion and prevention: Regulatory focus as motivational principle. *Advances in Experimental Social Psychology, 30*, 1–46.

Higgins, T. E. (2002a). How self-regulation creates distinct values: The case of promotion and prevention decision making. *Journal of Consumer Psychology, 12*(3), 177–191.

Higgins, T. E. (2002b). Making a good decision: Value from fit. *American Psychology, 55*(11), 1217–1230.

Hingle, M. D., Castonguay, J. S., Ambuel, D. A., Smith, R. M., & Kunkel, D. (2015). Alignment of children's food advertising with proposed federal guidelines. *American Journal of Preventive Medicine, 48*(6), 707–713.

Househ, M., Borycki, E., & Kushniruk, A. (2014). Empowering patients through social media: The benefits and challenges. *Healthier Informatics Journal, 20*(1), 50–58.

Idson, L. C., Liberman, N., & Higgins, T. E. (2000). Distinguishing gains from nonlosses and losses from nongains: A regulatory focus perspective on hedonic intensity. *Journal of Experimental Social Psychology, 36*(3), 252–274.

Institute of Medicine. (2013). Challenges and opportunities for change in food marketing to children and youth: Workshop summary. Retrieved from http://www.nationalacademies.org/hmd/Reports/2013/Challenges-and-Opportunities-for-Change-in-Food-Marketing-to-Children-and-Youth.aspx.

Ipe, M. (2008). An introduction. In M. Ipe (Eds.), *Advergaming and ingame advertising* (pp. 3–16). Hyderabad: Icfai University Press.

Izard, C. E. (1997). Emotions and facial expressions: A perspective from differential emotions theory. *The Psychology of Facial Expression, 2*, 57–77.

Keller, P. A. (1999). Converting the unconverted: The effect of inclination and opportunity to discount health-related fear appeals. *Journal of Applied Psychology, 84*(3), 403.

Keller, P. A. (2006). Regulatory focus and efficacy of health messages. *Journal of Consumer Research, 33*(1), 109–114. doi: 10.1086/504141.

Keller, P. A., & Block, L. B. (1996). Increasing the persuasiveness of fear appeals: The effect of arousal and elaboration. *Journal of Consumer Research, 22*(4), 448–459.

Kim, Y. J. (2006). The role of regulatory focus in message framing in antismoking advertisements for adolescents. *Journal of Advertising, 35*(1), 143–151.

Kitayama, S., Markus, H. R., & Matsumoto, H. (1995). Culture, self, and emotion: A cultural perspective on "self-conscious" emotions. In J. P. Tangney & K. W. Fischer (Eds.) *Self-conscious emotions: The psychology of shame, guilt, embarrassment, and pride* (pp. 439–464). New York, NY: Guilford Press.

Koteyko, N., Hunt, D., & Gunter, B. (2015). Expectations in the field of the internet and health: An analysis of claims about social networking sites in clinical literature. *Sociology of Health & Illness, 37*(3), 468–484.

Krebs-Smith, S. M., Guenther, P. M., Subar, A. F., Kirkpatrick, S. I., & Dodd, K. W. (2010). Americans do not meet federal dietary recommendations. *Journal of Nutrition, 140*(10), 1832–1838.

Larson, N., Story, M., Eisenberg, M. E., & Neumark-Sztainer, D. (2016). Secular trends in meal and snack patterns among adolescents from 1999 to 2010. *Journal of the Academy of Nutrition and Dietetics, 116*(2), 240–250.

Lee, A. Y., & Aaker, J. L. (2004). Bringing the frame into focus: The influence of regulatory fit on processing fluency and persuasion. *Journal of Personality and Social Psychology, 86*(2), 205–218.

Lee, A. Y., Keller, P. A., & Sternthal, B. (2010). Value from regulatory construal fit: The persuasive impact of fit between consumer goals and message concreteness. *Journal of Consumer Research, 36*(5), 735–747.

Lefebvre, R. C., & Bornkessel, A. S. (2016). Digital social networks and health. *Circulation, 127*(17), 1829–1836.

Liberman, N., & Trope, Y. (1998). The role of feasibility and desirability consideration in near and distant future decisions: A test of temporal construal theory. *Journal of Personality and Social Psychology, 75*(1), 5–18.

Lister, C., Royne, M. B., Payne, H., Cannon, B., Hanson, C., & Barnes, M. (2014). The laugh model: Reframing and rebranding public health through social media. *American Journal of Public Health, 105*(11), 2245–2251.

Lockwood, P., & Kunda, Z. (1997). Superstars and me: Predicting the impact of role models on the self. *Journal of Personality and Social Psychology, 73*(1), 91.

Malik, V. S., Schulze, M. B., & Hu, F. B. (2006). Intake of sugar-sweetened beverages and weight gain: A systematic review. *American Society for Clinical Nutrition, 84*(2), 274–288.

Markus, H. R., & Kitayama, S. (1991). Culture and self: Implications for cognition, emotion, and motivation. *Psychological Review, 98*(April), 224–253.

McLeroy, K. R., Bibeau, D., Steckler, A., & Glantz, K. (1988). An ecological perspective on health promotion programs. *Health Education & Behavior, 5*(4), 351–377.

Mink, M., Evans, A., Moore, C. G., Calderon, K. S., & Deger, S. (2010). Nutritional imbalance endorsed by televised food advertisements. *Journal of the American Dietetic Association, 110*(6), 904–910.

Moore, D. J., Williams, J. D., & Qualls, W. J. (1996). Target marketing of tobacco and alcohol-related products to ethnic minority groups in the United States. *Ethnicity and Disease, 6*, 83–98.

Nicovich, S. G. (2005). The effect of involvement on ad judgment in video game environment: The mediating role of presence. *Journal of Interactive Advertising, 6*(1), 29–39.

Obermiller, C., Spangenberg, E., & MacLachlan, D. L. (2005). Ad skepticism the consequences of disbelief. *Journal of Advertising, 34*(3), 7–17.

Ogden, C. L., Carroll, M. D., Kit, B. K., & Flegal, K. M. (2012). Prevalence of obesity and trends in body mass index among US children and adolescents, 1999–2010. *JAMA, 307*(5), 483–490.

Ogden, C. L., Carroll, M. D., Kit, B. K., & Flegal, K. M. (2014). Prevalence of childhood and adult obesity in the United States, 2011–2012. *JAMA, 311*(8), 806–814.

Park, H., Rodgers, S., & Stemmle, J. (2013). Analyzing health organizations' use of Twitter for promoting health literacy. *Journal of Health Communication: International Perspectives, 18*(4), 410–425. doi: 10.1080/10810730.2012.727956.

Pew Internet. (2015). Digital divides. Retrieved from http://www.pewinternet.org/2015/09/22/digital-divides-2015.

Piernas, C., & Popkin, B. M. (2010). Trends in snacking among US children. *Health Affairs, 29*(3), 398–404.

Pounders, K. R., & Mackert, M. S. (2015). Matching temporal frame, self-view, and message frame valence: Improving persuasiveness in health communications. *Journal of Advertising, 44*(4), 388–402.

Puhl, R. M., & Latner, J. D. (2007). Stigma, obesity, and the health of the nation's children. *Psychology Bulletin, 133*(4), 557–580.

Reisch, L. A., Gwozdz, W., Barba, G., De Henauw, S., Lascorz, N., & Pigeot, I. (2013). Experimental evidence on the impact of food advertising on children's knowledge about and preferences for healthful food. *Journal of Obesity, 2013*, 13. doi: 10.1155/2013/40852.

Rethinkbreastcancer.com (n.d.). http://rethinkbreastcancer.com/understanding-breast-health/your-man-reminder/

Rogers, R. W. (1983). Cognitive and physiological processes in fear appeals and attitude change: A revised theory of protection motivation. In J. T. Cacciopo & R. Petty (Eds.), *Social psychophysiology: A sourcebook* (pp. 153–176). New York, NY: Guildord Press.

Rosenheck, R. (2008). Fast food consumption and increased caloric intake: A systematic review of a trajectory towards weight gain and obesity risk. *Obesity Reviews, 9*(6), 535–547.

Royne, M. B., & Levy, M. (2011). Marketing for public health: We need an app for that. *Journal of Consumer Affairs, 45*(1), 1–6.

Seo, M., & Matsaganis, M. D. (2013). How interpersonal communication mediates the relationship of multichannel communication connections to health-enhancing and health-threatening behaviors. *Journal of Health Communication, 18*, 1002–1020.

Singelis, T. M. (1994). The measurement of independent and interdependent self-construals. *Personality and Social Psychology Bulletin, 20*(October), 580–591.

Spassova, G., & Lee, A. Y. (2013). Looking into the future: A match between self-view and temporal distance. *Journal of Consumer Research, 40*(1), 159–171.

Speck, P. S. (1987). *On humor in advertising.* Unpublished Doctoral Dissertation. Texas Tech University.

Stokols, D. (1996). Translating social ecological theory into guidelines for community health promotion. *American Journal of Health Promotion, 10*, 282–298.

Story, M., & French, S. (2004). Food advertising and marketing directed at children and adolescents in the US. *International Journal of Behavioral Nutrition and Physical Activity, 1*(3), 3–20.

Sutherland, E. R. (2008). Obesity and asthma. *Immunology Allergy Clinic of North America, 28*(3), 589–602.

Tangney, J. P., & Dearing, R. L. (2002). *Shame and guilt.* New York, NY: Guildford Press.

Tracy, J. L., Robins, R. W., & Tangney, J. P. (2007). *The self-conscious emotions: Theory and research.* New York, NY: Guilford Press.

Trope, Y., & Liberman, N. (2003). Temporal construal. *Psychological Review, 110*(3), 403–421.

Vashisht, D., & Sreejesh, S. (2015). Effects of brand placement strength, prior game playing experience and game involvement on brand recall in advergames. *Journal of Indian Business Research, 7*(3), 292–312.

Wade, W. (2004, February 26). Care and feeding of cyber-pets rivets tag-along marketers. *New York Times,* 87–100.

Wakefield, M. A., Loken, B., & Hornik, R. C. (2010). Use of mass media campaigns to change health behavior. *The Lancet, 376,* 1261–1271.

Walther, J. B., Carr, C. T., Choi, S. S. W., DeAndrea, D. C., Kim, J., Tong, S. T., & Van Der Heide, B. (2010). Interaction of interpersonal, peer, and media influence sources online. *A Networked Self: Identity, Community, and Culture on Social Network Sites, 17,* 17–38.

Ward, B. W., Schiller, J. S, & Goodman, R. A. (2014). Multiple chronic conditions among US adults: A 2012 update. *Preventing Chronic Disease, 11.* Retrieved from http://www. medscape.com/viewarticle/825839

Webb, T., Joseph, J., Yardley, L., & Michie, S. (2010). Using the internet to promote health behavior change: A systematic review and meta-analysis of the impact of theoretical basis, use of behavior change techniques, and mode of delivery on efficacy. *Journal of Medical Internet Research, 12*(1), e4.

World Health Organization. (2009). The extent, nature, and effects of food promotion to children: A review of the evidence to December 2008. Retrieved from http://www. who.int/dietphysicalactivity/Evidence_Update_2009.pdf.

Yoon, H. J. (2015). Humor effects in shame-inducing health issue advertising: The moderating effects of fear of negative evaluation. *Journal of Advertising, 44*(2), 126–139.

12

CONSUMERS' MOTIVATIONS FOR LURKING AND POSTING IN BRAND COMMUNITIES ON SOCIAL NETWORKING SITES

Marijke De Veirman, Verolien Cauberghe, Liselot Hudders, and Patrick De Pelsmacker

Introduction

Companies and brands increasingly interact with their audiences, especially via online communication and participation formats. One of these formats is the brand community. Online brand communities allow companies and brands to inform and interact with their customers. By creating brand communities in social networking sites (SNS brand communities), such as Facebook brand pages, companies deliver unique and interesting content to (potential) consumers and stimulate them to interact with each other, their fellow network contacts, and the brand (Jahn & Kunz, 2012). These (potential) customers have never been more enabled to engage online with brands and share their brand evaluations with others.

Motivations for participating in more "traditional" (i.e., non-SNS) virtual brand communities, online platforms where brands can interact with their current and potential customers, are fairly well documented (e.g., Nonnecke & Preece, 2001; Ridings & Gefen, 2004). However, these insights might not fully apply to SNS brand communities, as these are embedded in a larger network of social ties between people who usually do not share a common interest in and enthusiasm, or even love, for a brand (Boyd & Ellison, 2007). This might be advantageous for brands, as consumers' interactions are potentially visible for their entire social network and thus have much larger reach than interactions in traditional virtual brand communities. Consequently, SNS brand communities may contribute to the spreading of brand-related content and in this way increase the brand's visibility, brand awareness, and brand involvement (Jahn & Kunz, 2012). Moreover, consumers' interactions may guide the brand evaluations of their friends. This word-of-mouth is highly desirable as it appears to be more effective than traditional advertising tactics due to higher credibility of and lower resistance to peers in a SNS than company-originated sources (de Vries, Gensler, & Leeflang, 2012).

The purpose of this chapter is to explore the characteristics and marketing potential of SNS brand communities, how SNS users interact with these communities, and what motivates them to engage in different types of interaction. This will be done by providing an overview of research on these topics and by reporting the results of an empirical study in which the relationship between motivations to engage in brand related activities and performing different types of activities is investigated. First, we discuss how SNS brand communities differ from traditional online brand communities and in what ways they are valuable for brand communications. Next, we give an overview of research on how users engage in brand-related activities on SNSs and what motivates them to do so. We elaborate on the relationship between these motivations and brand-related activities and we report the results of the empirical study. We conclude with a discussion on managerial implications.

SNS Brand Communities

The first brand communities were developed offline. Members, usually devoted brand advocates, interacted with other members via social activities and events organized by the brand. The development of the internet facilitated the creation of virtual brand communities. A virtual brand community is a "specialized, non-geographically bound community, based on a structured set of social relations among admirers of a brand" (Muñiz & O'Guinn, 2001, p. 412). A virtual brand community, initiated by organizations as part of brand management strategies or by individual consumers, is as a group of individuals with common interests in a brand, who communicate with each other electronically about a specific brand, product, or service, unrestrained by time and space (Rothaermel & Sugiyama, 2001; Sicilia & Palazón, 2008).

Currently, the popularity of social networking sites (SNSs) provides virtual brand communities with new platforms (Kaplan & Haenlein, 2010), such as brand pages on Facebook or accounts on Twitter or Instagram. Social networking sites are defined as:

> Web-based services that allow individuals to construct a public or semi-public profile within a bounded system, articulate a list of other users with whom they share a connection, and view and traverse their list of connections and those made by others within the system.
>
> *(Boyd & Ellison, 2007, p. 2)*

Brand pages can be considered a new form of virtual brand community (Sung, Kim, Kwon, & Moon, 2010). A brand community has three core components: 1) consciousness of kind, the intrinsic connection that members feel toward one another, and the collective sense of difference from others not in the community, 2) shared rituals and traditions, and 3) a sense of duty to the community and its members (Muñiz & O'Guinn, 2001). These brand community characteristics can also be present in SNS brand communities. Members share a common interest, namely the brand, and SNS communities allow member-initiated interaction, as consumers can participate in the community through reading, liking, sharing, and posting content (Muñiz & O'Guinn, 2001). However, brand pages are immersed in SNSs, and the social context that surrounds brand pages may create important differences (Jahn & Kunz, 2012; Zaglia, 2013; Habibi, Laroche, & Richard, 2014a; 2014b). SNS brand communities are "open," since consumers can easily join and leave the community (Gruner, Homburg, & Lukas, 2014).

Individuals join a brand page by a simple click on the button "Like" on Facebook or "Follow" on Twitter or Instagram. This process requires a low effort and does not necessarily require high brand involvement. Individuals may easily engage in multiple memberships to different brand pages (Habibi et al., 2014b). Brand pages can reach a mass audience, while traditional virtual brand communities do not usually go beyond thousands of brand admirers. Importantly, SNSs allow easy information diffusion. By clicking "Like," "Share," "Retweet," or "Comment" on a post on Facebook, Twitter, or Instagram, the information may be distributed to the user's entire network. Traditional virtual brand communities are specifically established as a platform to facilitate brand-related conversations among owners and brand admirers. However, SNS brand communities are embedded in a network of social ties between people who are not necessarily all like-minded "fans" of the brand (Muñiz & O'Guinn, 2001; Boyd & Ellison, 2007).

Consequently, brand-related content posted to SNS brand communities has much larger reach, as consumers' interactions are potentially visible to their entire social network, most of which are not members of the brand page (Lipsman, Mudd, Rich, & Bruich, 2012). Members of the brand page may perform a bridging function with other individuals interested in the brand (Liao & Chou, 2012) and facilitate the interaction between the brand and the members' friends (Ellison, Vitak, Gray, & Lampe, 2014). SNSs partly transferred branding power from marketers to consumers (Muntinga, Moorman, & Smit, 2011; Chauhan & Pillai, 2013).

SNS brand communities are easily accessible as posted messages are automatically displayed on fans' personal "walls" and people may interact with the community without having to create a separate login for the community (Jahn & Kunz, 2012). In social networks, members often use their real identities to create a profile. This transparency in brand supporters' identities may positively impact on credibility, brand evaluation, and purchase intentions by members of their network (Habibi et al., 2014a).

On the other hand, as a consumer can become a fan of several brands at the same time and, thus, to become a member of several brand communities on one SNS, members might be less committed compared to members of traditional virtual brand communities, who have actively searched and signed up for a website that is especially established to discuss the brand (Pöyry, Parvinen, & Malmivaara, 2013).

The main motivation of SNS users is to be connected with friends and meet new friends (Raacke & Bonds-Raacke, 2008; Brandtzæg & Heim, 2009); for entertainment (Brandtzæg & Heim, 2009); or for self-presentation, self-expression, or self-esteem (Wilcox & Stephen, 2013). Therefore, information that is not oriented to these consumer motivations, such as commercially-oriented brand information, can be perceived as highly irritating (Taylor, Lewin, & Strutton, 2011). This irritation can lead SNS users to develop a negative attitude toward the company or the brand (Logan, Bright, & Gangadharbatla, 2012). Moreover, since brand posts may blend with other messages on consumers' walls, this implies that brand-related content has to compete with other updates in the consumer's social network, which may negatively affect levels of attention and consequently levels of interaction (Pöyry et al., 2013).

In general, SNS brand communities provide a number of opportunities for companies and brands. Members of SNS brand communities may post brand information that can then be seen by their contacts in the SNS. In that way, positive brand information is spread through the social network of the brand community members, and this may increase many people's commitment to the brand (Mattila & Wirtz, 2002; Ha & Perks, 2005). In SNSs, consumers build their own profile with their personal information. When they join a SNS brand community, companies can have access to their information and that of their social network (e.g., profiles, pictures, location, gender, and family status) (Ridings, Gefen, & Arinze, 2006; Habibi et al., 2014b). Companies can use this information to enhance communication effectiveness. The brand can plan posts to be seen by specific groups of fans or followers (Mata & Quesada, 2014; Tsimonis & Dimitriadis, 2014). Additionally, they can use this information to improve the messages they create, by analyzing the likes and dislikes of their members on other posts and on their own posts. Virtual brand communities often lead to better market performance (Rothaermel & Sugiyama, 2001; Bagozzi & Dholakia, 2006).

SNSs offer metrics that enable companies to measure the success of brand communities. For instance, brand awareness through SNSs can be measured as the numbers of fans the brand page has or the number of individuals who have seen their posts. Additionally, brand interactions can be measured by the number of times consumers liked, commented, or shared on Facebook or Instagram, or have retweeted or favored on Twitter, or by the posts consumers write on the brand page (Hoffman & Fodor, 2010; Yu, 2014). Finally, the sentiment of the comments about the brand can be measured. Sentiment refers to the tone of the conversation, the amount of positive and negative brand mentions.

Engaging in Brand-Related Activities on Social Networking Sites

Members of a brand community engage in brand-related activities in much the same way as they interact with other SNS content. On the one hand, there is the passive use of SNS information or "quiet membership" of a brand community. This refers to non-interactive behavior, i.e., people who rarely contribute to the community themselves, but mainly read posts from the brand and of other members of the community as they browse the brand page. This type of passive, less publicly visible engagement is called consuming behavior or "lurking." On the other hand, members may interactively engage in the community, by publicly liking and sharing posts, add content themselves, or react to comments of others. This "communicative membership" is called "posting" (Burnett, 2000; Hammond, 2000; Schlosser, 2005). Muntinga et al. (2011) distinguish two types of posting behavior: contributing behavior (e.g., sharing posts) and creating behavior (e.g., adding posts). Previous research on virtual brand communities found that only a small fraction of members publicly post comments (Nonnecke & Preece, 2001). The majority prefers to passively enjoy the benefits offered by the comments of the brand or others, without making any substantial contribution (Preece, Nonnecke, & Andrews, 2004).

Consumer Motivations for SNS Brand Community Participation

As motivations are consumers' needs or drives, which lead them to participate in the community, it is important for brands to gain understanding of these motivations. For brand communities to be successful, first of all they need to attract members. SNS users may be motivated to become members for different reasons: social interaction and integration, entertainment, informational, status enhancement, and economic benefits (e.g., promotional deals) (Bagozzi & Dholakia, 2006; Pentina, Prybutok, & Zhang, 2008; Park & Kim, 2014; Habibi et al., 2014a). These motivations fall into two classical categories that also apply to SNS use in general: utilitarian needs for knowledge and benefits, and intrinsic hedonic needs for enjoyment and self-enhancement (Huang, 2008; Pöyry et al., 2013; Yu, 2014). Similarly, Toubia and Stephen (2013) differentiate between what they call intrinsic and image-related motivations. Sukoco and Wu (2010) distinguish two main motives for consumers to join a virtual brand community: a self-related and a social-related motivation. The former refers to consumers' need for enjoyment, information, and maintenance of their self-esteem, while the latter is related to consumers' need for affiliation and social status. Nadkarni and Hofmann (2012) propose a similar distinction of motivations to engage in SNSs: the need to belong and the need for self-presentation.

Hennig-Thurau, Gwinner, Walsh, and Gremler (2004) find that consumers mainly participate in virtual brand communities to vent negative feelings, care for others, enhance their self-worth, seek advice, obtain social or economic benefits, obtain platform assistance, or help the company. Wiertz and de Ruyter (2007) point out that the most contributing members mainly engage out of feelings of commitment to the brand. Moreover, members take into account the perceived informational value of interacting with the community (Brodie, Hollebeek, Jurić, & Ilić, 2011). According to Zaglia (2013), people mainly participate in brand communities out of interest and passion for the brand, willingness to learn and improve skills, to build social relationships with others and enhance their social position, and to receive information that is tailored to their needs. Kwon, Kim, Sung, and Yoo (2014) distinguish four primary motivations for consumers to follow brands on Twitter: incentive seeking, social-interaction seeking, brand usage/likeability, and information seeking. Enginkaya and Yilmaz (2014) suggest five motivations to interact with and/or about the brand over social media: brand affiliation, conversation, opportunity seeking, entertainment, and investigation. Bernritter, Verlegh, and Smit (2016) make a distinction between consumer identity-related drivers, such as identity signaling (Hollenbeck & Kaikati, 2012) and self-expression (Wallace, Buil, de Chernatony, & Hogan, 2014); brand-related drivers, such as brand love (Bergkvist & Bech-Larsen, 2010; Batra, Ahuvia & Bagozzi, 2012); and consumer-brand identification (Stokburger-Sauer, Ratneshwar, & Sen, 2012), and, finally, community-related drivers such as group membership (Morandin, Bagozzi, & Bergami, 2013), or social identification with the community (Muñiz & O'Guinn, 2001; Bagozzi & Dholakia, 2006; Muntinga et al., 2011).

Muntinga et al. (2011) propose a framework of six motivations to engage in SNS brand communities: information, entertainment, remuneration, personal identity, integration and social interaction, and empowerment. In the next section, we will elaborate on the relationship between these six motivations and brand-related activities of SNS users.

Motivations as Antecedents of Engagement

The need for *information* is about seeking advice and opinions. Consumers derive information from what others think and share in the virtual brand community (Dholakia, Bagozzi, & Pearo, 2004). Muntinga et al. (2011) found that, as opposed to contributing to brand communities and creating content, consuming brand-related content is driven by the need for information. Nonnecke & Preece (2001) suggest that lurkers do not feel the need to participate (post) as their informational needs are satisfied without actively having to contribute.

The entertainment motivation is associated with pleasure-seeking, passing time, enjoyment, and relaxation. Previous research indicated entertainment to be an important motivation for both lurking and posting behavior (Goldsmith & Horowitz, 2006). Muntinga et al. (2011) indeed found that the need for entertainment is associated with all types of brand engagement activities.

The social interaction motivation covers various needs, such as the need to a sense of belonging, the need for social contact, etc. Daugherty, Eastin, and Bright (2008) found social interaction to be a motivation for creating user-generated content in general, and Muntinga et al. (2011) found it to be an important motivation for contributing to and creating brand-related content on social media, while this was not the case for merely consuming content.

Consumers who are driven by a remuneration motivation undertake a certain action because they expect to be rewarded for it (Ryan & Deci, 2000). Hennig-Thurau et al. (2004) found that online community members are more willing to participate when economic incentives are offered. Muntinga et al. (2011) found remuneration to be a motivation for consuming brand-related content and not for contributing to or creating brand-related content. However, it is a current practice of marketers to offer incentives to encourage their fans to engage and actively participate in brand-related activities rather than rewarding people for merely liking their brand page without any additional efforts. Therefore, it could be expected that primarily posting, and not lurking, behavior is motivated by the idea of a possible remuneration.

Self-presentation refers to the way people present their personal identity to others. Social media users present themselves through personalizing their profile and their activities on social media (Tüfekçi, 2007). Peluchette and Karl (2009) found that Facebook users purposely post content to present themselves in a certain way to others. Several studies (e.g., Jahn & Kunz, 2012; Wallace et al., 2014) showed that consumers participate in brand-related activities to fulfill the need to profile themselves to their personal network, manage their self-identities, reinforce their self-esteem and identify with and gain recognition from peers (Jahn & Kunz, 2012; Hollenbeck & Kaikati, 2012). It is an important motivation for contributing to and creating brand-related content, but not for merely consuming it (Muntinga et al., 2011).

Consumers may also use social media based on an empowerment motivation, i.e., to influence other consumers or the brand itself (Fournier & Avery, 2011). This idea of empowerment was found to be an important motivation for creating brand-related content in Muntinga et al.'s (2011) study.

Empirical Illustration

In the empirical illustration provided, we quantitatively explore the relationships between motivations to engage with brands on SNSs and the type of brand-related activities people engage in. We use Muntinga's et al. (2011) conceptual model of six motivations and predict which motivations can be linked to lurking and posting behavior on Facebook brand pages.

Method, Subjects, and Procedure

The study employed an online survey that was posted on Facebook. Participants were asked to share the survey link in their own social network. First, participants were asked if they liked any brand pages. Participants who indicated not to be a fan of any Facebook brand page were excluded from the study. Next, the 187 remaining participants (32.6% male; M_{age} = between 18 and 25 years; education: 33.2% secondary education, 66.8% higher education) were asked to write down one of the brand pages they "Like" on Facebook. After this, they were asked to indicate how they interacted with this brand page. Next, participants were asked about their motivations to perform brand-related activities. The last part of the survey collected demographic information of the participants.

Measures

First, participants had to indicate how often they performed a number of brand-related activities on the Facebook brand page, using a 7-point scale (1 = *never*, 7 = *always*). Five brand-related activities were included: 1) reading and viewing messages, photos, and videos of the brand, 2) liking messages, photos, and videos of the brand, 3) sharing messages, photos, and videos of the brand, 4) commenting on brand posts and others' contributions to the brand page, 5) posting messages, photos, and videos to the brand page (Muntinga et al., 2011; Gummerus, Liljander, Weman, & Pihlström, 2012). Next, participants were asked about their motivations to perform each of the above-mentioned activities, namely information, social interaction, entertainment, self-presentation, remuneration, and empowerment. The measurement scales are shown in Table 12.1.

TABLE 12.1 Measures (7-point scale)

Variable and items	Source	Alpha
Information motivation *I am looking for information about the brand.* *I want to know what other people think about or do with the brand.* *I want to know how to use the brand and how I can solve a problem with the brand.*	Muntinga et al. (2011)	.82
Entertainment motivation *Relax.* *Get entertained.* *Kill time when bored.*	Gummerus et al. (2012)	.80
Social interaction motivation *I can meet people like me on this fan page.* *I can meet new people like me on this fan page.* *I can find out about people like me on this fan page.* *I can interact with people like me on this fan page.*	Jahn and Kunz (2012)	.88
Remuneration motivation *Get a discount.* *Take part in a competition.*	Wallace et al. (2014)	.92
Self-presentation motivation *I can make a good impression on others.* *I can improve the way I am perceived.* *I can present to others who I am.* *I can present to others who I want to be.*	Jahn and Kunz (2012)	.93

Variable and items	Source	Alpha
Empowerment motivation *I want to give suggestions on new or existing products.* *I want to influence other people.* *I want to influence the brand.*	Muntinga et al. (2011)	.87

Measurement Model

Exploratory factor analysis confirmed two types of participation in Facebook brand pages: rather passive, less-publicly visible behavior or lurking, and more active, publicly visible behavior or posting. The two factors explained 78.27 percent of the total variance. Lurking included activities that are not or only merely visible for consumers' social network or other fans, namely reading and viewing brand posts and liking them. Sharing brand posts; reacting on brand posts or others' comments; and posting messages, photos, or videos on the brand page were considered more visible to one's social network or other fans and were therefore labeled posting. The mean scores of the items loading on each factor were used as dependent variables in further analysis. A paired sample t-test revealed that, as previously found, participants engaged far more in lurking behavior ($M = 3.63$, $SD = 1.31$) than in posting behavior ($M = 1.54$, $SD = .78$, $p < .001$).

Next, a structural equation model analysis was conducted to test the relationship between motivations and posting and lurking behavior. First, confirmatory factor analysis (CFA) using AMOS 22 was applied for testing the measurement model. Based on modification index and standardized residuals analysis, it was decided to allow co-variation between the motivation variables, a number of items were removed, and so was the "information" variable. After all these modifications, the model fit was acceptable: $\chi2/df = 1.61$, $GFI = .90$, $NFI = .91$, $CFI = .96$, and $RMSEA = .06$. Based on the criteria put forward by Fornell and Larcker (1981), the measurement model also showed satisfactory reliability, convergent validity, and discriminant validity.

Results

A structural equation model was tested, relating all the independent variables (motivations: social interaction, entertainment, empowerment, self-presentation, remuneration) to the two dependent variables (lurking, posting). The results are shown in Table 12.2.

There is a significant positive effect of the entertainment motivation ($b = .17$, $p = .04$) and the social interaction motivation ($b = .20$, $p = .04$) on lurking. The social interaction motivation has greater explanatory value than the entertainment motivation. The remuneration, self-presentation and empowerment motivations do not explain lurking behavior. There is a significant positive effect of the

TABLE 12.2 Structural Model Results

Path	Unstandardized effects	SE	p value
Lurking ← Social interaction	.20	.10	.04
Lurking ← Entertainment	.17	.08	.04
Lurking ← Empowerment	.08	.09	.38
Lurking ← Self-presentation	.03	.05	.47
Lurking ← Remuneration	.05	.04	.25
Posting ← Social interaction	.18	.08	.03
Posting ← Entertainment	−.07	.07	.28
Posting ← Empowerment	.21	.08	.01
Posting ← Self-presentation	.00	.04	.90
Posting ← Remuneration	.07	.04	.06

empowerment motivation ($b = .21, p = .00$) and the social interaction motivation ($b = .18, p = .03$) on posting. The empowerment motivation has a slightly greater explanatory value than the social interaction motivation. The self-presentation, entertainment, and remuneration motivation do not explain posting behavior.

Conclusion and Implications

SNS users engage with brands in much the same way they interact with other SNS content. In most cases they "lurk," meaning that they engage in rather passive, not publicly visible brand page viewing. In some cases they "post," i.e., they share brand posts with their own social network; react on brand posts or other fans' comments; and post messages, photos, or videos to the brand page. These are interactive and publicly visible brand engagements.

The motivations to engage with brands are partly similar to the reasons why SNS users engage with other content on social networks. They want to have fun, express their self-identity, get socially connected, be in control, get rewarded, and look for information. According to our empirical test, lurking and posting are partly driven by different motivations. Both lurking and posting are driven by the need for social interaction. Lurking is also (but to a lesser extent) motivated by the need for entertainment. Although we could not test it, it may be assumed that collecting information is also a prime motivator for lurking. Similar to Muntinga et al.'s (2011) findings, our study confirms that empowerment is an important motivation for posting. Consumers actively and publicly engage in brand-related activities in Facebook brand pages to exert influence on other consumers or the brand itself. Unexpectedly, in our study, the self-presentation motivation did not explain why consumers engage in posting behavior on brand pages. In other studies, however, this motivation has been found to be very relevant for active and public SNS use.

Based on previous research and our own—be it limited—empirical study, there are a number of managerial implications. First of all, SNS brand communities are interesting advertising tools. They provide brands with a lot of information about the characteristics, interests, and behaviors of community members and their social network. Positive brand-related messages from peers may enhance consumers' commitment to the brand. Companies can use this information to improve communication effectiveness because it allows more fine-grained targeting and the development of more relevant messages. On top of that, SNSs offer metrics that enable companies to measure the effects of brand community activities.

Members of SNS brand communities can engage with the community in a passive or an active way. In both cases, their motivation to do so is the need for social interaction. Consequently, it is important that marketers do not put too many restrictions on consumers' possibilities to interact and let anyone have the possibility to post (not harming) content to the brand page's timeline. For passive engagements, such as reading and liking brand-related posts, also providing relevant information in an entertaining way is important. Brand pages should be interesting and fun. The most important activity that brand communities should aim for is active engagement: members sharing posts, commenting on other posts, and adding content. Much like with any other SNS-related activity, brand page members express their self-identity through these active engagements.

Perhaps the most common motivation for SNS brand community members is self-empowerment. Community members actively engage with brand-related content to have an impact on brands and on other people. So, companies have to make sure they listen to their fans and respond to their questions and suggestions, thank them for their replies and sharing their opinions, since this may give them a sense of empowerment, encouraging them to further participate actively. Brand pages may even be used as a source for crowdsourcing. By asking fans' opinions, fans will feel valued and appreciated, and they may even provide strategic input. As previous research has shown that brand-specific factors can affect consumer engagement (Van Doorn et al., 2010), future research could delve into brand-specific participation behavior and take into account different product categories, for instance, hedonic versus utilitarian products, durables versus fast moving products, goods versus services, high versus low involvement products, etc.

References

Bagozzi, R. P., & Dholakia, U. M. (2006). Antecedents and purchase consequences of customer participation in small group brand communities. *International Journal of Research in Marketing, 23*(1), 45–61. doi: 10.1016/j.ijresmar.2006.01.005.

Batra, R., Ahuvia, A., & Bagozzi, R. P. (2012). Brand love. *Journal of Marketing, 76*(2), 1–16. doi: 10.1509/jm.09.0339.

Bergkvist, L., & Bech-Larsen, T. (2010). Two studies of consequences and actionable antecedents of brand love. *Journal of Brand Management, 17*(7), 504–518. doi: 10.1057/bm.2010.6.

Bernritter, S., Verlegh, P. W. J., & Smit, E. G. (2016). Consumers' online brand endorsements. In P. De Pelsmacker (Ed.), *Advertising in new formats and media: Current research and implications for marketers* (pp. 189–209). London, UK: Emerald Group Publishing Limited.

Boyd, D. M., & Ellison, N. B. (2007). Social network sites: Definition, history, and scholarship. *Journal of Computer-Mediated Communication, 13*(1), 210–230. doi: 10.1111/j.1083–6101.2007.00393.x.

Brandtzæg, P. B., & Heim, J. (2009). Why people use social networking sites. In A. A. Ozok & P. Zaphiris (Eds.), *Online communities and social computing* (pp. 143–152). Berlin Heidelberg: Springer.

Brodie, R. J., Hollebeek, L. D., Jurić, B., & Ilić, A. (2011). Customer engagement. *Journal of Service Research, 14*(3), 252–271. doi: 10.1016/j.jbusres.2011.07.029.

Burnett, G. (2000). Information exchange in virtual communities: A typology. *Information Research: An Electronic Journal, 5*(4), n.p. Retrieved August 24, 2015 from http://www.shef.ac.uk/~is/publications/infres/ircont.html.

Chauhan, K., & Pillai, A. (2013). Role of content strategy in social media brand communities: A case of higher education institutes in India. *Journal of Product & Brand Management, 22*(1), 40–51. doi: 10.1108/10610421311298687.

Daugherty, T., Eastin, M. S., & Bright, L. (2008). Exploring consumer motivations for creating user-generated content. *Journal of Interactive Advertising, 8*(2), 1–24. doi: 10.1080/15252019.2008.10788139.

De Vries, L., Gensler, S., & Leeflang, P. S. H. (2012). Popularity of brand posts on brand fan pages: An investigation of the effects of social media marketing. *Journal of Interactive Marketing, 26*(2), 83–91. doi: 10.1016/j.intmar.2012.01.003.

Dholakia, U. M., Bagozzi, R. P., & Pearo, L. K. (2004). A social influence model of consumer participation in network- and small-group-based virtual communities. *Journal of Research in Marketing, 21*, 241–263. doi: 10.1016/j.ijresmar.2003.12.004.

Ellison, N., Vitak, J., Gray, R., & Lampe, C. (2014). Cultivating social resources on social network sites: Facebook relationship maintenance behaviors and their role in social capital processes. *Journal of Computer-Mediated Communication, 19*(4), 855–870. doi: 10.1111/jcc4.12078.

Enginkaya, E., & Yılmaz, H. (2014). What drives consumers to interact with brands through social media? A motivation scale development study. *Procedia—Social and Behavioral Sciences, 148*, 219–226. doi: 10.1016/j.sbspro.2014.07.037.

Fornell, C., & Larcker, D. F. (1981). Evaluating structural equation models with unobservable variables and measurements error. *Journal of Marketing Research, 18*, 39–50. doi: 10.2307/3151312.

Fournier, S., & Avery, J. (2011). The uninvited brand. *Business Horizons, 54*(3), 193–207. doi: 10.1016/j.bushor.2011.01/001.

Goldsmith, R. E., & Horowitz, D. (2006). Measuring motivations for online opinion seeking. *Journal of Interactive Advertising, 6*(2), 3–14. doi: 10.1080/1525019.2006.10722114.

Gruner, R. L., Homburg, C., & Lukas, B. A. (2014). Firm-hosted online brand communities and new product success. *Journal of the Academy of Marketing Science, 42*(1), 29–48. doi: 10.1007/s11747–013–0334–9.

Gummerus, J., Liljander, V., Weman, E., & Pihlström, M. (2012). Customer engagement in a Facebook brand community. *Management Research Review, 35*(9), 857–877. doi: 10.1108/01409171211256578.

Ha, H., & Perks, H. (2005). Effects of consumer perceptions of brand experience on the web: Brand familiarity, satisfaction and brand trust. *Journal of Consumer Behavior, 4*(6), 438–452. doi: 10.1002/cb.29.

Habibi, M. R., Laroche, M.-O., & Richard, M. O. (2014a). Brand communities based in social media: How unique are they? Evidence from two exemplary brand communities. *International Journal of Information Management, 34*(2), 123–132. doi: 10.1016/j.ijrinfomgt.2013.11.010.

Habibi, M. R., Laroche, M.-O., & Richard, M. O. (2014b). The roles of brand community and community engagement in building brand trust on social media. *Computers in Human Behavior, 37*, 152–161. doi: 10.1016/j.chb.2014.04.016.

Hammond, M. (2000). Communication within on-line forums: The opportunities, the constraints and the value of a communicative approach. *Computers & Education, 35*(4), 251–262. doi: 10.1016/S0360–1315(00)00037–3.

Hennig-Thurau, T., Gwinner, K. P., Walsh, G., & Gremler, D. D. (2004). Electronic word-of-mouth via consumer-opinion platforms: What motivates consumers to articulate themselves on the internet? *Journal of Interactive Marketing, 18*(1), 38–52. doi: 10.1002/dir.10073.

Hoffman, D. L., & Fodor, M. (2010). Can you measure the ROI of your social media marketing? *Sloan Management Review, 52*(1), 41–49.

Hollenbeck, C. R., & Kaikati, A. M. (2012). Consumers' use of brands to reflect their actual and ideal selves on Facebook. *International Journal of Research in Marketing, 29*(4), 395–405. doi: 10.1016/j.ijresmar.2012.06.002.

Huang, E. (2008). Use and gratifications in e-consumers. *Internet Research, 18*(4), 405–426. doi: 10.1108/10662240810897817.

Jahn, B., & Kunz, W. (2012). How to transform consumers into fans of your brand. *Journal of Service Management, 23*(3), 344–361. doi: 10.1108/09564231211248444.

Kaplan, A. M., & Haenlein, M. (2010). Users of the world, unite! The challenges and opportunities of social media. *Business Horizons, 53*(1), 59–68. doi: 10.1016/j.bushor.2009.09.003.

Kwon, E. S., Kim, E. Y., Sung, Y., & Yoo, C. Y. (2014). Brand followers: Consumer motivation and attitude towards brand communications on Twitter. *International Journal of Advertising: The Quarterly Review of Marketing Communication, 33*(4), 657–680. doi: 10.2501/IJA-33–4–657–680.

Liao, S., & Chou, E. Y. (2012). Intention to adopt knowledge through virtual communities: Posters vs lurkers. *Online Information Review, 36*(3), 442–461. doi: 10.1108/14684521211241440.

Lipsman, A., Mudd, G., Rich, M., & Bruich, S. (2012). The power of "like": How brands reach (and influence) fans through social-media marketing. *Journal of Advertising Research, 52*(1), 40–52. doi: 10.2501/JAR-52–1–040–052.

Logan, K., Bright, L. F., & Gangadharbatla, H. (2012). Facebook versus television: Advertising value perceptions among females. *Journal of Research in Interactive Marketing, 6*, 164–179. doi: 10.1108/17505931211274651.

Mata, F. J., & Quesada, A. (2014). Web 2.0, social networks and e-commerce as marketing tools. *Journal of Theoretical and Applied Electronic Commerce Research, 9*(1), 56–69. doi: 10.4067/S0718–18762014000100006.

Mattila, A. S., & Wirtz, J. (2002). The impact of knowledge types on the consumer search process: An investigation in the context of credence services. *International Journal of Service Industry Management, 13*(3), 214–230. doi: 10.1108/09564230210431947.

Morandin, G., Bagozzi, R. P., & Bergami, M. (2013). Brand community membership and the construction of meaning. *Scandinavian Journal of Management, 29*(2), 173–183. doi: 10.1016/j.scaman.2013.03.003.

Muñiz, Jr., A. M., & O'Guinn, T. C. (2001). Brand community. *Journal of Consumer Research, 27*(4), 412–432. doi: 10.1086/319618.

Muntinga, D. G., Moorman, M., & Smit, E. G. (2011). Introducing COBRAs: Exploring motivations for brand-related social media use. *International Journal of Advertising, 30*(1), 13–46. doi: 10.2501/IJA-30–1–013–046.

Nadkarni, A., & Hofmann, S. G. (2012). Why do people use Facebook? *Personality and Individual Differences, 52*(3), 243–249. doi: 10.1016/j.paid.2011.11.007.

Nonnecke, B., & Preece, J. (2001). *Why lurkers lurk*. Paper presented at the Americas Conference on Information Systems, Boston.

Park, H., & Kim, Y. K. (2014). The role of social network websites in the consumer–brand relationship. *Journal of Retailing and Consumer Services, 21*(4), 460–467. doi: 10.1016/j.jretconser.2014.03.011.

Peluchette, J., & Karl, K. (2009). Examining students' intended image on Facebook: "What were they thinking?!" *Journal of Education for Business, 85*(1), 30–37. doi: 10.1080/08832320903217606.

Pentina, I., Prybutok, V. R., & Zhang, X. (2008). The role of virtual communities as shopping reference groups. *Journal of Electronic Commerce Research, 9*(2), 114–136. www.csulb.edu/journals/jecr/issues/20082/paper3.pdf.

Pöyry, E., Parvinen, P., & Malmivaara, T. (2013). Can we get from liking to buying? Behavioral differences in hedonic and utilitarian Facebook usage. *Electronic Commerce Research and Applications, 12*(4), 224–235. doi: 10.1016:j.elerap.2013.01.003.

Preece, J., Nonnecke, B., & Andrews, D. (2004). The top five reasons for lurking: Improving community experiences for everyone. *Computers in Human Behavior, 20*(2), 201–223. doi: 10.1016/j.chb.2003.10.015.

Raacke, J., & Bonds-Raacke, J. (2008). MySpace and Facebook: Applying the uses and gratifications theory to exploring friend-networking sites. *Cyberpsychology & Behavior, 11*(2), 169–174. doi: 10.1089/cpb.2007.0056.

Ridings, C. M., & Gefen, D. (2004). Virtual community attraction: Why people hang out online. *Journal of Computer-Mediated Communication, 10*(1), n.p. doi: 10.1111/j.1083-6101.2004.tb00229.x.

Ridings, C. M., Gefen, D., & Arinze, B. (2006). Psychological barrier: Lurker and poster motivation and behaviour in online communities. *Communication of Association for Information Systems, 18*, 329–354.

Rothaermel, F. T., & Sugiyama, S. (2001). Virtual internet communities and commercial success: Individual and community-level theory grounded in the atypical case of TimeZone.com. *Journal of Management, 27*(3), 297–312. doi: 10.1016/S0149-2063(01)00093-9.

Ryan, R. M., & Deci, E. L. (2000). Intrinsic and extrinsic motivations: Classic definitions and new directions. *Contemporary Educational Psychology, 25*(1), 54–67. doi: 10.1006/ceps.1999.1020.

Schlosser, A. E. (2005). Posting versus lurking: Communicating in a multiple audience context. *Journal of Consumer Research, 32*(September), 260–265. doi: 10.1086/432235.

Sicilia, M., & Palazón, M. (2008). Brand communities on the internet: A case study of Coca-Cola's Spanish virtual community. *Corporate Communications: An International Journal, 13*(3), 255–270. doi: 10.1108/13563280810893643.

Stokburger-Sauer, N., Ratneshwar, S., & Sen, S. (2012). Drivers of consumer–brand identification. *International Journal of Research in Marketing, 29*(4), 406–418.

Sukoco, B. M., & Wu, W. (2010). The personal and social motivation of customers' participation in brand community. *Journal of Business, 4*(5), 614–622.

Sung, Y., Kim, Y., Kwon, O., & Moon, J. (2010). An explorative study of Korean consumer participation in virtual brand communities in social network sites. *Journal of Global Marketing, 23*(5), 430–445. doi: 10.1080/08911762.2010.521115.

Taylor, D. G., Lewin, J. E., & Strutton, D. (2011). Friends, fans, and followers: Do ads work on social networks? *Journal of Advertising Research, 51*(1), 258–275. doi: 10.2501/JAR-51-1-258-275.

Toubia, O., & Stephen, A. T. (2013). Intrinsic vs. image-related utility in social media: Why do people contribute content to Twitter? *Marketing Science, 32*(3), 368–392. doi: 10.1287/mksc.2013.0773.

Tsimonis, G., & Dimitriadis, S. (2014). Brand strategies in social media. *Marketing Intelligence & Planning, 32*(3), 328–344. doi: 10.1108/MIP-04-2013-0056.

Tüfekçi, Z. (2007). Can you see me now? Audience and disclosure regulation in online social network sites. *Bulletin of Science, Technology & Society, 28*(1), 20–36. doi: 10.1177/0270467607311484.

Van Doorn, J., Lemon, K. N., Mittal, V., Nass, S., Pick, D., Pirner, P., & Verhoef, P. C. (2010). Customer engagement behavior: Theoretical foundations and research directions. *Journal of Service Research, 13*(3), 253–266. doi: 10.1177/1094670510375599.

Wallace, E., Buil, I., de Chernatony, L., & Hogan, M. (2014). Who 'likes' you. . . and why? A typology of Facebook fans. From 'fan'-atics and self-expressives to utilitarians and authentics. *Journal of Advertising Research, 54*(1), 92–109. doi: 10.2501/JAR-54-1-092-109.

Wiertz, C., & de Ruyter, K. (2007). Beyond the call of duty: Why customers contribute to firm-hosted commercial online communities. *Organization Studies, 28*(3), 347–376. doi: 10.1177/0170840607076003.

Wilcox, K., & Stephen, A. T. (2013). Are close friends the enemy? Online social networks, self-esteem, and self-control. *Journal of Consumer Research, 40*(1), 90–103. doi: 10.1086/668794.

Yu, J. (2014). We look for social, not promotion: Brand post strategy, consumer emotions, and engagement. A case study of the Facebook brand pages. *Journal on Media & Communications, 1*(2), 28–36. doi: 10.5176/2335–6618_1.2.17.

Zaglia, M. E. (2013). Brand communities embedded in social networks. *Journal of Business Research, 66*(2), 216–223. doi: 10.1016/j.jbusres.2012.07.015PMID23564989.

13

ASSESSING THE FINANCIAL VALUE OF DIGITAL ADVERTISING

An Event Study Approach

Chan Yun Yoo and Tae Hyun Baek

Introduction

Advertising practitioners are undergoing pressure to be more accountable for advertising and to communicate its added value to top management as well as to shareholders (Marketing Science Institute, 2004). Determining the value created by digital advertising has become a growing focus, which demands that both practitioners and scholars translate advertising resource allocations into measurable effects. Practitioners and scholars, however, have not adequately demonstrated digital advertising's impact on performance metrics that really matter to top management and shareholders, partly due to the lack of established effectiveness of measures (Marvin, 2013). Consequently, the perceived lack of accountability has threatened digital advertising's credibility or even standing in the media mix (Ha, 2008). Nonetheless, digital advertising continues to play an important role in many firms' advertising strategies.

Advertising practices that include digital advertising can help build long-term assets (e.g., brand equity, customer equity) and can be leveraged to deliver financial and firm value effects (Rust, Ambler, Carpenter, Kumar, & Srivastava, 2004). Although financial methods alone have proved inadequate for justifying advertising investments (Rust et al., 2004), the event study method, which assesses the financial impact of changes in any marketing strategy including digital advertising, seems particularly relevant in today's advertising environment where accountability is imperative. Therefore, the purpose of this chapter is: 1) to introduce the event study framework and procedure for assessing digital advertising accountability, especially, the effects of digital advertising on financial or economic value (i.e., shareholder returns), and 2) to present preliminary research examining the relationship between Fortune 500 firms' launching a digital advertising channel (i.e., Twitter) and shareholder values. This research finds that digital advertising investments may be linked to shareholder values.

Underlying Assumptions of an Event Study

Brown and Warner (1980) note the underlying assumptions of an event study:

> Event studies provide a direct test of market efficiency. Systematically nonzero abnormal security returns, which persist after a particular type of event are inconsistent with the hypothesis that security prices adjust quickly to fully reflect new information. In addition, to the extent that the event is unanticipated, the magnitude of abnormal performance at the time the event actually occurs is a measure of the impact of that type of event on the wealth of the firms' claimholders. Any such abnormal performance is consistent with market efficiency, however, since the abnormal returns would only have been attainable by an investor if the occurrence of the event could have been predicted with certainty.
>
> *(pp. 205–206)*

As such, the event study is based on three key theoretical and methodological assumptions (McWilliams & Siegel, 1997; Srinivasan & Bharadwaj, 2004): 1) Financial markets are efficient, and thus, the market's reaction to an event can be measured by stock returns over the event window; that is, the period during which the stock prices of the firm involved in the event will be studied, 2) the event is unexpected, and thus, abnormal (or excess) stock returns—the difference between an asset's actual return and its predicted return—indicate the market's reaction to the unexpected event, and 3) there are no confounding effects during the event window, and thus the effect of the event is isolated from the effects of other events.

In regard to the first assumption, a significant body of work in economics and finance has addressed the efficient market hypothesis (Fama, Fisher, Jensen, & Roll, 1969), suggesting that stock prices incorporate all relevant information available to investors and thus provide unbiased estimates of a firm's discounted future cash flow (Rappaport, 1997). Such an assumption provides a basis for using the event study method. Thus, any financially relevant information that is newly revealed to investors will be quickly reflected in stock prices, and an event is anything that results in new relevant information.

As for the second assumption, only an unexpected event can change stock prices. Because the market previously did not have information on the event, investors would gain information from the event or announcement. Abnormal stock returns can then be assumed to be the results of the stock market's response to new information. Thus, information that may result in a positive or negative change in expected future cash flows also will have a positive or negative effect on the stock price. An event, however, could have been expected, or information may have leaked out to the market prior to a formal event or announcement. Such information leakages may make the event study method challenging because determining when investors become aware of new information may be difficult.

The third assumption is based on researchers isolating the effect of an event from other confounding effects. McWilliams and Siegel (1997) have considered this assumption as the most critical for the event study method. Confounding events can include announcements of cash dividends, new products, unexpected earnings, mergers and acquisitions, stock buybacks, changes in key executives, lay-offs, restructurings, and local and federal regulations (McWilliams & Siegel, 1997; Wiles & Danielova, 2009). Any of these events might impact stock prices during the event window. Therefore, the length of the event window is very critical, because it is more difficult to control for confounding effects when long windows are used [e.g., ±90 days in Davidson, Worrell, and Dutia's CEO succession study (1993)]. Thus, an event window should be short enough to exclude confounding effects, and long enough to capture the significant effect of an event. Foster (1980) discussed methods that allow researchers to control for confounding events in an event study: 1) eliminating firms that have confounding events, 2) partitioning a sample by grouping firms that have experienced the same confounding events, 3) eliminating a firm from the sample on the day that it experiences a confounding event, and 4) subtracting the financial impact of the confounding effect when calculating the abnormal returns.

Research Design and Methods for the Event Study

Srinivasan and Bharadwaj (2004) suggested that an event study should follow these necessary steps: defining the event and specifying criteria for inclusion, calculating abnormal returns based on the normal performance model, testing statistical significance, and explaining significant abnormal returns.

Defining the Event as Well as Specifying Criteria for Inclusion

Events are typically found through extensive searches of databases such as Lexis-Nexis or Factiva to ensure the times and dates of the events are clearly identified. The event day is the date that the event actually occurred. In practice, the event window often includes up to one or more days after the event day to capture the price effects of the event and one or more days before the actual event to capture information leakages.

Then, it is necessary to specify the criteria for the inclusion of a firm's event in a study and to identify those firms that experienced confounding events during the event window. Researchers may elect to exclude certain cases from the study because of prior theoretical and methodological considerations. For example, in a study examining the effects of launching a Twitter channel on shareholder value, the launch date and time for a firm's Twitter account can be acquired on its official Twitter page by putting a cursor on the "joined" date. Firms with no stock information on the event day—because they are not publicly traded or because they have an initial public offering (IPO) after launching its Twitter accounts (e.g., Facebook)—would not be included in the study.

Calculating Abnormal Stock Returns

The next step is to assess an event's impact on a firm's shareholder value. It requires a measure of abnormal stock returns that was pioneered by Fama et al. (1969). The percentage change in the stock price is the stock return:

$$(1) \quad R_{it} = \frac{P_{it} - P_{it-1}}{P_{it-1}}$$

Where P_{it} is the stock price of asset i at time t. This stock return reflects market expectations of the financial impact of information arriving between t-1 and t. When this information deals with an event, such as launching a Twitter channel, an "important and relatively objective indication" (Kalyanaram, Robinson, & Urban, 1995, p. 14) of an event's anticipated financial consequences is obtained.

The link between an event and a firm's stock return would be examined by comparing the stock return R_{it} at the event day with $E(R_{it})$, that is, the return that would be expected if the event had not taken place. According to the market model (i.e., normal performance model), the expected return $E(R_{it})$ to asset i at time t can be expressed as a linear function of the returns from a benchmark portfolio of marketable assets R_{mt}:

$$(2) \quad E(R_{it}) = \alpha_i + \beta_i R_{mt}$$

Where α_i and β_i are the ordinary least squares (OLS) parameter estimates obtained from the regression of R_{it} on R_{mt} over an estimation period preceding the event, for example, 255 trading days, ending 46 days prior to the event. Typically, event studies using daily stock prices have used a 45-day window to separate the estimation period from the event window (Srinivasan & Bharadwaj, 2004).

A benchmark portfolio includes several broad-based stock indices, such as the Center for Research in Securities Price (CRSP) value-weighted index, the CRSP equal-weighted index, and the S&P 500 index. Removing the portion of the stock's return that is related to variations in the general market's return increases the possibility of detecting the event's effect on the stock's return. The difference between the actual return and the estimated expected return provides a measure of the "abnormal" return e_{it} for the shares of firm i and time t:

$$(3) \quad e_{it} = R_{it} - E(R_{it}) = R_{it} - (\alpha_i + \beta_i R_{mt})$$

This abnormal return, or prediction error, is the unexpected change in the stock price, which is then attributed to the event that took place at time *t*.

Testing Statistical Significance

Generally, significance tests for an event study can be grouped in parametric and nonparametric tests (Corrado, 1989; McWilliams & Siegel, 1997; Srinivasan & Bharadwaj, 2004; Kolari & Pynnonen, 2011). In a large-sample event study, abnormal returns (ARs) for the event generally are aggregated over time to produce cumulative abnormal returns (CARs) and then averaged over several firms to generate inferences about the event (i.e., Cumulative Average Abnormal Returns: CAARs).

A parametric test is based on the assumption of normal distribution of abnormal returns and depends on a classic t-test, which performs to specify if the abnormal effects in relation to the event are significantly different from zero and, thus, not the result of pure chance. In other words, the null hypothesis is that the event has no impact on firm value, whereas the alternative hypothesis is that the event increases or decreases the firm value. Parametric test statistics, however, tend to be very sensitive to outliers (McWilliams & Siegel, 1997). A useful and important control for outliers is for researchers to report nonparametric test statistics (Corrado, 1989).

Typically two nonparametric tests—a sign test and a rank test—are frequently employed in conjunction with a parametric test. The sign test (Cowan, 1992), such as the binomial Z statistic, tests whether the proportion of positive to negative returns exceeds the number from expected returns from the market model. However, a sign test is not robust in specifying whether the distribution of abnormal stock returns is skewed. To overcome this weakness, a nonparametric rank test, suggested by Corrado and colleagues (Corrado, 1989; Corrado & Zivney, 1992), transforms abnormal returns into ranks (i.e., ranking is done for all abnormal returns of both the event and the estimation period). It tests the null hypothesis that no abnormal return exists on the event day or during the event window.

Explaining Abnormal Returns

The final step of an event study is explaining abnormal returns. After determining the significance of the CAARs, researchers should explain abnormal returns by showing that the cross-sectional variation in abnormal returns is consistent with theoretical models. In order to examine any theoretically presumed association between the magnitude of abnormal returns and characteristics specific to the event, researchers have created a cross-sectional regression model of abnormal returns. Matrix of characteristics of an event and a firm become independent variables, while cumulative abnormal returns (CARs) become dependent variables in Ordinary Least Square (OLS) regression models. The t-statistics in OLS regression models will be used to assess whether or not independent variables are statistically significant.

Use of Event Studies in Assessing the Effects of Digital Advertising

Given that the total revenue of digital advertising is expected to reach about $60 billion in the United States by the end of 2015 (eMarketer, 2015), the effect of digital advertising on a firm's financial value has generated considerable interest. Searches through EBSCO Business Source Complete, using the keyword terms "advertising" and "event study," between 1997 and 2015, returned about 120 academic articles, but no such study has been conducted in the context of digital advertising.

Prior studies demonstrated that advertising decisions, such as changing an advertising slogan (Mathur & Mathur, 1995), changing ad spending before a recall announcement (Gao, Xie, Wang, & Wilbur, 2015), introducing celebrities as spokespersons (Agrawal & Kamakura, 1995), winning one or more Clio Awards (Tippins & Kunkel, 2006), and running Super Bowl commercials (Fehle, Tsyplakov, & Zdorovtsov, 2005), had significant impacts on the shareholder wealth of firms. These studies offer valuable insights into the financial effects of traditional advertising initiatives, but the financial or economic values of digital advertising practices, due to the lack of academic research, remains unclear.

When a firm launches a new digital advertising channel or initiates a new digital advertising campaign, investors could be expected to buy or sell stocks on the basis of their expectations of how the new channel or the campaign will affect the value of future cash flows. For example, investors may expect the firm to maintain its usual level of digital advertising, and thus, they could consider adding a new channel or launching a new digital advertising campaign as either an opportunity or threat.

Digital advertising developments that positively affect future cash flows should be expected to increase stock prices, whereas those that negatively affect cash flows should be expected to decrease them. Thus, an event in a digital advertising environment might have an impact on the financial performance of a firm and might produce an abnormal movement in stock prices. These hypotheses could be especially ripe for research given the increased emphasis among advertising practitioners and scholars on the accountability of digital advertising and the relationship between digital advertising investments and financial values of firms.

Accordingly, event studies could be designed in different ways to reflect specific research purposes and questions in the context of digital advertising. The event study method could be used in clinical studies as well as large sample studies. A clinical study could investigate the effect of a digital advertising event on stock prices of a single firm, such as an analysis of the market's reaction to a new Instagram sweepstakes campaign. Meanwhile, large sample studies could examine the impact of an important event (e.g., launching a new social media account as a digital advertising channel) on stock prices of different sample firms.

The following sections present how the latter (i.e., large sample event studies) could be conducted using steps suggested by Srinivasan and Bharadwaj (2004). Specifically, an exploratory event study, examining the relationship between launching a firm's Twitter account as a digital advertising channel and shareholder value, illustrates each step of the research procedure. Furthermore, the results of the study highlight how digital advertising investments could be linked to the expected financial value of a firm.

The Exploratory Event Study: Assessing the Financial Value of Launching a Twitter Channel

Information about a firm's launch of a Twitter channel is typically distributed to the market via cross-media campaigns through slogans such as "Follow us on Twitter" and other promotions (i.e., events and sweepstakes). This firm-initiated communication effort cues investors to the use of Twitter as a digital advertising channel. Therefore, launching a Twitter channel is considered an unexpected event controlled mainly by an advertiser, and it becomes a market signal directed at influencing the behavior of one or more investors of the firm. Information about a firm's decision to add a Twitter channel to its advertising portfolio should be expected to change investors' perceptions regarding a firm's future financial performance. Ultimately, information-based trading is expected in response to the event of launching a Twitter channel.

Identifying the Event and the Event Window

When research is interested in examining the financial value of launching a Twitter channel, the event is defined as launching an official Twitter account, and the event day is defined as the date when the Twitter account first appeared. Putting a cursor on the "joined" date on a Twitter account page obtains the accurate timing of the event. For example, Starbucks launched its official Twitter channel on November 29, 2006 at 11:19 a.m. In this study, however, the event windows were set, ranging from five days before through five days after the event, because of the potential for information leakage (e.g., advertisers' early press release about their launch of a Twitter channel) and the gradual dissemination of information via post-launch promotions.

Samples and Data

Fortune 500 companies are deemed to be appropriate as the sampling units for the study because they include firms from a variety of industries as well as the nations' largest firms with respect to revenues. Thus, they are more likely to adopt Twitter to interact with shareholders and customers (Culnan, McHugh, & Zubillaga, 2010), and their use of Twitter has been examined in the prior studies (Rybalko & Seltzer, 2010; Lee, Oh, & Kim, 2013). All Fortune 500 companies were searched through Twitter via typing each company name into the search box. A total of 96 firms (e.g., Energy Transfer Equity, World Fuel Service Corporation) were identified as not having official Twitter accounts at the time of searching, and they were dropped from the dataset.

Launch dates (i.e., event day) for those firms were recorded by checking the "joined" date of the official Twitter page. Daily stock-price returns for each firm were obtained from the CRSP databases, and 41 cases were dropped from the further analyses, because they were either privately held (e.g., State Farm Insurance, United Services Automobile Associations, etc.) or their stock-price data around the Twitter launching date were not available (e.g., Facebook, Vanguard Health Systems, etc.). These deletions reduced the sample to 363 cases.

Finally, a Factiva database was extensively searched to identify any case with confounding events during the event window. Firms with confounding events were removed, including those with announcements of cash dividend, new products, unexpected earnings, mergers and acquisitions, stock buybacks, changes in key executives, layoffs, restructurings, local and federal regulations, and lawsuits (McWilliams & Siegel, 1997) five days before and after the event day. This process retained 217 firms in the sample (see Appendix).

Results of the Event Study

The parameters of the market model for each firm were estimated during a window of 255 trading days, ending 46 days prior to the event, using the CRSP's equal-weighted index to model the market portfolio. All statistical calculations were performed using the EVENTUS program developed by Cowan Research, LLC. The sample firms' cumulative average abnormal returns (CAARs) and test statistics, five days before and after the event day, appear in Table 13.1.

Empirically determining the event window is standard practice in an event study to allow for any uncertainty regarding when the information was available to investors and to understand the cumulative effect of an event (Agrawal & Kamakura, 1995; Wiles & Danielova, 2009). No significant CAARs were found for the event windows prior to launching a Twitter channel (e.g., [−5 to −1], [−3 to −1], and [−1 to 0]), indicating information regarding the pending addition of a Twitter channel did not leak into the marketplace in a substantial enough manner to cause investors to reassess the firms. However, significant CAARs for the [0 to +3] event window were found. This event window fits the expectations that the market can become gradually aware of a launch of a Twitter channel via advertisers' post-promotions. The direction and pattern of the results for the post-event windows are similar, but further interpretations should be made for the statistically significant [0 to +3] event window.

TABLE 13.1 Cumulative Average Abnormal Returns (CAARs) of Launching a Twitter Channel for Fortune 500 Firms

Event Window	CAAR (%)	Sample Size (N)	The Number of Firms with Positive Abnormal Returns (%)	The Number of Firms with Negative Abnormal Returns (%)	Brown and Warner (1985) Portfolio t-Statistic	Patell (1976) Z-Statistic	Kolari and Pynnonen (2011) Generalized Rank t-Statistic
−5 to −1	.11	217	123 (56.7)	94 (43.3)	.25	.63	.29
−3 to 0	−.10	217	116 (53.5)	101 (46.5)	−.30	−.32	−.34
−1 to 0	−.21	217	110 (50.7)	107 (49.3)	−.78[a]	−.70	−.91
−1 to +1	−.31	217	108 (49.8)	109 (50.2)	−.91	−1.24	−.92
0 to +1	−.15	217	98 (45.2)	119 (54.8)	−.253	−1.11	−.58
0 to +3	−.58	217	94 (43.3)	123 (56.7)	−1.48*	−1.94*	−1.65*
0 to +5	−.25	217	100 (46.1)	117 (53.9)	−0.49	−.52	−.55

[a]$p < .10$, *$p < .05$

Results show that on average, sample Fortune 500 firms experienced -0.58 percent abnormal returns on [0 to +3] days after adding Twitter as their digital advertising channel. The associated binomial proportionality test statistic (Z) was significant, providing additional support for the robustness of the negative abnormal returns (123 of 217 abnormal returns are negative; $Z = -1.94$, $p < .05$). Furthermore, t-statistics for the crude dependence adjustment (CDA) time-series portfolio test ($t = -1.48$, $p < .05$) (Brown & Warner, 1985) as well as the generalized rank t-test ($t = -1.65$, $p < .05$) (Kolari & Pynnonen, 2011) were statistically significant, indicating that the results were not due to the outliers in the sample. Combining all together, launching a Twitter account as a firm's digital advertising channel negatively affected the shareholder's value.

Explaining Negative Abnormal Returns

Given that the use of Twitter is believed to generate positive consequences such as the co-creation and the speedy transmission of advertising content, and the potential to build relationships with millions of customers, the finding that the stock market reacted to the firm's launching Twitter channel in a negative manner was surprising. On average, launching a Twitter channel decreased the value of the firm by 0.58 percent.

Explaining the negative abnormal return is the necessary step of the event study. It is expected that the type of customers with whom the firm communicates should be relevant to the negative impact of a firm's Twitter launch. The buying process for consumer goods has been shown to be less rational, and it involves the exchange of smaller monetary amounts than the sale and purchase of industrial goods (Turley & Kelley, 1997). Furthermore, consumer goods firms tend to have a larger group of stakeholders (Jeong & Yoo, 2011), and they may need to send more market signals than industrial goods firms. Thus, if launching a Twitter channel has a positive effect on stakeholders' perception of the firm, then it is more likely with consumer goods, where brand images and brand relationships play important roles. Oppositely, the benefits of launching a Twitter channel should not be as great for industrial goods firms. Industrial goods are more likely to be tested and assessed in an objective manner, which makes industrial goods firms more prone to develop a sales orientation rather than a marketing orientation, leading to less appreciation of marketing intelligence and marketing communications (Avlonitis & Gounaris, 1997).

To examine the above scenario, a cross-sectional regression model was tested with the independent variable of industrial goods firms (i.e., dichotomously coded: 1 or 0) and two control variables (the firms' total assets and market value in millions of dollars). Note that the significant multicollinearity between consumer- and industrial-goods firms did not allow the entering of both as independent variables into the model. The model ($F_{3, 179}$ = 3.69, p < .01, adjusted R-square = .11) found that industrial goods firms yielded significantly negative abnormal stock returns to the firms' Twitter launch (β = -.18, t = -3.03, p < .01), suggesting that the overall negative abnormal returns on the [0 to +3] event window were attributable to industrial goods firms in the Fortune 500 list.

Conclusion

The exponential growth of digital advertising is intuitively understandable because digital media are especially powerful in facilitating real-time engagement with shareholders and customers, which has become critical for driving sales. Digital advertising's credibility, however, has been questioned and the pressing need has been also accentuated for advertisers to link digital advertising investment to financial performance. Furthermore, due to a lack of compelling empirical evidence, it remains unclear whether digital advertising investments, such as adding a new social media channel, will increase or decrease the financial value of a firm.

This chapter suggests that an event study would be a supplemental, but appropriate, method for evaluating the financial value effects of digital advertising practices. Event studies have been frequently employed to detect the effects of event-induced variance on abnormal returns in the field of finance and economics as well as in the past advertising studies, but have virtually never been used in the context of digital advertising. Acknowledging the gap, this chapter outlines the study framework and procedure for an event study and discusses how the event study method could be utilized to explain digital advertising's accountability and to examine the effect of digital advertising on the financial value of a firm. Furthermore, it demonstrates how the event study can be applied to the context of digital advertising, especially for examining the financial value of launching a digital advertising channel.

The exploratory event study found that launching a Twitter account as a firm's digital advertising channel has a negative impact on shareholder's value, and further analysis revealed that unexpected negative abnormal returns are attributable to a large number of industrial goods firms. A number of speculative reasons emerged: investors' fear in a new social media channel may play a role in generating negative market reactions, or their concern about increased security risk, which seemingly involve information leakage and inadvertent disclosure of internal corporate data (Waxer, 2011), may outweigh the expected benefits of using a Twitter channel.

Future studies, therefore, should examine in more detailed manner why industrial goods firms suffered negative abnormal returns upon launching a Twitter channel to provide further theoretical and practical explanations. Furthermore, digital advertisers should bear in mind that the results only reflect the short-term effect of launching a Twitter channel on the firm's financial performance for the [0 to +3] event window. While maintaining a Twitter presence, advertisers can harness its power by successfully implementing intended strategies, facilitating real-time communication and user engagement, and sharing knowledge with shareholders and customers. Thus, advertisers should not be discouraged by the overall negative abnormal returns found in the study. Further event studies, however, are recommended to examine whether the financial value effects of Twitter or other digital advertising channels could be enhanced or attenuated with continuous management and care.

References

Agrawal, J., & Kamakura, W. A. (1995). The economic worth of celebrity endorsers: An event study analysis. *Journal of Marketing, 59*(3), 56–62.

Avlonitis, G. J., & Gounaris, S. P. (1997). Marketing orientation and company performance: Industrial vs. consumer goods companies. *Industrial Marketing Management, 26*(5), 385–402.

Brown, S. J., & Warner, J. B. (1980). Measuring security price performance. *Journal of Financial Economics, 8*(3), 205–258.

Brown, S. J., & Warner, J. B. (1985). Using daily stock returns: The case of event studies. *Journal of Financial Economics, 14*(1), 3–31.

Corrado, C. J. (1989). A nonparametric test for abnormal security-price performance in event studies. *Journal of Financial Economics, 23*(2), 385–395.

Corrado, C. J., & Zivney, T. L. (1992). The specification and power of the sign test in event study hypothesis tests using daily stock returns. *The Journal of Financial and Quantitative Analysis, 27*(3), 465–478.

Cowan, A. R. (1992). Non-parametric event study tests. *Review of Quantitative Finance and Accounting, 2*(4), 343–358.

Culnan, M. J., McHugh, P. J., & Zubillaga, J. I. (2010). How large US companies can use Twitter and other social media to gain business value. *MIS Quarterly Executive, 9*(4), 243–259.

Davidson, W. N., Worrell, D. L., & Dutia, D. (1993). The stock market effects of CEO succession in bankrupt firms. *Journal of Management, 19*(3), 517–533.

eMarketer. (2015). US digital ad spending will approach $60 billion this year, with retailers leading the way: Retail industry will spend more on mobile, programmatic and video ads than any other sector. Retrieved from http://www.emarketer.com/Article/US-Digital-Ad-Spending-Will-Approach-60-Billion-This-Year-with-Retailers-Leading-Way/1012497.

Fama, E. F., Fisher, L., Jensen, M. C., & Roll, R. (1969). The adjustment of stock prices to new information. *International Economic Review, 10*(1), 1–21.

Fehle, F., Tsyplakov, S., & Zdorovtsov, V. (2005). Can companies influence investor behaviour through advertising? Super bowl commercials and stock returns. *European Financial Management, 11*(5), 625–647.

Foster, G. (1980). Accounting policy decisions and capital market research. *Journal of Accounting and Economics, 2*(1), 29–62.

Gao, H., Xie, J., Wang, Q., & Wilbur, K. C. (2015). Should ad spending increase or decrease before a recall announcement? The marketing-finance interface in product-harm crisis management. *Journal of Marketing, 79*(5), 80–99.

Ha, L. (2008). Online advertising research in advertising journals: A review. *Journal of Current Issues & Research in Advertising, 30*(1), 31–48.

Jeong, J., & Yoo, C. Y. (2011). Deceptive advertising and abnormal stock returns: An event study analysis. *International Journal of Advertising, 30*(3), 509–535.

Kalyanaram, G., Robinson, W. T., & Urban, G. L. (1995). Order of market entry: Established empirical generalizations, emerging empirical generalizations, and future research. *Marketing Science, 14*(3), G212-G221.

Kolari, J. W., & Pynnonen, S. (2011). Nonparametric rank tests for event studies. *Journal of Empirical Finance, 18*(5), 953–971. doi: http://dx.doi.org/10.1016/j.jempfin.2011.08.003.

Lee, K., Oh, W.-Y., & Kim, N. (2013). Social media for socially responsible firms: Analysis of Fortune 500's Twitter profiles and their CSR/CSIR ratings. *Journal of Business Ethics, 118*(4), 791–806.

Marketing Science Institute. (2004). Linking marketing to financial performance and firm value. *Journal of Marketing, 68*(October), 73–75.

Marvin, G. (2013, November 26). Despite soaring digital video ad spend, advertisers lack measurement tools. *Marketing Land*. Retrieved from http://marketingland.com/despite-soaring-digital-video-ad-spend-advertisers-lack-measurement-tools-study-66412.

Mathur, L. K., & Mathur, I. (1995). The effect of advertising slogan changes on the market values of firms. *Journal of Advertising Research, 35*(1), 59–65.

McWilliams, A., & Siegel, D. (1997). Event studies in management research: Theoretical and empirical issues. *Academy of Management Journal, 40*(3), 626–657.

Patell, J. M. (1976). Corporate forecasts of earnings per share and stock price behavior: Empirical test. *Journal of Accounting Research, 14*(2), 246–276.

Rappaport, A. (1997). *Creating shareholder value: A guide for managers and investors*. New York, NY: The Free Press.

Rust, R. T., Ambler, T., Carpenter, G. S., Kumar, V., & Srivastava, R. K. (2004). Measuring marketing productivity: Current knowledge and future directions. *Journal of Marketing, 68*(4), 76–89.

Rybalko, S., & Seltzer, T. (2010). Dialogic communication in 140 characters or less: How Fortune 500 companies engage stakeholders using Twitter. *Public Relations Review, 36*(4), 336–341.

Srinivasan, R., & Bharadwaj, S. (2004). Event studies in marketing strategy research. In C. Moorman & D. R. Lehmann (Eds.), *Assessing marketing strategy performance* (pp. 9–28). Cambridge, MA: Marketing Science Institute.

Tippins, M. J., & Kunkel, R. A. (2006). Winning a clio advertising award and its relationship to firm profitability. *Journal of Marketing Communications, 12*(1), 1–14.

Turley, L., & Kelley, S. W. (1997). A comparison of advertising content: Business to business versus consumer services. *Journal of Advertising, 26*(4), 39–48.

Waxer, C. (2011, February 11). CIOs struggle with social media's security risks: Facebook and other social networking sites help agencies interact with citizens but also present security threats. *Government Technology.* Retrieved from http://www.govtech.com/pcio/CIOs-Social-Media-Security-Risks-021111.html.

Wiles, M. A., & Danielova, A. (2009). The worth of product placement in successful films: An event study analysis. *Journal of Marketing, 73*(4), 44–63.

APPENDIX

Company	Event Day: Twitter Launch	SIC Code[a]	Confounding Event[b]
Starbucks Corporation	20061129	5810	0
Oracle	20070305	7372	0
Wells Fargo	20070314	6022	0
Intel	20070329	3679	1
Progressive Corporation	20070403	6331	0
JetBlue Airways Corporation	20070530	4512	0
United Technologies	20070611	3724	1
CarMax, Inc.	20070622	5521	1
Southwest Airlines	20070702	4512	0
Yum! Brands, Inc.	20070912	5812	0
Live Nation Entertainment, Inc.	20071023	7922	0
EMC Corporation	20071106	3572	0
Monsanto Company	20071130	2879	0
General Motors	20071204	3711	1
Hormel Foods Corporation	20080122	2011	0
Alaska Air Group	20080207	4512	0
Texas Instruments Incorporated	20080219	3674	0
Marriott International, Inc.	20080313	7011	0
Health Net, Inc.	20080324	6324	0
Allstate	20080401	6331	1
AT&T	20080501	4812	0
Home Depot	20080515	5211	1
Advanced Micro Devices	20080521	3674	0
DIRECTV	20080529	4899	0
Alcoa, Inc.	20080611	3334	1
Caterpillar	20080612	3531	1
Whole Foods Market, Inc.	20080616	5411	0
Nordstrom	20080618	5651	0
URS Corporation	20080702	8711	0

(Continued)

(Continued)

Company	Event Day: Twitter Launch	SIC Code[a]	Confounding Event[b]
SanDisk Corporation	20080708	3570	0
Lennar Corporation	20080711	1531	0
Ryder System, Inc.	20080721	7513	1
U S BANCORP DEL	20080723	6021	0
Ford	20080731	3711	1
Big Lots, Inc.	20080731	5331	0
Dow Chemical Company	20080801	2821	1
CSX Corporation	20080804	4011	0
Cisco Systems	20080806	3674	1
Marathon Oil Corporation	20080807	2911	0
Tyson Foods	20080813	2015	0
Northrop Grumman Corporation	20080813	3812	1
Genworth Financial	20080814	6311	0
The Southern Company	20080815	4911	0
NetApp, Inc.	20080818	3572	1
Synnex Corporation	20080822	7373	0
Raytheon CO	20080827	3812	1
PetSmart, Inc.	20080905	5990	0
Discover Financial Services	20080905	6141	0
Aetna	20080908	6324	0
Charter Communications	20081001	4841	1
Western Digital Corporation	20081027	3572	1
Windstream Holdings, Inc.	20081029	4813	0
Wal-Mart	20081103	5311	1
Harley-Davidson, Inc.	20081104	3751	0
Hewlett-Packard	20081105	3571	0
SLM Corporation	20081105	6141	0
Whirlpool	20081110	3633	0
Agilent Technologies, Inc.	20081110	3825	1
J. C. Penney Company	20081117	5311	1
Best Buy	20081118	5731	0
Symantec Corporation	20081118	7370	0
Henry Schein, Inc.	20081124	5047	0
Xerox Corporation	20081125	3577	0
Union Pacific Corp	20081125	4011	0
Waste Management, Inc.	20081125	4953	1
Travelers Companies, Inc.	20081125	6331	0
Coca-Cola Enterprises, Inc.	20081201	5651	0
Berkshire Hathaway	20081205	6331	0
Hertz Global Holdings, Inc.	20081209	7514	0
Gap	20081229	5651	0
Office Depot, Inc.	20090102	5943	1
Deere & Company	20090107	3523	0
IBM (International Business Machines)	20090114	3571	0
Micron Technology, Inc.	20090115	3674	1
Viacom, Inc.	20090115	4841	0
Baker Hughes, Inc.	20090122	3533	1
Con-way, Inc.	20090122	4213	0
The Williams Companies, Inc.	20090122	4922	0

Company	Event Day: Twitter Launch	SIC Code[a]	Confounding Event[b]
Lowe's	20090122	5211	0
AECOM Technology Corporation	20090123	8711	0
Sears Holdings	20090126	5331	1
Unum Group	20090127	6321	0
Hartford Financial Services Group	20090127	6331	0
eBay	20090129	7389	0
Northeast Utilities	20090202	4911	0
Automatic Data Processing, Inc.	20090203	7374	1
Consolidated Edison, Inc.	20090206	4931	0
J&J (Johnson & Johnson)	20090209	2834	1
Google	20090210	7375	0
Sempra Energy	20090211	4932	0
The Priceline Group, Inc.	20090211	7389	0
Tech Data Corporation	20090213	5040	0
Amazon.com	20090213	7370	1
Chevron	20090217	2911	0
Pepsico	20090219	2086	1
Avon Products, Inc.	20090223	2844	1
Discovery Communications, Inc.	20090226	4841	1
Foot Locker, Inc.	20090226	5661	0
American Airlines	20090302	4512	0
Owens Corning	20090304	2951	0
Starwood Hotels & Resorts	20090304	6798	0
Ball Corporation	20090305	3411	0
Dr Pepper Snapple Group	20090309	2086	1
ConocoPhillips	20090309	2911	1
Chubb Corporation	20090309	6331	0
BlackRock, Inc.	20090311	6211	0
DuPont	20090312	2821	0
Centene Corporation	20090312	6324	0
Humana	20090313	6324	1
Boeing	20090318	3721	0
Northwestern Mutual Life Insurance	20090320	4931	0
Anixter International, Inc.	20090320	5063	0
NCR Corporation	20090323	3578	0
Navistar International Corporation	20090323	3711	1
Coca-Cola	20090326	2086	0
CBS Corporation	20090326	4841	1
P&G (Procter & Gamble)	20090327	2841	1
Insight Enterprises, Inc.	20090327	5045	1
The Mosaic Company	20090330	2874	0
INTL FCStone	20090330	6211	0
Ingram Micro	20090401	5045	0
Amgen, Inc.	20090402	2830	1
DaVita HealthCare Partners, Inc.	20090403	8092	0
AGCO Corporation	20090406	3523	0
Safeway	20090406	5411	0
Mohawk Industries, Inc.	20090409	2273	1
PPG Industries, Inc.	20090409	2851	0

(Continued)

(Continued)

Company	Event Day: Twitter Launch	SIC Code[a]	Confounding Event[b]
First American Financial Corporation	20090409	7374	0
Western Union Company	20090413	6099	0
Wynn Resorts, Limited	20090414	7990	1
PG&E Corporation	20090415	4911	0
O'Reily Automotive, Inc.	20090415	5531	0
Freddie Mac	20090415	6111	1
Barnes & Noble, Inc.	20090416	5942	0
Bristo-Myers Squibb Company	20090421	2834	1
Ralph Lauren Corporation	20090422	2329	0
Entergy Corporation	20090422	4911	0
The Hershey Company	20090423	2066	1
CBRE Group, Inc.	20090423	6726	0
Merck & Co.	20090427	2834	1
J.B Hunt Transport Services, Inc.	20090427	4213	0
Kohl's	20090427	5311	1
Kelly Services, Inc.	20090428	7361	1
Kroger	20090429	5411	0
Exxon Mobil	20090430	2911	1
Campbell Soup Company	20090501	2032	1
Cigna	20090504	6324	1
Kindred Healthcare, Inc.	20090504	8062	1
AutoNation	20090512	5511	0
Dick's Sporting Goods, Inc.	20090519	5941	1
American Electric Power Company	20090520	4911	0
United Rentals, Inc.	20090522	7359	0
Occidental Petroleum Corporation	20090526	1311	0
American Express	20090526	6141	1
Lockheed Martin	20090527	3721	1
Express Scripts	20090527	8093	1
TJX Companies	20090528	5651	1
CenturyLink	20090602	4813	1
Rockwell Automation, Inc.	20090604	3829	1
Hess	20090605	2911	1
Walgreen	20090610	5912	1
Baxter International, Inc.	20090611	3841	1
WESCO International, Inc.	20090617	5063	0
Lincoln National Corporation	20090618	6311	1
Macy's	20090625	5311	0
The Pantry, Inc.	20090626	5411	0
Goodyear Tire & Rubber Company	20090701	3011	0
Medtronic	20090701	3845	1
Ameren Corporation	20090710	4931	0
Pfizer	20090713	2834	1
CONSOL Energy	20090714	1221	0
DTE Energy Company	20090714	4911	0
Apache Corporation	20090715	1311	0
Smithfield Foods	20090715	2013	0
United Natural Foods, Inc.	20090715	5140	0

Company	Event Day: Twitter Launch	SIC Code[a]	Confounding Event[b]
Laboratory Corporation	20090715	8071	1
Verizon Communications	20090723	4812	1
Sealed Air Corporation	20090724	2671	1
FirstEnergy Corp.	20090724	4911	1
Johnson Controls	20090730	1796	0
Emerson Electric	20090803	3629	1
Exelon Corporation	20090803	4931	1
Dillard's, Inc.	20090805	5311	0
Applied Material, Inc..	20090811	3550	1
ONEOK, Inc.	20090811	4923	0
Fidelity National Financial, Inc.	20090812	6361	0
Corning, Inc.	20090813	3357	0
Thermo Fisher Scientific, Inc.	20090814	3829	0
Norfolk Southern	20090817	4011	0
Walt Disney	20090820	7996	1
SunTrust Banks	20090824	6021	0
Cognizant Technology Solutions	20090828	7370	0
Mondelez International	20090831	2000	0
McDonald's	20090902	5812	0
Chesapeake Energy Corporation	20090903	1311	0
Apple	20090908	3571	1
Coach, Inc.	20090910	3911	0
Microsoft	20090914	7370	1
MasterCard, Inc.	20090917	7389	0
Quest Diagnostics, Inc.	20090922	8071	0
Advance Auto Parts	20090923	5531	0
Cliffs Natural Resources, Inc.	20090924	1011	0
Eastman Chemical Company	20090924	2821	0
Staples	20090930	5940	0
Metlife	20090930	6311	0
Citigroup	20091002	6021	1
Integrys Energy Group, Inc.	20091005	4931	0
UGI Corporation	20091005	4932	0
Fidelity National Information Services	20091007	7389	1
Duke Energy Corporation	20091009	4911	0
Dominion Resources, Inc.	20091019	4922	0
Qualcomm, Inc.	20091023	3663	0
Cummins, Inc.	20091103	3519	1
Harris Corporation	20091103	3663	0
NextEra Energy	20091103	4911	1
Target	20091110	5331	1
Comcast	20091112	4841	1
Casey's General Stores, Inc.	20091112	5331	0
Tenet Healthcare Corporation	20091119	8062	0
ConAgra Foods, Inc.	20091124	2096	0
Dollar Tree, Inc.	20091204	5331	0
Terex Corporation	20091209	3537	0
PNC Financial Services Group	20091211	6021	0
Mattel, Inc.	20091221	3942	1

(Continued)

(Continued)

Company	Event Day: Twitter Launch	SIC Code[a]	Confounding Event[b]
L Brands, Inc.	20091230	5651	0
Level 3 Communications, Inc.	20100106	4813	1
Kinder Morgan Energy Partners	20100108	4922	0
Xcel Energy, Inc.	20100121	4931	0
The Andersons, Inc.	20100126	5150	0
Air Products & Chemicals	20100129	2813	1
McGraw Hill Financial, Inc.	20100201	2731	1
CVS	20100202	5912	1
ADM (Archer Daniels Midland)	20100203	2046	1
The Sherwin-Williams Company	20100204	5231	1
Parker-Hannifin Corporation	20100208	3492	1
D. R. Horton, Inc.	20100210	1531	0
Heinz H J CO	20100216	2030	1
Fannie Mae	20100218	6112	0
V.F. Corporation	20100224	2325	0
Stanley Black & Decker	20100226	3423	0
CenterPoint Energy, Inc.	20100308	4931	0
Newell Rubbermaid, Inc.	20100309	3089	0
AIG (American International Group)	20100324	6331	1
Time Warner Cable, Inc.	20100330	4841	0
Colgate-Palmolive Company	20100401	2844	1
FMC Technologies, Inc.	20100405	3533	0
The Charles Schwab Corporation	20100413	6211	1
Rite Aid	20100416	5912	1
FedEx	20100419	4513	0
Spectra Energy Corp	20100507	4923	1
Family Dollar Stores, Inc.	20100517	5331	1
McKesson	20100527	5122	1
GameStop Corp.	20100527	5734	0
3M Company	20100601	3841	1
Kimberly-Clark Corporation	20100602	2676	1
Assurant, Inc.	20100604	6331	0
Biogen Idec, Inc.	20100614	2830	1
W.W. Grainger, Inc.	20100614	5063	1
UPS (United Parcel Service, Inc.)	20100621	4215	1
Ameriprise Financial, Inc.	20100707	6282	0
Principal Financial Group	20100708	6321	0
Allergan, Inc.	20100709	2834	0
LKQ Corporation	20100712	5015	0
Avery Dennison Corporation	20100713	2754	0
Bank of New York Mellon Corporation	20100716	6022	1
Fluor Corporation	20100824	1623	1
St. Jude Medical, Inc.	20100826	3845	0
TravelCenters of America LLC	20100826	5541	0
MeadWestvaco Corporation	20100910	2621	0
WellCare Health Plans, Inc.	20100913	6324	0
Sysco	20100914	5141	0
Motorola Solutions	20100927	3663	1

Company	Event Day: Twitter Launch	SIC Code[a]	Confounding Event[b]
Omnicare, Inc.	20101012	5912	1
Bank of America	20101025	6021	1
Boston Scientific Corporation	20101110	3841	0
Marsh & McLennan Companies, Inc.	20101119	6411	1
Masco Corporation	20101209	5211	0
Fifth Third Bancorp	20101227	6711	1
Public Service Enterprise Group Incorporated	20110106	4931	0
Republic Services, Inc.	20110110	4953	0
Community Health systems	20110110	8062	0
The Blackstone Group L.P.	20110118	6282	1
Gannett Co., Inc.	20110131	2711	1
Penske Automotive Group, Inc.	20110131	5511	0
Dean Foods company	20110203	2026	1
Ecolab, Inc.	20110211	2841	1
Goldman Sachs Group	20110216	6211	0
Cardinal Health	20110222	5122	0
Honeywell International, Inc.	20110225	3724	1
C. H. Robinson Worldwide, Inc.	20110301	4731	1
United Continental Holdings, Inc.	20110304	4512	0
Celanese Corporation	20110310	2869	0
Universal Health Services, Inc.	20110310	8062	0
General Electric	20110316	4813	1
Altria Group	20110317	2111	0
Erie Insurance Group	20110323	6410	0
J.P. Morgan Chase	20110330	6021	1
AutoZone, Inc.	20110406	5531	0
Las Vegas Sands Corp.	20110407	7011	0
General Mills	20110411	2043	0
Supervalu	20110414	5141	1
Halliburton Company	20110426	1389	1
AmerisourceBergen	20110427	5122	1
The Estee Launder Companies, Inc.	20110429	2844	0
Mylan, Inc.	20110505	2834	1
Ashland, Inc.	20110506	2819	0
Simon Property Group	20110519	6798	0
Edison International	20110524	4911	0
Gilead Sciences, Inc.	20110602	2830	0
The J.M. Smucker Company	20110610	2033	1
Celgene Corporation	20110628	2890	0
State Street Corporation	20110708	6022	0
Franklin Resources, Inc.	20110718	6282	0
Broadcom Corporation	20110719	3670	0
Core-Mark Holding Company, Inc.	20110720	5149	0
Dana Holding Corporation	20110727	3714	1
W.R. Berkley Corporation	20110802	6331	0
Ross Stores, Inc.	20110808	5650	1
Abbott Laboratories	20110822	2834	1
Nucor Corporation	20110824	3312	0

(Continued)

(Continued)

Company	Event Day: Twitter Launch	SIC Code[a]	Confounding Event[b]
Capital One Financial Corporation	20110829	6712	1
Bed Bath & Beyond	20110913	5700	0
Darden Restaurants	20110913	5812	0
Lear Corporation	20110915	3714	0
Weyerhaeuser Company	20110915	6798	0
BorgWarner, Inc.	20110919	3714	1
The Interpublic Group of Companies, Inc.	20110922	7311	1
Paccar	20111013	3711	0
UnitedHealth Group	20111024	6324	0
Morgan Stanley	20111101	6798	1
Dish Network	20111104	4841	1
ManpowerGroup, Inc.	20111107	7363	1
BB&T Corporation	20111108	6021	1
Nike	20111118	3021	1
PPL Corporation	20111129	4911	0
Domtar Corporation	20111206	2621	0
Airgas, Inc.	20111208	5084	1
WellPoint (Anthem, Inc.)	20111212	6324	0
Vanguard Health Systems, Inc.	20111212	8069	1
Newmont Mining corporation	20111215	1041	0
Loews Corporation	20111215	6331	0
Kellogg Company	20120103	2043	0
Prudential Financial, Inc	20120123	6311	1
Reynolds American, Inc.	20120207	2111	1
Jabil Circuit, Inc.	20120207	3672	1
The Clorox Company	20120301	2842	0
Ingredion, Inc.	20120305	2046	0
Visa	20120411	7389	0
Praxair, Inc.	20120418	2813	0
Sanmina	20120504	3672	0
Avis Budget Group	20120515	6531	1
Computer Sciences Corporation	20120604	7373	1
Arrow Electronics	20120725	5065	1
Expeditors International of Washington, Inc.	20120726	4730	0
Tractor Supply Company	20120806	5999	1
KKR & Co. L. P.	20120820	6282	1
Peabody Energy Corporation	20120828	1221	0
General Dynamics Corporation	20120906	3731	1
Philip Morris International	20121101	2111	0
Avnet	20121108	5065	1
Reliance Steel & Aluminum Co.	20121217	5051	0
Global Partners LP	20140624	5171	0

[a] 0-: Agriculture, Forestry, and Fishing, 1-: Mining and Construction, 2- or 3: Manufacturing, 4-: Transportation, Communications, Electric, Gas, and Sanitary Services, 5-: Wholesale and Retail Trade, 6-: Finance, Insurance, and Real Estate, 7- or 8-: Services, 9-: Public Administration
[b] 1 = Yes, 0 = No

14

BETWEEN AN AD BLOCK AND A HARD PLACE

Advertising Avoidance and the Digital World

Louise Kelly, Gayle Kerr, and Judy Drennan

You have done it and I have done it. We gravitate toward things that give us pleasure and avoid those which cause us pain. This basic human instinct is core to one of the oldest concepts in psychology, that of Approach-Avoidance. Our avoidance motivation is a "spring to action" that allows us to avoid negative stimuli in our environment, such as hot cooktops, boring lectures, or even advertising.

Avoidance behavior—or behavior withdrawal—is something well documented by neuroscience as lateralized in the right anterior cortical regions of our brains. At the core of this spring to action is emotion, and there is substantive empirical evidence of an association between negative affective evaluation and avoidance behavior (Chen & Bargh, 1999; Elliot & Thrash, 2002). That is, the pop-up ad annoys us, and we ignore it. Some researchers like Elliot and Thrash (2010) even suggest that approach and avoidance temperaments are basic dimensions of our personality. Perhaps you know someone who controls the remote in your household.

It might seem, therefore, that advertising avoidance is a part of human nature. But what do we know about it? And what triggers this avoidance? What challenges do advertisers face as they cope with empowered consumers, who control where and how they receive and share branded messages and increasingly choose not to receive any advertising at all? Perhaps, most importantly, how could this basic human instinct threaten free content online and potentially reshape digital advertising? Does this leave us between an ad block and a hard place? This chapter sets out to investigate these issues by defining advertising avoidance and exploring the ways in which it has been transformed in the digital world. To do this, it builds on the theoretical premise of promotional radiation to look at types of advertising avoidance, antecedents of advertising avoidance, and new research and industry trends shaping advertising avoidance in the digital world.

Advertising Avoidance Defined

Advertising avoidance is an important area of research, spanning traditional media (Speck & Elliott, 1997), online media (Edwards, Li, & Lee, 2002; Cho & Cheon, 2004), and more recently social media (Kelly, Kerr, & Drennan, 2010; Hadija, Barnes, & Hair, 2012; Barreto, 2013). Speck and Elliott (1997) created the most widely adopted definition of advertising avoidance, describing it as: "all actions that media users employ to reduce exposure to advertising content" (p. 61). This type of avoidance may be conceptualized as a spectrum, ranging from consumers not even noticing the advertisement (banner blindness) (Dreze & Hussherr, 2003; Hervet, Guerard, Tremblay, & Saber Chtourou, 2011) to users downloading ad blocking software to ensure that they do not receive any advertising (Kelly et al., 2010). This suggests that advertising can be both intentionally and unintentionally avoided (Duff & Faber, 2011).

Speck and Elliott (1997) investigated advertising avoidance across four media types (television, radio, magazines, and newspapers), concluding that avoidance is influenced by consumer characteristics, variables specific to the medium, as well as consumer perceptions toward the advertising. While they were first to include communication problems related to advertising, such as search hindrance, distraction, and disruption, as antecedents of avoidance, they found that attitude toward advertising in a medium explained the greatest variation in avoidance across all media types.

Advertising Avoidance and the Digital World

Researchers have explored advertising avoidance in the online environment since the turn of the 21st century, investigating why avoidance occurs on the various online platforms, and the role of technology in facilitating avoidance (Johnson & Kaye, 1998; Kiousis, 2001; Cho & Cheon, 2004; Obermiller, Spangenberg, & MacLachlan, 2005; Jin & Villegas, 2007; Kelly et al., 2010; Duff & Faber, 2011; Lorenzo-Romero, Constantinides, & Alarcon-del-Amo, 2011; Taylor, Lewin, & Strutton, 2011). Where once you had to leave the room to avoid advertising on television, now you can change channels with the remote, record or download or stream programs without advertising content, or even use software to mechanically block all advertising online.

As a result of these advances, advertising avoidance has become a $21.8 billion business globally. More than 198 million ad blockers globally, an increase of 41 percent in the past year, help people automatically avoid advertising (WARC, 2015). This ad block leaves the industry in a hard place with up to 27 percent of lost advertising inventory, posing a threat to free content online. It is predicted that without the revenue from online advertising, many of the marginally profitable websites offering free content will cease to exist (Naughton, 2015).

There are a number of reasons offered to explain ad blocking, which primarily relate to consumer empowerment and privacy. The most common reason cited in the literature for using ad blockers was related to privacy concerns about the misuse of personal information (WARC, 2015). On social network sites, for example, the increasing personalization of content sees advertising more specifically targeted to consumers based on their reported activities and their online behavior. For example, while Kelly et al. (2013) reported young consumer confidence in their own experience and ability to control privacy information, they still identified the "creepy line" that marketers and digital platforms sometimes cross.

Another reason for advertising avoidance in the digital world relates to consumer empowerment. As new technology has given consumers more power to actively seek out information online, they are no longer dependent upon advertising to provide product information (Dinev & Hart, 2004; Schultz, 2008; Hadija et al., 2012). This new empowerment has altered the way they perceive online advertising, and as such has made advertising avoidance much easier. In fact Schultz (2006) sees advertising avoidance as a consumer decision to participate or not in a brand conversation.

Types of Advertising Avoidance

Advertising avoidance has been described as being cognitive, affective, mechanical, or behavioral in nature (Speck & Elliott, 1997; Cho & Cheon, 2004; Kelly et al., 2010). Speck and Elliott (1997), for example, suggest that there are three types of advertising avoidance: cognitive (ignoring ads), behavioral (flip or skip), or mechanical (eliminating or blocking the ad). Cho and Cheon (2004), on the other hand, model avoidance on the three types of basic consumer responses (Vakratsas & Ambler, 1999), proposing affective (negative feelings or disliking the ad), cognitive (thought suppression or ignoring the ad), and behavioral (an action such as scrolling down to avoid advertising) responses.

One important difference between these two typologies reflects the division in the psychology literature as to whether affect and cognition are separate or interrelated systems (see Folkman, 1984; Zajonc, 1984). Some researchers suggest that cognition is a prerequisite for emotion, while others view affect and cognition as separate and partially independent systems. However, in the context of advertising avoidance, it would seem likely that the described affective avoidance (negative feelings or emotional beliefs about the advertising) still requires either cognitive avoidance (ignoring the ads) or behavioral avoidance (clicking away from the page) to enact it and to actually avoid the ad. Hence we suggest that affective avoidance is actually an affective response and often the catalyst for subsequent cognitive or behavioral avoidance.

The other difference in these two typologies is mechanical avoidance. Unlike Speck and Elliott (1997), Cho and Cheon (2004), who studied avoidance on the internet, do not propose mechanical avoidance as a type of advertising avoidance. This is interesting as mechanical avoidance is so easily achieved online through technology such as ad blocking software. It is conceivable though that mechanical avoidance could be seen as the ultimate behavioral avoidance. Indeed, Cho and Cheon's definition of behavioral avoidance, "consumer avoidance actions other than lack of attention" (2004, p. 91), could also describe mechanical avoidance. Notably, despite building these different typologies of advertising avoidance, Speck and Elliott (1997) and Cho and Cheon (2004) all still measured advertising avoidance as a single, higher-order construct.

Antecedents of Advertising Avoidance

In keeping with the idea of approach-avoid, it is likely that threats, punishment, and adverse stimuli will encourage avoidance in order to prevent harm or loss. Therefore, consumers will approach advertising that offers rewards or helps them fulfill their goals, and avoid advertising that disrupts or threatens them in some way, even if it is only a loss of time.

A number of different antecedents of advertising avoidance have been identified in the literature. These include negative stimuli: the absence of reward, such as lack of an incentive or irrelevance of the message; disruption, such as task interruption; clutter and threats, such as expectation of a negative experience; skepticism of the advertising; attitude toward the advertising medium; and privacy concerns and control (Cho & Cheon, 2004, Kelly et al., 2010).

Where there is no reward, there is little incentive to approach advertising. In the context of SNS, Kelly et al.'s (2010) exploratory study found that consumers avoided advertising on these sites when they felt that the advertising message was not relevant to them. Similarly, if consumers saw little value in the advertising, if there was no incentive for them to pay attention, then they were also likely to avoid it (Ducoffe & Curlo, 2000; Edwards et al., 2002).

Jin and Villegas (2007) also researched online advertising avoidance, considering the role of consumer ambivalence and consumer interactivity. Their study found that when consumers had low levels of interactivity and high levels of ambivalence toward the advertising, they were more likely to avoid or ignore the advertising. Hadija et al. (2012) propose that consumers on social networking sites (SNS) simply do not notice the advertising on their SNS.

Disruption to the online task also triggers advertising avoidance (Cho & Cheon, 2004). This could be caused by advertising clutter (or the belief that there is too much advertising), which is considered to disrupt media viewing and impact advertising avoidance in traditional (Speck & Elliott, 1997) and online media (Cho & Cheon, 2004). Research has shown that a low-clutter environment produces more desirable outcomes for advertisers (Nelson-Field, Riebe, & Sharp, 2012). Consumers are less likely to recall the advertising—especially if it is a lesser-known brand—if they feel that there are too many messages being directed at them (Nelson-Field et al., 2012).

In terms of threats, expectation of negative experience is likely to encourage advertising avoidance online (Cho & Cheon, 2004) and in SNS (Kelly et al.,

2010). When consumers perceive that advertising is deceptive, exaggerated, incorrectly targeted, or leads users to inappropriate sites (Cho & Cheon, 2004), they are likely to avoid the advertising. Similarly, as Kelly et al. (2010) suggest, if consumers have had a previous negative experience when they have clicked on advertising, they may be reluctant to click on advertising a second time.

In one of the earliest studies into advertising avoidance in the online environment, Edwards et al. (2002) examined negative responses and the avoidance of pop-up ads. They found that advertising intrusiveness infringed on consumer freedom online, encouraging consumers to avoid the advertising.

This perception of a negative experience may also be influenced by the believability or trustworthiness of an advertising medium. Moore and Rodgers (2005) found that trust in the advertising medium influences consumer perception of the advertising message and determines whether they ignore the message or not. Indeed, Speck and Elliott (1997) found that attitude toward advertising in a medium explained the greatest variation in avoidance across four traditional media types. Similarly, if consumers have a skeptical attitude toward the medium (e.g., Facebook) or are cynical about the advertising message, they are also more likely to avoid the advertising (Johnson & Kaye, 1998; Kelly et al., 2010).

A final threat is to one's privacy. Examining personalized advertising avoidance, Baek and Morimoto (2012) identified privacy concerns as having an impact on advertising avoidance. Building on this, Sheehan and Hoy (1999) found that consumers, if concerned, took control of their online information by participating in avoidance behaviors, such as providing incorrect information and removing themselves from mailing lists. More recently, behavioral targeting offers a visible manifestation of privacy concerns, and as a result many consumers turn to ad blocking software to protect themselves online (Johnson, 2013).

Models of Advertising Avoidance

Two studies have taken the research into antecedents of advertising avoidance and related these to the types of advertising avoidance online. These are discussed below.

Advertising Avoidance in the Online Environment: Cho and Cheon 2004

Cho and Cheon (2004) were first to develop a model of advertising avoidance for the online environment. As shown in Figure 14.1, it was built upon the three antecedents of advertising avoidance, identified earlier in this chapter: interruption of task, perceived clutter, and negative past experiences with internet advertising. When the speed of data retrieval and processing is reduced or interrupted by advertising, consumers may react in a negative way toward the advertisement or product (Cho & Cheon, 2004). Likewise, if perceived clutter is excessive,

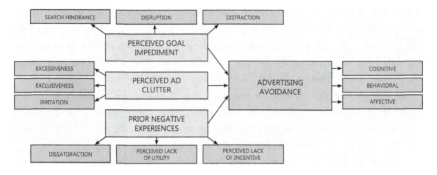

FIGURE 14.1   Advertising Avoidance in the Online Environment

Source: Cho and Cheon, 2004

consumers are likely to have difficulty in discriminating between messages, leading them to disregard all messages in this space (Cho & Cheon, 2004). Finally, past experience with online advertising that is deceptive, exaggerated, incorrectly targeted, or leads users to inappropriate sites, encourages advertising avoidance online (Cho & Cheon, 2004).

Advertising Avoidance on SNS: Kelly, Kerr, and Drennan 2010

In 2010, Kelly, Kerr and Drennan proposed a new model of advertising avoidance, by applying Cho and Cheon's (2004) research in the online environment to the more specific context of online SNS. In addition to the three antecedents that Cho and Cheon (2004) identified, Kelly et al. (2010) revealed other factors of influence and incorporated these into a model (see Figure 14.2).

Kelly et al. (2010) suggest that SNS users avoid advertising if they feel threatened when clicking on an advertisement. This could be a result of previous negative experiences with advertising on SNS or a warning from people in authority. Relevance of the advertising message was also found to be an antecedent of advertising avoidance. If the advertising message is not of interest to the receiver, then the information is likely to be ignored. This also supports Greenwald and Leavitt's (1984) early study on relevance, which found that consumer involvement with a message is dependent upon relevance. Skepticism of the advertising message and even skepticism of the advertising medium were also reasons for consumers to avoid advertising on SNS.

Toward a New Model of Advertising Avoidance

Previous models of advertising avoidance identified the antecedents of avoidance, yet measured advertising avoidance as a single construct. Kelly's (2014) quantitative study extended this knowledge of avoidance by testing whether some

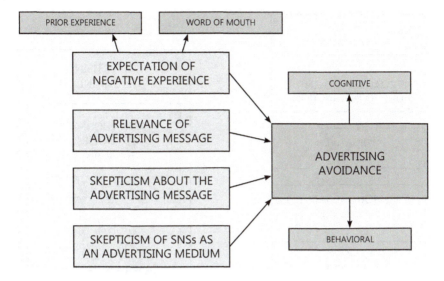

FIGURE 14.2   Model of Advertising Avoidance in Online Social Networking Sites

Source: Kelly et al., 2010

antecedents influenced some types of avoidance (such as cognitive or behavioral) but not others.

Their study found that attitude toward SNSs as an advertising medium, expectation of negative experiences with advertising owing to word-of-mouth and negative past experiences, and perceived goal impediments influence all types of advertising avoidance. When consumers had concerns about their privacy or control of their information on Facebook, they were likely to exhibit an affective response and cognitive avoidance, but not behavioral avoidance. If consumers saw no value or incentive in advertising, they were likely to exhibit cognitive and behavioral avoidance, with no affective response. Relevance of advertising message influenced how they felt and thought about advertising, but did not influence their action or behavior to avoid the advertising. Clutter influenced how consumers felt toward advertising, but not enough to trigger cognitive or behavioral avoidance. Skepticism toward the advertising message did not influence any type of advertising avoidance.

As shown in Figure 14.3, the results of this study suggest that SNS consumers have a strong emotional connection with their Facebook site, with eight of the ten tested antecedents creating an affective response. Only skepticism of advertising message and lack of incentive have no influence on how they feel toward the advertising. Likewise, cognitive advertising avoidance is also influenced by eight of the antecedents. Skepticism of advertising message again and advertising clutter had no impact. Finally, the study suggests that consumers will take action to behaviorally avoid advertising if they have a negative attitude toward it, if they

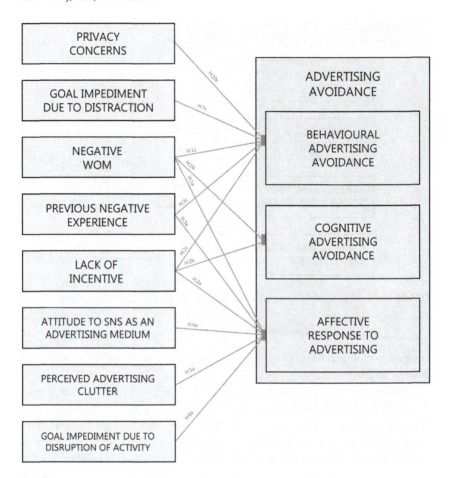

FIGURE 14.3 Antecedents of Cognitive Avoidance on Facebook

Source: Kelly, 2014

do not see value or incentive in the advertising, or if it distracts them from doing what they intended on Facebook.

The take-out for brands wanting to share this emotional space with their consumers is that understanding their expectations and being sensitive to the emotional nature of the medium may result in more engaging and more influential campaigns.

Advertising Avoidance Across Time

Maybe you are one of social network generation. Perhaps you grew up on MySpace, before migrating to Facebook, before going mobile. If so, you might find the longitudinal study by Kelly, Kerr, and Drennan (2013) a bit of déjà vu. In 2007, the cohort of teens aged 13 to 17 years were interviewed about their views on advertising on SNS. The majority of participants ignored the advertising (cognitive avoidance) and felt that the advertising on SNS (in this case mostly MySpace) was not targeted to them at all. Their parents had terrified them about the dangers of clicking on ads for fear of viruses and ending up in inappropriate websites, so even if they noticed an ad, they were hesitant to click. Thus, if the product was relevant to them it was a pure coincidence rather than receiving targeted advertising. They also thought if their site was set to private mode (which most of them were) then the SNS platform did not have access to their information for targeted advertising. Clutter was not an issue. They distrusted advertising and were reluctant to give out any personal details.

Four years later this same group was interviewed as mature 17–21 year olds who had abandoned MySpace in favor of Facebook. They had come to understand that advertisers used their information to target messages to them, but privacy concerns were flagged if this information became too personal. They understood the risks of being online and were strategic about the information they shared. Clutter of news feeds had become an issue, with brands vying for attention with their friend's messages, and this annoyed them. Their distrust of advertising on SNS had increased with maturity. And although they did not trust the advertising, they had faith that Facebook would protect their information.

The longitudinal study confirmed what many parents have long suspected: young people have mastered the art of avoidance. From ignoring things that do not attract them to an enviable proficiency with privacy settings, young people are well informed and well prepared to avoid advertising. Perhaps this is why they like advertising on Facebook, which is "just there," yet complain about more innovative engagement strategies such as "liking," which has become the new clutter. Increasingly, they rely on mechanical avoidance, which is easier and more automatic than cognitive avoidance, which at least requires some thought. Participants were confident in their own experience and their own ability to control their personal data. They are wary of unethical marketers and concerned about the "creepy line" that platforms such as Facebook continue to push. However, the delivery of more relevant advertising that consumers want to read could outweigh these concerns. Likewise, the need to socialize online might be greater than any privacy concern.

New Trends in Advertising Avoidance

What's next for this social network generation? Or even for the rest of the population who are now largely digitally enabled.

Mechanical Ad Blocking Threatens Free Content

The use of ad blocking software has rattled the advertising industry and threatens free content online. *The Wall Street Journal* reported that Randall Rothenberg, president of the Interactive Advertising Bureau (IAB) had blasted ad-blocking companies, calling them "profiteers" and charged them as standing in the way of free speech (Shields, 2016). Rather than blame the software that enables advertising avoidance, we need to better understand why it is happening in the first place.

This chapter has presented the antecedents as triggers of advertising avoidance. In addition, it has provided two overarching reasons why people avoid advertising: first for privacy reasons, and second, because they are empowered by technology to do so. They have the power to block advertising using all kinds of devices and software. They also have the power to find information when they require it, replacing the need for advertising, or perhaps changing the need for advertising from information to entertainment.

However, no research to date has looked at mechanical avoidance from a consumer perspective. Do consumers realize that, once blocked by mechanical means, all advertising, even that which is relevant or entertainment, is banished forever? And have consumers forgotten that advertising is the price you pay for free content? Future research is urgently needed to investigate the thinking behind the ad blocking.

Reckless Use of Content

Even if consumers block advertising, they still have a lot of clutter to contend with. Apart from advertising clutter, there's vendor clutter and consumer clutter. Jeff Charney, CMO, Progressive in *Ad Age* (January 11, 2016) suggests that this reckless use of content is one of marketing's biggest challenges. He says:

> Everyone's so concerned about ad blocking and time shifting, but we see a very different threat. Everybody is flooding the web with their own content, hour-by-hour, minute-by-minute. That's great, the web is democratized and the best stuff will usually rise up, but the clutter also makes it noisy. We're not just competing with our top competitors, or even other brands outside of our category, we're competing with people's friends, mothers and self-made celebrities on YouTube, Facebook, Twitter, etc. And it's just getting started.
>
> *(n.p.)*

So if we could control some of this other clutter, would consumers be less concerned with blocking ads? Certainly, research from the early days of social network sites suggested that clutter was not a problem (Kelly et al., 2010). However, research conducted shortly after noted that advertising on SNSs has the additional challenge of competing with user-generated content (Hadija et al., 2012). Undoubtedly, the popularity of the platforms and the reckless creation of content escalates the clutter.

Ad Blocking and Self-Regulation

Interestingly, it is not only consumers who are blocking ads online. In 2015, the number of ads blocked by Google increased by nearly 50 percent to 780 million advertisements. Typically, these ads contained malware, misleading messages, or somehow impacted the user experience. Amongst the culprits are 12.5 million pharmaceutical ads, 10,000 sites selling counterfeit goods, and 30,000 sites promoting weight loss scams (Hickman, 2016). Therefore, when used for the good of society, ad blocking can also be a form of advertising self-regulation, helping eliminate misleading, deceptive, or potentially dangerous advertising.

Conclusion

This chapter provided an explanation of the triggers for advertising avoidance and presented the challenges that advertisers face in order to cope with a new breed of empowered consumers who wield their power to control how, when, or even whether they receive online advertising.

Advertising avoidance has become so easy and, in many cases, automatic. We don't even have to make a cup of coffee or ignore the branded message in order to avoid advertising. However, the ease of using ad-blocking software is leaving the advertising industry, and publishers, between an ad block and a hard place. If left unchecked, it is likely to threaten the very premise of advertising to fund free media content.

References

Baek, T. H., & Morimoto, M. (2012). Stay away from me: Examining the determinants of consumer avoidance of personalized advertising. *Journal of Advertising, 41*(1), 59–76.

Barreto, A. M. (2013). Do users look at banner ads on Facebook? *Journal of Research in Interactive Marketing, 7*, 119–139.

Chen, M., & Bargh, J. A. (1999). Consequences of automatic evaluation: Immediate behavioral predispositions to approach or avoid the stimulus. *Personality and Social Psychology Bulletin, 25*(2), 215–224.

Cho, C.-H., & Cheon, H. J. (2004). Why do people avoid advertising on the internet? *Journal of Advertising, 33*(4), 89–97.

Dinev, T., & Hart, P. (2004). Internet privacy concerns and their antecedents—Measurement validity and a regression model. *Behaviour and Information Technology, 23*(6), 413–422.

Dreze, X., & Hussherr, X. F. (2003). Internet advertising: Is anybody watching? *Journal of Interactive Marketing, 17*, 8–23.

Ducoffe, R. H., & Curlo, E. (2000). Advertising value and advertising processing. *Journal of Marketing Communications, 6*(4), 247–262.

Duff, B. R. L., & Faber, R. J. (2011). Missing the mark: Advertising avoidance and distractor devaluation. *Journal of Advertising, 40*(2), 51–62.

Edwards, S. M., Li, H., & Lee, J.-H. (2002). Forced exposure and psychological reactance: Antecedents and consequences of the perceived intrusiveness of pop-up ads. *Journal of Advertising, 31*(3), 83–95.

Elliot, A. J., & Thrash, T. M. (2002). Approach–avoidance motivation in personality: Approach and avoidance temperaments and goals. *Journal of Personality and Social Psychology, 82*(5), 804–818.

Elliot, A. J., & Thrash, T. M. (2010). Approach and avoidance temperament as basic dimensions of personality. *Journal of Personality, 78*(3), 865–906.

Folkman, S. (1984). Personal control and stress and coping processes: A theoretical analysis. *Journal of Personality and Social Psychology 46*(4), 839–852.

Greenwald, A. G., & Leavitt, C. (1984). Audience involvement in advertising: Four levels. *Journal of Consumer Research, 11*(June), 581–592.

Hadija, Z., Barnes, S. B., & Hair, N. (2012). Why we ignore social networking advertising. *Qualitative Market Research, 15*(1), 19–32.

Hervet, G., Guerard, K., Tremblay, S., & Saber Chtourou, M. (2011). Is banner blindness genuine? Eye tracking internet text advertising. *Applied Cognitive Psychology, 25*, 708–716.

Hickman, A., (2016). Google blocked ads up by 50% in 2015. *AdNews*. Retrieved from http://www.adnews.com.au/news/google-blocked-ads-up-by-50-in-2015.

Jin, C. H., & Villegas, J. (2007). Consumer responses to advertising on the internet: The effect of individual difference on ambivalance and avoidance. *CyberPsycology and Behaviour, 10*(2), 258–266.

Johnson, J. P. (2013). Targeted advertising and advertising avoidance. *The RAND Journal of Economics, 44*(1), 128–144.

Johnson, T., & Kaye, B. K. (1998). Cruising is believing? Comparing internet and traditional sources on media credibility measures. *Journalism and Mass Communication Quarterly, 75*(2), 325–340.

Kelly, L., Kerr, G., & Drennan, J. (2010). Avoidance of advertising in social networking sites: The teenage perspective. *Journal of Interactive Advertising, 10*(2), 16–27.

Kelly, L., Kerr, G., & Drennan, J. (2013). *Advertising avoidance on social networking sites: A longitudinal study*. Presented at the American Academy of Advertising Annual Conference, New Mexico.

Kelly, L. M. V. (2014). *An exploration of advertising engagement, advertising avoidance and privacy concerns on social networking sites*. Doctoral Dissertation. Retrieved from http://eprints. qut.edu.au/79114/

Kiousis, S. (2001). Public trust or mistrust? Perceptions of media credibility in the information age. *Mass Communication & Society, 4*(4), 381–403.

Lorenzo-Romero, C., Constantinides, E., & Alarcon-del-Amo, M.-D.-C. (2011). Consumer adoption of social networking sites: Implications for theory and practice. *Journal of Research into Interactive Marketing, 5*(2/3), 170–188.

Moore, J. J., & Rodgers, S. L. (2005). An examination of advertising credibility and skepticism in five different media using the persuasion knowledge model. In *American Academy of Advertising Conference Proceedings* (p. 10).

Naughton, J. (2015). The rise of ad-blocking could herald the end of the free internet. Retrieved from http://www.theguardian.com/commentisfree/2015/sep/27/ ad-blocking-herald-end-of-free-internet-ios9-apple.

Nelson-Field, K., Riebe, E., & Sharp, B. (2012). What's not to "like?" Can a Facebook fan base give a brand the advertising reach it needs? *Journal of Advertising Research, 52*(2), 2–14.

Obermiller, C., Spangenberg, E., & MacLachlan, D. (2005). Ad skepticism. *Journal of Advertising, 34*(3), 7–17.

Schultz, D. E. (2006). IMC is do or die in new pull marketplace. *Marketing News, 40*(13), 7.

Schultz, D. E. (2008). Actions, not promises. *Marketing Management, 17*(2), 10–11.

Sheehan, K. B., & Hoy, M. G. (1999). Using e-mail to survey internet users in the United States: Methodology and assessment. *Journal of Computer Mediated Communication, 4*(3). Retrieved from http://www.ascusc.org/jcmc/vol4/issue3/sheehan.html.

Shields, M. (2016). IAB CEO continues to hammer ad blockers. *The Wall Street Journal.* Retrieved from http://www.wsj.com/articles/iab-ceo-continues-to-hammer-ad-bloc kers-1453849338.

Speck, P. S., & Elliott, M. T. (1997). Predictors of advertising avoidance in print and broad-cast media. *Journal of Advertising, 26*(3), 61–76.

Taylor, D. G., Lewin, J. E., & Strutton, D. (2011). Friends, fans, and followers: Do ads work on social networks? *Journal of Advertising Research, 51*(1), 258–275.

Vakratsas, D., & Ambler, T. (1999). How advertising works: What do we really know? *Journal of Marketing, 63*(1), 26–43.

WARC. (2015). Ad blocking a "viral phenomenon." Retrieved from https://www.warc. com/LatestNews/News/Ad_blocking_a_viral_phenomenon.news?ID=35212.

Zajonc, R. B. (1984). On the primacy of affect. *American Psychologist, 39*(2), 117–123.

PART IV

Digital Media—Radiating Voices

15

WHO CREATES BRAND-RELATED CONTENT, AND WHY? THE INTERPLAY OF CONSUMER CHARACTERISTICS AND MOTIVATIONS

Daniël G. Muntinga, Marjolein Moorman,
Peeter W. J. Verlegh, and Edith G. Smit

Introduction

Social media platforms such as weblogs, social networking sites, video sharing sites, and online communities facilitate a wide variety of ways for consumers to create brand-related content. Such content is central to the social media phenomenon (Smith, Fischer, & Yongjian, 2012). It gives consumers influence and credibility (Liu-Thompkins & Rogerson, 2012), and has strong potential to shape brand perceptions (Christodoulides, Jevons, & Blackshaw, 2011) and purchase behavior (Dhar & Chang, 2009). Marketers, therefore, seek to strategically inspire and cultivate the voluntary creation of brand-related content (Muñiz & Schau, 2011). To do so effectively, advertisers and marketers must be equipped with an understanding of who creates, and why they create brand-related content.

Identifying consumers who create brand-related content and exert influence over other consumers' attitudes and behaviors is critical to a successful social media strategy. It permits marketers to more precisely target and design their efforts to encourage brand-related content creation and leverage social media to the best advantage (Chatterjee, 2011; Godes, 2011; Hinz, Skiera, Barrot, & Becker, 2011). Because different types of consumers have different functions in the diffusion of information and behavior through online social networks (Watts & Dodds, 2007; Boster, Kotowski, Andrews, & Serota, 2011), different consumer characteristics may relate differently to their creation of brand-related content. However, researchers have not yet begun to examine the characteristics of consumers that create brand-related content, and the field remains largely unaware of who are the influential consumers.

In addition to knowing who creates, academics and practitioners need to understand why these potentially influential individuals create brand-related content. Muntinga (2013) shows that consumers' intrinsic motivations are important predictors of their creation of brand-related content. Little is known, however, about how intrinsic motivations are distributed across consumers. While it has repeatedly been suggested that different types of consumers have different motivations to engage with brands on social media (Porter, Donthu, MacElroy, & Wydra, 2011; Taylor, Lewis, & Strutton, 2011), this notion so far remains without academic evidence. Despite Godes et al.'s (2005) call for research on the "fundamental *motives* behind the individual's proclivity for communication as a function of the individuals' *characteristics*" (p. 418, emphasis added), little to no work in the realm of social media marketing has investigated the relationship between consumers' characteristics and their motivations to create brand-related content.

The objective of this study is, therefore, to examine the relationship between consumers' characteristics and motivations to create brand-related content while investigating the interplay of both factors in predicting brand-related content creation. The remainder of this chapter proceeds as follows. It begins by explaining this study's theoretical lens, the Uses and Gratifications (U&G) approach, followed by the introduction of three types of personality characteristics that are relevant for understanding the dynamics of social media. Next, prior research on consumers' motivations for creating brand-related content is discussed, and a research question is posed about the interplay of characteristics, motivations, and brand-related content creation. The chapter then describes the study's design, presents findings, and discusses how the findings can help strategic decision-making about how to encourage the creation of brand-related content. The chapter concludes with a brief discussion of the study's limitations and describes opportunities for further research.

Background

Uses and Gratifications Approach and Brand-Related Content

Brand-related content, when created by consumers (also "consumer-" or "user-generated content"), is defined as content that "is made available through publicly accessible transmission media such as the internet, reflects some degree of creative effort, and is created for free outside of professional routines and practices" (Christodoulides, Jevons, & Bonhomme, 2012, p. 55). The centrality of the consumer in this definition suggests the value of employing a user-centric research perspective for examining the drivers of brand-related content creation. The Uses and Gratifications (U&G) approach is the predominant user-centric theoretical framework for studying how and why individuals use media (McQuail, 2010). Commonly applied to traditional media, it is also an appropriate perspective for studying social media, as these compel the active participation of its users (Ruggiero, 2000; Nambisan & Baron, 2009; Taylor, Lewis, & Strutton, 2011; Eisenbeiss, Blechschmidt, Backhaus, & Freund, 2012).

U&G states that media use is the consequence of various factors working in concert (Katz, Blumler & Gurevitch, 1974; Rosengren, 1974). For U&G scholars, motivation is a central factor, as they assume that people purposely select and use media according to goals they actively aim to achieve. Research shows that people's motivations influence their selection, use, and sharing of different media and different content (e.g., Levy & Windahl, 1984; Rubin, 2002). But U&G also assumes that people's motivations for using media are shaped by their particular characteristics. In line with this, the present study proposes that 1) consumers' characteristics 2) influence their motivations, which 3) influence their creation of brand-related content.

Consumer Characteristics

Despite the relevance of an individual's characteristics for understanding social media dynamics (Li & Chignell, 2010), academics have not yet begun to examine how consumers' characteristics relate to their brand-related social media use. Scholars from other academic disciplines, however, have. Several studies employ the Five-Factor Model of human personality ("Big Five") to examine how user characteristics relate to the generic use of social network sites (SNSs). The majority of these studies show that the Big Five's elementary traits (extraversion, neuroticism, conscientiousness, agreeableness, and openness to experiences) exhibit limited ability to predict concrete behaviors on SNSs (e.g., Ross et al., 2009; Correa, Willard Hinsley, & De Zúñiga, 2010; Ong et al., 2011; Zhong, Hardin, & Sun, 2011; Hughes, Row, Batey, & Lee, 2012; Pettijohn II, LaPiene, Pettijohn, & Horting, 2012). It has been suggested that other, more social media-specific traits that are not defined by the Big Five may provide a better understanding of how characteristics affect social media use (e.g., Paunonen & Ashton, 2001; Baumgartner, 2002; Ross et al., 2009; Moore & McElroy, 2012; Skues, Williams, & Wise, 2012).

This study, therefore, uses three attributes that have been demonstrated to be relevant in social media contexts (Westerman, Spence, & Van der Heide, 2012): *mavenism, connectivity,* and *persuasiveness.* Taken together, these characteristics make up the personality components of being an opinion leader (Katz & Lazarsfeld, 1955; Chan & Misra, 1990; Gladwell, 2000; Boster et al., 2011). Many authors have contended that opinion leadership is an appropriate construct for dealing with social media marketing (e.g., Nisbet & Kotcher, 2009; Aral & Walker, 2011; Chu & Kim, 2011; Aral &Walker, 2012; Godes, 2011). Online opinion leaders, or "e-fluentials," (Sun, Youn, Wu, & Kuntaraporn, 2006) exercise great and frequent influence over other consumers' attitudes and behaviors (e.g., Hinz et al., 2011; Iyengar, Van den Bulte, &Valente, 2011). They have been shown to seek and forward more online information (Sun et al., 2006), make more use of the internet (Nisbet, 2006), and engage in more online word-of-mouth (Godes & Mayzlin, 2009) than less influential consumers.

But true opinion leaders are rare (Smith, Coyle, Lightfoot, & Scott, 2007). Few consumers exhibit high levels of all three characteristics of opinion leadership: most consumers who are high on mavenism, connectivity, or persuasiveness are low on the other two characteristics (Boster et al., 2011; Westerman et al., 2012). As a consequence, companies that wish to stimulate the creation of brand-related content may want to look beyond those consumers that are extremely influential, yet also extremely few in number (Katz & Lazarsfeld, 1955; Gladwell, 2000; Smith et al., 2007; Watts & Dodds, 2007; Fournier & Lee, 2009). As Boster et al. (2011) states, "influential members of social networks need not be viewed unidimensionally; indeed, it may be unprofitable to do so because different types of people fill different network functions" (p. 193). Thus, consumers high on mavenism, connectivity, and persuasiveness are influential in their own right, and accordingly, these three characteristics are interesting constructs for investigating how consumer characteristics relate to the creation of brand-related content.

Mavenism

The body of literature investigating mavens is extensive. Introduced by Feick and Price (1987), the maven predominantly features in marketing and consumer behavior research (Goldsmith, Clark, & Goldsmith, 2006). Mavens are understood as "information brokers" (Gladwell, 2000, p. 69): consumers who are well informed about products and brands, and who pass on their knowledge to other consumers. They are experts and are often consulted for advice in the real world (e.g., Goodey & East, 2008), as well as on social media (e.g., Lester, Tudor, Loyd, & Mitchell, 2012). Several studies link mavenism to increased internet usage (Barnes & Pressey, 2012), online search behavior (Belch, Krentler, & Willis-Flurry, 2005), and creating generic content (Laughlin & MacDonald, 2010).

Connectivity

Social media are "hyper-social" (Moran & Gossieaux, 2010), enabling users to connect with others online more than they can ever do offline. Some consumers are more connected than other consumers. For instance, they have a lot of Facebook friends, many followers on Twitter, or "500+" LinkedIn connections. Such well-connected consumers have a central position in their network and often link individual consumers and separate consumer collectives (Granovetter, 1973). As such, they allow for brand-related content to flow from one collective to another (Chatterjee, 2011). Well-connected consumers have been demonstrated to use SNSs more frequently (Lin & Lu, 2011), participate more in virtual marketing campaigns (Hinz et al., 2011), and contribute more to online platforms (Smith et al., 2007) than less well-connected consumers.

Persuasiveness

Some consumers are more effective at convincing others and frequently try to influence other consumers. They are skilled communicators and presenters, enjoy discussing issues, and usually have things their way (Boster et al., 2011). While research on the relationship between persuasiveness and content creation is largely absent in the literature, studies into what makes individuals, in the eyes of others, more or less persuasive (see Petty & Wegener, 1998) provide anecdotal evidence of a relationship. The Big Five trait openness to experiences is found to relate positively to the extent to which a person is perceived as persuasive: individuals low on openness to experiences are less persuasive (Rhodes & Wood, 1992), while individuals high on this personality trait are more persuasive (Gerber, Huber, Doherty, Dowling, & Panagopoulos, 2012). Additionally, research has demonstrated that openness to experiences relates positively to SNS use (Correa et al., 2010; Zhong et al., 2011) and online co-creation behaviors (Füller, Matzler, & Hoppe, 2009; Füller, 2010).

Motivations for Creating Brand-Related Content

Apart from knowing who are the consumers who create brand-related content, research on why these people create is also warranted (e.g., Moore & McElroy, 2012). "Why" in this regard refers to consumers' motivations. Research on motivations is rich and covers a wide range of academic disciplines. Although the body of literature on what motivates consumers to create specific brand-related content on social media is relatively small compared to other disciplines, it has been growing steadily over the past decade. Research has demonstrated that especially intrinsic motivations are an important factor underlying brand-related online word-of-mouth giving behavior (Hennig-Thurau, Gwinner, Walsh, & Gremler, 2004; Brown, Broderick, & Lee, 2007) and the creation of brand parodies (Berthon et al., 2008; Campbell, Pitt, & Berthon, 2011). Moreover, research demonstrates that consumers' passive-to-active brand-related activities on social media are, to a large extent, explained by the motivation types information, entertainment, personal identity, integration and social interaction, and empowerment and remuneration (Muntinga, 2013) (See Table 15.1 for a brief description of these motivations).

Muntinga (2013) shows that the activity of creating brand-related content is predominantly explained by intrinsic motivations rather than extrinsic motivations. Intrinsic motivations are driven by a strong interest and involvement in an activity itself. In the context of the current study, this indicates that consumers' creation of brand-related content is, to a large extent, dependent on the ability of that behavior to satisfy certain needs. Extrinsic motivations, on the other hand, stand apart from the performed activity. Behavior that is extrinsically motivated is usually driven by the prospect of gaining some kind of extrinsic reward, deadlines,

TABLE 15.1 Summary of Linear Regression for Consumer Characteristics Predicting Motivations, Controlling for Sex, Age, and Education (standardized regression coefficients (b^*) reported).

Characteristics	Motivations				
	Information	Entertainment	Integration and social interaction	Personal identity	Empowerment
Mavenism	.48**	.39**	.53**	.42**	.43**
Connectivity	.37**	.29**	.46**	.50**	.47**
Persuasiveness	.28**	.32**	.34**	.27**	.29**

Note. **$p < .01$.

time constraints, media availability, or competition (Ryan & Deci, 2000). While intrinsic and extrinsic motivations can both drive a consumer to create brand-related content and combinations of both are common (Kietzmann, Silvestre, & McCarthy, 2012), "one is likely to be primary for a given person doing a given task" (Amabile, 1997, p. 44). Muntinga (2013) demonstrates that creating brand-related content is primarily motivated by intrinsic motivations. Extrinsic motivation (Muntinga, Moorman, and Smit's (2011) "remuneration" motivation) was shown to have little predictive ability. Remuneration, then, is both theoretically and empirically unlikely to have much predictive ability in this particular study, so it is not taken into further account in this study.

Relating Characteristics and Motivations to Brand-Related Content Creation

Although it has been argued that online, different consumers may be driven by different motivations (Porter et al., 2011), previous social media marketing research has largely neglected how personality relates to motivations and how both factors interact to affect consumers' creation of brand-related content (Godes et al., 2005; Moore & McElroy, 2012).

Several theoretical perspectives concerned with drivers of human behavior, such as social cognitive theory (e.g., Dweck & Leggett, 1988) and self-determination theory (e.g., Deci & Ryan, 2000), suggest that particular personality features affect people's motivations, which in turn influence their behavior (Ryckman, 2004; Fang & Mowen, 2009). This study's theoretical foundation, U&G, assumes a similar path of influence, namely that media use is influenced by motivations, which in turn depend on personality (Haridakis & Hanson, 2009). This chapter, therefore, adopts the view that the influence of consumers' personality characteristics on their creation of brand-related content is mediated by their motivations. After all, as Baumgartner (2002) states, motivations are "more ideographic in nature, more closely tied to behavior" (p. 287) than personality.

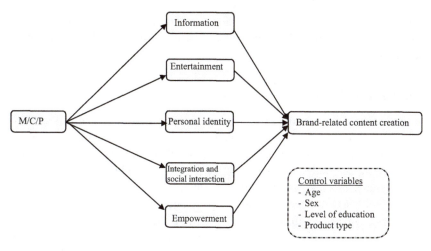

FIGURE 15.1   Conceptual Framework

Note. C = connectivity; M = mavenism; P = persuasiveness.

All human behavior is "multimotivated" (Maslow, 1970, p. 29) and so is brand-related social media use. While the relationship between motivations and brand-related content creation is increasingly well understood (see Muntinga et al., 2011), little theoretical guidance exists to predict which personality characteristics affect which motivations and how both factors interact to predict the creation of brand-related content. Because of the exploratory nature of this study, specific hypotheses were not formulated with respect to the exact nature of the proposed mediated relationship. Instead, the following research question was posed (see Figure 15.1 for a graphical representation):

RQ: How do consumers' motivations mediate the influence of consumer personality characteristics on consumers' creation of brand-related content on social media?

Research method

Social Networking Sites

A survey was developed and disseminated among the members of several brand profiles on a large social networking site (SNS). SNSs are the most prominent and important social media platforms and marketers' preferred online promotional tool (Moran & Gossieaux, 2010). Many of the profiles or pages on this platform revolve around brands. Initiated by the brand itself (the "official" brand page) or by its consumers (groups), these pages form a platform for consumers to engage in a wide variety of activities, including the creation of brand-related content. This feature makes SNSs interesting platforms for fielding this study's questionnaire.

Sample and Procedure

Respondents were recruited by soliciting the members of several of the SNS's brand pages. From a list of popular brand pages, only those pages were selected that centered on actual product brands. From the remaining brand pages, 100 brands were randomly selected; duplicates were avoided. The first author enrolled as a member of these brands' pages and observed whether they showed recent participation activity; those that did not were not selected.

Forty brand pages remained, and the questionnaire was tailored to each of these brands. Banner advertisements were created that contained links to the questionnaires, which were specifically targeted to the selected brand pages' members, aged 13 and older. In addition, the brand pages' administrators were requested to distribute the link to the questionnaire to their members; five administrators complied with this request. As an incentive to take part in this study, respondents were offered the prospect of winning a tablet computer of a popular brand. After removing the brands that yielded fewer than ten respondents, 28 product brands remained. For these brands, 2,495 respondents completed the survey (respondents between 13 and 78 years old, M_{age} = 24.88, SD = 12.93, 52% female).

Measures

For this study, the following variables were taken into account: the independent variable—namely, the three personality characteristics (mavenism, connectivity, and persuasiveness); five proposed mediators—namely, motivations (information, entertainment, personal identity, integration and social interaction, and empowerment); and, the dependent variable—brand-related content creation. All measures were provided on 7-point scales presented in a slider format, as slider scales may enhance measurement accuracy (Saris & Gallhofer, 2007).

Personality Characteristics

The measures of the personality characteristics mavenism, connectivity, and persuasiveness were taken from Boster et al. (2011), who developed a 15-item instrument to identify these three types of influential individuals based on self-reports. Because Boster et al.'s instrument was originally developed as a self-reported measure for identifying opinion leadership in health contexts, several minor modifications were made to the statements for current purposes. This is in accordance with Boster et al. (2011) who, in their future research directions section, encouraged utilization of their scales in contexts other than health. Principal component analysis with varimax rotation confirmed the three dimensions (each of five items), which were all sufficiently reliable. The items were then computed for each personality characteristic using their mean scores.

For mavenism, an example of an item is: "When I know something about a brand or a product, I feel it is important to share that information with others" (anchored by "strongly disagree" (= 1) and "strongly agree" (=7); $M_{mavenism}$ = 4.38, SD = 1.40, Cronbach's alpha = .82, R^2 = 58.78, EV = 2.93, normal distribution). For connectivity, an example of an item is: "I'm often the link between friends in different groups" (anchored by "strongly disagree" (= 1) and "strongly agree" (= 7); $M_{connectivity}$ = 3.82, SD = 1.57, Cronbach's alpha = .89, R^2 = 69.71, EV = 3.419, normal distribution). For persuasiveness, an example of an item is: "I am able to adapt my method of argument to persuade someone" (anchored by "strongly disagree" (= 1) and "strongly agree" (= 7); $M_{persuasiveness}$ = 4.71, SD = 1.40, Cronbach's alpha = .87, R^2 = 66.57, EV = 3.33, normal distribution).

Consumer Motivations

Using the motivation instrument adopted from Muntinga et al. (2011) and Muntinga (2013), the following motivations were taken into account: information (three items), entertainment (three items), integration and social interaction (four items), personal identity (three items), and empowerment (three items). All motivation scales were sufficiently reliable (Cronbach's alpha > .65), except for the entertainment scale (Cronbach's alpha = .23). The item "[because] I am bored" was found to decrease reliability of the scale and was subsequently removed (Cronbach's alpha = .65) (see Appendix 5.1 for the items for the motivation instrument).

Creating Brand-Related Content

The dependent variable, creating brand-related content, was measured with a single-item, adopted from Muntinga (2013): "I create weblogs, reviews, videos, music, pictures, and/or articles about [brand]" (anchored by "never" (= 1) and "very frequently" (= 7); $M_{creating}$ = 3.02, SD = 2.04, normal distribution).

Control Variables

In addition, several factors were measured as possible covariates, namely age, sex, level of education (primary education (elementary school) = 1, secondary education (high school) = 2, vocational education = 3, higher vocational education = 4, university education = 5), and product type. With regard to the latter, the 28 brands selected in the study were categorized as either a "search" or "experience" product according to Nelson's (1974) description of both product types. Search products are products that can be evaluated prior to purchase (N = 1,145; 46.4%).

Experience products are products that cannot be evaluated until purchase and use of the product ($N = 1,325; 53.6\%$). A dummy variable was computed to measure product type (search products = 0, experience products = 1).

Results

This study aimed to examine the relationship between consumer characteristics and intrinsic motivations to create brand-related content, but also adopted the view that the influence of characteristics on brand-related content creation is mediated by motivations. It also examined the interplay of characteristics and motivations. First, a description is given of those who are high on the three characteristics, based on their demographics, behavior, and motivations. Second, findings are reported that shed light on the motivational patterns underlying mavenism, connectivity, and persuasiveness. Third, the assumption is tested that creating brand-related content is influenced by specific motivations, which in turn are influenced by consumer characteristics.

Who? Mavens, Connectors, and Persuaders

According to Keller and Berry (2003), 10 percent of the population influences the thoughts and behaviors of the other 90 percent of the population. The present study focuses on three types of characteristics that may make a consumer, through his or her creation of brand-related content, potentially influential: mavenism, connectivity, and persuasiveness. Who are the consumers that are high on these characteristics? "High" in this regard is defined, in line with Keller and Berry (2003), as being within the highest 10 percent of the scale.

Mavenism

Findings revealed that 156 respondents were high on mavenism (scored between 6.18 and the scale maximum of 7). Analysis of variances showed that consumers high on mavenism did not significantly differ from consumers who scored relatively low on the scale (that is, within the lowest 90 percent of the scale) when it came to age and education. However, mavens tended to be male ($F(1,1434) = 16.107$, $p < .01$) and created significantly more brand-related content than consumers low on mavenism ($M_{create} = 4.46$, $SD = 2.33$ versus $M_{create} = 2.92$, $SD = 1.98$; $F(1,2493) = 86.416$, $p < .01$). Mavens also scored higher on the motivations than non-mavens: information ($F(1,1481) = 105.913$, $p < .01$), entertainment ($F(1,1481) = 58.715$, $p < .01$), personal identity ($F(1,1384) = 115.697$, $p < .01$), integration and social interaction ($F(1,1384) = 118.170$, $p < .01$), and empowerment ($F(1,1289) = 100.826$, $p < .01$). This suggests that mavens were more prominently driven by internal motivations than other consumers.

Connectivity

For connectivity, a similar pattern was observed. A total of 156 respondents scored high on connectivity (5.84–7), and these respondents did not differ significantly from their less well-connected counterparts in terms of age and education. Analysis of variance showed that those high on connectivity were predominantly male ($F(1,1434)$ = 4.368, p < .05) and created more brand-related content than respondents that scored relatively low on this scale: M_{create} = 4.56, SD = 2.33 versus M_{create} = 2.91, SD = 1.98; $F(1,2493)$ = 99.439, p < .01. In addition, consumers high on connectivity also scored significantly higher on each of the five motivations: information ($F(1,1481)$ = 99.879, p < .01), entertainment ($F(1,1481)$ = 66.909, p < .01), personal identity ($F(1,1384)$ = 146.097, p < .01), integration and social interaction ($F(1,1484)$ = 117.368, p < .01), and empowerment ($F(1,1289)$ = 114.892, p < .01). Again, this suggests that connectors were more prominently internally motivated than less well-connected consumers.

Persuasiveness

Of the respondents, 153 were within the highest 10 percent of the persuasiveness scale (6.46–7). Again, these respondents did not differ significantly from less persuasive respondents in terms of age and education. Analysis of variance showed that those high on persuasiveness were predominantly male ($F(1,1434)$ = 5.133, p < .05) and created significantly more brand-related content than respondents that score relatively low on this scale: M_{create} = 3.94, SD = 2.04 versus M_{create} = 2.96, SD = 1.99; $F(1,2493)$ = 33.469, p < .01. Respondents high on persuasiveness also scored significantly higher on the motivations information ($F(1,1481)$ = 63.560, p < .01), entertainment ($F(1,1481)$ = 58.813, p < .01), personal identity $F(1,1384)$ = 72.639, p < .01, integration and social interaction ($F(1, 1384)$ = 68.526, p < .01), and empowerment $F(1,1289)$ = 64.992, p < .01).

Overall

While respondents who were high on one characteristic tended to also score high on the other two characteristics, results demonstrate that few consumers were shown to exhibit high levels of all three characteristics. Sixty-three respondents scored within the highest 10 percent of the mavenism, connectivity, and persuasiveness scales. Effectively, then, these respondents were so-called opinion leaders. Such individuals were predominantly male ($F(1,1434)$ = 8.340, p < .01), created more brand-related content than all other respondents (M_{create} = 5.53, SD = 2.33 versus M_{create} = 2.95, SD = 2.00; $F(1,2493)$ = 101.837, p < .01), and—similar to mavenism, connectivity, and persuasiveness—scored significantly higher on intrinsic motivations than respondents that did not exhibit high levels of all three characteristics.

Different Consumers, Different Motivations?

While it has repeatedly been suggested that different consumers are motivated differently to engage with brands and brand-related content on social media, academic research on this topic is largely absent. Linear regression analyses were conducted to investigate the intrinsic motivations underlying the three consumer types in their creation of brand-related content (results are shown in Table 15.2).

Mavenism

Because the demographic variables of sex and age correlated significantly with mavenism and several of the five motivations (see Appendix 5.2), these variables were included in the analyses as covariates. The demographic variable education and the variable product type did not correlate with the motivations and therefore were not included. Controlling for the influence of age and sex, then, mavenism significantly predicted all motivations. This indicates that all motivations may play a role in mavens' creation of brand-related content. The integration and social interaction ($b\star = .53$), information ($b\star = .48$), and empowerment ($b\star = .43$) motivations, however, were the most prominent drivers of mavens' creation of brand-related content

Connectivity

Using identical analyses, the five motivations were regressed on connectivity. In this analysis, only sex was included as a covariate since age, education, and product type correlated significantly with neither connectivity nor motivations. Results showed that connectivity significantly and positively predicted all motivations, but most prominently the personal identity ($b\star = .50$), empowerment ($b\star = .47$), and integration and social interaction ($b\star = .46$) motivations.

Persuasiveness

Controlling only for the influence of sex and education, persuasiveness significantly predicted all the motivations. Persuasiveness was most prominently associated with the motivations integration and social interaction ($b\star = .34$), entertainment ($b\star = .32$), and empowerment ($b\star = .29$).

Motivations for Creating Brand-Related Content

Linear regression results showed that creating brand-related content was significantly driven by all of the five motivations taken into account: information ($b\star = .10, SE = .03, t = 2.92, p < .01$), entertainment ($b\star = .12, SE = .03, t = 3.75, p < .01$), integration and social interaction ($b\star = .13, SE = .04, t = 3.37, p < .01$), personal identity ($b\star = .11, SE = .03, t = 3.12, p < .01$), and empowerment ($b\star = .10, SE = .03, t = 3.13, p < .01$).

TABLE 15.2 Direct and Indirect Effects of Characteristics on Brand-Related Content Creation through Motivations, Controlled for Sex

	Direct effect		Indirect effect														
			Information				Entertainment				Integration and social interaction						
					95% CI				95% CI					95% CI		
Characteristics	De	SE	Ie	SE	LL	UP	Ie	SE	LL	UL	Ie	SE	LL	UL			
Mavenism	.02	.03	.05	.02	.01	.08	.04	.01	.02	.07	.07	.02	.03	.12			
Connectivity	.10**	.03	.03	.01	.01	.07	.04	.01	.02	.06	.05	.02	.01	.09			
Persuasiveness	.03	.03	.03	.01	.00	.05	.04	.01	.01	.06	.04	.01	.02	.07			

	Indirect effect									
	Personal identity					Empowerment				
			95% CI					95% CI		
Characteristics	Ie	SE	LL	UL		Ie	SE	LL	UL	
Mavenism	.05	.02	.01	.08		.05	.02	.02	.08	
Connectivity	.04	.02	.00	.09		.04	.02	.00	.08	
Persuasiveness	.03	.01	.01	.05		.03	.01	.01	.05	

Note: Standardized regression coefficients ($b\star$) reported; De = direct effect; Ie = indirect effect; LL = lower limit; SE = standard error; UL = upper limit; when 95% CI (confidence interval) contains zero the indirect effect is significant; $\star\star p < .01$.

Mediation Analyses

To verify the assumption that creating brand-related content was influenced by motivations, which in turn were influenced by characteristics, a bootstrapping approach was employed. This approach for assessing specific mediating relationships allows for the examination of multiple mediators (Zhao, Lynch, & Chen, 2010; Hayes, 2012). The indirect effects of mavenism, connectivity, and persuasiveness on brand-related content creation were examined through the proposed mediators: the intrinsic motivations information, entertainment, integration and social interaction, personal identity, and empowerment. Three bootstrapping analyses were conducted, one for each consumer characteristic. Each of these controlled for the influence of sex, which was shown to correlate significantly with the three independent variables, three out of five proposed mediators, and the dependent variable (see Appendix).

Results showed significant total effects for mavenism ($b\star = .25$, $SE = .02$, 95% CI [.21, .30]), connectivity ($b\star = .21$, $SE = .02$, 95% CI [.16, .25]), and persuasiveness ($b\star = .16$, $SE = .02$, 95% CI [.12, .20]). This indicates that mavens created more brand-related content than connectors and persuaders, and that connectors created more brand-related content than persuaders. As depicted in Table 15.2, there was also a significant direct effect for connectivity on creating ($b\star = .10$, $SE = .03$), but not for mavenism and persuasiveness. This means that connectivity also had an effect on creating independent of motivations. With regard to mediation, for all three models, the confidence intervals did not contain zero, which indicates that although small, as is common for mediated effects,[1] there was a significant indirect effect of all three characteristics on the creation of brand-related content through motivations.

Conclusion and Discussion

To inspire and cultivate consumers' creation of brand-related content on social media, academics and practitioners need to have an understanding of who are the consumers that create brand-related content, and why they create it (e.g., Godes et al., 2005). Little to no work in the realm of social media marketing, however, has previously investigated the relationship between consumer characteristics and consumer motivations, and how both factors interplay to predict consumers' creation of brand-related content on social media. The present study fills this gap in literature. It shows that different consumers have different motivations to create brand-related content and that the relationship between characteristics and brand-related content creation is mediated by motivations. Below, this study's results are discussed in light of the existing literature.

Different Consumers Are Differently Motivated to Create

Previous research has suggested that consumer characteristics that are highly relevant for a social media environment may help to better understand the dynamics of brand-related social media use (cf. Paunonen & Ashton, 2001; Baumgartner, 2002; Ross et al., 2009; Moore & McElroy, 2012; Skues et al., 2012). This study therefore employed three characteristics that have been demonstrated as highly relevant in a social media context: mavenism, connectivity, and persuasiveness. These three characteristics represent three consumer types that fill different network functions, and as such they are potentially very influential through their dissemination and creation of brand-related content (Boster et al., 2011). Because intrinsic motivations have been shown to have great ability to predict consumers' creation of brand-related content, it is important to understand the intrinsic motivations behind mavens', connectors', and persuaders' creation of brand-related content. This study is the first to investigate and demonstrate that different types of consumers have different motivations to create brand-related content on social media.

Mavenism

The first consumer characteristic, mavenism, has received great academic attention since the introduction of the market maven-construct by Feick and Price in 1987. Research on mavens, that is, "information brokers" (Gladwell, 2000, p. 69), has demonstrated that this trait is positively linked to a variety of off- and online behaviors such as increased use of the internet (Barnes & Pressey, 2012) and increased creation of generic content on social media (Laughlin & MacDonald, 2010). While the market maven-construct mainly features in marketing literature and while the concept has been shown relevant in social media contexts (Lester et al., 2012), to date, little was known about how mavenism related to consumers' creation of specifically brand-related content. By showing that mavenism can also be linked to consumers' increased creation of brand-related content, this study therefore both corroborates and extends previous research's findings. Mavens not only collect and share the brand-related information that companies and other consumer produce, but they also create a substantial amount of brand-related content themselves.

Little was hitherto known what drives the maven. There is some research that has investigated the psychological profile of mavens (Goldsmith et al., 2006), but what inspires a maven to create brand-related content thus far fully remained in the dark. This study demonstrated that mavens are primarily motivated by a need for integration and social interaction (belonging to a group, engaging in brand-related conversations), a need for information (for instance about where to buy products and brands or about their brand-related social environment), and a need for empowerment (influencing brands and/or other consumers).

Connectivity

Findings indicate that the second of the three social-media specific consumer characteristics, connectivity, also significantly relates to consumers' creation of brand-related content. Although the total effect of connectivity is less than that of mavenism, there is a significant direct effect of connectivity on creating. Connectivity is associated with consumers who have a great many connections and bridge different consumer collectives. Word-of-mouth and social media marketing commonly assumes that such highly connected consumers are likely to generate a large amount of influence as they occupy central positions in social networks (Libai, Muller, & Peres, 2013). Literature confirms this by demonstrating that highly connected consumers are particularly active in online environments (Rosen, 2009), make more use of social networking sites (Lin & Lu, 2011), and contribute more to online platforms than other consumers (Hinz et al., 2011). However, the connectivity characteristic was not earlier tied to brand-related content creation on social media. By doing so, this study not only adds to the field's understanding of the dynamics of interpersonal influence via social media, but also contributes to the ongoing discussion in literature about the efficacy of different network targeting strategies that suggest that targeting consumers in the presence of social influence can be very effective (e.g., Aral, Muchnik, & Sundararajan, 2012).

In addition, this study demonstrates that the connectivity characteristic can also be directly linked to brand-related content creation, that is, independent of motivations. This result attests to the special role of connectors in the context of social media and, in particular, social networking sites (SNSs). Social media enable people to easily keep in touch with a great many people from different countries and different periods of life. Making connections with other people is a basic element for individuals making use of SNSs (Boyd & Ellison, 2007). "Being connected," then, is a highly relevant characteristic for the social media phenomenon. In that regard, results from studies into the relationship between user personality and SNS use suggests that when a personality trait is highly relevant for a concrete behavior, it may well have some explanatory power for this behavior (Baumgartner, 2002; Ross et al., 2009; Amichai-Hamburger & Vinitzky, 2010; Moore & McElroy, 2012). This is why, in this study, it was chosen to employ three personality characteristics that were shown to be highly relevant for social media (Westerman et al., 2012). The direct effect of connectivity shows that indeed, when personality traits are highly relevant for concrete behaviors, they may explain additional variance independent of intrinsic motivations.

What motivates consumers who are highly connected? In the absence of such knowledge in the existing literature, this study set out to investigate connectors' motivations to create brand-related content. Results indicate that connectors are primarily motivated by a need for personal identity (portraying oneself in a preferred manner, self-expression, or gaining self-assurance), followed by a need for empowerment (influencing companies or other consumers), and a need for integration and social interaction (talking and connecting with like-minded others).

Persuasiveness

The third consumer characteristic that was taken into account, persuasiveness, stands for the ability to convincing other consumers effectively and regularly. Persuasiveness has been mentioned as a potentially influential personality trait with regard to social networks (Gladwell, 2000; Boster et al., 2011), but literature on persuasiveness as a specific trait is virtually absent (conversely, the body of research into what makes an individual persuasive in the eyes of other consumers is vast). Unsurprisingly, then, research on this characteristic in the context of consumers' creation of brand-related content so far did not exist, although Füller et al. (2009) and Füller (2010) showed that the Big Five trait "openness to experiences," associated with persuasiveness (Boster et al., 2011), relates to increased online co-creation activity. While previous research thus only provided anecdotal evidence for the influence of persuasiveness in online marketing contexts, this study empirically demonstrates that the more persuasive an individual reports to be, the more brand-related content he or she creates. Persuaders, however, create less brand-related content than mavens and connectors.

Why do persuaders create brand-related content? This study demonstrates that persuaders are primarily driven by a need for integration and social interaction (belonging to a group of like-minded people and engaging with them in brand-related conversations), a need for entertainment (enjoyment, relaxation), and a need for empowerment (influencing companies or other consumers).

The Interplay of Characteristics and Motivations

This study thus shows that different types of consumers have different motivations to create brand-related content. However, in line with the Uses and Gratification (U&G) premise that media use is driven by a variety of factors working in concert (e.g., Katz et al., 1974), it was also investigated whether the creation of brand-related content on social media results from the interplay of consumer characteristics and intrinsic motivations. Particularly, since motivations have previously been demonstrated to explain a large portion of variance in creating brand-related content (see Muntinga, 2013), it was examined whether motivations mediated the relationship between consumer characteristics and brand-related content creation.

Results show that, indeed, consumer characteristics affect consumer motivations, which in turn affect consumers' creation of brand-related content. By demonstrating that the effect of consumer characteristics on brand-related content creation is to a large extent mediated by intrinsic motivations, this study makes three important contributions to the literature. First, in demonstrating that a mediation model of personality and motivations is well able to predict concrete behaviors, it corroborates U&G's premise that media use is the result of the interplay of a host of factors. Second, it additionally validates U&G because it shows that the most important of these factors are dispositional, that is, stemming from a strong interest and involvement in the activity and needs within the individual—namely motivations. All media use, brand-related social media use no less, is actively directed toward fulfilling certain needs. Understanding these needs, then, is vital toward gaining an understanding of the dynamics of media use. This chapter thereby corroborates previous findings that beyond extrinsic factors, intrinsic motivation is a key element of creating brand-related content to be understood (cf. Muntinga, 2013). Third, this second contribution confirms Baumgartner's (2002) earlier mentioned statement that motivations are "more ideographic in nature, more closely tied to behavior" (p. 287) than personality.

With regard to this third contribution, this study's results have important implications for the growing body of research into the individual differences associated with the use of social media and social networking sites (SNSs) in particular. Arguing that personality is an important determinant of human behavior, an increasing number of authors investigate how the Big Five factors of human personality relate to the use of SNSs. The majority of these studies however demonstrate that such general personality traits explain little variance in SNS use (e.g., Ross et al., 2009). While the debate about the relevance of personality is ongoing (e.g., Amichai-Hamburger & Vinitzky, 2010), there is consensus among authors that other factors, such as consumer characteristics that are not captured by the Big Five, as well as motivations, may explain concrete behaviors in specific situations (Moore & McElroy, 2012). This study confirms this idea. It shows that motivation is a very important factor to consider when aiming to predict (brand-related) social media use, but it also shows that highly specific personality traits may explain additional variance in concrete behaviors independent of motivations when they are also highly relevant for those behaviors. Considering the growing academic interest in explaining SNS use, then, this study urges authors that wish to predict SNS use to employ more social-media specific personality traits. Most importantly however, this study aligns with prior research by making a strong case for including motivation in such research.

Practical Implications

The present study has implications for practitioners who wish to inspire and cultivate the voluntarily creation of brand-related content on social media. They can be guided by this study's results as follows. First, it is shown that targeting consumers who can be identified as mavens may be particularly beneficial. Consumers who often seek for and disseminate brand-related information create more brand-related content than other types of consumers, especially persuaders. As a result, strategically stimulating mavens to create may make brand-related content go viral and become "contagious" more quickly. Mavens can be identified by consulting demographic/usage profiles (Lester et al., 2012), psychological markers (Iyengar et al., 2011), or employing standard self-report methods such as that recently developed by Boster et al. (2011).

Second, yet more importantly, this study shows that the influence of personality on brand-related content creation is to a large extent mediated by motivations. For brand managers, this finding denotes an important practical implication, because motivations can be more easily addressed than personality factors (Ross et al., 2009) and because (as this study also shows) mavens, connectors, and persuaders do not differ very much in terms of demographics. Marketing and advertising practitioners currently remain predominantly reliant on sociodemographics, psychological profiles, and usage profiles when seeking to most effectively propagate brand-related content and behaviors. Intrinsic motivations, on the other hand, are commonly neglected as targeting factors. Based on this study's findings, it is argued that encouraging consumers' creation of brand-related content may be done best by helping consumers fulfill their intrinsic motivations. Practitioners that wish to stimulate mavens thus first need to understand why mavens engage in the creation of brand-related content. Findings from this chapter can particularly help them do so: mavens are shown to be primarily driven by needs for integration and social interaction, information, and empowerment.

Limitations and Future Research Directions

This research is subject to some limitations, which may provide interesting directions for future research. First, this study uses a sample of 28 brands and two product types: search and experience products. The type of product is not shown to affect the creation of brand-related content or the motivations underlying this behavior. The fact that the type of product has little explanatory power aligns with research demonstrating that brands themselves do not explain much variance in brand-related behaviors; as Ahuvia (2015) aptly states, "nothing matters more to people than people" (p. 122). Nevertheless, previous research on electronic word-of-mouth on social media demonstrates that the search/experience dichotomy holds value for explaining consumers' reactions toward brand-related content (Willemsen et al., 2011). In that respect, it is to some extent surprising to find that that this dichotomy does not hold for the current study. While it may well be that the explanatory value of the search/experience scheme only lies at the consequences-side of brand-related content, it would be interesting to examine why it has no explanatory value for the antecedents-side of brand-related content. Future research is therefore warranted to further investigate the conditions and situations in which the search/experience scheme does (not) hold value.

As a second and perhaps most potent avenue for future research, this study shows that motivations, in general, are a more prominent predictor of brand-related content creation than consumer characteristics. For those researchers that employ personality as the sole determinant of social media use, as there are many, this result implies that they should also begin to incorporate intrinsic motivation in their work. After all, by leaving out motivations, they neglect the most powerful driver of (brand-related) social media use. However, media use is the consequence of a host of antecedents, personality, motivations, and a great many others, working together. Future research on the antecedents of brand-related social media use should therefore ideally seek to integrate motivation and personality within one overarching framework. In that regard, this study can be considered as the first step toward that framework.

Note

1 See Preacher and Kelley (2011) for an extended discussion of the practical importance of effect size in the context of mediation.

References

Ahuvia, A. C. (2015). Nothing matters more to people than people: Brand meaning and social relationships. *Review of Marketing Research, 12*, 121–149.

Amabile, T. M. (1997). Motivating creativity in organizations: On doing what you love and loving what you do. *California Management Review, 40*(1), 39–58.

Amichai-Hamburger, Y., & Vinitzky, G. (2010). Social network use and personality. *Computers in Human Behavior, 26*(6), 1289–1295.

Aral, S., Muchnik, L., & Sundararajan, A. (2012). Engineering social contagions: Optimal network seeding in the presence of homophily. Retrieved from http://papers.ssrn.com/sol3/papers.cfm?abstract_id=1770982.

Aral, S., & Walker, D. (2011). Creating social contagion through viral product design: A randomized trial of peer influence in networks. *Management Science, 57*(9), 1623–1639.

Aral, S., & Walker, D. (2012). Identifying influential and susceptible members of social networks. *Science, 337*(6092), 337–341.

Barnes, S. J., & Pressey, A. D. (2012). In search of the "Meta-Maven": An examination of market maven behavior across real-life, web, and virtual world marketing channels. *Psychology & Marketing, 29*(3), 167–185.

Baumgartner, H. (2002). Toward a personology of the consumer. *Journal of Consumer Research, 29*(2), 286–292.

Belch, M. A., Krentler, K. A., & Willis-Flurry, L. A. (2005). Teen internet mavens: Influence in family decision making. *Journal of Business Research, 58*(5), 569–575.

Berthon, P. R., Pitt, L. F., & Campbell, C. (2008). AdLib: When consumers create the ad. *California Management Review, 50*(4), 6–30.

Boster, F. J., Kotowski, M. R., Andrews, K. R., & Serota, K. (2011). Identifying influence: Development and validation of the connectivity, persuasiveness, and maven scales. *Journal of Communication, 61*(1), 178–196.

Boyd, D., & Ellison, B. (2007). Social network sites: Definition, history, and scholarship. *Journal of Computer-Mediated Communication, 13*(1), 210–230.

Brown, J., Broderick, A. J., & Lee, N. (2007). Word of mouth communication within online communities: Conceptualizing the online social network. *Journal of Interactive Marketing, 21*(3), 2–20.

Campbell, C., Pitt, L. F., & Berthon, P. R. (2011). Understanding consumer conversations around ads in a web 2.0 world. *Journal of Advertising, 40*(1), 87–102.

Chan, K. K., & Misra, S. (1990). Characteristics of the opinion leader: A new dimension. *Journal of Advertising, 19*(3), 53–60.

Chatterjee, P. (2011). Drivers of new product recommendation and referral behavior on social network sites. *International Journal of Advertising, 30*(1), 77–101.

Christodoulides, G., Jevons, C., & Blackshaw, P. (2011). The voice of the consumer speaks forcefully in brand identity: User-generated content forces smart marketers to listen. *Journal of Advertising Research, 51*(1), 101–111.

Christodoulides, G., Jevons, C., & Bonhomme, J. (2012). Memo to marketers: Quantitative evidence for change. How user-generated content really affects brands. *Journal of Advertising Research, 52*(1), 53–64.

Chu, S.-C., & Kim, Y. (2011). Determinants of consumer engagement in electronic word-of-mouth (eWOM) in social networking sites. *International Journal of Advertising, 30*(1), 48–75.

Correa, T., Willard Hinsley, A., & De Zúñiga, H. G. (2010). Who interacts on the web? The intersection of users' personality and social media use. *Computers in Human Behavior, 26*, 247–253.

Deci, E. L., & Ryan, R. M. (2000). The "what" and "why" of goal pursuits: Human needs and the self-determination of behavior. *Psychological Inquiry, 11*(4), 227–268.

Dhar, V., & Chang, E. A. (2009). Does chatter matter? The impact of user-generated content on music sales. *Journal of Interactive Marketing, 23*(4), 300–307.

Dweck, C. S., & Leggett, E. L. (1988). A social-cognitive approach to motivation and personality. *Psychological Review, 95*(2), 256–273.

Eisenbeiss, M., Blechschmidt, B., Backhaus, K., & Freund, P. A. (2012). "The (real) world is not enough:" Motivational drivers and user behavior in virtual worlds. *Journal of Interactive Marketing, 26*(1), 4–20.

Fang, X., & Mowen, J. C. (2009). Examining the trait and functional motive antecedents of four gambling activities: Slot machines, skilled card games, sports betting, and promotional games. *Journal of Consumer Marketing, 26*(2), 121–131.

Feick, L. F., & Price, L. L. (1987). The market maven: A diffuser of marketplace information. *Journal of Marketing, 51*(1), 83–97.

Fournier, S., & Lee, L. (2009). Getting brand community right. *Harvard Business Review, 87*(4), 105–111.

Füller, J. (2010). Refining virtual co-creation from a consumer perspective. *California Management Review, 52*(2), 98–122.

Füller, J., Matzler, K., & Hoppe, M. (2009). Brand community members as a source of innovation. *Journal of Product Innovation Management, 25*(6), 608–619.

Gerber, A. S., Huber, G. A., Doherty, D., Dowling, C. M., & Panagopoulos, C. (2012). Big five personality traits and responses to persuasive appeals: Results from voter turnout experiments. *Political Behavior*, published online, doi: 10.1007/s11109-012-9216-y.

Gladwell, M. (2000). *The tipping point: How little things can make a big difference*. New York, NY: Little Brown.

Godes, D. (2011). Invited comment on "opinion leadership and social contagion in new product diffusion." *Marketing Science, 30*(2), 224–229.

Godes, D., & Mayzlin, D. (2009). Firm-created word-of-mouth communication: Evidence from a field test. *Marketing Science, 28*(4), 721–739.

Godes, D., Mayzlin, D., Chen, Y., Das, S., Dellarocas, C., Pfeiffer, B., Libai, B., Sen, S., Shi, M., & Verlegh, P. W. J. (2005). The firm's management of social interactions. *Marketing Letters, 16*(3/4), 415–428.

Goldsmith, R. E., Clark, R. A., & Goldsmith, E. B. (2006). Extending the psychological pro-file of market mavenism. *Journal of Consumer Behaviour, 5*(5), 411–419.

Goodey, C., & East, R. (2008). Testing the market maven concept. *Journal of Marketing Management*, *24*(3–4), 265–282.

Granovetter, M. S. (1973). The strength of weak ties. *American Journal of Sociology*, *78*(6), 1360–1380.

Haridakis, P., & Hanson, G. (2009). Social interaction and co-viewing with YouTube: Blending mass communication and social connection. *Journal of Broadcasting and Electronic Media*, *53*(2), 317–335.

Hayes, A. F. (2012). PROCESS: A versatile computational tool for observed variable mediation, moderation, and conditional process modeling. Retrieved from http://www.afhayes.com/public/process2012.pdf.

Hennig-Thurau, T., Gwinner, K. P., Walsh, G., & Gremler, D. D. (2004). Electronic word of mouth via consumer-opinion platforms: What motivates consumers to articulate themselves on the internet. *Journal of Interactive Marketing*, *18*(1), 38–52.

Hinz, O., Skiera, B., Barrot, C., & Becker, J. U. (2011). Seeding strategies for viral marketing: An empirical comparison. *Journal of Marketing*, *75*(6), 55–71.

Hughes, D. J., Rowe, M., Batey, M., & Lee, A. (2012). A tale of two sites: Twitter vs. Facebook and the personality predictors of social media usage. *Computers in Human Behavior*, *28*(2), 561–569.

Iyengar, R., Van den Bulte, C., & Valente, T. W. (2011). Opinion leadership and social contagion in new product diffusion. *Marketing Science*, *30*(2), 195–212.

Katz, E., Blumler, J. G., & Gurevitch, M. (1974). Utilization of mass communication by the individual. In J. G. Blumler & E. Katz (Eds.), *The uses of mass communications: Current perspectives on gratifications research* (Vol. 3, pp. 19–32). Beverly Hills, CA: Sage Publications.

Katz, E., & Lazarsfeld, P. F. (1955). *Personal influence*. Glencoe, IL: Free Press.

Keller, E. B., & Berry, J. L. (2003). *The influentials: One American in ten tells the other nine how to vote, where to eat, and what to buy*. New York, NY: Simon & Schuster.

Kietzmann, J. H., Silvestre, B. S., McCarthy, I. P., & Pitt, L. F. (2012). Unpacking the social media phenomenon: Towards a research agenda. *Journal of Public Affairs*, *12*(2), 109–119.

Laughlin, J. D., & MacDonald, J. B. (2010). Identifying market mavens online by their social behaviors in community-generated media. *Academy of Marketing Studies Journal*, *14*(1), 55–70.

Lester, D., Tudor, R. K., Loyd, D. D., & Mitchell, T. (2012). Marketing mavens' fusion with social media. *Atlantic Marketing Journal*, *1*(1). Retrieved from http://digitalcommons.kennesaw.edu/amj/vol1/iss1/6.

Levy, M. R., & Windahl, S. (1984). Audience activity and gratifications: A conceptual clarification and exploration. *Communication Research*, *11*(1), 51–78.

Li, J., & Chignell, M. (2010). Birds of a feather: How personality influences blog writing and reading. *International Journal of Human-Computer Studies*, *68*(9), 589–602.

Libai, B., Muller, E., & Peres, R. (2013). Decomposing the value of word-of-mouth seeding programs: Acceleration vs. expansion. *Journal of Marketing Research*, *50*(2), 161–176.

Lin, K.-Y., & Lu, H.-P. (2011). Why people use social networking sites: An empirical study integrating network externalities and motivation theory. *Computers in Human Behavior*, *27*(3), 1152–1161.

Liu-Thompkins, Y., & Rogerson, M. (2012). Rising to stardom: An empirical investigation of the diffusion of user-generated content. *Journal of Interactive Marketing*, *26*(2), 71–82.

Maslow, A. H. (1970). *Motivation and personality*. New York, NY: Harper & Row.

McQuail, D. (2010). *Mass communication theory* (6th ed.). London: Sage Publications.

Moore, K., & McElroy, J. C. (2012). The influence of personality on Facebook usage, wall postings, and regret. *Computers In Human Behavior*, *28*(1), 267–274.

Moran, E., & Gossieaux, F. (2010). Marketing in a hyper-social world: The tribalization of business study and characteristics of successful online communities. *Journal of Advertising Research*, *50*(3), 227–228.

Muñiz, A. M. Jr., & Schau, H. J. (2011). How to inspire value-laden collaborative consumer generated content. *Business Horizons*, *54*(3), 209–217.

Muntinga, D. G. (2013). *Catching COBRAs*. Amsterdam: SWOCC.

Muntinga, D. G., Moorman, M., & Smit, E. G. (2011). Introducing COBRAs: Exploring motivations for brand-related social media use. *International Journal of Advertising*, *30*(1), 13–46.

Nambisan, S., & Baron, R. (2009). Virtual consumer environments: Testing a model of voluntary participation in value co-creation activities. *Journal of Product Innovation Management*, *26*(4), 388–406.

Nelson, P. (1974). Advertising as information. *The Journal of Political Economy*, *82*(4), 729–754.

Nisbet, E. C. (2006). The engagement model of opinion leadership: Testing validity within a European context. *International Journal of Public Opinion Research*, *18*, 3–30.

Nisbet, M. C., & Kotcher, J. (2009). A two-step flow of influence? Opinion-leader campaigns on climate change. *Science Communication*, *30*, 328–354.

Ong, E. Y. L., Ang, R. P., Ho, J. C. M., Lim, J. C. Y., Goh, D. H., Lee, C. S., & Chua, A. Y. K. (2011). Narcissism, extraversion and adolescents' self-presentation on Facebook. *Journal of Personality and Individual Differences*, *50*, 180–185.

Paunonen, S. V., & Ashton, M. C. (2001). Big five factors and facets and the prediction of behavior. *Journal of Personality and Social Psychology*, *81*(3), 524–539.

Pettijohn II, T. F., LaPienne, K. E., Pettijohn, T. F., & Horting, A. L. (2012). Relationships between Facebook intensity, friendship contingent self-esteem, and personality in U.S. college students. *Cyberpsychology: Journal of Psychosocial Research on Cyberspace*, *6*(1), 1–8. Retrieved from http://www.cyberpsychology.eu/view.php?cisloclanku=2012042901.

Petty, R. E., & Wegener, D. T. (1998). Attitude change: Multiple roles for persuasion variables. In D. Gilbert, S. Fiske, & G. Lindzey (Eds.), *The handbook of social psychology* (4th ed., pp. 323–390). New York, NY: McGraw-Hill.

Porter, C. E., Donthu, N., MacElroy, W. H., & Wydra, D. (2011). How to foster and sustain engagement in virtual communities. *California Management Review*, *53*(4), 80–110.

Preacher, K. J., & Kelley, K. (2011). Effect size measures for mediation models: Quantitative strategies for communicating indirect effects. *Psychological Methods*, *16*(2), 93–115. doi: 10.1037/a0022658.

Rhodes, N. D., & Wood, W. (1992). Self-esteem and intelligence affect influenceability: The role of message reception. *Psychological Bulletin*, *111*, 156–169.

Rosen, E. (2009). *The anatomy of buzz revisited: Real-life lessons in word of mouth marketing*. New York, NY: Doubleday.

Rosengren, K. E. (1974). Uses and gratifications: A paradigm outlined. In J. G. Blumler & E. Katz (Eds.), *The uses of mass communications: Current perspectives on gratifications research* (pp. 269–286). Beverly Hills, CA: Sage Publications.

Ross, C., Orr, E. S., Sisic, M., Arseneault, J. M., Simmering, M. G., & Orr, R. R. (2009). Personality and motivations associated with Facebook use. *Computers in Human Behavior*, *25*(2), 578–586.

Rubin, A. M. (2002). The uses and gratifications perspective of media effects. In J. Bryant & D. Zillmann (Eds.), *Media effects: Advances in theory and research* (pp. 525–548). Mahwah, NJ: Lawrence Erlbaum Associates.

Ruggiero, T. E. (2000). Uses and gratifications theory in the 21st century. *Mass Communication & Society, 3*(1), 3–37.

Ryan, R. M., & Deci, E. L. (2000). Intrinsic and extrinsic motivations: Classic definitions and new directions. *Contemporary Educational Psychology, 25*(1), 54–67.

Ryckman, R. (2004). *Theories of personality.* Belmont, CA: Thomson/Wadsworth.

Saris, W. E., & Gallhofer, I. N. (2007). Estimation of the effect of measurement characteristics on the quality of survey questions. *Survey Research Methods, 1*(1), 29–43.

Skues, J. L., Williams, B., & Wise, L. (2012). The effects of personality traits, self-esteem, loneliness, and narcissism on Facebook use among university students. *Computers in Human Behavior, 28*(6), 2414–2419.

Smith, A. N., Fischer, E., & Yongjian, C. (2012). How does brand-related user-generated content differ across YouTube, Facebook, and Twitter? *Journal of Interactive Marketing, 26*(2), 102–113.

Smith, T., Coyle, J., Lightfoot, E., & Scott, A. (2007). Reconsidering models of influence: The relationship between consumer social networks and word of mouth effectiveness. *Journal of Advertising Research, 47*(4), 387–397.

Sun, T., Youn, S., Wu, G., & Kuntaraporn, M. (2006). Online word-of-mouth (or mouse): An exploration of its antecedents and consequences. *Journal of Computer-Mediated Communication, 11*(4), 1104–1127.

Taylor, D. G., Lewis, J. E., & Strutton, D. (2011). Friends, fans, and followers: Do ads work on social networks? How gender and age shape receptivity. *Journal of Advertising Research, 51*(1), 258–275.

Watts, D. J., & Dodds, P. S. (2007). Influentials, networks, and public opinion formation. *Journal of Consumer Research, 34*(4), 441–458.

Westerman, D., Spence, P. R., & Van der Heide, B. (2012). A social network as information: The effects of system generated reports of connectedness on credibility on Twitter. *Computers in Human Behavior, 28*(1), 199–206.

Willemsen, L. M., Neijens, P. C., Bronner, F. E., & De Ridder, J. A. (2011). "Highly recommended!" The relationship between message characteristics and perceived helpful-ness of online reviews. *Journal of Computer-Mediated Communication, 17*, 19–38.

Zhao, X., Lynch Jr., J. G., & Chen, O. (2010). Reconsidering Baron and Kenny: Myths and truths about mediation analysis. *Journal of Consumer Research, 37*, 197–206.

Zhong, B., Hardin, M., & Sun, T. (2011). Less effortful thinking leads to more social networking? The associations between the use of social network sites and personality traits. *Computers in Human Behavior, 27*(3), 1265–1271.

APPENDIX

Motivation	Items
Information	I am looking for information about [brand]
	I want to know what other people think about, or do with [brand]
	I want to know how to use [brand], or how I can solve a problem with [brand]
Entertainment	Just because I like it
	I am bored
	I think it is relaxing
Personal identity	I want to impress others with what I know or have of [brand]
	I want to express what kind of person I am
	It gives me self-confidence
Integration and social interaction	I feel a bond with other people that like [brand]
	I want to talk, discuss, and share information with people that also like [brand]
	I want to belong to a group of people that all like [brand]
	I want to meet new people that are also interested in [brand]
Empowerment	I want to make [brand] suggestions about new or existing products
	I want to influence other people
	I want to influence [brand] to do, or to leave, something

APPENDIX B Result of Bivariate Correlations Between the Observed Variables

	1	2	3	4	5	6	7	8	9	10	11	12	13
1. CRE	1												
2. MAV	.35**	1											
3. CON	.37**	.62**	1										
4. PER	.20**	.64**	.55**	1									
5. INF	.38**	.47**	.36**	.29**	1								
6. ENT	.37**	.35**	.28**	.29**	.51**	1							
7. PID	.41**	.41**	.48**	.25**	.50**	.48**	1						
8. ISI	.41**	.52**	.46**	.34**	.60**	.53**	.62**	1					
9. EMP	.38**	.43**	.45**	.28**	.50**	.40**	.63**	.59**	1				
10. AGE	.05	.10**	-.02	.05	.07*	-.04	-.10**	.04	-.14**	1			
11. SEX	.09**	.15**	.08**	.08**	.10**	.08**	.03	.13**	.02	.03	1		
12. EDU	-.04	.09**	.01	.09**	.04	-.04	-.05	.03	-.06*	.40**	.08**	1	
13. PRO	-.04	-.07**	-.06*	-.06*	-.04	.04	-.02	.00	-.00	-.12**	-.07**	-.03	1

Note. AGE = age; CON = connectivity; CRE = creating; EDU = education; EMP = empowerment; ENT = entertainment; INF = information; ISI = integration and social interaction; MAV = mavenism; PER = persuasiveness; PID = personal identity; PRO = product type; SEX = sex; * $p < .05$, ** $p < .01$.

16

SOCIAL MEDIA ADVERTISING

Unraveling the Mystery Box

Saleem Alhabash, Juan Mundel, and Syed Ali Hussain

Picture this. Candace Payne, a stay-home mom, buys a Chewbacca electronic mask from Kohl's for herself. She decides to take a selfie video with the mask on her face and share it with friends and family. Payne puts on the mask and dissolves into uncontrollable laughter. She posts the video to her Facebook page for her friends and family to view. Within a few days, and through electronic word-of-mouth (eWOM), Payne's selfie video was shared and viewed over 140 million times on Facebook, making it the most viewed Facebook Live video of all time (Guynn, 2016; Itkowitz, 2016). Payne's video is an excellent example of how social media work, how it facilitates brand and product evolution, and most importantly, how it continues to alter the rules of advertising, marketing, and public relations, mainly by dissolving the boundaries between advertising, marketing, and public relations (Scott, 2015). While the traditional advertising model generally applied a linear progression from ideation, strategic thinking, execution to evaluation; social media advertising is an amalgamation of iterative processes intertwined to galvanize advertisers' strategic input, public relations efforts, offline strategies (including point-of-purchase), mobile tactics, and most importantly, use of approaches that build on the organic nature of social media content. Social media amplify the importance of the human factor in that the highest salience is placed on understanding how consumers respond, react, and generate online content that fits (or modifies) an existing advertising strategy. As social media ad spending rapidly and exponentially increases, valued at $8.5 billion in 2014 and expected to hit $14 billion by 2018 (Hoelzel, 2014), social media advertisers are faced with two major questions. First, how can advertisers create genuine, unique, and viral experiences that affect consumers' attention, engagement, and hopefully, purchase behavior? Second, how can advertisers quantify return on investment (ROI) from social media advertising? Or, an even better question: how should advertisers think and rethink ROI from social media advertising given its nuances, intricacies, and complexities? Responses to these questions are detailed in the sections below.

Social Media and Advertising: Concepts

Compared to traditional media, social media provide users the ability to not only view and access information, but also share, engage with, and create multimodal content distributed privately, semi-privately, and publicly through networks of friends, followers, and users (Scott, 2015). We define social media advertising as any piece of online content designed with a persuasive intent and/or distributed via a social media platform that enables internet users to access, share, engage with, add to, and co-create.

Social media advertising can be grouped into paid, owned, and earned media (Hurrle & Postatny, 2015). Platforms like Facebook, Twitter, YouTube, and Instagram offer advertisers numerous ways to pay social media platforms for the exchange of behavior targeting to reach consumers through display ads, promoted content, and various applications and plug-ins. On the other hand, advertisers may resort to strategic tactics using organic presence, wherein the company directly disseminates content to their followers online. Finally, earned social media refers to instances where users engage with content either through eWOM or through user-generated content (UGC) related to the brand/service. In doing so, advertisers invest in and cultivate consumers as brand/service ambassadors and social media influencers, who will generate content and online engagement with the brand for dissemination among their online social network (Roman, 2015; mediakix.com, 2016).

The Chewbacca mom viral video discussed at the beginning of this chapter is a prime example of user-generated brand mentions that not only offer brand visibility (e.g., mentioning Kohl's, the Chewbacca electronic mask, association with the Star Wars brand) but also highlights the converged nature of the present advertising world. In the example, Kohl's responded immediately and posted a video in which they offered Payne and her family numerous gifts (Wahba, 2016). Facebook invited Payne to their headquarters to celebrate her video's 140+ million views. Instances like this further underscore the opportunities and affordances provided by social media for advertising, marketing, and public relations.

Digital ad spending has been constantly growing in the United States, and advertisers are increasingly allocating larger budgets to social media (Okazaki & Taylor, 2013; Saxena & Khanna, 2013; Olmstead & Lu, 2015). As of mid-2015, advertisers spent $23.68 billion on social media advertising, with a projected growth to $35.98 billion in 2017, representing 16 percent of all digital spending (eMarketer, 2015). These figures only include activities in which advertisers pay social media platforms for any form of advertising, excluding organic advertising activities. In 2015, advertisers allocated roughly $13 for every $100 spent on all forms of paid advertising, including TV, print, radio, out-of-home, directories, and other digital media, which is projected to grow to roughly \$18 per \$100 in 2017 (eMarketer, 2016).

This points toward two important insights. First, the salience of social media advertising is no longer a nuance. Second, as advertisers continue to invest in social media, then it must be garnering effectiveness, something that warrants further investigation. There are several reasons for the claim that advertising on social media is more effective than advertising via traditional media (Sass, 2015). First, placing ads on social media is much cheaper than traditional media (Bhanot, 2012). Second, advertisers now have the tools to better quantify and reach specific target audiences. Third, social media analytics provide improved accuracy to measure ad effectiveness through machine learning algorithms and data analytics, tracking not just views and impressions, but also different facets of online and offline forms of ad engagement.

Despite clear and evident advantages of social media for advertising, numerous challenges exist that we attempt to emphasize in the remainder of this chapter. First, success on social media is largely attributed to coincidental efforts and trial-and-error. Therefore, a theoretical discussion of the processes associated with social media advertising is critically important. Second, there are neither clear standards nor consistency in terms of what are the key outcomes to which advertisers should pay attention, and more importantly, what do these outcomes mean and how do they translate and redefine traditional advertising and marketing outcomes (e.g., purchase intention, purchase behavior, brand loyalty, etc.).

Re-Envisioning Persuasion Theories in a Social Media Context

Much social media advertising practice, while relying on strategic thinking processes, is the result of considerable trial-and-error. The nature of social media— how accessible, cheap (in most cases, free), and easy-to-use they are—has shifted industry standards in terms of the strategic ad production processes. The era of pre-tests, evaluations, and systematic consumer research has been replaced with systematic processes that reflect the "always-on" nature of social media and users. The new era is of *research as we go*. However, existing persuasion theories can still be applied to design and measurement of social media advertising. The next section details the ways in which three theoretical frameworks—often applied in advertising and persuasion research—can be used to unravel the phenomenon of social media advertising and its effects.

Dual Process Models of Persuasion

Among the multiple information processing models, the elaboration likelihood model (ELM, Petty & Cacioppo, 1981, 1986) and the heuristic systematic model (HSM, Chaiken, 1980, 1987; Chaiken, Liberman, & Eagly, 1989) have been widely adopted in advertising research. The premise of ELM and HSM is that processing of persuasive messages often occurs in two distinctive ways: activating either the central route (systematic) or the peripheral route (heuristic) processing. Central route or systematic processing involve heightened allocation of elaboration and thinking about a message's persuasive argument, while the peripheral route (heuristic) processing is less cognitively involving and rather superficial in that humans rely on heuristic cues and short-cuts to evaluate the message and subsequently their acceptance of arguments. Source (e.g., model attractiveness, expertise, trustworthiness), message (e.g., advertising appeal, argument quality), and receiver (e.g., involvement) attributes are thought to influence the method of processing that is guided by an individual's motivation and ability to process information.

ELM/HSM, stemming from the study of persuasive communication over the past four decades, envisioned the persuasive process as a linear one, similar to other communication models (e.g., Shannon & Weaver, 1949; Lasswell, 1971): a communicator develops a message, disseminates it through a channel to a receiver who is affected by that message with some instances of feedback. The uniqueness of social media persuasion lies in two areas: 1) information overload, and 2) blurring persuasive lines.

Information Overload

First, the persuasion process is increasingly gravitating toward non-linearity that is mainly fueled by information overload, content abundance, and multitasking. With the abundance of content to which social media users are exposed to, attention, comprehension, and retention of persuasive messages occur in parallel with other activities, while other entities (including competing advertisers) concurrently disseminate information to the user. Additionally, some users are rarely engaged in a single-medium or single-message use sessions (Kononova, 2013). Instead, they are often multitasking (though, in reality, it is frequent task-switching). Yeykelis, Cummings, and Reeves (2014) found that college student participants spent an average of 19 seconds on a single task, including writing term papers, answering emails, and checking social media, among other activities. Therefore, a significant challenge to advertisers and marketers is understanding how to effectively reach consumers and gain their attention toward persuasive messages disseminated via social media. Messages that *do* get noticed, liked, shared, and commented are either built on strong emotional appeals and/or display relevant information (Berger & Milkman, 2010; Eckler & Bolls, 2011; Alhabash et al., 2013; Alhabash, Baek, Cunningham, & Hagerstrom, 2015). These are basic psychological processes that shape our understanding of persuasive communication (Lang, 2006; Lang, 2014; Lang & Bailey, 2015). Humans allocate cognitive resources to processing external stimuli (i.e., persuasive message) through motivational activation that is responsive to novelty, emotionality, and motivational relevance (Lang, 2006). Messages that make it through the clutter filters are ones that strategically balance the three instigators of motivational processing. Think of the *Chewbacca Mom* video: it's novel in that an adult woman is trying on a children's toy, it's funny, and it relates to parenting experiences. Most importantly, the video has a persuasive effect for multiple brands (i.e., Kohl's, Star Wars, Chewbacca mask) that is seamless and unique from a traditional ad format. Even though this video was not originally created and disseminated as an advertisement, with its growing popularity and emphasis on the brand, it simulated an advertisement on social media. However, not all social media ads are created equal nor will they yield desired outcomes. Different message types might lead to different forms of online and offline behaviors. A study using psychophysiological measurement showed that the physiological responses (namely, heart rate and skin conductance) preceding the performance of online behaviors varied as a function of whether the participant pressed the Like, Share, or Comment buttons (Al-Riyami et al., 2016).

Blurring Persuasive Lines

Second, the distinctions made between the sender, message, channel, and user are blurring, if not fading away. In the present era of UGC and eWOM, distinguishing persuaders from persuaded is hard, if not impossible, with little certainty about channel-specific effects in the emergence of cross-platform advertising. For example, person X posts an ad for brand A to her Facebook page with the caption "I love this ad, celebrity Y is so cute . . . I love brand A." The ad featuring celebrity Y is seen by person Z, who presses the like button and writes a comment under the video, while person W shares it with his friends. Who is the source in this case? Who is the receiver? One may argue that these distinctions are contextual. Nonetheless, the traditional way of separating senders from receivers is no longer applicable. It is essential to redraw the lines between sources and receivers in the context of social media. The placement of individual consumers within this circular and iterative process of interchangeable roles and information could potentially influence processing of persuasive communication as well as any persuasive outcomes. A revised dual processing approach not only highlights the interconnectedness and interchangeable roles among senders, messages and channels, and receivers, but also signifies the interchangeability of processing routes and styles as consumers shift from one method to another as a function of direct effects and interactions, as well as magnitude of interconnectedness and interchangeability among the levels of influence (senders, message/channels, and receivers; see Figure 16.1).

Theory of Reasoned Action/Planned Behavior

The behavioral approach to persuasion effects can be understood through two related theories: the theory of reasoned action (TRA) and its extension, the theory of planned behavior (TPB). TRA/TPB explain what drives peoples'

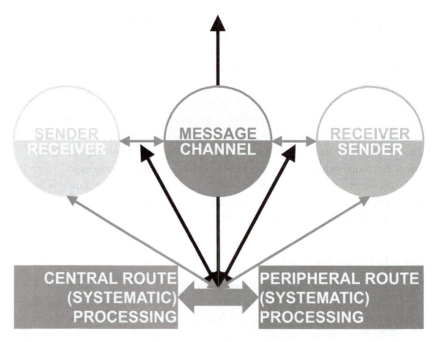

FIGURE 16.1 Integrating Social Media into Dual Process Models of Persuasion

volitional or voluntary behavior as a function of ways in which persuasive communication affects one's attitudes, and in turn influences their behavioral intentions, ultimately translating into behavior. This theoretical framework also posits that subjective norms, or the perceptions of the prevalence and acceptance of the behavior among one's social ties, as well as an individual's perceptions about his/her control over the behavior, also influence behavioral intentions and actual behaviors (Ajzen, 1985).

Within the context of social media, engagement with online persuasive messages (e.g., ad) in the form of viral behaviors: behaviors that contribute to online content's virality (see Alhabash & McAlister, 2014) can mediate the relationship between attitudes and (offline) behavioral intentions, and subsequently actual behaviors. Past research showed strong associations between viral behavioral intentions (e.g., intentions to like, share, and comment on a social media message) and offline behavioral intentions (Alhabash, McAlister, Lou, & Hagerstrom, 2015; Alhabash, McAlister, Quilliam, Richards, & Lou, 2015). Not only did viral behavioral intentions explain close to half of the variance in offline behavioral intentions, but also, variations among different levels of viral behavioral intentions have been documented. More specifically, Alhabash et al. (2015) showed that across four different experimental studies, expressing intentions to "like" a persuasive message was the strongest mediator between attitudes toward the message and offline behavioral intentions. While past research suggests a causal order for the

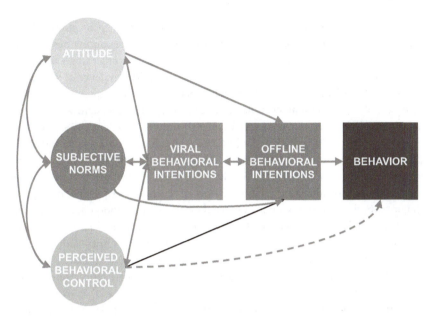

FIGURE 16.2   Integrating Social Media into Theory of Planned Behavior

relationship between attitudes, viral behavioral intentions, and offline behavioral intentions, respectively, arguments about reverse causality are also valid and need further study.

As viral behaviors directly affect offline behavioral intentions and behaviors, subsequently, they also mediate the relationship between attitudes toward the behavior, subjective norm, and perceived behavioral control, on one side, and behavioral intentions (offline), on the other. Holding (offline) behavioral intentions and behaviors as constant outcomes for persuasive communication, the revised TPB model should include viral behavioral intentions (as well as viral behaviors) as a factor influenced by and also influencing the three behavioral predictors (attitudes, norms, control), along with an interrelationship with offline behavioral intentions. While perceived behavioral control is a function of an individual's psychological traits and processes, subjective norms are especially important in the social media context.

Social Norms on Social Media

Social norms are perceptions that individuals have about the prevalence and acceptance of certain attitudes and/or behavior (Schultz, Nolan, Cialdini, Goldstein, & Griskevicius, 2007). Park and Smith (2007) identified five distinctive expressions of norms: subjective norms, personal descriptive norms, personal injunctive norms, societal descriptive norms, and societal injunctive norms. Per Park and Smith (2007), subjective norms have been articulated in TPB and refer to the perceptions of how others expect the individual to behave, and they argue that the concept of subjective norm has been at times reflective of descriptive norms and, at other times, of injunctive norms. Descriptive norms are defined as the perceived prevalence of the behavior among a social group (e.g., close friends, people who are important to me, the general public), while injunctive norms refer to the perceived approval or acceptance of the behavior among the social group (Perkins & Berkowitz, 1986; Berkowitz, 1997; Perkins, 2003; Park & Smith, 2007). The distinction between individual and societal levels of descriptive and injunctive norms stems from the anchoring of a reference group an individual is asked to evaluate. Individual level perceptions deal with an individual's perception of how prevalent (descriptive) and accepted (injunctive) the behavior is among people they believe are important. On the other hand, societal level norms are about perceptions of prevalence and acceptance of the behavior among a large group of people (e.g., Americans, university students).

Social norms-based marketing efforts provide specific information as a means for behavioral comparison. In doing so, descriptive norms reflect one's actual behavior versus one's beliefs about others. Research suggests that social norms advertising campaigns have been successful in preventing risky behaviors, such as alcohol abuse. The positive approach commonly used in these campaigns has largely led to positive outcomes (Wechsler et al., 2003).

The increasing prevalence of social media has also resulted in increased social network size of average users on platforms like Facebook and Twitter; not all of them may be close friends or frequent interactions. With that in mind, it becomes important to distinguish the influence of social norms on social media via strength of ties (Wellman, 1996; Haythornthwaite, 2002). The influence of strong versus weak ties—an expression of perceived social norms—can variably influence persuasive effects related to social media advertising, specifically in relation to UGC and eWOM. Chang, Chen, and Tan (2012) found advertisements endorsed by strong ties as more effective compared with those endorsed by weak ties when the product was hedonic as compared to being utilitarian. The study also found closely related people with similar values had a greater impact on purchase intentions. Li, Lee, and Lien (2012) observed similar results in that users receiving advertisements endorsed by related others found them more relevant.

Given that social media enable users to establish and maintain social connections with others, and that one's behavior is exposed to others, such publicity of an individuals' life can create normative perceptions about a person's behavior, both online and offline (Zeng, Huang, & Dou, 2009; Chu & Kim, 2011). Kim, Lee, and Yoon (2015) found that attitudes toward a reference behavior, subjective norms, and personal descriptive norms influence behavioral intentions to interact with "liking" public pages on Facebook.

Thus, a question arises: how are normative perceptions expressed and evaluated when consumers are interacting with branded content via social media platforms?

While considering descriptive and injunctive norms, social media affordances enable quantification of the norms that may influence behavioral perceptions among consumers. Descriptive norms can be expressed through access and sharing measures (e.g., number of views on YouTube, number of shares on Facebook), while injunctive norms can be inferred by looking at evaluative viral behaviors, such as the number of likes, as well as the tone of comments, and users' own posts related to the object of persuasion. Additionally, distinguishing between individual- and societal-level norms, social media users are able to see posts and interaction by their network of friends (with varying degrees of social tie strength) as well as general public posts. For example, a Twitter user can see that a particular brand-related hashtag is trending, which can express a societal-level norm. She can also see one of her close friends on Twitter using that hashtag, reflecting an individual-level norm.

Another means of social normative influence on behavior via social media deals with how consumers think about their friends on social media in terms of behavioral prevalence and acceptance (Wang & Yu, 2012; Hutter, Hautz, Dennhardt, & Füller, 2013). Within the context of social media, the number of "friends" a user has could reinforce the fear of sanctions by loss of reputation for disobeying what the user perceives to be customary (normative). Marwick and Boyd (2011) posited that content generators take into account different imaginary audiences when producing their material, and those users tend to self-censor themselves to avoid relationship problems and rants. Viken, Kim, Alhabash, and Smith (2016) also found that posts interacting with alcohol-related content on Facebook influenced self-reported drinking behavior and descriptive drinking norms among close friends and acquaintances. Viken et al. (2016) also found that the strongest predictor of self-reported drinking behavior is the perceived norms of how many drinks close Facebook friends had in a given time period.

Social Media Persuasion for Behavioral Change

The "million-dollar-question" in relation to social media advertising is: how can offline behaviors (e.g., purchase, consumption, etc.) be attributed to social media ads? Additionally, how can online behaviors translate to offline? As with previous models and studies of advertising effects, the most commonly used indicator of behavioral change is behavioral intentions. Per TRA/TPB, behavioral intentions are assumed to be the strongest predictors of actual behaviors. Therefore, research reviewed in this section looks mainly at effects of social media advertising and persuasion on behavioral intentions and, in some cases, proxies of actual behaviors. This section is organized by theme of effects. More specifically, we categorize social media advertising into: 1) incidental exposure effects, 2) engagement effects, and 3) UGC effects.

Incidental Exposure

Incidental exposure is defined as instances when an individual is exposed to secondary information at a time when he/she is paying attention to a different (primary) task (Janiszewski, 1988). It can be commonly observed that because of the clutter surrounding an individual in society, advertisements generally get only incidental attention from consumers (Pham & Vanhuele, 1997). However, research suggests that even though exposure to an ad might be brief and incidental, the pervasiveness of advertising influences ad recognition, familiarity, and recall (Hawkins & Hoch, 1992; Holden & Vanhuele, 1999), and helps build familiarity for the brand (Fang, Singh, and Ahluwalia, 2007). Kelly, Kerr, and Drennan (2010) studied attitudes and message avoidance toward social media advertising and found that participants did not mind excessive clutter as long as the SNS use was free of charge. While early studies on digital advertising and incidental exposure focused on participants' attention to banners within search engines (Manchanda, Dubé, Goh, & Chintagunta, 2006), the emergence of social media platforms brought a new level of research in investigating whether online social media users indeed registered the displayed ads. A 2013 study that tracked participants' visual attention found that online banners on Facebook attract less attention as compared with recommendations from friends (Barreto, 2013). However, this does not mean that ads went unnoticed. Instead, incidental exposure has been found to increase the likelihood of being considered for a future purchase (Shapiro, 1999). In a study by Alhabash et al. (2016), participants were exposed to Facebook ads that either featured an alcoholic (beer) or non-alcoholic (water) brand. Not only did participants indicate greater behavioral intentions to consume alcohol following exposure to beer than water ads, but they also were more likely to select a bar than a coffee shop gift card with which they were provided at the end of the study. Alhabash et al.'s (2016) findings offer an understanding of not only the important—and often the considerable—effect of exposure to ads on social media; once ads are noticed and processed, the potential for effectiveness is heightened.

Engagement Effects

Research on engagement effects also reveals strong relationships between behavioral intentions to like, share, and comment and expression of intentions to perform message-induced behaviors offline. In a number of studies, Alhabash and colleagues documented this strong effect among samples of college students (Alhabash et al., 2013; Alhabash, Baek et al., 2015; Alhabash et al., 2015). On a conceptual level, these effects can be explained by understanding different stages of behavioral change. Behavior change models that highlight the importance of readiness for change (e.g., Marcus, Selby, Niaura, & Rossi, 1992; Webb & Sheeran, 2006) offer a clear explanation for the online-offline behavioral intention relationship. That is, engaging with an online message comes with and is the product of certain levels of cognitive and affective mechanisms. Pressing the "like" button, sharing an ad, or commenting on someone else's brand-related post can indicate endorsement by the individual of the brand and behavior advocated in the advertisement. Thus, readiness for behavior change may increase. On the other hand, engaging in viral behaviors with branded content reflects higher-order mechanisms for information processing and enhances memory storage of the ad content and brand-related attributes.

UGC Effects

The relationship between generating persuasive content as consumers and whether or not consumers will buy or use the product or service has been documented in a number of studies. For example, Viken et al. (2016) showed that participants who reported posting about alcohol during a major celebration were ones that actually consumed more alcohol than their counterparts who did not post about alcohol on Facebook. Based on Viken et al.'s (2016) findings, we can see that the act of generating UGC may be strongly associated with offline behaviors. UGC can also signify the source of persuasion. Paek, Hove, Jeon, and Kim (2011) showed that PSAs that were produced by peer users (UGC) received more favorable attitude ratings than those produced by experts, mediated by involvement. Paek et al. (2011) argued that the effects of peer versus expert sources could be explained using the model similarity concept in relation to persuasive effects. Peer-generated messages appear more genuine and are perceived as less "ad-looking" than ones where the source is an expert or a professional model.

Social media advertising proposes three distinct levels of outcomes: exposure, engagement, and UGC—all of which are thought to influence attitudes and offline behaviors. Lee (2015) provides a guide for measuring return on investment (ROI) from social media, based on identification of social media advertising goals, data aggregation, and impact measurement. Nonetheless, these recommendations are limited only to assigning monetary values to online activities based on hypothetical assumptions. The task of valuing exposure to social media ads, online engagement, and UGC-engagement requires further investigation that not only relies on big data aggregation, but also triangulates data points from multiple sources, using multiple methodological approaches (e.g., combining server-level data with survey and experimental designs). Additionally, to maximize the value of social media advertising investment, one may need to revise the types of outcomes that are attainable, measurable, and meaningful. To sum, is the immediate post-exposure sale the most important revenue on social media? Or is it the relationship and loyalty that stems from conversation, co-creation, and engagement?

Summary

The current chapter reviewed theoretical frameworks, traditionally used in advertising and persuasion research, within the context of social media advertising. Additionally, we reviewed recent studies that tackled three areas of social media advertising effects: exposure, engagement, and UGC. The questions posed at the beginning of this chapter have been partially answered by prior studies. Advertising scholars and practitioners should strive to further explore ways to systematically produce persuasive effects using evidence-based and strategically-oriented advertising campaigns with an aim to transform investment of time, effort, and money into meaningful intentions and behaviors, both online and offline.

References

Ajzen, I. (1985). From intentions to actions: A theory of planned behavior. In J. Kuhl & J. Beckmann (Eds.), *Action control: From cognition to behavior* (pp. 11–39). Berlin Heidelberg, Germany: Springer-Verlag.

Alhabash, S., Baek, J. H., Cunningham, C., & Hagerstrom, A. (2015). To comment or not to comment? How virality, arousal level, and commenting behavior on YouTube videos affect civic behavioral intentions. *Computers in Human Behavior, 51*, 520–531.

Alhabash, S., & McAlister, A. R. (2014). Redefining virality in less broad strokes: Predicting viral behavioral intentions from motivations and uses of Facebook and Twitter. *New Media & Society, 17*(8), 1317–1339.

Alhabash, S., McAlister, A. R., Hagerstrom, A., Quilliam, E. T., Rifon, N. J., & Richards, J. I. (2013). Between likes and shares: Effects of emotional appeal and virality on the persuasiveness of anticyberbullying messages on Facebook. *Cyberpsychology, Behavior, and Social Networking, 16*(3), 175–182.

Alhabash, S., McAlister, A. R., Kim, W., Lou, C., Cunningham, C., Quilliam, E. T., & Richards, J. I. (2016). Saw it on Facebook, drank it at the bar! Effects of exposure to Facebook alcohol ads on alcohol-related behaviors. *Journal of Interactive Advertising, 16*(1), 44–58.

Alhabash, S., McAlister, A. R., Lou, C., & Hagerstrom, A. (2015). From clicks to behaviors: The mediating effect of intentions to like, share, and comment on the relationship between message evaluations and offline behavioral intentions. *Journal of Interactive Advertising, 15*(2), 82–96.

Alhabash, S., McAlister, A. R., Quilliam, E. T., Richards, J. I., & Lou, C. (2015). Alcohol's getting a bit more social: When alcohol marketing messages on Facebook increase young adults' intentions to imbibe. *Mass Communication and Society, 18*(3), 350–375.

Al-Riyami, A., Almutairi, N., Eisele, M., Johnson, E., Kim, W., Lou, C., & Alhabash, S. (2016). Psychophysiological responses to likes, shares, comments, and status updates on Facebook. *Psychophysiology, 51*(S1), S47.

Barreto, A. (2013). Do users look at banner ads on Facebook? *Journal of Research in Interactive Marketing, 7*(2), 119–139.

Berger, J., & Milkman, K. (2010). What makes online content viral? *Journal of Marketing Research, 49*(2), 192–205.

Berkowitz, A. D. (1997). From reactive to proactive prevention: promoting an ecology of health on campus. In P. C. Rivers & E. R. Shore (Eds.), *Substance abuse on campus: A handbook on substance abuse for college and university personnel* (pp. 119–139). Westport, CT: Greenwood Press.

Bhanot, S. (2012). Use of social media by companies to reach their customers. *SIES Journal of Management, 8*(1), 47–55.

Chaiken, S. (1980). Heuristic versus systematic information processing and the use of source versus message cues in persuasion. *Journal of Personality and Social Psychology, 39*(5), 752–756.

Chaiken, S. (1987). The heuristic model of persuasion. In M. P. Zanna, J. M. Olson, & C. P. Herman (Eds.), *Social influence: The Ontario symposium* (pp. 3–39). Hillsdale, NJ: Erlbaum.

Chaiken, S., Liberman, A., & Eagly, A. H. (1989). Heuristic and systematic processing within and beyond the persuasion context. In J. S. Uleman & J. A. Bargh (Eds.), *Unintended thought* (pp. 212–252). New York, NY: Guilford.

Chang, K. T., Chen, W., & Tan, B. C. (2012). Advertising effectiveness in social networking sites: Social ties, expertise, and product type. *IEEE Transaction on Engineering Management, 59*(4), 634–643.

Chu, S. C., & Kim, Y. (2011). Determinants of consumer engagement in electronic word-of-mouth (eWOM) in social networking sites. *International Journal of Advertising, 30*(1), 47–75.

Eckler, P., & Bolls, P. (2011). Spreading the virus: Emotional tone of viral advertising and its effect on forwarding intentions and attitudes. *Journal of Interactive Advertising, 11*(2), 1–11.

eMarketer. (2015). Social network ad spending to hit $23.68 billion worldwide in 2015. Retrieved from http://www.emarketer.com/Article/Social-Network-Ad-Spending-Hit-2368-Billion-Worldwide-2015/1012357.

eMarketer. (2016). US spending on paid media expected to climb 5.1% in 2016. Retrieved from http://www.emarketer.com/Article/US-Spending-on-Paid-Media-Expected-Climb-51-2016/1013739.

Fang, X., Singh, S., & Ahluwalia, R. (2007). An examination of different explanations for the mere exposure effect. *Journal of Consumer Research, 34*(1), 97–103.

Guynn, J. (2016, May 24). Chewbacca mask video star visits Facebook. *USA Today*. Retrieved from http://www.usatoday.com/story/tech/news/2016/05/24/candace-payne-chewbacca-

Hawkins, S. A., & Hoch, S. J. (1992). Low-involvement learning: Memory without evaluation. *Journal of Consumer Research, 19*(2), 212–225.

Haythornthwaite, C. (2002). Strong, weak, and latent ties and the impact of new media. *The Information Society, 18*(5), 385–401.

Hoelzel, M. (2014, November 13). The social-media advertising report: growth forecasts, market trends, and the rise of mobile. *Business Insider*. Retrieved from http://www.businessinsider.com/social-media-advertising-industry-trends-2014–11.

Holden, S. J., & Vanhuele, M. (1999). Know the name, forget the exposure: Brand familiarity versus memory of exposure context. *Psychology and Marketing, 16*(6), 479–496.

Hurrle, D., & Postatny, J. (2015). *Social media for scientific institutions: How to attract young academics by using social media as a marketing tool*. Berlin, Germany: Springer.

Hutter, K., Hautz, J., Dennhardt, S., & Füller, J. (2013). The impact of user interactions in social media on brand awareness and purchase intention: The case of MINI on Facebook. *Journal of Product & Brand Management, 22*(5/6), 342–351.

Itkowitz, C. (2016, May 23). Why "Chewbacca Mom" is the viral video we didn't know we needed. *The Washington Post*. Retrieved from https://www.washingtonpost.com/news/inspired-life/wp/2016/05/23/why-chewbacca-mom-is-the-viral-video-we-didnt-know-we-needed/

Janiszewski, C. (1988). Preconscious processing effects: The independence of attitude formation and conscious thought. *Journal of Consumer Research, 15*(2), 199–209.

Kelly, L., Kerr, G., & Drennan, J. (2010). Avoidance of advertising in social networking sites. The teenage perspective. *Journal of Interactive Advertising, 10*(2), 16–27.

Kim, S., Lee, J., & Yoon, D. (2015). Norms in social media: The application of theory of reasoned action and personal norms in predicting interactions with Facebook page like ads. *Communication Research Reports, 32*(4), 322–331.

Kononova, A. (2013). Multitasking across borders: A cross-national study of media multitasking behaviors, its antecedents, and outcomes. *International Journal of Communication, 7*, 1688–1710.

Lang, A. (2006). Using the limited capacity model of motivated mediated message processing to design effective cancer communication messages. *Journal of Communication, 56*(S1), S57–S80.

Lang, A. (2014). Dynamic human-centered communication systems theory. *The Information Society, 30*(1), 60–70.

Lang, A., & Bailey, R. L. (2015). Understanding information selection and encoding from a dynamic, energy saving, evolved, embodied, embedded perspective. *Human Communication Research, 41*(1), 1–20.

Lasswell, H. D. (1971). *Propaganda technique in World War I.* Cambridge, MA: MIT Press.

Lee, K. (2015, March 26). The delightfully short guide to social media ROI. Retrieved from https://blog.bufferapp.com/guide-calculate-social-media-roi.

Li, Y. M., Lee, Y. L., & Lien, N. J. (2012). Online social advertising via influential endorsers. *International Journal of Electronic Commerce, 16*(3), 119–154.

Manchanda, P., Dubé, J. P., Goh, K. Y., & Chintagunta, P. K. (2006). The effect of banner advertising on internet purchasing. *Journal of Marketing Research, 43*(1), 98–108.

Marcus, B. H., Selby, V. C., Niaura, R. S., & Rossi, J. S. (1992). Self-efficacy and the stage of exercise behavior change. *Research Quarterly for Exercise and Sport, 63*(1), 60–66.

Marwick, A., & Boyd, D. (2011). To see and be seen: Celebrity practice on Twitter. *Convergence: The International Journal of Research into New Media Technologies, 17*(2), 139–158.

Mediakix.com. (2016). The differences between brand ambassadors, influencers, & celebrities. Retrieved from http://mediakix.com/2016/06/brand-ambassadors-influencers-celebrities-differences/

Okazaki, S., & Taylor, C. (2013). Social media and international advertising: Theoretical challenges and future directions. *International Marketing Review, 30*(1), 56–71.

Olmstead, K., & Lu, K. (2015). Digital news revenue: Fact sheet. *Pew Research Center.* Retrieved from http://www.journalism.org/2015/04/29/digital-news-revenue-fact-sheet/

Paek, H.-J., Hove, T., Jeon, H. J., & Kim, M. (2011). Peer or expert? *International Journal of Advertising, 30*(1), 161–188.

Park, H. S., & Smith, S. W. (2007). Distinctiveness and influence of subjective norms, personal descriptive and injunctive norms, and societal descriptive and injunctive norms on behavioral intent: A case of two behaviors critical to organ donation. *Human Communication Research, 33*(2), 194–218.

Perkins, H. (2003). *The social norms approach to preventing school and college age substance abuse: A handbook for educators, counselors, and clinicians.* San Francisco, CA: Jossey-Bass.

Perkins, H. W., & Berkowitz, A. D. (1986). Perceiving the community norms of alcohol use among students: Some research implications for campus alcohol education programming. *International Journal of the Addictions, 21*(9–10), 961–976.

Petty, R. E., & Cacioppo, J. T. (1981). *Attitudes and persuasion: Classic and contemporary approaches.* Dubuque, IA: William C. Brown.

Petty, R. E., & Cacioppo, J. T. (1986). *Communication and persuasion: Central and peripheral routes to attitude change.* New York, NY: Springer.

Pham, M. T., & Vanhuele, M. (1997). Analyzing the memory impact of advertising fragments. *Marketing Letters, 8*(4), 407–417.

Roman, E. (2015, October 28). How brand ambassadors make social . . . more social. *The Huffington Post.* Retrieved from http://www.huffingtonpost.com/ernan-roman/how-brand-ambassadors-mak_b_8395432.html.

Sass, E. (2015, November 17). Survey: Social media more effective than traditional marketing. *MediaPost*. Retrieved from http://www.mediapost.com/publications/article/262819/survey-social-media-more-effective-than-tradition.html.

Saxena, A., & Khanna, U. (2013). Advertising on social network sites: A structural equation modeling approach. *Vision: The Journal of Business Perspective, 17*(1), 17–25.

Schultz, P. W., Nolan, J. M., Cialdini, R. B., Goldstein, N. J., & Griskevicius, V. (2007). The constructive, destructive, and reconstructive power of social norms. *Psychological Science, 18*(5), 429–434.

Scott, D. M. (2015). *The new rules of marketing and PR: How to use social media, online video, mobile applications, blogs, news releases, and viral marketing to reach buyers directly.* Hoboken, NJ: John Wiley & Sons.

Shannon, C. E., & Weaver, W. (1949). *The mathematical theory of communication.* Urbana, IL: University of Illinois Press.

Shapiro, S. (1999). When an ad's influence is beyond our conscious control: Perceptual and conceptual fluency effects caused by incidental ad exposure. *Journal of Consumer Research, 26*(1), 16–36.

Viken, G., Kim, W., Alhabash, S., & Smith, S. (2016). *An analysis of celebratory drinking and related Facebook activity on college campuses.* Poster presented to the 2016 Kentucky Conference on Health Communication, April 14–16, 2016, Lexington, KY.

Wahba, P. (2016, May 23). Kohl's reaps marketing bonanza from "Chewbacca Mom." *Fortune.* Retrieved from http://fortune.com/2016/05/23/kohls-chewbacca-marketing/

Wang, X., & Yu, C. (2012). Social media peer communication and impacts on purchase intentions: A consumer socialization framework. *Journal of Interactive Marketing, 26*(4), 198–208.

Webb, T. L., & Sheeran, P. (2006). Does changing behavioral intentions engender behavior change? A meta-analysis of the experimental evidence. *Psychological Bulletin, 132*(2), 249–268.

Wechsler, H., Nelson, T. E., Lee, J. E., Seibring, M., Lewis, C., & Keeling, R. P. (2003). Perception and reality: A national evaluation of social norms marketing interventions to reduce college students' heavy alcohol use. *Journal of Studies on Alcohol, 64*(4), 484–494.

Wellman, B. (1996). Are personal communities local? A Dumptarian reconsideration. *Social Networks, 18*(4), 347–354.

Yeykelis, L., Cummings, J. J., & Reeves, B. (2014). Multitasking on a single device: Arousal and the frequency, anticipation, and prediction of switching between media content on a computer. *Journal of Communication, 64*(1), 167–192.

Zeng, F., Huang, L., & Dou, W. (2009). Social factors in user perceptions and responses to advertising in online social networking communities. *Journal of Interactive Advertising, 10*(1), 1–13.

17

TARGETED DIGITAL ADVERTISING AND PRIVACY

Heather Shoenberger

Targeted digital advertising has grown rapidly and become increasingly sophisticated. The internet allows the collection, aggregation, and synthesis of clickstream data; purchase behavior; etc. to deliver advertisements tailored to previous online behavior (Barnes, 2002). Search engines, social media, and other types of digital content rank messages displayed to consumers based on algorithms or rules (Sullivan, 2002). Tailoring allows for potentially more relevant search results and accompanying advertisements based on consumer behavior in the digital context (e.g., past searches, clickstream activity, etc.) (FTC, 2007; Milne, Rohm, & Bahl, 2009). For example, consider the newly released Pokemon Go application. The app is based on geo-location technology, which has attracted millions of users within days of its initial launch. The app is able to capture email addresses, web pages viewed before entering the app, geographic location, IP address, Google profile information (if a person signed into the app using a Google account), and more (Bernstein, 2016). All of the information captured by this popular app could be used to design and serve digital advertising specifically tailored to a consumer based on his/her behavior in the digital context. However, as tailored messaging in the digital context grows, so too does the concern that consumer privacy expectations may not be met.

The editors of this book note in Chapter 2 that in the realm of digital advertising, there is a network of message movements across platforms. The issue of targeted digital advertising and privacy touches upon message curation, manipulation, and creation of messages as information about consumers' online behavior is stored, analyzed, and used to create personalized search results and serve targeted advertisements. There are clear benefits for advertisers and consumers in that personalized messages based on past consumer behavior are the advertising that consumers see. Advertisers are able to offer more relevant content and, subsequently, consumers receive more relevant messages.

As digital advertisers work to interpret and apply seemingly infinite amounts of data, curate the important pieces of information, and manipulate the information to provide messages to consumers, the issue of how to address consumer privacy concerns persists. What is the meaning and value of privacy in relation to the benefits of digital advertising? Do consumers receive adequate notification and/or options for controlling their data? Where should the line be drawn between consumer-reported anxiety over data privacy, and unfocused, rather nonchalant behavior regarding data protection?

In considering the above questions, this chapter will begin with a short discussion of privacy and digital advertising. In doing so, the current regulation of privacy in the digital advertising context will be discussed, and the literature on consumer concerns versus their actual behaviors online will be highlighted. The chapter concludes with some suggestions for future research to address the complex issue of privacy concerns as they relate to digital advertising.

Information and Privacy

People constantly negotiate a balance between privacy and the need to be stimulated by other human beings. Violation of expected privacy boundaries may harm the human psyche and cause emotional or even physical ailments to arise (Westin, 1967). Privacy is important to the emotional and cognitive functioning of people because it allows them to pursue self-actualization (Calo, 2015).

Privacy is easy to understand when considered analogous to a physical door that provides privacy for people in their homes. It becomes more complicated as it relates to how and when data about a person is used. It may not be as easy to grasp or protect privacy in a context that is not understood through physical boundaries. Companies involved in digital advertising have to grapple with defining an appropriate line between offering relevant messages based on profiles curated online and failing to respect the privacy expectations of the consumer. Privacy, in the digital advertising context, involves how the data collected about consumers is employed to deliver tailored advertisements. The tension is generated by what consumers *expect* advertisers to do with their personal information and what advertisers actually *do* the personal details that consumers provide online.

In the economic context, consumer advocates worry that unfettered data collection by companies for advertising purposes will be harmful to the consumer, incorrect digital profiles may be created, and using personal profiles may be used to discriminate against people and cause other harms (Podesta et al., 2014). The other side of the issue includes fear that stifling of data collection will result in stunted innovation and an inefficient marketplace (Calo, 2015).

Control over the information created by consumers in the digital context is controversial with some scholars advocating for the information to remain under the control of the consumer and others advocating for more control to be held by those who may curate and use the data for market purposes (Calo, 2015). Targeted digital advertising will be the focus of this chapter because the very existence of targeted digital advertising depends, in large part, on the data provided by consumers. While digital advertising could be any advertisement placed on digital media such as mobile devices or the internet, targeted digital advertising uses consumer data to serve ads to consumers based on their behavior online.

Respect for information privacy can be useful to the growth and maintenance of markets because it has the capacity to increase trust between consumers and companies. Trust on the part of consumers is necessary for digital commerce to prove satisfactory to consumers and grow (Pavlou, 2003). Trust is especially important in this context as consumers have little bargaining power when it comes to digital transactions of personal data (Beldad, De Jong, & Steehouder, 2010). The Federal Trade Commission enforces companies' privacy policies to mollify consumer trust issues and allow privacy to bolster an efficient marketplace (Calo, 2015). Privacy allows transactions online to take place based on relevant information (e.g., the price of a product) instead of based on entire profiles (e.g., information about the seller or buyer's spiritual practices) (Calo, 2015).

Some companies may keep consumer data collected via use of their website or application proprietary but may use the data in ways that violate consumer expectations of privacy. For example, Facebook holds consumer data proprietary within its own network to offer pieces of content such as news stories, friend photos, etc. to people based on their interests (Sutton, 2016). The idea of a consumer within Facebook's walls being served only stories interesting to them based on prior behavior is defended as a good business decision though some critics have noted the content may be biased toward Facebook leaders' sensibilities, especially in the news story realm (Sutton, 2016). Facebook also ran into trouble when its "People You May Know" feature was connected to geo-location data about people, although the company later denied it used geo-location data to suggest new friends (Burlacu, 2016). The feature, when based on geo-location and other information, may expose physical locations a consumer meant to keep private (Nicks, 2016). For example, one story included a consumer who received a friend suggestion based on an anonymous meeting he attended (Nicks, 2016). In both instances of companies housing vast amounts of consumer data, there is a concern over hacking. What if a hacker was able to expose nearly every aspect of someone's private life, including medical visits or anonymous meetings, with one successful attempt to access Facebook's data? Of course, once again, consumer control as a mechanism of privacy protection is paramount. In this and most digital advertising settings, the onus is on the consumer to opt-out of geo-location tracking via their mobile settings and other privacy settings within each respective application or device.

The integrity of consumer data privacy remains an important topic upon which regulators and scholars routinely discuss and debate as more information is collected about consumer behavior via better analytics and emerging technologies. The discussion involves balancing consumer privacy expectations against the interests of the market. A right to privacy was not explicitly included in the United States' law, thus regulators and privacy advocates are forced to search for ways to carve out such a right or institute safeguards to hold companies accountable for data use and distribution, and provide notice to consumers about how their data may be used.

Regulating Privacy in the Digital Advertising Context

The first mention of a right to privacy was spurred by technological advancement and a concern that the government may be able to conduct surveillance on citizens in ways that would chill behavior and information sharing (Solove, 2006). Warren and Brandeis (1890) noted that what was once whispered behind closed doors would one day be screamed from the rooftops. This sentiment of privacy, actions taken with no obvious onlooker, is relevant to the discussion of privacy in the context of digital advertising today.

Currently, the legal definition for privacy exists in the consumers' ability to show that they had an expectation of privacy in the matter at hand (Solove, 2006). If a consumer cannot show a reasonable expectation of privacy, there are few protections available under privacy law. Thus, the definition of privacy in the context of digital advertising is important.

Under the umbrella of digital advertising, privacy has often been synonymous with control (Solove, 2006; Brandimarte, Acquisti, & Loewestein, 2013). Thus, ensuring meaningful control over data in the digital context is the crux of the privacy debate in the digital advertising context. Privacy operationalized as control requires the consumer to carefully be aware of how online sites say they are using the customer's data (Milne, Labrecque, & Cromer, 2009). Consumers are obliged to digest each site or device's privacy policy, if available, and to decide whether to agree with the terms and conditions. The U.S. legal system holds consumers to "click-thru" contracts in the same way as contracts physically signed despite the differences in the motivation to read the digital contracts, the asymmetry of the bargaining relationships, etc. (Moringiello, 2014), and privacy law expects consumers to proactively protect their interests (Schlosser, White, & Lloyd, 2006; Moringiello, 2014; Shield, 2014).

The Federal Trade Commission (FTC), in its regulatory role, works to ensure consumer control over data. The FTC began its foray into privacy protection in the 1990s when it started enforcing companies' existing privacy policies in the interest of preventing unfair or deceptive acts that affect commerce (Calo, 2015). The theory behind the enforcement was to encourage trust among consumers that privacy policies presented by companies could be relied on (Solove & Hartzog, 2014).

The FTC encourages notice and choice, often in the form of a link or icon directing the consumer to a stated privacy policy, in an effort to allow control over data collection and use (Federal Trade Commission, 2007). In addition to icons and links, privacy information may pop up just before a consumer downloads an application or navigates through a site. The looming issue for privacy advocates and regulators is how to approach the issue of consumers' control over data/privacy in a meaningful way. Consumers' paradoxical behavior makes privacy protection via notice and choice challenging.

Consumers' Actual Behavior Versus Concerns

Both consumers' actual behavior and their voiced concerns are important to consider in addressing the issue of privacy and digital advertising. Those who collect and use consumer data must be aware of the concern or anxiety consumers have about how data is collected and used in the digital context. Such concern may lead to a lack of trust of e-commerce and result in lower engagement with the digital economy (e.g., Malhotra, Kim & Agarwal, 2004). However, even the most vigilant consumer advocate is faced with the reality of the "privacy paradox," which refers to the common observation that while people voice anxiety about their data privacy and security, they often freely offer personal information (LaRose & Rifon, 2007; Norberg, Horne, & Horne, 2007; Yap, Beverland, & Bove, 2009). The paradox between consumers' stated attitudes and behavior inconsistent with those attitudes makes the idea of equating consumer control of data with sufficient respect for privacy problematic.

Linking control over one's own data with privacy protection assumes (Kang, 1998; Solove, 2006) that a consumer's ability to control usage and dissemination of their personal information is integral to their ability to monitor privacy interests (Brandimarte, Acquisti, & Loewenstein, 2013). However, though consumers consistently indicate anxiety over privacy online, they show little interest in attending to such policies, rarely taking the initiative to control their data (Metzger, 2007; Joinson, Reips, Buchanan, & Schofield, 2010). While previous studies suggest consumers want additional regulation of privacy concerns in the digital context (Turow et al., 2009; McDonald & Cranor, 2010), a recent White House report stated that consumers agree to policies and terms of agreement without reading them, spurring privacy advocates and researchers to reflect on whether current privacy policies are effective at ensuring consumers have meaningful notice and choice/control over the use of their data (Leon et al., 2012; Sanger & Lohr, 2014). In fact, consumers appear apathetic in regard to privacy information offered, particularly when considering entertainment technologies, such as a shopping website or Snapchat. For example, Snapchat users were asked if they knew their snaps could be captured and saved. Almost 80 percent of the consumers queried said they knew that snaps could be captured and just over half noted that they did not care (Roesner, Gill, & Kohno, 2014).

This example magnifies the notion that consumers do want control over their personal information in a digital context but often do not use the various control mechanisms offered to them by advertisers or brands (such as opt in/opt out functions) (Milne & Rohm, 2000; Miyazaki & Fernandez, 2000; Milne & Culnan, 2002; Malhotra, Kim, & Agarwal, 2004; Okazaki, Li, & Hirose, 2009). The desire and ability to control ones' data requires knowledge and self-efficacy in the area of data collection and use online. The literature suggests consumers' lack of knowledge is linked to a lack of trust in the advertising that results from such collection (McDonald & Cranor, 2010). Additionally, some research suggests that consumers are likely to change their behaviors online upon realizing how data is collected and used to create tailored messages (Milne, Rohm, & Bahl, 2009). However, other research notes that higher belief in one's ability to control data online actually led to sharing more sensitive information (Brandimarte, Acquisti, & Loewenstein, 2013). The digital context is cluttered with advertising (see Chapter 5), so it is up to advertising scholars to understand how consumers navigate this clutter, and how data privacy and data management may be improved within a cluttered space (see Shoenberger & McNealy, 2016).

Another important factor is that of convenience. Consumer perceptions of convenience may vary depending on the context, and convenience is considered one of the most influential variables driving online shopping and engagement with activities in the digital context (Jiang, Yang, & Jun, 2013). In fact, convenience has been said to overshadow feelings of risk when engaging with online shopping (Bhatnagar, Misra, & Rao, 2000). Though consumers noted their concern about sending credit card and other personal information over the internet to shop online or participate in "for-pay" activities, the convenience of engaging in activities online outweighed those concerns (Horrigan, 2008). It is well established that consumers are often willing to exchange certain information for the benefits of free content or other kind of benefit (Milne & Gordon, 1993). In other words, they are willing to trade privacy for access to content (Calo, 2015). What other shortcuts do they rely on to navigate the digital context?

The use of cues in the digital context is paramount as consumers, with the desire for convenience, navigate a sea of information. This is especially true in the digital context (Mayer, Huh, & Cude, 2005; Sundar, 2008; Shoenberger & McNealy, 2016). Research on the use of heuristics or peripheral processing shows that most consumers do not engage in careful, cognitive processing to evaluate information and, instead, use design cues and website usability to make decisions about credibility of websites (Metzger, Flanagin, & Medders, 2010). In fact, "site presentation" is the first visual quality of a website that consumers use to determine credibility (Metzger et al., 2010, p. 416). Thus, there is an important link between visual aesthetics and perceived credibility (Robins & Holmes, 2008).

This is why researchers called for privacy logos early in the privacy and digital advertising context because they were believed to be important cues of trust given that people were not likely to read an entire policy online (Mayer, Huh, & Cude, 2005). Research confirmed the psychological link between logos and trust, finding that when people see a familiar logo (e.g., TRUSTe) they assume the site or app is safe without the provision of any additional investigation (Miyazaki &

Krishnamurthy, 2002; Mayer, Huh, & Cude, 2005; LaRose & Rifon, 2007; Shoenberger & McNealy, 2016). However, the existence of a logo may mean very little in reality, and the privacy policy underneath the logo may not offer any substantial protection. The challenging paradox of consumer desire for control over their data but lack of action with regard to that control is an interesting puzzle for regulators and researchers.

Conclusion

The concerns of data curation and manipulation by advertisers to provide tailored advertising to consumers is problematic, first of all, because of the consumer privacy paradox. That is, consumers seem to desire (even ask for) greater privacy and greater control over their privacy online but frequently (and sometimes freely) give out personal information to brands that request it. As we have seen in this chapter, there is much public concern over who controls the almost infinite amount of data generated in the communication digital network. At the same time, there is clear evidence that when people are in the network, they often divulge information without checking on how it will be used. Researchers and others have also pointed out how important it is in the digital marketplace to maintain consumer trust in the information and transactions they are presented with (Malhotra, Kim, & Agarwal, 2004; Richards & Hartzog, 2015).

This issue is further complicated when considering that search engines like Google, and social media sites, like Facebook, are becoming more and more adept at collecting, storing, and analyzing data. Although the algorithms these companies use are proprietary, it is clear that they are built on massive and detailed knowledge of what people are doing when they are in the digital communication network (see Chapter 2), and probably a lot of what they are doing outside their digital participation. Already a "creepy factor" exists for advertisements that follow people around on the internet based on previous search behavior (Sloane, 2015, n.p.). The question of how far companies should go with targeted advertising using the vast amount of data collected on consumer behavior online will loom large in the future (Sloane, 2015).

With respect to findings of consumer behavior in the privacy arena, future research must seek to find a way to understand what types of information being collected may harm consumers and with what effects. Additionally, based on consumer reliance on cues and their need for convenience in the digital context, more research is needed to discover how and when privacy policies/icons are processed and used by consumers.

Advertisers and regulators may seek to create uniform policies related to the type of information collected, perhaps to give consumers a visual cue of what the language of the policy contains without having to click through and digest a policy. Further research is needed to examine whether the implementation of more uniform policies delineated by icon type or color may decrease indications of privacy anxiety for consumers and increase social trust.

References

Barnes, S. J. (2002). Wireless digital advertising: Nature and implications. *International Journal of Advertising, 21*(3), 399–420.

Beldad, A., De Jong, M., & Steehouder, M. (2010). How shall I trust the faceless and the intangible? A literature review on the antecedents of online trust. *Computers in Human Behavior, 26*(5), 857–869.

Bernstein, J. (2016). You should probably check your Pokemon Go privacy settings. *Buzz-Feed.* Retrieved from https://www.buzzfeed.com/josephbernstein/heres-all-the-data-pokemon-go-is-collecting-from-yourphone?bffbmain&ref=bffbmain&utm_term=.gxW4E8169#.smLEJBWM.

Bhatnagar, A., Misra, S., & Rao, H. R. (2000). On risk, convenience, and Internet shopping behavior. *Communications of the ACM, 43*(11), 98–105.

Brandimarte, L., Acquisti, A., & Loewenstein, G. (2013). Misplaced confidences privacy and the control paradox. *Social Psychological and Personality Science, 4*(3), 340–347.

Burlacu, A. (2016). Facebook allegedly tracks phones' location to serve friend suggestions: How to turn this off. *TechTimes.com.* Retrieved from http://www.techtimes.com/articles/167397/20160629/facebook-allegedly-tracks-phones-location-to-serve-friend-suggestions-how-to-turn-this-off.htm.

Calo, R. (2015). Privacy and markets: A love story. *Notre Dame Law Review, 91*, 649. Retrievable from http://heinonline.org/HOL/LandingPage?handle=hein.journals/tndl91&div=19&id =&page=

Federal Trade Commission. (2007). FTC staff proposes online behavioral advertising privacy principles. Retrieved from https://www.ftc.gov/news-events/press-releases/2007/12/ftc-staff-proposes-online-behavioral-advertising-privacy.

Horrigan, J. (2008). Online shopping. Retrieved from http://www.pewinternet.org/2008/02/13/online-shopping/

Jiang, L., Yang, Z., & Jun, M. (2013). Measuring consumer perceptions of online shopping convenience. *Journal of Service Management, 24*(2), 191–214.

Joinson, A. N., Reips, U. D., Buchanan, T., & Schofield, C. B. P. (2010). Privacy, trust, and self-disclosure online. *Human-Computer Interaction, 25*(1), 1–24.

Kang, J. (1998). Information privacy in cyberspace transactions. *Stanford Law Review, 50*(4), 1193–1294.

LaRose, R., & Rifon, N. J. (2007). Promoting i-safety: Effects of privacy warnings and privacy seals on risk assessment and online privacy behavior. *Journal of Consumer Affairs, 41*(1), 127–149.

Leon, P., Ur, B., Shay, R., Wang, Y., Balebako, R., & Cranor, L. (2012). Why Johnny can't opt out: A usability evaluation of tools to limit online behavioral advertising. In *Proceedings of the SIGCHI Conference on Human Factors in Computing Systems* (pp. 589–598). ACM.

Malhotra, N. K., Kim, S. S., & Agarwal, J. (2004). Internet users' information privacy concerns (IUIPC): The construct, the scale, and a causal model. *Information Systems Research, 15*(4), 336–355.

Mayer, R. N., Huh, J., & Cude, B. J. (2005). Cues of credibility and price performance of life insurance comparison web sites. *Journal of Consumer Affairs, 39*(1), 71–94.

McDonald, A., & Cranor, L. F. (2010, August). Beliefs and behaviors: Internet users' understanding of behavioral advertising. *TPRC.* Retrieved from http://aleecia.com/authors-drafts/tprc-behav-AV.pdf.

Metzger, M. J. (2007). Making sense of credibility on the Web: Models for evaluating online information and recommendations for future research. *Journal of the American Society for Information Science and Technology, 58*(13), 2078–2091.

Metzger, M. J., Flanagin, A. J., & Medders, R. B. (2010). Social and heuristic approaches to credibility evaluation online. *Journal of Communication, 60*(3), 413–439.

Milne, G. R., & Culnan, M. J. (2002). Using the content of online privacy notices to inform public policy: A longitudinal analysis of the 1998–2001 US Web surveys. *The Information Society, 18*(5), 345–359.

Milne, G. R., & Gordon, M. E. (1993). Direct mail privacy-efficiency trade-offs within an implied social contract framework. *Journal of Public Policy & Marketing, 12*(2), 206–215.

Milne, G. R., & Rohm, A. J. (2000). Consumer privacy and name removal across direct marketing channels: Exploring opt-in and opt-out alternatives. *Journal of Public Policy & Marketing, 19*(2), 238–249.

Milne, G. R., Labrecque, L. I., & Cromer, C. (2009). Toward an understanding of the online consumer's risky behavior and protection practices. *Journal of Consumer Affairs, 43*(3), 449–473.

Milne, G. R., Rohm, A., & Bahl, S. (2009). If it's legal, is it acceptable? *Journal of Advertising, 38*(4), 107–122.

Miyazaki, A. D., & Fernandez, A. (2000). Internet privacy and security: An examination of online retailer disclosures. *Journal of Public Policy & Marketing, 19*(1), 54–61.

Miyazaki, A. D., & Krishnamurthy, S. (2002). Internet seals of approval: Effects on online privacy policies and consumer perceptions. *Journal of Consumer Affairs, 36*(1), 28–49.

Moringiello, J. M. (2014). Notice, assent, and form in a 140 character world. *Southwestern Law Review, 44*, 275.

Nicks, D. (2016). Facebook might be using your location to suggest friends: Here's how to make sure it doesn't. *Money.com*. Retrieved from http://time.com/money/4386138/facebook-friend-suggestions-privacy-concerns/.

Norberg, P. A., Horne, D. R., & Horne, D. A. (2007). The privacy paradox: Personal information disclosure intentions versus behaviors. *Journal of Consumer Affairs, 41*(1), 100–126.

Okazaki, S., Li, H., & Hirose, M. (2009). Consumer privacy concerns and preference for degree of regulatory control. *Journal of Advertising, 38*(4), 63–77.

Pavlou, P. A. (2003). Consumer acceptance of electronic commerce: Integrating trust and risk with the technology acceptance model. *International Journal of Electronic Commerce, 7*(3), 101–134.

Podesta, J., Pritzker, P., Moniz, E., Holdren, J., & Zients, J. (2014). Big data seizing opportunities, preserving values. *Executive Office of the President*. Retrieved from http://www.whitehouse.gov/sites/default/files/docs/big_data_privacy_report_may_1_2014.pdf.

Richards, N. M., & Hartzog, W. (2015). Taking trust seriously in privacy law. *SSRN*. Retrieved from http://ssrn.com/abstract=2655719.

Robins, D., & Holmes, J. (2008). Aesthetics and credibility in web site design. *Information Processing & Management, 44*(1), 386–399.

Roesner, F., Gill, B. T., & Kohno, T. (2014, March). Sex, lies, or kittens? Investigating the use of Snapchat's self-destructing messages. In *International Conference on Financial Cryptography and Data Security* (pp. 64–76). Berlin Heidelberg: Springer.

Sanger, D., & Lohr, S. (2014). Call for limits of web data on consumers. *The New York Times*. Retrieved from http://www.nytimes.com/2014/05/02/us/white-house-report-calls-for-transparency-in-online-data-collection.html?_r=0.

Schlosser, A. E., White, T. B., & Lloyd, S. M. (2006). Converting web site visitors into buyers: How web site investment increases consumer trusting beliefs and online purchase intentions. *Journal of Marketing, 70*(2), 133–148.

Shield Jr., J. J. (2014). Apple, Inc. v. Superior Court: Caveat emptor: The future of online credit card transactions. *DePaul Business & Commercial Law Journal, 13*, 529.

Shoenberger, H., & McNealy, J. (2016). Offline v. online: Re-examining the reasonable consumer standard in the digital context. Retrieved from https://www.ftc.gov/system/files/documents/public_comments/2015/10/00046-98087.pdf.

Sloane, G. (2015). 2016 year in preview: Ad targeting toes the creepy line. *Digiday.com*. Retrieved from http://digiday.com/brands/2016yearinpreview-targeting-ads-get-lot-creepier/

Solove, D. J. (2006). A taxonomy of privacy. *University of Pennsylvania Law Review, 154*(3), 477–564.

Solove, D. J., & Hartzog, W. (2014). The FTC and the new common law of privacy. *Columbia Law Review, 114*, 583–676.

Sullivan, D. (2002). How search engines work. *Search Engine Watch*. Retrieved from http://www. searchenginewatch.com/webmasters/work.html.

Sundar, S. S. (2008). The MAIN model: A heuristic approach to understanding technology effects on credibility. In M. J. Metzger & A. J. Flanagin (Eds.), *Digital media, youth, and credibility* (pp. 73–100). Cambridge, MA: The MIT Press, doi: 10.1162/dmal.9780262562324.073.

Sutton, K. (2016). With news feed values, Facebook pushes back against bias claims. *Politico.com*. Retrieved from http://www.politico.com/media/story/2016/06/with-news-feed-values-facebook-pushes-back-against-bias-claims-004634.

Turow, J., King, J., Hoofnagle, C. J., Bleakley, A., & Hennessy, M. (2009). Americans reject tailored advertising and three activities that enable it. *SSRN* 1478214. Retrievable from http://papers.ssrn.com/sol3/papers.cfm?abstract_id=1478214.

Warren, S. D., & Brandeis, L. D. (1890). The right to privacy. *Harvard Law Review, 4*(5), 193–220.

Westin, A. F. (1967). Privacy and freedom. *Washington and Lee Law Review, 25*(1), 166.

Yap, J. E., Beverland, M. B., & Bove, L. L. (2009). A conceptual framework of the causes and consequences of the privacy paradox. In *The Australian and New Zealand Marketing Academy Conference*.

18

EXPLORING PLAYER RESPONSES TOWARD IN-GAME ADVERTISING

The Impact of Interactivity

Laura Herrewijn and Karolien Poels

Introduction

Digital games are firmly ingrained in our culture. From the 1970s onwards, they have evolved into an extremely popular entertainment medium that is able to attract interest across genders, age groups, and cultures. In 2015, the global games industry generated software revenues of just over $80 billion; numbers are expected to rise even further, to $104 billion, by the end of 2018 (Juniper Research, 2015). Given this explosive growth, in-game advertising has emerged as a promising new advertising medium, sparking the interest of the advertising industry, game sector, and academic research. The aim of this chapter is twofold. First, it intends to give an introduction to this practice of in-game advertising: providing a definition, an overview of its benefits and drawbacks, and an outline of the (industry-commissioned and academic) research that has been conducted on its effectiveness. Second, it will bring together the gathered information and illustrate the potential impact of in-game advertising by drawing on a case study (Herrewijn, 2015). This case study was designed to investigate player responses toward different types of advertisements that are integrated into a digital game, with a focus on the inter-activity they allow.

In-game advertising (IGA) concerns the incorporation of advertisements into the environment of a digital game, a practice similar to the integration of product placements in movies or television shows (Herrewijn & Poels, 2014). IGA can take a lot of different forms, ranging from sponsorship deals to the use of real-world analogs (e.g., banner ads such as billboards and posters, radio spots, television commercials), brand placements (e.g., branded cars, clothing, food and drinks, buildings, accessories), branded music and sounds (e.g., the use of branded music, brand sound effects, the voices of licensed characters and sports commentators), branded characters (e.g., the use of mascots, celebrities), etc. (for an elaborate overview, see Herrewijn & Poels, 2014). Some of these placements merely appear as part of the game's scenery, serving as passive background props, while other placements can be meaningfully interacted with and constitute a major part of the player's gameplay (e.g., when the player has to actively use a brand in order to progress in the game) (Nelson, 2005; Skalski, Bracken, & Buncher, 2010). For instance, a large percentage of sports games are produced from licensed properties. Sporting leagues such as the International Federation of Association Football license sports games yearly, i.e., the FIFA game series (Electronic Arts, 1993–2015), and in these games, billboards for real products are placed around the sports stadium, the athletes' clothes are adorned with the logos of sponsors, and the voices of well-known sports commentators are heard in the background. Moreover, in racing games such as the Need For Speed series (Electronic Arts, 1994–2015), there are not only billboards placed around the race tracks, players can further choose from, and race with, a large range of real-world cars (including cars from Audi, Alfa Romeo, BMW, Ford, Honda, Jaguar, Nissan, Porsche, Toyota, Volkswagen, etc.).

It is important to note, however, that, unlike advergames (i.e., digital games that are specially made to promote a certain brand and thus act as de-facto ads in themselves), when IGA is incorporated in a digital game, the main purpose of the game remains the entertainment of the player and not the communication of the brand message (Herrewijn & Poels, 2014).

In-Game Advertising: Benefits and Drawbacks

From the early 2000s on, both the advertising industry and academia have been showing explicit and increasing interest in IGA, citing that digital games offer a wide variety of opportunities and benefits for the inclusion of advertisements.

For advertisers, the appeal of IGA lies first and foremost in the ability of digital games to reach an ever growing, diverse audience. Digital gaming has become one of the fastest growing and most popular forms of entertainment (Juniper Research, 2015). There is a global audience of over half a billion people playing digital games, and best-selling games such as World of Warcraft, Call of Duty: Modern Warfare 3, and Grand Theft Auto V have been among the highest revenue-generating entertainment products ever. Moreover, games have surpassed their status as being a pastime for adolescent boys and have grown into a mainstream medium that touches every segment of the population. According to the Entertainment Software Association (2015), 42 percent of U.S. citizens play digital games on a regular basis (three hours or more per week), 44 percent of all game players are women, and the average game player is 35 years old and has been playing games for 13 years.

Additionally, digital games are potentially interesting vehicles for the integration of advertising because they possess several unique characteristics that can give them advantages over other advertising media (e.g., print, radio, television, movies, the internet) (Nelson, 2002; Chambers, 2005). First of all, digital games have the benefit of a *long shelf life* and *high replay value*. Games typically take between 10 and 200 hours to complete, meaning that the chance of repeated and extensive exposure to integrated advertising is considerably high (Internet Advertising Bureau, 2007).

Additionally, where other media are often suffering from a lack of focused attention, games continue to demand more concentration (Internet Advertising Bureau, 2007). External stimuli can distract people from paying complete attention to medium content. People are often multitasking, eating, reading, talking, or doing household tasks while also consuming content from multiple media at the same time. For instance, it is possible, and not uncommon, for people to watch television while also catching up with their family members, eating dinner, checking their email, and/or surfing the internet on their laptop or mobile device. Gaming, however, is different. It is a medium where if the audience is not focused, there will be consequences for their progress in-game. In the majority of cases, if people are not concentrating while playing a game, there is a good chance that their performance will suffer, resulting in lower game scores and maybe even the death of their game character (Internet Advertising Bureau, 2007).

Further, it is more difficult to skip, block, or avoid the advertisements that are integrated as part of the game environment. Lately, popular advertising media such as television and the internet are increasingly disadvantaged by the emergence of technology and software that enables people to avoid advertising (Chambers, 2005). People can record movies or television programs using their digital video recorders (DVRs) and fast-forward through, or simply remove, commercials while watching these programs later on. Moreover, content filtering and ad-blocking software are becoming more and more popular among the internet-using population (Chambers, 2005). For example, ad block plugins are some of the most popular internet browser extensions worldwide. These plugins prevent advertisements from being displayed all over the web and currently count over 198 million users (PageFair & Adobe, 2015). Consequently, practices where advertisements are programmed within the entertainment context, such as product placement in television programs, movies, and games (i.e., IGA), offer advertisers the chance of promoting their brands in an environment where users cannot blatantly avoid them (Herrewijn, 2015).

Throughout the years, IGA has also advanced from a very static toward a more dynamic advertising medium (Schneider & Cornwell, 2005; Internet Advertising Bureau, 2007). In the beginning, IGA was hard-coded into a game in its development stage, resulting in static ads that could never be changed or updated once the game was released. However, from the mid-2000s onwards, IGA has become much more flexible. Due to the online capabilities of modern digital games, advertisements can now be dynamically embedded into games. Access to the internet enables advertisers to dynamically place and alter ad units in games and gather gameplay statistics. This way, ads do not have to be integrated in games in the form of static, unchanging images anymore but can be delivered and updated in-game based on multiple criteria, such as date, time of day, ad frequency, and players' demographic, regional, and gamer profile, providing brand campaigns with a great amount of flexibility (Schneider & Cornwell, 2005; Internet Advertising Bureau, 2007).

Finally, games can offer brands the opportunity to become an integral part of the digital game experience, reaching out to players in a highly vivid, interactive, and immersive entertainment environment. First of all, while other media rely primarily on one or two sensory channels (visual and/or auditory), digital games are able to produce a sensorial rich and vivid environment that is capable of presenting information to additional senses. Haptic technology, for instance, allows players to receive kinesthetic and tactile cues while playing a digital game, enabling them to feel vibrations in their game controllers when their game characters take damage or when their racing car collides with an obstacle, providing a sense of danger (Nelson, 2005). Moreover, digital games are an interactive medium that requires an active audience. They give players the ability to control their own actions and perceptions: players do not just observe a car race across the screen; they actively control it, feeling its speed, maneuvering it between obstacles and opponents (Nelson, Keum, & Yaros, 2004).

Lastly, digital games offer players a highly immersive experience; they provide a particular form of mediated experience that is able to create the feeling of being drawn into the game world represented on-screen (Calleja, 2011). These characteristics provide new and interesting ways to interact with the game environment altogether (Nelson, 2005), but more importantly, they offer a unique opportunity for the integration of advertisements; high degrees of player interactivity, immersion, and vividness can make players feel as if they are first-hand controlling and interacting with a brand in a lively and exciting environment (Nelson et al., 2004).

Advertisers are not the only party that can potentially benefit from IGA though. The practice is also attractive to game companies because it offers an additional revenue stream to subsidize the rising game development costs beyond the traditional model of revenue from retail sales (Chambers, 2005; Internet Advertising Bureau, 2007; Boyd & Lalla, 2009). This ultimately also benefits the *gamer* as end-user. Digital games are more and more expensive to make, but game players have not felt this increase; due to alternative revenue streams such as IGA, the retail prices of games have remained relatively static (Chambers, 2005; Internet Advertising Bureau, 2007; Boyd & Lalla, 2009). Finally, if the advertising fits naturally in the game and does not interrupt the player's game experience, it can even make the virtual environment more realistic and immersive (Internet Advertising Bureau, 2007).

Despite its promising new branding opportunities and growth potential, however, IGA also faces several obstacles. The most obvious manifestation of this can be found in the rise and subsequent fall of several IGA-related companies during the last decade. In the early- to mid-2000s, several companies were founded that focused exclusively on offering IGA services, such as Massive Incorporated (Microsoft), Adscape Media (Google), IGA Worldwide, and Double Fusion. By the end of 2010, however, the majority of these companies ceased to exist. This development can be primarily attributed to two factors.

First of all, both advertisers and game companies have been struggling with the audience's negative reactions toward IGA they deem to be too intrusive. Gamers are extremely protective of their passion. If they disapprove of the commercial messages within their favorite games (e.g., when the advertisements do not fit within the context of the game, disrupt their game experience, or simply start to annoy them), they will voice their discontent among the widespread gaming community, potentially resulting in *consumer backlash* or a negative impact on the popularity and sales of both the game and the incorporated brands (Internet Advertising Bureau, 2007; Shields, 2012).

Moreover, many advertisers still do not fully embrace digital games as a viable advertising vehicle because of the continuing difficulties in determining and optimizing the advertisements' effectiveness (Nelson, 2002; Internet Advertising Bureau, 2007; Boyd & Lalla, 2009; Shields, 2012). IGA and its effectiveness have attracted the attention of both industry-commissioned and academic research, which have repeatedly looked at the impact of IGA on people's cognitive response (i.e., brand awareness), affective (i.e., brand evaluation), and conative responses (i.e., purchase intention, buying behavior) to the brand(s) (Nelson, 2005; Skalski et al., 2010). However, most of these studies have produced mixed (and often contradictory) results.

In-Game Advertising Effectiveness

According to several industry-commissioned studies carried out by Nielsen Entertainment, IGA in sports and racing games helps to drive brand awareness and is able to significantly change consumer opinions in a positive way (Activision, 2005; Microsoft Corporation, 2007; GamesIndustry International, 2008). Research results show that average brand recall rates are considerably higher, with brands being spontaneously recalled by more than 40 percent of participants. Moreover, these industry reports state that a high percentage of gamers show a more favorable attitude toward the brands and ads after playing the game, and that in general, participants do not mind IGA and even think it contributes to the realism of the game (Activision, 2005; Microsoft Corporation, 2007; GamesIndustry International, 2008). For example, in a research study conducted by Nielsen on behalf of IGA Worldwide, 82 percent of participants felt that games were just as enjoyable with ads as without, and there was a 61 percent increase in consumers' favorable opinions toward the brands advertised in-game (GamesIndustry International, 2008).

Another study of Nielsen in collaboration with Electronic Arts builds on these results and expands them even further by studying the impact of in-game ads occurring in several sports games in a large-scale field experiment. Using its consumer panel of 100,000 U.S. households, Nielsen found that IGA also influences buying habits. The study focused on households that purchased at least one of six EA Sports games containing a variety of product placements of the brand Gatorade and compared them with households that did not purchase any of these games. Results show that the advertising integrated into the games increased household dollars spent on Gatorade by 24 percent (Guzman, 2010).

These Nielsen Entertainment studies have to be interpreted with caution though, since it concerns research by and in the interest of the industry. However, not only the industry has shown a growing interest in IGA research; academic studies have also increasingly turned their attention to the effectiveness of IGA in recent years.

In the first published academic study on IGA, Nelson (2002) explored the effectiveness of placing advertisements in racing games in two experimental studies. Participants were asked which brands they spontaneously recalled immediately after gameplay and after a delay of five months. On average, players were able to recall 25 to 30 percent of brands in the short-term and 10 to 15 percent in the long-term. However, results differed greatly depending on the type of IGA (e.g., passive billboard versus interactive product placement) and the type of brand (e.g., local versus (inter)national, relevant versus irrelevant) that were employed.

Since then, academic research has focused on the effectiveness of IGA in a wide variety of game genres and situations. Results of these studies have been mixed. Chaney et al. (2004), for example, looked at IGA effects in a first-person shooter game and observed brand recall rates that were rather low. Participants generally recalled going past billboards in the game, but they had little memory for the brands that were featured on them. More specifically, the brands that were integrated were only recalled by 5 to 20 percent of the participants. Further, the in-game ads had a very limited effect on players' purchase intentions of the featured brands. These findings oppose those of Mau, Silberer, and Constien (2008), however, who also looked at the effectiveness of advertising inside a first-person shooter game and found recall rates that were considerably higher. In their study, 68 percent of participants could recall the integrated brands correctly. Participants' attitudes toward the integrated brands depended greatly on the players' familiarity with the integrated brands; attitudes toward an unfamiliar brand were enhanced, while attitudes toward a familiar brand deteriorated.

Academic analyses such as these offer a more nuanced view on the practice of IGA than the one publicized by the industry; they show that the integration of IGA is a complicated matter that is subject to a wide variety of characteristics. Findings often parallel the results of research looking at the effectiveness of advertising in other media (e.g., print, television, and the internet), which has repeatedly demonstrated that ad effectiveness is dependent on a multitude of characteristics related to the advertisement (e.g., the type of brand that is featured, the prominence of the brand), the audience (e.g., gender, age, culture, prior experience with the medium), and the advertising context (e.g., the type of vehicle that is used, the amount of congruity between the context and the ad, a person's social environment, his subjective responses in reaction to the medium content) (Moorman, 2003).

Many of these factors have been shown to be of importance when examining the effectiveness of IGA as well (for an elaborate overview, see Herrewijn & Poels, 2014). For instance, concerning the characteristics of the advertisement that is integrated into the game, research has shown that IGA effectiveness greatly depends on the type of brand (e.g., local versus international brands) and the prominence of the brand placement (e.g., central versus peripheral location) that is being integrated. Furthermore, several studies argue that IGA effects are not only a function of the ad itself, since IGA is not encountered in a vacuum by a passive audience; the characteristics of the player, like his prior level of game experience, also seem to play an important role. Finally, research has demonstrated that the characteristics of the context in which the advertisement is embedded or encountered are crucial in light of its effectiveness as well, with examples including the congruity of the game and the ad (e.g., low versus high), the social setting in which the game is played (e.g., alone versus together with others), and the player's subjective experience during gameplay (e.g., enjoyment, immersion) (Herrewijn & Poels, 2014).

Theoretical Models

Academics studying IGA and its effectiveness generally use several theoretical models to ground their research. Two theoretical models are of particular importance when studying the impact of commercial messages in the context of digital games, namely, the limited capacity model of motivated mediated message processing (Lang, 2009) and the excitation transfer model (Zillman, Katcher, & Milavsky, 1972).

The limited capacity model of motivated mediated message processing (LC4MP) states that a person's ability to process information is limited, with people having access to only a limited pool of cognitive resources at a particular time (Lang, 2009). More specifically, the model implies that when people are oversaturated with stimuli, their processing capabilities (i.e., the encoding, storage, and retrieval of information) will diminish (Lang, 2009). This has important implications for the effectiveness of IGA in terms of brand awareness. Digital games are highly interactive and involve media that bombard the player with a multitude of tasks and stimuli that all vie for attention at the same time. Getting a brand noticed and remembered in such an involving game context is not self-evident, since people allocate their cognitive resources to those aspects of an activity that are most relevant to them at a particular time, namely their primary task. In a digital game context, the primary task consists of actually playing the game; the player tries to process and act on the information that is most essential to his progression in the game (e.g., shooting enemies, driving a car as fast as possible in a race). Since people will focus their attention primarily on the playing of the game, this leaves fewer mental resources available for secondary tasks, such as the processing of advertisements that are embedded into the background of the game (Lang, 2009). The LC4MP (Lang, 2009) is, thus, of great importance when studying the player's ability to cognitively process the advertising messages that are integrated into a digital game.

Furthermore, the excitation transfer model argues that affect evoked by one stimulus can transfer to, and even amplify, a person's affective response to another stimulus (Zillman et al., 1972). In an advertising context, the excitation transfer model has been applied to explain a transfer of affect from medium content (e.g., a television program) to advertising that is encountered in its context (e.g., a television commercial), influencing people's evaluation of the ads and featured brands (Singh & Churchill, 1987; Yoo & MacInnis, 2005). The model is also believed to have implications for IGA. Advertisements in games are encountered inside the game and are seen as part of the game environment. When this environment induces a certain affective response (e.g., arousal, involvement), the valence of this response might subsequently transfer to the in-game ads as well.

Case Study: The Impact of Brand Interactivity

The previous section gave an overview of the different studies that have been conducted on the effectiveness of IGA, simultaneously showing which factors might influence effectiveness and which theoretical models have been used to ground IGA studies.

Next, we take a closer, more elaborate look at the mechanisms that might underlie the effectiveness of an advertisement integrated into the world of a digital game. Consequently, we present a case study in which we consider the impact of one factor, in particular, that can affect the way an in-game brand placement performs: its *interactivity* (Herrewijn, 2015).

As mentioned earlier, interactivity is a crucial factor to consider in a digital game context. It is one characteristic that distinguishes digital games from other, more passive media (e.g., print, television). By using an input device or game controller, players can exert agency over the actions and movements of their avatar in the game world (Calleja, 2011): when they press a button (e.g., while playing computer or console games) or touch the screen (e.g., while playing mobile games), the game responds, and the avatar will act accordingly on the screen. They can control their avatar's movements and perceptions, and make their own choices. Players do not just observe a predetermined chain of events as they unfold; they can actively participate in them and decide their outcome (Nelson, 2002; Nelson et al., 2004). This feedback loop between players and their avatar in the game world makes up a vital and indispensable part of the digital game experience; without it, there would essentially be no game (Calleja, 2011).

The highly interactive environment offered by digital games also has important implications for IGA. Within such an environment, it becomes possible to let players interact with a brand in a meaningful way. Racing and sports games often contain a large range of branded vehicles and/ or clothing that the player can customize and compete with. Eating or drinking products and observing a certain effect on the player character (e.g., regaining a certain amount of health or energy points after drinking a can of soda) is also commonplace in games, as is the integration of products that can be used as tools, accessories, or media (e.g., using a certain brand of cellphone to communicate with other players or non-player characters). Finally, there have also been instances in which games let players actively engage with billboards, by unveiling more images and/ or information when the player touches or activates it (Herrewijn & Poels, 2014). Such brand interactions can elevate a brand from being a mere background prop to being a major part of the player's gameplay (Nelson, 2005; Skalski et al., 2010). However, the impact of brand interactivity on the effectiveness of brand placements in terms of brand awareness and evaluations has barely been touched upon in academic research.

An exception is Nelson's study (2002), which showed that varying degrees of brand interactivity could, indeed, have a significant impact on the effectiveness of IGA. She showed that in the context of a racing game, selecting and racing a branded car led to higher brand awareness than driving past passive billboards on the side of the road (Nelson, 2002). This finding can be framed in the context of the *LC4MP* (Lang, 2009) that was discussed earlier. Because the branded car constituted an essential part of the player's gameplay (i.e., driving it was crucial to the player's progress in the game), it was incorporated as a part of the player's primary task. As such, the brand in question demanded more explicit attention, resulting in a more elaborate processing. The passive billboards, on the other hand, were not imperative to the player's headway in the game and therefore remained part of the player's secondary task, receiving less attention.

Moreover, research shows that imagined interaction with a brand also leads to better brand attitudes. For instance, Escalas (2004) showed that when people imagine themselves using a product in a narrative context, they were distracted from its commercial nature and did not think critically about it. Moreover, in compliance with the *excitation transfer theory* (Zillman et al., 1972), if the imagined interaction evoked positive feelings, those feelings get transferred to the advertised product as well (Escalas, 2004). Surprisingly, this point-of-view has never been studied in an IGA setting before.

The goal of the current study was, therefore, to investigate the impact of brand interactivity on player responses toward IGA in greater detail, taking into account both brand awareness (i.e., brand recall, brand recognition) and brand evaluations (i.e., brand attitudes).

Method and Rationale

To accomplish this goal, we designed an experiment in which we asked participants to play a digital game containing IGA for approximately 20 minutes. We worked with the computer version of the action role-playing game, Fallout: New Vegas. We used the game's official editor to create our own game environment for use in the experiment. This made it possible to fully control the structuring of the gameplay (e.g., player perspective, spatial lay-out of the game level, game difficulty) and the creation and inclusion of IGA (e.g., types of brands, types of IGA, number of exposures) in the game environment, resulting in a highly authentic game scenario in which to analyze IGA effectiveness.

Within this game environment, we manipulated brand interactivity as a within-subjects factor. More specifically, we included two different types of IGA in the experimental game. We contrasted between brand placements that could be interacted with in order to gain an advantage in-game (and that thus constituted a central and active part of the player's gameplay) on the one hand, and poster advertisements with a passive role on the other.

Because the original game makes use of advertising for fictitious food and drinks (e.g., "Nuka-Cola," a soda brand), we decided to use these product categories as well. We chose to work with real brands that were unfamiliar to our experimental population (since they are not available in their country of origin), namely "Mello Yello," "Reese's Pieces," "Vernors," and "Baby Ruth." This was done to create a credible IGA scenario while avoiding effects of prior brand exposure or pre-existing brand attitudes. Familiarity with and attitudes toward the integrate brands were assessed beforehand, in a pre-test involving 43 people (32 male, 11 female; M_{age} = 22.23, SD_{age} = 4.02).

The brands "Mello Yello" and "Reese's Pieces" were integrated as interactive brand placements (i.e., bottles of soda, boxes of candy) in the game. These product placements were scattered around the level (see Figure 18.1) and were available from vending machines (see Figures 18.2 and 18.3).They could be picked up and consumed to gain health points (e.g., when the player got hurt). Since consuming these products was the only way to regain health in-game, people had to actively search for them and use them when needed. Moreover, the brands "Vernors" and "Baby Ruth" were integrated as passive poster ads, which were put against the walls of the game level (see Figure 18.4). Each brand was integrated into the experimental game level on six different locations and was encountered 7.25

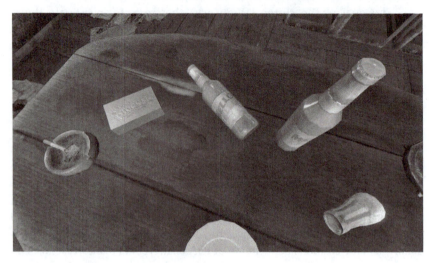

FIGURE 18.1   The Interactive Brand Placements ("Mello Yello," "Reese's Pieces") Integrated into the Game

FIGURE 18.2   A Vending Machine for the Interactive Brand Placement "Mello Yello" Integrated into the Game

FIGURE 18.3   A Vending Machine for the Interactive Brand Placement "Reese's Pieces" Integrated into the Game

FIGURE 18.4   The Passive Brand Placements ("Vernors," "Baby Ruth") Integrated into the Game

times on average ($SD = 1.73$), with no significant differences in the number of exposures between the different brands ($F(3, 162) = 2.35, p = .08$).

When participants finished playing the game, they were asked to fill in a self-report questionnaire. This questionnaire consisted of questions regarding the player experience (i.e., players' pleasure and arousal during gameplay were measured by means of Lang's (1980) 9-point self-assessment manikin), the effectiveness of the in-game ads (i.e., brand awareness was assessed by measuring brand recall and brand recognition; brand evaluations were assessed by measuring brand attitudes), and participants' socio-demographic (e.g., gender, age), and play-related characteristics (e.g., prior game experience, game frequency).

Sixty-two people (57 male, 5 female) between 18 and 37 years old (M = 22.32, SD = 3.21) and of Belgian nationality participated in the experiment. Most of the participants were experienced gamers who had been playing digital games for six years or more (6 to 8 years: 22.6%, 9 years or more: 74.2%) and played games on a weekly or daily basis (weekly: 30.6%, daily: 64.5%). On average, participants experienced a fair amount of pleasure (M = 5.48, SD = 1.20) and a moderate amount of arousal (M = 3.77, SD = 2.05) during gameplay.

Results and Conclusions

The findings of the study show that, as expected, the manipulation of brand interactivity resulted in significant differences in brand awareness and brand attitudes, with the interactive brands attaining significantly higher awareness scores and attitudes than brands that were integrated in a passive way (see Table 18.1).

Concerning brand awareness, results show that the interactive product placements were recalled ($F(3, 174)$ = 16.21, p < .001, η^2 = .22) and recognized ($F(3, 183)$ = 23.53, p < .001, η^2 = .28) significantly better than their passive counterparts.

In the case of interactive brand placement "Mello Yello," for instance, 27 percent of the participants spontaneously recalled the brand, while 73 percent recognized the brand logo afterwards. Taking into account that people were not familiar with the brands prior to participation in the experiment and only played the game for a short period of time, memory for the interactive placements can be considered to be remarkably high. The brand awareness scores of the passive poster advertisements, on the other hand, were much lower. For instance, passive placement "Vernors" was recalled by no one, although its logo was later recognized by 24 percent of the participants.

Additionally, we also found a significant difference in brand awareness between our two interactive brands, with "Mello Yello" attaining higher scores than "Reese's Pieces." This may have been a result of the way in which they were implemented into the game. Although both brands were integrated as interactive brand placements (i.e., bottles of soda, boxes of candy), they were also available from vending machines. The "Mello Yello" vending machine, however, featured an additional "Mello Yello" logo (see Figure 18.2), while the "Reese's Pieces" vending machine did not (see Figure 18.3). Apart from the interactive nature of the brand placements, their prominence thus also seems to play an important role in determining their effectiveness.

Regarding brand awareness, the results are, therefore, in line with the study of Nelson (2002) discussed earlier, and offer further support for the theory put

TABLE 18.1 The Impact of Brand Interactivity on IGA Effectiveness

	Brand interactivity		Passive brands		ANOVA			
	Interactive brands		Passive brands					
	Mello Yello (a)	Reese's Pieces (b)	Vernors (c)	Baby Ruth (d)				
IGA Effectiveness	Mean (SD)	Mean (SD)	Mean (SD)	Mean (SD)	F	(df)	p	η^2
Brand recall	.27 (.43)[b,c,d]	.09 (.27)[a,c,d]	.00 (.00)[a,b]	.02 (.13)[a,b]	16.21	(3, 174)	< .001	.22
Brand recognition	.73 (.45)[b,c,d]	.44 (.50)[a,c,d]	.24 (.43)[a,b]	.18 (.39)[a,b]	23.53	(3, 183)	< .001	.28
Brand attitude	3.37 (1.19)[c]	3.50 (1.10)[c]	2.98 (.92)[a,b]	3.14 (.92)	4.64	(3, 183)	.004	.07

Note. The results from Bonferonni post-hoc tests are indicated by the letters in superscript. Brand attitudes were measured by the means of three 7-point scales, with 0 being very negative and 6 being very positive.

forward by the LC4MP (Lang, 2009). That is, because the interactive brands make up an essential part of the gameplay, they are incorporated as a part of players' primary task, demanding more explicit attention than the passive brands and resulting in more elaborate processing.

Furthermore, the interactive placements also attained significantly higher brand attitudes than the passive poster ads ($F(3, 183) = 4.64, p = .004, \eta^2 = .07$). Participants remained neutral toward the passive brands but reported slightly more positive attitudes toward the interactive brands. Again, considering that people were unfamiliar with the brands beforehand and only played the experimental game for approximately 20 minutes, this positive change in attitudes for the interactive brands is noteworthy. This finding is in line with the expectations formulated by Escalas (2004) and the excitation transfer theory (Zillman et al., 1972). That is, interacting with a brand in a digital game context distracts players from its commercial nature, and if this interaction evokes positive feelings, these feelings can get transferred to the advertised brand as well.

In conclusion, the results of the study suggest that the integration of brand placements that can be meaningfully interacted with in-game is a far more effective IGA strategy than incorporating passive ads, both in terms of brand awareness and brand evaluations. Playing digital games is an interactive experience that offers new and interesting ways for the integration of advertisements. When the player is able to interact with a brand in-game and has to actively use it in order to successfully finish the mission, the brand will be closely tied to the primary task, demanding more of the player's attention and opening up possibilities for the transfer of positive feelings associated with the encounter. Brands that are simply used as props in a scene, however, are less meaningful to the player's overall experience, resulting in lower brand recall, brand recognitions, and brand attitudes. It, therefore, seems best for advertisers to avoid the passive banner ad approach and work together with game developers to develop interactive approaches that give the player the opportunity to feel, control, and/or interact with the brand in creative ways.

References

Activision. (2005). Activision and Nielsen entertainment release results of pioneering research on in-game advertising. Retrieved from http://investor.activision.com/relea sedetail.cfm?releaseid=181109.

Boyd, G., & Lalla, V. (2009). Emerging issues in in-game advertising. Retrieved from http://www.gamasutra.com/view/feature/3927/emerging_issues_in_ingame_.php.

Calleja, G. (2011). *In-game: From immersion to incorporation.* Cambridge, MA: London MIT Press.

Chambers, J. (2005). The sponsored avatar: Examining the present reality and future possibilities of advertising in digital games. In *Proceedings of DiGRA 2005 Conference.*

Chaney, I. M., Lin, K., & Chaney, J. (2004). The effect of billboards within the gaming environment. *Journal of Interactive Advertising, 5*(1), 54–69.

Entertainment Software Association. (2015). 2015 Sales, demographic and usage data. Essential facts about the computer and video game industry. Retrieved from http://www.theesa.com/wp-content/uploads/2015/04/ESA-Essential-Facts-2015.pdf.

Escalas, J. E. (2004). Imagine yourself in the product: Mental simulation, narrative transportation, and persuasion. *Journal of Advertising, 33*(2), 37–48.

GamesIndustry International. (2008). Landmark IGA-Nielsen study. Retrieved from http://www.gamesindustry.biz/articles/landmark-iga-nielsen-study—in-game-ads-are-effective-and-well-received-by-the-gaming-community—it-transpires.

Guzman, G. (2010). Video game advertising: Playing to win. . . and sell. Retrieved from http://blog.nielsen.com/nielsenwire/consumer/video-game-advertising-playing-to-win%E2%80%A6-and-sell/

Herrewijn, L. (2015). *The effectiveness of in-game advertising: The role of ad format, game context and player involvement.* Doctoral Dissertation. University of Antwerp.

Herrewijn, L., & Poels, K. (2014). Rated A for advertising: A critical reflection on in-game advertising. In M. C. Angelides & H. Agius (Eds.), *Handbook of digital games* (pp. 305–339). Hoboken, NJ: Wiley-IEEE Press.

Internet Advertising Bureau. (2007). *In-game advertising: The UK market.* Retrieved from http://kaznowski.blox.pl/resource/IAB_ingame_advertising__the_UK_Market_March_2007_1594.pdf.

Juniper Research. (2015). *Digital games revenues to pass $100 billion per annum by 2018.* Retrieved from http://www.juniperresearch.com/press/press-releases/digital-games-revenues-to-pass-$100-billion-per-an.

Lang, A. (2009). The limited capacity model of motivated mediated message processing. In R. L. Nabi & M. B. Oliver (Eds.), *The SAGE handbook of media processes and effects* (pp. 193–204). Thousand Oaks, CA: Sage Publications.

Lang, P. J. (1980). Behavioral treatment and bio-behavioral assessment: Computer applications. In J. B. Sidowski, J. H. Johnson, & T. A. Williams (Eds.), *Technology in mental health care delivery systems* (pp. 119–137). Norwood, NJ: Ablex Publishing.

Mau, G., Silberer, G., & Constien, C. (2008). Communicating brands playfully: Effects of in game advertising for familiar and unfamiliar brands. *International Journal of Advertising, 27*(5), 827–851.

Microsoft Corporation. (2007). *Massive study reveals in-game advertising increases average brand familiarity by up to 64 percent.* Retrieved from http://www.microsoft.com/en-us/news/press/2007/aug07/08–08InGameAdsPR.aspx.

Moorman, M. (2003). *Context considered: The relationship between media environments and advertising effects.* Doctoral Dissertation. Amsterdam: Universiteit van Amsterdam.

Nelson, M. R. (2002). Recall of brand placements in computer/video games. *Journal of Advertising Research, 42*(2), 80–92.

Nelson, M. R. (2005). Exploring consumer response to "advergaming." In C. Haugtvedt, K. Machleit, & R. Yalch (Eds.), *Online consumer psychology. Understanding and influencing consumer behavior in the virtual world* (pp. 156–183). Mahwah, NJ: Lawrence Erlbaum Associates, Inc.

Nelson, M. R., Keum, H., & Yaros, R. A. (2004). Advertainment or adcreep: Game players' attitudes toward advertising and product placements in computer games. *Journal of Interactive Advertising, 5*(1), 3–21.

PageFair & Adobe. (2015). *The cost of ad blocking. PageFair and Adobe 2015 ad blocking report.* Retrieved from https://downloads.pagefair.com/wp-content/uploads/2016/05/2015_report-the_cost_of_ad_blocking.pdf.

Schneider, L., & Cornwell, B. T. (2005). Cashing in on crashes via brand placement in computer games: The effects of experience and flow on memory. *International Journal of Advertising, 24*(3), 321–343.

Shields, M. (2012). When it comes to ads in games, these guys aren't playing around. Electronic arts is out to master the delicate dance of marketing and gaming. *AdWeek*. Retrieved from http://www.adweek.com/news/advertising-branding/when-it-comes-ads-games-these-guys-arent-playing-around-141158?page=1.

Singh, S. N., & Churchill, G. A. (1987). Arousal and advertising effectiveness. *Journal of Advertising, 16*(1), 4–40.

Skalski, P., Bracken, C. C., & Buncher, M. (2010). Advertising: It's in the game. In M. S. Eastin, T. Daugherty, & N. M. Burns (Eds.), *Handbook of research on digital media and advertising: User generated content consumption* (pp. 437–455). Hershey, New York, NY: Information Science Reference.

Yoo, C., & MacInnis, D. J. (2005). The brand attitude formation process of emotional and informational ads. *Journal of Business Research, 58*(10), 1397–1406.

Zillman, D., Katcher, A. H., & Milavsky, B. (1972). Excitation transfer from physical exercise to subsequent aggressive behavior. *Journal of Experimental Social Psychology, 8*(3), 247–259.

19

NEW METHODS FOR MEASURING ADVERTISING EFFICACY

Daniel McDuff

Introduction

Advertisements—from traditional print, radio, and TV ads, to internet banners and online video advertisements—are placing increasing emphasis on emotional content. By creating ads that surprise, engage, and entertain, advertisers aim to create memorable content that will help consumers remember the product and build positive associations with the brand that trigger at the point of decision to purchase and ultimately drive sales. In today's media landscape there are a number of additional benefits of emotional connections that were less prevalent in the past, including increasing the likelihood of pass-along sharing, message endorsement, and brand "fandom."

Advertisers have long striven to design ads that elicit emotion in viewers but have struggled to measure the extent to which they have been successful. Measuring advertising efficacy is important to help avoid costly mistakes associated with publishing material that harms a brand; it is therefore critical to provide effective and efficient ways to measure emotional, in addition to cognitive, responses. This chapter will illustrate how new technology for measuring emotional responses has been applied to evaluating digital advertising effectiveness.

The appreciation of the role of emotions in advertising is not new. Zajonc (1980) argued that emotion can function independently of cognition and can, indeed, override it. Emotions have been posited to be markers, mediators, and moderators of consumer responses (Bagozzi, Gopinath, & Nyer, 1999). Batra and Ray (1986) stressed the need to consider both the cognitive and affective aspects of responses to advertising, while Erevelles (1998) argued that advertising models that omit emotions do not adequately explain advertising effectiveness. Inevitably, advertisements will contain elements of both rational and emotional content, even if their creators intended to emphasize one element over the other. Emotions have been shown to play a significant role in increasing brand liking (emotional rub-off) (Biel, 1990) and brand attitude (Russell, 2002), influencing favorability (Heath, Brandt, & Nairn, 2006), persuading consumers (Batra & Ray, 1986; Johar, Maheswaran, & Peracchio, 2006), increasing respect and love (Roberts, 2005; Pawle & Cooper, 2006), and predicting purchase intent toward a brand (Morris, Woo, Geason, & Kim, 2002). Moreover, the key to branding is building an emotional connection between consumers and a brand (Mehta & Purvis, 2006). Emotions play a significant part in the decision-making process of purchasing, and advertising is often seen as an effective source of enhancement of these emotional associations (Mehta & Purvis, 2006).

Cognitive responses to advertisements can be captured quite effectively via surveys. However, one caveat in considering the strength of findings related to emotion is that most of the measures have also been obtained from self-report questionnaires involving post-hoc cognitive reflection. While questionnaires are easy to administer, their accuracy about emotion can be unreliable. Post-hoc reporting of an earlier emotion can be influenced by the current (end-state) emotion as well as by a person's ability to map remembered, possibly complex, feelings to the various choices on the questionnaire, which tend to be simple descriptors (Fredrickson & Kahneman, 1993). Consequently, self-reported feelings may or may not accurately describe the truly experienced trajectory of visceral emotions.

The development of new technology now enables us to measure people's physiological states and behaviors in a quantitative way. The technologies include the use of functional Magnetic Resonance Imaging (fMRI), electroencephalography (EEG), eye-tracking (ET), electromyography (EMG), automated facial coding (FC), and other physiological sensors (for measuring electrodermal activity (EDA), heart rate (HR), and heart rate variability (HRV)). These techniques allow measurement of responses in real-time without requiring subjects to complete another task (as is the case with survey or dial measurement). However, the interpretation of the data is often more challenging than with self-report responses. As an example, large individual differences in physiological parameters can exist. A person's heart rate will be influenced by their overall physical condition, posture, and preceding activities, in addition to their emotional response to content they are viewing. An early survey of many techniques for quantitative measurement of emotions in marketing research was published by Poels and Dewitte (2006). However, in the past decade, new measurement methods and frameworks have been developed and a great deal of new research has been performed.

In the past, the measurement of emotional responses to advertisements required subjects to be brought to a laboratory facility where experimenters could record their physiological or behavioral responses to content. The only alternative was for experimenters to travel to participants' homes, an extra effort and considerable expense that helped achieve greater ecological validity. However, constraints related to travel, scheduling, and staffing limit the number of participants and the geographical area that can be included, making experiments unscalable. Studies using such methods typically included fewer than 100 participants from one city.

In recent years, new scalable methods for measuring emotional responses to advertisements have been developed. This chapter discusses these approaches and how they have been applied in measuring advertising efficacy. Particular emphasis is placed on quantitative, scalable approaches of capturing emotional responses. These methods allow experiments to be performed in-situ (e.g., in the subject's home) and the passive capture of visceral responses to advertisements. Furthermore, they allow a broader and global demographic to be sampled than just those available in a close geographic locale; a global network of market research facilities is not required as people can be reached via the internet. Large-scale emotion measurement approaches have great potential for extending our ability to measure advertising effectiveness and naturally complement more controlled laboratory testing.

The following chapter discusses recent research in digital advertising that has applied these new research methodologies and how the data collected are related to common advertising effectiveness measures including ad recall, purchase intent, ad likeability, and ad zapping. The chapter also presents future directions for this research and suggests how new research methods might be used to programmatically deliver content based on emotional reactions in addition to being used for pre- and/or post-testing of advertisements.

Methods for Measuring Emotions and Engagement

As noted, the measurement of emotions in advertising is not a new concept. However, most methods for measuring emotional responses have relied on subjects' self-reports. Nevertheless, self-report is an imperfect measure of emotions. Emotions measured via behaviors, autonomic responses, and brain imaging solve several of the limitations associated with self-report by capturing changes related to emotion without cognitive bias and without interrupting one's attention. Common physiological measures in advertising include measurements of facial expressions, skin conductance, and heart rate, to reflect people's emotional changes in an objective way. In the following section, techniques are described for measuring emotional responses to advertisements.

Self-Report

Self-report methods remain the most commonly used means of measuring the efficacy of advertising, requiring essentially no training. Self-report includes questionnaires, verbal self-report, visual self-report, and moment-to-moment rating (such as turning a dial, or a pencil and paper approach, e.g., "warmth monitor" (Aaker, Stayman, & Hagerty, 1986)). Self-report is relatively simple, cheap, and quick. However, it is subject to bias from desire to please (or not) the interviewer, as well as from comfort with the context and other factors unrelated to advertising interests (Aaker, Stayman, & Hagerty, 1986).

Visual self-report methods can make reporting emotions easier and remove some of the cognitive effort that is required in verbalizing emotions. Self Assessment Mannequins (SAM) have proven to be a useful tool, with an advertising specific system (AD-SAM) being proposed (Morris et al., 2002). SAM uses a dimensional measure of emotions with axes of valence, arousal, and dominance. Another example of a visual self-report tool used in market research is an Emoticon approach for assessing emotional experience (Wood, 2012). These emoticons are images of facial expressions of discrete emotional states.

Dial methods allow subjects to report feelings continuously by turning a dial (or moving a slider, which is more common for web-based surveys). Continuous measurement is useful as emotions can change over time, and people may experience several "peaks" in emotional response when viewing an advertisement. In fact, many advertisements will have more than one scene that aims to elicit emotions.

However, it is becoming more and more apparent that self-report methods still have several weaknesses: 1) self-report methods (some more, some less) require the user to cognitively evaluate their experience; 2) subjects cannot easily perform another task at the same time, and their experience is interrupted; and 3) it is hard to get continuous measures of multiple states.

Eye Tracking

There is a sizeable body of literature using eye-tracking for assessing marketing effectiveness (Wedel & Pieters, 2008). Vision-based tracking systems allow the point of gaze of an individual to be estimated based on their eye position. Gaze patterns indicate whether people viewed a single point for a long time or viewed a range of points in quick succession. As an example, Teixeira, Wedel, and Pieters (2010) found that eye gaze patterns were linked to ad "zapping" behavior in an in-lab study. When focus was more consistent, subjects were less likely to "zap."

Most eye-tracking studies are performed using commercially available hardware systems, including a customized camera. However, eye-tracking solutions that utilize a standard webcam have been developed. These methods are less precise than eye-tracking solutions that use dedicated hardware. Even with some form of calibration, it remains challenging to isolate the point of gaze on a screen, in part because the position and dimensions of the screen and browser window are often not known but also because estimating eye positions and head pose with high accuracy is not trivial from a low resolution image. There remains little published evidence of the efficacy of these webcam approaches. Nevertheless, they present the possibility of in-field eye-tracking studies that can be performed at scale.

Facial Analysis

Facial responses provide a passive way of measuring someone's experience. Amongst other signals, the face communicates rich information about emotional experiences. The quantification of facial behavior has relied primarily on three approaches: 1) measurement of electrical muscle potentials on the face, known as electromyography (EMG), 2) manual coding of visible changes on the face from photographic images or video segments typically by a trained observer, and 3) automatic coding of visible changes on the face from photographic images or video segments by a computer. Neither of the first two approaches is easily scalable, as discussed below. However, automated coding presents a highly efficient method of coding facial behavior.

Electromyography involves the measurement of muscle potential using electrodes attached to the skin. The most commonly measured muscles are the *zygomatic major* (activated when people smile), the *corrugator* (activated when people furrow their brow), and the *orbicularis oculi* (activated when people raise their cheeks, as with a "Duchenne" smile). These capture elements of positive and negative emotional valence responses respectively (Cacioppo, Petty, Losch, & Kim, 1986). Facial EMG has been used to assess valence of emotional responses to messages (Bolls, Lang, & Potter, 2001) and is typically a more interpretable measure of valence than physiological responses (Micu & Plummer, 2010). Hazlett and Hazlett (1999) found that EMG measurements to advertising were related to ad recall, with advertisements that elicited greater amounts of *zygomatic major* (smiling) and *corrugator* (brow furrowing) muscle movements being more memorable.

EMG allows measurement of very subtle muscle movements that may not be visible to a human observer. However, they are also sensitive to head motion artefacts. As EMG measurements require specific, non-ubiquitous hardware and contact with the subject, it is not a scalable method of measuring responses. Furthermore, it requires sticky electrodes to be attached to the subject's face creating an unnatural viewing experience.

Facial coding is an observational method of capturing behavior on the face. Coding facial behavior can be based on "sign judgments" using an objective-coding scheme of facial actions (muscle movements) or "message judgments" using a subjective interpretation of emotion. Most objective coding uses the Facial Action Coding System (FACS) (Ekman & Friesen, 1978; Cohn, Ambadar & Ekman, 2007), the most comprehensive and widely used taxonomy of facial behavior. FACS describes the appearance of the face when muscle movements are present; allowing trained human coders to identify them from images or videos. Subjective judgments involve human observers assessing the emotion or cognitive state of a person from their facial expression.

Manual facial coding (whether using an objective or subjective approach) requires trained human coders and is a laborious and time-consuming task. It is not a scalable approach for capturing responses to media and certainly could not be used for any application that requires real-time results or even results within a short space of time. In recent years the development of computer-based algorithms for automatic coding of facial behavior has enabled scalable and repeatable analysis of responses. This technology involves a computer analyzing the texture and shape of the faces within a video and estimating the likelihood of particular actions or expressions being present.

The first example of facial coding used in advertising research was presented by Derbaix (1995). Derbaix found that the contribution of affective responses on ad attitude and brand attitude were evident in verbal responses but not facial measures. The facial coders assigned basic emotion labels to the frames of the viewer's response. However, basic emotions may not be a suitable taxonomy for this task as advertisements may not elicit prototypic displays of emotion. This study is in a minority, with many other examples showing utility in using facial expression measures to evaluate media success.

More recently, facial coding has been applied on a much larger scale thanks to automated techniques. Teixeira, Wedel, and Pieters (2012) analyzed facial expressions in response to video advertisements and found that "zapping" behavior was reduced when ads elicited expressions of emotion. Similar results were obtained by Yang, Kafai, An, and Bhanu (2014) who designed an automated system for predicting "zapping" likelihood from smile responses. Several subsequent studies have analyzed facial responses collected over the internet (Teixeira, Picard, & Kaliouby, 2014; Lewinski, Fransen, & Tan, 2014; McDuff, 2014; McDuff et al., 2015). Both Teixeira et al. (2014) and McDuff et al. (2015) found links between purchase intent and facial responses to advertisements. Other studies have linked facial responses to political debates to voting preferences (McDuff, Kaliouby, Kodra, & Picard, 2013).

Physiological Responses

EDA is one of the most reliable measures of sympathetic arousal (previously known as Galvanic Skin Response), which is associated with attention, arousal, cognitive overload, and memory. EDA has been typically measured through skin conductance at the fingertips using tethered systems. Measurement of EDA generally requires specialist hardware, although some commercial "wearable" devices (such as smartwatches) are able to measure EDA in addition to pulse rate. LaBarbera and Tucciarone (1995) argue strongly for the use of EDA in marketing research and present a number of studies to demonstrate the validity of physiological measurement in evaluating ad effectiveness. The strongest link found was between EDA and sales. Subsequent studies have found EDA to be a better predictor of memory (free-recall and brand recognition tests) than valence, as measured via EMG or self-report (Bolls, Lang, & Potter, 2001).

Inter-beat intervals (IBI) of the heart and breathing patterns are controlled by both the sympathetic nervous system (SNS) and the parasympathetic nervous system (PNS). Heart rate variability (HRV) captures changes in the autonomic response. Tonic and phasic changes in heart rate can be used to capture arousal and attention of viewers. This was demonstrated by Lang (1990) in a study of viewers watching TV ads embedded between two sitcoms to simulate a more realistic viewing experience. Negative messages may receive more attention than positive messages (Bolls, Lang, & Potter, 2001). Respiratory sinus arrhythmia (RSA) has been used as a measure of attention to business news messages. RSA was found to increase with emotional over neutral content—specifically, happy and angry faces (Ravaja, Kallinen, Saari, & Keltikangas-Jarvinen, 2004).

Recent research has presented methods of capturing cardiopulmonary parameters, including heart rate and heart rate variability, using a camera (Poh, McDuff, & Picard, 2011). Therefore, these signals could be measured in a scalable way using an online framework like the one described above. As video streaming and on-device analysis advance, the quality of these measurements will increase considerably. Combining heart rate and HRV measurements with facial expressions will eventually provide a much richer picture of a subject's emotional experiences. However, there is still some way to go before robust HRV measurements are possible from video recorded in unconstrained settings over the internet.

Brain Imaging

Neuromarketing is a growing area of research in the media and marketing industries (Lewis & Phil, 2004). Electroencephalography (EEG) is the measurement of electrical activity in the brain using electrodes placed on the scalp. One of the main advantages of EEG over other brain imaging techniques is that it is a non-invasive. However, it is not possible to measure activity below the cortex. Although it is non-invasive, it still requires subjects to wear a head-mounted device and, as with facial EMG, creates an unnatural experience for the subject. Commercial devices with less obtrusive form factors have recently been created, and these help make the experience more natural.

Functional magnetic resonance imaging (fMRI) is better suited to imaging subcortical brain structures more involved in emotion; however, it is very expensive, and a person has to lie on his or her back and try not to move while being placed in a scanner that makes a loud repetitive noise. Thus, fMRI measurement results in a very unnatural viewing experience.

Interesting research questions could be answered using brain imaging techniques, and there is potential for uncovering information not revealed using other measurement methods (Ariely & Berns, 2010). However, both EEG and fMRI are also highly sensitive to motion: all their measures can be easily corrupted by facial expressions or other movements. Telling a person they cannot move and having them lie on their back in a loud environment can interfere with emotional experience (e.g., if you are not permitted to laugh, you might try to suppress thinking that something is funny). Also, there is still no clear scientifically verified mapping between brain regions and emotions that can be used accurately across all individuals. The lack of accurate emotion mappings, the obtrusive nature, and the financial cost of using most brain-imaging methods makes it almost impossible to measure natural emotion responses of people over large populations or in real-consumption settings; however, there is still interesting basic research to be extended that is currently only possible in laboratory settings and with smaller groups, such as that by Ambler, Ioannides, and Rose (2000).

Frameworks for Studies

The collection and analysis of physiological data, in addition to self-report, requires suitable frameworks. In-lab and in-field data collection have a number of differences. Below is a summary of the state-of-the-art in both in-lab and in-field solutions.

In-Lab

Laboratory based studies have many benefits such as allowing highly accurate measurement of physiological parameters or muscle movements using hardware designed specifically for the task. However, there are also a number of challenges. Subjects can be influenced by the presence of an experimenter and/or their comfort with the situation and surroundings, factors that are unrelated to the stimulus of interest. These may impact the participant's emotional experience (Wilhelm & Grossman, 2010), and the influence is difficult to quantify. In addition, running such studies is labor-intensive and may not be cost effective.

In most cases, emotion measurement techniques are still used in laboratory settings. In-lab data collection can make use of custom hardware for detecting affective signals. These might include eye-tracking, EMG, contact physiology (e.g., ECG or EDA) or brain imaging (e.g., EEG or fMRI). There are still a number of physiological signals that can be measured only in in-lab settings (fMRI being the most obvious).

Simultaneously synchronizing, storing, visualizing, and analyzing data from many sensors can be challenging. Software platforms that help simultaneously collect signals from multiple inputs are useful. Examples of companies who produce systems for collecting sensor data include Innerscope and iMotions.

In-Field

Conducting experiments in-field, and without the use of expensive, obtrusive, and uncomfortable sensors, can avoid some of the problems associated with in-lab data experiments. However, this type of data collection also presents technical challenges. How can emotions be measured without physical contact with the viewer and by using devices that they already own? How can we collect data reliably and efficiently when the viewing environment is not controlled?

Whilst laboratory data collection has been applied in advertising research studies for several decades, in-field studies have been limited due to technical challenges associated with measuring physiological parameters and behaviors in real-world contexts. This state of affairs is largely due to the severely limited scalability of in-lab solutions used for data collection.

Several commercial companies (Affectiva, RealEyes, Kairos) now offer services for automated facial coding over the internet. The measurement of facial responses to content is now a standard procedure in copy-testing of advertising content; it is used on a daily basis to help evaluate whether an advertisement is achieving its intended goals. Many companies now use this methodology to test their content, including Mars, Kellogg's, Unilever, and CBS. Unilever now tests every ad the company develops with facial coding technology (over 3000 ads annually).

Emotion measurement frameworks that allow in-field collection of affective responses typically utilize the subject's webcam to capture their response. Viewers watching content online can choose to opt-in through a browser. Their response can be processed on the device or streamed to the cloud and processed there. As described above, facial actions and expressions, gestures, eye gaze, and physiological responses can be extracted from video data used computer-vision technology. As these computer vision technologies mature, the power of internet-based emotion measurement frameworks will grow considerably; at the time of writing, this technology is still evolving.

With the new scalability offered via in-field frameworks, companies have been able to collect far more emotion data than was possible previously. For example, at the start of 2016, Affectiva had a repository of over four million face videos. Data on this scale has enabled these companies to build normative databases for facial coding and other emotion measurement techniques (McDuff & Kaliouby, 2016). These are essential as the interpretation of emotional responses is complex and context-dependent. As an example, gender, culture, and age differences in expressiveness have all been observed, and it is unlikely that these variables are entirely independent.

Applications

There are a number of distinct applications for emotion measurement techniques in digital advertising. As discussed above, advertising effectiveness measurement can take the form of laboratory or field tests. The content evaluated can be display, video, banner, or interactive ads, and anything from concepts through to finished content or digital experiences. The tests can be performed before the campaign begins (pre-tests) or after the campaigns has begun (post-tests). In the following sections, specific examples are presented of applications of emotion measurement techniques in measuring advertising efficacy, with a particular focus on how scalable measurement is used.

Emotion data is used primarily in two ways: 1) quantitative analysis modelling the relationship between emotions and advertising outcomes, and 2) qualitative analysis of content to help diagnose elements that are successful in eliciting desired responses and those that are not. The techniques described are often applied in both pre-tests and post-tests. However, qualitative analysis is relied on more heavily in the pre-test phase to help optimize the media.

Concept Testing

Testing marketing concepts at early stages can help avoid wasting marketing resources, the idea being that at an early mock-up stage content can be edited to improve the likelihood of success. However, it is typically harder to capture and interpret emotional responses to concepts than finished media. The richer the media tested the more likely it is to elicit observable affective responses from viewers. Videos usually elicit more emotion than static images, and videos with audio elicit more obvious emotional responses than silent video. There is still much that is unexplored about emotional responses to concepts and how these predict the efficacy of finished material. Nevertheless, the use of facial coding in concept testing is now relatively common practice.

Copy Testing

The most common use of emotion measurement on a large-scale is in the copy-testing of advertisements, from traditional print and TV adverts to online video adverts. Figure 19.1 shows an example of a facial coding results dashboard for an

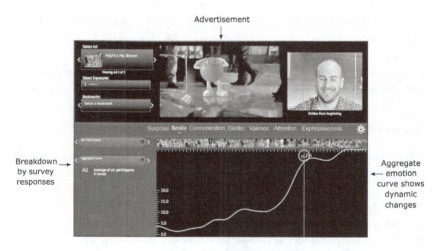

FIGURE 19.1   An Example of Aggregated Facial Expression Data Presented in a Dashboard. Emotion measurement techniques allow for passive and continuous measurement of responses—something that is difficult to achieve with self-report approaches. Dashboards are often used for diagnostic purposes.

Image: Affectiva, Inc.

advertisement. This type of interface is typically how emotion data is delivered in copy-testing. Teixeira et al. (2012) showed that inducing affect is important in engaging viewers in online video advertisements and to reduce the frequency of "zapping" (skipping the advertisement). It was found that joy was one of the states that stimulated viewer retention in commercials. Using an internet-framework, Teixeira, Picard, and Kaliouby (2014) collected facial responses from 178 participants to 82 commercials. Entertainment (as measured by smiling responses from the participants) affected purchase likelihood, with too little or too much entertainment being sub-optimal. Driving purchase intent is more complex than just making viewers smile: peak positive responses that are immediately preceded by a brand appearance are more likely to be effective (McDuff et al., 2015). Studies have found expressions of happiness (e.g., smiling) to be the most highly correlated with advertising effectiveness measures; for example, attitudes toward the ad and brand (Lewinski, Fransen, & Tan, 2014). This is to be expected, as generally speaking, ads intend to induce positive affect, and many are intentionally humorous.

These passive methods are particularly useful for studying wear-out effects of creative content. McDuff et al. (2012) showed examples of how facial responses to advertisements were significantly different in populations viewing for the first time versus not.

Digital advertising has yielded a number of new formats for presenting video content. For example, videos embedded in websites can autoplay (with or without audio), play on click, and auto resize on the screen. Which of these formats is optimal for viewer engagement is not clear. Measurement of emotions and gaze behavior has been used to test different video formats. However, much more work is required to fully evaluate which formats are best for engaging viewers.

Tracking Studies

One of the next big changes in emotion measurement within advertising is the use of longitudinal data from in-the-field campaign tracking studies. There are several challenges that need to be overcome to make this successful. First, participants will need to be incentivized to provide access to their webcam on an ongoing basis and allow it to be switched on during everyday browsing. Second, when subjects are viewing video media whilst browsing the web, rather than taking a market research survey, there is much less control over when the ad is seen and whether it is watched from start to finish. In addition, as described above, there are a number of different types of video formats and each will impact how the ad is viewed. Tracking studies will enable researchers to understand individual subjects' baseline responses much more effectively, as they will provide access to longitudinal data, something that is rarely available in copy-testing studies.

Single Source Studies

Are ads that are successful in evoking emotions also successful in driving sales? Understanding the answer to this question is ultimately the aim of much advertising effectiveness research. However, few studies have been able to address the question systematically due to the lack of emotion response data tied with sales measures. We conducted a large online ad study investigating the link between emotions expressed to advertisements and single-source sales data. We recorded facial responses over the internet to 240 ads in four countries (United Kingdom, United States, France, and Germany). The ads were for products in a number of consumer packaged goods (CPG) categories (chocolate, gum, pet foods, instant meals). The single source data was collected from a four-week period during which the ad was aired on TV and four weeks prior to airing. Participants were given a set-top box for tracking their exposure to ads, and their purchases were logged. This study found that in the category of chocolate and confectionery ads, there was a positive relationship between level of smiling (entertainment or humor response) and sales effectiveness of the ads. However, for other categories (such as instant foods), the relationship was much weaker. Certainly, smiling and positive emotion expressions are simpler to detect and interpret than negative expressions (McDuff et al., 2013). Beyond advertisements for CPG products, the relationships between expressed emotions and sales effectiveness is still unclear.

Future Directions

As emotion measurement and data collection frameworks mature, the collection of facial expression, eye gaze, and physiological data will be possible as part of many different types of in-field advertising effectiveness studies. With scalable methods of measuring audience engagement and emotional responses to content, real-time monitoring of a campaign's emotional impact will also be possible. Longitudinal panels will allow advertisers to track subjects' responses throughout a campaign by analyzing their reactions every time they are exposed to an advertisement on their computer. In addition, it may be possible to make use of these measurements to perform "emotion-based targeting." Audience segments that show higher levels of emotional engagement to specific types of content may be targeted with similar content.

Measuring audience reactions in focus groups, theatres, and public spaces requires the ability to capture responses from multiple people simultaneously. Computer vision-based methods of emotion measurement, such as facial coding, are particularly suited as measurements can be made from the same video source. There is also a growing interest for in-situ methods of measurement such as this.

There are still limitations in the measurement and interpretation of emotional responses. The meaning of physiological responses and behaviors are highly context-dependent and different types of ads intend to elicit different emotional responses. Therefore, the "effectiveness" of an ad cannot be evaluated without considering context. Building databases of emotional responses from which context dependent models can be built is a vital future direction.

Ethics and Privacy

Recording and analyzing affective responses of people is a sensitive topic, and there are many justified concerns related to potential invasions of privacy. As this form of measurement becomes more and more mainstream, using frameworks similar to those that we have described above, additional safeguards will become necessary. It is important as these technologies develop and become applied in field studies that social norms are developed around their use. Viewers should always be aware that their camera can be accessed in a study and should know when it is turned on. It is reasonable to argue that this will alter emotion responses; however, in the course of collecting many millions of videos, we have consistently found viewers' reactions to be highly naturalistic.

Methods of anonymizing emotion data would allow researchers to protect subjects whilst still being able to measure the emotional impact of online content. This could take the form of processing videos on the client's machine (therefore not requiring video data to be streamed to the cloud) or encrypting video data into an unidentifiable form from which the physiological and behavior signals are still recoverable.

Finally, as data collection moves to more longitudinal studies (rather than one-off copy-test surveys), it becomes more difficult to guarantee that the subject being analyzed is the subject who consented.

Conclusion

Advertisements—from traditional print, radio, and TV adverts to internet banner and online video advertisements—are increasingly placing more emphasis on emotional content. However, traditional methods of measuring responses to advertising have a number of limitations. In recent years, new scalable methods for measuring advertising efficacy have been developed. I have presented a summary of these approaches for measuring advertising efficacy with a particular focus on quantitative, scalable methods of capturing emotional and cognitive responses. The measurement of emotions and memory of advertising in real consumption contexts and across larger populations will undoubtedly lead to a more accurate understanding of digital advertising effectiveness.

References

Aaker, D. A., Stayman, D. M., & Hagerty, M. R. (1986). Warmth in advertising: Measurement, impact, and sequence effects. *Journal of Consumer Research, 12*(4), 365–381.

Ambler, T., Ioannides, A., & Rose, S. (2000). Brands on the brain: Neuro-images of advertising. *Business Strategy Review, 11*(3), 17–30.

Ariely, D., & Berns, G. S. (2010). Neuromarketing: The hope and hype of neuroimaging in business. *Nature Reviews Neuroscience, 11*(4), 284–292.

Bagozzi, R. P., Gopinath, M., & Nyer, P. U. (1999). The role of emotions in marketing. *Journal of the Academy of Marketing Science, 27*(2), 184–206.

Batra, R., & Ray, M. L. (1986). Affective responses mediating acceptance of advertising. *Journal of Consumer Research, 13*(2), 234–249.

Biel, A. L. (1990). Love the ad. Buy the product? Why liking the advertisement and preferring the brand aren't strange bedfellows after all. *Admap, 26,* 21–25.

Bolls, P. D., Lang, A., & Potter, R. F. (2001). The effects of message valence and listener arousal on attention, memory, and facial muscular responses to radio advertisements. *Communication Research, 28*(5), 627–651.

Cacioppo, J. T., Petty, R. E., Losch, M. E., & Kim, H. S. (1986). Electromyographic activity over facial muscle regions can differentiate the valence and intensity of affective reactions. *Journal of Personality and Social Psychology, 50*(2), 260.

Cohn, J. F., Ambadar, Z., & Ekman, P. (2007). Observer-based measurement of facial expression with the facial action coding system. In J. A. Coan & J. B. Allen (Eds.), *Handbook of emotion elicitation and assessment* (pp. 203–221). New York, NY: Oxford University Press.

Derbaix, C. M. (1995). The impact of affective reactions on attitudes toward the advertisement and the brand: A step toward ecological validity. *Journal of Marketing Research, 32,* 470–479.

Ekman, P., & Friesen, W. V. (1978). *Facial action coding system: Investigatoris guide.* Alto, CA: Consulting Psychologists Press.

Erevelles, S. (1998). The role of affect in marketing. *Journal of Business Research, 42*(3), 199–215.

Fredrickson, B. L., & Kahneman, D. (1993). Duration neglect in retrospective evaluations of affective episodes. *Journal of Personality and Social Psychology, 65*(1), 45.

Hazlett, R. L., & Hazlett, S. Y. (1999). Emotional response to television commercials: Facial EMG vs. self-report. *Journal of Advertising Research, 39,* 7–24.

Heath, R., Brandt, D., & Nairn, A. (2006). Brand relationships: Strengthened by emotion, weakened by attention. *Journal of Advertising Research, New York, 46*(4), 410.

Johar, G. V., Maheswaran, D., & Peracchio, L. A. (2006). Mapping the frontiers: Theoretical advances in consumer research on memory, affect, and persuasion. *Journal of Consumer Research, 33*(1), 139–149.

LaBarbera, P. A., & Tucciarone, J. D. (1995). GSR reconsidered: A behavior-based approach to evaluating and improving the sales potency of advertising. *Journal of Advertising Research, 35*(5), 33–54.

Lang, A. (1990). Involuntary attention and physiological arousal evoked by structural features and emotional content in TV commercials. *Communication Research, 17*(3), 275–299.

Lewinski, P., Fransen, M. L., & Tan, E. S. (2014). Predicting advertising effectiveness by facial expressions in response to amusing persuasive stimuli. *Journal of Neuroscience, Psychology, and Economics, 7*(1), 1.

Lewis, D. B. D., & Phil, D. (2004). Market researchers make increasing use of brain imaging. *Nature Neuroscience, 7*(7), 683.

McDuff, D. (2014). Crowdsourcing affective responses for predicting media effectiveness. Doctoral Dissertation. Massachusetts Institute of Technology.

McDuff, D., & Kaliouby, R. E. (2016). Applications of automated facial coding in media measurement. *IEEE Transactions on Affective Computing, 99*, published online, doi: 10.1109/TAFFC.2016.2571284.

McDuff, D., Kaliouby, R. E., Cohn, J. F., & Picard, R. W. (2015). Predicting ad liking and purchase intent: Large-scale analysis of facial responses to ad. *IEEE Transactions on Affective Computing, 6*(3), 223–235.

McDuff, D., Kaliouby, R. E., & Picard, R. W. (2012). Crowdsourcing facial responses to online videos. *IEEE Transactions on Affective Computing, 3*(4), 456–468.

McDuff, D., Kaliouby, R. E., Kodra, E., & Larguinet, L. (2013). Do emotions in advertising drive sales? Use of facial coding to understand the relationship between ads and sales effectiveness. In *ESOMAR Marketing Research Congress*.

McDuff, D., Kaliouby, R. E., Kodra, E., & Picard, R. (2013). Measuring voter's candidate preference based on affective responses to election debates. In *Affective Computing and Intelligent Interaction (ACII), 2013 Humaine Association Conference on* (pp. 369–374). IEEE.

Mehta, A., & Purvis, S. C. (2006). Reconsidering recall and emotion in advertising. *Journal of Advertising Research, 46*(1), 49.

Micu, A. C., & Plummer, J. T. (2010). Measurable emotions: How television ads really work. *Journal of Advertising Research, 50*(2), 137–153.

Morris, J. D., Woo, C., Geason, J. A., & Kim, J. (2002). The power of affect: Predicting intention. *Journal of Advertising Research, 42*(3), 7–18.

Pawle, J., & Cooper, P. (2006). Measuring emotion-lovemarks, the future beyond brands. *Journal of Advertising Research, 46*(1), 38–48.

Poels, K., & Dewitte, S. (2006). How to capture the heart? Reviewing 20 years of emotion measurement in advertising. *Journal of Advertising Research, 46*(1), 18–37.

Poh, M. Z., McDuff, D. J., & Picard, R. W. (2011). Advancements in noncontact, multiparameter physiological measurements using a webcam. *IEEE Transactions on Biomedical Engineering, 58*(1), 7–11.

Ravaja, N., Kallinen, K., Saari, T., & Keltikangas-Jarvinen, L. (2004). Suboptimal exposure to facial expressions when viewing video messages from a small screen: Effects on emotion, attention, and memory. *Journal of Experimental Psychology: Applied, 10*(2), 120–131.

Roberts, K. (2005). *Lovemarks: The future beyond brands*. New York, NY: PowerHouse Books.

Russell, C. A. (2002). Investigating the effectiveness of product placements in television shows: The role of modality and plot connection congruence on brand memory and attitude. *Journal of Consumer Research, 29*(3), 306–318.

Teixeira, T. S., Picard, R., & el Kaliouby, R. (2014). Why, when, and how much to entertain consumers in advertisements? A web-based facial tracking field study. *Marketing Science, 33*(6), 809–827.

Teixeira, T. S., Wedel, M., & Pieters, R. (2010). Moment-to-moment optimal branding in TV commercials: Preventing avoidance by pulsing. *Marketing Science, 29*(5), 783–804.

Teixeira, T. S., Wedel, M., & Pieters, R. (2012). Emotion-induced engagement in internet video advertisements. *Journal of Marketing Research, 49*(2), 144–159.

Wedel, M., & Pieters, R. (2008). A review of eye-tracking research in marketing. *Review of Marketing Research, 4*, 123–147.

Wilhelm, F., & Grossman, P. (2010). Emotions beyond the laboratory: Theoretical fundaments, study design, and analytic strategies for advanced ambulatory assessment. *Biological Psychology, 84*(3), 552–569.

Wood, O. (2012). How emotional tugs trump rational pushes. *Journal of Advertising Research, 52*(1), 31–39.

Yang, S., Kafai, M., An, L., & Bhanu, B. (2014). Zapping index: Using smile to measure advertisement zapping likelihood. *IEEE Transactions on Affective Computing, 5*(4), 432–444.

Zajonc, R. B. (1980). Feeling and thinking: Preferences need no inferences. *American Psychologist, 35*(2), 151–175.

PART V

Evaluating Digital Advertising

20

INTERNATIONAL DIGITAL ADVERTISING

Lessons from Around the World

Charles R. Taylor and John P. Costello

Introduction

Digital advertising has become an increasingly important element of the marketing mix for firms across the globe. Experts estimate that by 2019, online advertising will become the biggest segment of advertising budgets worldwide, surpassing television advertising with a forecasted annual spend of nearly $240 billion (PWC, 2015). The pivotal role of digital advertising in the marketing strategy of companies internationally is easy to take for granted today, but online advertising is still relatively young. Companies began advertising on the internet in the early 1990s, and the early years of interactive advertising was often marked with attempts to apply principles from other advertising domains (e.g., outdoor advertising, direct mail) with little success (Taylor, 2009). Even in the United States, digital technologies did not become a major medium until 2005. While researchers and managers have learned a great deal about digital advertising in the past few decades, the dynamic nature of the technologies used and the growth of online access worldwide reflects the need for continued exploration of digital marketing internationally.

In this chapter, we, first, briefly discuss some factors that have led to the rise of digital advertising across the globe. Next, we will discuss innovative research pertinent to international digital advertising from three perspectives. We organize the research and discuss international digital advertising related to 1) consumer considerations, 2) executional factors related to ads, and 3) general philosophy/goals behind advertising in building the brand in the long term. Within these sections, we propose general principles related to digital advertising internationally, based on the Taylor (2009) framework (see Figure 20.1) and the recent research in the international digital advertising literature. We conclude each section by summarizing major findings and outlining future areas of international digital advertising research.

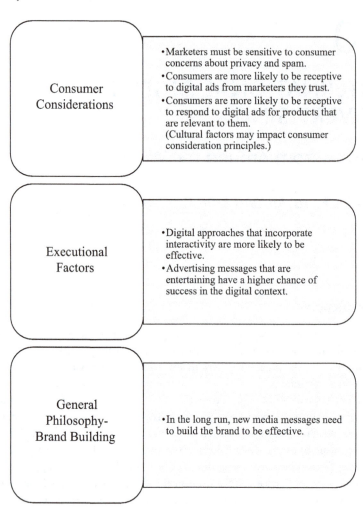

FIGURE 20.1 Principles of Digital Advertising

Adapted from Taylor, 2009

Factors Leading to the Growth of Digital Advertising Worldwide

Companies operating internationally can now reach more consumers online than ever before, making digital advertising viable when marketing to a diverse set of global markets. A number of issues have contributed to the success of digital advertising worldwide; however, none is more essential than growth in the number of people with access to the internet. This growth in access has taken place fairly rapidly both in the United States and many other nations across the world. According to the Pew Research Center, between 1995 and 2014, the percentage of U.S. adults with access to the internet grew from 14 percent to 87 percent (Pew Internet and American Life Project, 2014). This percentage is even higher among younger people, with 97 percent of U.S. adults ages 18–29 and 93 percent of adults ages 30–49 reporting having access to the internet in 2014 (Pew Internet and American Life Project, 2014).

This phenomenon is not unique to the United States alone. The International Telecommunication Union (ITU), a United Nations body, estimates that 3.2 billion out of the world's 7.2 billion people are now online, including 2 billion in the developing world (BBC News, 2015). In the year 2015, 80 percent of households in developed nations and 34 percent of households in developing nations will have access to the internet (BBC News, 2015). This growth has been fairly rapid in the past 10+ years, with more than eight times as many people online in the world today as in the year 2000 (BBC News, 2015).

Within the developing world, there is significant variance in terms of internet access. In the wealthiest emerging nations, such as China, Russia, and Chile, more than seven in 10 adults have access to the internet, but access is much lower in less wealthy countries such as India (20%), Uganda (15%), and Pakistan (8%) (Pew Global Attitudes and Trends, 2016). As in the United States, younger and more educated people across nations tend to have higher rates of access to the internet compared to their older and less educated counterparts (Pew Global Attitudes and Trends, 2016). For example, in Thailand, 83 percent of the 18–34 year old population is online versus only 27 percent of the population over 35 years of age (Pew Global Attitudes and Trends, 2016).

Another important factor in the growth of digital advertising internationally is increased access to broadband worldwide. Broadband allows for richer media in online advertising, which allows firms more options to create effective advertising (Taylor, 2009). This situation is also largely driven through mobile broadband access, as more consumers are accessing broadband through their phones. In the United States and Europe, 78 percent of people use mobile broadband and 69 percent of the world has 3G coverage—although this figure is only 17 percent in Africa (BBC News, 2015). Similar to internet access, ownership of a smartphone in many emerging nations is largely dependent on age. For example, in Malaysia, 72 percent of the population ages 18–34 has a smartphone, while the figure is 27 percent for those 35 and older (Pew Global Attitudes and Trends, 2015). This pattern is less prevalent in other countries like China, Thailand, and Vietnam (Pew Global Attitudes and Trends, 2016).

Other important factors in the growth of digital advertising include the emergence of social media and user generated content (UGC) sites (e.g., Facebook, Twitter, Wikipedia, blogs) and the realization that search engines can be effective advertising vehicles, leading to the sale of media space on sites such as Google and Yahoo. Paid search is the most established and understood advertising medium on the internet representing $54 billion worth of ad spending annually (PWC, 2015). This medium is forecasted to grow to $85 billion worldwide by 2019 and will represent about 35 percent of all online advertising worldwide (PWC, 2015). Social media remain an important area for advertisers across the globe as well, including nations that are fairly new to accessing the web. In a study of consumers across 32 developing nations, the Pew Research Center found that socializing with family and friends was the most popular activity online, with 86 percent of respondents using the internet to contact a relative or friend (Pew Global Attitudes and Trends, 2015).

The past decade has witnessed a shift from online access in only the most developed countries, to more and more nations gaining internet access across the globe. This opens the market for digital advertising and presents a number of challenges to digital advertisers internationally. For instance, international expansion of digital advertising makes it increasingly important for firms to understand what principles apply across borders and what must be localized to fit the particular targeted culture. Understanding what is important to consumers of digital advertising is paramount. Some of the most important considerations related to these consumers will be discussed in the following section. The analysis builds on Taylor's (2009) assertion that the primary principles of digital advertising are related to either consumer-related factors (i.e., consumer considerations) or executional factors. Additionally, we discuss some issues related to general philosophy toward digital advertising.

Consumer Considerations in International Digital Advertising

Taylor (2009) found that it is good practice in digital advertising to 1) understand and respond to consumer concerns about privacy, 2) build trust with the consumer, and 3) deliver messages that are relevant to the customer. To create and execute successful digital advertising campaigns internationally, firms must understand consumers' preferences. As a relatively new medium, it is understandable that consumers may be concerned about issues related to their own privacy and may vary in the level of trust they have in the firm's digital advertising targeting them. Additionally, given the importance of segmentation and targeting in marketing, it seems natural that the relevance of digital advertising content would largely impact the efficacy of an advertisement in the eye of the consumer. Research on consumers of digital advertising addresses these issues and has uncovered many of the ways in which consumer privacy, trust of the marketer, and relevance of advertisements impact advertising effectiveness. Also, a smaller stream of research has addressed how cultural differences between consumers may impact how they react to digital advertisements. Findings related to each of these issues are discussed in the following sections.

Consumer Privacy

As discussed, the proliferation of smartphones, globally, has given greater access online to a larger number of individuals, including individuals in developing nations. While this affords smartphone owners vast opportunities in the digital world, it also creates an "always on" culture. Compared to traditional media like television or radio, which are characterized by distinct blocks of consumption, users of smartphones tend to be constantly checking their devices and surfing the web throughout the day. Consumers also tend to view their mobile devices as a part of their personal space (Hart, 2008) and, as a result, are especially sensitive to digital advertisements that violate their privacy or risk being viewed as spam. Digital advertising that does not respect consumer privacy will likely result in low levels of success and may also create backlash toward the company.

A study by Barwise and Strong (2002) surveyed 1,000 mobile phone users from the greater London area and found that explicit permission for SMS advertising messages was essential for getting favorable responses from consumers. The authors found that this type of service was especially effective for selling lower ticket items to younger consumers (Barwise & Strong, 2002). In a multi-method study in New Zealand on mobile SMS advertising, Carroll, Barnes, Scornavacca, and Fletcher (2007) found that obtaining user trust and permission were necessities and suggested that privacy remains the biggest challenge facing digital marketing (see Chapter 17).

Unni and Harmon (2007) investigated the topic of location-based advertising in an effort to understand how this may impact consumers' feelings of privacy. Location-based advertising (LBA) is described as "targeted advertising initiatives delivered to a mobile device from an identified sponsor that is specific to the location of the consumer" (Unni & Harmon, 2007, p. 28). The authors used an experiment with a U.S. college student sample and found that LBA associated privacy concerns were high, and perceived benefits and value of LBA was low (Unni & Harmon, 2007). Further, the study found that LBA became more effective when the consumer granted permission to the marketer (Unni & Harmon, 2007). In a qualitative study of French consumers, Truong and Simmons (2010) found that consumers viewed a great deal of mobile advertising as intrusive. These consumers also expressed the desire for companies to ask permission before they began sending advertisements to consumers' mobile phones (Truong & Simmons, 2010). Another source of concern was a general mistrust of mobile operators, which created doubts that these advertisers were adhering to government regulations related to consumer privacy (Truong & Simmons, 2010).

Tucker (2014) investigated how social media users' perception over control of private information impacted their likelihood to click on targeted advertisements on social media sites. The study used a field experiment conducted by a U.S.-based nonprofit firm trying to optimize its advertising campaigns on Facebook. The nonprofit firm randomized whether or not users saw advertisements explicitly personalized to match information from their profiles; however, halfway through the study, Facebook introduced updates to its privacy policy that would simplify and improve privacy controls for users. Tucker (2014) found that after the addition of these policies, which provided users with an increased perception of privacy, consumers indicated they were twice as likely to click on personalized ads. This finding suggests that giving social media users control over their privacy could benefit advertisers on social media sites and increase consumer engagement with digital ads.

Trust

In addition to sensitivity to consumer privacy, research also suggests that trust of the marketer is important in the creation of effective digital advertising. The previously mentioned Carroll et al. (2007) study of SMS advertising found that consumers in New Zealand preferred to have their mobile service provider screen advertisers to ensure that advertising messages came from a trusted source. In a study of a Japanese mobile advertising campaign, Okazaki, Katsukura, and Nishiyama (2007) found that trust played a pivotal role in both message recall and advertising toward the ad. Choi, Hwang, and McMillan (2008) investigated mobile phone advertising and the potential cross-cultural differences between U.S. and Korean consumers. The study found that although a number of differences existed between the two cultures, advertising that was both fun *and* trustworthy prompted positive attitudes and purchase intentions for both Koreans and Americans (Choi et al., 2008).

In the previously mentioned Truong and Simmons (2010) study, the authors found that third parties can play a key role in developing trust of brands that advertise online. This study found that when brands had positive reviews from online experts and comparable sites, like Hotels.com or TripAdvisor.com, consumers tended to put greater trust in the legitimacy of those brands (Truong & Simmons, 2010). Another trust issue that emerged from this study was a concern that personal data would be misused, a consumer consideration closely tied to privacy. These findings have important implications for brands that want to be more trusted in the eyes of consumers and create successful digital advertising.

Past research has shown that trust in a mass medium impacts how consumers view the credibility of the information provided and can influence whether consumers pay attention to advertising on that medium (Johnson & Kaye, 1998; Moore & Rodgers, 2005). As social media has grown as an increasingly important medium for advertising, it is important to understand how much consumers trust content on social media websites. In a qualitative study of Australian teenage social media users, Kelly, Kerr, and Drennan (2010) found a general distrust of advertisers on social media sites. Subjects cited a lack of credibility in the medium and the lack of regulation on social media advertising as reasons for their lack of trust (Kelly et al., 2010). In a study of U.S. college students, Chu and Kim (2011) found that trust of a social networking site could enhance the chances that the consumer engaged in WOM on social media sites. Taken together, these studies show a general lack of trust from consumers, but social media has become more mainstream in recent years so future studies may need to account for this factor. For instance, the results of the Tucker (2014) study suggest that when credible social media sites (like Facebook) announce privacy improvements, consumers find these improvements to be credible and are more trusting of advertising on these sites as a result.

Relevance

Research on digital advertising has found that consumers are more likely to respond to products and services that are relevant to them. In research on the adoption of MMS advertising, Pagani (2004) conducted a pilot study featuring a sample of consumers from Italy and the United States consisting of a qualitative study conducted by Nokia with 24 focus groups across six nations (Brazil, Germany, Italy, Singapore, United Kingdom, United States), and a quantitative study conducted in Italy. The pilot study found that usefulness and relevance of messages were essential in acceptance of MMS messages by consumers (Pagani, 2004). Nasco and Bruner (2008) found that when using mobile devices, relevancy of content drove recall, perceived importance of the content, and behavioral intention to access content on a mobile device in the future. Carroll et al. (2007) also found that relevancy of mobile advertising was important in gaining the acceptance of consumers in New Zealand. Merisavo et al. (2007) studied SMS advertising on a sample of over 4,000 Finnish mobile phone users. The authors suggest, based on the results of the study, that effective mobile advertising should provide utility and have relevance to the targeted consumer (Merisavo et al., 2007). Truong and Simmons (2010) also found that French consumers were more likely to be accepting of digital advertisements they did not grant permission to receive if the advertisement presented a relevant value proposition.

Bart, Stephen, and Savary (2014) investigated mobile display advertising (MDA), which includes banner ads on mobile web pages and applications. This form of digital advertising is one of the fastest growing, from a $16.7 billion annual spend globally in 2013 to a forecasted spend of $62.8 billion by 2017 (Bart et al., 2014). In this study, the authors conducted a field experiment that spanned three years and 54 U.S. MDA campaigns, and included a sample of nearly 40,000 consumers (Bart et al., 2014). The results of this study suggest that advertisements for products that are higher involvement and utilitarian-oriented tended to result in more favorable attitudes and purchase intentions (Bart et al., 2014).

In a study of social media communities in China, Zeng, Huang, and Dou (2009) found that social media users' perceptions of advertising on the sites was dependent on the relevance and value of the advertising. The authors also found that the relevance and value of social media advertising was influenced by group identity and group norms related to social networking communities (Zeng, Huang, & Dou, 2009). The authors suggested that to increase advertising revenue, social media sites should foster a strong sense of community that promotes a strong identity among members (Zeng, Huang, & Dou, 2009).

Culture's Impact on Consumer Response

While privacy, trust, and relevance are presumed to be important when evaluating digital advertising in a number of national contexts, some research has also investigated how cultural differences may impact consumer response to ads. The Taylor (2009) framework does not specifically address the role that culture plays in consumer response to digital advertising; however, this is an important consideration for global marketers and an emerging area of research (see Chapter 24). Brettel and Spilker-Attig (2010) use a real data set from a bookseller operating in the United States and France with over 1.2 million transactions. The authors examined four online advertising channels: search advertising, affiliate price comparisons, affiliate coupon/loyalty, and newsletter/email and found that customers in each country should be targeted in different ways based on cultural differences (Brettel & Spilker-Attig, 2010). Study results showed that consumers from the United States, which is characterized as a masculine and individualistic culture, focused on advertising based on price, while French customers, who are characterized by high uncertainty avoidance, preferred advertisements that stressed brand familiarity (Brettel & Spilker-Attig, 2010). Results also showed that while search advertising has a limited impact on United States customers, it has a significant positive effect on French customers, which is explained by the French consumers' affinity to brand names. Additionally, the authors found that digital coupons and loyalty programs drove U.S. customers to the advertising, which is presumably explained by a culture of individual optimization (Brettel & Spilker-Attig, 2010).

Möller and Eisend (2010) studied the impact that national level culture has on banner advertising effectiveness, analyzing survey data from over 7,000 respondents in 34 countries as well as click-through rates of over 2,000 users in 26 countries. The authors found that banner advertising effectiveness varied based on Hofstede's cultural dimensions of individualism, uncertainty avoidance, power distance, and masculinity (Möller & Eisend, 2010). Specifically, consumers that came from individualistic countries were less accepting of banner advertisements, as measured by click behavior, as compared to consumers from collectivist cultures (Möller & Eisend, 2010). Together, these studies show that responses to digital advertising, at least in the form of banner ads, can be impacted by culture.

Although the previous section states that relevance improves digital advertising effectiveness for consumers, emerging research also suggests that cultural factors may impact whether a consumer perceives a particular digital advertisement as relevant. Maslowska, Smit, and van den Putte (2013) studied tailored advertising in the Netherlands, which has a long history with advertising, and Poland, which does not. Tailored advertising employs an individualized message with unique information about the recipient (Maslowska et al., 2013). Using a sample of online Dutch and Polish respondents, the authors used an experimental design with face cream advertisements as the stimuli that were either generic or tailored to the consumer. The authors found that Polish consumers perceived the tailored advertising as more relevant and subsequently "became more involved and were less skeptical toward the messages, which led them to have more positive attitudes" (Maslowska et al., 2013, p. 504). The authors suggest that, due to a lack of experience with advertising as a culture, level of persuasion knowledge for Polish consumers is lower than in a country like the Netherlands, and as a result, their level of susceptibility to advertising is higher (Maslowska et al., 2013).

Consumer Considerations: Conclusion and Future Research

In total, the existing literature from a number of international contexts found that consumers worldwide value their privacy thereby suggesting that advertising tends to be more effective when marketers respect consumers' privacy. Research also suggests that consumers tend to react more positively to advertising from marketers they trust. Also, advertising is more likely to be effective when it is relevant to the targeted user. These streams of research provide some guiding principles to better understand how digital consumers on a global scale may evaluate and respond to digital advertising.

As a relatively young area of research, there is still much to be studied related to how consumers react to digital advertising, including how national cultures may shape consumer response. Digital advertising is a global phenomenon, so it is important to understand the important role being part of different cultures may play in the evaluation of online advertising by consumers. Although research in this area has been conducted using samples from various nations such as Europe, North America, Asia, and Australasia, more research incorporating a diverse set of national cultures is needed. As the developing world is gaining increased access to the internet, it will be essential for researchers to investigate and understand the "new" consumer of digital advertising.

Executional Variables and International Digital Advertising

In addition to understanding how international consumers react to digital advertising, it is important to understand what elements of the advertisement itself influence success of the ad. The capabilities of digital advertising differ from more traditional forms of advertising in a variety of ways and, as a result, strategies that may have proven effective in other promotional contexts may not succeed online. Since marketers need to reach consumers in a variety of cultural contexts, it is important to understand which types of variables related to the advertisement translate across borders and which will not. Two variables that have emerged as especially important for effective international digital advertising in markets across the globe are interactivity and entertainment value.

Interactivity

Based on the advanced capabilities of the medium, digital advertisements are able to achieve levels of interactivity with the consumer that are generally not possible in traditional forms of advertising, such as television or radio (see Chapter 1). Research has shown that across the globe, digital advertisements that promote interactivity attempt to engage consumers and improve the effectiveness of digital advertisements. In a study that focused on website advertising, McMillan, Hwang, and Lee (2003) used a field study that included a sample of consumers that had recently used one of several hotel websites. The authors found that perceived level of interactivity was the best predictor of consumer attitudes (McMillan et al., 2003). Dickinger, Haghirian, Murphy, and Scharl (2004) conducted a qualitative study of SMS advertising on European mobile marketing experts from industry and academia to understand success factors for digital advertising. The authors found that interactivity was related to more effective SMS advertisements (Dickinger et al., 2004). Jelassi and Enders (2005) also found that when digital marketers incorporated interactivity into their advertisements, they achieved greater levels of success.

Interactivity also seemed to be important for social media advertising. Social media's inherent interactivity perhaps makes it well suited for one-on-one interactions with customers and may allow brands to provide highly personalized targeting in their advertisements (Okazaki & Taylor, 2013). Although this area of inquiry is still relatively new, there exists some preliminary research that suggests that interactive social media marketing can lead to positive outcomes for the marketer. For example, in a survey study of fashion brand consumers in Korea, Kim, and Ko (2010) found that interaction of social media marketing had a positive effect on purchase intentions for the product. In a follow up study that also employed a Korean sample, Kim and Ko (2012) again found that interactivity was an important variable for digital marketing and suggested that social media marketing is pivotal for companies attempting to build brand equity.

Although the personalized and interactive nature of social media advertising has likely contributed to its success as a marketing tool, it may also have stifled research in global contexts. Okazaki and Taylor (2013) note there is a relative dearth of global research on social media and argue that this may be the case, in part, because "the combination of global and social media may have been viewed as mismatched since social media is often considered as a very personalized, rather than global, medium" (p. 58). The authors argue that this must be overcome, and that issues such as similarities and differences in the effectiveness of social media across cultures needs to be addressed (Okazaki & Taylor, 2013).

Entertainment

Entertainment is another variable that has proven to be important in digital advertising globally. Digital advertisements that can entertain the consumer are more likely to be successful in achieving engagement and improving purchase intent. Raney, Arpan, Pashupati, and Brill (2003) studied the role of entertainment on websites of four automotive brands. Using an experimental design and a U.S.-based sample, the authors found that the website that was high in entertainment value and included a mini-movie had the most positive evaluations, greatest intent to return to the site, highest levels of arousal, and resulted in the highest levels of purchase intent (Raney et al., 2003). In a study that employed lab experiments with subjects in Thailand and Taiwan, Chen, Ross, Yen, and Akhapon (2009) investigated how type of banner ad, web localization, and involvement impacted the evaluation of a website. The authors found that both national samples preferred ads with animated and entertaining content as well as websites that had localized language (Chen et al., 2009).

In addition to advertising on websites, research suggests that consumers preferred mobile ads that are entertaining. In a study of Japanese teenagers, Okazaki and Taylor (2008) found that entertainment value in SMS messages tended to increase the chance consumers would respond to a promotion. Truong and Simmons (2010) also found in a French context that entertaining mobile ads tended to be preferred and were even expected by consumers. In a cross-cultural study of U.S. and Korean consumer responses to mobile advertising, Choi et al. (2008) found that entertaining ads led to positive attitudes toward the ad and purchase intention in both national contexts. The authors suggested that one way to increase entertainment in a mobile ad was to deliver the message in the context of an "advergame" (Choi et al., 2008). This suggestion gets further support from the research of Yeu, Yoon, Taylor, and Lee (2013), who found in an experiment using a Korean sample that banner ads shown in advergames had a higher chance of being remembered both implicitly and explicitly.

Cheng, Blankson, Wang, & Chen (2009) conducted a field study of four subtypes of digital advertising in Taiwan: SMS mobile, MMS mobile, email-based, and internet-based (e-advertising). They found that entertainment was important in digital advertising and that not all forms of digital advertising had the same potential for entertaining the consumer. Specifically, the authors found that Taiwanese consumers found e-advertising and MMS advertising more entertaining, and viewed email-based and SMS advertising less positively on this attribute (Cheng et al., 2009). The authors suggested, based on the results, that consumers preferred multiple rich media to text-only advertising (Cheng et al., 2009). This suggestion is consistent with research on banner ads that found that ads that employed visual cues tended to be more easily processed than ads that used only verbal or visual/verbal cues (Wang, Shih, & Peracchio, 2013).

Entertainment has also been identified as an important factor in social media marketing. In the previously mentioned Kim and Ko (2010, 2012) studies, entertainment was identified as an important element of any successful social media marketing strategy. Entertainment was found to positively influence purchase intention, strengthened customer relationships with the brand (Kim & Ko, 2010), and drove customer equity (Kim & Ko, 2012). This is an area in need of additional study, but early research seems to indicate that effective social media marketing has the potential to offer consumers novel and entertaining content that helps build the brand and increase purchase intent.

Executional Variables: Conclusion and Future Research

Research in a number of national contexts has continued to reinforce the importance of interactivity and entertainment value in effective digital advertising. However, a great deal still remains unknown in our understanding of what variables work best in digital advertising. While entertainment and interactivity have emerged as important factors, digital advertising can come in a number of forms and may enjoy greater flexibility in executional strategy than other forms of advertising because of technological capabilities. Future research should address the potential effectiveness of the different executional variables available at a firm's disposal.

Additionally, more cross-cultural work in this area is needed. Although some challenges certainly exist (see Okazaki & Taylor, 2013 for a discussion of the challenges related to international social media research), it is incredibly important for firms to better understand how different tactics may be more or less effective depending on the culture of the market in which the ad is placed.

General International Digital Advertising Principle: Build the Brand

Thus far we have discussed what factors have led to the growth of digital advertising worldwide, we identified important considerations that may lead to successful consumer responses to ads, and we provided findings related to which executional variables have been shown effective in international digital advertising. This final section suggests a general philosophical principle that the authors believe should apply to all digital advertising, and we discuss research that supports and relates to this principle.

The general principle is this: most digital advertising, no matter the national context, must build the brand in the long run to be effective. In an early conceptual piece, Chiagouris and Wansley (2000) identified the ability for marketers to create intense bonds with consumers over the internet to build the brand. The authors argue that "When it comes to building a brand on the internet, never have so many talked so little of what may be the internet's most stunning capability—strengthening the bond with customers and prospects" (Chiagouris &Wansley, 2000, p. 35). Although much has changed in the world of digital advertising since this article was published, the principle still holds true. No matter what technology is employed to reach consumers, the ultimate goal must be to build the brand. Research has supported the brand-building and sale-generating abilities of digital advertising in a variety of forms in markets around the world.

In a survey of marketing managers of multinational companies operating in Europe and based out of the United States, Japan, and Europe, Okazaki and Taylor (2008) investigated the factors associated with implementation of SMS advertising. The results of this study supported the idea that managers from the European Union, the United States, and Japan would be more likely to adopt SMS advertising as a strategy if it would help to build their company's brand (Okazaki & Taylor, 2008). The study suggests that managers seem to believe that through encouraging action and excitement that SMS advertising may help to build brand equity (Okazaki & Taylor, 2008).

In a study of banner advertising, Manchanda, Dubé, Goh, and Chintagunta (2006) used a general consumer data set of an online-only firm that sold healthcare and beauty products to consumers. The study established that exposure to banner ads did increase purchase probabilities, especially for current consumers of the brand (Manchanda et al., 2006). The authors also found that managers should expect effect sizes in banner advertising on the same order of magnitude for traditional advertising (Manchanda et al., 2006). Understanding how traditional and digital advertising work together to build brands is an essential issue for managers worldwide.

In a study that aimed to explore the connection between online and brick and mortar channels as well as digital and traditional advertising, Dinner, Van Heerde, and Neslin (2014) used data from a high-end clothing retailer in the United States. The authors found that the impact of advertising did not apply to just one purchase channel (i.e., online or brick and mortar) but rather applied across multiple channels (Dinner et al., 2014). They also found that online display and search advertising were more effective than traditional advertising due to cross channel effects on the offline channel (Dinner et al., 2014). The authors argued that firms may be underestimating the return on investment of online advertising because they are neglecting the impact it has on brick and mortar sales (Dinner et al., 2014). This is important, as studies of managers have reported frustration with the measurement tools and models available to assess the success of digital marketing campaigns in building a brand (Cheong, De Gregorio, & Kim, 2010).

Research has also found that social media has the potential to build brands. Kim and Ko (2012) found in a study of fashion brands with a Korean sample that social media marketing that incorporated entertainment, interaction, trendiness, customization, and word-of-mouth (WOM) was more likely to be effective. They also found that social media marketing had the potential to increase value equity, relationship equity, and brand equity (Kim & Ko, 2012). Both relationship equity and brand equity had the ability to drive purchase intention, making effective social media a good tactic to increase sales of a brand (Kim & Ko, 2012). In a survey that used a German-speaking subject sample from companies across three industries, Bruhn, Schoenmueller, and Schäfer (2012) found that social media communications had a stronger positive influence on brand image than traditional forms of advertising. In another survey that used a sample of Polish social media users, Schivinski and Dabrowski (2015) examined the role that both firm-created and user-created social media communications played in brand equity measures. The authors found that both firm- and user-generated social media brand communications positively impacted brand awareness and associations (Schivinski & Dabrowski, 2015). They also found that user-generated social media brand communications had a positive influence on brand loyalty and perceived brand quality (Schivinski & Dabrowski, 2015).

Conclusion and Future Research Directions

Digital advertising has become an essential promotional tool for firms operating in markets worldwide. As more individuals around the globe gain access to the internet and broadband connection through their computers and smartphones it is more important than ever to understand what matters most to consumers of digital advertising. Research suggests that consumers are concerned about their privacy, prefer marketers that they trust, and respond more positively to ads that are relevant to them. There is also evidence that national culture can influence responses to and preference for various forms of digital advertising. Consumers internationally also seem to have a preference for digital advertisements that are interactive and provide entertainment value. Most importantly, however, successful international digital advertising must work to build the brand in the long term.

As a fairly new area of inquiry, there is a need for additional research in the area of international digital advertising in general. There have been a number of studies on digital advertising using samples from different nations; however, most of these studies are from highly developed countries. As more of the developing world gains access to the internet, new studies should focus on these consumers and the challenges of applying digital advertising principles in these global markets. Additionally, more cross-cultural research is needed to better understand the role culture plays in the success of digital advertising internationally. A limited number of studies have employed samples from nations with differing national cultures but more work is needed in this area.

Digital advertising is in many ways driven by technological innovation, so the ways in which marketers reach consumers online is constantly changing. Early researchers primarily considered a firm's website when talking about digital advertising, but today and as noted in Chapter 2, the firm's digital strategy may include search advertising, a mobile strategy, and social media marketing, among others. Digital advertising now can take place on a mobile phone or on a computer, and consumers in markets that would have been unreachable through digital advertising not long ago are online and engaged. The dynamic nature of this topic makes it both exciting and challenging. New technologies must be investigated; researchers and managers cannot simply assume that new forms of digital advertising will work in exactly the same ways as previous methods in different cultures. However, while we must understand that each form of digital advertising has its own set of considerations, it is also important to look for unifying principles that hold true across different forms of digital media. These principles will allow for greater cohesion between the various forms of digital advertising that exist to marketers and for the creation of a unifying digital advertising theory that can be useful in a variety of markets across the globe.

References

Bart, Y., Stephen, A. T., & Sarvary, M. (2014). Which products are best suited to mobile advertising? A field study of mobile display advertising effects on consumer attitudes and intentions. *Journal of Marketing Research, 51*(3), 270–285. http://dx.doi.org/10.1509/jmr.13.0503.

Barwise, P., & Strong, C. (2002). Permission-based mobile advertising. *Journal of Interactive Marketing, 16*(1), 14–24. doi: 10.1002/dir.10000

BBC News. (2015). Internet used by 3.2 billion people in 2015. Retrieved from http://www.bbc.com/news/technology-32884867.

Brettel, M., & Spilker-Attig, A. (2010). Online advertising effectiveness: A cross-cultural comparison. *Journal of Research in Interactive Marketing, 4*(3), 176–196. http://dx.doi.org/10.1108/17505931011070569.

Bruhn, M., Schoenmueller, V., & Schäfer, D. B. (2012). Are Social Media replacing traditional media in terms of brand equity creation? *Management Research Review, 35*(9), 770–790. http://dx.doi.org/10.1108/01409171211255948.

Carroll, A., Barnes, S. J., Scornavacca, E., & Fletcher, K. (2007). Consumer perceptions and attitudes towards SMS advertising: Recent evidence from New Zealand. *International Journal of Advertising, 26*(1), 79–98. doi: 10.1080/02650487.2007.11072997.

Chen, J. V., Ross, W. H., Yen, D. C., & Akhapon, L. (2009). The effect of types of banner ad, web localization, and customer involvement on Internet users' attitudes. *CyberPsychology & Behavior, 12*(1), 71–73. doi: 10.1089/cpb.2008.0199.

Cheng, J. M. S., Blankson, C., Wang, E. S. T., & Chen, L. S. L. (2009). Consumer attitudes and interactive digital advertising. *International Journal of Advertising, 28*(3), 501–525. doi: 10.2501/S0265048709200710.

Cheong, Y., De Gregorio, F., & Kim, K. (2010). The power of reach and frequency in the age of digital advertising: Offline and online media demand different metrics. *Journal of Advertising Research, 50*(4), 403–415. doi: 10.2501/S0021849910091555.

Chiagouris, L., & Wansley, B. (2000). Branding on the internet. *Marketing Management, 9*(2), 34–38.

Choi, Y. K., Hwang, J. S., & McMillan, S. J. (2008). Gearing up for mobile advertising: A cross-cultural examination of key factors that drive mobile messages home to consumers. *Psychology & Marketing, 25*(8), 756–768. doi: 10.1002/mar.20237

Chu, S. C., & Kim, Y. (2011). Determinants of consumer engagement in electronic word-of-mouth (eWOM) in social networking sites. *International Journal of Advertising, 30*(1), 47–75. doi: 10.2501/IJA-30-1-047-075.

Dickinger, A., Haghirian, P., Murphy, J., & Scharl, A. (2004). An investigation and conceptual model of SMS marketing. In *Proceedings of the 37th Hawaii International Conference on System Sciences.* IEEE. doi: 10.1109/HICSS.2004.1265096.

Dinner, I. M., Van Heerde, H. J., & Neslin, S. A. (2014). Driving online and offline sales: The cross-channel effects of traditional, online display, and paid search advertising. *Journal of Marketing Research, 51*(5), 527–545. http://dx.doi.org/10.1509/jmr.11.0466.

Hart, K. (2008, March 10). Advertising sent to cellphones opens new front in war on spam. *Washington Post* (p. A1).

Jelassi, T., & Enders, A. (2005). *Strategies for e-business: Creating value through electronic and mobile commerce.* Upper Saddle River, NJ: Prentice Hall.

Johnson, T. J., & Kaye, B. K. (1998). Cruising is believing? Comparing Internet and traditional sources on media credibility measures. *Journalism & Mass Communication Quarterly, 75*(2), 325–340. doi: 10.1177/107769909807500208.

Kelly, L., Kerr, G., & Drennan, J. (2010). Avoidance of advertising in social networking sites: The teenage perspective. *Journal of Interactive Advertising, 10*(2), 16–27. doi: 10.1080/15252019.2010.10722167.

Kim, A. J., & Ko, E. (2010). Impacts of luxury fashion brand's social media marketing on customer relationships and purchase intentions. *Journal of Global Fashion Marketing, 1*(3), 164–171. doi: 10.1080/20932685.2010.10593068.

Kim, A. J., & Ko, E. (2012). Do social media marketing activities enhance consumer equity? An empirical study of luxury fashion brand. *Journal of Business Research, 65*(10), 1480–1486. doi: 10.1016/j.jbusres.2011.10.014.

Manchanda, P., Dubé, J. P., Goh, K. Y., & Chintagunta, P. K. (2006). The effect of banner advertising on internet purchasing. *Journal of Marketing Research, 43*(1), 98–108. http://dx.doi.org/10.1509/jmkr.43.1.98.

Maslowska, E., Smit, E. G., & van den Putte, B. (2013). Assessing the cross-cultural applicability of tailored advertising: A comparative study between the Netherlands and Poland. *International Journal of Advertising, 32*(4), 487–511. doi: 10.2501/IJA-32-4-487-511.

McMillan, S. J., Hwang, J.-S., & Lee, G. (2003). Effects of structural and perceptual factors on attitudes toward the website. *Journal of Advertising Research, 43*(4), 400–409. http://dx.doi.org/10.1017/S0021849903030393.

Merisavo, M., Kajalo, S., Karjaluoto, H., Virtanen, V., Salmenkivi, S., Raulas, M., & Leppäniemi, M. (2007). An empirical study of the drivers of consumer acceptance of mobile advertising. *Journal of Interactive Advertising, 7*(2), 41–50. doi: 10.1080/15252019.2007.10722130.

Möller, J., & Eisend, M. (2010). A global investigation into the cultural and individual antecedents of banner advertising effectiveness. *Journal of International Marketing, 18*(2), 80–98. http://dx.doi.org/10.1509/jimk.18.2.80.

Moore, J. J., & Rodgers, S. L. (2005, January). An examination of advertising credibility and skepticism in five different media using the persuasion knowledge model. In *American Academy of Advertising Conference Proceedings* (p. 10). American Academy of Advertising.

Nasco, S. A., & Bruner, G. C. (2008). Comparing consumer responses to advertising and non-advertising mobile communications. *Psychology & Marketing, 25*(8), 821–837. doi: 10.1002/mar.20241.

Okazaki, S., & Taylor, C. R. (2008). What is SMS advertising and why do multinationals adopt it? Answers from an empirical study in European markets. *Journal of Business Research, 61*(1), 4–12. doi: 10.1016/j.jbusres.2006.05.003.

Okazaki, S., & Taylor, C. R. (2013). Social media and international advertising: Theoretical challenges and future directions. *International Marketing Review, 30*(1), 56–71. http://dx.doi.org/10.1108/02651331311298573.

Okazaki, S., Katsukura, A., & Nishiyama, M. (2007). How mobile advertising works: The role of trust in improving attitudes and recall. *Journal of Advertising Research, 47*(2), 165–178. doi: 10.2501/S0021849907070195.

Pagani, M. (2004). Determinants of adoption of third generation mobile multimedia services. *Journal of Interactive Marketing, 18*(3), 46–59. doi: 10.1002/dir.20011.

Pew Global Attitudes and Trends. (2016). Smartphone ownership and internet usage continues to climb in emerging economies. Retrieved from http://www.pewglobal. org/2016/02/22/smartphone-ownership-and-internet-usage-continues-to-climb-in-emerging-economies/

Pew Internet & American Life Project. (2014). Internet use over time. Retrieved from http:// www.pewinternet.org/Shared-Content/Data-Sets/2000/April-2000-Survey-Data. aspx, http://www.pewinternet.org/data-trend/internet-use/internet-use-over-time/

PWC. (2015). Global entertainment and media outlook 2015–2019. Retrieved from http://www.pwc.com/gx/en/industries/entertainment-media/outlook/segment-insights/internet-advertising.html.

Raney, A. A., Arpan, L. M., Pashupati, K., & Brill, D. A. (2003). At the movies, on the web: An investigation of the effects of entertaining and interactive web content on site and brand evaluations. *Journal of Interactive Marketing*, *17*(4), 38–53. doi: 10.1002/dir.10064.

Schivinski, B., & Dabrowski, D. (2015). The impact of brand communication on brand equity through Facebook. *Journal of Research in Interactive Marketing*, *9*(1), 31–53. http://dx.doi.org/10.1108/JRIM-02–2014–0007.

Taylor, C. R. (2009). Editorial: The six principles of digital advertising. *International Journal of Advertising*, *28*(3), 411–418. doi: 10.2501/S0265048709200679.

Truong, Y., & Simmons, G. (2010). Perceived intrusiveness in digital advertising: Strategic marketing implications. *Journal of Strategic Marketing*, *18*(3), 239–256. doi: 10.1080/09652540903511308.

Tucker, C. E. (2014). Social networks, personalized advertising, and privacy controls. *Journal of Marketing Research*, *51*(5), 546–562. http://dx.doi.org/10.1509/jmr.10.0355.

Unni, R., & Harmon, R. (2007). Perceived effectiveness of push vs. pull mobile location based advertising. *Journal of Interactive Advertising*, *7*(2), 28–40. doi: 10.1080/15252019.2007.10722129.

Wang, K. Y., Shih, E., & Peracchio, L. A. (2013). How banner ads can be effective: Investigating the influences of exposure duration and banner ad complexity. *International Journal of Advertising*, *32*(1), 121–141. doi: 10.2501/IJA-32-1-121-141.

Yeu, M., Yoon, H. S., Taylor, C. R., & Lee, D. H. (2013). Are banner advertisements in online games effective? *Journal of Advertising*, *42*(2–3), 241–250. doi: 10.1080/0091 3367.2013.774604.

Zeng, F., Huang, L., & Dou, W. (2009). Social factors in user perceptions and responses to advertising in online social networking communities. *Journal of Interactive Advertising*, *10*(1), 1–13. doi: 10.1080/15252019.2009.10722159

21

A REVIEW OF INTERNET AND SOCIAL NETWORK ADVERTISING FORMATS[1]

Francisco Rejón-Guardia and Francisco J. Martínez-López

Introduction

In this day and age, large sums of money are dedicated to commercial communication on a global level. This budget tends to be divided into conventional media and nonconventional media. Very recently, nonconventional media used in communication has assumed large importance as far as its share of business budgets are concerned. Among the most-used advertising media during the last few decades, the internet is especially noteworthy. The analysis done by advertisers and marketers of the behavior and time dedicated by internet users is a testament to the level of the internet's pervasiveness, as well as the number of hours, which are continually increasing, that are dedicated to surfing the web, to the detriment of time dedicated to other means of communication. The main contribution of this paper is to offer a description of the theoretical framework of the subject of online advertising effectiveness, looking specifically at a variety of digital advertising formats.

Additionally, special attention is paid to the specific case of social network sites (SNSs), examining the main aspects of advertising effectiveness in this setting that have been studied in academic literature. We ought to be conscious of the fact that, in terms of the time spent by individuals connected to the internet, SNSs are the online platforms to which they dedicate the most time (Raacke & Bonds-Raacke, 2008; Hughes, Rowe, Batey, & Lee, 2012). Therefore, SNSs have become important places of high strategic value for placing advertisements. One analysis of time dedicated to the main social networks (Facebook, LinkedIn, etc.) shows elevated numbers of active user traffic. When faced with this situation, the SNSs must consider how to monetize their mass of users (e.g., Facebook has over one billion users already), as the main revenue source of SNSs is the sale of advertising space for publicity (Lipsman, Mud, Rich, & Bruich, 2012). This tendency is related to the exponential increase of online advertising investment that has occurred in recent years (Nielsen, 2012).

Companies are aware of the importance of running campaigns on SNSs that prove relevant for the users. To this end, advertisers must concentrate on improving advertising efficacy. With this backdrop, this review addresses specific questions in relation to this topic, such as: What is understood about advertising efficacy on SNSs? Is advertising on SNSs more effective than advertising in conventional media? What are the perceptions, beliefs, and attitudes of the consumer toward SNS advertisements? Are they more favorable than in other advertising-saturated media? Nevertheless, analysis of the literature indicates that many questions about advertising on SNSs remain unanswered. The popularity of social networks and their recognition as a potential medium of advertising have grown so quickly that research studies have not been able to keep up with the pace of industry. With this work, we are also endeavoring to offer an integrated revision of the topic of advertising on SNSs.

This chapter further aims to update the main works on online advertising in an environment as volatile as the internet, with a specific focus on the study of online and social network advertising formats. This chapter provides the reader with an understanding of the position of paid social tools that can contribute to a brand-spreadable media model. This study also assesses the efficacy of digital advertising on social networks, thus contributing to the creation of a theoretical framework for understanding effective brand campaigns. Finally, we make some theoretical conclusions and comment on noteworthy practices that are valid for practitioners, marketers, and researchers.

The remainder of the chapter is as follows: First, a starting approach to the online advertising framework is made, introducing a spectrum of advertising formats used on the internet, with specific descriptions of formats used by outstanding SNSs such as Facebook. Next, the topic of advertising effectiveness in the specific context of SNSs is addressed. Finally, some theoretical and practical concluding remarks about online advertising effectiveness are discussed, and interesting future lines of research are pointed out as well.

Literature Review of Online Advertising

In order to establish a starting point for the study of efficacy of advertising on the internet, and more specifically, on SNSs, an analysis of the main articles of advertising research has been performed. As a starting point, we examine the bibliometric study of advertising research on the internet by Kim and McMillan (2008), as well as the revision done by Ha and McCann (2008). Then we expand said analysis, incorporating recent studies that have emerged on the topic of online advertising messages published on the internet. We pay special attention to the analysis of the research focused on the topic of advertising on SNSs.

Like McMillan, we also analyze the main works related to the study of internet advertising. To this end, a selection of specialized journals was chosen, highlighting four main journals in the academic sphere related to advertising, marketing, and the internet. Journals were classified based on number of citations and impact factor, according to the Journal of Citations Report (JCR), from which *Journal of Advertising, Journal of Advertising Research, Journal of Current Issues and Advertising Research*, and *Journal of Interactive Advertising* were selected. The authors, by means of a statistical analysis of the citations that appear throughout these publications, discovered that the main topics dealing with advertising on the internet were categorized into six themes: 1) effectiveness of internet advertising, 2) interactivity, 3) electronic commerce, 4) advertising processes, 5) attitude toward the site/ad/ brand, and 6) comparisons to traditional media.

With the objective of updating the analysis performed by Kim and McMillan (2008), we did a revision of main contributions published on the subject of advertising research. We selected, first, the most cited magazines in the area of marketing and advertising according to JCR (2011 edition), ranked by impact factor on its JCR's subject. After the revision, articles were selected whose keywords included the terms advertising, internet, and social networks. Going forward from these works, a detailed classification of the apparent themes was elaborated and organized by year. The most relevant works were classified by themes based on their keywords and content, which most notably included advertising effectiveness, consumer behavior studies, effectiveness studies for different online advertising formats, internet and SNSs, electronic word of mouth (eWOM), user-generated content (UGC), and a neuroscience approach. The analysis period ranged from 2003 to 2016. The main trends and topics related to internet-based advertising include:

- The growth of social communication platforms on the internet. Here, the analysis of eWOM (electronic word of mouth) on the web is especially interesting. A number of important studies evaluate eWOM produced in social networks (Riegner, 2007; Smith, Coyle, Lightfoot, & Scott, 2007; Lee & Youn, 2009; Okazaki, 2009; Prendergast, Ko, & Yuen, 2010; Amblee & Bui, 2011; Chen, Wang, & Xie, 2011; Vázquez-Casielles, Suárez-Álvarez, & del Río-Lanza, 2013; Jin & Phua, 2014; López & Sicilia, 2014; Moran, Muzellec, & Nolan, 2014; Wallace, Buil, Chernotony, & Hogan, 2014; Kareklas, Muehling, & Weber, 2015; Shan & King, 2015; Wang, Cunningham, & Eastin, 2015). Special attention is paid to user-generated content (UGC) (Christodoulides, Jevons, & Bonhomme, 2012; Morrison, Cheong, & McMillan, 2013; Dickinson-Delaporte & Kerr, 2014) and the earned media (Nelson-Field, Riebe, & Sharp, 2012; Harrison, 2013; Spotts, Purvis, & Patnaik, 2014) on SNSs.
- The ease with which messages are propagated in the network and their bond with viral marketing. Specifically, it is proposed that the propagation

of messages is related to users' need to construct and express their identity (Taylor, 2012; Ewing, 2013; Chen & Lee, 2014; Hayes & King, 2014; Grant, Botha, & Kietzmann, 2015; Shan & King, 2015).

- The existence of a long line of studies focused on the different advertising formats employed on the internet. From amongst these works, the most studied format is the banner. The evaluation of measures of behavioral efficacy through CTR (click-through rate) stand out as noteworthy (Moore, Stammerjohan, & Coulter, 2005; Manchanda, Dubé, Goh, & Chintagunta, 2006; Fourquet-Courbet, Courbet, & Vanhuele, 2007; Robinson, Wysocka, & Hand, 2007; Yaveroglu & Donthu, 2008). Studies of the factors that affect the click-through keyword search ads are also important (Yoo, 2012). The next most-studied format was video (Cha, 2013; Chen & Lee, 2014; Goodrich, Schiller, & Galletta, 2015; Grant et al., 2015; Li & Lo, 2015), and the advertising formats used on mobile platforms, including the use of apps as advertising spaces (Kim, Lin, & Sung, 2013; Fulgoni & Lipsman, 2014; Limpf & Voorveld, 2015).

- Among the global SNSs, Facebook is the most dominant—and fastest growing—social medium, with more than 1.44 billion monthly active users as of March 2015. For marketers, Facebook's platform offers a different kind of mechanism for communicating with their potential audiences, which gives it a very important role in companies' IMC policies (LaPointe, 2012; Lipsman et al., 2012; Nelson-Field et al., 2012) and marketing strategies (LaPointe, 2012; Nelson-Field, Riebe, & Sharp, 2013; Logan, 2014; Wallace et al., 2014; Brettel, Reich, Gavilanes, & Flatten, 2015). Second comes Twitter, with 560 million active users in 2014 (Logan, 2014; Kinney & Ireland, 2015).

- The study of advertising efficacy through web-user behavior also emerged. Here, the focus of interest is on negative beliefs, attitudes, and behaviors that might arise when receiving and processing online advertising (Cho & Cheon, 2005; Taylor, Lewin, & Strutton, 2011; Wise, Alhabash, & Eckler, 2013; Goodrich, 2014; Grant et al., 2015).

- The study of emotions caused by advertisements allows for a more accurate prediction of its efficacy than evaluative measures of information processing such as persuasion, brand linkage, cut-through measures, and even message delivery (Wood, 2012). Here, we see the recent interest in neuro-scientific approaches (Bakalash & Riemer, 2013; Steele et al., 2013; Precourt, 2015).

- Of the actions that improve the efficacy of messages in a given social network, correctly predicting the criteria used to segment our target population proves crucial to increasing purchasing intent or product use in social networks (Dominic Yeo, 2012; Tucker, 2014).

Next, a description of high-relevancy advertising formats on the internet and SNSs is offered.

Advertising Formats on the Internet

In the beginning, internet advertising employed simple formats that achieved a strong response from users (Rae & Brennan, 1998). As bandwidth connections have increased, the possibilities to create online ads have grown exponentially, since greater bandwidth allows the user to download a greater amount of information. Furthermore, the technological development of programming languages and software has paved the way for a wide variety of internet advertising formats. This has led to current campaigns being composed of audio-visual and multimedia material. Therefore, advertisers are faced with the decision of which format best fits their creative content and advertising strategy needs.

In this day and age, one can find millions of websites that feature new advertising formats with integrated multimedia elements, such as on-demand audio or video streaming. These formats were called rich media by the IAB (2011, p. 16). As seen in Table 21.1, the principal advertising formats on the internet can be classified into four categories: integrated formats, floating formats, transitional formats, and the main mobile creative formats.

Among the integrated formats, the most important is undoubtedly the banner ad that, with more than 18 years of use, continues to be one of the most commonly used advertising formats on the internet. The first known banner on the internet appeared on the HotWired.com website in 1994 (Cho & Leckenby, 2003). Since then, it has become the most frequently used advertising format on the internet and has also consistently sustained the interest of researchers. The banner is essentially a form of display advertising within a website, similar to what it has historically been in print media. Its primary objective is to attract traffic to the page of the advertiser, who pays for the ad's inclusion on certain pages. Generally, banner ads are created with images (formats: GIF, JPEG, or PNG) or with animation developed through technologies such as Java, Adobe Shockwave and, most commonly, Flash. They are designed with the intention to grab attention and communicate the desired message. Therefore, banners do not necessarily need to conform to the graphics of their containing website. This explains the designers' effort to create attractive (or eye-catching) banners by combining different designs with high quality images, in 3D and with animation or movement.

Among the floating formats, the most studied are pop-ups and pop-unders. Pop-unders, in comparison with pop-ups, are less interruptive since they appear behind the main page that is being visited. However, for this same reason, they are not seen until the user closes the windows that they are using, making it more difficult for the navigator to determine which page activated the opening of the pop-under (Moe, 2006). Sometimes emerging formats of pop-ups activate new windows, occasionally creating an infinite loop, which, intentional or not, is normally very upsetting (Edwards, Li, & Lee, 2002; Quinones et al., 2008). Due to this, techniques and programs that block the appearance of this type of emerging window continually appear under the common names pop-up killers or pop-up blockers. In 2004, some of the most important websites (e.g., msn.com) began to

TABLE 21.1 The Most Used Advertising Formats on the Internet and Mobile Advertising

Advertising formats	Types		
	• Sponsored links • Ad sense • Banner • Expandable Banner • Leaderboard & Super Leaderboard—Provisional unit—970X 90 • Medium Banner • Medium rectangle—300x250 • Rectangle—180 x 150 • Mega Banner • Skyscrapers—Wide Skyscrapers—160 x 600 • Half page—300X600 • Button 2—120X60 • Micro Bar—88X31 • Buttons • Full page-ads • Sponsored sections • Billboard—970x250 (Rising Start 2016) • Filmstrip—300X600 (Rising Start 2016) • Portrait—300X1050 (Rising Start 2016) • Pushdown—970X90 (Rising Start 2016) • Sidekick—300X250–300X600–970X250 (Rising Start 2016) • Slider—970X90 (Rising Start 2016)		
Floating formats	• Interstitials		• Pop-up & Pop-up Large • Pop-under
Transitional formats	• Layers • Interstitials • Superstitials • Preloaders		
Advergaming Email Marketing— Direct Marketing	• Product or brand placement		
Rich Media	• In-Banner Video file-loaded—300x250 180x150 160x600 728x90 300x600 • In-Banner Video Streaming • Expandable/Retractable		
Electronic Bulletins Mini-sites Viral Marketing Sponsorship			
Mobile Marketing		Image Ads	• Smartphone Static Banner—300x50 • Smartphone Static Wide Banner—320x50 • Smartphone Interstitial—300x250 • Feature phone Small Banner—120x20 • Feature phone Medium Banner—168x28 • Feature phone Large Banner—216x36
		Mobile Rich Media Ads	• Smartphone Rich Interstitial—300x250

(Continued)

TABLE 21.1 (Continued)

Advertising formats	Types
Rising Starts	• Smartphone Rich Banner Expandable—300x50 • Smartphone Rich Wide Banner Expandable—320x50 • Adhesion Banner—320x50 • Pull—320x50 • Slider—320x50 • Filmstrip (Tablet)—300x600 • Filmstrip Full Screen—320x50 • Full Page Flex (Interstitial or Inline)—320x50

Source: Elaborated from Rejón-Guardia & Martínez-López (2014) and IAB (2016)

limit the use of emerging windows, considering them overly intrusive for users. The pop-up format has fallen out of use recently, as users consider it to be one of the most irritating and undesired features on the internet, according to IAB (2015).

Other commonly used formats on the internet fall into the category of transitional formats, in which the formats known as interstitials and superstitials are found. This type of ad bears great resemblance to television advertising. The fundamental difference is that interstitials appear between two web pages of content. They are therefore referred to as transitional advertisements; in other words, the user sees the ad while they navigate between web page "a" and page "b." Superstitials correspond to an interactive advertising format similar to a television spot, developed for sending a message from a single sender to a single receiver. Next, the formats employed by the main SNSs are highlighted due to the businesses' increasing investment in these new media.

Advertising Formats on SNSs

SNSs provide advertisers with a large amount of information from its millions of users (Hughes et al., 2012). When the quantity of users and the time dedicated to participation is high, SNS spaces begin to be attractive to companies, as they are able to use them to introduce their products or services through advertisement. The social networks' interactive features also facilitate management of relations between brand and client by means of likeable experiences (Gensler, Völckner, Liu-Thompkins, & Wiertz, 2013).

Text, video, audio, and other multimedia-based content on the web (rich media) can be included in SNSs' structure. The aim of businesses is to increase the number of followers a brand has, promote a network, share a promotion, generate notoriety, introduce a new product, etc. This makes SNSs especially interesting to advertisers, since they are in possession of larger space and greater flexibility than conventional advertising media, expressed in terms of interactivity, personalization, and feedback (Benevenuto, Rodrigues, Almeida, Almeida, & Ross, 2009). In traditional channels, users maintain a reactive attitude, meaning they are passive and open to suggestions; this includes advertising. In contrast, in social media, users participate with a proactive attitude, providing content, photographs, and opinions. Because of these unique characteristics of social media and its users, conventional advertising actions normally obtain inferior results when compared to those that are launched on SNSs. Advertising becomes a fundamental axis on which the main SNSs base their strategies for monetizing their activity; they possess space, audience, and information about their users, through which communication campaigns can articulate effectively and, most importantly, efficiently.

Table 21.2 presents some of the advertising formats employed by the most important social networks worldwide based on marketing campaign objectives.

TABLE 21.2 Social Network Sites—Advertising Objectives and Best Ad Formats

Social Network Site

Objectives and Goals	Social Network	Formats	
Branding and dissemination	*Twitter*	Promoted tweets	
		Promoted trends	
	Facebook	Promoted posts and content ads	
		Logout experience	
	LinkedIn	Promoted posts	
		Targeted display	
	YouTube	Masthead standard or expandable or lite	
	Spotify	Leaderboard ads	Brand app
		Homepage takeover	Branded experiences
		Audio	
		Video takeover	
	Google+	+Post ads	
		Engagement ads	
Audience creation	*Facebook*	Like ads and sponsored stories	
	Twitter	Promoted accounts	
	YouTube	Promoted channel ads	
Link	*Facebook*	App ads and app sponsored stories	
		Event ads	
	YouTube	TrueView in search and TrueView in stream	
Sales or downloads	*Facebook*	Facebook exchange (retargeting and remarketing)	
		Facebook offers	
		Apps download	
Register and database improvement	*Facebook*	Registration plugin	
		Lead generation	
		Lead manager	
		Share content ads	
	Twitter	Twitter cards	
	LinkedIn	LinkedIn ads	
		LinkedIn slide	
		LinkedIn Inmail	

Source: Own elaboration

Facebook, considered to be the world's largest social network (Darvell, Walsh, & White, 2011; Lipsman et al., 2012), presents the following advertising formats as part of its business strategy: sponsored pages, sponsored ads, sponsored stories, and the use of complementary material that can be incorporated into any web page and that can bring content and social features to any network. Amongst these, we find examples of "premium" advertising such as a like ad, poll ad, event ad, and comment ad. The advertising formats used by Facebook are fundamentally based in the use of promoted links with text and images, which can be located anywhere on the pages seen by the user, even the profile page. Advertisers are able to promote their own network and obtain registers/records of users through a landing page. Furthermore, these advertising formats allow detailed segmentation by sex, age, geographic location, job type, company, even by the users' behavior in the social network.

Twitter, the number one microblogging social network in the world, has also developed unique advertising formats. It makes use of promoted tweets, which are comprised of advertising messages in the format of "tweets" (short messages of 140 or fewer characters) that appear in the search results for certain key words. These messages are labelled "promoted" to indicate that they are advertisements, although the properties of a classic "tweet," such as the ability to retweet (i.e., a message that is duplicated or mentioned by another user), are preserved. Another of the unique formats employed by Twitter is known as "promoted trends," i.e., promoted topics that subscribers use to spread information of interest, daily, weekly, or monthly. Known as "spreadability" (see Chapter 2), what is "spread" as a trend would be an advertising message pre-established by Twitter as a trend. When users search for current trends, they find the promoted trend displayed among the search results. However, Twitter does not accept all types of content to be promoted, and it solely permits those tweets that, at the time, are already enjoying certain popularity on the network. The most recent advertising innovation that has been incorporated into the network is known as a promoted account and consists of recommending an account or profile in the "who to follow" section. These accounts must have a relationship with someone whom the user already follows. In this way, the odds that a user of a social network will follow a promoted account are increased. This allows advertisers to become familiar with the information shared on the social network that, from a communications standpoint, could prove interesting/useful. For example, a business like Coca-Cola would have a vested interest in its profile being visible in the zones of social networks that are dedicated to suggesting who to follow.

LinkedIn is a social network for businesses and professionals whose members can create and develop a list of contacts with information on people and companies with whom they have formed a link or work connection. The main advertising formats used here are promoted posts and targeted displays, both of which allow the company to reach potential clients based on the orientation of the advertising content, which in turn is adapted to the recipient's profile on that social network. The variables that tailor the product to the potential client are the type of work the client does, the industry in which they work, education, skills, etc.

YouTube is the most widely used social network for video sharing, with millions of subscribers who upload millions of videos per minute to the site. YouTube offers various formats, the most important being the YouTube homepage masthead, with three variations: 1) standard masthead, 2) expandable masthead, and 3) masthead lite. These executable formats are located beneath the tool bar on the main page. YouTube deploys TruView technology to direct advertising only to the audience with most potential interest in the product, thus increasing cost efficacy. The formats that use this advert orientation include TruView in-display, which presents the advertisement simultaneously with YouTube videos, as well as on search pages or on Google's display network, so that the advertiser only pays when the viewer decides to watch the video and clicks on the ad.

Spotify is a music streaming service whose business model is based on subscriptions and freemiums; the latter offers a free service to customers in return for exposure to advertising. The most widely used advertising formats are leaderboard, homepage takeover, audio (spot, cover art, and clickable campaign name), and video takeover.

Finally, Google+ is an interest-based social network owned and managed by Google. Its most popular advertising formats include +Post Ads and engagements. Next, we delve deeper into the efficacy of online advertising, in particular the banner format, due to its being the most commonly employed advertisement strategy on the internet.

Effectiveness of Advertising in Social Networks

As mentioned, businesses use social networks to promote their products, improve communication with customers, and gain knowledge about the market. According to what has been observed, from the use of SNSs as an advertising medium, the following noteworthy phenomena occur: 1) an action-focused communication strategy unique to the business, which materializes in the exhibition of products or services and the creation of events and activities and 2) a communication distribution strategy, which provides and spreads content that is relevant for web users, but that is not exclusively produced by the company. The latter is more interesting to users that consult businesses' profiles on social networks because the business makes content available that is not exclusively related to its own products or events, but is about news related to the sector or information relevant to the consumer.

Therefore, businesses, regardless of the strategy they decide to follow, must always concern themselves with spreading attractive and "impactful" content to the consumer. To do this, they make use of audio-visual content, promotions, discounts, updates, gifts, contests, etc. These tactics must be adapted to the unique possibilities offered by each of the social networks to allow businesses to project themselves publicly. Regardless of the business's intended use of the social network, the true asset of these media lies in the number of users interacting with them. Precisely for the scope of their social reach, social networks are increasingly catching the attention of researchers in online advertising.

Likewise, the rapid growth of SNSs fuels advertisers' search for new advertisement options (Hart, 2007). This growing industry finds itself in a difficult position, as it has to find a balance between its need to generate profits through publicity and the users' need to have uninterrupted experiences (Nutley, 2007). However, there are still few studies that deal with the unique characteristics of advertising on social networks. Specifically, advertisements on social networks possess certain features that differ from other media due to the responses that are not considered strictly as personal actions, but rather as actions shaped by the characteristics of the community (Zeng, Huang, & Dou, 2009). In this sense, there are several factors that influence individuals' responses to the advertisement. For example, the influence the social and group norms have on the attitudes of its members and, therefore, on how the individuals of the group express themselves. The identity of members in relation to the group and its social norms will moderate the intention to accept advertising within the group. Thus, in groups where the members have a strong sense of identity, social norms will have a positive effect on the users' intentions. The greater the sense of self held by the group members of an online community, the more likely the group will be to form an opinion about the advertisement (Zeng et al., 2009). Therefore, if businesses want to receive positive responses to their advertisements within SNSs, they must consider two factors that are key to the responses and behavior of the individuals who belong to the SNS: the ad's relevance and value within the community. Specifically, when users perceive the advertising message as relevant to the theme of the community as well as aligned with the representation of their social identities, the ad's presence will be seen as positive. This will garner more positive results (Fue et al., 2009).

In line with earlier considerations, studies like Nielsen's (2010) have examined the value of advertising in communities on SNSs. To do this, an important distinction between formats was made to look at ads that were intended for the social network Facebook. This is the case with the ad on the landing page, composed of a creative graphic combined with an ad in text form. Nielsen (2010) also studied the use of ads on the home page that include social content allowing information about members of the social network to be added. Additionally, a format known as organic impression was used, which presents some claim or information about some of the members of the social network's preferences regarding the advertising campaign. These last two advertising formats are based on what is known as earned media or publicity, a concept that has been used in the evaluation of public relations for years. Historically, publicity has corresponded with the number of times that a brand or brand-related image appeared in the nightly news, the front page of a newspaper, a movie, or a television program. Publicity's key lies in the brand not having paid for the exposure in any way. This means that the communication has been sufficiently interesting, entertaining, and has sufficient journalistic interest for the media to continue repeating the ad voluntarily. Therefore, in social media with social content, like SNSs, the consumer is invited to broadcast or sanction the brand to their online contacts through actions such as becoming a fan or by showing their approval of an action by liking, retweeting, or favoriting—a process Chapter 2 refers to as "spreadability." This tendency of spreadability makes the brands resort to advertising tools that come from means of social communication known as organic impressions. With this in mind, hybrid-advertising formats are being developed between paid and earned media communication (Nielsen, 2010).

The results obtained by Nielsen (2010) indicate that, in terms of advertising efficacy, when paid ads contain some form of social content, they produce a higher rate of recall, awareness, and purchase intentions. Furthermore, it has been observed that users exposed consecutively to a paid ad and an ad containing organic content show a three-fold increase in remembering the ad in addition to elevated purchase intent. Additionally, the extent of advertising efficacy was evaluated exclusively in terms of the organic formats, based on the number of exposures (frequency) necessary to produce a response from the user. It was found that knowledge and purchase intention continue to grow after 10 or more exposures to the message. Specifically, there is a gap in brand familiarity between consumers exposed to the message three to nine times compared to those exposed 10 times or more, with positive significant differences showing in this last category. This reflects the strong impact that organic impressions have on users, increasing the users' disposition to continue processing the messages during long periods of time. Therefore, the takeaway from this study is that, in order to maximize profit and potential positive responses from earned media, it is necessary to invest in advertising on social networks. After investment, one must pursue positive actions on the part of users of the social network, as this adds social value. Moreover, there is a strong relationship between the users of a social networks' rate of participation in a campaign and the number of organic impressions that said users make (Nielsen, 2010).

Additionally, to generate a reaction of some kind to the advertising message in any of its formats, it is essential to capture the social network user's attention, keeping in mind the limitations of their attention. Specifically, some studies indicate that social network users do not notice advertising in the conventional forms that are used in other media (Soares, Pinho, & Nobre, 2012). Up until now, users accepted a symbiotic relationship with conventional media (radio, television, or press), in which the presence of advertisements in the medium was the price or remuneration for receiving content either free or at a reduced cost (Taylor et al., 2011). However, in SNSs, this remuneration does not exist. This relationship has been modified because the advertisement intrusively interrupts the flow of the consumer's activity. This explains why a high degree of trust is given to advertisements that arrive via word-of-mouth (WOM) between users (Steyn, Wallström, &

Pitt, 2010). Subsequently, the options provided by social networks such as Facebook include promoting ads or suggesting ads to friends (Murdough, 2009). The benefits of positive WOM are important. It is estimated that each client who gets involved in the chain of WOM doubles the value of investment allocated to promoting a product or brand in comparison to ads sponsored by the brand. This behavior is able to convince twice as many clients to try or purchase the product. Nonetheless, businesses must be aware that negative WOM will have an inverse impact, potentially even more powerful than positive WOM. It is therefore imperative to avoid negative WOM (Trusov, Bodapati, & Bucklin, 2010).

Recent research on advertising efficacy has focused on advertisements in social networks. Specifically, Wood (2012) notes that perceived emotions through the advertisements are predictive of the message's efficacy, in terms of outperformed persuasion, brand linkage, and cut-through measures. And Brettel et al. (2015) analyzed which Facebook advertising formats determine short-term and long-term impact on sales.

Concluding Remarks

Advertising online assumes a strategic role for many businesses that use the internet. In advertising, the approach to the evaluation of objectives is fundamental. Objectives should not solely be approached in terms of sales, as the effect of advertising on individuals is not always reflected in direct sales. Other variables, such as the improvement of attitudes or future preferences toward the brand, are worth outlining and obtaining. This chapter points out the importance digital advertising has taken on in the academic sphere, with the evaluation of certain online advertising formats (e.g., banner) being especially prolific. Moreover, several lines of research have been highlighted for their relevancy and interest. Next, theoretical conclusions and noteworthy practices are provided.

First, as far as specific advertising formats go, the banner and its variants are the most commonly used on the internet today. Based on the literature review that we have performed, some recommendations can be made to practitioners so that they may properly use banner ads:

- Moderate use of banner animation. Excessive animation of the banner's content can awaken negative attitudes toward the ad that, in turn, unleash undesirable behaviors, such as advertising avoidance.
- Banners must be located in the most visible zones of the web page. The eye-tracking technique has proven to be revealing on this idea. In occidental cultures, where the people read from left to right, the most-seen zones are located in the right margin. Moreover, the first pages of the navigation menu are preferable to the pages that require deeper navigation within a website.
- The banner's content must be relevant to the user and should, therefore, be chosen based on their interests. Furthermore, the banner must be designed with the right kind of creativity.

- Forced exposure to the banner should be reduced. It is recommended to encourage voluntary exposure to the banner. The literature shows that voluntary exposure produces a greater probability of the message being processed in a conscious and favorable form by the user. This increases other behaviors, such as the level of attention paid to the message; the likelihood of clicking, recognizing, and remembering the brand; and generally improving the attitudes and behaviors of the users in relation to the banner and brand. This allows the navigator to obtain more information about a product or service, thereby increasing the possibilities of a future purchase.

As for advertisement on SNSs, the key for businesses resides in exposure time and in the information offered by users. Currently, advertisements on SNSs are also essential for the execution of integrated-marketing communication campaigns. Below, we present some practical suggestions:

- Using SNSs as a means to grab the client's attention or to house and centralize FAQ is crucial. It is advisable to develop a climate that promotes the participation of consumers in the recommendation of products or services.
- SNSs prove to be especially interesting as a tool for exploring the market. They are valid for product testing, launching new products or services, and analyzing options.
- Social networks can provide information on the direction and tendencies of the market based on the changes observed in consumers' likes.
- Due to the strategic value of these relationships, management and control of the SNSs should be assumed by professionals; hence, the *importance of the community manager* (see Garrigos-Simon, Lapiedra Alcamí, & Barberá Ribera, 2012). In this respect, businesses should engage with consumers once they have initiated activities in this setting. In other words, their strategies and actions must be planned and constant (Murdough, 2009).
- Relevance and strength in relations is key. One of the social networks' main advantages is that the development of personal connections with consumers leads to an increase in the number of revisits and time dedicated to the social networks. For consumers, the creation of connections and content is very important, which indicates that sellers are making good use of targeted advertising to raise the communicative efficacy of social advertising by using user profile data.

From the standpoint of greater monetization of SNSs through advertisements, the key is offering messages based on content that is both interesting and relevant to the user. The advertising innovation and creativity on SNSs can lead to voluntary and viral propagation of the advertiser's messages, increasing the impact on the business' target population. It is also important that SNSs make innovations in the use of metrics, allowing for better evaluation and control by businesses of their campaigns on social networks.

With respect to the academic sphere and advertising research, there is a definite gap between what is being investigated and the real problems faced by businesses in the world of internet advertising. This gap is being increased by the current staggering proliferation of SNSs, which makes advertising research in SNSs especially interesting. In relation to these practical suggestions, we point out some possible research suggestions:

- Establishing differences with regard to which categories of products are especially suited to be promoted via social networks must be done. Another approach would be to establish if there are types of products or services not particularly fit for or not easily promoted through social networks.
- Determining what the key is to creating a message that will go viral and being spread in the interest of the advertiser is essential. Advertising clutter in conventional media is one of the main causes for lack of advertising efficacy since it increases the probability that users will not process the message. In this vein, it is fundamental to identify if the user perceives social networks as a medium with excessive advertising clutter and, if that is the case, to what extent this excessiveness affects the processing and efficacy of the advertisement.
- Evaluating the beliefs and attitudes generated by internet and SNS advertising is necessary. There is a wide variety of advertising formats available on the internet and in SNSs. It would be useful to identify which of them could help achieve the proposed advertising goals, as well as which are more fitting for each proposed objective.

Companies must note the users' type of access to the internet and to SNSs. Soon, mobile devices and mobile-adapted environments are going to become crucial for reaching consumers. For example, there is a clear tendency toward accessing SNSs on the go, through brief connections by means of mobile devices (i.e., smartphones and tablets). It is therefore of interest to analyze the efficacy of the advertisement in a mobile setting. Through mobile devices, the advertiser can obtain precise information about the user's location by using technologies like geolocalization. Information about the user's whereabouts can provide an advantage to contextual advertising. In the same way, the noticeably smaller screen size of mobile devices constitutes a limitation that should be studied, keeping various aspects in mind with regard to the message's perceived intrusiveness, the possibility of message evasion, the improvement of advertising creativity, as well as the possible limitations of advantages that mobile technology can offer.

Note

1   This article is a shorter updated version of: Rejón-Guardia, F., and Martínez-López, F. J. (2014), "An Integrated Review of the Efficacy of Internet Advertising Concrete

Approaches to the Banner Ad Format and the Context of Social Networks," in F.J. Martínez-López (Ed.) *Handbook of Strategic e-Business Management*, Springer, pp. 523–564. Springer has kindly given permission to publish the article in this book.

References

Amblee, N., & Bui, T. (2011). Harnessing the influence of social roof in online shopping: The effect of electronic word of mouth on sales of digital microproducts. *International Journal of Electronic Commerce, 16*(2), 91–114. doi: 10.2753/JEC1086–4415160205.

Bakalash, T., & Riemer, H. (2013). Exploring ad-elicited emotional arousal and memory for the ad using fMRI. *Journal of Advertising, 42*(4), 275–291. http://doi.org/10.1080/00913367.2013.768065.

Benevenuto, F., Rodrigues, T., Almeida, V., Almeida, J., & Ross, K. (2009). Video interactions in online video social networks. *ACM Transactions on Multimedia Computing, Communications, and Applications, 5*(4), 30:1–30:25.

Brettel, M., Reich, J. C., Gavilanes, J. M., & Flatten, T. C. (2015). What drives advertising success on Facebook? An advertising-effectiveness model: Measuring the effects on sales of "likes" and other social-network stimuli. *Journal of Advertising Research, 55*(2), 162–175. http://doi.org/10.2501/JAR-55-2-162–175.

Cha, J. (2013). Do online video platforms cannibalize television? How viewers are moving from old screens to new ones. *Journal of Advertising Research, 53*(1), 71–82. http://doi.org/10.2501/JAR-53-1-071–082.

Chen, T., & Lee, H.-M. (2014). Why do we share? The impact of viral videos dramatized to sell: How microfilm advertising works. *Journal of Advertising Research, 54*(3), 292–303. http://doi.org/10.2501/JAR-54-3-292–303.

Chen, Y., Wang, Q., & Xie, J. (2011). Online social interactions: A natural experiment on word of mouth versus observational learning. *Journal of Marketing Research, 48*(2), 238–254.

Cho, C. H., & Cheon, H. J. (2005). Cross-cultural comparisons of interactivity on corporate web sites: The United States, the United Kingdom, Japan, and South Korea. *Journal of Advertising, 34*(2), 99–115. http://doi.org/10.1080/00913367.2005.10639195.

Cho, C. H., & Leckenby, J. (2003). The effectiveness of banner advertisements: Involvement and click-through. *Journalism and Mass Communication Quarterly, 80*(3), 623–645.

Christodoulides, G., Jevons, C., & Bonhomme, J. (2012). Memo to marketers: Quantitative evidence for change. How user-generated content really affects brands. *Journal of Advertising Research, 52*(1), 53–64. doi: 10.2501/JAR-52-1-053–064.

Darvell, M. J., Walsh, S. P., & White, K. M. (2011). Facebook tells me so: Applying the theory of planned behavior to understand partner-monitoring behavior on Facebook. *Cyberpsychology, Behavior, and Social Networking, 14*(12), 717–722. doi: 10.1089/cyber.2011.0035.

Dickinson-Delaporte, S., & Kerr, G. (2014). Agency-generated research of consumer-generated content: The risks, best practices, and ethics. *Journal of Advertising Research, 54*(4), 469–478. doi: 10.2501/JAR-54-4-469–478.

Dominic Yeo, T. E. (2012). Social-media early adopters don't count. *Journal of Advertising Research, 52*(3), 297–308. doi: 10.2501/JAR-52-3-297–308.

Edwards, S. M., Li, H., & Lee, J. H. (2002). Forced exposure and psychological reactance: Antecedents and consequences of the perceived intrusiveness of pop-up ads. *Journal of Advertising, 31*(3), 83–95. doi: 10.1080/00913367.2002.10673678.

Ewing, M. T. (2013). The good news about television: Attitudes aren't getting worse. Tracking public attitudes toward TV advertising. *Journal of Advertising Research, 53*(1), 83–89. http://doi.org/10.2501/JAR-53-1-083-089.

Fourquet-Courbet, M. P., Courbet, D., & Vanhuele, M. (2007). How web banner designers work: The role of internal dialogues, self-evaluations, and implicit communication theories. *Journal of Advertising Research, 47*(2), 183–192. http://doi.org/10.2501/S0021849907070213.

Fulgoni, G., & Lipsman, A. (2014). Numbers, please: Digital game changers: How social media will help usher in the era of mobile and multi-platform campaign-effectiveness measurement. *Journal of Advertising Research, 54*(1), 11–16.

Garrigos-Simon, F. J., Lapiedra Alcamí, R., & Barberá Ribera, T. (2012). Social networks and Web 3.0: Their impact on the management and marketing of organizations. *Management Decision, 50*(10), 1880–1890. http://dx.doi.org/10.1108/00251741211279657.

Gensler, S., Völckner, F., Liu-Thompkins, Y., & Wiertz, C. (2013). Managing brands in the social media environment. *Journal of Interactive Marketing, 27*(4), 242–256. http://doi.org/10.1016/j.intmar.2013.09.004.

Goodrich, K. (2014). The gender gap: Brain-processing differences between the sexes shape attitudes about online advertising. *Journal of Advertising Research, 54*(1), 32–43. doi: 10.2501/JAR-54-1-032-043.

Goodrich, K., Schiller, S. Z., & Galletta, D. (2015). Consumer reactions to intrusiveness of online-video advertisements do length, informativeness, and humor help (or hinder) marketing outcomes? *Journal of Advertising Research, 55*(1), 37–50. http://doi.org/10.2501/JAR-55-1-037-050.

Grant, P., Botha, E., & Kietzmann, J. (2015). Branded flash mobs: Moving toward a deeper understanding of consumers' responses to video advertising. *Journal of Interactive Advertising, 15*(1), 28–42. http://doi.org/10.1080/15252019.2015.1013229.

Ha, L., & McCann, K. (2008). An integrated model of advertising clutter in offline and online media. *International Journal of Advertising, 27*(4), 569–592. doi: 10.2501/S0265048708080153.

Harrison, F. (2013). Digging deeper down into the empirical generalization of brand recall: Adding owned and earned media to paid-media touchpoints. *Journal of Advertising Research, 53*(2), 181–185. doi: 10.2501/JAR-53-2-181-185.

Hart, K. (2007). Online networking goes small, and sponsors follow. *The Washington Post.* Retrieved from http://search.proquest.com/docview/410179234.

Hayes, J. L., & King, K. W. (2014). The social exchange of viral ads: Referral and coreferral of ads among college students. *Journal of Interactive Advertising, 14*(2), 98–109. http://doi.org/10.1080/15252019.2014.942473.

Hughes, D. J., Rowe, M., Batey, M., & Lee, A. (2012). A tale of two sites: Twitter vs. Facebook and the personality predictors of social media usage. *Computers in Human Behavior, 28*(2), 561–569. doi: 10.1016/j.chb.2011.11.001.

IAB. (2011). IAB internet advertising revenue report. Retrieved from http://www.iab.com/wp-content/uploads/2015/05/IAB_Internet_Advertising_Revenue_Report_FY_2011.pdf.

IAB. (2015). Rising stars ads and brand equity. Retrieved from http://www.iab.com/insights/rising-stars-ads-and-brand-equity/

IAB. (2016). IAB display advertising guidelines. Retrieved from http://www.iab.com/guidelines/iab-display-advertising-guidelines/

Jin, S. A. A., & Phua, J. (2014). Following celebrities' tweets about brands: The impact of Twitter-based electronic word-of-mouth on consumers' source credibility perception, buying intention, and social identification with celebrities. *Journal of Advertising, 43*(2), 181–195. http://doi.org/10.1080/00913367.2013.827606.

Kareklas, I., Muehling, D. D., & Weber, T. J. (2015). Reexamining health messages in the digital age: A fresh look at source credibility effects. *Journal of Advertising, 44*(2), 88–104. http://doi.org/10.1080/00913367.2015.1018461.

Kim, E., Lin, J. S., & Sung, Y. (2013). To app or not to app: Engaging consumers via branded mobile apps. *Journal of Interactive Advertising, 13*(1), 53–65. http://doi.org/10.1080/152 52019.2013.782780.

Kim, J., & McMillan, S. J. (2008). Evaluation of internet advertising research: A bibliometric analysis of citations from key sources. *Journal of Advertising, 37*(1), 99–112. doi: 10.2753/JOA0091–3367370108.

Kinney, L., & Ireland, J. (2015). Brand spokes-characters as Twitter marketing tools. *Journal of Interactive Advertising, 15*(2), 135–150. http://doi.org/10.1080/15252019.2015.1101357.

LaPointe, P. (2012). Measuring Facebook's impact on marketing. *Journal of Advertising Research, 52*(3), 286–287. doi: 10.2501/JAR-52-3-286-287.

Lee, M., & Youn, S. (2009). Electronic word of mouth (eWOM): How eWOM platforms influence consumer product judgment. *International Journal of Advertising, 28*(3), 473–499. doi: 10.2501/S0265048709200709.

Li, H., & Lo, H.Y. (2015). Do you recognize its brand? The effectiveness of online in-stream video advertisements. *Journal of Advertising, 44*(3), 208–218. http://doi.org/10.1080/00 913367.2014.956376.

Limpf, N., & Voorveld, H. A. M. (2015). Mobile location-based advertising: How information privacy concerns influence consumers' attitude and acceptance. *Journal of Interactive Advertising, 15*(2), 111–123. http://doi.org/10.1080/15252019.2015.1064795.

Lipsman, A., Mud, G., Rich, M., & Bruich, S. (2012). The power of "like": How brands reach (and influence) fans through social-media marketing. *Journal of Advertising Research, 52*(1), 40–52. doi: 10.2501/JAR-52-1-040-052.

Logan, K. (2014). Why isn't everyone doing it? A comparison of antecedents to following brands on Twitter and Facebook. *Journal of Interactive Advertising, 14*(2), 60–72. http://doi.org/10.1080/15252019.2014.935536.

López, M., & Sicilia, M. (2014). eWOM as source of influence: The impact of participation in eWOM and perceived source trustworthiness on decision making. *Journal of Interactive Advertising, 14*(2), 86–97. http://doi.org/10.1080/15252019.2014.944288.

Manchanda, P., Dubé, J. P., Goh, K. Y., & Chintagunta, P. K. (2006). The effect of banner advertising on Internet purchasing. *Journal of Marketing Research, 43*(1), 98–108. http://doi.org/10.1509/jmkr.43.1.98.

Moe, W. W. (2006). A field experiment to assess the interruption effect of pop-up promotions. *Journal of Interactive Marketing, 20*(1), 34–44. doi: 10.1002/dir.20054.

Moore, R. S., Stammerjohan, C. A., & Coulter, R. A. (2005). Banner advertiser-web site context congruity and color effects on attention and attitudes. *Journal of Advertising, 34*(2), 71–84. doi: 10.1080/00913367.2005.10639189.

Moran, G., Muzellec, L., & Nolan, E. (2014). Consumer moments of truth in the digital context: How "search" and "E-word of mouth" can fuel consumer decision making. *Journal of Advertising Research, 54*(2), 200–204. http://doi.org/10.2501/JAR-54-2-200-204.

Morrison, M. A., Cheong, H. J., & McMillan, S. J. (2013). Posting, lurking, and networking: Behaviors and characteristics of consumers in the context of user-generated content. *Journal of Interactive Advertising, 13*(2), 97–108. http://doi.org/10.1080/15252019.2013.826552.

Murdough, C. (2009). Social media measurement: It's not impossible. *Journal of Interactive Advertising, 10*(1), 94–99. doi: 10.1080/15252019.2009.10722165.

Nelson-Field, K., Riebe, E., & Sharp, B. (2012). What's not to "like?" *Journal of Advertising Research, 52*(2), 262–269. doi: 10.2501/JAR-52-2-262-269.

Nelson-Field, K., Riebe, E., & Sharp, B. (2013). More mutter about clutter: Extending empirical generalizations to Facebook. *Journal of Advertising Research, 53*(2), 186–191. doi: 10.2501/JAR-53-2-186-191.

Nielsen. (2010). Advertising effectiveness: Understanding the value of social media ad impressions. Retrieved from http://www.nielsen.com/us/en/insights/news/2010/nielsenfacebook-ad-report.html.

Nielsen. (2012). The social media report 2012. Retrieved from http://www.nielsen.com/us/en/insights/reports/2012/state-of-the-media-the-social-media-report-2012.html.

Nutley, M. (2007). It's the influencers, not the social media, that brands need to target. Retrieved from http://www.marketingweek.co.uk/its-the-influencers-not-the-social-media-that-brands-need-to-target/2056151.article.

Okazaki, S. (2009). Social influence model and electronic word of mouth. *International Journal of Advertising, 28*(3), 439–472. doi: 10.2501/S0265048709200692.

Precourt, G. (2015). How does neuroscience work in advertising? *Journal of Advertising Research, 55*(2), 112–113. http://doi.org/10.2501/JAR-55-2-112-113.

Prendergast, G., Ko, D., & Yuen, S. Y. V. (2010). Online word of mouth and consumer purchase intentions. *International Journal of Advertising, 29*(5), 687–708. 10.2501/S0265048710201427.

Quinones, P-A., Vora, J., Steinfeld, A., Smailagic, A., Hansen, J., Siewiorek, D. P., Phadhana-Anake, P., & Shah, A. (2008). The effects of highlighting and pop-up interruptions on task performance. *Proceedings of the Human Factors and Ergonomics Society Annual Meeting, 52*(3), 177–181. doi: 10.1177/154193120805200306.

Raacke, J., & Bonds-Raacke, J. (2008). MySpace and Facebook: Applying the uses and gratifications theory to exploring friend-networking sites. *Cyberpsychology and Behavior, 11*(2), 169–174. doi: 10.1089/cpb.2007.0056.

Rae, N., & Brennan, M. (1998). The relative effectiveness of sound and animation in web banner advertisements. *Marketing Bulletin, 9*, 76–82.

Rejón-Guardia, F., & Martínez-López, F. J. (2014). An integrated review of the efficacy of internet advertising: Concrete approaches to the banner ad format and the context of social networks. In *Handbook of strategic e-business management* (pp. 523–564). Berlin Heidelberg: Springer. Retrieved from http://link.springer.com/chapter/10.1007/978-3-642-39747-9_22.

Riegner, C. (2007). Word of mouth on the web: The impact of web 2.0 on consumer purchase decisions. *Journal of Advertising Research, 47*(4), 436–447. doi: 10.2501/S0021849907070456.

Robinson, H., Wysocka, A., & Hand, C. (2007). Internet advertising effectiveness: The effect of design on click-through rates for banner ads. *International Journal of Advertising, 26*(4), 527–541. doi: 10.1080/02650487.2007.11073031.

Shan, Y., & King, K. W. (2015). The effects of interpersonal tie strength and subjective norms on consumers' brand-related eWOM referral intentions. *Journal of Interactive Advertising, 15*(1), 16–27. http://doi.org/10.1080/15252019.2015.1016636.

Smith, T., Coyle, J. R., Lightfoot, E., & Scott, A. (2007). Reconsidering models of influence: The relationship between consumer social networks and word-of-mouth effectiveness. *Journal of Advertising Research, 47*(4), 387–397. doi: 10.2501/S0021849907070407.

Soares, A. M., Pinho, J. C., & Nobre, H. (2012). From social to marketing interactions: The role of social networks. *Journal of Transnational Management, 17*(1), 45–62. doi: 10.1080/15475778.2012.650085.

Spotts, H. E., Purvis, S. C., & Patnaik, S. (2014). How digital conversations reinforce super bowl advertising: The power of earned media drives television engagement. *Journal of Advertising Research, 54*(4), 454–478. http://doi.org/10.2501/JAR-54-4-448-453.

Steele, A., Jacobs, D., Siefert, C., Rule, R., Levine, B., & Marci, C. D. (2013). Leveraging synergy and emotion in a multi-platform world: A neuroscience-informed model of engagement. *Journal of Advertising Research, 53*(4), 417–430. doi: 10.2501/JAR-53-4-417-430.

Steyn, P., Wallström, Å., & Pitt, L. (2010). Consumer-generated content and source effects in financial services advertising: An experimental study. *Journal of Financial Services Marketing, 15*(1), 49–61. doi: 10.1057/fsm.2010.3.

Taylor, D. G. (2012). Self-enhancement as a motivation for sharing online advertising. *Journal of Interactive Advertising, 12*(2), 13–28. doi: 10.1080/15252019.2012.10722193.

Taylor, D. G., Lewin, J., & Strutton, D. (2011). Friends, fans, and followers: Do ads work on social networks? *Journal of Advertising Research, 51*(1), 258–275. doi: 10.2501/JAR-51-1-258-275.

Trusov, M., Bodapati, A. V., & Bucklin, R. E. (2010). Determining influential users in internet social networks. *Journal of Marketing Research, 47*(4), 643–658. http://dx.doi.org/10.1509/jmkr.47.4.643.

Tucker, C. (2014). Social networks, personalized advertising, and privacy controls. *Journal of Marketing Research, 51*(5), 546–562. http://dx.doi.org/10.1509/jmr.10.0355.

Vázquez-Casielles, R., Suárez-Álvarez, L., & del Río-Lanza, A. B. (2013). The word of mouth dynamic: How positive (and negative) WOM drives purchase probability: An analysis of interpersonal and non-interpersonal factors. *Journal of Advertising Research, 53*(1), 43–60. http://doi.org/10.2501/JAR-53-1-043-060.

Wallace, E., Buil, I., De Chernotony, L., & Hogan, M. (2014). Who "likes" you . . . and why? A typology of Facebook fans: From "fan"-atics and self-expressives to utilitarians and authentics. *Journal of Advertising Research, 54*(1), 92–109. doi: 10.2501/JAR-54-1-092-109.

Wang, S., Cunningham, N. R., & Eastin, M. S. (2015). The impact of eWOM message characteristics on the perceived effectiveness of online consumer reviews. *Journal of Interactive Advertising, 15*(2), 151–159. doi: 10.1080/15252019.2015.1091755.

Wise, K., Alhabash, S., & Eckler, P. (2013). "Window" shopping online: Cognitive processing of general and specific product windows. *Journal of Interactive Advertising, 13*(2), 88–96. http://doi.org/10.1080/15252019.2013.826550.

Wood, O. (2012). How emotional tugs trump rational pushes: The time has come to abandon a 100-year-old advertising model. *Journal of Advertising Research, 52*(1), 31–39. doi: 10.2501/JAR-52-1-031-039.

Yaveroglu, I., & Donthu, N. (2008). Advertising repetition and placement issues in online environments. *Journal of Advertising, 37*(2), 31–44. http://doi.org/10.2753/JOA0091-3367370203.

Yoo, C.Y. (2012). An experimental examination of factors affecting click-through of keyword search ads. *Journal of Current Issues & Research in Advertising, 33*(1), 56–78. doi: 10.1080/10641734.2012.675559.

Zeng, F., Huang, L., & Dou, W. (2009). Social factors in user perceptions and responses to advertising in online social networking communities. *Journal of Interactive Advertising, 10*(1), 1–13. doi: 10.1080/15252019.2009.10722159.

22

MEASURING THE EFFICIENCY OF DIGITAL ADVERTISING

Albena Pergelova and Fernando Angulo-Ruiz

Introduction: Digital Advertising, Empowerment, and the Continuous Impetus for Efficiency

The rise of digital advertising is no surprise since it offers advertisers more precise targeting, (Edelman, 2009) and consumers get more personalized messages. In an era of constantly increasing clutter and competition for the audience's attention, better targeting is especially important for advertisers because it means increased cost effectiveness (achieving the goal for less or achieving more under the same level of input). Better targeting is arguably important for the increasingly more empowered consumer. Armed with information and knowledge, consumers can now be co-creators or even sole creators of messages—instead of recipients—and appreciate (or so advertisers hope) tailored and more personalized communication (De Keyzer, Dens, & De Pelsmacker, 2015). While research has suggested that online advertising can, indeed, help advertisers by increasing the overall advertising efficiency (e.g., Pergelova, Prior, & Rialp, 2010), there is also research indicating that we should be careful when assessing the effects of digital advertising. Even though personalization decreases ad avoidance (Baek & Morimoto, 2012), online ads could lead to negative brand attitudes if they are perceived as distractors (e.g., Duff & Faber, 2011). Digital advertising campaigns typically employ multiple sources and can lead to multiple outcomes (both positive and negative, such as negative eWOM, negative brand attitudes, etc.); therefore, the methods for assessing the effectiveness and efficiency of advertising should ideally be able to reflect this reality and incorporate the multitude of potential results.

Rodgers and Thorson (2000), in their Interactive Advertising Model (IAM), directed the attention of researchers to the consumer-controlled and advertiser-controlled elements of the model. The importance of thinking about both aspects—and carefully considering the new multiplicity of consumer-controlled aspects—has only increased since the publication of the original IAM in 2000. Consumer-controlled aspects are increasingly not only at the level of outcomes (e.g., click on ad, form attitude), but at the level of input into the communication through, for example, consumer-generated advertising, consumer-generated advertising parodies, and even consumer-generated websites designed to praise a brand or spread negative eWOM about a brand. While interactive media have presented advertisers with opportunities for more precise targeting and communication, they have also made them cede control over messages about their brands (Campbell, Pitt, Parent, & Berthon, 2011) through consumer-generated advertising, eWOM, and brand communities, among others. Conceptual developments in communications, advertising, and marketing literatures suggest that we are moving toward greater appreciation and preference for more participative, dialogue-based communication between companies/brands and consumers that are mutually controllable and responsive (Yadav & Varadarajan, 2005; Deighton & Kornfeld, 2009; Jenkins, Ford, & Green, 2013). While such a view is intuitively appealing given the shift of power to former consumer-audiences (which are now co-creators), the challenges of measuring digital advertising effectiveness and efficiency are only compounded. Against this backdrop, this chapter's objective is to synthesize the digital advertising effectiveness/efficiency literature, propose a model that incorporates a broader set of metrics, including consumer empowerment, and outline a methodological measurement approach that can capture the diversity of inputs and outputs (both consumer and advertiser-controlled) generated as a result of digital advertising campaigns.

Current Ways to Measure Digital Advertising Effects

In this section, we provide a review of the digital advertising effectiveness literature, organizing it around two themes: advertiser-controlled inputs into the ad campaign and consumer-controlled inputs (Rodgers & Thorson, 2000), with the caveat that the distinction is fluid because of the consumer-advertiser interaction and interdependence in the process (Stewart & Pavlou, 2002). The review is not meant to be exhaustive, but rather is to illustrate the types of inputs into and outcomes from digital advertising campaigns.

Digital Advertising Effectiveness Metrics from the Perspective of Advertiser-Controlled Elements

The ad type, ad format, and ad features are all advertiser-controlled elements of digital communication campaigns (Rodgers & Thorson, 2000). Looking at the digital advertising effectiveness literature from this perspective generates a picture of the diversity of ad formats/features and their (relative) effectiveness. Studies within this stream of literature have examined display (e.g., banner) ads, paid search, social media advertising, mobile advertising, etc., either in isolation or in combination, including comparing digital and traditional advertising. The variables, considered as outcomes (i.e., variables measuring how effective ads are), tend to be slightly different depending on whether the study takes a broader marketing perspective or focuses on advertising-specific theoretical approaches. From an advertising point of view, the effectiveness variables used typically fall within the cognition (e.g., recall), affection (e.g., attitude toward the ad or brand), or behavior (e.g., purchase intention) (CAB) model in advertising. Given that marketing's key contribution to the organization is to stimulate demand for organizational products or services (Clark, Key, Hodis, & Rajaratnam, 2014), current literature on digital advertising effectiveness from this perspective studies the impact of firm controlled digital advertising inputs on consumers' mindset metrics (e.g., brand awareness, liking) and on firm top-line performance (e.g., sales).

In the topic about the relative effectiveness of digital advertising, literature studies the impact of digital and traditional advertising on sales, brand recall, and customer spending and cross-buying behavior. Danaher and Dagger (2013) studied the impact of advertisements in television, newspapers, radio, magazines, catalogs, mail, search, and email on sales of an Australian upscale department store and found that television ads, catalogs, and mail had higher sales elasticity than search and email. In a similar study, Dinner, Van Heerde, and Neslin (2014) examined the impact of traditional advertisements, online display ads, and paid search ads on sales in a high-end clothing retailer in the United States, but the authors disentangled sales into offline and online as well as the cross–effects of digital advertising on offline sales. Interestingly, Dinner et al. (2014) found that paid search had larger elasticity compared to traditional advertising when both direct and cross–effects were taken into consideration. Draganska, Hartmann, and Stanglein (2014) studied the impact of television ads, banner ads, rich media, and video on brand recall. The authors' findings indicate that digital advertising showed the same effects as television advertisements if pre-existing knowledge of a brand was taken into consideration. Kumar, Bezawada, Rishika, Janakiraman, & Kannan (2016) studied the impact of social media on customer spending and cross-buying behavior of a wine and spirit specialty retailer. They found that the positive effect of social media was moderated by television ads and emails. However, current literature is not yet conclusive with regard to the advantage of digital advertising.

For example, literature on paid search assesses digital advertising's impact on click-through rates, brand evaluations, and conversion. Agarwal, Hosanagar, and Smith (2011), for instance, studied the impact of paid search position in pure online retailers and found that although top positions increased click-through rates, bottom positions tended to increase conversions, revenues, and profits. On the contrary, Rutz, Bucklin, and Sonnier (2012) found that top position of paid search advertising positively impacted conversion in the case of a lodging chain. Yoo (2014) found that top-ranked keyword search ads for unknown brands generated greater recognition and more favorable brand evaluations along the primed attribute than those ranked lower than well-known brands. Jerath, Ma, and Park (2014) studied the impact of keyword popularity on click behavior and found that more popular keywords increased the click behavior in organic search, while less popular keywords were associated with more clicks in paid search. Rutz and Bucklin (2011) found that generic keywords led to branded keywords, which in turn led to click conversions, and posited that research needs to focus on the chain of effects of generic and branded keywords.

Online display advertising seems to create awareness and recognition. Hoban and Bucklin (2015) examined the impact of online display advertising on impressions of an online financial tools provider and found that these ads impact impressions of new visitors (serving as an awareness tool) and of authenticated and converted users (serving as a reminder tool). Li and Kannan (2014) found that display ads and emails impacted conversion in the short-term while paid search and emails impacted conversions in the long-term. Chun, Song, Hollenbeck, and Lee (2014) examined contextual banner ads (in which marketers strive to develop customized images or texts more relevant to customers based on the content of web pages) on brand memory and attitudes toward the advertisement and brand, and demonstrated that contextual advertisements enhanced brand recognition and induced favorable attitudes toward the ad. Li and Lo (2015) studied the effects of ad length, ad position, and ad-context congruity on brand name recognition in an online in-stream video advertising context. Baron, Brouwer, and Garbayo (2014) compared the effectiveness of large-canvas display formats, full-screen interactive "takeover" formats, and "skin" or wrap formats, and found that consumers exposed to large-canvas display and full-screen takeover formats were more likely to exhibit shopping behaviors, such as going to the brand's site to learn more or looking for the product in stores.

Social media advertising has attracted a lot of research attention because of the high personalization possibilities of advertising on social networking sites (SNSs). For instance, De Keyzer, Dens, and De Pelsmacker (2015) demonstrated that personalized advertising on SNSs led to more positive consumer responses than non-personalized advertising, mainly because personalized ads were perceived as more relevant. Thus, when an ad was perceived as personally relevant, attitude toward the brand and click intention improved (De Keyzer, Dens, & De Pelsmacker, 2015).

The mobile advertising literature focuses on the impact of mobile advertising on attitude, intention, coupon redemption, and on locational targeting. For example, Bart, Stephen, and Sarvary (2014) found that mobile display ads positively affected attitudes and intentions but only for utilitarian and high involvement products. Danaher, Smith, Ranasinghe, and Danaher (2015) assessed the impact of mobile phone coupon characteristics on redemption and found that location—in addition to face value, expiry length, and timeliness—affected coupon redemption of snack foods. Mobile phones can also be used for location-based marketing. Fong, Fang, and Luo (2015) studied the impact of locational targeting for a movie theater and found that, in the case of mobile discounts, competitive locational targeting (placing mobile ads near competitors' locations) was more effective than own-location targeting (near a firm's own location).

One important emerging stream of literature focuses on the potential negative effects of firm-controlled aspects of digital ad campaigns. For instance, Duff and Faber (2011) examined the effect of banner ads on affective evaluation rating for brands (e.g., like/dislike), and found that when ad viewers were engaged in a task unrelated to the ad, and ads were actively ignored, a negative impact occurred, even in the absence of any explicit memory of having been exposed to the brand. Goldstein, Suri, Macfee, Ekstrand-Abueg, and Diaz (2014) studied the role of annoying ads and found that these ads increased the tendency of consumers to abandon the website. Baek and Morimoto (2012) focused on the potential determinants of advertising avoidance in the context of personalized advertising media, including unsolicited commercial email, postal direct mail, telemarketing, and text messaging. The authors found that privacy concerns and ad irritation had a direct positive effect on ad avoidance, while perceived personalization led to decreased ad avoidance. Goodrich, Schiller, and Galletta (2015) investigated intrusive online video advertisements and found that they negatively affected attitudes and intentions toward both the advertised brand and the host website. Higher intrusiveness in their study was associated with greater abandonment of the advertisement, less favorable brand attitudes, and reduced purchase intention for the advertiser, as well as negative website attitudes and reduced revisit intentions for the website, and informative or humorous advertisements were perceived as less intrusive (Goodrich, Schiller, & Galletta, 2015). Cho, Huh, and Faber (2014) included both potential positive (perceived informativeness, entertainment) and negative (perceived risk, irritation) effects of viral advertising in their study, and found that advertiser trust influenced perceived informativeness and perceived risk.

Thus, the inclusion of both potential positive and negative effects in measurement models is important because, as Duff and Faber (2011) postulate, the majority of advertising studies assume that ads that are not fully processed will either result in no impact or may have a positive effect on the consumer due to mere exposure. Yet, this view does not reflect the reality of many consumers that are annoyed by ads online and actively try to avoid them. To understand this, we review the literature on digital advertising metrics from the perspective of consumer-controlled inputs.

Digital Advertising Effectiveness Metrics from the Perspective of Consumer-Controlled Inputs

Consumer engagement has been suggested as an antidote to consumers that are empowered and connected in digital spaces, and that—by and large—want to avoid digital ads. Studies suggest that two-thirds of U.S. adults reject behavioral targeting based on their prior search and browsing behavior (Turow, King,

Hoofnagle, Bleakley, & Hennessy, 2009). Thus, many authors have emphasized that to succeed in the new digital world, brands must relinquish control (e.g., Fournier & Avery, 2011). An implicit recognition of the need for more participative, mutually controllable, and responsive view toward digital advertising would inform studies that focus on consumers' inputs into the communication process. Such studies typically investigate consumer-generated ads and eWOM/forwarding messages (viral advertising) that sometimes consist of ad parodies/spoofs and/ or online consumer reviews.

Consumer-Generated Ads (CGA)

Motivated by the contention that consumer-generated ads (CGA) may be more effective than traditional company ads and the scant empirical evidence on the topic, Lawrence, Fournier, and Brunel (2013) studied whether there is a performance advantage for CGAs across a set of accepted measures of ad persuasion: attitude toward the ad, attitude toward the brand, brand interest, and purchase intent. The authors found that it is the fact that CGAs were made by people, not companies, that drove responses to them. Lawrence et al. (2013) posited that CGAs engaged viewers more on cognitive, personal, emotional, and behavioral grounds because of the presence of credible, authentic, and non-corporate consumer source. Orazi, Bove, and Lei (2016) showed that the disclosure of consumer participation in the ad creation process resulted in positive ad evaluations. In addition to CGA, scholars have examined ad parodies. For instance, Bergh, Lee, Quilliam, and Hove (2011) investigated key dimensions of ad parodies (humor, truth, mockery, and offensiveness) and examined how they influence brand attitudes, attitudes toward the parodies, and intention to pass along the parodies. In their study, humor and truth were positively related to attitudes toward the parodies and intention to pass them along, while offensiveness was negatively related to attitudes toward the parodies; brand attitudes, however, were not impacted.

Viral Advertising and Electronic Word-of-Mouth (eWOM)

Viral advertising and electronic word-of-mouth (eWOM) have also received a good deal of research attention. Although viral advertising initiates with a marketer-designed ad, it is consumers' decisions to pass along the ad and spread eWOM that is the essence of virality. Alhabash and McAlister (2015) define virality through 1) viral reach (volume of message sharing and forwarding by internet users, e.g., shares), 2) affective evaluation (internet users' explicit affective responses to online messages, e.g., likes and dislikes), and 3) message deliberation (internet users' active and public deliberation of online messages, e.g., comments).

Cho, Huh, and Faber (2014) examined the influence of sender trust and advertiser trust on four stages of viral advertising effects, and demonstrated that sender trust influenced a wider range of viral advertising effects as compared to advertiser trust. Kareklas, Muehling, and Weber (2015) investigated the influence of perceived source credibility on the effectiveness of health-related public service announcements (PSAs) and eWOM communications. Their results suggest it is not the advertising message alone that influences consumers' responses but rather the commenters' reactions to the claims presented in the PSA that also independently contribute to consumers' attitudes and behavioral intentions. Thus, Kareklas et al. (2015) demonstrated that online comments impacted effectiveness in a similar way as other user-generated opinions, such as product reviews. Hennig-Thurau, Wiertz, and Feldhaus (2015) studied the impact of Twitter reviews on revenues in the case of an instant success product: movies. They found that negative Twitter reviews on Fridays reduced movie revenues of Saturday and Sundays by 15 percent. Alhabash, McAlister, Lou, and Hagerstrom (2015) reported a mediating effect of viral behavioral intentions (e.g., likes, shares, comments) on the relationship between attitudes toward the message and offline behavioral intentions. Schulze, Schöler, and Skiera (2014) studied the effectiveness of viral marketing and found that sharing mechanisms that used direct messages from friends and broadcast messages from strangers were significantly more effective for utilitarian products. Stephen and Galak (2012) studied the effect of traditional and social earned media on sales and found that although both traditional and social earned media impact sales, the elasticity of community rating—social earned media—were higher than those of traditional.

In addition to consumer-generated content (CGC) and eWOM, studies have examined the effects of consumers choosing to self-disclose information in interactive advertising campaigns. According to van Noort, Antheunis, and Verlegh (2014), consumers' self-disclosure to the brand stimulates favorable attitudinal (campaign and brand attitude) and behavioral (purchase and forwarding intentions) consumer responses, especially for individuals who had relatively low online privacy concerns in the social network sites context.

Toward a More Inclusive Model of Effectiveness: Consumer Empowerment, Long-Term Company Performance, and Cost-Effectiveness of Digital Advertising

The common tie among studies cited above is that they look at digital advertising through the "stickiness" lens, i.e., they apply a traditional marketing "funnel" approach in which companies produce marketing communications content, deliver it to consumers, and use the marketing tools with the higher probability of making consumers "stick" with the ad and consequently make a purchase decision. Even when researchers look at consumer-initiated and consumer-controlled aspects of the communication, such as eWOM, the research question is typically concerned with the issue of how to increase such behavior for the benefits of the marketer, instead of how to maximize positive outcomes for both/all parties involved. This is surprising given the advancement in conceptual developments focused on participative, dialogue-based, co-creation approaches in both communications and marketing (Deighton & Kornfeld, 2009; Jenkins et al., 2013).

For instance, Yadav and Varadarajan (2005) suggested that interactivity should be defined as the degree to which computer-mediated communication is perceived by each of the parties involved to be bidirectional, timely, mutually controllable, and responsive. This definition recognizes the need for a dialogue stance and takes a more dynamic and balanced approach where both the firm and the consumer exercise an influence on the process. Stewart and Pavlou (2002) suggest a focus on continuous interaction among actors where consumers and marketers are interdependent and influence each other's development and evolution.

Empirical literature has provided an indication of consumers' motivation to engage in social media from a uses and gratifications (U&G) approach, to explain why and how people use certain media to gratify their needs. As Kwon, Kim, Sung, and Yoo (2014) summarize, consumers are motivated by needs for social support, reinforcement of self through social interactions, and psychological well being, which includes self-esteem and life satisfaction. Yet, digital advertising effectiveness studies only approach these issues as motivations, and do not take into consideration those measures as outputs for the consumer (i.e., does a participant's self-esteem increase as a result of the interaction online?). Some studies have included consumers' perceptions of interactivity (the degree to which the consumer perceives the website to be controllable, responsive, and synchronic), suggesting that if consumers perceive more control over their online purchase decision, more communication with the online store and other consumers, this would lead to favorable attitudes toward the site (Cui, Wang, & Xu, 2010).

Tucker (2014) studied the impact of online targeted ads (or more personalized ads) on clicks and found that—in the case of a not-for-profit organization— targeted ads were more effective when more privacy control was given to users. Additionally, Schumann, von Wangenheim, and Groene (2014) indicated that targeted online ads may increase the willingness of users to disclose personal information in free websites if normative reciprocity appeals were used (e.g., "Your support is required! Our service is free of charge for you—targeted ads help us fund it").

These studies suggest that consumers appreciate openness, transparency, and the opportunity to have more control over the communication process. Consumers' appreciation for companies that engage in digital advertising from this stance will likely result in better and longer-term relationships and support (e.g., loyalty) to the organization. Thus, we advocate the use of metrics that reflect not only effectiveness for the advertiser but also desirable effects for consumers such as consumer-perceived value (Dao, Le, Cheng, & Chen, 2014), firm-consumer relationships that are beneficial to both parties (Kwon et al., 2014), and measures that empower consumers to make decisions and participate on their own terms, e.g., privacy control features.

On a broader level, empowerment requires mechanisms for individuals to gain control over issues that concern them (Pires, Stanton, & Rita, 2006). For instance, Leung (2009) uses a three dimensional model of psychological empowerment in the context of civic engagement and user-generated content (UGC) with items reflecting self-efficacy and desire for control over one's life and decisions, in addition to perceived competence (knowledge). Such measures can be usefully imported and used as a supplement to traditional company-centered effectiveness measures.

We postulate that if organizations are effective in generating outputs that empower consumers, this will lead to increased cost-effectiveness (efficiency) of advertising campaigns because of earned (not paid) media and increased willingness of consumers to engage with and respond favorably to companies that voluntarily cede control and provide avenues for openness and dialogue. Only a few studies have looked at efficiency of digital advertising compared to other media (e.g., Pergelova et al., 2010; Cheong, de Gregorio, & Kim, 2014). Yet, it is important to keep the relationship in mind, as well as the difference between effectiveness and efficiency. While effectiveness measures the achievement of objectives, efficiency looks at the inputs (e.g., advertising dollars spent) in relation to the outputs/objectives achieved. Cheong et al. (2014) studied advertising spending efficiency among top U.S. advertisers from 1985 to 2012 and found that the more recent 2008–2012 period (the period during which the internet has become core advertising medium) has seen a distinct increase in inefficiency. Thus, the authors argue that despite the internet's lower overall cost and greater audience tracking capabilities, online spending must be carefully tracked and managed for gains in efficiency coupled with achievement of objectives in relation to the efficiency levels.

Proposed Measurement Approach: How DEA Matches Developments in Theory and Offers an Assessment of Digital Advertising Efficiency

The new reality (message movement across platforms, UGC, and empowerment of participants, i.e., formerly the "audience") necessitates a new way of measuring the effect of digital advertising that can capture the diversity of inputs and outputs generated as a result of digital advertising campaigns. Figure 22.1 presents an integrative model incorporating both advertiser-controlled and consumer-controlled inputs, intermediate outputs (including those related to consumer empowerment), and long-term company performance. While one can envision different methodological approaches for empirically testing this model (e.g., structural equation modeling), we present data envelopment analysis (DEA) as a method that easily incorporates multiple inputs and outputs and offers efficiency estimation.

The challenge of assessing the effectiveness of diverse digital advertising measures comes from the fact that such measures usually have multiple objectives,

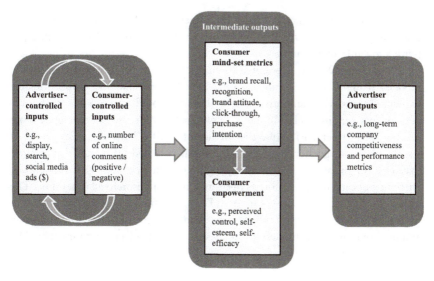

FIGURE 22.1 Integrative Model of Digital Advertising Efficiency

related not only to build awareness, consideration, and preference, but also to enhance performance. We argue that this chain of effects should be addressed as a whole: digital advertising performance (advertiser-controlled and consumer-controlled elements), mind-set metrics, and consumer empowerment.

One limitation of the techniques typically used in extant literature (e.g., regression analysis) is the restriction of the number of dependent variables possible to evaluate. In that sense, as we are working with constructs composed by multiple variables, we suggest DEA. This method is able to identify a specific best-performing decision-making unit (e.g., a firm or a firm-time unit), and it is able to assist those units in setting goals in specific aspects considered in the analysis. In the DEA literature the term "decision-making unit" (DMU) refers to a productive entity, which can be a firm, a business unit within the firm, a non-profit organization, a region, a country, or all entities that use inputs to produce certain outputs. Moreover, DEA is also relevant because it provides a single measure of overall efficiency computed for every unit under analysis and compared with the other units under analysis.

DEA was first proposed by Charnes, Cooper, and Rhodes (1978) as an evaluation tool for measuring and comparing productivity of DMUs. DEA has been extensively used in operations management (Banker, Charners, & Cooper, 1984), and has also been applied to advertising (e.g., Pergelova et al., 2010). DEA is a non-parametric, linear programming-based technique designed to measure the relative performance of DMUs, where the presence of multiple inputs and outputs poses difficulties for comparisons. DEA uses the ratio of weighted inputs and outputs to produce a single measure of productivity (relative efficiency). Efficient

DMUs are those for which no other DMU generates as much as—or more of—every output (with a given level of inputs) or uses as little or less of each input (with a given level of outputs).

In designing DEA, it is essential to choose an appropriate orientation of the model. An input-oriented model would look for efficiency by proportionately reducing inputs, while an output-oriented model would focus on increasing outputs given a certain level of inputs. The efficient DMUs have an efficiency score of one (or 100 percent), while the inefficient DMUs have efficiency scores of less than one but greater than zero in an input-oriented DEA model, and more than one (or more than 100 percent) in the output-oriented DEA model. The efficiency of each unit, therefore, is measured in comparison to all other units. The model we suggest is an output-oriented DEA. The rationale is that we intend to maximize mind-set metrics and their performance consequences (intermediate and final output in our model) given a level of digital advertising initiatives. The model is provided below:

Model 1:

$Max. \beta_t$,

$s.t.$:

$$\sum_{k=1}^{K} \lambda_k \cdot y_{ikt} \geq \beta_t \cdot y_{it}^o, \qquad i=1,...,I,$$

$$\sum_{k=1}^{K} \lambda_k \cdot x_{jkt} \leq x_{jt}^o, \qquad j=1,...,J,$$

$$\sum_{k=1}^{K} \lambda_k = 1,$$

$$\lambda_k \geq 0.$$

Where β_t is the efficiency coefficient for the unit under analysis in period t ($\beta_t = 1$ indicates that the unit under analysis is efficient and $\beta_t > 1$ that this unit is inefficient). β_t-1 determines the output growth rate required to reach the frontier), y_{it}^o is the observed outputs vector of the unit under analysis in period t, x_{jt}^o is the observed inputs vector of the unit under analysis in period t, y_{ikt} and x_{jkt} refer to outputs and inputs vectors for the k $(k=1, ..., K)$ units forming the total sample, and λ stands for the activity vector.

Our model for capturing digital advertising cost effectiveness is different from basic DEA models because the generation of performance is the result of two consecutive and interdependent stages. Basic DEA methods treat the organization under assessment as a black box, meaning just taking into account the inputs consumption and the output created. In the case of the proposed model, a more complex problem is defined, and the basic DEA may be insufficient. Indeed, as a relationship between the intermediate output (customer mind-set metrics) and the final (long-term) output (competitiveness, sustainability) has to be established, network DEA is necessary. Therefore, a good approach of DEA for the proposed model can be based on network DEA. During stage one, digital advertising efforts (expended in t), are oriented toward the fulfillment of customer mind-set metrics or consumer empowerment maximization (in t). In stage two, the optimal level of customer mind-set metrics or consumer empowerment is added to the previous resources (marketing resources, expended in t) to optimize the level of long-term performance (in t). A firm oriented toward the optimization of long-term performance should manage efficiently both stages in order to guarantee the achievement of the final goal. More details on network DEA can be found in Sexton and Lewis (2003), Lewis and Sexton (2004), and Angulo-Ruiz, Donthu, Prior, and Rialp (2014).

Another aspect that needs consideration is the role of undesirable outputs. Examples of such outputs can be negative reviews, negative word-of-mouth, and others. Directional distance function (DDF) based on DEA can help measuring efficiency of digital advertising taking into consideration desirable and undesirable outputs. Literature employs DDF in the cases of firms in industries that face environmental regulations (Diaz, 2009), since the "costs of abatement capital would typically be included on the input side, but no account would be made of the reduction in effluents on the output side" (Chung et al., 1997, p. 229). DDF aims to increase the desirable outputs while simultaneously decreasing the undesirable outputs. Chung et al. (1997) model the Malmquist–Luenberger productivity index, which can be helpful to measure efficiency of digital advertising, including desirable and undesirable outputs.

To summarize, advancements in the DEA method make it especially suitable for assessing digital advertising: the method can accommodate multiple inputs and outputs, including undesirable ones, it can provide a measure of efficiency, and it is able to work with complex multi-stage models.

Conclusion

The quest to find the next best digital advertising tool and the newest metric to measure advertising's short-term impact (e.g., Did yesterday's Twitter campaign bring enough participants to our online contest?) could leave advertisers with little time to stop and think about the big picture and consider the strategic considerations and the broader implications of their work. Yet, such implications are crucial for the long-term sustainability of any organization. The model presented here takes as a conceptual basis the idea of interactivity as mutually controllable, responsive, and open to dialogue environment, in which consumers will reward openness, transparency, and relinquishing of control on behalf of organizations. From a strategic, long-term perspective, we suggest that such a stance toward digital advertising will bring competitive advantage and enhanced performance outcomes for companies, as it brings about greater levels of consumer empowerment.

With the advancement of technology, interactions are no longer limited to face-to-face encounters. "Interactiveness" includes technology and infrastructure that permits two-way communication and ongoing dialogue between firms and consumers, but it goes far beyond this technical aspect. Interactiveness implies a change in the managerial mindset, moving away from one-way marketing and control and toward collaboration and value co-creation. Interactiveness, thus, can be seen as a dialogue of equals for joint problem solving, taking into consideration the interests of all involved parties. Looking at interactiveness from this perspective, it is neither a tactical solution nor a technological solution to help or complement traditional push/pull marketing activities. It is a philosophy, a culture, and as such, it should be built throughout the organization. A truly interactive approach, then, explicitly considers the different actors involved in market exchanges in their settings—as parts of the whole—as active participants in the system and in the value creation. Such an approach recognizes that the effectiveness of the interactive communication "hinges not only on how the marketer's message influences the consumer but also on how the consumer shapes the interaction" (Stewart & Pavlou, 2002, p. 380). We, therefore, propose that a digital advertising measurement approach from this perspective should incorporate both consumers' and advertisers' efforts (inputs) and consequences (outputs). It is our hope that the model and the measurement approach presented here will stimulate debate and advance research in digital advertising.

References

Agarwal, A., Hosanagar, K., & Smith, M. D. (2011). Location, location, location: An analysis of profitability of position in online advertising markets. *Journal of Marketing Research, 48*(6), 1057–1073. doi: http://dx.doi.org/10.1509/jmr.08.0468.

Alhabash, S., & McAlister, A. (2015). Redefining virality in less broad strokes: Predicting viral behavioral intentions from motivations and uses of Facebook and Twitter. *New Media and Society, 17*(8), 1317–1339. doi: 10.1177/1461444814523726.

Alhabash, S., McAlister, A., Lou, C., & Hagerstrom, A. (2015). From clicks to behaviors: The mediating effect of intentions to like, share, and comment on the relationship between message evaluations and offline behavioral intentions. *Journal of Interactive Advertising, 15*(2), 82–96. doi: 10.1080/15252019.2015.1071677.

Angulo-Ruiz, F., Donthu, N., Prior, D., & Rialp, J. (2014). The financial contribution of customer-oriented marketing capability. *Journal of the Academy of Marketing Science, 42*, 380–399. doi: 10.1007/s11747-013-0353-6.

Baek, T. H., & Morimoto, M. (2012). Stay away from me. *Journal of Advertising, 41*(1), 59–76. doi: 10.2753/JOA0091-3367410105.

Banker, R., Charnes, A., & Cooper, W. (1984). Some models for estimating technical and scale inefficiencies in data envelopment analysis. *Management Science, 30*, 1078–1092. http://dx.doi.org/10.1287/mnsc.30.9.1078.

Baron, S., Brouwer, C., & Garbayo, A. (2014). A model for delivering branding value through high-impact digital advertising. *Journal of Advertising Research, 54*(3), 286–291. doi: 10.2501/JAR-54-3-286-291.

Bart, Y., Stephen, A. T., & Sarvary, M. (2014). Which products are best suited to mobile advertising? A field study of mobile display advertising effects on consumer attitudes and intentions. *Journal of Marketing Research, 51*(3), 270–285. http://dx.doi.org/10.1509/jmr.13.0503.

Bergh, B., Lee, M., Quilliam, E., & Hove, T. (2011). The multidimensional nature and brand impact of user-generated ad parodies in social media. *International Journal of Advertising, 30*(1), 103–131. doi: 10.2501/IJA-30-1-103-131.

Campbell, C., Pitt, L., Parent, M., & Berthon, P. (2011). Understanding consumer conversations around ads in a web 2.0 world. *Journal of Advertising, 40*(1), 87–102. doi: 10.2753/JOA0091-3367400106.

Charnes, A., Cooper, W., & Rhodes, E. (1978). Measuring the efficiency of decision making units. *European Journal of Operational Research, 3*, 429–444. doi: 10.1016/0377-2217(78)90138-8.

Cheong, Y., de Gregorio, F., & Kim, K. (2014). Advertising spending efficiency among top U.S. advertisers from 1985 to 2012: Overspending or smart managing? *Journal of Advertising, 43*(4), 344–358. doi: 10.1080/00913367.2014.884955.

Cho, S., Huh, J., & Faber, R. (2014). The influence of sender trust and advertiser trust on multistage effects of viral advertising. *Journal of Advertising, 43*(1), 100–114. doi: 10.1080/00913367.2013.811707.

Chun, K.Y., Song, J. H., Hollenbeck, C., & Lee, J. H. (2014). Are contextual advertisements effective? The moderating role of complexity in banner advertising. *International Journal of Advertising, 33*(2), 351–371. doi: 10.2501/IJA-33-2-351-371.

Chung, Y. H., Fare, R., & Grosskopf, S. (1997). Productivity and undesirable outputs: A directional distance function approach. *Journal of Environmental Management, 51*, 229–240. doi: 10.1006/jema.1997.0146.

Clark, T., Key, T. M., Hodis, M., & Rajaratnam, D. (2014). The intellectual ecology of mainstream marketing research: An inquiry into the place of marketing in the family of business disciplines. *Journal of the Academy of Marketing Science, 42*, 223–241. doi: 10.1007/s11747-013-0362-5.

Cui, N., Wang, T., & Xu, S. (2010). The influence of social presence on consumers' perceptions of the interactivity of web sites. *Journal of Interactive Advertising, 11*(1), 36–49. doi: 10.1080/15252019.2010.10722176.

Danaher, P. J., & Dagger, T. S. (2013). Comparing the relative effectiveness of advertising channels: A case study of a multimedia blitz campaign. *Journal of Marketing Research, 50*(4), 517–534. http://dx.doi.org/10.1509/jmr.12.0241.

Danaher, P. J., Smith, M. S., Ranasinghe, K., & Danaher, T. S. (2015). Where, when, and how long: Factors that influence the redemption of mobile phone coupons. *Journal of Marketing Research, 52*(2), 710–725. http://dx.doi.org/10.1509/jmr.13.0341.

Dao, W., Le, A., Cheng, J., & Chen, D. (2014). Social media advertising value: The case of transitional economies in Southeast Asia. *International Journal of Advertising, 33*(2), 271–294. doi: 10.2501/IJA-33-2-271-294.

Deighton, J., & Kornfeld, L. (2009). Interactivity's unanticipated consequences for marketers and marketing. *Journal of Interactive Marketing, 23*, 4–10. doi: 10.1016/j.intmar.2008.10.001.

De Keyzer, F., Dens, N., & De Pelsmacker, P. (2015). Is this for me? How consumers respond to personalized advertising on social network sites. *Journal of Interactive Advertising, 15*(2), 124–134. doi: 10.1080/15252019.2015.1082450.

Diaz, G. (2009). *Determinant factors of urban waste eco-efficiency in Catalunya: An institutional approach*. Doctoral Dissertation. Retrieved from http://tdx.cesca.cat/handle/10803/1491.

Dinner, I. M., Van Heerde, H. J., & Neslin, S. A. (2014). Driving online and offline sales: The cross-channel effects of traditional, online display, and paid search advertising. *Journal of Marketing Research, 51*(5), 527–545. http://dx.doi.org/10.1509/jmr.11.0466.

Draganska, M., Hartmann, W. R., & Stanglein, G. (2014). Internet versus television advertising: A brand-building comparison. *Journal of Marketing Research, 51*(5), 578–590. http://dx.doi.org/10.1509/jmr.13.0124.

Duff, B., & Faber, R. (2011). Missing the mark. *Journal of Advertising, 40*(2), 51–62. doi: 10.2753/JOA0091–3367400204.

Edelman, B. (2009). Who owns metrics? Building a bill of rights for online advertisers. *Journal of Advertising Research, 49*(4), 401–403. doi: 10.2501/S0021849909091028.

Fong, N. M., Fang, Z., & Luo, X. (2015). Geo-conquesting: Competitive locational targeting of mobile promotions. *Journal of Marketing Research, 52*(5), 726–735. http://dx.doi.org/10.1509/jmr.14.0229.

Fournier, S., & Avery, J. (2011). The uninvited brand. *Business Horizons, 54*, 193–207. doi: 10.1016/j.bushor.2011.01.001.

Goldstein, D. G., Suri, S., Mcafee, R. P., Ekstrand-Abueg, M., & Diaz, F. (2014). The economic and cognitive costs of annoying display advertisements. *Journal of Marketing Research, 51*(6), 742–752. http://dx.doi.org/10.1509/jmr.13.0439.

Goodrich, K., Schiller, S., & Galletta, D. (2015). Consumer reactions to intrusiveness of online-video advertisements. *Journal of Advertising Research, 55*(1), 37–50. doi: 10.2501/JAR-55–1–037–050.

Hennig-Thurau, T., Wiertz, C., & Feldhaus, F. (2015). Does Twitter matter? The impact of microblogging word of mouth on consumers' adoption of new movies. *Journal of the Academy of Marketing Science, 43*, 375–394. doi: 10.1007/s11747–014–0388–3.

Hoban, P. R., & Bucklin, R. E. (2015). Effects of internet display advertising in the purchase funnel: Model-based insights from a randomized field experiment. *Journal of Marketing Research, 52*(3), 375–393. http://dx.doi.org/10.1509/jmr.13.0277.

Jenkins, H., Ford, S., & Green, J. (2013). *Spreadable media: Creating value and meaning in a networked culture.* New York, NY: New York University Press.

Jerath, K., Ma, L., & Park, Y. H. (2014). Consumer click behavior at a search engine: The role of keyword popularity. *Journal of Marketing Research, 51*(4), 480–486. http://dx.doi.org/10.1509/jmr.13.0099.

Kareklas, I., Muehling, D., & Weber, T. J. (2015). Reexamining health messages in the digital age: A fresh look at source credibility effects. *Journal of Advertising, 44*(2), 88–104. doi: 10.1080/00913367.2015.1018461.

Kumar, A., Bezawada, R., Rishika, R. Janakiraman, R., & Kannan, P. K. (2016). From social to sale: The effects of firm-generated content in social media on customer behavior. *Journal of Marketing, 80*(1), 7–25. http://dx.doi.org/10.1509/jm.14.0249.

Kwon, E. S., Kim, E., Sung, Y., & Yoo, C. Y. (2014). Brand followers: Consumer motivation and attitude towards brand communications on Twitter. *International Journal of Advertising, 33*(4), 657–680. doi: 10.2501/IJA-33–4–657–680.

Lawrence, B., Fournier, S., & Brunel, F. (2013). When companies don't make the ad: A multimethod inquiry into the differential effectiveness of consumer-generated advertising. *Journal of Advertising, 42*(4), 292–307. doi: 10.1080/00913367.2013.795120.

Leung, L. (2009). User-generated content on the internet: An examination of gratifications, civic engagement and psychological empowerment. *New Media and Society, 11*, 1327–1347. doi: 10.1177/1461444809341264.

Lewis, H. F., & Sexton, T. R. (2004). Network DEA: Efficiency analysis of organizations with complex internal structure. *Computers & Operations Research, 31*(9), 1365–1410. doi: 10.1016/S0305–0548(03)00095–9.

Li, H., & Kannan, P. (2014). Attributing conversions in a multichannel online marketing environment: An empirical model and a field experiment. *Journal of Marketing Research, 51*(1), 40–56. http://dx.doi.org/10.1509/jmr.13.0050.

Li, H., & Lo, H. Y. (2015). Do you recognize its brand? The effectiveness of online in-stream video advertisements. *Journal of Advertising, 44*(3), 208–218. doi: 10.1080/00913367.2014.956376.

Orazi, D., Bove, L., & Lei, J. (2016). Empowering social change through advertising co-creation: The roles of source disclosure, sympathy and personal involvement. *International Journal of Advertising, 35*(1), 149–166. doi: 10.1080/02650487.2015.1096101.

Pergelova, A., Prior, D., & Rialp, J. (2010). Assessing advertising efficiency. *Journal of Advertising, 39*(3), 39–54. doi: 10.2753/JOA0091–3367390303.

Pires, G. D., Stanton, J., & Rita, P. (2006). The internet, consumer empowerment and marketing strategies. *European Journal of Marketing, 40*(9/10), 936–949. http://dx.doi.org/10.1108/03090560610680943.

Rodgers, S., & Thorson, E. (2000). The interactive advertising model: How users perceive and process online ads. *Journal of Interactive Advertising, 1*(1), 42–61. doi: 10.1080/15252019.2000.10722043.

Rutz, O. J., & Bucklin, R. E. (2011). From generic to branded: A model of spillover in paid search advertising. *Journal of Marketing Research, 48*(1), 87–102. http://dx.doi.org/10.1509/jmkr.48.1.87.

Rutz, O. J., Bucklin, R. E., & Sonnier, G. P. (2012). A latent instrumental variables approach to modeling keyword conversion in paid search advertising. *Journal of Marketing Research, 49*(3), 306–319. http://dx.doi.org/10.1509/jmr.10.0354.

Schulze, C., Schöler, L., & Skiera, B. (2014). Not all fun and games: Viral marketing for utilitarian products. *Journal of Marketing, 78*(1), 1–19. http://dx.doi.org/10.1509/jm.11.0528.

Schumann, J. H., von Wangenheim, F., & Groene, N. (2014). Targeted online advertising: Using reciprocity appeals to increase acceptance among users of free web services. *Journal of Marketing, 78*(1), 59–75. http://dx.doi.org/10.1509/jm.11.0316.

Sexton, T. R., & Lewis, H. F. (2003). Two-stage DEA: An application to major league baseball. *Journal of Productivity Analysis, 19*(2–3), 227–249. doi: 10.1023/A:1022861618317.

Stephen, A. T., & Galak, J. (2012). The effects of traditional and social earned media on sales: A study of a microlending marketplace. *Journal of Marketing Research, 49*(5), 624–639. http://dx.doi.org/10.1509/jmr.09.0401.

Stewart, D., & Pavlou, P. (2002). From consumer response to active consumer: Measuring the effectiveness of interactive media. *Journal of the Academy of Marketing Science, 30*(4), 376–396. doi: 10.1177/009207002236912.

Tucker, C. E. (2014). Social networks, personalized advertising, and privacy controls. *Journal of Marketing Research, 51*(5), 546–562. http://dx.doi.org/10.1509/jmr.10.0355.

Turow, J., King, J., Hoofnagle, C. J., Bleakley, A., & Hennessy, M. (2009). Americans reject tailored advertising and three activities that enable it. Retrieved from http://repository.upenn.edu/cgi/viewcontent.cgi?article=1138&context=asc_papers.

Van Noort, G., Antheunis, M. L., & Verlegh, P. W. (2014). Enhancing the effects of social network site marketing campaigns: If you want consumers to like you, ask them about themselves. *International Journal of Advertising, 33*(2), 235–252. doi: 10.2501/IJA-33–2-235-252.

Yadav, M., & Varadarajan, R. (2005). Interactivity in the electronic marketplace: An exposition of the concept and implications for research. *Journal of the Academy of Marketing Science, 33*(4), 585–603. doi: 10.1177/0092070305278487.

Yoo, C. Y. (2014). Branding potentials of keyword search ads: The effects of ad rankings on brand recognition and evaluations. *Journal of Advertising, 43*(1), 85–99. doi: 10.1080/00913367.2013.845541.

23

HEALTH ADVERTISING IN THE DIGITAL AGE

Future Trends and Challenges

Tim K. Mackey and Bryan A. Liang

Introduction

Over the past 15 years, use of information and communication technologies has grown exponentially. This includes a rapid increase in global internet users, who made up a mere 6.5 percent of the world's population in 2000, but in 2015 represent an unprecedented 43 percent of the entire global populace (ITU, 2015). This nearly seven-fold increase equates to some *3.2 billion* people now online, according to the International Telecommunication Union, a United Nations' specialized agency (ITU, 2015). All these individuals are potential consumers in a growing and diverse globalized digital marketplace. Accompanying this growth, opportunities and challenges to harness the immense promise of digital advertising have proliferated, especially as information communication technologies have evolved from Web 1.0 (static websites and "readable" content) to Web 2.0 (interaction between web users and websites and "writable" content) to Web 3.0 (a.k.a., "the intelligent Web" emphasizing machine-facilitated understanding of information) and now to a ubiquitous presence of the mobile web (i.e., internet connected mobile devices).

Within this rapid rise of "all things digital," pharmaceutical and health marketing has emerged as a key industry segment in digital media. This growth is driven by a simple fact: More internet users means more people searching for, interacting with, and consuming health information online. In fact, according to the Pew Research Center's Pew Internet Project, 72 percent of U.S. adult internet users have searched for health information online within the past year. The most common searches sought information about specific diseases or conditions, explored available treatments and/or procedures, and queried for information about healthcare professionals (Pew Internet, 2014).

For example, many internet users turn to "Dr. Google" in order to look up health information for others (including caregivers who commonly use technology to aid with decisions regarding a wide-range of health activities), use internet-obtained information to try to self-diagnose a medical condition, or attempt to learn about the experiences of other users as a potential guide for their own health concerns (a.k.a., peer-to-peer healthcare). Additionally, about one-quarter of internet users watch online videos about health or medical issues and have consulted online reviews to gauge opinions about drugs or medical treatments (Fox, 2011). Finally, another emerging trend is the phenomenon of tracking health indicators using mobile devices or other online tools, with surveys estimating that seven out of 10 people track at least one health indicator such as weight, exercise, blood pressure, or sleeping habits (Pew Internet, 2014).

Importantly, this growth in digital health offerings has required healthcare professionals, hospitals, and marketers to develop tools, strategies, and campaigns targeted toward a new and growing segment of "e-patients," i.e., those health consumers using e-communication tools to source information about medical issues impacting themselves or their families. This market has been estimated at some $1.8 billion in U.S. measured media according to a global marketing research firm (Rodriguez, 2014).

However, health is uniquely situated compared to other forms of commercial and consumer-based advertising. Thus, digital health marketing can have broad societal implications that go far beyond consumer product and service promotion, since it directly impacts the health of individuals, communities, and populations. Because of this heightened importance and its potential to both positively *and* negatively impact health and wellness, the evolution of digital health marketing has been marked (and marred) by unique challenges.

To understand these challenges and the opportunities they present to better promote health, the broader network of marketers and message movements occurring across digital platforms must be assessed. This includes the complex process, touched on in Chapter 2, of "promotional radiating," except in health marketing, this process includes changing existing dynamics between consumers, patients, healthcare professionals, institutional providers, pharmaceutical manufacturers, and health marketers themselves.

Hence, in this chapter we provide a review of e-marketing in health. We begin with a brief history of health and pharmaceutical marketing, a longstanding focus of global policymakers regarding the potential dangers of health marketing, and how challenges faced more than a century ago continue to reverberate in today's continuously shifting digital media landscape. We then discuss some of the unique attributes of health and pharmaceutical marketing (including examining the current debate over direct-to-consumer (DTC) advertising of prescription drugs), explore the evolving role of social networking in health promotion and services, and discuss the quality and policy implications of having a lack of reliable data on health marketing expenditures. We also explore emerging trends, strategies, and future challenges for digital health marketing that loom on the horizon, including an examination of patient engagement portals, prescription drug coupons, health internet domains, and the criminalization of illicit online health marketing. Finally, we conclude with a discussion of how rapid changes in the media landscape that are being fueled by digital technologies and media are also changing the dynamics between patients, healthcare providers, and drug manufacturers, and what this could mean for the future of health marketing.

Pulp to Digital: A Brief History of the Evolution of Health and Pharmaceutical Marketing

Health marketing is in no way a recent phenomenon. In fact, the history of health, and more specifically, pharmaceutical marketing, begins prior to the advent of the modern concept of prescription drugs. Early pharmaceutical marketing traces its origins back to the early 19th century when "Nostrum-mongers" (i.e., dealers or suppliers of quack remedies) pioneered questionable marketing practices for their "health products" through the use of traditional media formats including print advertising, packaging, trademarks thereon, and even traveling medical shows (Applbaum, 2006, p. e189). This early and unregulated form of consumer health marketing came at the direct expense of patients and can be viewed as an extension of fraudulent medical "quackery" practices that sprung up in the 17th and 18th century (Rodgers, 1927, p. 1502). Promotion and sale of nonprescription "nostrums," "patent medicines," "elixirs," or "cures" were simply sales of amalgamated materials with no proof of efficacy, often containing dangerous ingredients (including cocaine and heroin, intentionally added, and antifreeze, unintentionally added). Such marketing exposed the public to harmful health effects, drug addiction, and death (Till, 2009).

It was not until the 1906 Pure Food and Drug Act by the U.S. Congress that policymakers recognized the health concerns with unfettered marketing. The Act mandated labeling of drug ingredients and monitoring of purity levels while also paving the way for the creation of the U.S. Food and Drug Administration (FDA) to enforce these rules. This eventually led to the landmark U.S. Food, Drug, and Cosmetic Act of 1938 (FDCA), which imbued the FDA with its current regulatory authority to approve and oversee the safety of new drugs and medical devices. Although earlier suspect marketing was a consideration, the legislative response was heavily influenced by the tragic deaths in 1937 of greater than one hundred patients due to poisoning from adulterated sulfanilamide elixir (a crude antibacterial) (Mackey & Liang, 2012). This policy set the ground for decades of rapid growth in new prescription drug approvals and products introduced to the U.S. market. It also resulted in a concomitant shift in pharmaceutical marketing practices away from patient-directed promotion to a physician focus, since they now acted as gatekeepers for both sale and use of prescription drugs (Wazana, 2000).

As a result, physician-directed pharmaceutical marketing skyrocketed, hitting its peak in the mid-2000s, when drug company marketing expenditures experienced more than triple digit growth of $11.4 billion in 1996 to $29.9 billion in 2005

(Mackey & Liang, 2013c). This growth was accompanied by a nearly 600 percent increase in U.S. prescription drug spending during a broader overlapping period: $40.3 billion in 1990 to $234.1 billion in 2008 (Mackey, Cuomo, & Liang, 2015).

Drug marketing aimed at physicians manifested itself through various promotional strategies, including the deployment of many thousands of pharmaceutical sales representatives who engaged in "detailing" the virtues of their particular prescription drug products one-on-one with physicians. It also included financial inducements to physicians in the form of gifts, direct monetary payment (e.g., consulting arrangements, speaking fees, and excessive honorariums), compensation for continuing medical education, free meals (for physician and staff), travel expense reimbursement, and other forms of financial conflicts of interest (Mackey et al., 2015). The objective was simple: influence a physician to prescribe a company's drug and, thus, generate sales and profits.

However, in the late 2000s, record-breaking billion-dollar civil and criminal penalties were levied against some of the largest multinational pharmaceutical firms for illegal drug marketing practices. This also led to increased public scrutiny over physician-directed promotion and the conflicts of interest these activities generated (Liang & Mackey, 2010). From a policy perspective, physician-directed promotion was criticized as leading to more expensive drug prices and unnecessary healthcare spending. Indeed, aggressive marketing can lead to inappropriate drug claims, uses, prescribing behavior, minimization of risks, shift to more expensive drugs, and lower utilization of generic prescription drugs (Wazana, 2000; Brennan et al., 2006; Mackey & Liang, 2013c). Recognizing that physician-directed health marketing could lead to suboptimal outcomes in patient care and contribute to increasing health expenditures, several states, and the (then) Federal government passed "sunshine laws" in an attempt to increase transparency to industry-physician relationships and ultimately curb this practice (see below).

As a result of this increased attention and policymaking, health marketing is undergoing a pendulum swing. A shift in focus is moving away from physicians and back to consumers, as in the days of the nostrums, occurring through the medium of direct-to-consumer advertising (DTCA) (Mackey & Liang, 2013c). Specifically, DTCA provides an opportunity for manufacturers and marketers to influence their consumer audiences directly (instead of marketing to a physician intermediary in hopes that he/she will prescribe the drug to the patient).

Most recently, pharmaceutical sector recognition of the changing marketing landscape in health has resulted in their entry into new media forms. Consequently, it also provides fertile ground for exploring the advantages and technologies for health product promotion afforded by the new digital age of advertising.

Digital DTCA: Controversy, Trends, and a Case Study of Marketing Globalization

DTCA (direct to consumer advertising), loosely translated, is direct marketing and promotion of products and services straight to a patient/consumer. It may seem like an obvious approach in mainstream promotion and advertising strategies. However, in the healthcare industry, DTCA of pharmaceutical drugs and other prescription healthcare products is a highly scrutinized and altogether unique phenomenon. In fact, of developed country markets, only two countries, the United States (the largest global spender on prescription drugs) and New Zealand legally permit prescription drug advertisements targeted toward the consumer (Liang & Mackey, 2011a).

There is a clear clinical and public policy rationale for what is nearly a world-wide ban on prescription drug DTCA. Fundamentally, pharmaceuticals are not like other consumer products, as they are not available for direct purchase by consumers and require professional, licensed consultation before being dispensed using a valid prescription. This arguably renders DTCA incompatible with highly regulated healthcare systems focused on quality and patient safety, as prescribing healthcare professionals, not patients, are the individuals tasked with deciding if a prescription drug should be used.

Because of fundamental conflicts underlying DTCA in healthcare delivery, there has been much debate about the pros and cons of DTCA in the United States as well as other countries that have sought to legalize it. Though proponents may claim DTCA acts as a vehicle to educate consumers about treatment options, more recently, the vast majority of public health and medical professionals argue DTCA not only creates concerns about accurate portrayal of drug risks and inappropriate prescribing, but it also presents higher risk today since newer approved drugs that are often aggressively advertised using DTCA have been found to be unsafe. For example, the heavily DTCA advertised "blockbuster" painkiller Vioxx was ultimately banned from most global markets (Wolfe, 2002; Donohue, Cevasco, & Rosenthal, 2007; Frosch, Grande, Tarn, & Kravitz, 2010).

Despite ongoing debates and the fact that consumers cannot directly purchase prescription drugs like other consumer products, the DTCA business is booming. It has experienced significant increases in its share of promotional expenditures since the first U.S. print DTCA in 1981 (Palumbo & Mullins, 2002). In fact, since the FDA began liberalizing the practice of DTCA by issuing permissive guidance in the late 1990s, growth in DTCA expenditures have far outpaced that of other forms of pharmaceutical marketing, though it continues to represent a smaller share of the overall total pharmaceutical promotional spending (Kornfield, Donohue, Berndt, & Alexander, 2013). Importantly, growth of DTCA has been estimated at a whopping 330 percent increase between 1996 and 2009, equating to an estimated $4.3 billion in expenditures in 2009, primarily used on traditional advertising mediums of television, print, and radio (Liang & Mackey, 2011b).

However, the rise in DTCA as an influential form of health marketing is also experiencing its own evolution, specifically in conjunction with the growth and proliferation of digital technologies and online channels to more broadly disseminate DTCA. In fact, a recent study reviewing publicly available data from several marketing firms found that internet-based DTCA ("eDTCA") increased expenditure by 109 percent from 2005 to 2009 (Mackey et al., 2015). The study also found that other sub-categories of DTCA (including TV, radio, outdoor ads, and print) either experienced declines or single digit growth over the same period (see Figure 23.1) (Mackey et al., 2015).

This eDTCA growth should come as no surprise. The rapid increase of health-information seekers online and the ability of digital health advertising to more broadly disseminate campaigns, messages, and paid advertisements across a full spectrum of online platforms (including websites, social media platforms and social sharing sites, mobile apps/devices, etc.) propagates message movement much more efficiently than traditional media. Hence, opportunities afforded by eDTCA have clear advantages over traditional DTCA message distribution and can also be more cost effective (Liang & Mackey, 2011c).

Indeed, the opportunity to actively engage directly with consumers and invest in eDTCA content was recognized early by pharmaceutical manufacturers, their consultants, and their marketing agencies. For example, a study conducted in 2011 that examined the top 10 highest grossing pharmaceuticals found that 90 percent had dedicated website product pages that advertised the drug online (Liang & Mackey, 2011c). However, by migrating DTCA from traditional media that is, for the most part, geographically limited in placement to digital advertising distribution channels, DTCA through eDTCA is effectively globalized to areas outside

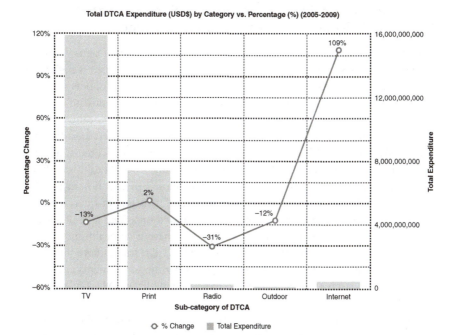

FIGURE 23.1 Total DTCA Expenditures (2005–2009)

the United States. This is important given, again, that DTCA is only legally permitted in the United States and New Zealand, but prohibited elsewhere. Yet digital advertising now allows unfettered transmission of this health marketing content across country borders (Liang & Mackey, 2011a). In this sense, the rise of eDTCA has not only vastly increased available marketing channels and venues for manufacturers to tap into, but has also allowed them to catalyze on a strategy of promotional radiation across different networks of internet users while also expanding the footprint of DTCA outside of the U.S. market.

Finally, from a policy perspective, unlike other countries that have historically banned the practice, DTCA as an advertising medium for prescription drug sales in the United States is likely here to stay. This is due to the fact that U.S. courts have granted significant protections for commercial free speech, of which DTCA qualifies (Liang & Mackey, 2011b). Though professional medical associations, such as the influential American Medical Association, as well as others, have called for a ban on DTCA, these efforts are likely to fail due to current U.S. constitutional jurisprudence (Stange, 2007; "AMA Calls for Ban on Direct to Consumer Advertising of Prescription Drugs and Medical Devices," 2015). Hence, DTCA and more importantly, its rising sub-category of eDTCA, are likely to experience continued growth and investment, and are poised to have a profound impact on the modern landscape of digital advertising.

Social Health? Challenges and Opportunities Associated with Social Media and Pharmaceutical Marketing

Social networking sites (such as the popular platforms Facebook, Twitter, Google+, YouTube, Pinterest, Instagram, LinkedIn, and Tumblr) have emerged as both innovative and disruptive forces that now—as Chapter 2 notes—profoundly influence the way individual users create, share, interact, and process health information. Reflecting the growing importance of social media platforms on health behavior, surveys have found that 23 percent of social networking site users have followed a friends' personal health updates or posts, 17 percent have used a social network site to remember or memorialize a person's suffering from a health condition, 14 percent have used a social network site to raise money or attention to a health-related cause, 11 percent have posted comments, information, or queries regarding health or medical matters, 9 percent have started or joined a health-related group on a social media platform, and 15 percent have used health information directly from a social networking site (Fox, 2011). Other studies have found that terminally-ill patients and their families aggressively use social media and online petitions in an attempt to gain access to experimental drugs (Mackey & Schoenfeld, 2016).

Within the realm of digital health marketing, the environment of health information seekers provides significant and, often, unique opportunities to engage in a more direct relationship with consumers via social media. Although of great potential, this arena is a matter of ongoing consternation for pharmaceutical manufacturers. Apprehension is largely due to the fact that the FDA has struggled with developing meaningful industry guidance on acceptable pharmaceutical manufacturer marketing activities engaging consumers on social networking sites (SNSs) (Mackey, 2016).

Complexities and uncertainties abound, including concerns regarding how to ensure privacy of medical and health-related information generated/discussed on SNSs, appropriately correcting misinformation about drug safety issues (such as an adverse drug reaction) contained in user-generated content (UGC), dealing with user questions about unapproved drug uses (i.e., off-label drug use information), and ensuring promotion appropriately balances the benefits and risks of a drug (Mackey, 2016). These substantive issues go beyond infrastructural limitations (such as Twitter, with its 140 character message limit). These challenges are further complicated by the fact that social media technologies are in constant flux. New forms of interaction, modes of sharing information and media, and formal commercial channels available for sponsored advertising within these sites are in a process of continuous development and change.

Despite these uncertainties, pharmaceutical manufacturers have not waited for uncertain FDA guidance, given that potential customers now spend so much of their time on health issues and SNSs. A 2011 study found that 40 percent of the top 10 global pharmaceutical corporations had dedicated social media corporate websites (that centralized all corporate social media accounts and assets), 100 percent had a corporate Facebook page, 100 percent had a sponsored blog/RSS feed, 80 percent had a YouTube channel, and 80 percent had developed at least one healthcare-related mobile application (Liang & Mackey, 2011c). Similarly, when examining the social media presence of the top 10 grossing pharmaceutical drugs in 2009, 70 percent were detected as having product-specific Facebook pages and 80 percent had a DTCA TV broadcast advertisement uploaded for global viewing on YouTube (Liang & Mackey, 2011c). The main findings of this early study indicated that pharmaceutical firms were actively creating and using social media as a strategic part of their online marketing campaigns/presence (Liang & Mackey, 2011c).

An update and expansion to this study published in 2015 found increasing trends of pharmaceutical industry engagement on SNSs (Tyrawski & DeAndrea, 2015). The study looked at two distinct social media content types: company-specific content (measured by examining the social media accounts and content of the top 15 global pharmaceutical firms) and drug-specific content (measured by examining social media content by searching for the top 20 drugs from 2013 on popular social media sites) (Tyrawski & DeAndrea, 2015). Unsurprisingly, it reported pharmaceutical companies were active on SNSs, with 93 percent operating a Twitter account, 66 percent using a Facebook page, 66 percent maintaining a YouTube Channel, 60 percent on LinkedIn, and lower levels of engagement (less than 26 percent) on platforms such as Pinterest, Instagram, Flickr, and Google+.

It also found that consumers were active in engaging with pharmaceutical social media content, with close to one-quarter (24 percent) of users commenting on posts generated by the industry (Tyrawski & DeAndrea, 2015). When examining company-specific content, "help-seeking" DTCA advertisements (i.e., reminders to consumers to seek treatment by mentioning a particular disease but not a specific treatment) were far more common than product-specific claims (i.e., explicitly mentioning a drug by name). The authors concluded that this clearly indicated continued drug company trepidation about directly engaging in DTCA product promotion via social media (Lurie, 2009; Tyrawski & DeAndrea, 2015).

On the other hand, when examining drug-specific social media content, researchers found quite a different trend, with 69 percent of the Facebook posts, tweets, and YouTube videos reviewed, including DTCA with drug product claims (Tyrawski & DeAndrea, 2015). Mirroring previous concerns about the balance of information presentation in DTCA, eDTCA posts only mentioning benefits of a drug were far more common than posts discussing benefits and risks or posts mentioning only risk information (Tyrawski & DeAndrea, 2015). Interestingly, while the main posts reviewed often highlighted the benefits of a drug promoted DTCA, comments in user-generated responses to these posts often did not follow the same pattern, with these comments often offering contrasting views or opinions (Tyrawski & DeAndrea, 2015).

Importantly, the process of promotional radiating was evident, as a combination of individuals and non-pharmaceutical organizations comprised more than 99 percent of all drug-specific posts (only 0.6 percent of content was controlled by accounts of pharmaceutical companies.) This indicates that social media-based DTCA is often subject to large and complex message movements across different user networks, and that message functionalities can often diverge from those intended by message creators (i.e., pharmaceutical companies).

Overall, there are only a handful of studies that have used empirical methods to examine the use of DTCA, eDTCA, and engagement processes by pharmaceutical firms on social networking sites. Initial findings indicate that much remains unknown about digital practices for marketing prescription drugs. The lack of transparency is unsurprising, given the paucity of information on how much the industry spends on pharmaceutical promotion. Guidance on this area would provide policymakers with a potential roadmap for assessment in designing recommendations and best practices.

Health Marketing Expenditures: The Who, What, and Where

Globally, it is estimated that worldwide spending on pharmaceuticals will grow by double digits, reaching $1.4 trillion by 2020 (IMS, 2015a). Though much of this future growth will come from *pharmemerging* markets including India, China, and Brazil, the United States nevertheless continues to be the top worldwide spender on prescription drugs (IMS, 2015b). National prescription drug spending is driven by an astounding $3 trillion (equivalent to $9,523 per person) in U.S. healthcare spending in 2014 (the highest of any country), which also equates to an estimated $374 billion spent on prescription drugs in the same year (Mackey, 2016). Yet, despite the billions of dollars spent on healthcare in the United States, precise estimates on exact amounts, characterization, and distribution of health and pharmaceutical marketing activities that drive much of this demand have been elusive.

Gagnon and Lexchin (2008) attempted to tease out how much is spent on drug marketing using data available from market research companies CAM and IMS to estimate pharmaceutical promotion expenditures in 2004. This study found major variations in reported aggregate amounts spent, methods of calculating costs, and gaps in overall reporting (Gagnon & Lexchin, 2008). A more recent study published in 2013 used a similar approach, examining pharmaceutical promotion expenditures for DTCA, as reported by Kantar Media and IMS Health and SDI, for provider-targeted promotion for a much longer period from 2001 to 2010 (Kornfield et al., 2013). This study found that total pharmaceutical promotion hit an all-time high in 2004 at $36.1 billion, but experienced declines thereafter, with similar trends of increases and declines for DTCA expenditures. These general trends are also supported by results from a 2015 study that found a similar slight decline (-8%) in aggregate DTCA expenditures from 2005 to 2009, largely attributable to the global recession and its impact on corporate marketing budgets (Mackey et al., 2015).

Despite early uncertainty, a light is finally shinning on how much is spent on certain pharmaceutical promotion activities. Given widespread public scrutiny over financial conflicts of interest arising from industry-provider relationships, in 2010, legislative provisions in the Patient Protection and Affordable Care Act, for the first time, legally mandated the public disclosure of certain forms of financial relationships and payments made by industry to physicians (Mackey & Liang, 2013c).

The Centers of Medicare and Medicaid Services implemented these provisions through its online Open Payments program, which now houses data on physician-directed promotion activities for half of 2013 and all of 2014, comprising a total of 15.67 million records and payments valued at some $9.92 billion (see https://openpaymentsdata.cms.gov). Hence, this public disclosure provision will allow for a more accurate estimation of total pharmaceutical promotion and enable the identification of macro and micro trends of the "who" (identification of variation in medical specialties receiving payments), "where" (temporal data and geographic locations of spending), and "what" (frequency, amounts, and the types of payments), as has already begun to be analyzed (Jarvies, Coombes, & Stahl-Timmins, 2014; Marshall, Jackson, & Hattangadi-Gluth, "Disclosure of Industry Payments to Physicians," 2016).

However, several pieces of information are missing that would help to provide a more complete picture of total health and pharmaceutical marketing spending. Specifically, the Open Payments program does not collect information about certain types of physician-directed promotion (e.g., free drug samples, amounts under $10 and that do not exceed $100 in the aggregate, certain educational materials, rebates, and some forms of indirect payments) and also does not include reporting of marketing expenditures directed toward non-physicians (i.e., other healthcare professionals such as nurses, physician assistants, pharmacy benefit managers, and healthcare payers) or consumers (Mackey & Liang, 2015). Critically, this means that DTCA expenditures are *not* included in this mandatory reporting, despite the fact that increased transparency on physician-industry relationships is leading to a shift in marketing strategies that now focus on the consumer-patient (i.e., DTCA). Even more uncertainty surrounds estimating amounts spent on eDTCA, as data collection and sampling methodologies to monitor digital advertising used by marketing research firms appears to vary widely.

Critically, without accurate data on pharmaceutical promotion both offline and online, it is impossible to accurately identify important trends occurring in health marketing and assess its potential impact on healthcare utilization, quality, outcomes, and cost. As the media landscape continues to move to digital technologies, getting better data and conducting "real-time" analysis of online marketing that is now widespread on social media and other online platforms will be crucial for marketers, their clients, public health professionals, and policymakers alike.

Future Trends and Challenges

In this final section, we identify several future trends and emerging challenges that have accompanied the rise in digital health marketing. Specifically, we discuss the use of online prescription drug coupons, the recent approval by the Internet Corporation for Assigned Names and Numbers (ICANN) of new generic top-level health domains, and the understudied phenomenon of commercial online patient engagement portals. We also discuss the dark side of digital health advertising, examining how the internet has enabled the criminalization of health marketing by illicit online pharmacies and other suspect online providers. All of these trends and challenges demand greater attention, scrutiny, and sufficient research to determine their place in the future of digital advertising for health.

Prescription Drug Coupons: Getting Twice the Value for DTCA?

One unique form of pharmaceutical marketing that has taken advantage of digital technologies is the prescription drug coupon (PDC). A PDC (also known as a prescription drug discount card) is exactly what it sounds like, a coupon or discount that markets cost-savings and rebates that reduce the out-of-pocket expenses or insurance co-payment consumers must pay when they are prescribed a branded (i.e., non-generic) prescription drug (Grande, 2012).

PDCs are an innovative extension of DTCA. PDCs serve the dual purpose of providing short-term savings to the customer *and* as an attractive medium to directly promote the use and benefits of a drug. Importantly, this dual use allows PDCs to generate brand awareness, create more favorable attitudes toward PDC drugs, and establish customer loyalty, especially for top-selling branded drugs that are on the verge of losing patent protection and market exclusivity (Bhutada, Cook, & Perri, 2009; Mackey, Yagi, & Liang, 2014b).

For example, Pfizer Inc.'s PDC program for its blockbuster cholesterol-lowering drug Lipitor, first launched in December 2010, which was a direct response to impending patent expiration and generic competition. Lipitor's PDC advertised a "$4 co-pay" that would cover the cost of a co-pay up to a maximum amount of $100 per month, leaving the consumer responsible for a remaining amount of only $4 (exact amount owed by the consumer is dependent upon the exact co-pay share). As a reflection of this market opportunity, the number of PDC drug programs grew more than four-fold from 86 in 2009 to 362 in 2012, and a study conducted in 2012 found that 9 out of 10 of the top selling pharmaceuticals in 2010 operated a PDC program (Mackey, Yagi, & Liang, 2014b).

PDCs are also available in several marketing mediums, including traditional forms of physical collateral (e.g., printed coupons, pamphlets, marketing inserts) that are left at physicians' offices to be picked up by patients (Mackey, Yagi, & Liang, 2014b). However, PDCs have also made the leap to digital advertising, with manufacturer and third-party websites that enable consumers to sign up for discounts using virtual discount cards and eCoupons. Advertising of PDC programs is similarly disseminated across common eDTCA marketing channels including Facebook promotional pages, YouTube videos, Tweets hyperlinking to PDCs, and even the use of mobile phone applications that allow users to search for and download coupons from the palm of their hand (Mackey, Yagi, & Liang, 2014b).

Though coupons may seem innocuous in other consumer and retail product industries, in healthcare, they are extremely controversial. Most importantly, PDCs distort the actual cost of prescription drugs, as insurance companies, *not* their customers, end up paying a higher bill for more expensive drugs. This can ultimately lead to higher long-term healthcare expenditures due to overutilization and consumers favoring branded version over generic equivalents. Estimates vary, but trade associations like the Pharmaceutical Care Management Association have estimated that PDC programs could lead to an estimated $32 billion in additional costs for commercially insured patients over the span of a decade (Mackey, Yagi, & Liang, 2014b). Concerns also arise from risks that consumers will not fully redeem coupons, that savings may be less than advertised (each PDC has different terms and conditions, and savings are dependent upon insurance status), and concerns surrounding patient care when a PDC ends (Mackey, Yagi, & Liang, 2014b). Due to these factors, the debate on PDCs is likely to continue, pitting temporary consumer savings against larger concerns over the rise in overall healthcare costs.

New Health Domains: The Future of Internet-Based Health Promotion?

Though only now becoming more widely known to the general public, a host of new generic top-level domain names (gTLDs) are starting to appear on the internet. gTLDs are part of a new program launched by ICANN, a non-governmental organization that controls naming of the internet to vastly expand the footprint of the web by introducing nearly a thousand new top-level domain names (i.e., names in the root zone, or simply put, everything after the final "dot" in a web address). Commonly recognized existing top-level domains include .com, .org, and .edu, which prior to ICANN's new gTLD program, were limited to 21 top-level domains that distinguished different name spaces on the World Wide Web. All this is set to change, with the ongoing approval of 948 new gTLDs, comprised of virtually any name, including in different languages, corporate brands: ".microsoft"; .communities: ".irish"; locations: ".london"; and other terms: ".store" and ".sexy." All are now in the process of being introduced to the internet hierarchy. Importantly, successful applicants/registrars are then given the *exclusive* rights to sell second-level domain names (i.e., everything before the top-level domain: "www.[name].com") to virtually anyone who wants to buy one.

Within this wave of new gTLDs are also several for health-related terms (including ".health," ".healthcare," ".doctor," ".hospital," and ".diet"—to name a few) that have been applied for and awarded to various for-profit companies. This exclusivity could very well shape the future of how health information is organized, presented, and viewed online, and possibly in a negative way (Mackey et al., 2014a).

These new health-related gTLDs, rather than serving as a signal of trustworthy and reliable health information, will create dedicated industry-specific spaces on the internet for health topics that will be largely unchecked for quality of content. Consequently, if previous activities are any guidance, their potential to create a much needed safe, evidence-based, and credible source of health information online is in serious question (Mackey, Liang, Attaran, & Kohler, 2013).

Indeed, concerned parties, such as the World Health Organization (WHO), national governments, medical professional societies, and non-governmental organizations have expressed grave concerns that without appropriate safeguards, these gTLDs will instead be populated by poor quality, inaccurate, misleading, and unreliable information that could adversely impact people's health (Mackey et al., 2014a). These concerns remain unanswered and poorly addressed as several health gTLDs are set to become active and available to the public for domain name purchase and registration. For policy purposes, this area of digital expansion requires close scrutiny, as websites using sensitive gTLDs such as ".health" should be subject to appropriate oversight systems in order to ensure that consumers can rely upon these domains for accurate and reliable health information.

Patient Portals: Creating Marketing Opportunities in a Controlled Environment

Patient portals operated by pharmaceutical manufacturers, medical device companies, and other healthcare service providers are a relatively new and understudied phenomenon. They use internet technology for raising disease awareness and support healthcare decision-making, but also to market health products. In the context of digital advertising, corporate patient engagement portals used by pharmaceutical and medical device companies can come in the form of branded and unbranded websites, with some operated under the exclusive control of a pharmaceutical firm and others by third-party marketing intermediaries (who may not disclose their funding sources). These patient-directed portals create structured online environments where manufacturers can provide a plethora of services. For example, they may raise consumer awareness regarding diseases/conditions of interest (similar to reminder advertisements used in DTCA), offer advice about seeking diagnosis and treatment (including DTCA about their own products), offer tools for disease management, offer online patient coaches/advocates, while also acting as online platforms to directly market to a desired, indeed, self-selected consumer segment (Collier, 2014).

Consumers join these portals by registering directly on the website or via email registration. In turn, users receive the benefits and services (often at no cost) described above, but also often opt in to allowing direct marketing regarding a company's updates, news, products, and promotions. Most importantly, consumer registration data provides a wealth of information on consumer segmentation that is extremely valuable and can be mined for future marketing research purposes (Mackey, 2016). Little is known about the makeup or key characteristics of commercial patient engagement portals from a research perspective, though use of these portals as an additional strategy in health and pharmaceutical marketing appears to be growing. The potentially hidden nature of sponsorship and possible insidious nature of advertising on these purported patient-oriented sites requires significant oversight to ensure exploitation of vulnerable patients and caregivers is not promoted by this digital health approach.

Digital Dangers: Criminalization of the Health Marketing

Though digital advertising tools carry the promise of new, innovative ways to interact and provide consumers with valuable health information, these same technologies introduce vulnerabilities that can be exploited by criminal actors (WHO, 2011). As a loose connection of networks, the internet is poorly regulated, and its technology is agnostic to "good" and "bad" actors. Hence, those engaged in the promotion and sale of questionable health products and services have equal if not greater flexibility in engaging in illegal activities. A clear example that personifies this risk is the illicit online pharmacy, defined as a website that fails to meet national or international pharmacy regulations, that often sell prescription drugs that are of dubious quality, authenticity, and safety (Tu & Corey, 2008). Indeed, more bluntly, these are eDrugDealers.

Tens of thousands of these illicit online pharmacies now thrive in an e-commerce environment that is convenient, easily accessible, anonymous, and that can leverage digital advertising channels to promote fraudulent and misleading health claims (Henney, 2001; Orizio, Merla, Schulz, & Gelatti, 2011). A telltale sign of an illicit online pharmacy is the marketing of their services as "no prescription," with these sites advertising the sale of prescription drugs direct to the consumer but never requiring a valid prescription during the checkout process (Orizio et al., 2011; Mackey & Liang, 2013b).

Risks abound from these websites. They sell anything from lifestyle drugs (e.g., erectile dysfunction treatments) to life-saving vaccines to drugs of abuse (e.g., prescription pain killers), all without the need to consult a healthcare professional. Importantly, these sites undermine the patient safety filter that a learned intermediary is designed to provide (Forman, 2003; Liang & Mackey, 2012). Unfortunately, these patient safety risks have been tragically demonstrated, with documented cases of consumers suffering adverse events and even death after purchasing prescription drugs illegally online (Liang & Mackey, 2009).

From a digital advertising perspective, online pharmacies are savvy and sophisticated, often using argument-driven marketing combined with fraudulent claims to appeal to their customers. For example, illicit online pharmacies have been reported as using "selling arguments" (Orizio et al., 2010, p. 971) that enhance attractive characteristics of their products and services that are of value to consumers (e.g., lower prices, shorter delivery times, greater privacy from purchasing online, convenience), while at the same time deemphasizing clear signs of risk (Levaggi et al., 2009; Orizio et al., 2010).

Illicit online pharmacies are also experts at message movements across platforms, with studies detecting illegal "no prescription" online marketing using search engine marketing/optimization, social networking sites (SNSs), marketing affiliate networks, and other emerging digital mediums to target consumers directly where they seek health information and advice: on the internet (Liang & Mackey, 2011c; Mackey & Liang, 2013c; Tyrawski & DeAndrea, 2015). In fact, a study published in 2013 demonstrated how easy it was to create an illegal online pharmacy advertisement on popular social media platforms by creating a fictitious "no prescription" ad and link to a website that was used to monitor user traffic and location (see Figure 23.2) (Mackey & Liang, 2013a).

Hence, illicit online pharmacies represent the dark side of digital advertising, with cybercriminals exploiting the internet to reap profits at the expense of the health and safety of consumers. These quickly moving criminals will continue to exploit extant offerings in digital marketing, necessitating continued empirical study and policy assessment.

FIGURE 23.2 A Fictitious Illicit Online Pharmacy Ad Posted to Social Media Sites

Conclusions

The digital marketing landscape today is in many ways similar to the plethora of unregulated nostrum vendors the FDA, and its first Commissioner Dr. Harvey Wiley, faced in 1907. The challenge of the distinct and critical nature of the health products and services, the need for greater patient/consumer education and access to reliable health information, the large amounts of resources spent on the healthcare industry, and the inevitable criminal element, all create important considerations for the future of digital health advertising. Through the process of understanding where health marketing has been and the challenges it has faced, we can be guided on approaches needed to ensure that the current revolution in digital health offerings and technologies primarily benefit consumers by, first and foremost, promoting their health and wellness and broader societal health.

References

AMA calls for ban on direct to consumer advertising of prescription drugs and medical devices. (2015, November 17). *Ama-Assn.org*. Retrieved from http://www. ama-assn.org/ama/pub/news/news/2015/2015–11–17-ban-consumer-prescription-drug-advertising.page.

Applbaum, K. (2006). Pharmaceutical marketing and the invention of the medical consumer. *PLoS Medicine, 3*(4), e189. doi: 10.1371/journal.pmed.0030189.

Bhutada, N. S., Cook, C. L., & Perri, M., III. (2009). Consumers responses to coupons in direct-to-consumer advertising of prescription drugs. *Health Marketing Quarterly, 26*(4), 333–346. doi: 10.1080/07359680903315902.

Brennan, T. A., Rothman, D. J., Blank, L., Blumenthal, D., Chimonas, S. C., Cohen, J. J., Goldman, J., Kassirer, J. P., Kimball, H., Naughton, J., & Smelser, N. (2006). Health industry practices that create conflicts of interest: A policy proposal for academic medical centers. *Journal of the American Medical Association, 295*(4), 429–433. doi: 10.1001/jama.295.4.429.

Collier, R. (2014). Patient engagement or social media marketing? *Canadian Medical Association Journal, 186*(8), E237–E238. doi: 10.1503/cmaj.109–4739.

Donohue, J. M., Cevasco, M., & Rosenthal, M. B. (2007). A decade of direct-to-consumer advertising of prescription drugs. *The New England Journal of Medicine, 357*(7), 673–681. doi: 10.1056/NEJMsa070502.

Forman, R. F. (2003). Availability of opioids on the Internet. *Journal of the American Medical Association, 290*(7), 889. doi: 10.1001/jama.290.7.889.

Fox, S. (2011, May 11). The social life of health information. Retrieved from http://www. pewinternet.org/2011/05/12/the-social-life-of-health-information-2011/

Frosch, D. L., Grande, D., Tarn, D. M., & Kravitz, R. L. (2010). A decade of controversy: Balancing policy with evidence in the regulation of prescription drug advertising. *American Journal of Public Health, 100*(1), 24–32. doi: 10.2105/AJPH.2008.153767.

Gagnon, M.-A., & Lexchin, J. (2008). The cost of pushing pills: A new estimate of pharmaceutical promotion expenditures in the United States. *PLoS Medicine, 5*(1), e1.

Grande, D. (2012). The cost of drug coupons. *Journal of the American Medical Association, 307*(22), 2375–2376. doi: 10.1001/jama.2012.5603.

Henney, J. E. (2001). Cyberpharmacies and the role of the US Food and Drug Administration. *Journal of Medical Internet Research, 3*(1), e3. doi: 10.2196/jmir.3.1.e3.

IMS. (2015a). Global medicines use in 2020: Outlook and implications. Retrieved from http://www.imshealth.com/en/thought-leadership/ims-institute/reports/global-medicines-use-in-2020.

IMS. (2015b). Medicines use and spending shifts: A review of the use of medicines in the U.S. in 2014. Retrieved from http://www.imshealth.com/en/thought-leadership/ims-institute/reports/medicines-use-in-the-us-2014.

ITU. (2015, May 26). ITU releases 2015 ICT figures. Retrieved from https://www.itu.int/net/pressoffice/press_releases/2015/17.aspx.

Jarvies, D., Coombes, R., & Stahl-Timmins, W. (2014). Open payments goes live with pharma to doctor fee data: First analysis. *British Medical Journal, 349*, g6003–g6003. doi: 10.1136/bmj.g6003.

Kornfield, R., Donohue, J., Berndt, E. R., & Alexander, G. C. (2013). Promotion of prescription drugs to consumers and providers, 2001–2010. *PLoS ONE, 8*(3), e55504. doi: 10.1371/journal.pone.0055504.

Levaggi, R., Orizio, G., Domenighini, S., Bressanelli, M., Schulz, P. J., Zani, C., Cami, L., & Gelatti, U. (2009). Marketing and pricing strategies of online pharmacies. *Health Policy, 92*(2–3), 187–196. doi: 10.1016/j.healthpol.2009.03.010.

Liang, B. A., & Mackey, T. (2009). Searching for safety: Addressing search engine, website, and provider accountability for illicit online drug sales. *American Journal of Law & Medicine, 35*(1), 125–184. doi: 10.1177/009885880903500104.

Liang, B. A., & Mackey, T. (2010). Confronting conflict: Addressing institutional conflicts of interest in academic medical centers. *American Journal of Law & Medicine, 36*(1), 136–187. doi: 10.1177/009885881003600103.

Liang, B. A., & Mackey, T. (2011a). Direct-to-consumer advertising with interactive internet media: Global regulation and public health issues. *Journal of the American Medical Association, 305*(8), 824–825. doi: 10.1001/jama.2011.203.

Liang, B. A., & Mackey, T. (2011b). Reforming direct-to-consumer advertising. *Nature Biotechnology, 29*(5), 397–400. doi: 10.1038/nbt.1865.

Liang, B. A., & Mackey, T. K. (2011c). Prevalence and global health implications of social media in direct-to-consumer drug advertising. *Journal of Medical Internet Research, 13*(3), e64. doi: 10.2196/jmir.1775.

Liang, B. A., & Mackey, T. K. (2012). Vaccine shortages and suspect online pharmacy sellers. *Vaccine, 30*(2), 105–108. doi: 10.1016/j.vaccine.2011.11.016.

Lurie, P. (2009). DTC advertising harms patients and should be tightly regulated. *The Journal of Law, Medicine & Ethics, 37*(3), 444–450. doi: 10.1111/j.1748–720X.2009.00405.x.

Mackey, T. K. (2016). Digital direct-to-consumer advertising: A perfect storm of rapid evolution and stagnant regulation comment on "trouble spots in online direct-to-consumer prescription drug promotion: A content analysis of FDA warning letters." *International Journal of Health Policy and Management, 5*(4), 271–274. doi: 10.15171/ijhpm.2016.11.

Mackey, T. K., Cuomo, R. E., & Liang, B. A. (2015). The rise of digital direct-to-consumer advertising? Comparison of direct-to-consumer advertising expenditure trends from publicly available data sources and global policy implications. *BMC Health Services Research, 15*(1), 236. doi: 10.1186/s12913–015–0885–1.

Mackey, T. K., Eysenbach, G., Liang, B. A., Kohler, J. C., Geissbuhler, A., & Attaran, A. (2014a). A call for a moratorium on the health generic top-level domain: Preventing the commercialization and exclusive control of online health information. *Globalization and Health, 10*(1), 62. doi: 10.1186/s12992–014–0062-z.

Mackey, T. K., & Liang, B. (2012). Globalization, evolution and emergence of direct-to-consumer advertising: Are emerging markets the next pharmaceutical marketing frontier. *Journal of Commercial Biotechnology, 18*, 58–64. doi: 10. 5912/jcb.564.

Mackey, T. K., & Liang, B. A. (2013a). Global reach of direct-to-consumer advertising using social media for illicit online drug sales. *Journal of Medical Internet Research, 15*(5), e105. doi: 10.2196/jmir.2610.

Mackey, T. K., & Liang, B. A. (2013b). Pharmaceutical digital marketing and governance: Illicit actors and challenges to global patient safety and public health. *Globalization and Health, 9*(1), 45. doi: 10.1186/1744–8603–9–45.

Mackey, T. K., & Liang, B. A. (2013c). Physician payment disclosure under healthcare reform: Will the sun shine? *Journal of the American Board of Family Medicine, 26*(3), 327–331. doi: 10.3122/jabfm.2013.03.120264.

Mackey, T. K., & Liang, B. A. (2015). It's time to shine the light on direct-to-consumer advertising. *The Annals of Family Medicine, 13*(1), 82–85. doi: 10.1370/afm.1711.

Mackey, T. K., Liang, B. A., Attaran, A., & Kohler, J. C. (2013). Ensuring the future of health information online. *Lancet, 382*(9902), 1404. doi: 10.1016/S0140–6736(13)62215–1.

Mackey, T. K., & Schoenfeld, V. J. (2016). Going "social" to access experimental and potentially life-saving treatment: An assessment of the policy and online patient advocacy environment for expanded access. *BMC Medicine, 14*(1), 17. doi: 10.1186/s12916–016–0568–8.

Mackey, T. K., Yagi, N., & Liang, B. A. (2014b). Prescription drug coupons: Evolution and need for regulation in direct-to-consumer advertising. *Research in Social & Administrative Pharmacy, 10*(3), 588–594. doi: 10.1016/j.sapharm.2013.08.002.

Marshall, D. C., Jackson, M. E., & Hattangadi-Gluth, J. A., (2016). Disclosure of industry payments to physicians: An epidemiologic analysis of early data from the open payments program, *Mayo Clinic Proceedings, 91*(1), 84–96. doi: 10.1016/j.mayocp.2015.10.016.

Orizio, G., Merla, A., Schulz, P. J., & Gelatti, U. (2011). Quality of online pharmacies and websites selling prescription drugs: A systematic review. *Journal of Medical Internet Research, 13*(3), e74. doi: 10.2196/jmir.1795.

Orizio, G., Rubinelli, S., Schulz, P. J., Domenighini, S., Bressanelli, M., Caimi, L., & Gelatti, U. (2010). "Save 30% if you buy today." Online pharmacies and the enhancement of peripheral thinking in consumers. *Pharmacoepidemiology and Drug Safety, 19*(9), 970–976. doi: 10.1002/pds.2007.

Palumbo, F. B., & Mullins, C. D. (2002). The development of direct-to-consumer prescription drug advertising regulation. *Food and Drug Law Journal, 57*(3), 423–443.

PewInternet. (2014). Health fact sheet. Retrieved from http://www.pewinternet.org/fact-sheets/health-fact-sheet/

Rodgers, W. C. (1927). Nostrums and quackery. *Journal of the American Medical Association, 88*(19), 1502–1503. doi: 10.1001/jama.1927.02680450046032.

Rodriguez, A. (2014, September 16). Why digital marketing has become the health-care industry's Rx for revenue. *Adage.com*. Retrieved from http://adage.com/article/digital/digital-health-care-industry-s-rx-revenue/294940/

Stange, K. C. (2007). Time to ban direct-to-consumer prescription drug marketing. *The Annals of Family Medicine, 5*(2), 101–104. doi: 10.1370/afm.693.

Till, M. (2009). Secret remedies: What they cost and what they contain. *BMJ, 338*(3), b1624–b1624. doi: 10.1136/bmj.b1624.

Tu, H. T., & Corey, C. G. (2008). State prescription drug price web sites: How useful to consumers? *Research Brief*, 1, 1–16.

Tyrawski, J., & DeAndrea, D. C. (2015). Pharmaceutical companies and their drugs on social media: A content analysis of drug information on popular social media sites. *Journal of Medical Internet Research*, *17*(6), e130. doi: 10.2196/jmir.4357.

Wazana, A. (2000). Physicians and the pharmaceutical industry: Is a gift ever just a gift? *Journal of the American Medical Association*, *283*(3), 373–380. doi: 10.1001/jama.283.3.373.

WHO. (2011). Safety and security on the internet: Challenges and advances in member states. *Who*. Retrieved from http://www.who.int/goe/publications/goe_security_web.pdf.

Wolfe, S. M. (2002). Direct-to-consumer advertising—Education or emotion promotion? *New England Journal of Medicine*, *346*(7), 524–526.

PART VI

Future Research Trends and Opportunities

24

THE ROLE OF CULTURE IN ELECTRONIC WORD-OF-MOUTH COMMUNICATION

Shu-Chuan Chu

Introduction

With online technologies facilitating the exchange of product-related information, the internet is recognized as a global space that could reduce consumers' information search costs. This chapter builds on the theoretical premise of the book by examining how internet users pass along or share information, namely electronic word-of-mouth (eWOM) but does so from a cultural perspective.

According to Internet World Stats (2015), the number of global internet users reached more than 3.36 billion in 2015. Meanwhile, digital advertising spending worldwide is forecasted to reach $252.02 billion by 2018, more than double that of $104.58 billion in 2012 (Statista, 2016). Today, the internet allows ordinary people to easily create and disseminate content about brands and services, namely user-generated content (UGC) (Smith, Fischer, & Chen, 2012; Bahtara & Muda, 2016). Major social networking sites such as Facebook, YouTube, Twitter, and Instagram made a large portion of the profit with UGC (O'Neill, 2011). For example, revenues of Facebook from UGC reached $1.86 billion in 2010, and YouTube earned $945 million the same year (Statista, 2010). With the proliferation of UGC, eWOM has gained increased prominence among researchers and professionals (Lee & Youn, 2009; You, Vadakkepatt, & Joshi, 2015; Baker, Naveen, & Kumar, 2016).

Primarily through the internet, eWOM has been categorized as consumer-to-consumer interactions (Yadav & Pavlou, 2014) that play an important role in influencing consumer decision-making (Goodrich & de Mooij, 2014; You et al., 2015). Studies have found eWOM to be more trustworthy than corporate-driven information (Goldsmith & Horowitz, 2006; Lee & Youn, 2009), and companies are increasing their marketing budgets to generate and shape eWOM. With increased focus on eWOM by industry, eWOM has led to a growing research stream whereby researchers examine antecedents and consequences of eWOM (Phelps, Lewis, Mobilio, Perry, & Raman, 2004; You et al., 2015; Baker et al., 2016). Despite this, little is known about the cross-cultural differences in the effectiveness of eWOM and its international applicability (Chu & Choi, 2011; Goodrich & de Mooij, 2014).

Park and Jun (2003) demonstrated differences in internet usage and perceived risks of internet shopping between Korean and American consumers. Dobele, Lindgreen, Beverland, Vanhammed, and van Wijk (2007) argued that culture is a determining factor in influencing recipients' emotional responses to viral marketing campaigns and subsequent forwarding behavior. Given the influence of nationalities in the acceptance of viral marketing campaigns, cultural values and backgrounds need to be taken into account in this context (Dobele et al., 2007). It is likely that incongruities also exist in how people from various nationalities differ in terms of their engagement with eWOM. An interesting question arises: do different cultural values (such as individualism vs. collectivism) have varying effects on eWOM? It would be theoretically interesting to examine cross-cultural differences in the context of eWOM, as culture has been identified as a key managerial consideration in online consumer behavior (Christodoulides, Michaelidou, & Argyriou, 2012).

The global nature of eWOM indicates that an understanding is also needed of how cultural values moderate the effects of eWOM on consumer product evaluation. Therefore, the goal of this chapter is twofold: 1) to review the current literature on the role of cultural values in eWOM, and 2) to provide directions for future academic research on eWOM by offering managerial implications for online marketing communications. Through improved understanding of the effects of global cultural differences on eWOM, this chapter contributes to research on digital advertising by identifying an under-investigated yet important research topic. It is hoped that this chapter will generate increased research interest in eWOM across cultures and help international advertisers develop their eWOM strategy to better target internet users in different countries, thereby building long-term consumer-brand relationships.

Electronic Word-of-Mouth and Culture

In Hennig-Thurau, Gwinner, Walsh, and Gremler's (2004) seminal study, eWOM is defined as "any positive or negative statement made by potential, actual, or former customers about a product or company, which is made available to a multitude of people and institutions via the Internet" (p. 39). eWOM has been found to have an impact on online customer value and loyalty (Gruen, Osmonbekov, & Czaplewski, 2006), sales (Chevalier & Mayzlin, 2006), eWOM elasticity (You et al., 2015), and virtual consumer communities (Hung & Li, 2007). What differentiates eWOM from offline WOM is that eWOM could lead to higher retransmission intentions than offline WOM conversations due to the easy accessibility of finding new people to generate online conversations with on a global scale (Christodoulides et al., 2012; Baker et al., 2016). As a result, eWOM is considered to be more influential than offline WOM, and has been recognized as an important marketing technique in online global branding (Chu & Choi, 2011).

According to Hofstede's (2001) definition, culture is "the collective programming of the mind, which distinguishes the members of one group from another" (p. 9). Culture has been found to influence consumer behavior and aspects of traditional WOM, such as WOM referral in relational service exchange (Schumann et al., 2010) and in the purchase of industrial services (Money, Gilly, & Graham, 1998), the relationship between self-relevance and WOM (Chung & Darke, 2006), and the effects of consumers' cultural values on WOM transmission patterns (Lam, Lee, & Mizerski, 2009). Cultural values have also been found to influence the nature of online communication, but there is little empirical research that has examined the impact of culture on the eWOM process. Because internet users from different cultures may use different channels and methods to disseminate messages, eWOM is expected to relate to international contexts and cultural values.

Fong and Burton (2008) examined United States-based and China-based electronic discussion boards and showed that differences in WOM across cultures can be extended to the online environment. Using the individualism-collectivism dimension, which explains the extent to which individuals value group membership in a given society (see Hofstede, 2001, for a detailed discussion on the individualism/collectivism dimension), Fong and Burton (2008) found that Chinese participants engaged in higher levels of information-seeking behavior, while posts from American counterparts involved information-giving behavior. In another study, Christodoulides et al. (2012) found that Chinese consumers were more susceptible to eWOM comments regardless of their valence, while UK consumers place more emphasis on negative eWOM. These studies revolve around the individualism/collectivism dichotomy (Hofstede, 2001) and highlight the importance of the cultural context by examining the relationship between cultural values and consumers' eWOM. The results of both aforementioned studies are consistent with the general assumption that internet users from a collectivistic culture, such as China, are more likely to reply to information transmitted in the form of eWOM due to their greater emphasis on reference groups and group norms.

With the introduction of social networking applications, social media have recently gained tremendous popularity, and research on eWOM in social media has received increasing attention (Chu & Kim, 2011; Goodrich & de Mooij, 2014; Lien & Cao, 2014; He & Pedraza-Jiménez, 2015). Chu and Choi (2011) examined social relationship variables between the United States and China with a focus on social capital, tie strength, trust, and interpersonal influence as potential predictors of eWOM in online social platforms. The results of their study suggested that culture did play a role in determining consumers' engagement in eWOM on social media in the two countries. Goodrich and de Mooij (2014) examined international differences in the use of social media and compared the effects of eWOM on consumer decision-making across 50 countries. Applying the cultural dimension framework (Hofstede, 2001), Goodrich and de Mooij (2014) found that individuals from a collectivistic culture tended to rely more on social media than people from an individualistic culture, suggesting that social media has become an alternative for offline WOM. Such findings provide evidence that the effects of eWOM on online purchase decisions may vary by culture, which opens the door for future research.

Directions for Future Research

Over the past few years, digital and social media have enabled consumers to share their brand experiences that may assist others (e.g., followers and friends) in making a more informed purchase decision. Through the examination of the moderating role of culture on the effect of eWOM on product evaluations, the following suggestions for future research are proposed. First, while social media provide the potential to advance eWOM research, limited empirical studies have investigated how and why consumers, across cultures, use social media and eWOM within social media. Thus, research could examine eWOM in a social media context through a "Uses and Gratifications" cultural lens to discover whether cultural differences exist. Second, future academic research could look into specific countries of interest and consider cultural differences within a country. Third, additional studies could use an integrated approach to study eWOM by incorporating cultural factors, message factors (e.g., positive or negative eWOM), and individual factors (e.g., level of self-concept and personality traits). The complex nature of culture's influence on eWOM and consumer decision-making requires continuous attention from researchers and practitioners. From a practical perspective, the cultural differences observed in eWOM would provide meaningful insights that help global advertisers adopt different strategies to better target consumers across cultures.

References

Bahtara, A. Z., & Muda, M. (2016). The impact of user-generated content (UGC) on product reviews towards online purchasing: A conceptual framework." *Procedia Economics and Finance, 37*, 337–342.

Baker, A. M., Naveen, D., & Kumar, V. (2016). Investigating how word-of-mouth conversations about brands influence purchase and retransmission intentions. *Journal of Marketing Research, 53*(2), 225–239.

Chevalier, J. A., & Mayzlin, D. (2006). The effect of word of mouth on sales: Online book reviews. *Journal of Marketing Research, 43*(3), 345–354.

Christodoulides, G., Michaelidou, N., & Argyriou, E. (2012). Cross-national differences in e-WOM influence. *European Journal of Marketing, 46*(11/12), 1689–1707.

Chu, S., & Choi, S. M. (2011). Electronic word-of-mouth (eWOM) in social networking sites: A cross-cultural study of the U.S. and China. *Journal of Global Marketing, 24*(3), 263–281.

Chu, S., & Kim, Y. (2011). Determinants of consumer engagement in electronic word-of-mouth (eWOM) in social networking sites. *International Journal of Advertising, 30*(1), 47–75.

Chung, C. M., & Darke, P. R. (2006). The consumer as advocate: Self-relevance, culture, and word-of-mouth. *Marketing Letters, 17*(4), 269–279.

Dobele, A., Lindgreen, A., Beverland, M., Vanhammed, J., & van Wijk, R. (2007). Why pass on viral messages? Because they connect emotionally. *Business Horizons, 50*(4), 291–304.

Fong, J., & Burton, S. (2008). A cross-cultural comparison of electronic word-of-mouth and country-of-origin effects. *Journal of Business Research, 61*(3), 233–242.

Goldsmith, R. E., & Horowitz, D. (2006). Measuring motivations for online opinion seeking. *Journal of Interactive Advertising, 6*(2), 2–14.

Goodrich, K., & de Mooij, M. (2014). How "social" are social media? A cross-cultural comparison of online and offline purchase decision influences. *Journal of Marketing Communications, 20*(1–2), 103–116.

Gruen, T. W., Osmonbekov, T., & Czaplewski, A. (2006). eWOM: The impact of customer-to-customer online know-how exchange on customer value and loyalty. *Journal of Business Research, 59*(4), 449–456.

He, X., & Pedraza-Jiménez, R. (2015). Chinese social media strategies: Communication key features from a business perspective. *El Profesional de la Información, 24*(2), 200–209.

Hennig-Thurau, T., Gwinner, K. P., Walsh, G., & Gremler, D. D. (2004). Electronic word-of-mouth via consumer-opinion platforms: What motivates consumers to articulate themselves on the Internet? *Journal of Interactive Marketing, 18*(1), 38–52.

Hofstede, G. (2001). *Culture's consequences: Comparing values, behaviors, institutions, and organizations across nations* (2nd ed.). Thousand Oaks, CA: Sage Publications.

Hung, K. H., & Li, S. Y. (2007). The influence of eWOM on virtual consumer communities: Social capital, consumer learning, and behavioral outcomes. *Journal of Advertising Research, 47*(4), 485–495.

Internet World Stats. (2015). World internet users and 2015 population stats. Retrieved from http://www.internetworldstats.com/stats.htm.

Lam, D., Lee, A., & Mizerski, R. (2009). The effects of cultural values in word-of-mouth communication. *Journal of International Marketing, 17*(3), 55–70.

Lee, M., & Youn, S. (2009). Electronic word of mouth: How eWOM platforms influence product judgment. *International Journal of Advertising, 28*(3), 473–499.

Lien, C. H., & Cao, Y. (2014). Examining WeChat users' motivations, trust, attitudes, and positive word-of-mouth: Evidence from China. *Computers in Human Behavior, 41*, 104–111.

Money, R. B., Gilly, M. C., & Graham, J. L. (1998). Explorations of national culture and word-of-mouth referral behavior in the purchase of industrial services in the United States and Japan. *Journal of Marketing, 62*(4), 76–87.

O'Neill, M. (2011). How much do Facebook & YouTube profit from user-generated content? Retrieved from http://www.adweek.com/socialtimes/user-generated-content-infographic/69916.

Park, C., & Jun, J. (2003). A cross-cultural comparison of Internet buying behaviour: Effects of Internet usage, perceived risks, and innovativeness. *International Marketing Review, 20*(5), 534–553.

Phelps, J. E., Lewis, R., Mobilio, L., Perry, D., & Raman, N. (2004). Viral marketing or electronic word-of-mouth advertising: Examining consumer responses and motivations to pass along email. *Journal of Advertising Research, 44*(4), 333–348.

Schumann, J. H., Wangenheim, F., Stringfellow, A., Yang, Z., Blazevic, V., Praxmarer, S., Shainesh, G., Komor, M. Shannon, R. M., & Jiménez, F. R. (2010). Cross-cultural differences in the effect of received word-of-mouth referral in relational service exchange. *Journal of International Marketing, 18*(3), 62–80.

Smith, A. N., Fischer, E., & Chen, Y. (2012). How does brand-related user-generated content differ across YouTube, Facebook, and Twitter? *Journal of Interactive Marketing, 26*(2), 102–113.

Statista. (2010). Social network revenue through user-generated content in 2010. Retrieved from http://www.statista.com/statistics/253651/social-network-revenue-through-user-generated-content/

Statista. (2016). Digital advertising spending worldwide from 2012 to 2018. Retrieved from http://www.statista.com/statistics/237974/online-advertising-spending-worldwide/

Yadav, M. S., & Pavlou, P. A. (2014). Marketing in computer-mediated environments: Research synthesis and new directions. *Journal of Marketing, 78*(1), 20–40.

You, Y., Vadakkepatt, G. G., & Joshi, A. M. (2015). A meta-analysis of electronic word-of-mouth elasticity. *Journal of Marketing, 79*(2), 19–39.

25

IMMERSION IN GAMES EXEMPLIFIES WHY DIGITAL MEDIA CREATE COMPLEX RESPONSES TO ADS

Mike Schmierbach

Digital advertising requires consideration of many platforms where traditional theories of advertising may not apply and where researchers must employ theories and concepts taken from other literatures. Video games are an excellent example of such a platform, and the study of them shows there is much to be learned. The growth in the popularity of video games has been accompanied by growth in using games as a platform for advertising. Because games provide a platform wherein individuals can interact directly with virtual representations of the product as well as view advertisements in a more immersive virtual environment, it is not surprising that research consistently demonstrates the effectiveness of linking brand messages with games. But future research in this area will require thinking more carefully about how features of the game-player experience shape responses to the brand message, and this means a more nuanced understanding is required of the games themselves. As an illustration of this point, I briefly consider the role of immersion in games as a factor that may exert a non-linear influence on message effectiveness and which may also interact with brand and message characteristics in unexpected ways.

Immersion is a broad term that comprises variables such as spatial presence, flow, and narrative transportation (or presence). These ideas are not interchangeable and some potential distinctions are considered at the end of this essay. In the context of advertising research, however, few studies consider more than one of these factors at a time, and this limits our understanding of how the factors may interact with each other. The importance of immersion is well-established from Nelson's seminal work establishing presence as a relevant mediator (e.g., Nelson, Yaros, & Keum, 2006) to research showing that optimal challenge (a component of flow) enhances the effectiveness of advertising (Waiguny, Nelson, & Terlutter, 2012), and demonstrating that difficulty in games may foster negative emotions and hinder brand effectiveness (Dardis, Schmierbach, Sherrick, & Luckman, 2013).

However, future research needs to probe the limits of immersion as a means to enhance branding effectiveness. First, more immersive games may also be more demanding. Lee and Faber (2007) provided relatively early data on the application of the limited capacity model to the effectiveness of game advertising, showing that "focal" brands requiring less attention were more readily remembered. Subsequent research parallels this, establishing not only a role for focal brands but also a complex influence of brand congruency and the presence of competing brands (e.g., Lee & Faber, 2007; Kim & Eastin, 2015). In these studies, the authors generally infer from ad characteristics the relative mental attention required to notice, process, and absorb brand messages. But game characteristics themselves are arguably also an important determinant of the capacity to process brand messages, as these may influence outcomes when branding is inserted in a game with naturalistic but unfamiliar controls (Dardis, Schmierbach, & Limperos, 2012). Facing the attentional demands of an unfamiliar control scheme, players may have been unable to put as much mental energy into processing brand messages.

As such, there is every reason to predict a non-linear relationship between immersion and advertising effectiveness. Low-immersion games may not draw the attention of players and, therefore, may not provide either the eyes-on-screen or the positive mood needed to make in-game product placement and advertising effective. But highly immersive games are cognitively demanding and may narrow the attention or focus of players to the point where they might miss all but the most intrusive of messages.

Variations in the game are only half of the picture, though. As Terlutter and Capella (2013) point out, variations in the advertisements also matter. Earlier, I noted that both the product-game congruency and placement of the advertisement have been the focus of several studies. In the case of congruency, at least, the picture is incomplete. Congruent ads seem less likely to reduce immersion, but they may also be less memorable. Furthermore, the meaning of congruency is incomplete. Congruency in the context of a racing game may involve car-related products, but in real-life auto sports, many advertisers are common brand names. Is Budweiser "congruent" when placed on a stock car? Similarly, billboards in a city-based shooter could depict a range of brands while still being perceived as congruent or at least not disrupting immersion. When immersion is high, individuals may not be capable of in-depth processing and, thus, may not even notice the congruency of certain brand messages. In short, there is little reason to expect that all "congruent" ads are equally effective or to expect high immersion to automatically enhance or reduce the effects of congruent ads.

Nor is congruence the only ad feature that matters. When actual ads appear in or alongside games, they may vary in the complexity of the message or in their emotional impact. A complex message would be difficult to process while playing a highly immersive game, but if it interrupts the immersive experience, the resulting greater focus may well increase the likelihood of attending to the ad. A player highly absorbed in a sad story might respond well to an ad that matches this emotional tone. Obviously, immersion is not the only aspect of the game or player experience that matters, but the fundamental point is that we need to move beyond the prominence and congruence of advertisements to think about other advertising features, and how features of digital advertising are likely moderated by the context in which they appear—context that is far more varied and less controlled than is often the case for traditional media.

Finally, we must return to a point referred to at the beginning of this essay. As noted, research to this point has most frequently focused on presence, but in a way that does not effectively distinguish it from other components of immersion. However, better theorizing in the future requires greater precision with these variables. It makes sense, for example, that spatial presence would amplify the effectiveness of advertisements within the focal area of the player; presence in this context represents a sense of being "in" the game that directly relates to "seeing" the ads themselves in that same environment. But flow is at least ostensibly a discrete experience from presence, and a player experiencing a high level of flow may actually have *less* focus on the game environment and physical details, being absorbed instead in the activities of play. What's more, both presence and flow are correlated with other game characteristics that may better explain why they have been related to the influence of advertising. Greater visual detail or vividness can generate presence; they can also make messages easier to see. Increased player performance is associated with flow; it might also be linked to positive moods and favorable impressions of in-game brands used in the play experience.

In summary, the future of research addressing digital advertising in games (and likely elsewhere) is going to need to move beyond establishing single-variable, linear-effect patterns. It needs to be more mindful of the nuanced meaning of ideas taken from media psychology (such as presence and flow). It needs to consider how those game-experience variables function in non-linear ways, as some imply an optimal state that is neither too low nor too high. It needs to address not only the features of advertisements but the ways they interact with the game experience, as the same ad will be encountered and processed in very different ways depending on the game state.

References

Dardis, F. E., Schmierbach, M., & Limperos, A. M. (2012). The impact of game customization and control mechanisms on recall of integral and peripheral brand placements in videogames. *Journal of Interactive Advertising, 12*(2), 1–12. doi: 10.1080/15252019.2012. 10722192.

Dardis, F. E., Schmierbach, M., Sherrick, B., & Luckman, B. (2013, August). *The impact of videogame-induced affect and ad type on memory of in-game advertisements.* Paper presented at the annual meeting of the Association for Education in Journalism and Mass Communication, Washington, DC.

Kim, E., & Eastin, M. S. (2015). External brand placement: The effects on game players' processing of an in-game brand. *Journal of Promotion Management, 21*(3), 391–411. doi: 10.1080/10496491.2014.996803.

Lee, M., & Faber, R. J. (2007). Effects of product placement in on-line games on brand memory: A perspective of the limited-capacity model of attention. *Journal of Advertising*, *36*(4), 75–90. doi: 10.2753/JOA0091–3367360406.

Nelson, M. R., Yaros, R. A., & Keum, H. (2006). Examining the influence of telepresence on spectator and player processing of real and fictitious brands in a computer game. *Journal of Advertising*, *35*(4), 87–99. doi: 10.2753/JOA0091–336735040.

Terlutter, R., & Capella, M. L. (2013). The gamification of advertising: Analysis and research directions of in-game advertising, advergames, and advertising in social network games. *Journal of Advertising*, *42*(2–3), 95–112. doi: 0.1080/00913367.2013.774610.

Waiguny, M. K., Nelson, M. R., & Terlutter, R. (2012). Entertainment matters! The relationship between challenge and persuasiveness of an advergame for children. *Journal of Marketing Communications*, *18*(1), 69–89. doi: 10.1080/13527266.2011.620766.

26

THE ADVENT OF VIRTUAL DIRECT EXPERIENCE (VDE) RESEARCH IN VIDEO GAMES

Integrating, Augmenting, and Informing Brand-Communication Strategies in Digital/Interactive Media

Frank E. Dardis

Research into in-game advertising has reached a stage that can incorporate many variables and concepts currently important to brand communication in the broader context of digital media. The purpose of this chapter is to briefly explain how examination of virtual direct experience (VDE) with brands through video games is uniquely suited to inform both in-game advertising and digital media research efforts.

Like any field that began as a nascent phenomenon, advertising research into video games began by focusing on attributes of the ads themselves. Early studies led by Nelson (2002) and others investigated features like ad size, location, duration, screen prominence, display mode (static vs. dynamic), and so on. This provided a great first understanding of how physical message characteristics could be manipulated to produce differing, important outcomes like brand recall and recognition, attitude toward the brand, and purchase intent. This line of valuable research—much of which is still being done today—would treat gaming platforms as analogous to traditional media in which advertising effectiveness is seen as trying to determine the best places, times, locations, modes, etc., in which to place advertisements in and around the main media content.

Another phase of gaming research began to consider the impact of game-produced and player-based factors on in-game advertising effects. Many of these studies would find that such factors either moderated or mediated the direct relationships between physical message attributes and brand-related outcomes. For example, players who had to spend too much cognitive effort on game play would not remember ads as well as those who spent less effort (Lee & Faber, 2007). These effects could be further moderated when ad location (e.g., focal vs. peripheral) was introduced (Dardis, Schmierbach, & Limperos, 2012). Other studies of this type focused on the presence or flow-like state achieved by the players, and how this influenced advertising effects, while some focused on other experience-based variables like enjoyment, immersion, performance ("winning vs. losing"), game-induced mood or affect, and so on. Much like the research into message attributes described above, this line of research also is valuable, necessary, and informative to academics and practitioners alike. However, the approach still conceptualizes gaming as a "traditional" platform, in the sense that it investigates the intersection of message-attribute effects with media-experience-produced or media-consumption-produced effects; most of the time in which players are told to simply play a game without much control over game attributes or features, other than trying to do their best.

This is not to suggest, of course, that gaming does not have its own unique attributes and media-produced effects that differentiate it from other types of media—digital or traditional. What this means is that understanding ad effects in gaming requires much more research into uncovering and precisely understanding effects from the gaming experience itself. But it is the next phase of gaming research—virtual direct experience (VDE)—that I believe can allow gaming research to uniquely also speak to and inform the much larger realm of digital media effects in general. The construct VDE is based on traditional foundations of brand integration and also on digital-media concepts of interactivity.

Besharat, Kumar, Lax, and Rydzik (2013) categorized three types of brand placements in video games: 1) billboarding, or simple, passive brand placements unassociated with game play, 2) product placement, in which brands are placed within a game for potential usage (e.g., eating a bag of Doritos while playing a jungle survival game), and 3) product integration, in which, to play the game, branded objects need to be used in the realistic way in which they are actually experienced in the real-world (e.g., Dardis et al., 2015). This thereby ostensibly makes the brand central to game playing, mimicking VDE as conceptualized in other non-gaming, interactive-media research, experiencing the product in a simulated or an online context as if in the real world (Griffith & Chen, 2004).

Early inquiry into VDE focused on how internet browsing allowed consumers to interact with brands or products in new ways, such as allowing for 3D product visualizations versus typical 2D ads (Li, Daugherty, & Biocca, 2001, 2003). Studies generally found that virtual experience could influence information processing (Schlosser, 2003), product knowledge (Jiang & Benbasat, 2007; Daugherty, Li, & Biocca, 2008), and brand attitudes and purchase intention (Li et al., 2003), due largely to increased interactivity. Further, Hang and Auty (2011) suggested that player interactivity with in-game brand placements can lead to enhanced "conceptual fluency" (i.e., ease of processing information in the advertising stimuli), which results in higher memory and brand choice among players than do mere brand placements. Besharat et al. (2013) showed that pleasant virtual experiences with product attributes led to greater memory of and attitudes toward brands that were associated with the attributes. Finally, Dardis, Schmierbach, and Limperos (2012) showed that allowing customization of the integral brand needed for game play led to higher brand recall rates, and Dardis et al. (2015) demonstrated that the in-game performance of the branded, integral product needed for game play (a Volkswagen racecar) predicted players' attitudes toward the real-world brand. We have just scratched the surface: there are many more factors to uncover as more is learned about VDE and in-game brand placements or advertisements.

The best part about examining VDE effects in video games is that it can be based very similarly upon the same two-pronged research approach described above: it entails a strategic communications decision (e.g., how and to what extent to allow a brand to be integrated into a game—which, in essence, becomes the "brand communication" itself—versus simply placing brand messages within or around a game). It also entails media-consumption based on game-produced effects within players that can influence the overall effectiveness of the strategy. But the difference in VDE is that the player is getting some "experience" with the brand as well as the gaming experience. This can lead to much more perceived interactivity, control, customization, and personalization with regard to the brand, all of which are factors that typically can speak more broadly to general digital-media effects than simply describing gaming effects.

With digital spending consistently increasing within media advertising budgets, such insight would seem to further validate gaming research as more critical than it already is to the larger fields of digital and interactive media. And when one considers the limitless interactivity that playing a VDE game allows the media user, such findings could be informative toward the understanding of whole new theories or methods of marketing communication of brands to consumers.

In sum, the research discussed here is obviously necessary and informative to move video game advertising forward. As brands continue to pump more marketing dollars into video game placements and experiences, researchers will need to pursue increased understanding of how each component makes the advertising efforts worthwhile or not. We are nowhere near "knowing it all." This is true in most any advertising forum. However, I believe that VDE through video games is an intriguing topic that is ripe for empirical examination, and one that is ostensibly and uniquely well-suited for integrating and adding to academic knowledge within the broader field of digital/interactive media.

References

Besharat, A., Kumar, A., Lax, J. R., & Rydzik, E. J. (2013). Leveraging virtual attribute experience in video games to improve brand recall and learning. *Journal of Advertising, 42*(2–3), 170–182. doi: 10.1080/00913367.2013.774593.

Dardis, F. E., Schmierbach, M., Ahern, L., Fraustino, J., Bellur, S., Brooks, S., & Johnson, J. (2015). The effects of in-game virtual direct experience (VDE) on reactions to real-world brands. *Journal of Promotion Management, 21*(3), 313–334.

Dardis, F. E., Schmierbach, M., & Limperos, A. (2012). The impact of game customization and control mechanism on recall of integral and peripheral brand placements in video games. *Journal of Interactive Advertising, 12*(2), 1–12. doi: 10.1080/15252019.2012.10722192.

Daugherty, T., Li, H., & Biocca, F. (2008). Consumer learning and the effects of virtual experience relative to indirect and direct product experience. *Psychology & Marketing, 25*(7), 568–586. doi: 10.1002/mar.20225.

Griffith, D. A., & Chen, Q. (2004). The influence of virtual direct experience (VDE) on on-line ad message effectiveness. *Journal of Advertising, 33*(1), 55–68. doi: 10.1080/00913367.2004.10639153.

Hang, H., & Auty, S. (2011). Children playing branded video games: The impact of interactivity on product placement effectiveness. *Journal of Consumer Psychology, 21*(1), 65–72. doi: 10.1016/j.jcps.2010.09.004.

Jiang, Z., & Benbasat, I. (2007). The effects of presentation formats and task complexity on online consumers' product understanding. *MIS Quarterly, 31*(3), 475–500.

Lee, M., & Faber, R. J. (2007). Effects of product placement in on-line games and brand memory: A perspective of the limited-capacity model of attention. *Journal of Advertising, 36*(4), 75–90. doi: 10.2753/JOA0091–3367360406.

Li, H., Daugherty, T., & Biocca, F. (2001). Characteristics of virtual experience in electronic commerce: A protocol analysis. *Journal of Interactive Marketing, 15*(3), 13–30. doi: 10.1002/dir.1013.

Li, H., Daugherty, T., & Biocca, F. (2003). The role of virtual experience in consumer learning. *Journal of Consumer Psychology, 13*(4), 395–407.

Nelson, M. R. (2002). Recall of brand placements in computer/video games. *Journal of Advertising Research, 42*(2), 80–92.

Schlosser, A. E. (2003). Experiencing products in the virtual world: The role of goal and imagery in influencing attitudes versus purchase intentions. *Journal of Consumer Research, 30*, 184–198. doi: 10.1086/376807.

27

ADVERTISING IN VIDEO GAMES

An Overview and Future Research Considerations

Anthony M. Limperos

In-Game Advertising: Promising Future or Passing Fad?

In today's media landscape, advertising has reached a whole new level of ubiquity. One can argue that consumers expect to see advertising on TV, in print, outdoors, and on any kind of networked device, but not necessarily in video games. In fact, video games are often not the first thing that comes to mind when consumers and practitioners think about venues for advertising. Though no comprehensive history regarding advertising in video games exists, most studies and commentaries that trace the evolution of this form of advertising seem to suggest that games (e.g., *Kool-Aid Man* and *Avoid the Noid*) made for the Atari 2600 and the personal computer (PC) in late 1970s and early 1980s represent some of the earliest examples of what is now commonly referred to as in-game advertising (Skalski, Campanella-Bracken, & Buncher, 2010). Even though in-game advertising was once considered a niche market, analysts estimate that the industry is currently worth $7 billion, and companies like Zynga have reported making as much as $153 million in revenue from in-game advertising in one year (Entertainment Software Association, 2014; Jordan, 2015). Despite their great value and potential, the reality is that most video game players are not making in-app or in-game purchases from advertising, leading some to question the real value of in-game ads (Robinson, 2016). Therefore, the purpose of this essay is to briefly synthesize in-game advertising research and discuss what researchers can do in the future to enhance understanding of the effectiveness of this form of advertising.

Common Types of In-Game Ads

There are many different forms of game-related advertising, but static in-game advertisements, dynamic in-game advertisements, and branded games (also known as "advergames") are the three most common.

Static advertisements in games are those that reside in the software, appearing during the course of game play. Sports and racing games contain a lot of static advertising. For example, *FIFA 16*, which is the most successful soccer video game franchise of all time, contains many different static ads ranging from team sponsors (e.g., Adidas, Nike, & Etihad) to ads for the game maker itself (EA Sports).

Dynamic in-game advertising is similar to static advertising in terms of the way it is displayed. However, online capabilities allow advertisers to serve ads in games based on the time of the day or location. For example, I used to routinely play a boxing game called *Fight Night* (EA Sports). There were a number of static advertisements in the game, but EA also sold dynamic ad space on the ring canvas within the game, and ads would change based on when people were playing. When playing one evening, I can vividly remember an ad for a new HBO show being prominently displayed in the ring. The ability to change an advertisement within a game due to networking capabilities captures the essence of dynamic in-game ads.

In 2006, Burger King worked with Blitz Games to create three different branded Xbox games that were sold at Burger King franchises (Barnes, 2016). These games were created with the idea of being another brand contact point for Burger King's meats campaign and were relatively successful at the time. Branded games represent a third form of in-game advertising known as advergames. Though console-based advergames are not that common, many companies currently use web-based advergames in support of their marketing and communication objectives (Lee & Youn, 2008).

Video Game Advertising Research: A Picture of Mixed Effectiveness

While video game advertising has been around for quite some time, research on the subject first began to appear in communication and related marketing journals about 15 years ago. Early studies in this area illustrated that simply playing a game with embedded brand messaging is enough to impact simple recall of that brand, but not for all players (Nelson, 2002; Yang, Roskos-Ewoldsen, Dinu, & Arpan, 2006). As a result of this varied effectiveness, scholarship moved in a direction toward gaining a better understanding of the conditions and processes under which brand messaging in games can be effective. Unlike forms of passive media like television and print, video games are interactive and place demands on the players' attention, which could ultimately be detrimental to information processing.

As a result of this shift toward understanding psychological process, researchers have examined how individual differences variables (Sparks & Chung, 2016), different types of games (Lull, Gibson, Cruz, & Bushman, 2016), and technological features like customization and game control mechanisms (Dardis, Schmierbach, & Limperos, 2012) affect recall of brand messages and advertisements in games. Perhaps unsurprisingly, both the early and more current research in this area paint a rather complex picture of how individuals process ads in games.

As is the case with most research focused on understanding the cognitive processing of media and persuasive messages, there is no all-encompassing theory or set of studies that can definitively explain both the value and effectiveness of forms of video game advertising. Almost all of the studies referenced above, and a good majority of research focused on advertising in games is experimental in nature taking place in a laboratory setting. Even though research has shown that individual, graphical, and technological differences, as well as the placement of ads in a game, impact recall and recognition, relatively few studies have been able to explain how these ad buys in games translate into purchase intentions or actual purchase of products or services advertised in the games. This is not to say that the theoretically driven laboratory studies are deficient in any way. In fact, without these studies, practitioners would merely be taking a shot in the proverbial dark in terms of message design for branded games and in-game advertising efforts. Research just needs to go a step further.

Future Research Considerations

In one of the most comprehensive essays focusing on digital games advertising, Terlutter and Capella (2013) provide a synthesis of the theories most often applied in the advertising and games context and provide a framework that highlights the key variables of interest that are often found in these studies. For anyone hoping to conduct research on the effectiveness of in-game advertising, this article provides a great road map of the literature, complete with future research suggestions. In the Terlutter and Capella (2013) article, there is a small section regarding the potential influence of "technical platform" on game advertising effectiveness. Based on my own research, and the fact that communication technologies continue to change and evolve, I believe that future research should place greater emphasis on isolating and explaining how variations in technology (e.g., different modalities) contribute to or detract from the effects of video game advertising. While individual differences, context, and types of games certainly matter, playing a console game on a 70-inch TV is fundamentally different than playing a mobile game on an 8-inch tablet or smartphone. Additionally, a game advertisement with sound and moving graphics is different than an advertisement that does not contain these elements. Therefore, understanding how variations in technology influence the effectiveness of in-game advertising will likely remain an important question for years to come.

Although video games have reached critical mass and are very popular with a wide audience, tracking the return on in-game advertising expenditures is not as clear-cut. The more that researchers can do to bridge the gap between what is theoretically and what is practically relevant, the more promising the future will be for both researchers and practitioners concerned with understanding the effectiveness of in-game advertising. On a final note, although it will continue to be important to research questions related to in-game advertising, the recent boom of e-sporting events and e-sports TV shows (which allow people to watch others play video games) presents a somewhat novel and vibrant area for future research consideration, especially since traditional elements of TV advertising are likely to be mixed with in-game advertising for multiple audiences.

References

Barnes, K. (2016). 10 oddities that found a home on Xbox. *PureXbox*. Retrieved May 26, 2016 from http://www.purexbox.com/news/2016/05/feature_10_oddities_that_found_a_home_on_xbox.

Dardis, F. E., Schmierbach, M. G., & Limperos, A. M. (2012). The impact of game customization and control mechanism on videogame advertising effects. *Journal of Interactive Advertising, 12*, 1–12.

Entertainment Software Association. (2014). Games: In-game advertising. *ESA*. Retrieved May 26, 2016 from http://www.theesa.com/wp-content/uploads/2014/11/Games_Advertising-11.4.pdf.

Jordan, J. (2015). Zynga generated $153 million of revenue from in-game ads in 2014. *Pocketgamer*. Retrieved May 26, 2016 from http://www.pocketgamer.biz/chart-of-the-week/60848/zynga-generated-153-million-of-revenue-from-in-game-ads-in-2014/

Lee, M., & Youn, S. (2008). Leading national advertisers' use of advergames. *Journal of Current Issues & Research in Advertising, 30*, 1–13. doi: 10.1018/10641734.2008.10505243.

Lull, R. B., Gibson, B., Cruz, C., & Bushman, B. J. (2016). Killing characters in video games kills memory for in-game ads. *Psychology of Popular Media Culture*, Advance online publication. doi: 10.1037/ppm0000108.

Nelson, M. R. (2002). Recall of brand placements in computer/video games. *Journal of Advertising Research, 42*, 80–92.

Robinson, M. (2016). Understanding in-game advertising's crisis of confidence. *Adweek*. Retrieved May 26, 2016 from http://www.adweek.com/socialtimes/deltadna-mark-robinson-guest-post-in-game-advertising-crisis-of-confidence/639056.

Skalski, P. Campanella-Bracken, C., & Buncher, M. (2010). Advertising: It's in the game. In M. S. Eastin, T. Daugherty, & N. M. Burns (Eds.), *Handbook of research on digital media and advertising: User generated content consumption* (pp. 437–455). Hershey, PA: Information Science Reference.

Sparks, J. V., & Chung, S. (2016). The effects of psychobiological motivational traits on memory of in-game advertising messages. *Psychology of Marketing, 33*, 60–68. doi: 10.1002/mar.20840.

Terlutter, R., & Capella, J. N. (2013). The gamification of advertising: Analysis and research directions of in-game advertising, advergames, and advertising in social network games. *Journal of Advertising, 42*, 95–112. doi: 10.1080/00913367.2013.774610.

Yang, M., Roskos-Ewoldsen, D. R., Dinu, L., & Arpan, L. M. (2006). The effectiveness of "in-game" advertising: Comparing college students' explicit and implicit memory for brands. *Journal of Advertising, 35*, 143–152. doi: 10.2753/JOA0091-3367350410.

28

EASY LOVING

Understanding Affect in Social Media

Attila Pohlmann and Qimei Chen

The act of Liking online content has become a routine task in our day-to-day interactions with family, friends, colleagues, and companies who advertise online. Facebook's emblematic thumbs-up button and a variety of similar heart-shaped mechanisms across social media platforms woo us to signal positive affect toward online content. Given the ease with which reactions are formed and communicated on social media, advertisers are cautioned against interpreting a Like as proxy for emotional engagement with online advertisements. Consequently, traditional advertising models such as response hierarchy models should be translated cautiously to social media contexts.

Whether thoughts or feelings are the better predictor of consumer intention is a highly debated topic in advertising and marketing research. Cognitive theories propose that viewers' attitude formation toward the object of an ad is mediated by their cognitive elaboration of the arguments presented in a persuasive communication (e.g., Greenwald & Leavitt, 1984; Tsal, 1985). The introduction of emotional response as a mediator for attitude formation (e.g., Batra & Ray, 1986) and as a predictor of behavioral outcomes (e.g., Smith, Haugtvedt, & Petty, 1994) indicates that focusing exclusively on cognitive processes impedes our understanding of consumer behavior in its entirety (Allen, Machleit, & Kleine, 1992). Affect has always played a central role in attitudinal research (e.g., Edell & Burke, 1987; Burke & Edell, 1989; Morris, Woo, Geason, & Kim, 2002). Given the increasing amount of stimuli that are competing for attention on social media, we discuss the theoretical implications of these developments for advertising and marketing research.

During the first decade of social media's evolution, the Like button was repurposed by many users: Liking bad news—public or private—was to be understood as a signal of empathy or concern; Liking an article about movie spoilers was to signal a real-world conversation topic to others. Often, the Like serves as an indicator of personal relevance, to validate others, or to simply acknowledge that a message was received, heard, or seen rather than being an expression of true fondness.

Recognizing this development, Facebook introduced an augmented Like button in 2016 that offers universal cultural emotional expressions, namely Love, Haha, Wow, Sad, and Angry, in addition to Like. These additional buttons allow users a more nuanced expression of emotions toward online advertisements and can provide marketers with valuable quantitative insight regarding consumer attitudes when they interact with an ad. In fact, marketers have access to an abundance of digital metrics, such as the number of Likes, followers, shares, co-creation attempts, and video views, to name a few (Hoffman & Fodor, 2010). Market research companies aggregate these data and build consumer profiles that transcend the boundaries of their activity on a single platform or device. Such structured data allow the tracking of the spread of information through networks and gauges user engagement, but more involved qualitative approaches, such as web scraping and sentiment analysis, are still needed to extract the emotional context and valence of these activities.

So, what insights can marketers hope to glean in the future from the expanded *reaction set* now available to Facebook users? What are some of the theoretical implications of social media users when they give their hearts away so easily online without really feeling the love? How will advertising researchers respond to this proliferation of quasi-emotion in a post-emotional society (Mestrovic, 1996; Wade, 2015) where social media users share a lighthearted Haha without moving a single facial muscle, least of all rolling on the floor? Would emotional responses perhaps be less diluted if there were an emotional allowance built into social media accounts prompting users to consider the allocation of their emotional bandwidth? And among how many emotions can one truly oscillate in a single minute without the risk of going numb while scrolling through the unpredictable emotional potpourri of updates from friends, news feed subscriptions, and sponsored advertisements?

While we cannot answer all of the questions, these questions hold important implications for advertising researchers regarding how consumers' experience and intensity of emotions affect various behavioral outcomes. Among these questions, and of particular relevance is how traditional advertising models—such as response hierarchy models—should be refurbished to capture these new developments in social media advertising. In what follows, we first review the challenges traditional response hierarchy models are facing and then propose a new interactive response model for advertising in the era of social media.

Traditional Response Hierarchy Models

Traditional response hierarchy models (e.g., Strong, 1925; Lavidge & Steiner, 1961; McGuire, 1978) of marketing communication propose that consumers move through at least three stages that can be aggregated into 1) the cognitive stage, where the consumer is exposed to an ad and cognitively becomes aware of its existence and content; 2) the affective stage, where persuasion occurs and an attitude or evaluation is formed; and 3) the behavioral stage, where consumers act on an intention or positive attitude, most often referring to purchase behavior.

Considering that most internet users try to avoid and ignore online ads (Drèze & Hussherr, 2003; Cho & Cheon, 2004)—merely processing them at pre-attentive levels (Schweizer, 2001; Yoo, 2007)—it is unlikely that users of social media will pause to carefully consider the persuasive appeals of an ad that they encounter in their social media stream. It is more likely that they remain swept up in the emotional flurry delivered by the next post in the eternal vertical scroll of their social media feed. Thus, consumer reactions communicated by employing the new reaction emojis are indicative of ad exposure, and their attitudes are likely based on peripheral cues rather than constituting the formation of a lasting attitude bonded with the object of the ad.

Toward a New Response Model in the Era of Social Media

These challenges are not necessarily a bad thing for advertisers. Given the limited attention and low motivation needed to process online ads, the elaboration likelihood model (ELM) (Petty & Cacioppo, 1986) predicts that consumers are not motivated to commit mental resources to cognitively process the stimuli they haphazardly encounter online. Instead, their attitude formation is based upon peripheral cues, such as attractiveness and credibility of the source of the message, or its perceived production quality, for instance.

For example, Goodrich (2011) found that when consumers browsed a website, lower levels of attention were positively correlated with brand attitude toward the advertised product, supporting prior findings that low attention positively affects attitude (Bornstein, 1989; Heath, Brandt, & Nairn, 2006). The reason for this outcome is that liking judgments are spontaneously made when attention is low, whereas the formation of disliking judgments requires a more involved cognitive process (Herr & Page, 2004). However, advertisers need to consider the implications of attitude persistence in social media under low-involvement conditions (Sengupta, Goodstein, & Boninger, 1997). Attitude persistence is of primary concern when attitude formations and purchase decisions are temporally delayed (Shen & Chen, 2007) or when attitude decays after the purchase (He, Chen, & Alden, 2016). Traditional conversion marketing in e-commerce aims to optimize the direct route to persuasion, from ad exposure to an online purchase behavior, compressing the temporal delay, and thereby reducing the need to foster attitude persistence for the sake of purchase behavior. Yet, managed without the proper diligence in an online context, the exposure to self-serving sales pitches of the business can easily be interpreted unfavorably by the viewer as single-sided, since such messages neglect the conversational and relational nature of social media (Hoffman & Fodor, 2010; Ramsay, 2010).

Furthermore, the evolution of technology profoundly alters the parameters of online customer attitude formation (e.g., Chen & Wells, 1999) and now allows for complex real-time interactions between customers and firms, facilitating the delivery of elaborately targeted communications. Issues that require attention are contagion effects, such as spreading attitude effects (Walther, 2002). Such effects occur when negative affect from user-generated content (UGC) is transferred onto the object of a sponsored ad or even from one ad to another. For example, reading about a friend's fear of flying or negative holiday experience can taint attitude toward the subsequently encountered advertisement for an airline or hotel chain. In traditional advertising media, such unfortunate occurrences used to be largely outside of the scope of marketers influence, but context-aware dynamic ad delivery systems need to be carefully configured to distribute global ad impressions accordingly.

Based on the discussion above, we propose a new interactive response model, shown in Figure 28.1, to help address the challenges associated with the traditional

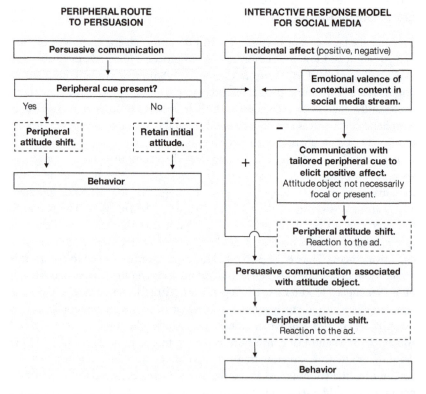

FIGURE 28.1 Peripheral Route, Only of the Elaboration Likelihood Model (ELM), on the Left (adapted from Petty & Cacioppo, 1986). Proposed Interactive Model of Attitude Formation for Social Media on the Right.

response hierarchy models in a landscape of changing technology. This proposed model for social media takes into account that advertisers can quantitatively gauge social media users' incidental affect and emotional reactions to ads from the expanded reaction set. To prevent unfavorable attitudes toward advertisements, an extended understanding of social media users' dynamic affective states is required that takes into account the interaction with UGC and provides for the delivery of communications with tailored peripheral cues to prime positive affective states. Once attained, such positive affective states can be associated with the attitude object of persuasive communications to elicit a desired behavior, such as making a purchase or otherwise supporting the formation of a brand relationship.

Compared to the traditional peripheral route to persuasion purported by ELM (e.g., Petty & Cacioppo, 1986), we believe that this new interactive response model more adequately captures the dynamics of consumer interactions and emotional processes. Marketers can employ this conceptual route to facilitate favorable consumer behaviors.

Nonetheless, ethical concerns with regard to consumer privacy require careful attention (see Chapter 17), considering that a substantial number of sensitive personality attributes (e.g., political views, personality traits, sexual orientation, use of addictive substances, general happiness, etc.) can be predicted with substantial accuracy from a digital record of about 50 Likes (Kosinski, Stillwell, & Graepel, 2013). Thus, an ad that is overly tailored can be perceived as outright uncanny. Especially in social media contexts where consumers expect an equitable relationship that they wish to form with a brand, the behavior of the business is evaluated according to social norms and human interaction etiquette. Consequently, norm violations or transgressions of a brand may ultimately be penalized by consumers (Aggarwal, 2004).

References

Aggarwal, P. (2004). The effects of brand relationship norms on consumer attitudes and behavior. *Journal of Consumer Research, 31*(1), 87–101.

Allen, C. T., Machleit, K. A., & Kleine, S. S. (1992). A comparison of attitudes and emotions as predictors of behavior at diverse levels of behavioral experience. *Journal of Consumer Research, 18*(4), 493–504.

Batra, R., & Ray, M. L. (1986). Affective responses mediating acceptance of advertising. *Journal of Consumer Research, 13*(2), 234–249.

Bornstein, R. F. (1989). Exposure and affect: Overview and meta-analysis of research, 1968–1987. *Psychological Bulletin, 106*(2), 265.

Burke, M. C., & Edell, J. A. (1989). The impact of feelings on ad-based affect and cognition. *Journal of Marketing Research, 26*(1), 69–83.

Chen, Q., & Wells, W. D. (1999). Attitude toward the site. *Journal of Advertising Research, 39*(5), 27–38.

Cho, C.-H., & Cheon, J. H. (2004). Why do people avoid advertising on the internet? *Journal of Advertising, 33*(4), 89–97.

Drèze, X., & Hussherr, F. X. (2003). Internet advertising: Is anybody watching? *Journal of Interactive Marketing, 17*(4), 8–23.

Edell, J. A., & Burke, M. C. (1987). The power of feelings in understanding advertising effects. *Journal of Consumer Research, 14*(3), 421–433.

Goodrich, K. (2011). Anarchy of effects? Exploring attention to online advertising and multiple outcomes. *Psychology & Marketing, 28*(4), 417–440.

Greenwald, A. G., & Leavitt, C. (1984). Audience involvement in advertising: Four levels. *Journal of Consumer Research, 11*(1), 581–592.

He, Y., Chen, Q., & Alden, D. L. (2016). Time will tell: Managing post-purchase changes in brand attitude. *Journal of the Academy of Marketing Science, 43*(3), 1–15.

Heath, R., Brandt, D., & Nairn, A. (2006). Brand relationships: Strengthened by emotion, weakened by attention. *Journal of Advertising Research, 46*(4), 410–419.

Herr, P. M., & Page, C. M. (2004). Asymmetric association of liking and disliking judgments: So What's not to like? *Journal of Consumer Research, 30*(4), 588–601.

Hoffman, D. L., & Fodor, M. (2010). Can you measure the ROI of your social media marketing? *MIT Sloan Management Review, 52*(1), 41.

Kosinski, M., Stillwell, D., & Graepel, T. (2013). Private traits and attributes are predictable from digital records of human behavior. *Proceedings of the National Academy of Sciences, 110*(15), 5802–5805.

Lavidge, R. J., & Steiner, G. A. (1961). A model for predictive measurements of advertising effectiveness. *The Journal of Marketing, 25*(6), 59–62.

McGuire, W. J. (1978). An information-processing model of advertising effectiveness. In H. L. Davis & A. J. Silk (Eds.), *Behavioral and management science in marketing* (pp. 156–180). New York, NY: Ronald (Wiley).

Mestrovic, S. (1996). *Postemotional society*. London: Sage.

Morris, J. D., Woo, C., Geason, J. A., & Kim, J. (2002). The power of affect: Predicting intention. *Journal of Advertising Research, 42*(3), 7–17.

Petty, R. E., & Cacioppo, J. T. (1986). The elaboration likelihood model of persuasion. In L. Berkowitz (Ed.), *Advances in experimental social psychology*, (Vol. 19, pp. 1–24). Orlando, FL: Academic Press, Inc.

Ramsay, M. (2010). Social media etiquette: A guide and checklist to the benefits and perils of social marketing. *Journal of Database Marketing & Customer Strategy Management, 17*(3–4), 257–261.

Schweizer, K. (2001). Preattentive processing and cognitive ability. *Intelligence, 29*(2), 169–186.

Sengupta, J., Goodstein, R. C., & Boninger, D. S. (1997). All cues are not created equal: Obtaining attitude persistence under low-involvement conditions. *Journal of Consumer Research, 23*(4), 351–361.

Shen, F., & Chen, Q. (2007). Contextual priming and applicability: Implications for ad attitude and brand evaluations. *Journal of Advertising, 36*(1), 69–81.

Smith, S. M., Haugtvedt, C. P., & Petty, R. E. (1994). Attitudes and recycling: Does the measurement of affect enhance behavioral prediction? *Psychology & Marketing, 11*(4), 359–374.

Strong, E. K. (1925). *The psychology of selling and advertising*. New York, NY: McGraw-Hill Book Company.

Tsal, Y. (1985). On the relationship between cognitive and affective processes: A critique of Zajonc and Markus. *Journal of Consumer Research, 12*(3), 358–362.

Wade, L. (2015). What is a world in which commercials make you cry? *The Society Pages.* Retrieved from https://thesocietypages.org/socimages/2015/12/28/what-is-a-world-in-which-commercials-make-you-cry/

Walther, E. (2002). Guilty by mere association: Evaluative conditioning and the spreading attitude effect. *Journal of Personality and Social Psychology, 82*(6), 919–934.

Yoo, C.Y. (2007). *Preattentive processing of web advertising.* Youngstown, NY: Cambria Press.

29

CONSIDERATIONS FOR APPLICATION OF COMPUTATIONAL SOCIAL SCIENCE RESEARCH APPROACHES TO DIGITAL ADVERTISING RESEARCH

Jisu Huh

Advertising is an inherently interdisciplinary field, situated primarily at the intersection of mass communication, marketing, and psychology. With the evolution of digital technologies and availability of massive datasets containing extensive information about consumer participation in brands' promotional radiation through an interconnected network of paid, earned, social, and owned media channels, a new stream of advertising research has emerged in collaboration with unlikely research partners: data scientists. Such a research approach is often referred to as big data analytics or, more generally, computational social science research.

Computational social science research is a fast-growing research approach across various disciplines. The expansion of its application to advertising research has been facilitated by the advancement of digital media technology, tracking online activities of large numbers of consumers, and increasing computing capacities enabling analysis of such massive datasets. Ranges of activities, including search, content viewing, product purchasing, connecting, liking, sharing, forwarding, and game-playing, can be captured and analyzed by marketers for targeting, ad development and placement strategies, and effect assessment.

With the profound shift in digital advertising focus to viral spread of ads through consumer activities and interactions, and availability of big data capturing them, computational advertising research has huge potential for revealing new insights and building theories explaining and predicting consumers' participatory behaviors related to advertising. As advertising researchers take an interest in, and gain familiarity with, computation social science research and its application to the advertising field, there is rising interest and engagement in multidisciplinary collaboration with researchers from computer science, statistics, and information and decision science fields. Like any multidisciplinary research, while having great advantages, computational advertising research presents unique challenges stemming from differences among disciplines. This think piece is aimed at presenting important considerations in multidisciplinary computational advertising research and proposing directions for future research.

Importance of Theory-Building Research

The current state of computational advertising research, in both industry and academe, seems to be dominated by primarily exploratory, data-driven approaches with pattern-drawing motivations. Big data are mined and explored often without a clearly focused theoretical framework, and patterns emerging from the mined data are often subjectively interpreted by the researcher, opening the possibility that similar data patterns might be interpreted differently by different researchers and different conclusions might be drawn.

For effective and fruitful computational advertising research, both exploratory research and theory-based research are important and should be properly implemented. Exploratory research can contribute to theory building by discovering new patterns of advertising phenomena leading to new theory development and testing the new theory by rigorous testing and retesting. On the other hand, for many of the new phenomena (e.g., analyzing traffic details for various devices to provide consumers with relevant advertisements), a clear and focused theoretical framework would be critically important. Researchers need to make strong connections between existing theories and the new research method, and to test old theories using the computational research approach.

In developing a theoretical framework for computational advertising research, an important consideration is to understand the limitations of the computational social science research approach. Overly complicated models with too many concepts, and constructs with multiple sub-dimensions, cannot be adequately modeled and tested in a computational system (Golbeck, 2005). Another limitation is that some of the important constructs in advertising theory represent individual consumers' internal mental state (e.g., involvement, motivation) and cannot be adequately measured by indicators obtained from big data, although evolution of neuroscience and other physiological measurements, and longitudinal computational research, show great promise to address this limitation (see Hofacker, Malthouse, & Sultan, 2016). With the consideration of such limitations, for computational advertising research, researchers should develop a simplified theoretical model with a small set of variables that are clearly and narrowly defined and measurable through quantitative data computation.

Matching between a Concept and Indicators, and Importance of Concept Explication

As concepts are the fundamental building blocks of theory, for viable application of the computational research approach to the advertising field, rigorous concept explication and measurement validation would be absolutely critical. Most of the concepts and constructs in advertising research have traditionally been measured by consumers' self-reported data collected using questionnaires or manipulated by researchers. As an alternative to the traditional approach, the biggest advantage of computational research is its ability to collect and analyze machine-observable activities performed by hundreds of thousands (sometimes millions) of individuals in a natural setting, and to overcome the limitations of questionnaire-based measurements, including sampling error, nonresponse error, and resource demand (e.g., time, financial). On the other hand, computational research's primary challenge is that abstract concepts and human mental events are not directly observable, and researchers need to identify valid proxy measures to be used for mathematical calculation of abstract concepts. Thus, the fundamental premise of computational social science research is scientifically justified linking or mapping between abstract concepts and appropriate indicators or proxies (Roy, Borbora, & Srivastava, 2013).

To make it possible to examine advertising phenomena, abstract concepts must be converted to observable data, and computational research requires selecting certain indicators representing each concept. In relation to this inherent challenge in computational research, a crucial issue in the current computational research in marketing/advertising industry and academe is a lack of rigorous concept explication guiding the concept-to-indicator mapping, resulting in confusion and discrepancies in the operationalization of concepts. Especially when research is conducted by those unfamiliar with the particular concepts and theories related to the observed phenomena, terms are often used imprecisely and can mean different things, the same concept is represented by different indicators, different concepts are measured by the same set of indicators, or sometimes wrong indicators are used. In multidisciplinary research involving scholars from different fields, another related issue is the communication gap, where concepts are understood differently and the same concept is represented by different terminologies in different fields.

Such an example is observed in the computational trust research and computational social influence research. For example, computational research on social influence has been fast growing with the rise of social media and eWOM phenomena (e.g., Leenders, 2002; Cha, Haddadi, Benevenuto, & Gummadi, 2010; Trusov, Bodapati, & Bucklin, 2010; Kaiser, Kröckel, & Bodendorf, 2012; Zhang, Zhao, & Xu, 2015; Subbian, Aggarwal, & Srivastava, 2016). Common social network indicators used to represent influence in a social media context include number of followers, number of friends, number of retweets, number of mentions, and frequency of online activities (e.g., Cha et al., 2010; Guo, Pathak, & Cheng, 2015; Zhang et al., 2015). Indicators for social influence vary across studies, and while some studies provide very cursory discussion of a conceptual definition, many of the studies cited do not offer concept explications of social influence.

As a concept developed in social psychology, social influence is generally conceptualized as a phenomenon that "occurs when an actor adapts his behavior, attitude, or belief, to the behavior, attitudes, or beliefs of other actors in the social system" (Leenders, 2002, p. 26). Given its theoretical origin and conceptual definitions, social influence is clearly an effect concept referring to influence of one entity on another. Thus, influence should be measured in terms of a causal link between the thoughts and actions of the influential and the influenced. This raises questions about the validity of using number of followers, number of friends, number of retweets, number of mentions, and frequency of online activities as indicators of social influence.

Moreover, very similar social media metrics are also used as indicators of trust between individuals in computational trust research (e.g., Adali et al., 2010; Roy, 2015). Trust is a concept that has been defined and examined in many different social science fields, including advertising (e.g., Cho, Huh, & Faber, 2014). Computational trust research, which examines trust between human actors mediated through computers, has evolved over the past decade primarily by researchers in the computer science field. This line of research focuses on discovering patterns of computer-mediated trust formation between individuals in social networks and explaining and predicting human trust formation in the real world (Golbeck, 2005; Roy, 2015). Some of the computational trust studies provide conceptual definitions of trust, while others lack solid conceptualization and theoretical justifications for selection of indicators for the concept.

The use of the same metrics as indicators for different concepts like influence and trust, or use of different indicators for the same concept, causes confusion and hinders cohesive theory development. Comparing trust and influence—since influence is an effect concept whereas trust is a relationship concept referring to the nature of a relationship between one individual and another (e.g., Mayer, Davis, & Schoorman, 1995; McKnight & Chervany, 2001; McKnight & Chervany, 2002)—it can be argued that social media metrics indicating interpersonal links are more suitable indicators for trust than influence, because they fit the conceptual definition of trust better than that of influence.

In order to move the computational advertising research forward, rigorous concept explication should guide the selection and justification of right indicators for a concept that are valid representations of the concept the way it is conceptually defined. Computational social science research needs the same measurement development procedures as the traditional social science research to develop and validate measures (see Chaffee, 1991; MacKenzie, Podsakoff, & Podsakoff, 2011). It will help especially in the multidisciplinary research context, to bring everyone together in terms of thinking about research questions and procedures, and disciplined and consistent use of terms. Additionally, it is important to carefully consider the existing discrepancies in matching between a concept and its indicators in reviewing previous computational research. As stated by Chaffee (1991), "our measures will be improved more by evaluation of what they are intended to measure than by technical tinkering" (p. 5).

Proposed Directions for Computational Research in Advertising

Computational social science research has great potential for examining and understanding consumers' interactions with and responses to digital advertising and advertising effects. Evolving digital technologies, such as social media, mobile devices, wearable technology, virtual reality, and the internet of things, will continue to produce more massive data, capturing every aspect of human behaviors mediated by computers. Such data are a gold mine of information for advertising researchers developing and testing theories, as well as for advertising practitioners devising more effective advertising strategies. Exploratory computational research offers valuable new insights about consumer behavior and effects of various marketing activities. However, purely exploratory research has limitations in its theoretical contributions, and, without theoretically grounded research frameworks and rigorous concept explication, simply following descriptive patterns or mistakenly believing that data patterns show objective truth can be problematic.

Given the technological challenges in conducting computational research with big datasets, multidisciplinary collaborations between advertising and computer science and decision science fields would be imperative. For meaningful and fruitful multidisciplinary collaborations contributing to advertising theory building, a strong theoretical framework and rigorous concept explication that makes theoretically sound matching between a concept and valid indicators would be crucial. Also, clear communication is absolutely critical among members of the multidisciplinary project team to bridge the differences among disciplines in understanding and using theoretical concepts and terms. With these considerations, several research directions are proposed for future research.

First, some theories or theoretical constructs seem to be especially more suitable than others for the computational research approach. Aforementioned social influence and trust constructs are such examples. Many digital advertising phenomena involve consumer-to-consumer and consumer-to-brand interactions and relationships, and computational trust research seems to have great potential for mapping, explaining, and predicting such phenomena.

Second, just like the traditional measurement scale development, thoughtful and rigorous research is needed to develop and test the right indicators for various concepts examined in advertising theory. For each concept-indicator mapping, thorough measurement validity tests should be conducted for face, content, criterion-related, and construct validity.

There are also many other possibilities and new avenues for research that can contribute to digital advertising theory building. New technology and complex social networks will constantly bring new types of data that will reveal some aspects of human psychological and behavioral phenomena. Datasets with edges (links or connections between network actors) representing human relations are very common in social media (e.g., network links indicating liking, friending, or following someone). However, the true meaning of edges in different networks is not clear and calls for more research. For example, friending someone or liking something on Facebook, following or retweeting someone on Twitter, liking or commenting on a video on YouTube—these actions might all represent different concepts and should not be assumed as the same network edges. In exploring social media data, expanding the theoretical scope from the individual-level psychology theory to social-level theory would be especially useful. Also, new theories could emerge from exploratory computational research, but, more importantly, rigorous causality testing should follow to test and validate the new theories.

The scope of computational advertising research could be further expanded beyond the current suggestions. Among the various interactive advertising response outcomes proposed in Rodgers and Thorson's (2000) Interactive Advertising Model (IAM), there are variables that are readily observable and currently measured in computational research, such as product purchase, but other more abstract and hard-to-measure concepts could be also captured. Researchers are encouraged to explore if some of the important theoretical concepts that are not currently examined in computational research (e.g., attention, involvement, attitude) could be captured through specific web metrics. Such potential for computational research is thoughtfully discussed in a recent article by Hofacker, Malthouse, and Sultan (2016), where the authors propose numerous possibilities for researchers to infer consumers' psychological characteristics and responses (e.g., attitude, satisfaction, dissatisfaction, pleasure) from behavioral big data.

A noticeable example of attempting to capture an abstract advertising-related concept using big data is research on engagement. Noting wide disagreements in the conceptual definition of engagement and inconsistencies in its operationalization in the previous engagement research literature, Maslowska, Malthouse, and Collinger (2016) proposed a new engagement model with four distinctive customer engagement components, with a conceptual definition and operationalizational approaches for each of them: 1) customer brand experience, 2) brand dialogue behaviors, 3) brand consumption, and 4) shopping behaviors. While big data cannot capture the psychological aspect of customer brand experience, they offer ample indicators for the other three components. Particularly, brand dialogue behaviors, defined as "all brand-related non-purchase behaviors" (Maslowska et al., 2016, p. 483), can be measured by tracking, counting, and analyzing a wide range of consumer actions, such as liking or following brand pages on social network sites (SNSs), downloading branded apps, playing branded games, and viewing/sharing/posting/creating brand-related user-generated content (Maslowska et al., 2016). Future research is encouraged to empirically test the proposed engagement model and measurement approaches.

Finally, expanding the source of big data beyond the current website browsing and social networking data would open new possibilities for computational advertising research. For example, virtual reality (VR) and online games are especially interesting environments where human psychology and behaviors can be observed in a virtual environment that mimics the real-world social atmosphere. Especially promising is massively multi-player online games (MMOGs), microcosms of real worlds, where various forms of digital advertising can be easily placed, and human interactions with and responses to them, as well as interpersonal trust and other types of relationships, can be tracked, stored, and analyzed (Roy, 2015). Researchers should also explore how unstructured data in forms of text, image, audio, and video can be analyzed to reveal new insights about consumer behavior and advertising phenomena.

References

Adali, S., Escriva, R., Goldberg, M. K., Hayvanovych, M., Magdon-Ismail, M., Szymanski, B. K., Wallace, W. A., & Williams, G. T. (2010). Measuring behavioral trust in social networks. In *Proceedings of the IEEE International Conference on Intelligence and Security Informatics (ISI)* (pp. 150–152), Vancouver, Canada, May 23–26. Retrieved from http://www.cs.rpi.edu/~szymansk/papers/isi.10.pdf.

Cha, M., Haddadi, H., Benevenuto, F., & Gummadi, K. P. (2010). Measuring user influence in Twitter: The million follower fallacy. In *Proceedings of the Fourth International AAAI Conference on Weblogs and Social Media* (pp. 10–17). Retrieved from https://www.google.com/url?sa=t&rct=j&q=&esrc=s&source=web&cd=1&ved=0ahUKEw iwtiCv_vNAhXFPCYKHRGoCTkQFggeMAA&url=https%3A%2F%2Fwww.aaai.org%2Focs%2Findex.php%2FICWSM%2FICWSM10%2Fpaper%2Fdownload%2F15 38%2F1826&usg=AFQjCNGNx7BiOl2YEc0B0HVjPQ-1RpoH-Q.

Chaffee, S. H. (1991). *Communication concepts I: Explication*. Newbury Park, CA: Sage.

Cho, S., Huh, J., & Faber, R. J. (2014). The influence of sender trust and advertiser trust on multistage effects of viral advertising. *Journal of Advertising, 43*(1), 100–114.

Golbeck, J. A. (2005). *Computing and applying trust in web-based social networks*. Doctoral Dissertation. University of Maryland. Retrieved from http://drum.lib.umd.edu/bit stream/handle/1903/2384/umi-umd-2244.pdf?sequence=1.

Guo, H., Pathak, P., & Cheng, H. (2015). Estimating social influences from social networking sites: Articulated friendships versus communication interactions. *Decision Sciences, 46*(1), 135–163.

Hofacker, C. F., Malthouse, E. C., & Sultan, F. (2016). Big data and consumer behavior: Imminent opportunities. *Journal of Consumer Marketing, 33*(2), 89–97.

Kaiser, C., Kröckel, J., & Bodendorf, F. (2012). Simulating the spread of opinions in online social networks when targeting opinion leaders. *Information Systems and e-Business Management, 11*(4), 597–621.

Leenders, R. T. A. (2002). Modeling social influence through network autocorrelation: Constructing the weight matrix. *Social Networks, 24*(1), 21–48.

MacKenzie, S. B., Podsakoff, P. M., & Podsakoff, N. P. (2011). Construct measurement and validation procedures in MIS and behavioral research: Integrating new and existing techniques. *MIS Quarterly, 35*(2), 293–334.

Maslowska, E., Malthouse, E. C., & Collinger, T. (2016). The customer engagement ecosystem. *Journal of Marketing Management, 32*(5–6), 469–501.

Mayer, R., Davis, J., & Schoorman, F. D. (1995). An integrative model of organizational trust. *The Academy of Management Review, 2*, 709–734.

McKnight, D. H., & Chervany, N. L. (2001–2002). What trust means in e-commerce customer relationships: An interdisciplinary conceptual typology. *International Journal of Electronic Commerce, 6*(2), 35–59.

Rodgers, S., & Thorson, E. (2000). The interactive advertising model. *Journal of Interactive Advertising, 1*(1), 41–60.

Roy, A. (2015). *Computational trust at various granularities in social networks.* Doctoral Dissertation. University of Minnesota. Retrieved from http://conservancy.umn.edu/bitstream/handle/11299/177102/Roy_umn_0130E_16776.pdf?sequence=1&isAllowed=y.

Roy, A., Borbora, Z. H., & Srivastava, J. (2013, August). Socialization and trust formation: A mutual reinforcement? An exploratory analysis in an online virtual setting. In *Proceedings of Advances in Social Networks Analysis and Mining (ASONAM), 2013 IEEE/ACM International Conference* (pp. 653–660). IEEE.

Subbian, K., Aggarwal, C., & Srivastave, J. (2016). Mining influencers using information flows in social streams. *ACM Transactions on Knowledge Discovery from Data (TKDD), 10*(3), 1–28.

Trusov, M., Bodapati, A. V., & Bucklin, R. E. (2010). Determining influential users in internet social networks. *Journal of Marketing Research, 47*(4), 643–658.

Zhang, L., Zhao, J., & Xu, K. (2015). Who creates trends in online social media: The crowd or opinion leaders? *Journal of Computer-Mediated Communication, 21*, 1–16.

INDEX